GOD, CREATION, AND REVELATION

NCMC
BT 046
75.2
.J488
1991

God, Creation, and Revelation

A NEO-EVANGELICAL THEOLOGY

Paul K. Jewett

with sermons
by Marguerite Shuster

WILLIAM B. EERDMANS PUBLISHING COMPANY

GRAND RAPIDS, MICHIGAN

23252985

Copyright © 1991 by Wm. B. Eerdmans Publishing Co.
255 Jefferson Ave. S.E., Grand Rapids, Mich. 49503
All rights reserved

Printed in the United States of America

Library of Congress Cataloging-in-Publication Data

Jewett, Paul King.
God, creation, and revelation : a neo-evangelical theology /
Paul K. Jewett with sermons by Marguerite Shuster.
p.   cm.
Includes bibliographical references.
ISBN 0-8028-0460-8
1. Theology, Doctrinal. I. Shuster, Marguerite. II. Title.
BT75.J488   1991
230'.046 — dc20   91-9778
                                                      CIP

Unless otherwise noted, all Scripture references are from the
Revised Standard Version of the Bible, copyrighted 1946, 1952 © 1971, 1973
by the division of Christian Education of the National Council of
the Churches of Christ in the U.S.A., and used by permission.

To Edward John Carnell
Former Colleague
and
Esteemed Friend

Contents

UNIT TWO
HOW WE KNOW GOD: REVELATION AND SCRIPTURE

UNIT THREE
WHO GOD IS: THE DIVINE NATURE

UNIT FOUR
WHAT GOD IS LIKE: THE DIVINE ATTRIBUTES

CONTENTS

UNIT FIVE
WHAT GOD HAS DONE: CREATION

Preface

"Of making many books there is no end, and much study is a weariness of the flesh" (Eccl. 12:12). These words of the seer can haunt the theologian. The problem is not just that there is no end of the many books the theologian makes, but when the effort is made to contain the subject of theology in one book, life ends before the book does. And so the theologian never gets to the end of his book. (While writing his *Summa Theologiae,* Thomas Aquinas died at the fourth sacrament.) If by chance the systematician should enjoy length of days, the result is a book so long that the *reader* never gets to the end. (Few have read all thirteen volumes of Barth's *Church Dogmatics;* and even those who have were taken no further than the first sacrament, which is where he laid down his pen.) Like many before me, I have not managed to condense the materials of a Christian systematics into a single volume. My original purpose to do so I have long since abandoned.

Yet there is one purpose that I have not abandoned and, I hope, have not betrayed too egregiously, namely, the resolve to avoid the esoteric jargon and abstruse style that so often leave theologians talking to themselves. Whereas they may, perhaps, be pardoned for the length of their books (since there is much that needs to be said), they are without excuse when they make the reading of their books an exercise in endless boredom. Though theologians cannot avoid the technical aspects of their discipline altogether, they are ill-advised to smile condescendingly when an Erasmus complains that theirs "are a thousand sublimated and refined niceties of notions, relations, quantities, formalities, quiddities, haecceities, and such like abstrusities, as one would think no one could pry into except he had not only such cat's eyes as to see best in the dark, but even such a piercing faculty as to see through an inch board, and spy out what never existed."[1] In this regard, I have tried to keep in mind what Heinrich Ott once said:

> Theology's inspiration is the passionate struggle for clarity, for illuminating and expressing the depths of faith, so that in the compact and well thought through formulation the basic words and themes of theology begin, as it were, to shine, so that they—and through them and in them the "kernel" itself, the one Subject matter of all theology—really becomes perceptible. [When this happens] there takes place in theology the *joy* of faith beholding itself in the medium of thought.[2]

Of course, a theologian's struggle for clarity does not arise out of a desire to clarify for clarification's sake. Rather, she seeks to illumine the Christian faith as she has been given to understand that faith. Since I devote the opening portion of the first unit of this study to locating my own position on the spectrum of theological possibility, I need say only a word at this juncture about my approach to the faith I seek to expound. I do theology from a traditional Protestant and Reformed point of view. The ecumenical creeds of the early church and the major confessions of the Protestant Reformation furnish the basic paradigms of thought with which I work. Though I consider my conclusions to be orthodox and evangelical, one could describe my position as "*neo*-evangelical" because what I write not only arises out of my understanding of the Bible as a divine revelation, but also reflects what I have read in the daily newspaper. That is to say, I am concerned both to expound the "faith once delivered to the saints," and to do so in a way that will clarify that faith for saints who are living in the twentieth century.

This does not mean—I hasten to add—that I have any thought of accommodating the exposition of the Christian faith to the canons of modernity. I have no desire to indulge in "creative thinking" so as to come up with something "essentially new." It was C. S. Lewis's demon, Screwtape, who counseled his nephew to cultivate in his patient a "horror of the Same Old Thing," so that nonsense in the intellect might reinforce corruption in the will. Such theological faddism makes one a dilettante of the latest possibilities rather than an expositor of the Word of God. I repudiate, in other words, the assumption that "modern thought is superior to all past forms of understanding reality, and is therefore normative for Christian

---

1. *In Praise of Folly,* as cited in Clyde L. Manschreck, ed., *A History of Christianity* (Englewood Cliffs: Prentice-Hall, 1964), p. 11.

2. "What is Systematic Theology," in *The Later Heidegger and Theology,* ed. James M. Robinson and John B. Cobb (New York: Harper, 1963), p. 97 (italics his).

faith and life."[3] Such a thesis leads one to do theology on the premise that the best is the newest. Congregations who sit under the preaching that such theology inspires become proud of their "pluralism" and "openness." They have supposedly been liberated by the insight that it really doesn't matter what one believes so long as one is tolerant of all beliefs.

By contrast, I seek to theologize as though theology does matter. My concern is not with a different theology, but with a theology that makes a difference. While it would be presumptuous to suppose that everyone believes that theology makes a difference, I write as one who does so believe. But theology is sometimes not given the chance to make the difference that it ought to make because it is crowded out by the practical concerns of life and society. The church sponsors seminars on divorce, suicide, disability, child abuse, mid-life crisis, and dying with dignity. It makes pronouncements on hunger, nuclear war, minority rights, labor relations, environmental concerns, and so on. Thus theology is lost in the shuffle, an incalculable loss in my judgment. I say this because I believe that it is the knowledge of theology that guides the church in saying and doing the right things in all of these worthy areas of personal and social concern. When we visit the sick and imprisoned, we need to know not only those to whom we do these things, but him in whose name we do them and to whom, in the last day, we shall be judged to have done them. And such knowing has an essential theological component.

Turning to other matters, the reader will notice that from time to time I refer to masterpieces of literature and especially to the hymns that the poets of the church have taught us to sing. Samuel Johnson defined poetry as "the art of uniting pleasure with truth by calling imagination to the help of reason." "The power of poetry," says Michael Lewis, "is the ability to express the inexpressible . . . in terms of the unforgettable."[4] Having taught in a seminary that has tended to ignore the place of church music and hymnody in the training of ministers, and having encountered a new generation of students who are more familiar with computers than with belles lettres, I have felt the need to do theology not only with the Bible and the newspaper in hand, but also with an occasional glance in the direction of the hymnal and our literary heritage. While theology cannot be done without a knowledge of philosophy and science, it cannot be done *well* without some knowledge of literature, for in literature matters of profound

---

3. "A Statement of Theological Affirmation," Theme 1. See *The Reformed Journal* 25 (March 1975): 8.

4. Louis Untermeyer, *A Treasury of Great Poems* (New York: Simon and Schuster, 1955), pp. v-vi.

theological substance are given magnificent verbal expression. After all, it was not to philosophy but to literature that Luther turned. "I am persuaded," he wrote to Eben Hess, "that without the knowledge of literature pure theology cannot at all endure. . . ."[5] Philosophy, to be sure, disciplines the mind and science enriches the understanding; but literature cultivates taste and improves the heart. It "teaches us by delighting" and so moves us to "take up good things."[6] Since I am not trained in either literature or hymnology, I am sure that others more knowledgeable than I could improve on this aspect of my work. Nonetheless, I hope that what I have written will give the reader some appreciation for the theological treasures of our literature and especially our hymnal.

Finally, a word concerning the decision to include sermons in a book of systematic theology. When studying with Emil Brunner, then professor of dogmatics at the University of Zurich, I was surprised to discover that he also held professorial rank in the department of preaching. As I became acquainted with his thought, I came to understand why this was so. The church's commission, Brunner argued, is the proclamation of the message which the apostles preached, as that message is preserved in Scripture. Dogmatic theology, therefore, arises out of the preaching of the church. In fact, the church existed for nearly two hundred years without such a discipline as dogmatics. This does not prejudice the church's right to do dogmatics nor deny the necessity that it should do it; but it does remind us that dogmatics is, by definition, the self-reflection of the church on the content and meaning of the message proclaimed in the gospel. This being the case, the discipline of dogmatics is not an end in itself. Its purpose is rather to clarify the message that the church proclaims.

In a similar vein, and more recently, Paul Holmer, for many years a divinity school professor, notes that his perspective on church and seminary made him critical of the divisions that are standardized in seminary curricula. On the one side stands theology, and on the other preaching: "As if preaching is something independent of theology and as if preaching is optional and only certain people do that, whereas I would think that having the word of faith on your lips is one of the ways to be a Christian. There is something artificial about the contemporary seminary's rubrics. Letting the rubrics construe the teachings is really baleful. The more deeply you get into the subject the less the rubrics fit."[7] Convinced by Brunner's

---

5. Letter to Eben Hess, March 29, 1523, as quoted by Roland Fry, *Perspectives on Man, Literature and the Christian Tradition* (Philadelphia: Westminster, 1961), p. 13.

6. Ibid., pp. 173, 178.

7. Mark Horst, "Disciplined by Theology: A Profile of Paul Holmer," *The Christian Century,* 12 Oct. 1988, 891-92.

argument and sharing Holmer's conviction that theology and preaching go together, I have long since concluded that theology done in such a way that it cannot be preached is like the salt of which our Lord speaks: having lost its savor, it is really good for nothing. Theology, in a word, is authenticated by the fact that it is preachable.

Perhaps to reassure myself that what I have written passes this litmus test, and, in any case, to help the reader hear what theology sounds like when it is preached, I submitted my materials to a former student now in the pastorate, Dr. Marguerite Shuster, and asked her to preach from time to time on several of the theological themes discussed in the ensuing volume. Her natural instinct for theology and her considerable skills in preaching have produced results that speak for themselves. While I can only hope that what I have written is readable, I am confident that what she has spoken is not only readable but edifying.

As I close, a word of appreciation for assistance rendered is due to my secretary, Dolores Loeding, my teaching assistants, Roger Van Horsen and Wayne Herman, and to Sandy Underwood Bennett, director of the seminary's word processing services, together with her associates, David Sielaff, Jan Gathright, and Anita Berardi Maher. I am also grateful to Fuller Theological Seminary for the privilege of teaching systematics and the opportunity afforded by sabbatical leaves to pursue the unfinished task of writing a systematic theology.

Pasadena, California, 1990 Paul K. Jewett

UNIT ONE

INTRODUCTION:
A PROLEGOMENON TO DOGMATICS

A creed, that is, a set of propositions which are believed, is the backbone of religious faith, though the backbone needs to be clothed with the flesh and blood of emotion, of spiritual fervour and faith. The church, then, must believe something. . . . The central core of the Christian faith is either absolute truth or it is nonsense.

C. E. M. Joad, *The Recovery of Belief*

I. Definition of Terms: Theology as Christian, Systematic, and Dogmatic

"Let all the house of Israel therefore know assuredly that God has made him both Lord and Christ, this Jesus whom you crucified" (Acts 2:36). Thus Peter, a Jew, speaking to Jews about Jesus' resurrection, concluded the first Christian sermon ever preached. Later Paul, apostle to the Gentiles, wrote: "If you confess with your mouth that Jesus is Lord and believe in your heart that God raised him from the dead, you will be saved" (Rom. 10:9). "Jesus Christ is Lord" (Phil. 2:11). This confession is the primary theological affirmation of the New Testament. Led through many circumstances to pursue the implications of this affirmation, early Christians came eventually to embrace many other affirmations, affirmations about God, humankind, and the world in which they lived. They even affirmed that the kingdoms of this world would pass away and "become the kingdom of our Lord and of his Christ" in the day when God makes "all things new" (Rv. 11:15; 21:5).

Naturally there was a need to interpret these primal affirmations, preserved in Scripture, that new converts might be initiated into the Christian faith and that this faith itself might be clarified over against competing options. This led the church to the formulation of Christian doctrine. Inevitably the believing community reflected, in turn, on the implications of these doctrines of "the faith . . . once for all delivered to the saints" (Jude 3). As Christian thinkers sought to relate one doctrine to another and thus bring the several parts into a larger whole, Christian theology as we know it today was born. In this particular book we shall be concerned with Christian theology in its systematic and dogmatic expression, beginning with the question, How do we understand and define these terms? What do we mean when we speak of *Christian, systematic,* and *dogmatic theology*?

First, a word on the noun *theology.* This is a book about theology because the ultimate subject of our study is God. Even when we are not speaking directly of him in the mystery of his being and attributes, we shall seek to address whatever subject is before us from the perspective of his self-revelation. Such an approach does not mean, of course, that we will ignore the insights of reason or the data of sense perception. Whenever the church has sought to theologize in a way that ignores such truths, it has done so to its own hurt. But we are saying that truth in this immanent sense, truth that we can discover for ourselves as we rationally transcend, reflect upon, and learn from our experience, is not the primary concern of theology. Theology, rather, has to do with truth that comes to us from God, and therefore it rests on revelation.

Hence, to use an illustration, when we affirm the doctrine of creation, we will simply affirm what the church has always taught, namely, that the world cannot be understood and explained in terms of itself. Rather, it must be understood in terms of its origin in the purpose of God, a purpose mysteriously actualized in a mighty act of divine power that we call "creation." Yet if we are adequately to express such a doctrine in our day, we must reckon with current scientific thought. We cannot speak as though scientists who postulate an expanding universe never lived. Advances in the areas of astrophysics, geology, and the like do impinge upon our theological understanding of the origin and nature of the world. Therefore we are bound to reflect these scientific advances when we seek to frame a doctrine of the creation of the world.

And the same is true of the doctrine that humankind is created in the divine image. Such a theological understanding of the human species does not mean that we can ignore the question of biological evolution, as though Darwin had never written *On the Origin of Species.* By the same token, we cannot ignore the evidence for fossil races of which we learn in physical anthropology, even though our concern is not with the morphology of ancient hominids but with the unity and antiquity of the human race in sin and grace, an obviously theological matter. Again, when we discuss the subject of salvation we shall be concerned with God's mighty acts of salvation culminating in Jesus Christ and in the redeeming work of his Spirit, the Spirit who unites sinners in a fellowship called the church. But what we have to say concerning these matters cannot be said apart from considerations related to the critical use of history, psychology, and sociology. Nevertheless, this is a book about theology, not history, psychology, or sociology. We are ultimately concerned not with the truths discovered by reason but with the truth revealed by God, truth that comes to us in Jesus Christ, to whom the Scriptures bear witness.

We have qualified our study of theology as the study of *Christian* theology. The adjective *Christian* distinguishes the theology we shall do from those theologies done from other religious perspectives. This is not to say that we deny the possibility of truth in other religions, but it is to say that we look upon efforts to find the final meaning and purpose of life outside the circle of Christian faith as inadequate at best. Of course, we do not make such a judgment simplistically. Christian thought will, for example, reflect much more affinity with Jewish thought than with Muslim thought. The larger part of the Christian Bible is made up of the Jewish Scriptures, and he whom Christians confess as Lord was a first-century Palestinian Jew. So also were his apostles, who first proclaimed the message on which the Christian church is founded. Indeed, the members of the parent church in Jerusalem not only acknowledged that their faith was Jewish in its antecedents, but considered themselves Jews in the ongoing practice and confession of their faith as Christians. And rightly so! It is unfortunate that Christian theologians have thought and written as though a Jew could not be a Christian and at the same time a Jew. A truly Christian theology will rather acknowledge that Christian thought bears a unique relationship to Jewish thought, since it accepts the Jewish Scriptures as containing that revelation which anticipates and gives meaning to the final revelation of God in Jesus Christ. Thus this final revelation of God is a revelation of the God of the Jews, the God who himself became incarnate as the Jew, Jesus of Nazareth. Obviously, Christian thought has no such relation with Islamic, Buddhist, or Hindu thought, or, for that matter, with any other religious thought.

However, to speak of Christian theology is to reflect a perspective that differs from that of other theologies, even Jewish theology.[1] Though we acknowledge these differences, we do not see it as a function of a book on Christian theology to engage in the eristic (apologetic) task of demonstrating the truth of Christian theology over against these other theological options. Not that Christians should avoid the challenge of giving a reason for the hope that is in them (1 Pt. 3:15); but we conceive the theologian's task as elaborating rather than defending the content of the Christian faith. We simply assume, then, when we describe our subject as *Christian* theology, that God has uniquely and finally revealed himself in Jesus Christ, and that our theology is but a reasoned elaboration of our confession of Jesus as the Christ. Christian theology is thought from within the circle of

---

1. For a normative statement of Jewish theology, see Franz Rosenzweig, *The Star of Redemption* (Boston: Beacon Press, 1972), translated from the 1930 edition.

faith in Christ. It is thought; but it is believing thought, thought which reflects commitment to Christ as well as reflection upon the implications of that commitment. Christian theology is an elaboration of the implicit content of the original confession that makes one a Christian. It is, in other words, the spelling out of the larger meaning of that primary affirmation with which Christian theology began in the first place: Jesus Christ is Lord!

We have further qualified our study as Christian *systematic* theology. Here we describe our task with a term that is troublesome to many. They would not object to doing theology—they believe in God. Nor would they hesitate to describe the theology that they do as Christian—they freely confess themselves believers in Jesus Christ. But "systematic" has over-tones of system-building, a project in which one easily succumbs to a (supposed) Greek, in contrast to a biblical, ideal of truth. The Greeks were the first logicians and philosophers, and as such they sought to achieve an overarching, all-inclusive, rational understanding of life and the universe. Granted, that is a noble ideal; it is still, many would argue, a deceptive one insofar as Christian theology is concerned. For it is an ideal that does not rest upon divinely given revelation but rather assumes the competence of autonomous reason to discover whatever truth can be known. Others have even gone so far as to charge that the dream of containing the truth in a rational system, such as the philosophers have sought to construct, is an instance of hubris, "original sin at the intellectual level" (Brunner). To try to contain the truth of the Christian faith in a logical system is, in any case, to lose it; it is to change theology into philosophy. Furthermore, it is argued, at the practical level such system-building has tended to fracture the church, as one system is pitted against another in unending controversy.

Along with these traditional hazards, many would further insist that the vast expansion of knowledge in our own day has made it impossible to write a systematic theology, despite our intention. We must, then, have a more modest agenda that does not aspire to encompass the whole of Christian faith in a system. This more modest agenda is reflected in the way contemporary theology is done: it takes the form of many theologies— "black," "feminist," "liberation," "narrative," "relational," "liturgical," and so on. Theology in our day is the theology *of* this or that. It may be the theology of hope, of play, of work, of death and dying; but whatever it is, it can no longer be systematic theology.

While we would readily admit there is truth in much of the above argument, we would also have to register a demur. First of all, even in the days of Catholic (and Protestant) scholasticism, dominated by "sys-tematic" theology, there was never one theology, but only theologies written from different perspectives, whether these perspectives were

Greek (Eastern) or Roman (Western); and beginning with the Reformation they became Lutheran, Calvinist, Anglican, Arminian, Liberal, etc. Protestants, moreover, never have canonized any system as such. While they have subscribed to the authority of biblical revelation, they have never acknowledged the final authority of any theologian's interpretation of that revelation. Systematic theology did not arise out of an ill-advised attempt to say the last word on the meaning of biblical revelation. It rather arose out of an ongoing need in the church: expounding and relating the doctrines Christians have confessed, in order that believers may be better instructed and the Christian vision more clearly defined over against other religious options.

In this regard it is interesting to note that Calvin, the great systematician of the Reformation, was not inspired by the ideal of Greek philosophy. Consequently he did not attempt, as did St. Thomas, to construct a *Summa Theologiae.* His *Institutes of the Christian Religion,* which first appeared while he was in his mid-twenties, was a little book with a more modest agenda. Its purpose was to set forth the truths of the gospel in an orderly (systematic) way so that the common folk might know what the Scriptures taught and so that those who had heard what heretics the Protestants were might better understand what they actually believed. True, Calvin reworked the *Institutes,* till in the final edition the book attained the size generally expected of treatises on systematic theology. But he really never changed the essential nature of the work. It remained an effort to set forth the content of the Christian faith in an orderly manner for purpose of instruction in the Christian church. And this is the meaning we are giving the adjective *systematic* when we speak of theology not only as Christian but as systematic.

Of course, setting forth Christian doctrines "in an orderly fashion" means, for the systematician, more than simply listing various doctrines seriatim, like so many beads on a string. It is inevitable, given the nature of the human mind, that Christians, who believe in the God revealed in Christ, should reflect on the implications of their faith by seeking to show how the several aspects of Christian truth are related to one another. If God is one, how is he related as the Father to the Son and to the Spirit in whom he reveals himself? If God really does sovereignly rule over his creation, how is this divine freedom related to our human freedom? If sinners are justified freely by God's grace, how are we to understand this "salvation by grace alone" in the light of the many scriptural admonitions to good works and the pursuit of "holiness without which no one will see the Lord" (Heb. 12:14)? Can it be that we are unable to do the good (Rom. 8:8) and yet somehow responsible for failing to do it

(Mk. 12:30)? These and many more illustrations that could be given raise inevitable questions of order, not simply in terms of sequence, but of a deeper coherence that makes the many doctrines Christians embrace parts of the one faith they confess.

But as soon as one sets oneself the task of suggesting how these various affirmations—such as divine sovereignty and free will; salvation by grace and good works—are related, one is on the way to becoming a "systematic" theologian. Not, to be sure, in the sense that philosophers have striven to achieve a system without paradox or mystery; but in the sense that one perceives the multifaceted nature of Christian truth and seeks to express that truth in such a way that the various parts of which it is made up are seen in the light of the larger whole, a whole that gives the parts their larger, *in situ* meaning.

Finally, we have qualified our study not only as Christian, not only as systematic, but also as *dogmatic* theology.[2] If the word "systematic" is problematic to many, surely the word "dogmatic" is more so. We live, as we are often reminded, in a day of tolerant pluralism, not of dogmatic narrowness, especially in matters theological. In looking back on our historical antecedents, as the heirs of the Western world and especially as members of the Christian church, we see how the fellowship of the church has been torn apart by dogmatic controversies, even to the shedding of blood and the loss of life.

> Torquemada's name with clouds o'ercast
> Looms in the distant landscape of the past
> Like a burnt tower upon a blackened heath,
> Lit by the fires of burning woods beneath.[3]

Besides being involved in such internecine controversy, too often the church has also imperiled its reputation as the custodian of the truth by its ill-advised and dogmatic opposition to the scientific enterprise. Not that the church has a corner on dogmaticism—science too has its dogmaticisms—but it sometimes seems that the more wrong the church has been, the more dogmatic it has become in defending itself. One is reminded of the preacher who wrote in the margin of her sermon notes, "Here argument

2. The adjectives "systematic" and "dogmatic" are sometimes used synonymously. What is dogmatic theology on the European side of the Atlantic is systematic theology on the American side. The indigenous theology of the Asian and African churches does not reflect a marked preference at this point. This may be due in part to the fact that the theologizing of the younger churches has often had other agendas.

3. Henry W. Longfellow, *Tales of a Wayside Inn,* conclusion of "The Theologian's Tale, Torquemada."

is weak, increase volume in presentation."[4] Yet the word "dogmatic" need not connote the arrogant, magisterial, and opinionated.

The noun "dogma" has been used in the church to refer to a doctrine or body of doctrines held by many, over a long period of time, to be true and authoritative, and therefore to be proclaimed with conviction. Such definitive and authoritative statements, though of long standing, are not so far infallible, for the Protestant at least, as to be beyond revision. Yet to speak of Christian theology as *dogmatic* is to acknowledge that any effort to revise the content of the Christian faith in terms of the present without regard to the past is simply a veiled rejection of Christian theology. There is no such thing as Christian theology that is simply a now-for-the-time-being theology. Christian theology is concerned with Jesus Christ; not the Jesus Christ remade in our contemporary image but the Jesus Christ who is the same "yesterday and today and for ever" (Heb. 13:8). Therefore, Christian theology is concerned with truths that escape their times, even the historical times and cultures in and out of which the theologians defending these truths have spoken.

To the extent, therefore, that theological formulations of the past have sustained the test of time, they constitute guidelines that help succeeding generations in their thinking about God. We would not press the claim of those widely believed theological truths to the extreme of simply identifying Christian truth with a given historical expression of it; yet neither would we so contextualize the truth that the context becomes the message. While everything that is said theologically is said in a certain way, the *way* it is said is not synonymous with *what* is said. Christian theology rests not on the context (history and culture) of the theologian doing theology, but on the revelation of the one Lord Jesus Christ whom we confess in faith, a faith that is one and that is sealed by a baptism that is one (Eph. 4:5). Hence, beneath the relativities of the many statements of the faith confessed by the church one can discern an underlying, ongoing continuity. Theology has to do not with the subjective perspective that the theologian brings to her work—at least not primarily—but with the objective body of truth with which she works. And it is the task of theology to articulate this truth

4. Throughout this study we shall ordinarily use the feminine pronoun of the human subject, rather than the generic masculine, not to exclude men but to highlight the inclusion of women in the contemporary task of theologizing. We shall revert to the traditional masculine usage when dealing with the divine attributes, since in that discussion we shall use feminine nouns and pronouns of the Deity. See below, Unit Four. For a brief discussion of our reservations with the latter usage, see this Unit, III, Addendum: A Comment on Sexist Language, pp. 44ff. Also Unit Three, IV, E, Sexist Language and the Doctrine of the Trinity, pp. 323ff.

so that it is both a legacy of the past, a faith once delivered, and at the same time a word for the present, a truth that we hold because it is the truth by which we are held.

> There is an out-thereness of biblical truth which is to be seen, whatever the angle of vision, and however the view of it is affected by the glasses we are wearing. . . , a hard core of information at the center of our perceptions and interpretations.[5]

EXCURSUS:
CONCERNING THEOLOGY AND THEOLOGIES

In the above discussion of the sense in which we consider "systematic" to be a legitimate description of Christian theology, we rejected what might be called the "*Summa* complex." This propensity for system-building is by no means dead. (In this regard the student may read with profit Kenneth Hamilton's strictures on Tillich's *Systematic Theology* in his *The System and the Gospel,* Grand Rapids: Eerdmans, 1967.) However, though system-making, which turns theology into philosophy, is still with us, proliferation rather than system-making is in vogue today. We have deemed it worthwhile, therefore, to comment briefly here on various types of theology, in the interest of further clarifying our own position. As we have already intimated, no one can escape doing theology from some perspective. As soon as an adjective is used to describe the noun "theology," even though it be as inclusive as the adjective "Christian," a choice has been made that says a great deal about the character of one's theology. Of the many possible perspectives, some make more difference in the end, and some less; and some are more exclusive of other options than others. And while many may be easy to describe, they can be hard to classify in terms of a larger schematization. Therefore we shall make no effort, in the ensuing comments, to enter into all the questions that might be raised or even to mention all the possible perspectives from which theology is done. We rather wish simply to say a word about those perspectives that help to focus our own, so that the reader may understand whence we come as we embark on the task of theologizing.

*   *   *   *   *

We begin with the term *evangelical.* Our approach may be described as evangelical in two senses of the word. First of all, it is evangelical in the traditional sense that we

---

5. Gabriel Fackre, *The Christian Story*, vol. I (Grand Rapids: Eerdmans, 1978), p. 15. One here recalls the comment of Dorothy Sayers that theology is not like science when it comes to "making progress." The old metaphors are not superseded any more than Agamemnon is superseded by Hamlet. See Dorothy Sayers, *The Mind of the Maker* (San Francisco: Harper, 1941), p. 44.

believe that saving grace is mediated by the Spirit primarily through the proclamation of the *evangel,* that is, the gospel. The spoken word takes precedence over the visible word of the sacraments as a "means of grace." Our theological perspective, therefore, may be called "evangelical" in contrast to "sacramental." Second, our approach is "evangelical" in the contemporary sense that it assumes: (*a*) a high view of Scripture as the Word of God written and of the person of Christ as the eternal Son of God; (*b*) the mandate to preach the gospel to the whole world; (*c*) the need of personal conversion, evidenced by the confession of Jesus as Lord; and (*d*) a commitment to social justice. When we use "evangelical" in this sense to describe our theological stance we mark it off from one that may be called "liberal."

Liberal theology, as grounded in the thought of Kant and Schleiermacher (see the latter's *The Christian Faith,* Edinburgh: Clark, 1928), has been given its most consistent expression in the works of such German theologians as Ritschl and Harnack. This liberal theological tradition differs from our own primarily in its view of Christ and the Scriptures that bear witness to him. As for Christ, theological liberalism understands the Incarnation not as an act of the Son of God, a divine person who assumed our humanity, but as a description of the unique quality of Jesus' life as a first-century Palestinian Jew. That special quality was Jesus' openness to God as his Father and his love of neighbor, a love in which the kingdom of God is manifested. In this openness to God, Jesus actualized the potential for the divine that we all possess. As we emulate his example, we too achieve salvation and bring in the kingdom of God by social progress. Jesus, then, is the first Christian and for this reason may be called God's "Son" by way of preeminence.

As for Scripture, theological liberalism understands the Bible, as it understands the person of the Redeemer, primarily in human categories. The Bible is essentially a human book whose message is *inspiring*—insofar as it is consonant with contemporary thought-categories—but not *inspired* in the sense that the authors were guided in a unique way by God's Spirit in what they wrote. This means that liberal theologians are open to the more radical conclusions of biblical criticism, though even they have drawn the line on the historicity of Jesus (S. J. Case, et al.), defending the proposition that Jesus of Nazareth actually lived and died. (As H. J. Cadbury, the late Hollis Professor of Divinity at Harvard, once observed in class, "crucified under Pontius Pilate" is the one statement in the creed [we all] can affirm.) Liberal theologians, of course, are devout believers in God; this one God, however, has many names. In our day, such theology frequently draws its philosophical inspiration not only from German Idealism but also from Process philosophy, viewing "process" rather than "being" as the ultimate category of thought. Given such an approach, even God is in some sense "in process," not only living but growing and learning as he lures the process (history) to ever new and creative possibilities.

*   *   *   *   *

Liberation theology is theology done from the perspective of the "existential" situation in which the author lives and works. It may be either evangelical or liberal, Protestant or Catholic. The primary instance today is the theology done mainly by Catholic but also Protestant theologians in South America. These theologians seek to speak a liberating word on behalf of the poor and oppressed. While the authors themselves are generally not among the disinherited for whom they speak, they have identified with them, as did Walter Rauschenbusch and others in North America who at the turn of the century stressed the social implications of the gospel. The various expressions of liberation theology, of course, reflect significant differences of nuance. The more radical make the concrete situation rather than the Scripture the "text" with which theology begins, though the latter is not ignored. Thus the traditional methodology, which begins with Scripture and applies it to the situation, is reversed.

Many expressions of liberation theology, in South America but increasingly in North America as well, also repudiate capitalism and seek to draw insight from Marxist economic theory. This use of Marxist thought is understandably difficult for many (especially North Americans) to accept. But it should be remembered that the use of insights gained from one part of Marxist thought does not entail accepting all the anti-Christian elements of Marxism as well. Nor should we allow our justifiable repudiation of Marxism as a worldview to obscure the truth that fundamental elements of liberation theology arise out of the Christian doctrine of God. The God of the Christian is the God of justice and compassion who in Scripture reveals himself as the Liberator of the poor and the captive. He is the God who identifies with them in that he himself became incarnate as a peasant having no place to lay his head (Mt. 8:20). Liberation themes, therefore, can be found, at least implicitly, in all theologies that are authentically biblical. (For a general statement of Latin American liberation theology see Gustavo Gutiérrez, *A Theology of Liberation,* Maryknoll, N.Y.: Orbis, 1971. See also Robert McAfee Brown, *Theology in a New Key,* Philadelphia: Westminster, 1978.)

*   *   *   *   *

Besides liberation theology, which in its various South American expressions protests the exploitation of the poor, there are other expressions of liberation theology, especially in North America, which protest oppression in the form of racism and patriarchalism. As a protest against racism, *black* theology was given its first concrete expression at the time of the American civil rights struggle in the sixties; but it has its roots in the much older struggle of the black church in America, the church that gave the people of God the spirituals. As done today, black theology is theology written from the perspective of the black experience in America. Some of its themes have also surfaced in African theology. (The initial book on black theology, as such, was James Cone's *Black Theology and Black Power,* New York: Seabury, 1969. See also C. Salley and R. Behm, *Your God is Too White,* Downers Grove: InterVarsity, 1970, and especially Cone's *God of the Oppressed,* New York: Seabury Press, 1972.) Black theology, like all liberation theology, has its more conservative and its more radical exponents; but its message cannot be ignored by any who seek to do theology from a biblical point of view.

When we speak of that liberation theology which protests patriarchalism, we are referring to what is commonly called *feminist* theology. This theology is also done from an existential perspective, namely, that of being a woman in a male-dominated society. Christian feminists have compelled many male systematicians to restate the doctrine of anthropology so as to transform the hierarchical pattern of sexual relationships into one of mutual enablement and service. So far as the doctrine of the church is concerned, this implies the right of women to ordination. At a more fundamental level it also involves one's doctrine of God and the need to struggle creatively with the basic language of theology, which has projected the masculinity of the theologian on the God of whom he speaks.

In its more radical forms, feminist theology goes beyond this worthy agenda and works with traditions outside the Judeo-Christian faith altogether. Such efforts often draw on the female symbolism of ancient religions and reject the masculine language and symbols used in Scripture of God and of Christ. In the words that Mary Daly used to entitle her well-known book (Boston: Beacon Press, 1973), the task of theology is to get "Beyond God the Father."

These more radical forms of feminist thought should not blind the evangelical student of theology to the valid biblical word being spoken by feminist theologians concerning the equal place of women with men inside and outside the church. (The first to hear this word, by the way, were the Quakers, who also pioneered in the struggle against slavery in antebellum America. In 1667, Margaret Fell, the wife of George Fox, founder of the Society of Friends, wrote a pamphlet entitled *Women's Speaking Justified, Approved and Allowed of by the Scriptures.* See Patricia Wilson-Kastner, *Faith, Feminism and the Christ,* Philadelphia: Fortress, 1983, for an able contemporary statement of feminist perspectives within an orthodox frame of reference.) Progress, however, has not come easily. Women have had to face not only the traditional chauvinism of white theologians but also the machismo of Latin theologians. Furthermore, as blacks have been restricted to the balcony of white churches, so women have been kept in the pews of black churches.

Liberation theology, black theology, feminist theology—all are forms of protest theology. From them many positive lessons can be learned. After all, Protestant theology gets its very name from the "protest" lodged by certain German Reformed princes at the Diet of Speier in 1529. But along with the positive there are also the negative lessons. In any theology of protest, whether it be against political and economic oppression of the poor, male oppression of the "other" sex, or racial oppression of ethnic minorities, there is the danger that one will be enticed by "the issue" away from the true center and concern of all Christian theology, namely, the God revealed in Jesus Christ. This is what happens when salvation is reduced, with the help of Marxist analysis, to economic liberation here and now; or when faith can no longer confess that Jesus is Lord because Jesus is a male and the male is the enemy; or when Jesus becomes a black revolutionary who died to liberate black Jews from white Romans, etc.

*   *   *   *   *

Along with these theologies reflecting the existential circumstances in which theology is done, there are also theologies, such as *historical* and *biblical* theology, whose perspective is shaped by the materials of the discipline. Of course, the methodological approach that a given scholar brings to such disciplines is not without consequence for the conclusions reached. Because this is so, we must comment on our own understanding of the relationship of these two disciplines to systematic theology. As for biblical theology, it should not, in our judgment, be loosed from its moorings in systematic theology. A biblical theology that is not in the service of systematics, but in lieu of it, is not a theology really free to hear what the Bible has to say. And why? Because biblical theology, done in conscious rejection of systematics, will gravitate away from normative to descriptive statements. It will turn biblical theology into theologies—Pauline theology, Petrine theology—and these, in turn, will become sub-categories of the history of religions. By contrast, when biblical theology is done in the service of systematics, it lays the foundation for the latter discipline, which is viewed as the orderly setting out of the teachings of Scripture. Thus systematics builds upon and integrates that which is done in biblical theology. The two disciplines, then, have a complementary rather than an adversative relationship. (The student may consult with profit in this regard the works of G. Ernest Wright, such as his *God Who Acts,* London: SCM Press, 1952.)

The same is true of the relation of *historical* theology to systematic theology. The discipline of historical theology is essential to systematics, for no systematician can ignore the past. Even the most sincere effort to be faithful to the Protestant principle of *sola Scriptura* is but pious arrogance if one attempts to do a theology of the Word without knowing how that Word has been understood in the past. (Otto Weber begins his dogmatics with an entire section on the history of dogmatics. See his *Foundations of Dogmatics,* Grand Rapids: Eerdmans, 1981-83 and the five-volume series of Jaroslav Pelikan, *The Christian Tradition,* Chicago: University of Chicago Press, beginning in 1971.) The Holy Spirit did not cease to be present in the world when the canon of Scripture was closed. Nor does the Spirit's effectual calling whereby we are made "contemporaneous" with the Christ of the first century (Kierkegaard) mean that we can ignore the ongoing work of the Spirit in the intervening centuries of church history, for the church is the mother of us all, the theologian as well as others. Systematic theology, in other words, though it rests on Scripture, must be informed by tradition.

* * * * *

To "define" further our own position, a few concluding remarks of a somewhat mis-cellaneous character are in order. Those who do biblical theology in the way we have advocated it should be done—that is, in the service of systematic theology—have used such concepts as "covenant" (Walter Eichrodt, *Theology of the Old Testament,* London: SCM Press, 1967) and "history," qualified as "salvation history," *Heilsgeschichte* (Oscar Cullmann, *Salvation As History,* New York: Harper, 1967), to integrate the biblical data. As for the "covenant approach," it has been used by systematicians also. This covenant theology—or "federal theology," as it is sometimes called—when given systematic form, has influenced our own thinking. We look upon God's redeeming act in Jesus Christ as fulfilling the covenant of grace, as making good God's gracious promise and engagement to save his people from their sins.

The "salvation history" approach has also influenced our thinking. God's covenan-tal acts are events in history. Inasmuch as this salvation history, which moves in and through ordinary history, is a matter of events (acts of God) and their interpretation, systematic theology betrays its Christian trust if it shifts the ground of theologizing from history to the realm of ideas (metaphysics). "Jesus died" is the event that the New Testament reports; "for me" is the interpretation that the New Testament gives to the event reported. Event and interpretation together constitute the bedrock revelation on which further theological interpretation is based as the church reflects upon its faith. We cannot say, with Albert Schweitzer, that though Jesus was an "incomparably great man," it would make no difference for Christian faith, in the last analysis, had Jesus never lived. In our own theologizing, the historical character of the Jesus event, as reported in the Gospels, makes all the difference in the world.

Hence, when we draw insights from "narrative" or "story" theology, we will assume that the biblical story is to be understood historically, in contrast to those who accept the more radical conclusions of historical criticism. The story that unfolds in the Bible is "true to life" not only in that it awakens a response in the hearer whose perception of authentic existence is deepened by the story; it is also true in the traditional sense that it rests upon objective events. This does not mean that we will look upon the Bible as a simple reporting of historical fact from cover to cover. Such an approach, in our judgment, is fraught with difficulty, especially when applied to the primal history of Genesis 1–11 with which the Bible begins, and to the Apocalypse with which it ends. We do not understand the opening chapters of Genesis as science nor the book of Revelation as Monday morning's headlines on Sunday. But neither is the biblical story, for us, a fiction like the myths of ancient Greece. The story that the Bible tells always has, in its beginning as well as in its denouement, contact with history unfolding in this world of time and space. Hence the fall of humankind is a story of a fall *in* history, not *into* history (as with the Greeks). Furthermore, sinners are redeemed by One who was not only "crucified under Pontius Pilate" but who also was raised "on the third day" and appeared to his disciples over a period of forty days (Acts 1:3).

Finally, the theological approach we shall advocate will be recognized as "orthodox" in the sense that it is rooted both in the old catholic tradition (Nicaea, Chalcedon) and in the Reformation, particularly the Genevan Reformation, with its emphasis on the Augustinian and Calvinistic understanding of Paul. We do not believe that the older orthodoxy has been dissolved in the acids of modernity (Walter Lippmann). At the same time it will be recognized that our statement of this older orthodoxy has been impacted by the thought of the modern world in which we live.

While it is orthodox theology, it is orthodox theology consciously done in the context of life and thought in the contemporary world. That is to say, it is "contextualized orthodoxy," an orthodoxy which, like all contextual theology, seeks to listen as well as to affirm.

"Contextualized" theology, "charismatic" theology, "proclamation" theology, "propositional theology," "remnant" theology, "relational" theology, and so on. We could go on listing theology's many adjectives, but were we to do so, time would fail us. Like the author of Hebrews, therefore, we must go on to other things.

II. Theological Method:
Philosophy, Science, and Theology

In the foregoing section we have had occasion to allude to both philosophy and science, and with reason, for these are among the great enterprises of the human spirit. From what we have said, it is obvious that we believe they are somehow related to theology. Just how is a matter we hope to clarify as we probe the question of theological method.

We begin with *philosophy*. Though we have mentioned many kinds of theology, one we have not mentioned is "philosophical" theology. The reason is that philosophical theology addresses the introductory, foundational issues of the discipline; hence it involves, among others, the question of methodology, the subject with which we are now concerned.[1] Our previous discussion reflects the fact that many theologians have viewed philosophy as the enemy. Probably the most jaundiced view was that of Luther, who came to regard Aristotle as the bane of all theology, and who said he would have held him to be the devil himself had he not had flesh. In more modern times it has been the vogue (especially in biblical theology) to compare and contrast Greek thought with biblical thought in such a way as to echo Tertullian's defiant question: What has Athens to do with Jerusalem?

But if the marriage of theology and philosophy has proven stressful, their divorce has never been final. The reason is not hard to see. Both Jews and Greeks, theologians and philosophers, are, by the theologian's own admission, creatures of one and the same God, whose image they bear.

---

1. What we here allude to as "philosophical" theology is called "fundamental" or "foundational" theology by many Roman Catholics. Since Ebeling, such terms have also been used by Protestants to describe the method and task of theology.

How, then, can the thought of the one be completely antithetical to that of the other? Furthermore, the questions philosophers and theologians address are of the same ultimate character. It is quite impossible, then, that theologians should pursue their task wholly without recourse to the tools of thought which the philosophers have honed. Augustine was, after his conversion, no longer a Neoplatonist, but a Christian who did theology as a Christian. Yet the influence of Platonic and Neoplatonic thought on his theologizing is obvious enough. And who can read Thomas without hearing what "the Philosopher" (Aristotle) has to say on many things. Even Luther and Calvin, for all their emphasis on Paul, reflect a familiarity with the major thinkers of Greek and Roman antiquity. And one can hardly understand Schleiermacher if one knows nothing of Kant. In more recent times, theologians have had much to say about Existentialism (whose father was the Danish philosopher Kierkegaard) as well as the Neo-Personalism of Ebner and Buber. Likewise, the Process thought of such philosophers as Whitehead and Hartshorne has spawned an entire school of contemporary theology called "Process Theology," which rests on the axiom that "becoming," not "being," is the ultimate category of reality. Hence, God himself is a part of the process, as we have observed, luring history to ever new and creative possibilities.

Yet for all its influence on theology, philosophy is not theology, and theology—when rightly done—is not philosophy. Though both philosophers and theologians are lovers of wisdom, the wisdom the philosopher seeks is quite different from that of which the theologian speaks. That is to say, philosophy and theology differ in a fundamental way. Philosophy is the human quest for truth. It begins with the thinking self (*cogito ergo sum*—Descartes) seeking for itself answers about itself and its world, the world of time and space. For philosophy, humanity's unique powers of rational transcendence, which make such a quest possible, are autonomous. Therefore philosophy seeks, apart from revelation, to construct a system of truth that will be self-consistent and self-contained, giving meaning to the world and to our lives in the world. True, this dream of *Geist* has become less grandly speculative since the triumph of the natural sciences, but the truth that concerns philosophers remains truth about the ultimate meaning of reality that is discovered by the thinking self. The question of how one comes to know this ultimate reality (the question of epistemology) and what the nature of this reality is (the questions of ontology and metaphysics) have evoked many different answers. But at bottom the method is the same: philosophy is concerned with truth accessible to reason alone. By contrast, the truth of which the theologian speaks is that truth given by divine revelation and received by faith. And if the theologian is a Christian theologian, it is the truth revealed *in Christ,* the truth that "destroys the wisdom of the world." The theologian's "truth," in other words, is a divine wisdom that makes foolish the wisdom of the world and appears foolish, in turn, to this world (1 Cor. 1:18ff.).

Yet for the theologian there is no *sacrificium intellectus,* no abandoning of reason to make room for the faith that embraces this truth. Rather, reason becomes a reason open to the truth given in revelation, truth that comes to us in a divine self-disclosure. While such truth does not conflict with truth discovered by rational inference working with the data of sense perception, to speak of truth "given," in distinction to truth "discovered," is nonetheless to speak in a way that entails a different methodology. To speak thus is to gain the insight that came to the young Augustine, while listening to Ambrose preach, that the Christian message is not about the ascent of the human spirit to God, but God's descent to humankind. In other words, the methodologies of philosophy and theology move in opposite directions. This present world is not perceived by the theologian, as it is by the philosopher, as having its own immanental meaning to be discovered by reason. Such a rational quest leads in the end to the conclusion of the Preacher, "Vanity of vanities! All is vanity" (Eccl. 1:2). Rather than having its meaning in itself, the world has its meaning in the purpose and counsel of God. And to live in the hope that this purpose will be fulfilled in the manifestation of God's glorious kingdom, the new heaven and the new earth, is, for the theologian, what it means to live meaningfully.

The ambivalence in the ongoing relationship between philosophy and theology makes it inevitable that some theologians will be more inclined, some less, to use philosophic tools in doing theology. Furthermore, there is bound to be a great difference in the philosophical orientation a given theologian will find helpful. (Some philosophic orientations—materialism, nihilism, atheism—are, of course, of no help to any who do theology. This is not to say, however, that they are of no concern to the theologian. See, for example, Helmut Thielicke's nearly two hundred pages devoted to "Theology in Self-Grounded Secularity" in his *The Evangelical Faith,* Grand Rapids: Eerdmans, 1974, vol. II, pp. 219ff.) Because of the different ways theologians employ philosophic concepts, we will try to locate ourselves, for the reader's benefit, on the broad spectrum of methodological possibility.

It goes without saying that as we do theology we will reflect a general affinity with Idealism rather than Naturalism because of the recognition in the former tradition that the human spirit is related to the eternal world of the Ideas (Plato) and is therefore grounded, in some sense, in the realm of the transcendent, what the Germans have called *"das Jenseits der Welt."* More particularly, we have been helped in doing theology by the insights of Existentialism and Neo-Personalism. To do theology in a proper way, in our judgment, is to think existentially, that is, in terms of one's concrete, individual, sinful, human existence. So far as doing Christian theology is concerned, this means that the theologian is placed before the same choice which the early Christians faced, a choice for (or against) Jesus Christ. Such a choice, when positively made, means that one's thought as a theologian is believing thought, thought from within the circle of faith. Christian faith, as Kierkegaard once said, is the cross on which speculation is crucified. (He had in mind the system of Hegel.) Since theology, if it is evangelical, arises out of the evangel, the good news that God in Christ is the reconciled God, a proper study of theology must embrace a positive response to this God, a "divine/human encounter," as Brunner would say. Faith, then, is not simply one of the loci of theology; it is theology's preface, its *prolegomenon*. And theology is faith's implication, faith's thinking itself out, faith's ongoing decision.

Given such a theological method, the student of theology will no longer view the doctrine of the divine omnipresence (to use a random illustration) as a mere theory; rather, in Jeremy Taylor's phrase, she will "practice the presence of God." In other words, the end of all true theology will be morality. It is our persuasion that as a methodology, Existentialism illumines the truth that what we should believe and what we should do are two sides of the same coin. To be sure, since the use of Existentialism is, for the theologian, methodological, it may be used also by those who have little in common with evangelical theology or, for that matter, with theology of any sort. (See J. Rodman Williams, *Contemporary Existentialism and Christian Faith*, Englewood Cliffs: Prentice-Hall, 1965, where the author deals with the thought of prominent existentialists like Sartre, Jaspers, Heidegger, Tillich, and Bultmann—and their concerns with such affirmations as "the Centrality of Humankind," the "Obscurity of God," the "Finality of Death," etc., hardly the leading motifs of an evangelical theology!)

While the impact of Existentialism will be evident in our theological method, that of certain other philosophical perspectives will be less so. Process thought, for example, has little to contribute to the way in which we will do theology. True, at the heart of the Christian faith is the doctrine of the Incarnation; God enters into our history in such a way that he too is in our process. But process theologians have in mind no such traditional view of the Incarnation when they speak of the God who is in process. There is no other "realm" or "dimension" whence the eternal Son was sent by his Father when he assumed our humanity and so entered our world of time and space. Rather, for the process theologian God is assumed to be in process as God, not as the Word who became flesh. To our way of thinking this is to deny that God is the Holy One; it is to forget, as Barth would say, that God is in heaven and we are on earth.

The relation between theology and philosophy is not only long-standing but subtle and complex in nature. We have likened it to a marriage that has often been unhappy but never ends in divorce. As we turn to the relation of theology to *science*, we have to do with an encounter not only more recent— and sometimes more acrimonious—but also, in our judgment, more easily defined. The problem, in the final analysis, does not have to do with such particulars as the six days of Genesis 1 versus the vast drafts of time assumed by astronomy and geology to account for the condition of planet earth. Nor is the problem primarily a matter of the evolutionary development of hominid antecedents to homo sapiens as postulated by biologists and anthropologists. The ultimate problem is rather the assumption, made by some (not all) scientists, that the single ontological plane accessible to telescope and microscope is the only plane of reality that exists.

When this point of view is reinforced by the human sciences, matters become intolerable for the theologian. Critical history then reduces revelation to a mere human quest for the divine; psychology shows that this quest for God is but the projection of the human psyche; and sociology shows that our views of reality are the result of cultural consensus. As history posits relativity as a *fact* of the human condition, so the sociology of knowledge posits its *necessity*. The only absolute left is John Dewey's: "Absolutely no Absolutes." God has become, in the blasphemous words of Ernest Haeckel, a "gaseous vertebrate." This loss of transcendence, in the name of science, threatens the entire universe of the theologian (and of everyone else for that matter) with irrelevance. Nevertheless, it is taken to be the only possibility open to those who understand the implications of the scientific method, which calls for rigorous adherence to mathematical law (reason) as verified by appeal to the data of sense perception. Even the imaginative and creative revolutions in science, from Copernicus to Einstein, rest ultimately, it is said, on this sure foundation. This method boasts of the dazzling achievements of modern technology and offers, at last, truth objectively demonstrable and therefore accessible to all.

Needless to say, we do not agree with such Scientism; we do not believe with Laplace that the "God-hypothesis" is unnecessary; we cannot embrace Russell's philosophy of "unyielding despair." Yet, on the other hand, we cannot dismiss an enterprise that leaves human footprints on the moon, banishes smallpox from the land of the living, and, for weal or woe, unlocks the power in the nucleus of the atom. Because we look upon the adversarial relation that has too often prevailed between science and theology as unfortunate, we shall, in our approach, seek to theologize in a way that is open to science, insofar as science has not "left its proper province." Thus we shall try to construct a theology that makes more modest claims than was the case when theology was recognized as the "queen of the sciences." Such a theology will be concerned not with what science says but with what God says. Yet it will be open to science and done with an awareness of what science says, for the truths of science and the truths of theology are ultimately the one truth of the one God.

We might picture this effort in terms of concentric circles on a target. As the circles move out from the truths of revelation at the personal center (God's self-disclosure in Jesus Christ) to the relatively less personal spheres of knowledge, reason becomes more competent and faith less essential.[2] Of course, even when concerned with the formal sciences of logic and mathematics, which are farthest removed from the personal center, the foundational questions will still be illumined, for the Christian, by the revelational center. The insights of reason (math, logic) are a reflection of the Logos, the Light lighting everyone who comes into the world (Jn. 1:9). However, there is no Christian logic or Christian mathematics as such. For theologian and scientist alike, two and two equal four. But matters become more complicated as one moves in toward the personal center of the circle. To affirm that two and two are four is one thing; to affirm that what theologians have called "sin" is simply neurosis is another. It is for this reason that we will increasingly appeal to revelation and faith as we move from the issues raised for theology by astrophysics, geology, and the like to those raised by history, psychology, and sociology.

In implementing the claims of faith and reason, our approach will reflect the distinction between "I-it" and "I-thou" truth. The former is truth gained by the personal self, the I, searching, probing the realm of objects. The latter is truth gained when an "I" relates to a "thou" as to another self in mutual disclosure. Since we analyze objects but meet persons, the difference between "I-it" truth and "I-thou" truth is dimensional in nature (Griesbach).[3] And when this meeting between an I and a "thou" is an encounter between the human "I" and the divine "Thou," the result is truth *given*, in the most ultimate sense, by revelation, in distinction from truth discovered by the human subject. It is truth that is received, therefore, by faith, not inferred by reason and verified by the senses. Such an approach means, of course, that we will seek no black-and-white solutions, equally satisfying in all instances, to the science-faith question. We will rather recognize that the degree of probability attaching to the truth claims of science is greater in some instances and less so in others. To be specific, for us the view of astrophysics that the universe is very old is acceptable to faith. On the other hand, the critical, historical view that Jesus is no more than a religious genius is not acceptable to faith. For faith, the former is settled by measured observation, not by the exegesis of the genealogies in Genesis; the latter by revelation, not by the pontifications of scientific historicism.

2. Emil Bruner has suggested this approach. For a summary of his thoughts at this juncture, see our *Emil Brunner's Concept of Revelation* (London: James Clarke & Co., 1954), especially the section on the law of contiguity (*Beziehungsnähe*), pp. 98-101.

3. Speaking of "dimensional" differences, it is here assumed that what we are saying applies to the macrocosm not the microcosm, where, since Planck and Heisenberg, the division of the world into subject and object seems no longer adequate.

Michael Polanyi, in his *Personal Knowledge* (Chicago: University of Chicago Press, 1958), has reminded us that *all* knowledge has a personal character, since knowers are persons. As for the distinction between "I-it" and "I-thou" knowledge, we have found helpful Ferdinand Ebner's *Das Wort und die geistigen Realitaten, Pneumatologische Fragmente* (Innsbruck: Brenner, 1921), a pioneering work that has been likened to a Copernican revolution in its implications. Also, the well-known *I and Thou* of Buber, which appeared in the original, *Ich und Du,* just two years after Ebner's book (Leipzig: Insel, 1923). No theologian in modern times has more fruitfully pursued this Neo-Personalism as a theological method than Emil Brunner. In fact, his Uppsala Lectures, under the title *Wahrheit als Begegnung* (Zurich: Zwingli, 1963), have, in their English translation, given theology the familiar expression "the divine-human encounter."

From this brief review it can be seen that, when compared to theology, both philosophy and science share a common methodology. To be sure, philosophy is more speculative than science, more given to system-building. But both are concerned with truth that the thinker can discover and validate, whereas theology is concerned with truth received by faith and to which the church bears witness on the basis of divine revelation.

To the age-old question, Is, then, theology a science, or is it not? the answer is obviously no, if one uses the word "science" as it is commonly used today. Yet in another sense it is, inasmuch as it recognizes the validity of both reason and experience, the same reason and experience to which science appeals. As we have intimated, the theologian does not oppose reason in the name of faith, but rather calls upon reason to be open to the truths of faith. And in so doing she imposes limits, not only upon reason in the name of faith, but also upon faith in the name of reason. She recognizes what Luther, standing before the emperor at Worms, called "right reason" (*"helle Grunde,"* sometimes translated "clear arguments") and reminds herself that no one ever broke logic but what logic broke her (McTaggart). The theologian also knows, this side of Copernicus and Galileo, the folly of denying the plain evidence of sense perception. The psalmist may say, "Yea, the world is established, it shall never be moved" (Ps. 96:10); nonetheless the earth moves both on its axis and around the sun. *The theologian, therefore, has no right to affirm something to be true for faith which is false for reason or manifestly contrary to the evidence of sense data.* Hence, theology that is good theology respects the method of science. In fact, it is itself a science in the sense that it is a "branch of systematized knowledge considered as a distinct field of investigation or as the object of study."[4] Though the truths of faith may transcend reason (e.g., the Trinity), and often cannot be verified by observation (e.g., the

---

4. *Webster's New International Dictionary,* 2nd ed., s.v. "science."

presence of the resurrected Christ with his people gathered as a worshipping congregation), yet their theological exposition neither defies reason nor ignores the data of experience. At least it ought not to.[5]

We are constrained to make this last disclaimer because theologians, even great ones, have their unfortunate moments. Thomas, for example, defends the doctrine of transubstantiation by insisting that "the presence of Christ's true body and blood in this sacrament [the Eucharist] cannot be detected by sense, nor understanding, but by faith alone which rests upon divine authority." Of course we would agree that something may be perceived by faith that cannot be perceived by sense; but what of the fact that our senses do clearly perceive bread and wine in the sacrament of communion so that faith does not transcend the sense world in this instance, but denies it? To this he answers that "in this sacrament he [Christ] shows us his flesh in an invisible manner," and quotes Ambrose to the effect that "although the figures of the bread and the wine be seen, still, after the Consecration, they are to be believed to be nothing else than the body and blood of Christ." He goes on to explain that the bread and wine are not present inasmuch as their *substance* is not present. What then do we see, smell, and taste? The accidents only, "for the accidents as discerned by the senses are truly present" (*Summa Theologiae,* New York: Benziger, vol. II, pt. 3, Q. 75, arts. 1, 2, passim). Thus the truth of faith not only transcends, but contradicts sense. Thomas, of course, would not agree. Citing Aristotle, *De Anima* III, that the proper object of the intellect is *substance,* he affirms that the intellect is preserved from deception by faith. "And this serves as answer . . . because faith is not contrary to the senses, but concerns things to which sense does not reach" (ibid., art. 5).

Such unfortunate theological sophistry is known to Protestant theology as well. At Marburg, embroiled in controversy over the presence of Christ in the Supper, Luther declared: "I believe that Christ is in heaven, but also in the sacrament, as substantially as he was in the Virgin's womb. I care not whether it be against nature and reason, provided it be not against faith." Zwingli responded, "Christ ascended to heaven, therefore he cannot be on earth with his body. A body is circumscribed and cannot be in several places at once." Luther: "I care little about mathematics." (See Schaff, *History of the Christian Church,* vol. VII, Grand Rapids: Eerdmans, 1953, p. 642.) And so the truth of faith, as it is made to contradict the senses for Thomas, is also made to contradict reason ("mathematics") for Luther.

---

5. Here Wesley's Quadrilateral—Scripture, faith, experience, reason—comes to mind, each having its part in shaping Christian belief and ordering Christian life.

III. Speaking of God

A. INTRODUCTION

Along with the question of methodology, the theologian faces the question of language. She claims to make affirmations about truths given in revelation and received by faith. When she does so, however, she uses the same words arranged in the same grammatical sentences that philosophers and scientists use when making affirmations about the mundane world, affirmations that are subject to rational proof and empirical verification. How can this be? If God and the world are qualitatively different, is it possible to stretch the language of the creature so as to speak meaningfully of the Creator? Can one build a bridge that will span the gap between earth and heaven?

Some linguistic (analytic) philosophers have answered such questions in the negative. Citing the meaning of language as used by mathematicians and scientists, they have charged that the sentences of theologians are meaningless. This is so, they allege, because the sentences of theologians do not correspond to the two recognized possibilities of all meaningful speech. All sentences are either analytic or synthetic; either their predicate is contained in the subject by a logical inference or they can be verified or falsified by empirical observation. "Rain is a form of precipitation" is an analytically true statement, as anyone can see by checking the dictionary. But the statement "God subsists as three persons eternally" is not analytically true. If we look in a dictionary, the meaning of the word "God" does not entail threeness. Again, the synthetic statement "Rain is falling outdoors" is true (or false) depending on the evidence upon looking out the window. But if there is no window to look out of because there is no world "outside" the house in which

I find myself, then the statement "Rain is falling outdoors" becomes literally nonsensical. That is to say, one can neither verify nor falsify it. So it is with such a statement as "God is present with his people when they gather to worship." It is a statement without meaning.

What shall we say to these things? For one, while a theologian can never verify the affirmations she makes on a positivist's terms, neither can a positivist falsify those affirmations on a theologian's terms. The reason is that the positivist's universe of discourse is really quite different from that of the theologian. The positivist is concerned with the realm of the senses, a realm amenable to rational analysis and empirical observation. Of course, the theologian does not deny that there is such a realm; in fact, the doctrine of the creation of the sensible world of time and space is a major locus of theology. The parting of the ways comes, rather, because the positivist claims that there is no realm other than that of the senses. While granting that one may make such a claim, the theologian would contend that to do so is simply to lose oneself in one's round globe (Calvin). It is, in fact, to embrace a metaphysical assumption as incapable of demonstration as the assumption that the theologian herself makes.[1]

And what is the assumption that the Christian theologian makes? Simply that a transcendent dimension of reality has broken into this mundane world of time and space in the person of Jesus Christ. Because this is so, the theologian speaks of this transcendent realm as one that is real—indeed, more real—than that of sight and sound. In other words, the affirmations of theology are not an illusion (Freud), the subjective exercise of projecting what reality *would* be like if there *were* a God. Theological affirmations assert, rather, what the world *is* like since there *is* a God. Hence, it is the claim of the theologian that her language is definitely cognitive; it deals with the *knowledge* of *God*. In fact, "God" is the key word in the theologian's universe of discourse. Without it, theology would be like Shakespeare's *Hamlet* without a Prince of Denmark![2]

Finally, as a result of God's act of self-disclosure in Christ, theologians (and all Christians) know from experience what it means to break out of the circle of immanence and to become aware of another "dimension," the realm of the transcendent. They therefore proceed to plot and map the

---

1. See the so-called "Hartford Affirmation," signed by eighteen Protestant, Roman Catholic, and Orthodox theologians, especially the repudiation of Theme 2: Religious statements are totally independent of reasonable discourse. Also theme 3: Religious language refers to human experience and nothing else, God being humanity's noblest creation. *The Reformed Journal* 25 (March 1975): 8-9.

2. See John Macquarrie, *God Talk: An Examination of the Language and Logic of Theology* (New York: Seabury, 1979), pp. 99-100.

landscape of this other realm even though they have no celestial language at their disposal, only the language used to describe this present, sensible world of time and space. Obviously this is no simple task! It is, in fact, the root problem of theological language. It is the reason why, in this introduction, we have felt compelled to ask the question, How are we to understand such an extraordinary use of ordinary language?

We begin by observing that the meaning of language always involves the context in which it is used. The reason words with mundane meanings take on new meanings when used theologically is that the theologian speaks from within a different context, a different universe of discourse, than that of the philosopher and scientist. Therefore her language is inevitably transposed into a new key. William Hordern draws upon the world of sports to illustrate what we have in mind. Human language is like a game. Just as the rules of one game cannot be made normative for all others, so it is with language games. Since the meanings of words depend on their context, we cannot make the rules of one context normative for all others.[3] But this is what positivists do when they view the world of empirical observation as the only world in which meaningful discourse is possible. Naturally, therefore, they complain that theological statements do not satisfy the criteria they use to ascertain the meaning of language. But to theologians such a complaint seems naive. Why should they stop talking just because their statements cannot be verified within a positivist frame of reference? This would be like arguing that one should stop playing the game of basketball because she is not playing by the rules of softball.

When we speak of theologians transposing language into a different key, it must be remembered that this is not the same thing as playing a different tune. Too often the effort to translate the meaning of classical theological language into its contemporary equivalent results, for all practical purposes, in the denial of all that such language means. Note, for example, John Dewey's definition of "God" as "the ever-enlarging ideal, projected out of the experiences of humankind until it becomes the harmonizing principle for everything" (*A Common Faith,* as summarized in C. L. Manschreck, *A History of Christianity,* Englewood Cliffs: Prentice-Hall, 1964, p. 513). One is reminded of Thielicke's complaint that efforts since Schleiermacher to make the gospel credible to contemporary men and women result in the message becoming the victim of its altered conceptual schematization. Thus, in modern theology the gospel of the kerygma is subtly transposed into another gospel. Ritschl's theology is a kind of Kantianism, Biedermann's theology a kind of Hegelianism, Bultmann's theology a kind of Heideggerianism. And this change is not simply a misimpression evoked in the minds of untrained readers by the terminology such theologians employ. "It is [rather] the revolt of the very pattern of human language against the task for which it is conscripted and

3. See his *Speaking of God* (New York: Macmillan, 1964), chap. 5.

its usurption of sovereignty over the message expressed thereby." (See Helmut Thielicke, *Der evangelische Glaube,* Tübingen: Mohr, 1968, vol. I, par. 7.)

But if the criteria of verification for theological statements differ in certain respects from those of philosophy and science, what are these criteria and what is the warrant for introducing them? As theologians have endeavored to answer these questions and so justify their "strange" way of speaking, they have approached their task both "from below" and "from above." When working with the problem from below, they have sought to analyze the language they use by probing the meaning and function of such terms as "myth," "symbol," "parable," and "analogy." When working with the problem from above, they have appealed to "revelation" as given by God's Spirit and have spoken of the need to be "obedient" to this word whose source is transcendent. When so doing they have described this word of revelation as a "convictional" or an "existential" word in contrast to ordinary words that are "descriptive" or "emotive." Both approaches, from below and from above, are helpful, even necessary, and therefore both are used interchangeably. In fact, they can hardly be separated, except in discussing their distinctions. This is because they constitute aspects of the larger question of the context, the frame of reference or universe of discourse, in which theological (including biblical and devotional) language is used.

In the ensuing discussion we shall begin with analysis of and comment on certain terms used to describe the nature of theological language. We shall then concern ourselves with efforts to justify such language as language from above, language, that is, which is revelatory when used in a context of faith. This latter discussion will lead us, finally, into the question of how theological language functions, the question of the "grammar" or "logic" of theological discourse.

B. CONCERNING MYTH, SYMBOL, AND ANALOGY

Of the several terms used to describe contemporary theological discourse, none is given greater prominence in present-day literature than *myth.* Theological language is said to be "mythological." Bultmann defines myth as "the use of imagery to express the other worldly in terms of this world and the divine in terms of human life, the other side in terms of this side."[4]

---

4. "New Testament and Mythology," in *Kerygma and Myth: A Theological Debate,* ed. Hans Werner Bartsch (New York: Harper, 1961), p. 10, n. 2.

Probably the greatest difficulty with using "myth" to describe theological statements is simply that ever since early Christians rejected the religious myths of Greek antiquity, the word has been used to describe stories about gods, human heroes, and animals as they are involved in momentous events in some remote past. But these heroes never lived and the events never really happened, and therefore they are not true. (Note how "myth" is contrasted with "truth" in 2 Tm. 4:4. People "will turn away from listening to the truth and wander into myths.") The erudite efforts of some to insist that such stories, even though the events never happened, are nonetheless "true" because of their evocative, dramatic, and primordial power, is to press language beyond reasonable limits. This problem becomes especially acute when one speaks of "the myth of God Incarnate," since the Jesus event is not only an historical event but a *recent* event: he was "crucified under Pontius Pilate." This is not to deny that the problem of theological language, which many have tried to solve or at least moderate with such a term, is a genuine one. The question is, Does the term "myth" aggravate more than it alleviates the problem?[5]

A second, less problematic term theologians use when describing the nature and meaning of theological language is *symbol*. Theological language is said to be "symbolic." It is helpful in finding one's way through the vexed question of symbolism to distinguish between *conventional* and *natural* symbols. The former, as Dorothy Sayers reminds us, is simply a sign

> to represent or stand for something with which it has no integral connection: thus the scrawl "X" may, by common agreement, stand in mathematics for an unknown quantity; in the alphabet for a sound . . . ; at the end of a letter for a fond embrace. The figure "X" is not, in itself, any of these things and tells us nothing about them. Any other sign would serve the same purpose if we agreed to accept it so.[6]

The symbols which primarily concern the theologian, when she speaks of theological language as symbolic, are what Sayers calls *natural* symbols, that is, things (or persons) that "image forth a greater reality of which they are themselves an instance."

---

5. Note the series of essays under the title *The Myth of God Incarnate,* ed. John Hick (London: SCM Press, 1977).

6. Dorothy L. Sayers, trans., *The Divine Comedy,* I: *Hell,* "Introduction" (Baltimore: Penguin, 1949), p. 12.

It should be noted that not all symbols the theologian uses are natural symbols. The cross, for example, is plainly a *conventional* one. That is why it can symbolize such different things to different people: to the ancient Romans, shame and condemnation; to many Jews (unfortunately), anti-Semitic hatred; to Christians, sacrificial love. To say that the cross is a conventional symbol is not, of course, to imply that it is insignificant to the Christian faith. In fact, though it is not used in the earliest expression of that faith, it has become its most ecumenical symbol, having a profound significance.

The color "black" has been widely used, even by black Christian authors, as a symbol of sin and evil. James Weldon Johnson refers to "black-hearted Judas" ("The Crucifixion," *God's Trombones,* New York: Viking, 1957, p. 40). See also Margaret Abigail Walker's poem "Molly Means"—"the evil look in her coal black eyes" (*Kaleidoscope,* ed. Robert Hayden, New York: Harcourt, Brace, 1967, p. 142). Black is also a conventional, not a natural, symbol—save for those white racists for whom black people really do image forth a greater reality of sinister evil. In the light of its current racist overtones, such symbolism will have no place in our own statement of Christian theology. The Bible does not separate black sheep from white sheep, but sheep from goats (Mt. 25:33). Grace does not turn our sins from *black* to white, but from *scarlet* to white (Is. 1:18).

Biblical language is replete with symbols of the sort commonly used by theologians. To speak of the "eye" of the Lord (Ps. 33:18) is to use a natural symbol of his knowledge. When Christians say that they "see the hand of God" in something that happens, they mean that they understand the event from the perspective of God's will and power that brought it about, working through the natural order. Obviously such a symbolic statement is not subject to empirical verification; no one literally sees God's hand. Nor do symbolic statements satisfy the rules of logical consistency. This is apparent from the fact that Christians call Jesus both the "Lamb of God" (Jn. 1:29) and the "good shepherd" (Jn. 10:11), whereas in the logical world of the positivist, lambs are lambs by definition and shepherds are shepherds, but never is a lamb a shepherd.

But to say that such symbolic language is not subject to the rules of verification used in matters mundane is not to admit that theological language is meaningless, much less untrue. The question, however, remains: If such language is subject neither to empirical nor logical verification, how then is it to be verified? The answer to this question involves an analysis of still another term widely used by theologians to describe their language, namely, "analogy." When theologians speak of their discourse as analogical in nature they postulate between God and creature a likeness-in-unlikeness. This raises the obvious question: If God is qualitatively different from the creature (as the theologians have affirmed), then what is the likeness that warrants the analogical use of language about the creature when speaking of the Creator? It would seem either that we can say nothing about God, or that we end up speaking not about the God who is infinite and transcendent but about a superlative creature. In the former case we do not talk; in the latter, we talk, but not about God.

Thomas, in seeking to resolve this problem, acknowledged that the language used by theologians to describe God is never univocal. But it does not follow, he argued, that it is therefore equivocal; such a conclusion would rule out theological discourse altogether. Therefore, it must be *analogical* in keeping with Paul's dictum, "The invisible things of God are clearly seen, being understood by the things that are made" (Rom. 1:20).[7] In other words, according to Thomas, in the use of certain terms to describe both God and the creature, a mean between pure equivocation and simple univocation may properly be assumed. In analogies, the meaning is not one and the same, as in univocals; yet neither is it wholly diverse as in equivocals. So, from the admission that as creatures we do not speak univocally of God and the affirmation that we do not speak equivocally of him, we must conclude that we speak of him analogically.[8]

In the ongoing debate over the use of "analogy" to describe theological language, attention has been focused on the basis of Thomas's assumption of a community of meaning (univocal element) in terms used of both God and the creature. That there must be such has often been acknowledged; but what might this shared element be and in what sense may it be predicated both of the creature and of God? The answer often given is just "being itself." God *is* and the creature *is*. Tillich goes so far as to argue that the statement "God is Being-itself" is really the only nonsymbolic (nonanalogical) statement about God that can be made. "Any concrete assertion about God [as that he is "just" or "good"] must be symbolic [analogical], for a concrete assertion is one which uses a

7. Thomas Aquinas, *Summa,* Q. 13, art. 5, pt. 1.

8. Thomas's appeal to the "analogical," as standing between the "univocal" and the "equivocal," might be illustrated as follows. Suppose one were to say to an Indian in the jungles of the Amazon, "The *SS Queen Mary* is like that rock"; such an affirmation would constitute a false analogy, for there is no likeness (no univocal element) in a comparison between a rock and an ocean liner. To speak thus is to engage in equivocation. But were one to say, "The *SS Queen Mary* is like that canoe you have hollowed out from a log," such an affirmation would constitute a true analogy. The univocal element in the analogy is that both objects float on water and carry people. Obviously, however, in many respects, the *SS Queen Mary* is *not* like a hand-hewed canoe. Hence, to speak of the former in terms of the latter is to speak in a way that is neither univocal nor equivocal, but analogical. What the Indian knows of the *SS Queen Mary* is true, though far from adequate in the sense of full and complete. And so it is with our language about God. The problem—to stay with the illustration—is that both the *SS Queen Mary* and the Indian's canoe are immanent objects in this world. No one ever said that there is an "infinite qualitative difference" between them, as have theologians when speaking of God and the world. But more of this presently.

segment of finite experience in order to say something about him [who is infinite]."[9] When, therefore, we say that God is Being-itself, we establish the basis for making finite being the ground of other assertions about God who is Infinite Being. This is so, Tillich reasons, because everything that is finite participates in Being-itself.

What is to be said to this argument? Does it justify the claim that we can close the gap between the creature and the Creator so as to speak of him meaningfully by way of analogy? Whatever the difficulties, Tillich's argument shows that theologians cannot avoid the question of the connotative definition of the verb "to be" when used of God. They must not only ask, but also seek to answer the question, What does it mean to say "God is"? Thomas, in giving his answer, assumed that *being* is the category of maximal significance since it includes "all the perfection of being," that is, all the differences and determinators whereby we distinguish one being from another. Furthermore, not only do all created beings have their being in common, but even God and the creature have "being" in common.

But here, just when it would seem that we have laid our finger on the univocal element in the analogical language of theology that would constitute a bridge between the finite and the Infinite and provide a reasoned basis for the use of language about God, we run into trouble. Thomas is constrained to warn us that when we say that God and the creature have their being in common, we must not understand this affirmation pantheistically, as though the world of manifold being is the unfolding of the ultimate divine Being. (One is reminded of the pantheistic overtones in the affirmation of Tillich, noted above, that everything finite "participates in" Being-itself.) Rather, all beings other than God are created beings because they are called into being by an act of his will and differ from one another according to the qualities that he has given them.

This is an important point for our discussion. All created beings differ from God in the fundamental sense that their being is bestowed upon them by the Creator, whereas his being has no cause outside himself. His being is Necessary Being, which means, to speak with Thomas, that his existence is identical with his essence. The Creator *must* be (or there would be no being whatever, only nothingness), whereas the creature *may* be, if God wills. Because the creature's being is contingent, that is, dependent on the will of the Creator, her existence as a creature is distinct from her essence. In other words, the creature *has* being, God *is* being. And so the verb "to

9. Paul Tillich, *Systematic Theology,* vol. I (Chicago: University of Chicago Press, 1951), p. 239. In this passage in Tillich there appears to be no substantial difference between the terms "symbolic" and "analogical."

be" really does not mean the same thing in the sentence "God is" that it means in the sentence "The creature is." The univocal element on which all analogy rests is threatened; while the unlikeness is clear, the likeness is questionable.

Confronted with this problem and convinced that the analogy of being (*analogia entis*) is, as a matter of fact, the basis of a natural theology that threatens the otherness of God, Barth and his followers have rejected it as a denial of the divine transcendence. And such a denial of the transcendent God is a denial (it is alleged) of the God of the Bible, who, as the thrice-holy One, is other than the creature and hence not to be likened to the creature. As early as *Der Römerbrief,* Barth reasserted the transcendence of God in reaction to a century of theological liberalism. He charged liberalism, in its efforts to reconcile religion and modern thought, with postulating an underlying oneness of the divine and the human. In brief, liberalism forgot that God is in heaven and the theologian on earth.

To speak, then, of an analogy of being is to subsume God and humankind under the genus "Being" as horses and zebras are subsumed under the genus "Equus." Speaking to this point, Barth registers the complaint that "an *analogia entis* between Creator and creature presupposes . . . a higher category or universal, the *genus*, 'Being,' that includes God and the creature."[10] This would mean that God is reduced to the same space-time continuum as the creature and so *becomes* a creature. Hence, Barth repeatedly warned that an analogy of being between Creator and creature means that we are ever in danger of clandestinely thinking (and speaking) about ourselves when we think we are thinking (and speaking) about God.

Barth, however, soon came to realize that his stress on the qualitative difference between God and the world had to be balanced by some sort of likeness or else God, in his revelation, could not be even partially understood by the creature. Were there no likeness at all, our awe of God would be but ignorance of him; our reverence would not praise but deny him. Therefore, along with otherness we must postulate likeness when we speak of God as revealed to the creature. But it is not a likeness of being (*analogia entis*); rather, it is a likeness of relation (*analogia relationis*).[11] Such an analogy is a true analogy, for it is based on a similarity; but the similarity

---

10. *Die kirchliche Dogmatik* (hereafter, *K.D.*) (Zurich: Evangelischer Verlag, 1947-67), III/3, p. 116 (cf. *C.D.*, III/3, sec. 49.2).

11. Barth styles the *analogia entis* "the invention of the Antichrist"; *K.D.*, I/1, p. x. As for the *analogia relationis* (analogy of relationship), this is simply a description of the position we will elaborate presently when we speak of God's act in the Incarnation as his breaking into the circle of immanence, making possible Christian speech in a faith context as the language of encounter and obedience.

is one of relationship, not of being. The divine "I" is to the divine "Thou" (God is a triune fellowship) what the human "I" is to the human "thou" (humankind is a fellowship of male and female). Hence the human creature is the image of God, and therefore the language of the creature may be used of God. This relational analogy between the Creator and the creature Barth sometimes calls an *analogia gratiae* or *revelationis* because it is established by the gracious act of the Creator and known to the creature through revelation rather than demonstrated by reason. And by the same token it may be called an *analogia fidei,* for all the truths of revelation come to us by faith in him who is the source of revelation.[12]

And so theology is not concerned with general, or universal "Being" (the philosophic question of ontology), but with *God's* being, the being that he gives us to see in his Word and works. In answering the question "Who is God?" and in interpreting the sentence "God is," we must never allow our thoughts to stray from his self-revelation. We must rather bring our thoughts into captivity to God's acts, that is, to his revelation, since God is who he is in his revelation; his revelation is never apart from himself. To say, in this sense, that God is his act is to say that he is the subject who acts freely in himself (as a trinitarian fellowship) and freely in distinction from himself (as our Creator and Redeemer). Thus, the being of God is not that of an abstract Universal, but that of a self-moved Being, a free Spirit, a personal Self who says, "I AM WHO I AM."[13]

C. THE REVELATION/FAITH CONTEXT OF THEOLOGICAL LANGUAGE

As our analysis of the symbolic and analogic character of theological discourse has shown, such discourse does not rest on rational, empirical demonstration but on revelation. Our speaking about God presupposes his having spoken to us. Hence, even the learned theologian cannot demonstrate to an unbeliever, in terms of a neutral, universally recognizable

---

12. *K.D.,* II/1, p. 275; *K.D.,* III/3 (cf. *C.D.,* III/3, sec. 48.3), p. 59. This use of *analogia fidei* differs, of course, from the common use, where "faith" refers to doctrine. Barth is speaking of an analogy between Creator and creature that is known by the fact of revelation and accepted by an act of faith.

13. We have summarized Barth's thinking on this point largely from *K.D.,* II/1, pp. 288-305, the section entitled "Gottes Sein in der Tat" ("The Being of God in Act"). We have sought to do so in a way that focuses the question of the divine Being in terms of our affirmation that God's Being is Personal Being, the first affirmation with which we shall presently begin our discussion of the divine nature.

principle of verification, that what she says about a world that is other than the world of time and space is true. She must acknowledge, therefore, that the meaning of theological discourse can be adequately perceived only within a context of faith. This is the "frame of reference," the "universe of discourse," that gives significance to theological language. In saying as much we are simply recognizing what is commonly assumed of all language, that the context in which one speaks determines the meaning of what one says. As Ramsey has remarked:

> We use our words significantly and naturally only in a particular context, and then we do it just as naturally as we move the mouth when eating. . . . It is the context in which words are used, which in all its richness and complexity gives to those words all that is involved in "understanding" them.[14]

It may be that the context in which we speak is scientific or legal or whatever. Regardless, we always speak in a context, and the context determines the ultimate "logic" or "grammar" of the sentences we use. When it comes to speaking theologically, the context of such discourse is faith—faith in Jesus Christ in whom God reveals himself and to whom Scripture bears witness. For this reason, the statements that the theologian makes are faith statements, for theology's task, as Rudolph Otto has reminded us, is to mirror faith in thought. Theological statements, therefore, are not essentially different from the confessional statements of worship. This is why a theologian who is a confessing Christian cannot speak truly about the faith that the church confesses, and at the same time do so in the objective, descriptive language of the natural scientist. Her sentences are somewhere between the affirmation, "Water boils at 212 degrees Fahrenheit at sea level," and the confession, "My Lord and my God!" (Jn. 20:28), with which the apostle Thomas acknowledged the risen Christ. And they are much nearer the latter than the former.[15] Their frame of reference is not the

14. *Words About God,* ed. Ian T. Ramsey (New York: Harper, 1971), p. 11.

15. Nearer because theology arises out of worship. (Hence the theologian has constantly to struggle for the right balance between the pulpit and the lectern.) True theological sentences are second-degree commitment sentences, not neutral, descriptive sentences. They are like the sentence in the marriage ceremony: "I do [take this man/woman to be my lawful husband/wife]." Such a sentence is not simply descriptive of one's inner inclination or feeling; it is a spoken *act,* a commitment. It was to Martin Kähler's credit, we might observe in passing, that he recognized the sentences in the gospels for what they are: the expression of the faith of the church; thus he understood them as faith statements, not statements that simply convey biographical information, a view that leads to the frustrating effort reflected in the "lives-of-Jesus" literature. See his *Der sogenannte historische Jesus und der geschichtliche biblische Christus* (Leipzig: George Böhme, 1896).

immanent world of the logical positivists for whom the empirical realm of space and time is the only one there is. Christians claim to have broken out of this world of immanence, in the sense that they have seen beyond it. As one of their poets has said,

> Who looks on glass
> On it may stay his eye,
> Or if it pleaseth through it pass,
> And then the heavens espy.[16]

True, we see through this glass darkly, not face to face (1 Cor. 13:12). Yet we do see, having the eyes of our understanding enlightened (Eph. 1:18) to look through the earthly glass to the heavenly reality beyond.

But, as we have observed, this is just to say that we have broken out of the circle of immanence, or better, that our circle of immanence has been broken into by Another. The God who first said, "Let light shine out of darkness," has shown in our hearts "to give the light of the knowledge of the glory of God in the face of Christ" (2 Cor. 4:6). We have had disclosed to us that which does not lie within the scope of human, rational possibility. Rather, it is that which awakens faith, a faith wherein we are open "to an encounter with the truth of God coming to us from out of transcendence."[17] This, obviously, is not to say that the sentence "God is love" is a sentence without meaning for want of an empirical referent. But it is to say that it is a faith statement. As Paul Holmer has observed, "Learning to use the word 'God' referentially does not come about through any special science; rather it is both the sign and the consequence of faith."[18]

To say that theological statements cannot be verified empirically is not, however, to say that they are indifferent to empirical reality. Though such statements cannot be forced into the procrustean bed of strict empirical language (that is, language open to testing by the observation of facts), they have, in some instances, what might be called empirical "fallout." The empty tomb, for example, is the empirical side of Jesus' resurrection. Therefore, to say "The Lord is risen!" is to imply that his tomb is empty. While the resurrection appearances to chosen witnesses took place in what might be called "Easter" time and space, the empty tomb is a fact in our *empirical* time and space. That is why a hypothesis such as "the body was

---

16. George Herbert, as quoted by Ian Ramsey, *Religious Language* (London: SCM Press, 1957), p. 77.

17. Peter Stuhlmacher, as cited by Anthony Thiselton, *The Two Horizons* (Grand Rapids: Eerdmans, 1980), p. 325.

18. "Contra the New Theologies," *The Christian Century,* 17 March 1965, 330.

stolen" (used in ancient times), or "the empty tomb story is the late invention of the church" (used in modern times) is the inevitable response of those who insist on some form of the verification principle used in logical empiricism. If one is going to use that principle to confirm one's lack of faith, one must make sure that the facts (like an empty tomb) that favor an affirmation of faith are not real but contrived. Only then can the resurrection be rejected as nonverifiable for "want of evidence."

Other theological statements that do not have such specific empirical implications do have what Ramsey has called an empirical or cosmic "fit." If "God is love" is a true statement, while it cannot be empirically verified as scientific statements are verified (the Holocaust should make that obvious), yet there must be *some* events in the world of time and space that can be interpreted as fitting such an affirmation. Otherwise, all our language about God would simply give comfort in sermons but have no epistemological or ontological worth. In other words, while the Holocaust makes empirical verification of God's love impossible, the existence of "righteous Gentiles" makes its empirical falsification likewise impossible.[19]

When we say that theological statements are faith statements or judgments, we do not mean what Albrecht Ritschl meant by "value judgments." We grant that Christian doctrines, expressed in theological statements, have value for the Christian (or the Christian community, as Ritschl would say). But we would not affirm that the value that such faith affirmations have for our moral and spiritual well-being make the question of their theoretical truth indifferent. To say that Jesus is the Son of God is not to describe the value he has for us because of his unique God-consciousness. Rather, it is to describe who he is, the Son of God eternally begotten of the Father, who therefore has value for us as our only Savior. In other words, Jesus is not the Son of God because he has value for us. On the contrary, he has value for us because he is the Son of God. (See A. Ritschl's *Theologie und Metaphysik,* Bonn: A. Marcus, 1887, for an exposition of his thought in these matters.)

19. See, for example, Philip Paul Haillie's moving account of the French Protestant town of Le Chambon that sheltered thousands of Jews in World War II under the leadership of Pastor Andre Trocme, *Lest Innocent Blood be Shed* (New York: Harper, 1979). Haillie is himself a Jew. Also Corrie Ten Boom, *The Hiding Place* (Old Tappan, N.J.: Revell, 1971). A small group of Jewish intellectuals believe that the history of the Holocaust has been distorted by a preoccupation with its horrors and a failure to tell the story of the Christians who helped the Jews. Their effort to tell that story is gaining support. See "Rabbi Leads Search for 'Righteous Christians' Who Helped Save Jews," *Los Angeles Times,* 24 Oct. 1987.

D. CONCLUSION

The use of human language in a theological sense is easy for those who stand within the circle of faith, which is its proper context. (One recalls Ramsey's observation that we do it as naturally as we move our mouths when eating.) In this regard it is interesting to note how the writers of Scripture simply assume without question that such usage is meaningful. They often link this human language about God to everyday life; it is the language of the home, the family, and the nation, language used in work and warfare. This is true of both the Old Testament and the New. (Witness Jesus' use of such earthly language in his parables about the heavenly kingdom.)

This example of the authors of Scripture has been followed by the Christian community as a whole. When Christians gather for worship they sing the hymn "Spirit of God, Descend upon My Heart," and speak of their heart as an "altar" on which the "flame" of God's love burns—"my heart an altar and your love the flame"—without asking how a structure of stone on which an animal is immolated can be a metaphor of the heart (or of what "heart" in this instance is a metaphor), or how meaning can be transferred from the literal referent (fire) to the intended referent (the divine love) in a way that illumines the nature of the latter. As a child naturally learns a language by using it, so it is with the language of faith. The Christian is one who confesses, "Jesus is Lord," and it is in the context of this confession that she knows the meaning of the sentence. In the ordinary use of language one does not learn to pronounce a word and then seek to find a meaning to go with it. So it is with the language of faith; the meaning and the language go together. And the meaning is learned in the context of faith in which the language is used.

One might also say that as one learns her mother tongue in a given culture, in a larger community where others speak the same language, so it is with the language of faith. It is the language spoken in the community of faith—the church—where in contrition and gratitude the assembled people of God speak the language of wonder and awe, that is, the language of worship. In other words, we come to speak *about* God by speaking *to* him; and we speak *to* him because we are spoken to *by* him. As in the natural order we do not fully know how we learn to speak—a child's first word is something of a miracle—so it is in the realm of faith. Theologians refer to this mystery as "effectual calling," by which term they describe the work of the Spirit speaking in the heart by and with the Scripture. As God the Son became incarnate ("the Word became flesh," Jn. 1:14) and thus made our human nature his own, so God the Spirit becomes the Spirit of adoption and thus makes our human language his own by teaching us to call God "Father" (Rom. 8:15-16). Christians can more easily witness *that* he has done this, than explain *how* he has done it.

> I know not how the Spirit moves,
>> Convincing us of sin,
> Revealing Jesus through the word,
>> Creating faith in him. (Nathan)

Yet the theologian's efforts to explain how Christians learn to speak the language of faith do shed some light on the subject. We shall, then, conclude our discussion of theological language with a brief summary of these efforts.

We begin by reiterating our conclusion that God is not reached by our analogies, based as they are on the experience of the finite created world. Though we necessarily speak of God in analogies, metaphors, symbols, and parables taken from this world, we do not find him out *by* these. Rather, we find him *in* these because he stoops to reveal himself to us in them. Not that we know God antecedently and independently of our analogies, but it is "in, with, and under" these that he discloses himself. While it may appear that the solid, tangible, empirical world from which our symbols and analogies are drawn is the ultimate reality, for one whose understanding has been illumined by faith this worldly reality is only penultimate, not ultimate. The ultimate reality is the world of faith rather than the world of sight.

Noting that in the Incarnation we have a divine self-disclosure that lays claim to what is in the world, Thielicke admits that this can only mean that God bears witness to himself in worldly analogies. But, he is careful to note, this does not mean that these analogies constitute a logical bridge from the reality of the world to the reality of God. "The analogy," he insists,

> cannot replace the testimony of the Spirit. Analogies can be appreciated only when the light is kindled in which we see light. The lilies of the field and the fowls of the air remain silent (Matthew 6:26, 28) and cannot of themselves proclaim to me the fact that I need not be anxious. Pagans see them too and are still anxious (6:32). Only when I know the one who adds other things to those who seek first the kingdom of God (6:33, Luke 12:30) do the lilies add their voice and the analogies begin to shine forth. Stained-glass windows glow only in the sanctuary.[20]

Furthermore, because God is a personal God who discloses himself to us "in, with and under" the tangible realities of his creation, and because we,

---

20. Helmut Thielicke, *The Evangelical Faith,* vol. I (Grand Rapids: Eerdmans, 1974), p. 370.

to whom he discloses himself, are persons who respond in faith to his revelation, theologians have sometimes (appropriately) described the language Christians use in talking about God as the language of encounter and obedience.

Encounter is the obvious universe of discourse in which the authors of Scripture speak. In human words they witness to encounters continuing between God and humankind. God revealed himself to Abraham and Sarah, and continues to reveal himself to their offspring throughout the course of Israel's history. And the same may be said of the new Israel made up of those who hear the call of Jesus and his Spirit. Hence the Bible may be viewed as an ongoing history of encounters between God and humans; and through the reading and hearing of the Bible further such encounters occur. Thus the church is perpetuated as the community of those who speak the language of faith and seek to live the life of love and reconciliation revealed supremely in Jesus Christ.

Of course, such encounters with God cannot be neutrally validated; they are self-validating. When Saul of Tarsus, on the road to Damascus, encountered the risen Christ, he could not dispute his identity. Yet, on the other hand, he did not return to Jerusalem to demonstrate that identity to his former associates. He made no effort to prove to them by some argument learned in Athens that Stephen was right after all, in his witness before the Sanhedrin, when he insisted that Jesus was the Righteous One (Acts 7:52). Though they are analogous to everyday I/thou encounters experienced at the human level, the "validation" of those encounters Christians have with God rests not upon analogy but upon the fact that they are human encounters with *God*. It is God the Spirit who enables us to cry, "Abba! Father!" (Rom. 8:15), and so God validates his own revelation.

Furthermore, when one is thus encountered by God, the response of faith that such an encounter evokes has aptly been described by theologians as the language of obedience. Paul said on the Damascus road, "What shall I do, Lord?" (Acts 22:10). To factor obedience into the meaning of theological discourse is perhaps the clearest evidence of all that such language is anything but that of a supposedly neutral philosophy or science. To speak of theological discourse as the language of obedience is to say that autonomous reason—that is, reason working solely with its own internal categories—is not adequate to cope with the divine Reality revealed in Christ to whom the Scriptures bear witness. The only appropriate response to such a revelation is an act described as "the obedience of faith" (Rom. 16:26). Not that faith demands that reason be abandoned, but it does require that reason be open (obedient) to the truth which it cannot verify either in terms of its own immanent norms of coherence or in terms of empirical observation. Reason that is thus open to God's Word is truly objective, not in the sense of an alleged neutrality, but in the sense of a capacity to be conformed to the transcendent Object—or better, Subject—disclosed in revelation.

This capacity to be *truly* rational, to conform one's reason to God's self-revelation, requires a fundamental change in one's mental makeup, namely, the recognition that reason is not autonomous. In fact, it involves the recognition that autonomous, self-sufficient reason is really the "Fall" at the intellectual level. Faith, by contrast, is reason that is obedient to revelation; it is the supreme instance of Luther's "right reason." It is the acknowledgment that Jesus is the Lord Jesus Christ, the Word of God. It is a listening, therefore, not in the sense of "hearing voices within," but in the sense of obedient response to the revelation that comes from without.

This response of obedience, to be sure, is expressed in the words of rational speech. When Paul says, "What shall I do, Lord?" (Acts 22:10), he is speaking not in an unknown tongue but in the words of reason. And the same is true of the words of theologians — indeed, of the entire Christian community in every age. But this common vocabulary and syntax that the Christian shares with the unbeliever does not mean that the Christian shares a language with the unbeliever in any ultimate sense. Though a Christian's language is reasonable, in that it is made up of coherent sentences, its ultimate meaning derives from the fact that it is spoken *by faith* in a community that lives and acts *in faith*.[21] To appeal, then, to the rational character of such language at the surface level to validate that language would be to beg the question, given an unbeliever's standpoint. Hence, though theology uses the language of rational understanding, it must be admitted that it is really giving not a demonstration, but a reason-oriented expression to the "faith . . . once for all delivered to the saints" (Jude 3).

Of course the question of the meaning of *any* language is an odd question, since it requires language to answer it. But when it comes to theological language, not only is the question of its meaning an odd question, but the language itself by which the question is answered sounds odd to those outside the circle of faith. Two reasons why this is so, implicit in our foregoing discussion, come immediately to mind; one is theoretical, one practical. On the theoretical side, theological language sounds odd to an unbeliever because it is talking about one thing in terms of another; it is talking about God in terms of this world. On the practical side, the

---

21. The author is reminded of a young woman who had sung in the *Messiah* each year at college. Converted in her last year, she observed that for the first time she "understood" the meaning of the words she had so frequently sung.

oddness of theological language is related to the oddness, from the world's point of view, of the Christian life as such.[22] It is not so much the intrinsic obtuseness of faith's language in itself as the demands that the Christian faith makes on one's life, including one's thought life, that constitutes the real obstacle to "understanding." Christian faith demands that one's thought life correspond to the subject matter. Old things must pass away so that all things may become new (2 Cor. 5:17).

When we speak thus, we are talking again about the fact that theological language has its genesis in the redeemed community, which is the worshipping community. And to the unredeemed, worship is an empirically odd event. It is something having to do with emotions and is akin to magic and superstition.[23] But for the believer, worship is a discernment/commitment situation, an "aha" moment. As Macquarrie has observed, the nonsense of theological language is like Samson's riddle (Jgs. 14:14); when we hit on the solution—or, we should say, when the solution hits us— then it all comes together. But when it "comes together," no one is more aware than the theologian that, while the Reality perceived is true, the language used to describe that Reality is inadequate. How quickly in theology is the limit of human discourse reached! This inadequacy of the theologian's language, however, is not due to the failure of her discourse to meet some principle of verification required by one who stands outside the community of faith; rather, it is due to the nature of the subject of discourse. Theological discourse is discourse about God, whom we know because he has disclosed himself to us. But this disclosure is given us in the human words of Scripture. And because the Spirit lisps to us in Scripture as a nurse to a child (Calvin), the doctrines of the church, even when faithful to Scripture, are but "rules for significant stuttering."[24]

In other words, we who are recipients of revelation are not thereby translated out of our finite and imperfect understanding. Revelation is rather God's coming to us *in* our finitude and imperfection.[25] Hence we perceive the truth from beyond our finitude *in* our finitude. As a result, when theologians speak of these truths they use paradoxes. But these paradoxes of faith are not logical contradictions. They are rather to be seen as arising

---

22. Noting the contrast in lifestyle between Christians and non-Christians, Peter observes that the latter think it strange ("odd," ξενίζονται) that Christians no longer join them in their way of living (1 Pt. 4:4).

23. Admittedly, much that has been called worship appears, even to many Christians, to be largely emotion based on superstition.

24. Ramsey, *Words About God,* p. 219.

25. The paradigm of revelation is always, for the Christian, incarnational rather than docetic.

out of a recognized inadequacy in human language to encompass the divine Subject with which theological discourse has to do—namely, God in his relationship to us. Donald Baillie has compared these paradoxes to the distortions of a mercator projection. We know that distortion is inevitable when we represent a spherical surface by drawing a map on a flat, two-dimensional plane. So we correct our geographical maps by the empirical experience of exploration. Likewise, we "correct" our theological "maps" by the vital experience of worship. Yet, as the inadequate maps in geography remain helpful and necessary to the explorer, in like manner the paradoxical doctrines in which faith expresses itself remain helpful and necessary to the worshipper.[26]

The sum of the matter, it would seem, is that theological language will always remain inadequate yet necessary. Due to its inadequacy, the theologian has no language guaranteed to work; she cannot perform semantic magic. To speak biblically, she cannot take the place of the Holy Spirit. Her speech is not in the plausible words of human wisdom but in the demonstration and power of the Spirit (1 Cor. 2:4). Anyone who sees what the camera "sees" will find this sentence meaningful: "And over his head they put the charge against him, which read, 'This is Jesus the King of the Jews'" (Mt. 27:37). But only those who "see" with the eye of faith can say,

> Inscribed upon the cross I *see*
> In shining letters, *God is love:*

> He bears my sins upon the tree;
> He brings me mercy from above. (Kelley)

To "see" with the "eye" of such faith, to be sure, involves decision, the decision to be a Christian. But then, all life that is human forces one to make decisions. And these decisions, which we all make, including the positivists and the analysts, reflect a deeper, if unconscious, decision about the nature of ultimate reality. Such a deeper decision always goes beyond the tautologies of mathematics and the securities of sense observation. This is so whether one confesses ultimate reality to be the God revealed in Jesus Christ or simply quanta of energy without purpose or intrinsic value. In the ensuing discussion, therefore, we will pursue further the implications of the Christian decision that there is, indeed, a God and that he has revealed himself in Jesus Christ. In doing so we shall endeavor to frame a theological statement that embraces all the essential doctrines of the Christian faith.

---

26. On the use of paradox in the exposition of a specific doctrine, see our *Election and Predestination* (Grand Rapids: Eerdmans, 1985), pp. 61ff.

FIRST ADDENDUM: A COMMENT ON SEXIST LANGUAGE

We have concluded that using human language in a theological sense is easy for those who stand within the circle of faith. However, like most conclusions theologians come to, this one needs a postscript. There is one area in which the use of human language in a theological sense has become increasingly difficult, rather than easy, for many who seek to articulate the implications of their faith. We refer, of course, to the use of masculine language with reference to God. Short answers appeal to many in such matters. One such is to argue that if one accepts Scripture as normative revelation—and we do—then one must simply use the language of Scripture in doing theology. On the other side are those who point out, as we have just done, that all language about God, even the language of Scripture, is analogical. Therefore theology is not bound in perpetuity in this matter but is free to use the analogies of Scripture in new and different ways. In our judgment, the truth is spoken on both sides, but not the whole truth. Hence, the question of God and sexist language is perhaps as difficult as any language problem the church has ever faced.

When we come to our exposition of the doctrine of God, the first (and fundamental) affirmation that we shall make is just that God is a personal God. We find it quite impossible, therefore, to avoid the use of personal pronouns altogether when referring to this personal God.[27] Obviously a new pronoun—which we do not have—is needed. The masculine "he," the feminine "she," and the neuter "it" are all problematic. The last ("it") is ultimately so, as designating the impersonal; the other two ("he" and "she") penultimately so because of their sexual connotation. In speaking thus, we imply, to be sure, that the use of the feminine pronoun is no more problematic than the use of the masculine. Theologically speaking, this is so because the woman as well as the man is the image of God (Gn. 1:27). Furthermore, God is like a mother (Is. 49:15) as well as a father (Ps. 103:13). Both figures can be used of God analogically, since God is to us all what both a mother and a father should be. Hence, Faber is correct when he teaches us in the beautiful hymn, "My God, How Wonderful You Are," to sing:

---

27. Even linguistically the avoidance of the personal pronoun is difficult: "And God will dwell with them, and they shall be God's people, and God himself (Godself?) shall be with them" (Rv. 21:3).

No earthly father loves like you,
　No mother, e'er so mild,
Bears and forbears as you have done
　With me, your sinful child.

Yet it is one thing to draw the theological conclusion that the feminine pronoun may be used of God as well as the masculine; it is another to resolve the implications of such a conclusion with satisfying consistency. Such a dual usage—God is "he/she" or "(s)he" or alternately "he" in one paragraph and "she" in the next—would require not only a departure from the usage of Scripture but would leave us with what Jean Caffey Lyles once called "the disturbing image of a God-Who-Suffers-From-Gender-Confusion."[28]

We have chosen, therefore, to refer to God as "he," though in the section on the attributes we will use the feminine pronoun "she," not to resolve but to highlight the problem created by the exclusive use of masculine language in speaking of God.[29] In this section the reader will, we hope, gain an appreciation of how the traditional masculine pronouns, when used of God, sound to an increasing number of women. We also hope that such usage, though unfamiliar, will be seen as by no means impossible, especially since many of the divine perfections of which we shall speak have been associated with the woman, even by the traditionalists.

We are well aware of the detailed difficulties and even inconsistencies such an effort entails. Not only will we have to change the pronouns of the hymn writers and other authors cited, but also the pronouns of Scripture itself.[30] And the linguistically sensitive ear will hear subtle, and sometimes not so subtle, tensions, as when we use the feminine pronoun while retaining the masculine "Lord," a name used throughout our discussion, especially in our treatment of the personal character of God as disclosed to Israel by the name "Yahweh," the "I AM WHO I AM."

A further evidence that we have not resolved the problem is our decision to retain the masculine pronoun when referring to Christ because of the character of the Incarnation. Although the second person of the Godhead is not literally the "Son" of the "Father," this eternal "Son" was

28. "The God-Language Bind," *The Christian Century,* 16 April 1980, 430-31.

29. See below, Unit Four, What God Is Like: The Divine Attributes, pp. 333ff.

30. The warrant for changing the scriptural pronouns used of God is found in the analogical nature of biblical language concerning which we have just spoken. On the other hand, we are about to argue that the use of the trinitarian name, Father, Son, and Holy Spirit, is essential to making a theological statement about God that is genuinely Christian. So, admittedly, we are involved in a *sic et non.* Our yes to such a procedure is confronted with a no that is equally cogent.

incarnate as the son of Mary in the most literal sense of the word. Hence, one can hardly use any other pronoun than the masculine when speaking of him whose name is Jesus of Nazareth. This is not to imply that the masculine character of God's incarnate humanity is essential to the very idea of incarnation. It is Christ's *genuine* humanity, not his *male* humanity, that is essential to the Incarnation. The evangelists are concerned, therefore, with Jesus as the Savior of all, men and women alike, not with Jesus as a male of the species. Yet it is a fact of redemptive history that in the Incarnation God became a man, not a woman. Hence, while this may be of no ultimate theological consequence, it determines our use of language at this point.

When we speak of the eternal "Son" of God as incarnate in the literal son of Mary, we are closing in on the heart of the problem of God and sexist language. We believe that God is a *personal* God (not a philosophic Monad or a religious Absolute) because he names himself and so reveals himself as personal in an act of self-disclosure. While the original Hebrew form of this name (יהוה, Yahweh) is sexually neutral, its New Testament equivalent (κύριος, Lord) is not. Furthermore, on this side of the Incarnation and Pentecost the full name of the God whom Christians confess as Lord is Father, Son, and Holy Spirit, the triune name into which they are baptized. So while the original name of the God of Israel is sexually neutral, the name of the God whom Christians worship as the one, true, and living God is not.

At this point one may ask, What's in a name? The essentials of the doctrine of the Trinity are that: (*a*) God is a personal God (subject, not object); (*b*) this personal God is a fellowship of Holy Love; and (*c*) the ineffable distinctions in God, whereby God is a fellowship, are persons. Therefore, we need only to find ways to speak of this triune God that are faithful to these essentials, ways that, at the same time, are not masculine in connotation.

While we are quite open to such a possibility, for the present we can only consider some of the efforts being made to speak of the Trinity in a nonsexist way and indicate why we find them less than satisfactory. Take, for example, the suggestion that for "Father, Son, and Spirit" we substitute "Creator, Savior, and Sanctifier." For those who do not accept the traditional doctrine that all God's works outside himself *(ad extra)* are one because God is one, such a substitution may be easy enough. But for those who do, the second as well as the first person of the Godhead is "Creator." He is the Logos by whom all things were made (Jn. 1:3). And the same may be said of the Spirit, the third person of the Godhead. "When," says the psalmist, speaking of God's many creatures, "you send your Spirit, they are created; and you renew the face of the earth" (Ps. 104:30 NIV). Hence Christians have, for centuries, sung the great *Veni Creator Spiritus:*

> Come, O *Creator* Spirit blest,
> And in our souls take up your rest. (Caswall)

In brief, orthodox Christian doctrine teaches that all three persons of the Godhead are and should be called (by appropriation) "Creator." And the same is true of such titles as "Savior" and "Sanctifier," as the data of Scripture make plain. But only the first person is called "the Father"; only the second, "the Son"; and only the third, "the Holy Spirit." In other words, the nature of the biblical data has compelled theologians who would be faithful to those data to distinguish between the essential and the economic Trinity. Not that there are two trinities, but the God who *is* (eternally) triune—as Father, Son, and Spirit—has become by a voluntary act of his will our Creator, Savior, and Sanctifier. Hence, to substitute "Creator," "Savior," and "Sanctifier" for "Father," "Son," and "Spirit" is to confuse rather than illumine what Scripture says about God as he is and as he has revealed himself to be.[31]

A similar confusion results when one substitutes "child" for "Son." "God so loved the world that God gave God's only *Child . . .*" (Jn. 3:16). True, the New Testament calls Jesus not only God's Son (υἱός, Jn. 3:16) but also God's *child* (παῖς, Mt. 12:18; Acts 4:27, 30). But the latter is a messianic title used by the first Christians because they understood the Suffering Servant songs of Isaiah messianically and so applied them to Jesus. The *Sitz im Leben* of such usage is the apologetic use of the Jewish prophetic Scriptures to explain the meaning of Jesus' death as the Messiah. It is a usage having to do, in other words, with the role the Son assumed in accomplishing our salvation. It takes little theological acumen to see that the problem the first Christians faced (If Jesus is the Messiah, how is it he was crucified?) is quite different from the problem we are now discussing: Since God transcends all sexuality, why speak of the second person of the Trinity as the Son? Again, we only confuse matters when we appropriate the vocabulary used to resolve one problem in order to resolve an entirely different problem.

An unsatisfactory result is likewise obtained by stressing the feminine character of the Spirit in the Godhead. While the Hebrew word for "spirit" (רוּחַ) is feminine in gender, its New Testament equivalent (πνεῦμα) is neuter. Although certain early Gnostic sects (the Mandaeans and Ophites) identified the Spirit with the Mother Principle in God, the church never accepted this doctrine, not because the canonical Scriptures were chosen by men, but because such teaching does not conform to what the apostles taught. Furthermore, to make the Spirit the locus of the feminine in the Godhead leaves the

---

31. For a fuller discussion of the economic Trinity, see below, Unit Three, IV, D, 4, The Trinity of Revelation, pp. 305ff.

masculine clearly in the acendency. The Trinity becomes Father, Son, and Mother. Thus, the Godhead is conceived of as like a human family, and a patriarchal one at that, since the Father is the *first* person and fountainhead of the Trinity, of whom the Son is "begotten" and from whom the Spirit "proceeds."

The problem of sexist language, when we take its full measure, is exceedingly complex. And the various efforts at resolution in our judgment leave something to be desired. Nonetheless, we can only confess that, of all the problems with "God-talk," none is more humbling than this one, for it reflects not only our inadequacy as finite but also our perverseness as sinners, insofar, at least, as males have appealed to the masculine language used of God to disinherit "the other sex" of their full rights as human and as citizens of the kingdom of heaven. Hence, no language problem in all theology demands and will continue to demand more attention than this one.

SECOND ADDENDUM: ON DICTION AND STYLE IN THEOLOGICAL DISCOURSE

Having reflected on the nature of theological language in a theoretical way, we shall conclude our comments with brief observations of a more practical sort. Our thesis is that theologians should write not so that they *may* be understood but so that they *may not* be *mis*understood. If they are misunderstood, at least it should not be due to their abstruse style. Of course, clarity is not synonymous with simplicity. In a subject like theology, an easy style wed to a profound thought may actually becloud the argument. In the name of "popular" writing an enormous amount of theologizing occurs in our day that is admittedly nothing if not fuzzy. Our plea is not for pop theology, but for theological discourse that is clear and precise.[32] Such clear and precise writing does not require one to use in-house language that obfuscates rather than illuminates the argument. Too often theologians, in the name of precision, have lapsed into professional jargon that intimidates the uninitiated. Helmut Thielicke felt it necessary to warn beginning students in theology not to become like the young theologue who returned from seminary to a Bible study group and pelted a questioning layperson

---

32. Precise writing is the antidote to that verbiage which Spurgeon once referred to as the fig leaf of theological explanation that covers a multitude of theological sin. Dorothy Sayers, a master of the art of precise writing, observes that there is a place for every word— though she notes that there are a few whose right place is in hell or some dictionary of barbarisms. See Sayers, *The Mind of the Maker* (New York: Harper, 1941), p. 103, n. 9.

with "synoptic tradition," "realized eschatology," and many other such phrases, till the questioner retreated behind a white flag.[33]

Along with clarity and precision, theological language should also reflect a robust forcefulness and energy. We say this because theology should, by definition, concern itself with thought that comes home to the reader. It is not meant simply to inform or entertain; its true function is rather to set forth and reflect upon those truths by which Christians live and in the hope of which they die. We can only deplore the anathemas with which the ancients threatened anyone who dared to disagree with their dogmas, and the epithets with which the Protestant Reformers sometimes loaded their theological opponents are likewise offensive.[34] Yet we cannot but commend the enthusiasm, power, and eloquence with which they wrote on the grand themes of "the faith once delivered to the saints."[35] In a day of religious tolerance and theological pluralism, there are still some things that need to be said with vigor and conviction.

33. Thielicke, *A Little Exercise for Young Theologians* (Grand Rapids: Eerdmans, 1963), pp. 13-14. A parishioner once handed the writer a scrap of paper on which was written: "And Jesus said to them, 'Whom do you say that I am?' And they replied, 'You are the eschatological manifestation of the Ground of Being, the kerygma manifested in conflict and decision in the humanizing process.' And Jesus said, 'Huh?' "

34. At the close of his life Luther called his sacramental opponents, including the Swiss, "heretics," "hypocrites," "liars," "blasphemers," "soul-murderers," "sinners unto death," "bedeviled all over." According to Schaff, he not only overwhelmed his detractors with such terms of opprobrium but coined new ones "which cannot be translated into decent English." *History of the Christian Church,* vol. VII (Grand Rapids: Eerdmans, 1953), p. 656. Though Calvin was more moderate, he did not hesitate to style his defamers "a stye of swine."

35. The writer recalls his experience in seminary on reading for the first time Luther's *Tractates* and the preface to Calvin's *Institutes.* The sheer energy of conviction manifest in such writing is contagious.

IV. Alternatives to Christian Theism

Given our understanding of theological method and the way in which theologians use language, it is evident that we consider theological affirmations to be faith judgments. While these faith judgments do not, or should not, violate the canons of rational thought or the data of sense perception, yet they cannot be verified by such criteria. Hence, for the Christian theology can never be adequately done apart from faith. The student of theology is involved by the very nature of her subject in an act of faith, decision, and choice. To be sure, philosophy and science, too (as Aristotle has shown us), rest ultimately on some postulate that cannot be demonstrated but is rather chosen as supposedly self-evident. Yet such a postulate, whatever it may be, differs radically from the postulate on which theology done by a Christian rests. Christian theology postulates a God whose name is Yahweh, who has revealed himself in Jesus Christ. Such a postulate is no self-evident truth, but a truth given in a divine self-disclosure, a truth that evokes a response of faith. Hence, in all matters theological, faith and knowledge, decision and understanding are so related that we cannot say where one leaves off and the other begins. The theologian can neither say simply, "I believe," nor simply, "I understand," but only (with Anselm), "I believe in order to understand" *(credo ut intelligam)*. The truths of theology, in other words, are never rightly perceived and understood apart from faith. And faith is an act of decision in which "the heart has its reasons that reason does not know" (Pascal).

The decision that makes one a Christian is, as we have said, the confession "Jesus Christ is Lord." It is out of this theological (confessional) statement that all other theological statements have come, insofar as they are Christian theological statements. Therefore, these derivative, penulti-

50

mate statements also involve decision and choice in their own way. Unlike the study of geometry in which the theorems are logically entailed in the axioms, and unlike the study of chemistry in which a hypothesis is confirmed by the data, the study of theology continually places the student before decisions and choices. On the theological map there are many forks in the road. Depending on the choice one makes, one will be a Trinitarian or a Unitarian, a Pelagian or an Augustinian, a sacramentalist or an evangelical, a liberal or a conservative, and so forth. In short, there is no way to do theology so as to arrive at a final system that is self-evident to all.

The above discussion of the nature of theological statements bears on the fact that the church has been called the church militant. While it is true that Christians believe the church is marked by oneness and therefore they can sing

> The church's *one* foundation
> Is Jesus Christ her Lord,

still, this side of the eschaton, it is also true that they must acknowledge that

> . . . with a scornful wonder
> Foes see her sore oppressed;
> By schisms rent asunder,
> By heresies distressed. (Stone)

Though we may deplore these schisms and heresies, we should not forget that it has been through controversy, not accommodation, that the church has made its greatest theological advances. What would Athanasius have been without Arius, or Augustine without Pelagius, or Luther without Leo X? Surely Arius contributed to our understanding of the Trinity and Pelagius to our understanding of grace. And did not Leo X help Luther to become a teacher of us all and not just a disturbed German monk?

The teacher of theology will also recognize that the nature of theological truth bears on the classroom experience. Some students take systematics in the expectation that the course will provide them with final answers to all the basic issues of the Christian faith, answers that are ready-made and simply to be accepted. Such an approach reduces dogmatics to a handing down of infallible definitions that are simply restated in contemporary language. (In this respect, for a Protestant at least, Hans Küng's chapter "Freedom in Theology," in his *Freedom Today,* New York: Sheed and Ward, 1966, makes for interesting reading.) Other students take a course in systematics having arrived at their final answers even before they begin the course. But the student who has a sense for the subject will be aware that she is ever standing, to some degree at least, at Kierkegaard's "crossroads of time and eternity." It is only by engagement in the great debate, by standing at the forks in the road and committing oneself, that one enters into the inner sanctum of systematic theology. And when one so commits herself, a course in dogmatics is no longer a smorgasbord catering to the individual "taste" of the student; it is rather a course that helps one not only to know what truths to hold, but so to hold those truths as to be held by them.

In July of 1946, Charles E. Park, minister of Boston's First Church, Unitarian, confessed his faith in the *Christian Register,* by reading the Apostles' Creed "between the lines" as follows:

> I believe in a single, eternal, all-inclusive, all-pervading Life Principle, who is the prototype of every grace, power and nobility found in his creation, and whom I call God; the Father almighty, Maker of heaven and earth, and in Jesus Christ, not his only son, for whose son am I, but our Lord, because he is a more nearly perfect embodiment of the Life Principle than anyone I know; who was neither conceived by the Holy Ghost nor born of the virgin Mary, but was conceived and born as we are all conceived and born; who suffered under Pontius Pilate, was crucified, dead and buried. . . . The third day some eager women found his tomb empty and jumped to the conclusion that in the night he rose from the dead. He ascended into no heaven, for since heaven is not a place but a spiritual condition, he never left heaven. . . . I believe in the Holy Spirit, the spirit in which God works, the holy, catholic church, so long as it tries to be holy and is catholic. . . , the resurrection of the body, if the body means personality—not if the body means this mortal frame, for I am sick to death of my mortal frame and hope to be rid of it soon—and the life everlasting, meaning a chance to finish the interrupted opportunities of this life. Amen.

Such an obvious rewriting of the faith of the church, as it has been traditionally confessed, illustrates in a rather striking way that one's theological conclusions involve decision and choice from the first to the last article. But striking as such an instance may be, it is by no means as radical as some. One perceives what the real alternatives are when one considers the choices that have been made by those who have left the Christian tradition altogether. As citizens of a post-Christian world, many have become agnostics and skeptics convinced that there is no sufficient reason to hold either that God exists or that he does not, though it seems likely to them that he does not. Such a state of ultimate mental suspension, however, places the mind in the position of Noah's dove that had no place to rest her feet. She must return to the ark or perish.[1]

---

1. William James observes: "When I look at the religious question . . . then this command that we shall put a stopper on our heart, instincts, and courage, and *wait*—acting, of course, more or less as if religion were *not* true—till doomsday, or till such time as our intellect and senses working together may have raked evidence enough,—this command, I say, seems to me the queerest idol ever manufactured in the philosophic cave. . . . Indeed, we *may* wait if we will, . . . but if we do so, we do so at our peril as much as if we believed. In either case we *act*, taking our life in our hands." *The Will to Believe,* as cited in Clyde L. Manschreck, ed., *A History of Christianity* (Englewood Cliffs, N.J.: Prentice-Hall, 1964), p. 451.

Little wonder, then, that Western thought since Schopenhauer has reflected a deep strand of pessimism. A secular humanist may indeed declare that life is meaningful apart from any transcendent dimension even as a tone is beautiful that does not endure; but such a position is really a whistling in the dark. It is like savoring a vase of beautiful flowers that soon must wither, cut off from their roots; it is like admiring the scenery as one canoes down a river, hearing ever more distinctly the roar of the cataracts in the distance. Death has the last word, whether it be the death of the individual or of the universe.

Pessimism, then, arises not from the recognition that there is really no living without choosing, but rather from the realization that the post-Christian choice is a losing one. We may choose with Bertrand Russell to build the soul's habitation on the principle of "unyielding despair."[2] We may say that "we stand on a mountain pass in the midst of whirling snow and blinding mist, through which we get glimpses now and then of paths which may be deceptive." Yet we must " 'be strong and of a good courage,' " for "if we stand still we shall be frozen to death."[3] Quite so! But then why not, as Pascal has urged us to do, wager that God is and "that he rewards those who seek him" (Heb. 11:6)? If we lose, we lose nothing; but if we win we gain all.[4]

And so we begin the theological task having made a choice. Finding ourselves already set out on the voyage of life, we have wagered. What we shall say as we seek to elaborate our theology in a Christian, systematic, and dogmatic way rests on the fundamental faith postulate that there is a personal God who has revealed himself to us in Jesus Christ our Lord. Unbelief will reject such a choice as a pious substitute for ignorance. However, unbelief cannot make good the claim that to choose the Christian postulate by faith is to act in an irrational way, for so to act is to act as do unbelieving philosophers and scientists. To be sure, the character of the Christian's postulate is not self-evident to reason; rather, it is authenticated by God himself in an act of self-disclosure. In this act he reveals himself in such a way that they who believe know they can believe, will believe, indeed, must believe. But the philosophers and scientists who begin their task by appealing to some postulate or hypothesis that they believe to be self-evident are also acting on what they believe, not on what they can demonstrate.

2. See below, Unit Three, II, C, The Divine Transcendence, pp. 198ff.
3. Fritz James Stephen in C. L. Manschreck, ibid., p. 451.
4. See *Pensées*, III, frag. 234, on the wager.

Some, of course, will hold that science will one day render such a postulate of faith, resting on revelation, unnecessary; but for us such confidence in science is overweening. As many have observed, the more the horizons of knowledge are pushed out in every direction, the more mysterious the universe and our place in it becomes. For every question science answers, new and deeper questions are opened up. As we probe and penetrate the disguises of our environment, the more evident it becomes that there is another dimension of truth that autonomous reason cannot elucidate. "Can you find out the deep things of God?" the author of Job asks (Job 11:7). To the confident answer of autonomous reason, "Not yet," the Christian responds, "Nor ever."

We therefore begin the theological enterprise not in the hope of finding God in the philosophical Absolute nor in the quest for some sort of Unified Field Theory. Such a concept of the mind, such a god whom we have discovered by searching him out, would not be the God of Christian theology. Rather, we begin with the confession that we have to do with the God who, as the good shepherd, has searched us out and found us in Jesus Christ. And from the beginning of the Christian era this confession has moved Christians to share their faith. Hence, having defined our terms and having indicated how we shall go about our task, we invite our readers to cast their lot with the Christians who "walk by faith, not by sight" (2 Cor. 5:7), to join Bunyan's pilgrim in his journey to the celestial city, to set their feet, in the words of C. E. M. Joad, "on the steep and slippery path that leads to heaven."[5]

ADDENDUM: CONCERNING THE THEISTIC PROOFS

The theological method to which we have committed ourselves makes it obvious that we will not seek to build the house of revealed theology on the foundations of natural theology. Yet we can hardly ignore the efforts to frame a theistic proof inasmuch as such efforts have engaged some of the profoundest theological minds in the church. For this reason, along with the general remarks we have already made concerning the faith character of theological affirmations, we need to say a word as to why we cannot accept the attempt to base such affirmations of faith on

5. For an arresting account of the distinguished philosopher's return to the Christian faith, see his *Recovery of Belief* (London: Faber and Faber, 1955).

a rational demonstration that God exists. (The word "demonstration" is used here in the sense of a valid conclusion drawn from incontrovertible premises.)

The first such effort is Anselm's ontological argument.[6] Anselm seeks to deduce the existence of God from his very being as the One than whom none greater can be conceived. Since none greater than God can be conceived, to argue that such a Being is no more than a thought in our minds is, Anselm argues, to defend a logical impossibility. If the One than whom none greater can be conceived exists in the understanding alone, the very Being than whom none greater can be conceived is One than whom a greater *can* be conceived. For to be in reality as well as in the understanding is to have more being and therefore to be greater. So, to speak with the psalmist, one is indeed a fool who says there is no God (Ps. 14:1), for such a one is involved in an intolerable contradiction. As Descartes would say, to conceive of a God who has no existence is like conceiving of a mountain that has no valley.[7]

The profoundest critic of Anselm's argument was Immanuel Kant. Casting the argument in a syllogistic form brings the Kantian critique of the argument into focus:

Major: I can conceive of a Being, than whom none greater can be conceived, a Being having all perfections.

Minor: Existence is a perfection.

Conclusion: Therefore such a Being exists.

Kant attacked this argument in its minor premise. Existence, he reasoned, cannot be regarded as an attribute or property whose addition enriches and whose subtraction impoverishes a concept of the mind. To use an illustration—since Kant is short on illustrations—the difference between a hundred silver dollars conceived in my mind and a hundred silver dollars stacked on a gaming table is not that they have different qualities. They do not. Both are round, gray, smooth, thick, and heavy; otherwise I would not be conceiving one hundred silver dollars but something else. The difference is rather that the silver dollars on the table, unlike those in my mind, engender sensations that are organized by the mind through the forms

6. *Proslogium,* sec. 2, 3. While it may be, as Barth has insisted, that Anselm intended simply to illumine the reasonable nature of belief in God, his argument, as taken up and restated by many thinkers after him, has commonly been understood as an attempt to prove God's existence in the strict sense.

7. See his *Discourse on Method,* pt. IV and his *Meditations on the First Philosophy,* III and IV.

and categories the mind brings to all sense data.[8] Therefore we cannot extrapolate from a concept of the mind to the necessary existence of a Being corresponding to that concept. With Kant's conclusion we agree. Hence we have chosen to base our doctrine of God on revelation rather than on a reasoned demonstration of the sort attempted by Anselm.[9]

Thomas, while he did not accept the ontological argument, still shared with Anselm the conviction that the basic sentence in theology, "God exists," can be established apart from revelation. For this reason, he began his *Summa Theologiae* with five variations of the cosmological argument, which together comprise the other great reasoned effort to establish the existence of God. In this way he comes to the same conclusion as Anselm, though from the opposite direction. Rather than *deduce* God's existence from his being, he *inferred* it (as a *tabula rasa* empiricist) from the nature of the world as an effect requiring an intelligent First Cause. Of the five forms of the argument—from motion to an Unmoved Mover, from effect to Cause, from mutable to necessary Existence, from degrees of perfection to absolute Perfection, and from design to a Designer—the last, the so-called teleological argument, has had great influence not only among Catholic but also among Protestant thinkers. (Paley's *Evidences,* with its argument that a watch implies a watchmaker, was on the Oxford required reading list for over 100 years!)

Many have admitted the force of Thomas's argument that an infinite regression of causes is absurd and that there must, then, be a First Cause. But it is one thing to say that, as an effect, the universe implies a First Cause and another to say that this First Cause is to be identified with the God of the theologians. Hume has made us all aware of the fallacy of such reasoning. In his *Dialogues Concerning Natural Religion* he observes that one can never, in strict logic, argue for a cause greater than is required to account for an effect. This is the fundamental weakness in all forms of the

---

8. The above illustration is from *Types of Religious Philosophy,* ed. E. A. Burtt (New York: Harper, 1951), pp. 256-57. Kant's argument is found in his *Critique of Pure Reason.*

9. At the same time, we must remember that the memorial Name of God in the Old Testament is יהוה, the Hebrew root meaning "to be." We must also remember that when God gives his name, he expounds it as "I AM WHO I AM" (Ex. 3:14). This means that God reveals himself to us as the One who *is* in the absolute sense. The creature can say "I am" only because of a creative act of God. Therefore she can overcome the *Angst* (dread, anxiety) of ceasing to be only by faith in a future act of God, the gift of life beyond death harbingered in the resurrection of Christ. But God's being is neither derived being nor being threatened by non-being. It is rather *necessary* being. Hence in the sentence "God exists," the Subject and the predicate are related in a way that illuminates the wonder of being itself, the mystery that *anything* is. Even Thomas Aquinas, who made no use of Anselm's argument, admitted that such a unique relationship is the implication of the Tetragrammaton.

cosmological argument for the existence of God. The effect (the universe) is finite, as the theologians themselves teach, while the God whose existence they infer from this finite effect is infinite. But a finite effect cannot entail an infinite Cause. In our judgment Hume has put his finger on the Achilles' heel of all forms of the cosmological argument. As for the teleological argument in particular, while many who do not stand among those embracing the Christian faith have acknowledged manifold instances of particular design in the physical realm—as the scale of a fish for swimming or the wing of a bird for flying—they have reasoned that the physical phenomena of the universe as a whole are so varied that the argument from design must be selective in its use of the data. Therefore the conclusion that there is a cosmic Designer remains moot.

We can only conclude, then, that it is because God has endowed the creature with the knowledge of himself that she perceives in the phenomenal world the evidence of the noumenal or, in the language of the apostle, that she perceives in things visible ("the things that have been made") God's invisible nature (his "power and deity"). So one may say with the apostle that sinners are without excuse before their Maker; but this is not because they deny the assured results of a reasoned demonstration that God exists but because they suppress the truth that God has made plain to them through natural revelation (Rom. 1:18ff.). One may also say with the psalmist that the world, when seen through the eyes of faith, evokes praise: "The heavens declare the glory of God" (Ps. 19:1 NIV). But neither the truth of natural revelation nor the praise it evokes in the believer entails the conclusion that the world, as an effect, constitutes a rationally compelling proof that the God revealed in Christ exists as its infinite First Cause. In this regard it should be noted that the Bible begins not with a proof of God's existence, but with a declaration of what he has done in creating heaven and earth (Gn. 1:1). The existence of God is not the conclusion of a syllogism, but the assumption behind all that the Bible says. By the same token, it is the assumption behind all that theology says as it pursues its task of spelling out the implications of biblical revelation.

Speaking of the arguments for the existence of God, there is a type of theology concerned with these arguments we have not mentioned — namely, humorous theology (not to be confused with a theology of humor, of which we shall speak in due course). As a specimen of such theology, we note the proofs for the existence of Santa Claus found in Robert McAfee Brown's *Hereticus Papers*.[10] The first (ontological) proof rests

10. Robert M. Brown, ed., *Hereticus Papers* (Philadelphia: Westminster Press, 1979), vol. 2, pp. 11ff.

on the idea I have in my mind of a perfect Santa Claus, a Santa Claus "than which no greater can be conceived." This most perfect Santa Claus, out of his infinite supply of toys, gives each girl and boy beyond all they can ask or even think. Moving with and even exceeding the speed of light, he never finds a chimney, whatever its size, that he cannot negotiate. "Indeed, it is easier for him to get down even the tiniest chimney than for a camel to go through the eye of a needle." But obviously such a Santa Claus must exist in reality outside my mind and not simply as an idea in my mind. Otherwise "the idea in my mind would *not* be the most perfect Santa Claus, since it would lack one of the attributes of perfection, namely, existence."

A long time ago, "Immanuel Kant (note the name Immanuel) said that he could imagine a perfect $100 bill in his pocket, but that did not mean that the $100 bill actually existed. There was no necessary transfer from idea to reality." Obviously this objection on Kant's part rests on a false premise, for "no professor has ever had, let alone been able to imagine having, $100 in his pocket at one time. The invalidity of Kant's premise already threatens the validity of Kant's conclusion."

The second proof for the existence of Santa Claus is an argument from a first clause. In developing this argument we are moving from Anselmic to Thomistic presuppositions. "As I look about the world I am aware of the existence of many clauses: subordinate clauses, dependent clauses, sanity clauses, and so forth. Does the existence of any of these clauses assume the status of a self-explanatory phenomenon? Of course not." However, in our effort to explain these clauses we end up in an infinite regress which does not really solve the problem at all. Who can abide such an infinite regress? And so "we are forced to posit the existence of a First Clause, itself unclaused," and this First Clause everyone calls "Santa Claus, the holy or sacred clause."

Another form of this argument for the existence of Santa Claus is one which reasons from effect (presents under the Christmas tree) to the one who put them there. This argument is known as "the clausmological argument."

Veiling

A Sermon Preached by Marguerite Shuster
at Knox Presbyterian Church, Pasadena, California,
Lord's Day, February 14, 1988.

And even if our gospel is veiled, it is veiled only to those who are perishing. In their case the god of this world has blinded the minds of the unbelievers, to keep them from seeing the light of the gospel of the glory of Christ, who is the likeness of God. For what we preach is not ourselves, but Jesus Christ as Lord, with ourselves as your servants for Jesus' sake. For it is the God who said, "Let light shine out of darkness," who has shone in our hearts to give the light of the knowledge of the glory of God in the face of Christ.

2 Corinthians 4:3-6

Paul had a problem. Well, if you insist on being thorough about it, Paul probably had lots of problems, just like the rest of us. But at the moment he penned my text, he had a particular problem. And, if I'm reading him correctly, he was at least momentarily frustrated and irritated by it. It wasn't a little, unimportant problem, one he could brush off or push aside. No, it had to do with the center of his whole calling as an apostle, with the one thing he was supposed to do in life—namely, to proclaim the gospel. People were apparently telling him that as a preacher, he was a loser. He was obscure. His gospel didn't make sense. No rational person could buy what he was saying because it would be like buying a pig in a poke—too much risk. In short, he preached a "veiled" gospel, in which many essential things were covered up and couldn't be seen. If he wanted them to take him seriously, he ought to do better at presenting his arguments; or he should talk sensibly about virtue and morality, which everybody at least understood, regardless of whether he could measure up or not; or something like that. Sticking to a story about a crucified God just wouldn't do, said the sophisticated unbeliever.

What should Paul say? Do you sense the temptation he must have felt? Perhaps, indeed, you have felt it yourself when you were struggling to witness to someone who thought anyone who believed as you did must not be very bright. Humanly speaking, at those points one longs for the Ultimate Argument, the syllogism that provides a definitive, inexorable proof of Christian truth, the intellectual karate chop that will reduce one's condescending challenger to awed assent.

A few weeks ago I heard a senior student, with only one quarter of seminary to go, preach to fellow students a very apt sermon in which he described the experience of starting each quarter with the sense of anticipation that *this time* there would be a class that would at last provide him with The Answers—the answers that would confute all doubters and be the badge of his authority as a minister of the gospel. The whole class burst out in sympathetic—and somewhat nervous—laughter. Everyone knew exactly what he was talking about. They all knew the moments of self-doubt and feelings of inadequacy. Time was running out. They were all about to be thrust out into the unbelieving world without that ultimate intellectual weapon. It's scary. They won't, however, be the first to arrive. As I already said, Paul was already there a couple thousand years ago.

Note what Paul does. He doesn't take the bait of his critics at all. He refuses even to begin an argument on their ground. Instead, he speaks what reasonable, tolerant, pluralistic, and inclusive people, people who wish to keep debate politely confined to grounds everyone can accept, must have heard as provocative, fighting words. He says, "If our gospel is veiled, it is veiled only to those who are perishing. In their case the god of this world has blinded the minds of the unbelievers, to keep them from seeing the light of the gospel of the glory of Christ." In other words, he says to his readers, the fault lies not in the gospel that he, Paul, is preaching, but with them. If they don't understand, that in itself is evidence that they are in danger of going to hell, that they are in the snares of Satan, and that Satan is preventing them from seeing what anybody with eyes could see. Not a very friendly way to begin an evangelistic conversation. I can't say that I would recommend it as a standard approach.

Nonetheless, I think we do need to take seriously the kind of choices implicit in Paul's polemic. Not to believe, he implies, is not really to be free, autonomous, and fully and gloriously human. Not to believe in a transcendent God will instead inevitably lead one to believe all too absolutely in this world. There is no neutral ground. We will either look up or down, to speak metaphorically, for our explanations of things.

Is a house explained by its basement, or is a basement explained by the fact that someone built a house? Are there human emotions because of a peculiar chemical reaction in human bodies and brains, or is there such a chemical reaction because of human emotions? Is there light because of electrons, or electrons because of light? Do some humans believe in God because they project into the universe a bigger model of themselves, or do they believe in God because he made a finite model of himself? It all depends on how you look at it. How you look at it *matters,* says Paul; because if you look down, if you look only at the world, you will become blind to any other way of seeing things, and the gospel will sound like nonsense. "The god of this world has blinded the minds of the unbelievers." That Paul speaks of a *god* of this world—meaning Satan—suggests that this world is not really the only thing to which we become subject; but that the Devil is the god *of this world* suggests that we may be aware only of the world and not of the further spiritual significance of our choices.

How can it be that we become blinded by the god of this world? Well, we have to be honest about the power and plausibility of worldly ways of looking at things. Leave aside the undoubted immediacy of sensual gratification as contrasted with hopes of heaven. Leave aside the pressing societal need for public virtues and well-enforced laws if all is not to turn to chaos, as contrasted with a superficially antinomian message of forgiveness and grace. Leave aside, I say, these significant worldly considerations and consider for the moment just the world's way of knowing.

I would suggest that we like the world's way of knowing for two reasons. First, it enables us to do things that we want done, like build airplanes and develop medicines and design computers—things that give us tremendous power. Second, it gives us a sense of control, since we basically, if we are scientists, at least understand *why* airplanes fly, *why* certain drugs kill certain bacteria, or *how* computers spit out reams of data. There are rules, there are formulas, there are self-consistent sets of axioms that we can understand and that lead to necessary conclusions. If an airplane crashes, we seek after causes in mechanical failure or aerodynamics or pilot error. We do not waste time exorcising demons from the engine. To do the latter—to import a spiritual cause—would actually interfere with solving the problem. Looking down is necessary if we are to function at all in these realms. No point in denying that.

But let us take an example of a different sort. Let us consider light. In order to do certain things with light, we need to know when it behaves like a wave and when like a particle; we need to know characteristics of certain parts of the spectrum, and so on. But notice something curious here. Presumably a blind person could *know* all of these things and yet never have seen light. Something has been lost along the way. The actual seeing of light, so critical to our experience, is totally foreign to that person. I had a conversation with a very bright, well-read young man the other day who held that what some would call the spiritual gift of discernment was actually the product of a particular, not-very-healthy pattern of relationships with one's mother during one's infancy. Well, perhaps. Still, what the young man didn't seem to see was that *even if the explanation was in some sense correct,* it was very much smaller than the thing it explained. I was reminded of one of my favorite of G. K. Chesterton's remarks. He says, "Contemplate some able and sincere materialist. . . . He understands everything, and everything does not seem worth understanding. His cosmos may be complete in every rivet and cog-wheel, but still his cosmos is smaller than our world."[1]

By looking down, we continue to explain things by principles that are less than we are—that do, again, provide tremendous power and control and plausibility, but through which we lose big chunks of the reality we actually experience. As soon as we make the intellectual commitment that what is *most real* is what we can explain, demonstrate, prove, or make work according to one or another of our reductionistic principles, we have in the most literal possible sense lost our souls. We are "the perishing," those who have sold out to the god of this world—namely, to Satan in one of his many disguises, for he is always at work to reduce us to what is lowest in our own natures.

It's no use protesting that we are simply noble seekers of truth, and that God will surely be found wherever we look with sufficient earnestness. It's no use implying that any respectable God would be willing to be reasonable and make himself manifest according to our formulas. We might as well bring our chemistry teacher a canister of helium and a lump of carbon and earnestly demand that she "be reasonable" and show us how to make water out of those components. We might as well go to New York Harbor and demand a train ticket to London. If we insist on hanging on to our presuppositions and conditions, we can't get there from here, and that's all there is to it. Indeed, if we insist on hanging on to our presuppositions and conditions, we will increasingly doubt that there is any "there" to get to, for our every effort will be resoundingly defeated. Our choice will continually confirm itself.

1. *Orthodoxy* (New York: Image Books, 1959), p. 23.

All this impotence, this blindness, Paul attributes quite flatly to un-belief—unbelief that Jesus Christ is Lord, with all that implies about a whole new order of things not governed by the god of this world, not confined by the limits of our own reason. What we need, then, is not arguments but eyes; what we need is not answers but light. If God's glory is not something we can figure out or deduce from our experiments, then it must be something with power to impress itself upon us as undeniably as the blazing sun, something to which, though we cannot explain it, we can yet point. And those who have eyes will see. The answer to the question, "Is it eyes or light, faith or revelation, that we really need?" is No. It is not eyes *or* light, faith *or* revelation. It is both: eyes *and* light, faith *and* revelation.

The skeptic wavers. He says, "I want sufficient reasons to believe." And we're right back at our initial problem, for sufficient evidence comes only after the fact. If one wishes to understand an obscure language of which one has never heard, one has to believe that it means something and set oneself to learning it *before* one will receive convincing evidence. If one born deaf wishes to know what sound is like before deciding to have surgery to give him hearing, those seeking to help him will be absolutely thwarted. As David Lloyd George is quoted as saying, sometimes nothing but a big step will do. You can't cross a chasm in two small jumps.[2] And as St. Anselm said much earlier, "I believe in order that I may understand." Belief and understanding go together and can in no way be torn apart, any more than can the faculty of vision from the light by which one sees. Again, our choice will be self-confirming. As surely as we believe, the veil will be ripped away and we will be given light—not, perhaps, all at once; not, perhaps, in an overwhelming blaze that would blind us all over again; but light enough to see nonetheless.

And what will we see? "The light of the gospel of the glory of Christ, who is the likeness of God. . . . For it is the God who said, 'Let light shine out of darkness,' who has shone in our hearts to give the light of the knowledge of the glory of God in the face of Christ." When we see rightly, we see that the one God is responsible for all light—the light by which we see natural things in the natural world as well as the light by which we see spiritual things.[3] He who gives us the means of knowing atoms and acorns is the same One who gives us the means of knowing himself. When we see rightly, what we see is a created cosmos with value and meaning

2. Source unknown.

3. C. K. Barrett, *The Second Epistle to the Corinthians* (New York: Harper & Row, 1973), p. 135.

and purpose; and what we see first is the transcendent glory of it all—the glory of Christ, the glory of God. Glory—divine and heavenly radiance, loftiness, majesty, power, splendor, honor—knowledge of the glory is what we receive as we believe. We are called to live our lives by the light that comes from knowledge of the divine glory.

That casts a new light on everything. Think about it for a moment. Don't things, even the most ordinary things, look different when seen by the light of the knowledge of glory? In one way, of course, they look smaller and dimmer and less attractive as gods. But in another way, they look infinitely more important because their meaning is not limited to themselves alone, much less to their lowest determinants. Imagine this whole world illumined by a transcendent glory. Wonderful!

Something more wonderful still must yet be seen, though; for while glory may awe and inspire us, it does little to win our love. Abstract, overpowering glory may command our minds, but it does not in itself gain our hearts. So Paul does not leave us with the glory absolutely distant and unapproachable. He does not leave us knocked over by a God "in light inaccessible hid from our eyes," as God of course is in himself. Much less does he leave us struggling incoherently to believe in the virtues of believing. No; in the most astounding phrase in this whole passage, Paul tells us that the glory of God has a human face. "We preach not ourselves [or our theories or our demonstrations or our virtues] but Jesus Christ as Lord." "God . . . has shone in our hearts to give the light of the knowledge of the glory of God *in the face of Christ*." "Veiled in flesh the Godhead see," says the carol—a veil lifted momentarily in the glory of the Transfiguration, which we celebrate today. Then the veil of flesh dropped down again, and we see only a Galilean carpenter. That is where we must look. The glory of God with a human face—the face of Jesus. See him, and believe. Believe, and see. Glory!

UNIT TWO

HOW WE KNOW GOD: REVELATION AND SCRIPTURE

He sang of God—the mighty source
of all things—the stupendous force
    On which all strength depends;
From whose mighty arm, beneath whose eyes,
All period, power, and enterprise
    Commences, reigns, and ends.

.   .   .   .   .

Glorious—more glorious, is the crown
Of him that brought salvation down
    By meekness, called thy Son
Thou at stupendous truth believed,
And now the matchless deed's achieved,
    DETERMINED, DARED, and DONE.

Christopher Smart, *A Song to David*

I. God's Self-Disclosure in Creation and Providence

In our remarks on theological method we noted that theology, in contrast to philosophy and science, postulates a truth given by divine revelation. Theologically speaking, revelation is not simply abstract information supernaturally communicated, and much less is it immediate awareness of the divine through mystical union and religious ecstasy. It is rather God's act of disclosing himself, his act of making himself and his will known to the creature who bears his image.[1] When speaking of this divine disclosure in a general way, the older theologians referred to the seed of religion (semen religionis) or sense of divinity (sensus divinitatis), by which they meant that God has so impressed the thought of himself on our minds and hearts that an innate awareness of his will is inseparable from our very constitution as human.[2]

This "general" or "natural" revelation, as it is sometimes called,[3] is what Paul speaks of in Romans 1:18f. when he affirms that God's wrath is justly provoked against the Gentiles for their transgression of his will, which he has made known to them. They suppress (κατεχόντων, literally, "keep at arm's length" or "keep down," that is, "hold the lid on") the truth revealed to them so that it cannot properly develop in terms of righteous living. This truth that the Gentiles suppress is, says the apostle, "what can be known about God . . . because God has shown it to them" (v. 19).

---

1. The Greek word for revelation (ἀποκαλύπτω) literally means an "uncovering," a "laying bare" of something hid from view.
2. So Calvin, Institutes, I, 2 and 3, passim.
3. "General," that is, given generally to all the members of the human family; "natural," that is, endemic to the human condition.

The apostle elaborates the same thought in Romans 2:14-15. "When Gentiles who have not the law do by nature what the law requires, they are a law to themselves . . . they show that what the law requires is written on their hearts, while their conscience also bears witness and their conflicting thoughts accuse or perhaps excuse them." Though these Gentiles do not have the law, that is, the revelation rooted in the law promulgated at Sinai and elaborated in the Jewish Scriptures, yet, says the apostle, they are not wholly without the knowledge of God and his will, as is evident from the fact that they do by nature things concerning which the law speaks. Though they by no means keep the law perfectly, they cannot plead ignorance to excuse their sinful behavior.

Perhaps Paul uses the circumlocution, "who show that what the law requires is written on their hearts," rather than just saying, they "show the *law* written on their hearts," because "writing the law on their heart" is the way the prophets speak of the blessings of salvation guaranteed in the new covenant (Jer. 31:31-33; see also Ez. 36:26). The apostle surely does not wish to imply that the Gentiles enjoy by *nature* the covenant blessings bestowed on Israel by *grace*. He is rather concerned to show that Gentiles, who are apart from special revelation—namely, the covenant promise of salvation—are yet sufficiently aware of the divine will, aware of the difference between right and wrong, the difference between what God approves and disapproves; that they are, so to speak, "a law to themselves." Not that they are free to do whatever they please with impunity; on the contrary, they are "a law to themselves" in the sense that their very lives evidence an ineluctable awareness of God's will. They can no more escape their responsibilities as moral selves than they can escape their shadows as physical selves.

It is difficult to say how the apostle thought of this innate knowledge of the divine will. He simply says that the conscience of the Gentiles "bears witness along with" (συμμαρτυρούσης τῆς συνειδήσεως). Along with what? Perhaps along with the inner "writing" of the Creator on their hearts. If this is his meaning, then we may restate his argument as follows: God's creating all members of the human family in his image involves the "writing" of his will on their hearts after the analogy of his writing on tables of stone at Sinai. This inner "writing" of the Creator manifests itself at the noetic level as the faculty of conscience whose witness confirms, that is, "witnesses along with," the innate knowledge of the divine will given in our creation as moral agents. As a result of this witness of conscience, even Gentiles who never have heard of the Ten Commandments are yet aware that some things are right and others wrong. Or Paul could mean that the conscience, as the inner faculty that distinguishes right from wrong, bears its witness along with the outer deeds that the Gentiles do, condemning some of those deeds and excusing others. As a result, when Gentiles contemplate the way they live, their thoughts reveal an unending tension between condemnation and approbation.

However we may interpret what Paul says precisely, it is obvious that this inner knowledge with which all are endowed from birth is no full-blown system of divinity. It is rather a potential, actualized as we live out our lives in the world of time and space—specifically in that particular time and space that God has given each of us (Acts 17:26). Hence, there will be an enormous difference between the God-awareness of a Mayan Indian of the Old Empire, a graduate of the University of Cambridge, and a survivor of Auschwitz. The Scriptures, then, warrant only the broadest of judgments. All have some knowledge of God—or gods, as Luther would say; consequently all are sinners who come short of his glory to the extent that they knowingly do that which is contrary to the divine will (Rom. 3:23).

Speaking of what God has shown to all concerning himself, the apostle says nothing of God's grace and mercy but speaks only of his "eternal power and deity." In a paradox, he speaks of these as God's "invisible nature" perceived by the visible things he has made (Rom. 1:20). In other words, the phenomenal world discloses the noumenal world. When the creature endowed with the divine image contemplates the creation, she cannot escape the impression of a higher Power "in, with, and over" the tangible world of the senses. Under such circumstances, as Carlyle once observed, were one not to wonder and worship, one would be like a pair of spectacles behind which there are no eyes.[4] To be sure, our awe in the presence of the mystery of creation is muted by our very familiarity with the world.[5] And, being sinners, we even use our knowledge as the occasion for greater sin. As Paul observes, when sinners turn their backs on God, they not only refuse to honor him as God but become vain in their reasonings, even going so far as to exchange the glory of the immortal God for the image of mortals, birds, four-footed creatures, and even creeping things.[6]

By contrast, those whose minds have been illumined by faith will resonate with the words of the psalmist, "The heavens are telling the glory

---

4. Thomas Carlyle, *Sartor Resartus,* chap. X.

5. Luther observes that the smallest flowers show God's wisdom and might, yet, he complains, we trample on lilies like so many cows. One wonders what he would say to our present-day ravaging of the environment wherein we not only "trample on (individual) lilies" but destroy whole species of them—forever!

6. Romans 1:22-23. The descending scale reflects Paul's awareness of idolatry as practiced in Greece, Rome, and Egypt in his day.

of God; and the firmament proclaims his handiwork." The nature psalms, of course, are an expression of Israel's faith in YAHWEH, the God of the covenant.[7] But this does not mean that the revelational character of the creation is simply in the eye of the believer and that the creation reveals nothing to the unbeliever. It means rather that the *response* to that revelation differs greatly depending on whether one views the created order with or without the eye of faith.[8] But respond one must, whether negatively or positively, for the human subject can never, like the beast of the field, merely react to the natural order in a religiously neutral way. Of course the relation of animals to their environment is both significant and informative, as the fascinating study of animal behavior shows, but they neither acknowledge nor deny God in any of his works. To be human, on the other hand, is to be not only a part of the created order but uniquely involved with the Creator of that order.

In his *Mere Christianity* (New York: Macmillan, 1952), C. S. Lewis, a lay theologian "with a rare gift to make righteousness readable," uses the argument we have just summarized to begin his case for Christianity. When it comes to right and wrong, he observes, people always act as though such behavior were obvious to everyone. Otherwise, what was said about the Nazis during and after the war would be nonsense. "What was the sense in saying the enemy were in the wrong unless right is a real thing which the Nazis at bottom knew as well as we did and ought to have practiced?" (ibid., pp. 18-19). Otherwise we should not blame them for what they did anymore than we would blame them for the color of their hair. Imagining a country where one is praised for double-crossing those who have been kindest to her is like imagining a country where the sum of two and two is five.

Lewis goes on to observe that while most of us agree that right and wrong are not a matter of mere taste, yet we do not live the way we believe. It is this disparity between what we know and what we do that reflects the difference between the so-called laws of nature and the laws of morality. The former simply describe what happens, but the latter do not describe "what humans, in fact, do" (ibid., p. 26). When it comes to morality, we must distinguish between what *is* and what *ought* to be, a distinction applying nowhere else, whether we think of electrons or galaxies. So it appears that there is another reality than that of the senses. Such a reality, says Lewis, implies

---

7. Here one should read Christopher Smart's great poem *A Song to David,* inspired by the nature psalms of the Old Testament. Louis Untermeyer calls it "sheer magnificence . . . revealing new meanings and far reaching glories with each reading." *A Treasury of Great Poems* (New York: Simon and Schuster, 1955), p. 566. We have prefaced this section with two stanzas from Smart's poem.

8. "At my meal just now I was gladdened by the beautiful design of a laurel leaf floating on my soup. . . . Thus does God remind us of the beauties of his kingdom even in an environment lacking in everything that is lovely and harmonious." So wrote Ludwig Steil, pastor of the Evangelical Church of Holsterhausen, Wanne-Eichel, Germany, in a letter to his wife from Dachau sometime before he died there, Jan. 17, 1945. See *Dying We Live.*

something behind the universe and this Something is like a Someone, a Director, a Guide. This Someone is by no means necessarily the God of Christian theology; but given the bind we are in—we know what we ought to do and we know that we do not do it—the Christian diagnosis and solution of the human problem is as plausible as any.

Not only in creation, but also in his providential care God has revealed himself, as Paul reminded his hearers at Lystra: "Yet he did not leave himself without witness, for he did good and gave you from heaven rains and fruitful seasons, satisfying your hearts with food and gladness" (Acts 14:17). Speaking of this "second species" of God's revelatory work—the first being creation—Calvin observes that God providentially rules human society so as to exhibit his clemency to the pious and his severity to the wicked. Of course, Calvin speaks as a believer to believers; he was not oblivious to the ambiguities of history. He follows Augustine in reasoning that we should not be perplexed beyond all hope when God allows good people to be harassed with adversity while the ungodly exult for a time with impunity. Rather, we should conclude that his punishment of one sin implies that he is angry with all sins and, though he passes by many sins for the present, there will be a judgment hereafter.[9] As in creation, so in providence unbelievers rarely perceive God's works for what they are, that is, disclosures of his wisdom and power.

> Blind unbelief is sure to err
>   And scan his works in vain;
> God is his own interpreter
>   And he will make it plain. (Cowper)

But to the believer, when the young lions roar after their prey, they are "seeking their food from God" (Ps. 104:21); it is God who arrays the lilies of the field with a glory beyond Solomon's (Mt. 6:29-30), feeds the raven (Lk. 12:24), and knows of a fallen sparrow (Mt. 10:29-30).

Our injection of the belief factor into the discussion leads inevitably to the question of that "special" revelation wherein God discloses himself, not only as the Creator and Ruler over all, but as the Redeemer reconciled to sinners through faith in Christ. This revelation is, in the words of Christopher Smart, that "stupendous truth" at which David believed (i.e., reached toward with ardent aspiration), a truth "determined, dared, and

---

9. Speaking of Augustine and God's revelation through providential circumstances, witness the good bishop's poignant lament that he failed, in his youth, to hear God's word (though he spoke in his very ear) in and through the admonitions of his mother Monica, when she enjoined upon him a life of chastity (*Confessions* II [III], 7).

done" by him who is called God's Son. It is he who brought salvation down to this lost world. We must now turn to this second aspect of the Christian doctrine of revelation, the revelation of God in Christ Jesus.

The question is often raised: Should general revelation be understood simply in terms of its negative effect of rendering those who resist it without excuse (Rom. 1:18-20)? Or is there the possibility, since God the Creator and God the Redeemer are one and the same God, that some may be savingly related to him apart from any knowledge of that revelation of mercy given to Israel and in these last days fulfilled to us in his Son (Heb. 1:1-2)? Though we cannot subscribe to Schleiermacher's "religion-in-the-religions" approach (nor that of Lessing in *Nathan the Wise*), we would point out that since the Christian doctrine of revelation includes God's witness to himself in creation and in history, it is not necessary to deny the saving efficacy of this witness, in every conceivable instance, in order to secure the ultimate truth claims of Christianity. There is a righteousness of the law which, if practiced, one shall live by (Rom. 10:5, citing Lv. 18:5). But we cannot get beyond this conditional statement. One thing is clear, in any case, and that is that knowledge and responsibility are closely related in Scripture. Hence the Gentiles, who have no knowledge of Christ, are not accountable for their ignorance of him in whose name salvation is proclaimed (Acts 4:12). If one cannot believe in him of whom one has not heard (Rom. 10:14), neither can one disbelieve. The Gentiles, then, who have never heard of Christ, are accountable to God only insofar as they know his will apart from Christ, and fail to live by the light of that knowledge. The degree of their accountability is God's, not ours, to determine. (For Dante's solution to the age-old question of the "noble heathen," see *The Divine Comedy,* bk. III: Paradise, Canto 20.)

II. God's Self-Disclosure in Jesus Christ

A. INTRODUCTION

As we move in our thinking from general to special revelation, the first question we face is, How are these two forms of revelation related?[1] In traditional Roman Catholic thought, following Thomas, there are not strictly speaking two forms of revelation to be related, but two ways of knowing God. There is that knowledge of God resting on reason alone and that resting on revelation. While the former—the knowledge that God exists—can be rationally demonstrated, the latter—that God is a Trinity, that he is our Maker and Redeemer, and so on—can be known only by revelation. Since we have already indicated the problems we have with the theistic proofs, we shall not pursue the approach of natural theology further at this time.[2] Rather, because we believe the knowledge of God to rest entirely on his self-disclosure, we shall assume a continuity of revelation qualified as general and special and address ourselves to the question of how these two types of revelation are related.

Calvin, in his response to this question, uses the homely illustration of spectacles. As dimness is removed from the eyes of the elderly by

---

1. In making the distinction between general (natural) and special (redemptive) revelation, we part company with Deists, who acknowledge no special revelation and therefore make no distinction of the sort we use here. "There is a word of God; there is a revelation. . . . *The Word of God is the Creation We Behold:* and it is *in this word* . . . that God speaketh universally to man. . . . In fine, do we want to know what God is? Search not the book called the scripture, which any human hand might make, but the scripture called the Creation." Tom Paine, *The Age of Reason;* italics his, as cited in Clyde L. Manschreck, *A History of Christianity* (Englewood Cliffs, N.J.: Prentice-Hall, 1964), p. 257.

2. See above, Unit One, IV, Addendum: Concerning the Theistic Proofs, p. 54.

spectacles, "so the Scriptures, collecting in our minds the otherwise confused notions of Deity, dispel the darkness and give us a clear view of the true God."[3] This traditional Reformed view of the matter occasioned a heated controversy between Barth and Brunner early in this century. Brunner argued that though sin has darkened the understanding, enslaved the will, and even seared the conscience, there yet remains a "broken natural knowledge" of God in the human heart that is the point of contact *(Anknüpfungspunkt)* for the preaching of the gospel. Barth reacted vehemently to this idea in his *No! An Answer to Emil Brunner.* This broken natural revelation, this point of contact for the gospel, is, Barth alleged, nothing more than the camel's nose of liberalism in the tent door of evangelical theology. Granted the plausibility of Brunner's appeal to Calvin, the latter would have spoken differently had he lived in our times.[4] Were we to adopt such a view, Barth said, theology would be compelled once more to acknowledge the essential continuity between nature and grace; to postulate a spark of divinity in every human breast that needs only to be fanned into a flame by education and culture. Given such, the kingdom will be brought in by the creature who is competent to achieve her own salvation. By contrast, Barth insisted, salvation is a perpendicular from above; it is the work of the Lord, the Spirit. And the Spirit does not need any "point of contact" within nature; he creates his own point of contact. Salvation is a miracle; it is absolutely by grace. Away, then, with the effort to lay the foundations of grace within the possibilities of nature.[5]

John Baillie, commenting on Barth's argument in his Gifford Lectures, observes:

> I had of course always believed that there is no ultimate salvation for mankind save in Jesus Christ, but when I began to read Dr. Barth's books, what struck me at once as unfamiliar was his insistence that mankind had no knowledge of God save in Jesus Christ. This is new teaching, and it is precisely what I have never been able to accept. I still believe, as I have always done, that at all times God "left himself not without witness" (Acts 14:17) but has revealed something of his holy nature to men through creation.[6]

3. *Institutes,* I, 6, 1.

4. Barth had in mind specifically the "German Christians" who had capitulated to the Nazis, failing to recognize the truth that Jesus Christ is the *"one* word of God." See the *Barmen Declaration.*

5. See Barth's *Natural Theology* (London: Bles, 1936) for the text of the main documents of the debate, translated into English by Fraenkel, with a preface by John Baillie.

6. John Baillie, *The Sense of the Presence of God* (New York: Scribner's, 1962), p. 255.

For ourselves, we can only applaud Barth's zeal to preserve a theology of grace alone. Only such a theology can do justice to the language of radical discontinuity with which Scripture speaks concerning nature and grace. The natural heart is a sinful heart, a "heart of stone" that must be replaced with a "heart of flesh"; the natural man or woman must be "born again," must become "a new creature in Christ." But, like Baillie, we believe that Brunner speaks some truth too. Even though fallen, alienated from God, and incapable of achieving her own salvation, the sinner is never wholly unrelated to God and thus wholly without the knowledge of God.

True, there are not two sources and norms of this knowledge; God alone is the source and norm of all our knowledge of him. True, his self-revelation does not stand under our reason, history, and experience. Yet the theology of the first article of the Apostles' Creed ("I believe in God . . . Maker of heaven and earth") implies that there is no reality, even though it is outside the bounds of special revelation, that is empty and meaningless. God is not just the Creator of those who confess him as Creator, but the Creator of heaven and earth and all therein, whether they confess him or not. Furthermore, though we confess that this creation is flawed by sin, yet as Christians we affirm that God's response to sin is the man Christ Jesus. If this is the case, then

> *either* this man only appeared to be a man and revelation [in this man] was itself just an appearance, *or* this man Jesus Christ, without sin to be sure, really was a man, and *then*, it would appear, we must conclude that human existence, human nature *as such*, possesses a passive capacity for revelation. But this cannot be asserted if (from the perspective of [redemptive] revelation) everything is meaningless before and outside of [this] revelation. Therefore there must be a continuity between "nature" and "grace."[7]

We shall, as we have noted, assume this continuity between nature and grace as we turn to consider the special revelation God has given of himself in the witness of Scripture to Christ, a revelation by which we know him as the God who is love, the God whose purpose in Christ is to show mercy to the sinner.

---

7. Weber, *Grundlagen der Dogmatik*, vol. I (Neukirchen-Vluyn: Neukirchener Verlag, 1955), pp. 127-28. English translation, *Foundations of Dogmatics*, vol. I (Grand Rapids: Eerdmans, 1981), p. 207. As time went on, Barth's rejection of a natural knowledge of God became less severe, as can be seen in his extensive treatment of the doctrine of the Word of God, *K.D.*, I/2. See especially par. 17, "The Revelation of God as the Abolition of Religion," *Church Dogmatics*, I/2 (Edinburgh: T. & T. Clark), 1956.

B. THE MODES (MODALITIES) OF SPECIAL REVELATION

Throughout our discussion so far, we have spoken of revelation as God's disclosure of himself and his will. Assuming this general understanding of revelation, we must now enlarge on it as we turn to the subject of special revelation. John Baillie once observed that in disclosing himself God "does not give us information by communication; he gives us himself in communion."[8] The thought of revelation as "communion" takes us beyond the general revelation given in nature and history to that revelation of which we now speak, a revelation that, in the mystery of the divine purpose, brings sinners into communion with God as their Redeemer. The beneficiaries of this revelation not only are aware of God's "eternal power and deity"; they also know him by name. He is "Yahweh," the "Lord." The recipients of such revelation are in covenant fellowship with him whose grace and mercy, first revealed to Israel, has in these last days been manifest to us in Christ. It is with revelation in this sense that theologians have been primarily concerned.

This special revelation is commonly called the "word of God." Due perhaps to the fact that this "word" comes to us as we read and hear what God says in Scripture, the term "special revelation" is often understood as synonymous with Scripture and construed as the sum total of the words that make up the propositions in the Bible. (In the contemporary debate over inerrancy, some insist that belief in "propositional revelation" is the touchstone of orthodoxy.) Such an approach is understandable, for the Bible is the word of God and the minister is quite correct when, in a service of worship, she introduces the reading of Scripture with, "Let us hear the word of God." Furthermore, as she begins to read, she is reading sentences, that is, propositions. So revelation does take the form or mode of words organized as propositions. Yet it is quite misleading, in our judgment, to reduce the doctrine of revelation to the single mode of written propositions, even though Scripture is made up of such, a fact no one can doubt.

The Bible itself, in fact, speaks of revelation not as so many sentences, but as God's making known the mystery of Christ (Eph. 3:1-6).[9] Revelation, then, is God's making himself known in and through the disclosure of his

---

8. John Baillie, *The Idea of Revelation in Recent Thought* (New York: Columbia University Press, 1956), p. 47.

9. When in this passage Paul speaks of the mystery of Christ as not made known in other generations, we should remember the qualifying phrase which he adds: "as it has been revealed to his holy apostles. . . ." Paul is no Marcionite. The God revealed in Christ is the God who made covenant with Israel, a covenant fulfilled, not set aside, in Christ (Gal. 3); he is the God revealed by the Spirit at Pentecost, the Spirit who moved the prophets of old to speak his word.

purpose, a mystery that would otherwise have remained unknown, since none has known the mind of the Lord but the Lord himself. This purpose is first intimated in the promise made to Abraham, Sarah, and their descendants (Rom. 4:13-25), a promise fulfilled in the coming of the Christ (Gal. 3:16) and in the outpouring of his Spirit (Acts 2:15-21). In other words, God does what he has engaged to do (Rom. 4:21); he is "the God who acts." This revelation in the mode of divine action in history has led to the familiar description of revelation as "salvation history," or "holy history" *(Heilsgeschichte)*. All history has the potential to mediate revelation in a general way; the history recorded in the Old and New Testaments, however, mediates revelation in a special way. And because this holy history moves, like all history, from past to present to future, biblical theologians sometimes speak of this revelation in the historical mode as promise (the history of Israel), fulfillment (the Jesus event), and consummation (the Second Coming).

Understanding revelation in terms of God's self-disclosure to his people as the God who promises salvation (and threatens judgment), and as the God who fulfills these promises (and threats) in history, we are in a position to understand in what sense the Bible is revelation. The Bible is revelation in the mode (form) of written words. In these words the human authors of Scripture, inspired by God's Spirit, reiterate the promises and warnings, record the events in which they are fulfilled, and preserve the interpretation of these events as events in which God has and will make himself known. Thus the Bible is taken up, as it were, into the constellation of revelation. And so it preserves special revelation for the church in all ages.

But special revelation is not simply synonymous with the Bible. God revealed himself in leading Abraham and Sarah out of Ur of the Chaldees to a land they had never seen, and in the deliverance of Israel from Egypt by the hand of Moses, long before the scriptural account of these events was written. Likewise, the Jesus event and the apostolic heralding of that event are prior to the record found in the gospels and Acts and received by the church as the word of God in the mode (form) of canonical Scripture. By the same token there is revelation still to come, promised, to be sure, in Scripture (1 Pt. 1:5-7), but still to occur in the future though the canon has long since been completed.

We would affirm, then, by way of summary, that special revelation occurs in the mode of events in history—past, present, and future—and in the mode of inspired witness to, and interpretation of, these events by prophets and apostles. Preserved for the church in the words of Scripture, this written revelation becomes effectual as the Spirit bears witness to Jesus Christ through the church's ongoing proclamation of the gospel.

Following his general introduction to theology, Barth begins his *Church Dogmatics* with a major opening section, of over a thousand pages, on "the Doctrine of the Word of God." At the heart of revelation, as he understands it, is a double act of God: Incarnation/Pentecost. The former (Incarnation) discloses God's freedom for humankind; the latter (Pentecost) humankind's freedom for God. This divine act of self-disclosure is to revelation what the bull's-eye is to the target. In the Incarnation, God's Word is present *in persona* as the Logos, the Word who became flesh. At Pentecost, the Spirit bears witness to this incarnate Word who is the Lord Jesus Christ. (No one can say "Jesus is Lord" but by/in the Holy Spirit, 1 Cor. 12:3.) Immediately around this center of revelation is Scripture, which is both a witness to the living Word and itself the word of God written. Finally, on the outer ring of the target, as it were, is the word of God in the form of the church's proclamation. Thus, for Barth, the word of God has a triple modality *(Gestalt)* as divine act in history, written testimony of Scripture, and ongoing proclamation by the church.

C. FAITH, HISTORY, REASON—AND REVELATION

Though Scripture is not the primary mode of revelation, it has become for the church a most necessary one, "those former ways of God's revealing his will to his people [by the inspired voices of prophets and apostles] being now ceased."[10] Because this is so, we shall devote an entire section to Scripture as the word of God written. But we must first say a word in anticipation of our discussion of Scripture concerning revelation as it relates (*a*) to faith, (*b*) to history, and (*c*) to reason.

First, a word about *revelation and faith.* We have viewed revelation from the perspective of God's acts in history by which he discloses himself as a God of mercy and of judgment. But what Christians perceive as "divine acts" in history are, for many, mere "mundane events." The Exodus of Israel out of Egypt to certain people is no more a divine revelation of God's covenant faithfulness than was the migration of the Huns out of Mongolia; Jesus is no more God in our midst than any other religious genius. To the Christian, such people are like those who are color-blind or tone-deaf; they hear but they do not understand, they see but they do not perceive (Is. 6:9). By the same token, to such folk Christians are visionaries, even fanatics, who see and hear the projections of their own imaginations.[11]

In the course of our prior discussion, we anticipated this problem when

---

10. *Westminster Confession,* chap. 1, sec. 1.
11. On the way in which the same events may be differently perceived, see Colin Brown, *History, Criticism and Faith* (Leicester, England: InterVarsity Press, 1976), pp. 195-96.

we noted that the truth that concerns the theologian is truth given by revelation and received by faith. This close conjunction of revelation and faith is so significant that it would be impossible to do justice to the doctrine of revelation without a special word on the place of faith in the event of revelation. Is God revealed in Jesus if no one recognizes him as the Christ? When Peter confessed, "You are the Christ," did not our Lord speak of this confession itself as an experience of revelation from the Father in heaven (Mt. 16:16-17)? Peter's confession did not rest on rational insight, but on divinely given insight. Such a view is in keeping with our understanding of special revelation as a disclosure on the part of the divine Subject to the human subject that eventuates in an I/thou fellowship, a communion with God the Redeemer. One may, with Kierkegaard, liken the recipient of such revelation to one who stands at the crossroads of time and eternity. The point at which eternity intersects time is the moment of decision par excellence for the recipient of revelation; it is the "now" *(Augenblick)* of "behold, now is the acceptable time; now is the day of salvation" (2 Cor. 6:2; Is. 49:8).

In biblical theology this thought is sometimes expressed in terms of the distinction between χρόνος (time as enduring) and καιρός (time as decisive—Lowell's "*once* to every man and nation"). Jesus weeps over Jerusalem because "you did not know the time (καιρός) of your visitation" (Lk. 19:44). While the Christian life takes place in "chronos" time, it is really lived as "kairos" time. Of course, some moments are more evidently "kairos" time than others. Witness the effect on Beyers Naudé of the fatal shooting by the police of 69 blacks in Sharpeville, South Africa, on March 26, 1960. For Naudé this event became the "moment" that decisively brought his doubts as a white Christian Afrikaner of impeccable pedigree into focus. It was the moment that turned him into a fierce opponent of apartheid.

Revelation, then, is not simply an objective event but a transitive one, an event in which the Spirit bears witness to the Son in the heart of the believer. No one, as Paul says, can call Jesus Lord but by the Holy Spirit (1 Cor. 12:3); and when this happens revelation is consummated. In other words, even as the Christ event is the turning point (decision) of history in general, so faith in Christ is the turning point (decision) of individual history in particular. The God who through Jesus Christ reveals himself as the God-who-is-*for*-us reveals himself through the Spirit as the God-who-remains-*with*-us-and-dwells-*in*-us.

Therefore, these two, revelation and faith, are not to be separated, as though the former were a divine act and the latter a merely human act. Yet they must be distinguished, since the one presupposes the other. There is first the revelation that happened in Jesus Christ, and only then is there the revelation that happens in the Holy Spirit. But it is the two together, the coming of the Son from the Father to accomplish God's redemptive purpose and the coming of the Spirit from the Father and the Son to bear witness to Jesus as Lord, that constitute the one act of self-disclosure on the part of the triune God, Father, Son, and Holy Spirit.[12]

Leaving the question of revelation and faith, we turn next to that of *revelation and history.* History has always worn the mean garment of contingency that makes any claims to absoluteness seem overweening and presumptuous. Between the accidental truths of history and the necessary truths of reason, Lessing has reminded us, there is an "ugly ditch" many have deemed impossible to cross. That is to say, because Christianity grounds the revelation of salvation in historical events—Christ was "crucified under Pontius Pilate"—it places itself under the rubric of history. Thus Christianity is of this world; and like all that lives in this world, it lives only to die. In the interest of preserving the truth of revelation, it is very tempting to seek to escape this threat of historical relativism by taking one's flight into some form of Idealism, whether it be the affirmation of the eternal Ideas of the Platonists, the rational proofs of the metaphysicians, the ethical postulate (categorical imperative) of the Kantians, the religious experience of the mystics, or even the aesthetic experience of a Beethoven. But for the Christian the answer to historical relativism (Positivism) can never be some form of Idealism or mysticism, for then revelation would lose the massive character of objective events in history. To put it simply, were one to say (with Fichte) that only the metaphysical, never the historical, can save, then one could never commit her soul for time and eternity to "a little Lord Jesus asleep in the hay."[13] Holy history would become nothing but the husk of immutable Being shining through the manifold of particular historical events. Jesus would become the concretion of the moral Ideal, a hero, a religious genius, the high point in the religious evolution of the human race—in short, everything but what he really is, the transcendent Son of God who became incarnate as a first-century Palestinian Jew. To steer the ship of faith between the Scylla of Idealism (with its flight

---

12. While the place of faith is integral to an evangelical doctrine of revelation, evangelicals generally teach the salvation of dying infants who are incapable of confessing faith. (Jesus declared that "of such is the kingdom," Lk. 18:15-17.) Likewise the severely retarded are deemed the objects of divine mercy. By his grace the God who makes the blind to see, the lame to walk, and the deaf to hear (Mt. 11:4-5) will also release these anonymous ones from their bondage in a better land and a better life.

13. Nor could she sing with Luther,

> O Lord! the Maker of us all!
> How hast thou grown so poor and small,

from the time-space continuum into the realm of eternal ideas, thus rendering impossible a revelation in *history*) and the Charybdis of historical positivism (with its denial of a transcendent dimension, thus rendering impossible a *revelation* in history) is primarily the task of philosophical theology. Yet it is of paramount importance to the dogmatician as well; hence we have included the question of revelation and history in our discussion of the doctrine of revelation. The least (and perhaps the most) that one can do in the discipline of dogmatics is to describe the way, or ways, in which Christian thinkers have approached this question and indicate the paradigms of thought they have used.

Some have sought to resolve the problem by defining the historical basis of revelation in minimal terms. Kierkegaard, for example, thought it sufficient to say that "we believe that in such and such a year God appeared among us in the humble figure of a Servant, that he lived and taught in our community and finally died."[14] The majority of Christian thinkers, however, have affirmed that a much broader basis in history is required if one is to do justice to the Christian doctrine of revelation. This is not to say that there is no difference between history and revelation but rather that history is the primary *medium* in which God has chosen to reveal himself. For the Christian church, this historical revelation culminates in the "Jesus event," an event in which God himself enters history as Jesus of Nazareth. In Jesus, revelation impinges uniquely on time like a "perpendicular from above" (Barth), like a "parabola from beyond history whose vortex touches history" (Brunner). In Jesus the Infinite becomes finite, the Eternal temporal. Hence, in Jesus revelation is historical in the most objective sense of the word. Revelation is the story of Jesus: the story of his birth, life, death, and resurrection in a given place on the map and at a given time on the calendar. Such a view of revelation as events in history that are grounded in eternity is quite different from the view that revelation is simply history as it evolves toward the utopian ideal of the kingdom of God. Revelation, in the Christian view, is not synonymous

---

That there thou liest on withered grass,
The supper of the ox and ass.

Luther's Christmas hymn, "From Heaven High I Come to You," 1534-35, stanza 9 in MacDonald's translation.

14. Søren Kierkegaard, *Philosophical Fragments,* trans. D. Swenson, ed. H. V. Hong (Princeton: Princeton University Press, 1936), p. 86. Such an approach reminds one of Bultmann's later emphasis on the Christ of the kerygma, encountered in the crisis of faith, in distinction to the Jesus of history. Of the latter we can know virtually nothing, except that he lived. The gospels are not history but *Gemeindetheologie,* the theological reconstruction of the early church.

with social progress; it is not the actualizing of the immanent possibilities of history. Rather, in the person of Jesus God has broken into history in a way that transcends the possibilities of history as such.[15]

Those who affirm the historical character of revelation walk by faith and not by sight. There is no way one can bring together, in a rational synthesis, the God who "is who he is" and the process of history in and through which he reveals himself to *be* who he is. Only faith can transcend the paradox of being and becoming; only faith can penetrate the incognito of that ordinary history in and through which God has chosen to reveal himself. Since God has created the boundary between eternity and time, faith affirms that he is free to step across that boundary and enter into time. But how he does so is beyond the creature's ken. Such acts of revelation are, as Kierkegaard would say, "indirect" rather than "direct" communication of the truth.

If the God with whom the Christian is concerned is the God who acts, if revelation is historical, then one can see why the thought of "story" or "narrative" has had such a prominent place in the Christian tradition. One nurtured in that tradition will remember the Bible stories first heard in Sunday School and such songs as Fanny Crosby's

> Tell me the story of Jesus,
> > Write on my heart every word.
> Tell me the story most precious,
> > Sweetest that ever was heard.

In preaching, the story has been told over and over again. (The great black preachers have been especially skillful in telling the biblical stories in a way that impacts the lives of their hearers.) As William Hordern has observed, instead of saying simply that God is a loving God, Christians tell the story of a man who died on a cross (*Speaking of God,* pp. 164ff.). The question that present-day "story" or "narrative" theology raises for the dogmatician, therefore, cannot be that of the validity of the form as such. Witness the use of Jesus' parables to convey Christian truth. Rather, it is a question of the extent to which the Christian story is historical not only in form but also in content. Obviously our own view is that the story concerns events that actually occurred. As Walter Lippmann once observed, to be indifferent to the historical character of the biblical narrative and at the same time enthusiastic about its truth is like commending a lover for the charm of his passion while assuring him there is no such lady as the one he adores (*Preface to Morals,* New York: Time, Inc., 1964, pp. 32-33).

---

15. This understanding of history from the perspective of revelation in Christ means that history is not, as the Greeks believed, cyclical, but is moving toward a goal from the history of Israel—anticipatory and messianic—to the Incarnation and on to the parousia, the final consummation. Hence the Bible knows nothing of reincarnation, of metempsychosis or transmigration of souls. The cyclical character of Greek history has been, in Christian thought, bent out into a straight line moving from creation to consummation.

As for *revelation and reason,* it is obvious from the development of our doctrine of revelation that we do not think of the truth given in revelation as we think of the truth discovered by reason. The truth of reason is truth that can be demonstrated. It is truth which we say to ourselves rather than the truth God says to us. The basic criterion of such truth is coherence. Hence rational thought strives to set aside contradiction and thus achieve coherence by grounding itself in continuity with itself. Herein lies its power. The truth of revelation, by contrast, is truth that must be appropriated — or rejected; in no case can it be demonstrated. It is truth coming through a divine self-disclosure, truth that encounters the creature in a way that calls for decision. In revelation God tells us his name; he stoops as a tall person to a child, lowering himself on his knees so that the child can look into his face (Brunner). Revelation concerns truth that leads to fellowship through obedience to the voice of God. It is truth that engages the heart and not just the head, as Pascal has reminded us.[16]

But though we distinguish head and heart, yet we know from the very experience of living that were the acceptance of revelation to set head and heart at odds, the result would be intolerable. Hence the question of how the truth of revelation is related to that of reason can never be answered in terms of an either/or but only a both/and. In the Christian vision, at least, the faculty of reason, like all our other faculties, is the gift of the Creator; it is, as it were, the image and reflection of God's own Mind as the Logos. It is only because we are endowed by the Creator with his image that we are able to think God's thoughts after him. Reason, then, rather than being opposed to revelation, gives us the capacity for revelation. It is because we have the powers of reason that we are enjoined to love God not only with all our heart but also with all our mind (Mk. 12:30). So to love God with the mind does not entail climbing up to God by rational arguments; but it does entail receiving with our mind as with open arms the God who comes down to us in Jesus Christ. The real problem, then, is not reason, but a would-be autonomous reason that turns the both/and of revelation and reason into the either/or of revelation or reason. Such autonomous reason will not accept the wisdom of God given in revelation. It opposes the venture of faith because it will accept only the necessities of rational

---

16. *Pensées,* sec. IV, par. 277. Pascal, of course, was no despiser of reason. A genius in mathematics and physics, he completed his work on the conic sections before he was sixteen and later solved the problem of the cycloid on which Galileo, Descartes, and others had exhausted their skills in vain. Nor did he cease to use reason when doing theology, as can be perceived from the elegant, incisive arguments found in the *Provincial Letters.* See, for example, Letter II.

thought. The only antidote to such proud autonomy is a reason aware of its limitations, a reason open to truth that is given rather than discovered.

Such a view of reason's place, however, does not make the theologian's task easy. If she allows the claims of reason along with, though subordinate to, those of revelation, she must take up the cross of living in two worlds. She must live in the world of faith *and* the world of reason, in the world of revelation *and* the world of thought. She must work with the categories of reason, yet curb the proud aspirations of fallen reason to achieve a final system. She must be not only a thinker, but a believing thinker, opposed to the sinful absolutizing of human thought, including human theological thought. Thus she will be careful to defend, with all the clarity that reason can afford, such paradoxes of faith as a unity in plurality (Trinity), the letter and the Spirit (Scripture), the divine that became human (Incarnation), a foolish wisdom (the atonement), a gift received that is an act performed (faith), and the freedom of divine servitude (salvation). In so doing she will be using reason to illumine the meaning of revelation and of faith in revelation to bring her thoughts (reason) into captivity to Christ (2 Cor. 10:5).[17]

ADDENDUM: GOD HIDDEN IN HIS REVELATION: THE DOCTRINE OF THE DIVINE INCOMPREHENSIBILITY

It might seem anomalous in the extreme to include in our discussion of divine revelation the affirmation that God remains hidden even in his self-disclosure. Yet theologians in all ages have felt constrained to speak this way, echoing the words of the early Christian confession, "And confessedly great is the *mystery* (μυστήριον) of godliness, who was manifest (ἐφανερώθη) in the flesh, justified in the Spirit . . ." (1 Tm. 3:16 — author's trans.). This juxtaposition of mystery and manifestation is remarkable indeed and calls for comment.[18]

---

17. Heresies may be viewed as the truths of revelation pressed to their logical extremity; thus the freedom (sovereignty) of God becomes fatalism; the freedom (responsibility) of the creature, Pelagianism, etc.

18. We have rendered the text of 1 Timothy 3:16 literally to underscore the point that is obscured in the usual translation when a colon is placed after "godliness" requiring that the ὅ be construed as "he" or "he who," rather than simply "who." Literally the text says that Christ *is* the mystery manifested and the manifested mystery.

As we turn to the question of the divine mystery in manifestation, we should note that we are not using the word "mystery," when speaking of God in his revelation, as it is sometimes used of phenomena in the natural order. True, one might see a parable of the divine mystery in the mysteries of the world of which we are a part. But the mystery of divine being is not of the same order as the riddles of nature—what makes sap go up a tree, what makes cancerous cells proliferate, etc. Such riddles will be resolved as science closes the lacunae in human knowledge. But God's mystery will never give way to our analysis and investigation. We cannot, by searching, find out God (Job 11:7). There is, as Kierkegaard would say, an infinite qualitative difference between the creature and the Creator. Our concern, then, is simply to observe that, being who he is and we being who we are, God, even in his revelation, is the God of whom we are aware as the Transcendent One, whose Being and purpose are such that we can only exclaim with the psalmist, "Great is the LORD, and greatly to be praised, and his greatness is unsearchable" (Ps. 145:3).

To speak of the hiddenness of God (the traditional doctrine of the divine incomprehensibility) is not to contrast the mystery of God's being in himself with the revelation of his purpose in creation and redemption. God is, in himself, the God whom he has revealed himself to be. Some in the Nominalist tradition, thinking of God in terms of absolute Power, have gone so far as to speak of God in himself as the hidden God *(Deus absconditus)* in contrast to the God revealed in Christ *(Deus revelatus)*. This is an unfortunate way of approaching the doctrine of the divine mystery, for it suggests that actually there are two Gods, one hidden in transcendent majesty and the other revealed in incarnate love. The teaching of Scripture is rather that even as revealed, God is far from fully revealed; God remains free in his revelation, transcendent in his condescension.

We might put it this way: God has revealed himself and consequently we know him; but though we know him truly, we do not know him fully, as he knows us. In the words of Watts's paraphrase of Psalm 139:1-5,

> My thoughts before they are my own,
>   Are to my God distinctly known.
> He knows the words I mean to speak,
>   Ere from my opening lips they break.

The psalmist goes on to confess, "Such knowledge is too wonderful for me; it is high, I cannot attain it" (v. 6). In Isaiah 55:8-9, we read, "For my thoughts are not your thoughts, neither are your ways my ways, says the LORD. For as the heavens are higher than the earth, so are my ways higher than your ways and my thoughts than your thoughts." We cannot, in other words, encompass God in our systems; we cannot put our mental arms around him. We can but touch the hem of his garment. Paul, reflecting upon Israel's election and rejection, probes the mystery of the divine purpose in the light of the revelation of God in Christ. But as he does so, he can only marvel at the depth of the divine wisdom; even as revealed in Christ, God remains the God whose judgments are unsearchable and his ways past finding out (Rom. 11:33-34).

This paradox that God's revelation involves hiddenness, that he remains the God who dwells in light unapproachable that no one has seen or can see (1 Tm. 6:16), though he is the God who has come to us in Jesus Christ, cannot be resolved by contrasting the Old Testament with the New. The hidden God is not the God of the Old Testament in contrast to the revealed God of the New. No, the paradox remains even this side of the Incarnation and Pentecost, and it will remain until faith is turned to sight. That is why Paul, though he believed that God had revealed himself in Christ, tends to give the phrase "the revelation of Jesus Christ" a forward, eschatological reference. The Corinthians are those "who wait for the revealing of our Lord Jesus Christ" (1 Cor. 1:7; see also 1 Thes. 1:10; 1 Pt. 1:7; 1:13). While our salvation is a historical reality in Christ, yet this salvation remains, for the present, a life "*hid* with Christ in God." At the last day, "when Christ who is our life appears, then you also will appear with him in glory" (Col. 3:3-4). Then, and only then, will the veil finally be lifted; then, and only then, shall we see him as he is (1 Jn. 3:2).

The thought that God is hidden in his revelation bears on how the gospels report the life of Jesus. They do so in a way that makes it evident that Jesus' presence did not constitute the presence of God in a direct and immediate sense. Many who saw Jesus and spoke to him concluded that at best he was a carpenter's son (Mt. 13:55), at worst one who was demon possessed (Jn. 7:20). Even the disciples who did recognize him as "the Christ, the Son of the living God" did so because their minds were enlightened by the Father (Mt. 16:16-17). Only thus did they penetrate the incognito of his humanity and perceive his essential divinity. While it is true that God himself was present in Christ, yet the divine person of the Son was perceptible in the historical personality of Jesus, a first-century Palestinian Jew, only in a mysterious and indirect way. Hence, though the revelation in the Son is God's final Word, it is yet a veiling, a revelation that can be misread. Were God not present in Christ in this hidden way, were he present in power and glory as at the last day, then the incognito would be lifted, then there would be no possibility of decision for or against him.

Because God remains hidden in his revelation, the incomprehensible God, all our theologizing should reflect a sense of the divine mystery. We do theology rightly only when we do it with a profound awareness of the awesome mystery of the divine being. Theological statements, we must remember, first came out of the doxological statements of the worshipping community. Therefore, the study of theology should reinforce the fundamental attitude that informs worship. When it inspires reverence for God, its proper Subject, theology best serves the church; and in such service it fulfills its true purpose.

Revelation

A Sermon Preached by Marguerite Shuster
at Knox Presbyterian Church, Pasadena, California,
October 2, 1988

In many and various ways God spoke of old to our fathers by the prophets;
but in these last days he has spoken to us by a Son, whom he appointed the
heir of all things, through whom also he created the world. He reflects the
glory of God and bears the very stamp of his nature, upholding the universe
by his word of power. When he had made purification for sins, he sat down
at the right hand of the Majesty on high, having become as much superior
to angels as the name he has obtained is more excellent than theirs.

Hebrews 1:1-4

God has spoken. Without that affirmation, and the fact behind the affirmation, there could be no such thing as Christian faith as we know it. Christianity, you see, is a *revealed* religion, not something that a talented scientist or mystic figured out by diligence and self-discipline and superior rational powers, but something simply *given* to us that we could not otherwise have known. It comes from beyond us, as that which gives meaning to the whole always must.

If there were nothing beyond us, our lives and achievements—whether scientific or religious—would be in the most absolute possible sense absurd, as the atheistic existentialists of another generation rightly perceived. That which is not part of something bigger, that which has no future, may appear glorious for a moment; but it's hard to rejoice for long if honesty forces one to admit that the open mouth of the grave is but an individual manifestation of the indifferent yawn of the universe, soon to swallow up everything in memoryless, indifferent darkness.

But if there is something beyond us, surely it is not at our beck and call. How, then, can we know—know not only that something is out there, but also, and more importantly, know the expression on its face? How can we know God unless God reveals himself? Hence, the critical nature of the basic assertion of my text: God has spoken. Revelation is unnecessary unless something is hidden. Revelation is impossible unless God speaks. Revelation is, as far as we are concerned, futile unless God speaks to us.

Revelation is unnecessary unless something is hidden. "Truly, thou art a God who hidest thyself," said the prophet Isaiah (45:15). "Canst thou by searching find out God? canst thou find out the Almighty unto perfection?" asks one of Job's friends (Job 11:7 KJV). Throughout Scripture, the implied answer is not a hopeful "not yet," but rather a firm "no, not ever."

In Isaiah's exclamation we hear something of the ambiguity of God's self-manifestation in creation and history. While the person who already believes sees evidence of God's handiwork everywhere, the person who does not believe sees sufficient evil in "nature red in tooth and claw" and in the monstrous acts of individuals and nations to provide a fairly persuasive intellectual argument against any benevolent design for the universe. I occasionally pull myself up short when I examine my own interpretation of events in my life or my attitude as I read Scripture: I become aware that the way I process things depends almost unconsciously upon a whole set of assumptions integral to my being a Christian. I cannot even imagine what it would be like, at this point, to try to function without those assumptions about God's activity. My worldview would surely fall apart. Then I consider that the majority of people in the world are not Christians. The facts of their daily experience do not, in themselves, make Christian claims self-evident. In the words of Pascal, who is arguing against supposed proofs of God from nature.

> [I]t is certain that those who have the living faith in their heart see at once that all existence is none other than the work of the God whom they adore. But for those in whom this light is extinguished, . . . to tell them that they have only to look at the smallest things which surround them and they will see God openly, to give them, as a complete proof of this great and important matter, the course of the moon and planets, and to claim to have concluded the proof with such an argument, is to give them ground for believing that the proofs of our religion are very weak. And I see by reason and experience that nothing is more calculated to arouse their contempt.

It is not after this manner that Scripture speaks. . . . It says, on
the contrary, that God is a hidden God. . . .[1]

In the question from the book of Job, we see criticism of the thought
that although he may be hidden, we have the capacity, by some heroic
bootstrap operation, to discover God. Do we suppose we can think our way
to an understanding of him, or that by exploring every nook and cranny of
the atom and the universe we will at last arrive at the necessary evidence
for his existence and the necessary and exhaustive description of his nature?
We deceive ourselves. The effort is doomed from the beginning. By definition, anything discovered in that way would not be a God who transcends
us and the world. It would not be a God who could tell us his purpose for
us, his plans for humanity and for the world. It would not be a God who
could say in a definitive way what counts and what is of no account, what
he expects of us and what are the consequences of belief and unbelief,
obedience and disobedience. In a strange way, only a God who is, in
himself, hidden from us can help, for only such a God is big enough to
speak to our most fundamental concerns.

If revelation is, then, necessary because something essential about God
is hidden, revelation is impossible unless God speaks. If we cannot climb
up to him, he must condescend to us and make himself known. And when
he does, his very act of self-revelation itself declares his hiddenness:[2] to
lift a veil is to acknowledge that there is a veil to be lifted. We see
something, but we do not see everything. One theologian remarks,

The language about God these days tends to be a curious combination
of modesty and extravagance—modesty at how little some people
claim to know about him, extravagance at the degree of assurance
with which others claim we can know little or nothing.[3]

My text shows a combination of modesty and extravagance too, but
of quite a different sort—modesty in acknowledging the varied and fragmentary ways in which God has chosen to reveal himself, extravagance in
exulting over the fully adequate finality of his self-revelation in Jesus
Christ: "In many and various ways God spoke of old to our fathers by the
prophets; but in these last days he has spoken to us by a Son. . . ."

Take the modesty of the first text. God has not left himself without a
witness throughout history. He has not done one thing and one thing only

1. *Pensées,* #242.
2. K. Barth, *Church Dogmatics,* I/2 (Edinburgh: T. & T. Clark, 1956), p. 84.
3. R. M. Brown, *The Pseudonyms of God* (Philadelphia: Westminster, 1972), p. 69.

to make himself known, but has spoken in a variety of ways "by" the prophets, which should be understood to include not only those whose writings have been handed down to us in the prophetic books of the Bible, but all of God's spokespersons—all writers of Scripture, all those to whose testimony the Scriptures attest, and very possibly others in whose lives and words God was actively communicating his will for humankind. Not equally at all times and places, you understand; there's nothing automatic about it. But sometimes God chooses human vehicles to speak not just their own words, but God's word. The revelation comes fundamentally as word—personal address, to persons, by which God communicates not bits of information about himself, but simply himself. By speaking, we give ourselves to others. And God's self-revelation is all of a piece, from the earliest primal history of Genesis to the present. Fragmentary, yes; incomplete, yes; but the word of the one God, in his own recognizable voice.

Now for the extravagance of this text. In seven descriptions—seven being a symbolic number representing completeness—it describes the Son, Jesus Christ, as the ultimate revelation of God (and it does not really say, "by *a* Son," as if any son would do, but simply and definitely "by Son"). It takes us from the beginning—"through whom . . . he created the world"—to the end—"whom he appointed the heir of all things," including the middle—he "uphold[s] the universe by the word of power." It establishes his identity as God: Christ radiates (better than "reflects") God's glory as the sun's rays convey the sun's light; he bears the exact likeness of God as a coin bears the exact imprint of a die. It tells the efficacy of his work on our behalf: he made purification for our sins (that is, he dealt with the evil that is usually the unbeliever's primary argument against faith) and then sat down at the right hand of the Father—unlike the Aaronic priests, who remained standing because their sacrificial service never came to an end. He is thus the prophet through whom God spoke his final word, the priest who accomplished the perfect cleansing, and the king enthroned in the place of chief honor.[4] Nothing more needs to be said, or, indeed, can be said, that is necessary for our salvation. Thus, with the coming of Christ, the Word of God in the fullest sense of the term, the Word that says all we need to know about God, the former days of imperfect knowledge are over and we enter the last days, the time of fulfillment of what the prophets promised.

To one who complains that even if these things be so, and even if God has spoken in a final way in Christ, so much yet remains unrevealed, unspoken, C. S. Lewis makes this reply:

4. F. F. Bruce, *The Epistle to the Hebrews* (Grand Rapids: Eerdmans, 1964), *in loc.*

Christians . . . have a bad habit of talking as if revelation existed to
gratify curiosity by illuminating all creation so that it becomes self-
explanatory and all questions are answered. But revelation appears to
me to be purely practical, to be addressed to the particular animal,
Fallen Man, for the relief of his urgent necessities—not to be the
spirit of inquiry in man for the gratification of his liberal curiosity.
We know that God has visited and redeemed His people. . . . What
we must do, which road we must take to the fountain of life, we know,
and none who has seriously followed the directions complains that
he has been deceived.[5]

Much is hidden. Much remains hidden even when God has spoken in Christ
to reveal all we need to know; though Lewis insists that no one who
seriously pursues what she knows will be disappointed.

But the plain fact remains that many do not appear to hear what God has
said; many do not seriously pursue even what we might suppose is no longer
hidden but clearly manifested in Christ. And that goes to show once again
that even in the cross of Christ, the supreme self-revelation of his righteousness and love, God remains in some sense hidden. God does not reveal
himself in such a way as to take away the necessity of decision and belief.
And so revelation is futile until we hear God's Word as a word to *us*.

"In many and various ways God spoke of old to our fathers by the
prophets; but in these last days he has spoken to us by a Son. . . ." He
spoke to *our fathers;* he has spoken *to us.* This story, implies the writer of
the letter to the Hebrews, is not just a story, to be evaluated impartially
and distantly as to its merits. No; it is *our* story. Our foreparents heard it,
in their time and way; and now it is addressed to us, inviting us to respond,
inviting us to participate in it. We can decline the invitation, fail to acknowledge that, supremely in the Scriptures, God still speaks. He speaks
to *us,* as surely as he spoke to our foreparents by the Old Testament
Scriptures and as surely as he spoke to the author of Hebrews, who, like
us, had never personally known Christ. And we can shut our ears.

The story is told of a royal messenger unsuccessful in accomplishing
his mission.

The king had sent a letter to a wise but skeptical man, who, in his
faraway province, refused to accept it. He was one of those men who
think too much, who complicate their lives by complicating small
things. He couldn't understand, not in the slightest, what the king
might want of him: "Why would the sovereign, so powerful and so

5. *God in the Dock* (Grand Rapids: Eerdmans, 1970), p. 43.

rich, address himself to me, who am less than nothing? Because he takes me to be a philosopher? There are more important ones. Could there be another reason? If so, what reason?

Unable to answer these questions, he preferred to believe the letter a misunderstanding. Worse, a fraud. Worse yet, a practical joke. "Your king," he said to the messenger, "does not exist." But the messenger insisted: "I am here, and here is the letter; isn't that proof enough?" "The letter proves nothing at all; besides, I haven't read it. And by the way, who gave it to you? The king in person?" "No," confessed the messenger. "It was given to me by a royal page. In his name." "Are you sure of that? And how can you be sure that it comes from the reigning sovereign? Have you ever seen him?" "Never. My rank does not permit or warrant it." "Then how do you know that the king is king? You see? You don't know any more than I."[6]

A very different story is told by John Bunyan, author of *Pilgrim's Progress*. Walking through the streets of Bedford one day, he overheard three or four poor women conversing about God as they sat in the sun in a doorway.

> I drew near to hear what they said, for I was now a brisk talker . . . in the matters of religion; but I may say, I heard but understood not. . . . Their talk was about a new birth, the work of God in their hearts. . . ; they talked how God had visited their souls with His love in the Lord Jesus. . . . They were to me as if they had found a new world. . . . At this I felt my own heart begin to shake. . . .[7]

Suddenly, empty words became God's word to him personally. He heard, so to speak, the King's own voice made present to him in human speech. And his shaking heart made response.

That is what revelation is finally about—a shaking human heart saying Yes to the God made known in Jesus Christ; Yes, this is the king's own voice; Yes, this is the King's very likeness; Yes, this is the same One who spoke through the prophets of old and to all those believers who have gone before; Yes, he has shown me his gracious purpose that I could never have guessed from looking just at the world; Yes, he speaks to me.

6. Elie Wiesel, *Souls on Fire* (New York: Summit Books, 1972), pp. 172-73.
7. Quoted in Leland Ryken, *Worldly Saints* (Grand Rapids: Zondervan, 1986), p. 211.

III. God's Self-Disclosure in the Witness of Scripture to Jesus Christ

A. THE CANON OF SCRIPTURE AND THE SCRIPTURE AS CANON

God, who spoke an anticipatory word by the prophets, has, in these latter days, spoken a final word by a Son (Heb. 1:1-2); special revelation culminates in the person of Jesus Christ. The meaning of the Jesus event having been disclosed through the preaching of the apostles, who were "eyewitnesses of his majesty" (2 Pt. 1:16), there is no need of further revelation this side of the parousia. However, there is every need, in the interim, that this revelation in Christ should not be lost to the people of God. Furthermore, in a culture where writing is known (and the capacity for an oral transmission of corporate memory consequently lost), the obvious way to preserve such revelation is by committing it to writing.[1] This, in the common confession of the church, is what happened under the guidance of God's Spirit. Hence, Scripture becomes most necessary in securing to the church the Word of God; it becomes the norm of its proclamation and life until faith becomes sight and we know as we are known. The word that the church has used to designate this written word as normative revelation is "canon."[2] As a designation of the writings acknowledged by the church

---

1. For a striking instance of preserving the truth by oral tradition in a culture that has no writing, see Alex Haley's fascinating account of his encounter with an African griot in *Roots* (New York: Dell, 1976), chap. 120.

2. From the Greek κανών, meaning "measuring rod," "standard," "model." First used of apostolic teaching viewed as the *regula fidei* of the church and subsequently (fourth century onward) in the specialized sense of the documents containing that teaching.

as authoritative, the canon is just the denotative definition of written revelation. It lists all the items that belong to a class, namely, the 39 books of
the Jewish Scriptures and the 27 books of the Christian Scriptures that
together make up the Bible.

It is a well-known fact that the church has never agreed on the exact denotative definition
of Scripture. The *Apocrypha* ("hidden things") of the Old Testament were written
between 300 B.C. and the beginning of the Christian era. Though never a part of the
original Jewish Scriptures, they were included in an appendix to the Septuagint, the
Greek translation of the Old Testament. Since the Greek-speaking Gentile church used
the Septuagint from the beginning, and since the first Latin Bible of the Western Church
was a translation of the Septuagint, the apocryphal books—Tobit, Judith, the long
version of Esther, etc.—came to be a part of the Bible of the ancient church. When
Jerome, the author of the Vulgate, discovered that the books of the Apocrypha were
not in the Hebrew Bible, he questioned their authority. However, Augustine's insistence
that they were a part of Scripture prevailed. At the time of the Reformation the
continental Reformers rejected them, while the English Reformers gave them a deutero-
canonical status. (Archbishop Temple rejected the Bible offered by the American Bible
Society to be used at the coronation of Edward VII as "mutilated" and "imperfect"
since it did not contain the Apocrypha.) The Council of Trent, reacting to the Reformation, officially gave these books equal standing in the Roman Catholic Church with
the other books of the Bible.

The *New Testament Apocrypha,* of Christian origin, were authored between A.D.
100 and 300. They include all the genre of the New Testament: gospels, Acts, epistles,
and apocalypses, such as the Gospel of the Hebrews, the Acts of Paul and Thecla, etc.
Some were read as Scripture for a time in parts of the ancient church, but they have
never been received by the Christian community as a whole. In recent times, however,
individual scholars have thought to find in them original Christian teaching omitted,
or even suppressed, in the New Testament. Elisabeth Schüssler-Fiorenza, for example,
argues: "Methodologically . . . it will be necessary to go beyond the limits of the New
Testament canon since it is the product of the patristic church, that is, a theological
document of the 'historical winners.' " "The textual and historical marginalization of
women is . . . a by-product of the 'patristic' selection and canonization process of
Scripture." (*In Memory of Her, A Feminist Theological Reconstruction of Christian
Origins,* New York: Crossroads, 1985, pp. xv and 53.)

The *Pseudepigrapha* are books of Jewish, and some of Christian, origin, written
between 200 B.C. and A.D. 200 and named from the fact that their authors use pseudonyms. Though never accepted by the church, they have been the object of study and
interest, especially because two of them, *Enoch* and the *Assumption of Moses,* are cited
in the canonical book of Jude (vv. 9, 14).

The *Antilegoumena* (from the Greek "to speak against") are the books disputed
for a time but finally accepted, as canonical. In the Old Testament they included Esther,
Job, Ecclesiastes, Ezekiel, and the Song of Solomon, all finally recognized by the rabbis
and never seriously disputed by the church. Probably first used by Origen (ca. A.D.
180), the term "antilegoumena" also describes Christian writings questioned in some

parts of the ancient church but finally recognized, namely, Hebrews, James, 2 Peter, 2 and 3 John, and Revelation. The controversy over Hebrews is intriguing since it was principally rejected in the West, where its author was known. When in due time it came to be ascribed to Paul and was thus properly credentialed, it was accepted. Quite possibly the problem was that it was written by a woman and, considering its affinity of thought with the writings of Paul, Priscilla is as good a candidate as any. The *Homolegoumena* (in distinction to the Antilegoumena) are the books on which there was basic agreement from the beginning, such as the four gospels and the Pauline epistles.

The earliest major list of books received by the church is the Muratorian Fragment (A.D. 170); the first complete list, including the Apocalypse, is that of the Council of Carthage, A.D. 397. By this time the familiar sequence of the books we now have was also fixed. The chapter divisions, however, were not introduced until 1200 by Stephen Langton, archbishop of Canterbury. Later still (1523) a system of verse divisions was applied to the Old Testament by Rabbi Isaac Nathan. His idea of verse divisions was adapted to Robert Stephens's Greek New Testament in 1551.

The expression "New Testament" *(Novum Testamentum),* implying an "Old Testament," first occurs in the writings of Tertullian, ca. A.D. 200. *Testamentum,* a legal term (Tertullian was a lawyer), was later chosen by Jerome to translate the Greek διαθήκη. In this way it became common Christian usage to describe the two parts of the Christian Bible as the Old and the New "Testaments." Actually, the Greek word means "covenant," so that correctly speaking we should say the Scriptures consist of the books of the Old and New Covenants; or the books of the Covenant, first administered to Israel and newly administered to the church in Christ.

A theology of canonicity obviously involves more than a denotative definition, that is, a listing of a given number of books received by the church as authoritative revelation. Connotatively defined, the canon designates those documents acknowledged by the church to be inspired by the Spirit, documents in and through which God has spoken, and still speaks, his word to his people. Divine inspiration is the common property of all the books of the canon by virtue of which they are united into one book, the Bible. Such a concept of the canon was never contested in the ancient church. The first Christians simply inherited the thought of an inspired Scripture—known to us as the "Old Testament"—from the Jewish synagogue in which they had been nurtured and in which they oftentimes continued to worship.

Following the disasters of 721 and 587 B.C., Jewish exiles in Babylon remained in contact with their prophets (Jer. 29; Ez. 14:1; 18:1ff.; 33:30ff.). Being closely knit together by the trauma of their experience, a remnant returned to the land and rallied around Ezra the scribe, who brought back from Babylon "the law of the God of heaven" (Ezr. 7:12-26). Binding themselves to do the will of Yahweh as recorded in their sacred writings, Jews both in the land and in the dispersion survived against incredible odds and so maintained their identity, an achievement that reflects their unique destiny as God's people.

As the number of their sacred writings increased, they came to be not only displayed in the synagogue, but also read and expounded each Sabbath (Acts 15:21), a practice in which Jesus took part (Lk. 4:15, 44) and which Paul used repeatedly in his Gentile mission as an occasion to preach Christ (Acts 13:13-14). This public reading of the Jewish Scriptures was simply taken over in the early Christian assemblies so that one may say the church was born with a canon in its hand.

Though united in accepting the concept of a canon, the church has not achieved a like consensus in the theological understanding of how this came about. At the time of the Protestant Reformation the issue became especially acute. The Roman Catholic Church regarded the ancient conciliar pronouncements concerning which books belonged in the canon to be magisterial in nature, not just declaratory. In other words, the authority of the canon, as the norm of faith and life, rested on the authority of the church. Obviously, the Reformers could not accept such a view, for they had judged the church and found it wanting in the light of Scripture. When Luther was asked at the Diet of Worms whether he would or would not renounce what he had written against the church, he answered that his conscience was held fast by the Scriptures he had adduced. Unwittingly perhaps, yet certainly, he thus made the authority of Scripture the formal definition of the Reformation.

It was Calvin, however, who first worked out the implications of the thought that there is no authority of the church over or even along with the Scripture. Scripture authenticates *itself* as the Word of God; or better, God authenticates the Scripture as his word, through his Spirit. In what is perhaps the most original piece of theologizing in the *Institutes,* Calvin asks (I, 7): "Who can persuade us which books are and are not to be received in the sacred number of the canon?" Calling the Roman Catholic Church's claims to be the arbiter of such questions an "impious fiction," he cites the apostle's testimony that the church is built on the foundation of the apostles and prophets (Eph. 2:20), whose authority is therefore antecedent to that of the church.[3] He thus concludes that it is not the outer (historical) testimony of the church, but the inner testimony of the Holy Spirit *(testimonium Spiritus Sancti internum)* that assures us of the divine character of Scripture. The way we recognize Scripture as not simply a human but a divine word is analogous to the way we recognize the difference between light and darkness, white and black, sweet and bitter. The persuasion, therefore, that

3. The Reformers recognized, of course, that Christians as a whole accept the Bible as God's Word on the basis of the teaching they have received from the church. In this practical sense the canon may be said to rest on tradition. Our concern here is with a deeper theological issue.

the Bible is the Word of God can be grounded in no higher authority than the testimony of the Spirit himself. This is not to say that for Calvin the Spirit's inner testimony makes the Scripture the Word of God, as though apart from that testimony it were simply a human word. The Scripture, as the inspired, objective witness to Christ, is in itself the Word of God, normative for the faith and life of the church. But it is only as the Spirit testifies to this truth in our hearts that we are persuaded that Scripture is God's Word.

Because the Scripture is what the Spirit testifies that it is, it contains in itself evidence of its divine character. This is why Calvin, having spoken of the Spirit's testimony in the *Institutes,* I, 7, went on to speak of the marks *(indicia)* of Scripture in I, 8. Had he been familiar with the historical-critical studies we now have, he would no doubt have argued differently on the specific phenomena of Scripture; but there is no warrant for saying he would have concluded that historical criticism has reduced the Bible to a merely human book that becomes divine only in the crisis of faith. His point is rather that while only God can authenticate his word (I, 7), once our eyes are enlightened by his Spirit we perceive evidences in Scripture itself of its divine character (I, 8). Calvin has in mind especially the unity-in-diversity of Scripture, but also its abiding power to change the lives of those who hear and heed its message.

The language used in the *Westminster Confession* in its listing of the *indicia* of Scripture (chap. I, v)—the "heavenliness of the matter," the "efficacy of the doctrine," the "majesty of the style," the "consent of all the parts," the "scope of the whole," the "full disclosure that it makes of the only way of salvation"—is obviously in need of qualification in certain respects. Not all of Scripture's matter is exactly heavenly, nor is its style uniformly majestic, etc. But details that easily come to mind in this regard for any who have studied the Bible critically should not become the trees that make us lose sight of the forest. Behind this language of another century the truth can still be discerned. The Scripture is indeed heavenly in its matter because it is about God and the salvation of sinners. It does not hawk for flies. What, for example, does it matter if the pharaoh of the Exodus is not named? Scripture is concerned with Yahweh's mighty act of delivering Israel from bondage in Egypt, whoever the pharaoh may have been.

There are, then, two extremes to be avoided if we would understand Calvin aright. On the one hand, we must not suppose that the inner testimony of the Spirit to the divine character of Scripture is pure subjectivity, as though Calvin should have written only the seventh chapter of Book One of the Institutes and omitted the eighth chapter altogether. On the other hand, neither should we suppose that the doctrine of inspiration means that the Bible is divine literature in the sense of a supernatural book that fell, as it were, from heaven. Such a view implies that the recognition of Scripture as God's Word rests on a rational demonstration that makes the inner testimony of the Spirit all but superfluous. Obviously this is not Calvin's view, as can be seen from the fact that he not only speaks of the inner testimony of the Spirit, but does so before he speaks of the marks of Scripture. The order Calvin gives his materials in this matter is significant.

The doctrine of the inward testimony of the Spirit has been called "the Achilles' heel of the Protestant system" (D. F. Strauss), for it seems, on an initial reading, to ground the authentication of Scripture in the subjective experience of the reader. Furthermore, the Roman Catholic position that the church, led by the Spirit, gives Scripture its unique authority by conciliar decision, seems to correspond to the simple fact that, had the church not regarded these books as authoritative, there would have been no canon in the first place. But upon a closer look interesting considerations emerge in this regard.

First of all, to say that the church establishes the canon is a circular piece of reasoning. A final authority (the church) cannot establish a final authority (Scripture) over itself. The decrees of church councils, then, do not *establish* the canon, but *acknowledge* it for what it is, the authoritative norm that confronts the church in all it teaches and does. Thus, the Scripture as canon is in an entirely different category from "canon law" or, as Protestants would call it, "church polity." All ecclesiastical communions make normative rules to govern their life, discipline, and worship; but these rules have authority only until such time as the institutions that make them decide to change them. But the church has no such authority over Scripture. To speak of the canon of Scripture is rather to confess that a standard outside itself has been given to the church by which it is to be defined and is to define itself.

It is worthwhile also to note that the recognition of the canon coincides, historically, with the rise of the episcopal office. This means the church recognized the objective authority of Scripture at the very time that it was beginning to finalize its institutional form along hierarchical, authoritarian lines. In fact, Paul's writings were recognized by this emerging episcopal institution as having a central place in the canon even though aspects of their message was little understood until the time of Augustine. The authority of the Scripture as canon, then, is clearly antecedent to the authority of the church.

As for the criteria used in acknowledging the books belonging to the canon, the church looked back to its origin. So far as the Jewish Scriptures were concerned, in recognizing this canon the church acknowledged its own origin within the covenant community of Israel. It recognized that, with Israel, it was the heir of the covenant promise (Eph. 3:6). As Ruth had said to Naomi, "Your God shall be my God," so the church acknowledged Israel's God to be its God, thus affirming that Israel's election was its own raison d'être. In its subsequent recognition of Christian Scriptures, along with the Jewish Scriptures, the church also looked back to its origin. Though the recognition of Christian Scriptures was given a fillip by Marcion's formation of a canon to supplant the Jewish Scriptures, the real reason the church came to acknowledge the books of the Christian canon was their apostolic character. The apostolicity of the Christian Scripture was not understood narrowly as meaning that every document in the New Testament was written by an apostle. It rather meant that the church acknowledged the apostolic witness to Jesus as the Christ, contained in these documents, to be a divinely inspired witness which was therefore normative. In acknowledging the canonical character of the documents of the New Testament, the church confessed itself to be no other than the church established by the apostles. The canon, in other words, was the objective guarantee that the church would remain apostolic. The teaching of the apostles, then, is not simply primary in the church's history, chronologically speaking, but also normative, theologically speaking.[4]

FIRST ADDENDUM: THE CANON AS CLOSED

The Reformers, as we have noted, rejected the Old Testament Apocrypha, favoring the Palestinian canon, which Jesus used, over the Hellenistic canon.[5] They also raised questions about some books of the New Testament—Luther had reservations about Hebrews, James, Jude, and the Apocalypse, while Calvin was silent, as a commentator, concerning the Apocalypse. These views of the Reformers have had a lasting effect only on the Old Testament canon. But they have implications for the New as well. The freedom claimed to reject certain books traditionally received by the church

---

4. It is in this sense that "apostolicity" should be understood as a mark of the church. Because the church acknowledged the apostolic witness to be the only reliable and normative witness to the Jesus event, it rejected the claims of the Gnostics and others to possess esoteric knowledge based on oral tradition differing in content from the witness of the apostles.

5. For a recent vindication of the Reformers' view, see Roger Beckwith, *The Old Testament Canon of the New Testament Church* (Grand Rapids: Eerdmans, 1986). Beckwith challenges the position of H. E. Ryles that the Jewish canon was not closed until the Synod of Jamnia, about A.D. 90. He marshals evidence that the Jewish canon was closed not only in Jesus' day but as early as Judas Maccabaeus in the second century B.C.!

implies the freedom to accept others, such as Paul's letter to the Laodiceans (Col. 4:16), which have been lost to the church. Were such authentic apostolic materials discovered, they should have a normative place in the witness of the church. The canon thus remains open, one might say, as a loose-leaf notebook from which sheets may be removed or added.[6] However, for the Protestant evangelical the canon is closed in the sense that the apostolic witness to God's Word in Jesus Christ is definitive. The ancient criterion of apostolicity remains normative to perpetuity for the proclamation of the church. Hence, there is no need to add a volume three (a *Book of Mormon* or *Science and Health*) to the Old and New Testament Scriptures to supplement and complete biblical revelation.

SECOND ADDENDUM: THE SUFFICIENCY (PERFECTION) OF SCRIPTURE[7]

To affirm that the church needs no other revelation than that given in Jesus Christ implies not only that the canon of Scripture is complete, but also that the message it contains is sufficient for the ongoing life and preaching of the church. Hence, one of the properties of Scripture is that of "sufficiency." To say that Scripture is "sufficient" is to say that all we need to know concerning God's will for our salvation, faith, and life is either expressly contained in Scripture or may be inferred from Scripture.

At the time of the Reformation, the sufficiency of Scripture was argued in the context of the debate with Rome concerning the normative character of tradition. Protestants have, of course, always recognized the indispensable nature of tradition. Jesus himself wrote no books, and everything the gospels say of him rests on tradition. In an early letter, Paul admonishes his readers to hold to the traditions (παραδόσεις) that they had been taught by him (2 Thes. 2:15); and by the time of the Pastorals there is a recognized "deposit" or "trust" presupposed as the basis of the Christian message. Furthermore, Protestants have recognized the great value of patristic learning in the ongoing exposition of that message by the church. Since the

---

6. By contrast, given the Tridentine view of the authoritative character of conciliar decisions on the canon, one might liken the canon to a bound volume in which every sheet is fixed.

7. The "sufficiency" of Scripture is virtually synonymous with the "perfection" of Scripture, though, for some, the latter refers to the preservation of the text of Scripture from error and falsification, especially in the Hebrew and Greek original. See Heinrich Heppe, *Reformed Dogmatics* (London: Allen & Unwin, 1950), pp. 28ff.

Reformers sought to *reform* the church, obviously they were not interested in founding a church de novo. The tendency, therefore, which can be observed in some Protestant circles, of not thinking back beyond 1517 is unevangelical because it is unchurchly.[8]

It should be remembered, therefore, that at the time of the Reformation the Protestant doctrine of the sufficiency of Scripture was directed not against tradition, but against the Roman Catholic principle of tradition. That principle was clearly enunciated at the Council of Trent. Speaking of the source of "all saving truth and the rule of conduct," the theologians of Trent declared it to be contained in the written books *and* the unwritten traditions that have come down to us from Christ and his apostles. The church "receives and venerates with the same sense of loyalty and reverence all the books [of the Bible] . . . *together with* all the traditions concerning faith and morals . . . preserved in continuous succession in the Catholic Church."[9] The "together with" by which Rome links Scripture and tradition has been made more palatable by the efforts of contemporary Catholic scholars to ground many disputed points of their tradition in Scripture. If, for instance, one doubts the biblical basis of the bodily assumption of the Virgin (the dogma promulgated Nov. 1, 1950, by Pius XII in the Apostolic Constitution *Magnificentissimus Deus*), who then is the woman in heaven, "clothed with the sun, the moon under her feet" (Rv. 12:1)?[10] In spite of such exegetical endeavors, however, a substantive difference remains between Catholicism and Protestantism on this score. The Dogmatic Constitution *Dei Verbum,* of the Second Vatican, explicitly declares that "both sacred Scripture *and* sacred Tradition are to be accepted and venerated with the *same* sense of loyalty and reverence."[11] The problem then is not tradition as such, but the Roman Catholic principle of tradition that binds Scripture

---

8. See Otto Weber, *Grundlagen der Dogmatik* (Neukirchen-Vluyn: Neukirchener Verlag, 1955), vol. I, p. 304. It must be admitted that Protestantism has fostered the tendency to look upon the individual, with her Bible in hand, as needing no other help than the illumination of the Spirit, an extreme and, therefore, unfortunate expression of the doctrine of the *sufficientia Scripturae*.

9. Dupuis Neuner, *Christian Faith, Doctrinal Documents in Catholic Faith* (Westminster, Md.: Christian Classics, 1975), p. 70. Italics added.

10. Karl Rahner, borrowing a leaf from Protestant theology, argues that if there can be no "I" without a "thou," then we may suppose there can be no resurrected "I" without a resurrected "thou." If the glorified Christ remains truly and fully human, does he not need a human counterpart? And who better qualifies for this honor than his mother, whose flesh he shared while here on earth? See our "Can We Learn From Mariology?" *The Christian Century,* 9 Aug. 1967, 1019ff. The original argument is in Rahner's *Schriften zur Theologie,* I, pp. 239ff.

11. *Christian Faith,* p. 86. Italics added.

and tradition together in a way that makes both alike normative for faith and life.

While the Reformers respected tradition, they opted for Scripture as the judge of tradition because they recognized it as the inspired source of the church's teaching. They also perceived that the later traditions dominating medieval thought were so manifold and contradictory that there was no way to work through the confusion other than to hold to the primary tradition as fixed in Scripture. The only other option was simply to accept the teaching office of the Church as that which infallibly determines what Scripture really means and which tradition is really valid. Had they chosen this option, the Reformers would have ended up with a doctrine of the sufficiency of the church rather than the sufficiency of Scripture, which is but a step toward the thought that the church is the ongoing, living presence of Christ in the world.

For the contemporary student of theology, the doctrine of Scripture's sufficiency has been transposed into quite another key by the vast proliferation of human knowledge. Since the doctrine teaches us to frame our answers to questions of atomic warfare, human engineering, euthanasia, and the like in the general light of Scripture, how are we to manage this? The authors of Scripture lived in other times and places and obviously never addressed such questions. We are compelled by such considerations to admit our limitations and to remember that the sufficiency of Scripture affirms that the Bible contains what we need to know of God's will for his glory and our salvation. The Bible is not a supernatural encyclopedia that never needs a supplement, a moral code for all possible contingencies. It is rather a lamp to our feet and a light to our path (Ps. 119:105) as we make our pilgrim journey to the celestial city.

The doctrine of the sufficiency of Scripture has been applied in interesting ways. "Hard-shell" Baptists and others have questioned Sunday schools, mission societies, etc.—since Scripture does not mention such things—as though God could leave nothing concerning the worship and government of the church to Christian common sense. And what shall we say of those who go to the Bible to find where to drill for oil and spend millions of (Texas) dollars on dry holes in Israel because the Bible says that Asher shall "dip his foot in oil" (Dt. 33:24)? (See *The Wall Street Journal*, 22 Aug. 1985. See also "The Temple Mount and the New Apocalypse," *The Christian Century*, 25 Sept. 1985, 820-21, where comment is made on the dubious efforts of American fundamentalists to aid and abet the rebuilding of the temple in Jerusalem in fulfillment of Old Testament prophecy.)

B. THE PRESERVATION (TEXT) AND TRANSLATION OF SCRIPTURE

1. THE CHURCH AS THE CUSTODIAN OF SCRIPTURE

The Westminster divines emphasized God's "singular care and providence" in preserving the text of Scripture; and well they might, for without the preservation of Scripture the church could not survive. Hence an adequate theology of Scripture includes not only the thought that Scripture is God's written Word but also that he has providentially secured this written revelation to his church throughout its history. While the account of how this has happened has not been given a prominent place in dogmatics, it is a heroic chapter in the story of God's people and worthy of inclusion in the teaching of the church. Only through such teaching will Christians appreciate their heritage.

The story begins with the Jewish Scriptures. When one contemplates the calamities that have overtaken God's people in their dispersion among the nations, it is nothing short of a second-degree miracle that their Scriptures (which are also ours) should have survived. Having lost their land, their temple, their priests, and their sacrifices, the Jews yet have preserved their sacred writings at great sacrifice and thus survived as the Lord's covenant community. This is an event unparalleled, it would seem, in the history of the world.

The same heroism was found among the early Christians. The Romans perceived that to destroy the church they had to destroy its sacred writings. While some Christians, under the duress of persecution, handed over these writings (the *traditores*) to the inquisitors, others paid with their lives to keep the sacred scrolls from the flames. Nor should we forget the anonymous legion of faithful copyists, many of them monks, whose patient labors preserved and disseminated the Scripture before the printing press changed the history of the world. A word also should be said of those textual critics whose labors in more recent times have rendered the text of the Greek New Testament so near the original as to put the church forever in their debt. In all these—the faithful remnant of the Jewish people, the Christian martyrs, the secluded monks, the modern scholars—the Christian sees the providential hand of God securing to his people through the ages a text sufficiently near the original to guarantee that the ongoing proclamation of the church will be an authentic and apostolic witness to the gospel.[12]

12. In the light of what happened before the Reformation as well as after the rise of Protestant liberalism, perhaps the word "guarantee" is too strong. Yet it was because of the

The generally received text (textus receptus), the Hebrew and Greek basis of the great versions coming out of the Reformation, was drawn entirely from handwritten manuscripts. So far as the Old Testament is concerned, the text is that of the Masoretes who, beginning in the seventh century of the Christian era, edited the Hebrew in the light of the Talmudic tradition. To this text they added vowel points, giving extravagant care to every detail in copying, that no "jot" or "tittle" of the law should be lost in transmission. (They knew, for example, without the aid of a computer, that the letter א occurs 43,377 times in the Old Testament.) Since the oldest extant manuscripts in the Masoretic tradition are as recent as the ninth century, an understandable wave of excitement greeted the discovery in 1947 of the Qumran library. Although a part of the Masoretic text could be traced back to the second century A.D., now there was a text available not later than the second century B.C.!

This pre-Masoretic text, however, proved in many respects to be simply a proto-Masoretic text. While gains were made in reconstructing the text of the LXX, the Hebrew text of the Old Testament coming out of Qumran has not proved superior to that of the Masoretes in any essential way. The restoration of the original, therefore, that would offer scholars a critical text of the Old Testament comparable to the current Greek New Testament text remains a desideratum.

As for the New Testament, the results of critical research have been more satisfying. With the discovery of Greek manuscripts going back to the major uncials of the fourth century and the fragmentary papyri of an even earlier date, scholars have, for all practical purposes, restored to the church the original Greek text of the New Testament. F. J. A. Hort, speaking of the difference between the original and our present Greek text, ventures that the amount of what can, in any sense, be called substantial variation "can hardly form more than a thousandth part of the entire text" (*The New Testament in the Original Greek,* London: Macmillan, 1896, Intro., p. 2).

No significant theological questions have been raised by the critical study of the Hebrew and Greek texts; no fundamental doctrine of the Christian faith has been called into question. The Trinity does not rest on the disputed reading of 1 John 5:7 or the resurrection of Jesus on the long ending of Mark's Gospel. At the beginning of the critical reconstruction of the New Testament text, however, many scholars struggled—understandably—with the rejection of the textus receptus, much as astronomers struggled for some time with the rejection of Ptolemy in favor of Copernicus. We mention this little-known chapter of past history because of its bearing on the so-called "inerrancy debate," a theological issue vigorously discussed in evangelical and conservative circles today.

It will be remembered that between the establishment of the received text of the Hebrew and Greek Bible and the emergence of the critical text

---

Bible's being there that the Reformers were able to lead the church out of the "Babylonian Captivity" (Luther) and, in more modern times, that Barth and others, trained as liberals, were able to return to a "theology of the word."

of the New Testament, the view that the Bible was dictated by the Spirit and therefore inerrant in every respect underwent a vigorous development in Protestant orthodoxy. It is from this era that we hear of "Holy Ghost Greek" and "inspired Hebrew vowel points." Naturally it was assumed that the inerrant Bible was, for all essential purposes, the Hebrew and Greek Bible to which the church had access in the textus receptus. This text, with which the Reformers worked, was looked upon as the original of God's inspired word over against the many translations based upon it. This was the text that the Westminster Divines had in mind when they spoke of the Hebrew and Greek as not only "immediately inspired of God" but "by his singular care and providence *kept pure in all ages.*"[13]

Theologians assumed, in other words, that the Hebrew and Greek Bible that they possessed, if not an exact replica of the original, was so nearly so that it constituted the inspired Bible as God had originally given it to the church. That is to say, they not only had a high theology of the inspiration of Scripture but also a high theology of its preservation. (For this reason they paid little attention to the distinction, so carefully maintained by present-day inerrantists, between an original, inerrant Bible [the autographs], which the church does not have, and the errant Bible in Hebrew and Greek, which it does have.) But more of this presently. For now we would only note that knowledge of the history and transmission of the original text of the Old and New Testaments, opened up to us by the science of textual (lower) criticism, confirms the traditional doctrine of the preservation of Scripture. That doctrine, essential to an evangelical theology, simply affirms that the text of Scripture is sufficiently reliable to ground the faith and life of the church as the people of God. Since the church could not survive without Scripture, it is cause for gratitude to know that the present critical text is the most reliable the church has had since ancient times.

2. THE CHURCH AS THE TRANSLATOR OF SCRIPTURE

Though the preservation and the translation of Scripture are quite different matters, they obviously go hand in hand theologically. For of what value to the church as a whole is a well-preserved original text of the Bible if it is not made accessible to all through translation? So obvious is the answer

---

13. *Westminster Confession*, I, 8. Italics added. For an erudite defense of the textus receptus as the authentic original, see Edward F. Hills, *The King James Version Defended* (Des Moines: The Christian Research Press, 1956).

to this question that one is surprised to learn that for centuries the Vulgate was the only version allowed in the West, even when Latin had become a dead language.[14] As Latin was considered the sacred language of the Mass, the Latin Bible was considered the sacred book of the church, belonging to the clergy rather than to the laity. For hundreds of years, no eminent teacher urged the right of the common people to read the Word of God for themselves. Reacting to the Reformation, the Council of Trent even declared the Latin Bible to be the only authentic text for preaching, lectures, and public disputation.[15]

With the final establishment of the Reformation, the Bible was put back into the hands of the common people, a radical and daring decision on the part of the Reformers, given the circumstances. Even before the Reformation, the church's mandate to translate the Scriptures into the language of every nation to which the gospel came had been urged by John Wycliffe. Appealing to the fact that Christ himself spoke in the tongue best known to his hearers and that at Pentecost the Spirit gave the apostles the gift to declare the Word of God to people of many tongues, he asked why the people of England should be denied Christ's word in their mother tongue.[16]

The great genius who was first in truly achieving the vision of Wycliffe was Martin Luther. Convinced that if the Reformation were to survive the people must have a Bible they could read for themselves, he began his translation at the Wartburg Castle in 1521. The problems he faced seem to ordinary mortals insuperable, but Luther was no ordinary mortal. He learned Greek and Hebrew as a mature man (without modern aids) and decided what dialect of German to use in translation. Though he never mastered the biblical languages with anything like perfection, when it came to the German tongue he was without a peer. Choosing the dialect of Saxony, he became the father of modern literary German. His rough draft

---

14. Having abandoned the bishop of Rome's original request for a revision of the Old Latin Bible, Jerome made a fresh start, working directly with the Greek and Hebrew. (He learned the latter with the help of an anonymous Jew while an ascetic in the Syrian desert.) After twenty years of labor (A.D. 385-405), he bequeathed to the church the Vulgate Bible. One of the three greatest versions ever achieved, it gradually made its way on its own merits, without official backing, until it became the only Bible in the West.

15. Fourth Session: Decree Concerning the Canonical Scriptures: Concerning the Edition and the Use of the Sacred Books.

16. The efforts of Wycliffe (the "morning star of the Reformation") were hardly appreciated by the Church. Archbishop Arandel of Canterbury cited him as "a pestilent wretch of damnable memory, yea, the forerunner and disciple of Antichrist, who, as the compliment of his wickedness, invented a new translation of the Scripture into his mother tongue." (See Schaff, *History of the Christian Church*, vol. VI, p. 344.) Tyndale, a consummate translator who shared Wycliffe's dream, was subsequently caught and burned at the stake (1536) for smuggling copies of his translation of the Bible into England.

of the German New Testament was finished in less than four months and sent off to Melanchthon for editing. In the more demanding task of translating the Old Testament he sought the help of Jewish acquaintances and had the assistance of his *Collegium Biblicum,* a group of scholars who met with him on a weekly basis. His essential qualifications as a translator were his intuitive insight into the substance of the biblical message and his sympathetic grasp of the content of the Bible as a whole.

Like all translations, even the great ones, Luther's German Bible reflected a theological *Tendenz.* The most notable instance was in his translation of Romans 3:28. "For we reckon one to be justified by faith" (δικαιοῦσθαι πίστει), writes the apostle. "By faith *alone" (allein durch den Glauben),* translates Luther. This, of course, brought Paul into a collision course with James, who declares (2:24) that one is justified by works and not by faith *alone.* Luther not only dismissed James as an "epistle of straw," but added: "If your papist makes much useless fuss about the word *sola, allein* [in Rom. 3:28], tell him at once, Dr. Martin Luther will have it so. . . ." (See Schaff, *History of the Christian Church,* vol. VII, p. 362. Schaff goes on to observe that he had an old copy of Luther's New Testament in which the word *allein* is printed in large type with a marginal finger pointing to it.)

Luther's example was followed wherever the Reformation went, resulting in many translations, including the King James Bible, the third and last of the great versions. The Protestant multiplication of vernacular translations compelled the Roman Catholic Church to provide translations for Catholics in Protestant countries, such as the Douay Version for those whose native tongue was English.

Since Vatican II all has changed in this regard. The Dogmatic Constitution *Dei Verbum* (1965) is surely one of the most hopeful documents produced by the Council so far as Protestants are concerned. Not only does the Constitution advocate that easy access to Scripture be provided for all the faithful, but also that suitable translations be made from the original texts, a task that (with the approval of the Church) may be pursued in cooperation with the "separated brethren" (non-Catholic Christians). The supreme fruit of this volte-face is the great French translation of L'École Biblique de Jerusalem, *La Bible de Jerusalem.*[17]

---

17. See *The Documents of Vatican II,* ed. Walter M. Abbott (Piscataway, N.J.: New Century Publishers, 1966), p. 125. To the stipulation of the Council that all the faithful shall have easy access to the Scripture, the editors add the footnote: "This is perhaps the most novel section of the Constitution. Not since the early centuries of the Church, has an official document urged the availability of the Scriptures for all."

Protestants, of course, continue to translate Scripture, not only for the benefit of the Christian "faithful," but also to evangelize non-Christians, especially on the mission field. The Herculean efforts of the Wycliffe Bible translators are worthy of special mention and have helped to make at least portions of the Bible available in over a thousand tongues. On the American scene, the effort to reach those who seldom read the Bible has spawned a veritable cornucopia of modern speech translations—some amplified, some paraphrased, some good, some not so good—until the American church is threatened by what Alvin Toffler has called "overchoice," a "peculiarly super-industrial dilemma" that paralyzes by surfeit. (See his *Future Shock,* New York: Random House, 1970, chap. 12.) The end will come, it seems, only when publishers have made all the money they can.

The translation of Scripture into any number of languages can—as we have seen—be adequately based, theologically, on the divine example; and it is a cause of rejoicing that our Roman Catholic brothers and sisters have come to agree. There is, to be sure, some loss of the original meaning in every translation effort since translation requires interpretation. Even placing a period at the end of Genesis 1:1 involves interpretation, for there is no period in the original.[18] It is the gulf between the culture of the original authors and that of their contemporary readers that compels the translator to become an imperfect interpreter and so risk a loss or change of meaning. She may, for example, be compelled to translate "we men" or "we women," "we two" or "we three or more," though the original is indefinite and uncommitted. Yet, though there is inevitable loss of meaning in translation, there is never essential loss. Had God placed us on a flat planet, who can say, as we evolved culturally away from one another, what might have happened. Perhaps a language gulf would have emerged between the various families of the human race that even the best of translators could hardly cross. But, as Teilhard de Chardin has reminded us, God has placed us on a sphere, not a plane. Thus socialization guarantees the ultimate unity of human speech, despite all the differences that have challenged missionaries, past and present, in their translation efforts.

While loss or change of meaning is inevitable in translation, this does not excuse the way specific translations sometimes reflect a manipulation of the text. Consider, for example, some of the translations of the enigmatic admonition that women should cover their heads when they pray, "because of the angels" (1 Cor. 11:10). All these translations, of course, are supposedly in the interest of "clarifying" the text. The Greek reads: διὰ τοῦτο ὀφείλει ἡ γυνὴ ἐξουσίαν ἔχειν ἐπὶ τῆς κεφαλῆς διὰ τοὺς ἀγγέλους. Very literally,

---

18. Note the NEB translation of the "waw" consecutives in the Hebrew: "In the beginning of the creation, *when* God made heaven and earth, and *when . . .*"

this says: "On this account the woman ought to have authority (power) on the head on account of the angels." Any responsible translator may add "sign," so that the text reads: ". . . sign of authority (i.e., a veil) on her head because of the angels." But what shall we say of the *Living Bible* translation: "So a woman should wear a covering on her head as a sign that she is under a man's authority, a fact for all the angels to notice and rejoice in." Charles Kraft (*Christianity and Culture,* Maryknoll, N.Y.: Orbis Books, 1979, p. 142) assures us that the admonition that women should cover their heads when praying means, in our American culture today, that women "should not wear their clothes too tight." This, supposedly, is translating with "dynamic equivalency." There are times when the study of dogmatics requires one to have a sense of humor to survive.

*   *   *   *   *

Unavoidable changes of meaning in translation are quite different from deliberate ones. The latter are theologically more problematic, and can be adjudicated only on an individual basis. Should one, for example, translate such verses as 1 Pt. 1:19 and Rv. 7:14, "blood of a *seal*" for Eskimos who have never seen a lamb? As a general rule, it seems to us, such renderings belong to the expositor rather than the translator, though changing the meaning of a text at the lexical level may at times preserve the meaning at a deeper level for certain readers. If calling Herod a "fox" (Lk. 13:32) means to certain native Americans in Mexico that he spoke in a "high falsetto voice," then the name of some other animal that is "sly" should be used. Furthermore, some renderings are not meant to be translations, strictly speaking. Everyone understands what Clarence Jordan is doing in his *Cotton Patch Version* (New York: Association Press, 1970) when he translates Paul's Epistle to the Romans as his "Letter to the Christians in Washington"; or when, in his paraphrase of Luke 10:27-35, he depicts the Good Samaritan as a black man. (At a meeting we once attended to discuss the publication of a Bible in Black street English—an effort that never materialized—Genesis 1:1 was rendered: "At the start of things the Man upstairs got the whole show on the road.")

As we conclude our discussion of the preservation and translation of Scripture, we should not overlook the implications of what has been said for the doctrine of the authority of Scripture. We have in mind, specifically, the definition of that doctrine in terms of verbal inerrancy. Though the church does not have liberty over the words of the Bible (since the Bible is God's word *to* the church), the task of translating these words involves, as we have seen, considerable freedom. While laypeople therefore have the written word of God in their Bibles, they never have it in more than an approximate way. Some translations are nearer the original, some less so, depending on the skill of the translators and the obstacles they have had to overcome in pursuing their task. Actually, what is true of the translations that the church uses is also true of the original from which they are made. Even in Greek and Hebrew the church does not possess God's Word in a verbally exact sense. As we have seen, slips of the copyist's hand and eye have left the church without the possibility of reconstructing the autographs word for word.

Furthermore, these errors of transmission and translation are not the only limitations facing the church in pursuing its mission of proclaiming the gospel to all people. The very concept of revelation in human words ties the revelation by which the church lives to a given culture, since language is the supreme achievement of any culture. But cultural history, like all history, moves down the stream of time. Thus the church finds itself ever in new cultures, in new times. No scholarship can so transcend this flow of time as to secure to the church a perfect understanding of the original text, even at the lexical level. This would be true even if textual critics and archaeologists were able to put the church in possession of the autographs themselves. The hapax legomena (unique occurrences of words) in the New Testament are notable for their difficulty. But the difficulties in understanding (and therefore in translating) obscure texts in the New Testament pale by comparison with the Old. Here not only isolated words, like those used by the erudite author of Job, are of unknown meaning, but a considerable portion of the Hebrew text of the Old Testament in general remains obscure as well.[19]

To know its Lord's will, therefore, and to know what it should proclaim to the world and how it should witness in the world, the church has relied upon, appealed to, and been judged by a Scripture more or less accurately translated from a text more or less faithfully transmitted from an original more or less clearly understood. Fortunately, however, these problems do not affect any essential doctrine of the church. Not that we would value a secondary over a primary text or place a premium on shoddy workmanship in translation. As a matter of fact, so far as Scripture is concerned, the church has a better preserved text, a more accurately translated text, and a better understood text, than it has ever had. For this we can only be grateful. But it does not have and never will have an inerrant original text. The implications of this fact will engage us further when we discuss the inspiration and authority of Scripture, a subject to which we shall turn shortly.

19. Some modern English versions reflect this fact in the footnotes. Not only are alternative translations with quite different meanings given, but often the note will simply say, "Heb. obscure." Our point is that one should not suppose that if we had the "inerrant" original text all obscurities would vanish. We are simply too far removed in time and place from the context of the original authors and their readers to do more than make scholarly conjectures as to the original meaning of many texts.

ADDENDUM: THE KING JAMES VERSION: A COMMENT ON THE PLACE OF BEAUTY IN THE WORSHIP OF GOD

In some respects, at least, the Vulgate and the King James are similar. Their use in the church began without official sponsorship and they established themselves over all rivals by their sheer intrinsic worth. Indeed, they became so well established that in both instances parting with them has occasioned pain and controversy in the church. Of course there is a great difference between them in that Latin is a dead language, while English is a living language; hence the King James Version is far from dead, even for the lay Christian. In fact, as late as 1971 it outsold all other English versions two to one, and it remains to the present day on the best-seller list. Its modern competitors have had the advantage of being translated from a more accurate critical text by scholars who have had the help of archaeological "light from the ancient East." Yet the King James, like "old man river, just keeps rolling along," though it has not been revised in over two hundred years, even to the conversion of a semicolon or the dropping of a comma.[20] Though we have requisitioned all the arts of fine bookmaking to render the King James attractive—it is published in large and small print; bound in red, white, blue, brown, and black leather; its India linen pages are gilded with gold, adorned with thumb indices and decked out with silken book markers—yet we have left it to groan under its Lilliputian burden of colons and semicolons, verse and chapter divisions, antique forms, archaic expressions, and antiquated spellings. Were it not the Gulliver of all versions, the greatest single literary achievement of the English-speaking church, it would long since have sunk down under such a load into a moldy oblivion.

The survival power of the King James is primarily due to its superior literary qualities; it is a work of art. True, the main purpose of any version is to make the Word of God intelligible and thereby accessible to God's people in their native language. But it is an egregious mistake to suppose that Bible translation is indifferent to the question of the beauty of language. To say that we have in the Bible a revelation of truth and therefore, in translating it, need concern ourselves only with accuracy of thought, not felicity of expression, is as false as it is common. Such an affirmation

---

20. There is *The New King James Bible* (New York: Thomas Nelson, 1979), which is not without merit. However, the translators—presumably all of them Americans—seem to have been convinced that the work of revising the King James could be entrusted only to those adhering to the textus receptus and the doctrine of inerrancy, hardly the prime qualification of a great translator! See *The New KJV,* Intro., v.

presupposes that truth has nothing to do with beauty, which is the judgment of an uneducated mind.[21] Delicacy of shading, fitness of word, grace of rhythm, and cadence are not the white gloves that encumber the hands of truth as it reaches out for our hearts. As Matthew Arnold, who understood these things so well, once observed, the power of poetry is generally admitted, though the soul of this power often eludes us. "It resides chiefly in the refining and elevation wrought by the great style."[22] In other words, if truth matters, then the clothes in which it is dressed also matter. To divorce truth from beauty is to put asunder what the Creator has joined together.[23]

While we shall not attempt to analyze in an in-depth way what constitutes beauty of language, we venture that it involves rhetoric understood as the skillful adaptation of speech to the subject and the hearer.[24] Such adaptation involves language that evokes emotion as inevitably as it communicates ideas. This is the key to the immortality of the King James: its language possesses the power not only to express thought but also to release feeling, not only to convince the mind but also to stir the heart. James Weldon Johnson tells us, in the preface to his *God's Trombones*, that he did not cast the black folk sermon in dialect but in the English of the King James because the original black preachers, men of unusual talent, used its language so skillfully to move their congregations. "The old-time Negro preacher," Johnson says, "loved the sonorous, mouth-filling, ear-filling

---

21. It seems especially easy for Americans to divorce truth from beauty. We cannot understand how Phidias (of whom we have never heard) could persuade Pericles (of whom we have never heard either) to divert naval funds, which would "threaten the national security," to build the Parthenon. True, the Parthenon was beautiful, perhaps the most beautiful building ever built; but it served no practical use. The Colosseum in Rome, on the other hand, makes sense. Though the subtleties and well-nigh invisible refinements of proportion are gone, *here* is something big and useful; people could sit in it, 100,000 at a time, and watch the circus!

22. Matthew Arnold, *Essays in Criticism* (New York: Macmillan, 1924), second series, pp. 63ff.

23. "Truth," "goodness," and "beauty" are the great triumvirate of fundamental values in Western thought. Since Darwin especially, arguments have been set forth to reduce beauty to the subjectivity of taste and times. But such arguments inevitably draw the temple roof down on the head of goodness and beauty. "Beginning in the sphere of beauty, subjectivism or relativism spreads first to judgements of good and evil, and then to statements about truth, never in the opposite direction. . . . What is good or true is held to be just as much a matter of private taste or customary opinion as what is beautiful." *Great Books* (Chicago: Encyclopedia Britannica, Inc., 1952), Synopticon, p. 113.

24. Rhetoric, of course, like all art can be prostituted to the cause of falsehood and error. This is no doubt why Plato condemned it as a form of flattery. But Plato's judgment was too sweeping. Witness Pascal's *Provincial Letters*, which are not only clear but persuasive because of the magnificence of their literary style. His flawless diction—portions of

phrase because it gratified a highly developed sense of sound and rhythm in himself and his hearers."[25]

As for the evocative power of the great style, Miles Smith, in his preface to the original 1611 edition of the King James, speaks in a way that reveals how the translators were carried beyond themselves because they viewed the text with which they worked as "being from heaven, not from earth; the author being God not humankind, the inditer, the Holy Spirit, not the wit of the apostles or prophets."

> Translation it is, [he continues,] that opens the windows, lets in the light; that breaks the shell that we may eat the kernel; that puts aside the curtain that we may look into the most holy place; that removes the cover of the well that we may come to the water.

How, then, did the King James translators come to their work? Did they trust in their own knowledge and depth of judgment? By no means. "They trusted in him who has the key of David, opening and no one shutting; they prayed to the Lord."[26] We would not argue, as some, that commitment to a liberal theological creed necessarily renders the work of a translator untrustworthy; indeed, we would say that liberal scholarship has illumined many questions of translation. But though a learned translation may be achieved without faith and though faith cannot achieve *any* translation without learning, yet one cannot account for the achievement of the King James translators and be indifferent to the fact that they added to their knowledge a faith as vital as their learning was sound. In other words, they had the qualifications that Martin Luther laid down as essential to a good translator, namely, "a truly devout, faithful, diligent, Christian, learned, experienced, and practiced heart."

Together with their faith, the King James translators displayed an uncanny sense of how to use the work of their predecessors. With sensitive ears and sure instinct they worked over the vast and varied materials at

---

the letters were rewritten dozens of times—lifted a subtle theological controversy out of the obscurity of the Port Royal Monastery and made it the common property of the world of letters. See also Augustine, *On Christian Doctrine,* Bk. IV, where he treats eloquence, style, and expression and their place in conveying truth.

25. James W. Johnson, *God's Trombones* (New York: The Viking Press, 1955), p. 9. The old-time black preachers not only used big words, but grappled with big themes. Johnson alludes to one who read a cryptic passage, closed the Bible with a bang, took off his glasses and began: "Brothers and sisters, this morning I intend to explain the unexplainable—find out the undefinable—ponder the imponderable—and unscrew the inscrutable." Ibid., pp. 4-5.

26. As quoted in Gustavus S. Paine, *The Learned Men* (New York: Crowell, 1959), pp. 172-76.

their disposal. It has been estimated that 60 percent of the text of the English Bible had been fixed before the King James was produced and that another 20 percent was approximately fixed.[27] But this only enhances their achievement.

Take, for example, Proverbs 3:17. They had before them not only the Hebrew text but the following translations: "Her ways are pleasant ways and all her paths are peaceable" (Coverdale, The Great Bible, the Bishop's Bible). Then there was the translation of the Geneva Bible that the Puritans brought to New England: "Her ways are ways of pleasure and all her paths are prosperity." The King James simply takes up these translations into a tactful balance and alliteration that results in perfect melody: "Her ways are ways of pleasantness and all her paths are peace." Consider the opening lines in the familiar passage in Matthew 11:28-30. Wycliffe translated: "Come unto me, all ye that labor and are laden, and I will rest you." The Geneva Bible reads: "Come unto me, all ye that are uneasy and laden, and I will ease you." The Bishop's Bible reads: "Come unto me, all ye that labor sore and are laden, and I will ease you." It remained for the King James to balance the rhythm with the word "heavy" and to add the lovely cadence at the end: "Come unto me, all ye that labour and are heavy laden, and I will give you rest," an invitation that cannot be surpassed, expressed in language that cannot be improved.

Of course there are errors in the King James, but none that threaten the faith of the church and few that could not be easily corrected. Of course the text on which the King James is based is an inferior text, but it is not a perverse text. The real problem with the King James, in our judgment, is not its mistakes but its archaisms. It is time, more than anything else, that has taken its toll on the venerable English Bible of our forebears and will continue to do so. If we continue to rope it off and admire it as a treasure in a museum, then the inexorable movement of time will put it on the shelf with Chaucer and the other great books of the Western world, and justly so, for as it becomes increasingly unintelligible to the layperson it will obscure rather than convey the Word of God. We find it anomalous in the extreme that the English-speaking church should leave the greatest of English versions untouched and so allow it to slip from its fingers. We spend millions to restore our cathedrals and yet we do not restore our Bible, more beautiful than any cathedral. We spend enormous amounts of time and money in promoting ecumenical understanding, and the one thing we have in common, the truest symbol of ecumenism in the English-speaking

---

27. See C. Butterword, *The Literary Lineage of the King James Bible* (Philadelphia: University of Pennsylvania Press, 1941), pp. 230ff.

church, we are deserting to the ravages of time. What the church needs to do, on both sides of the Atlantic and wherever English is spoken, is to do what the Germans have wisely done with their Bible — change it but not supplant it. Such versions as Luther's German Bible and the King James Bible escape their times; they are sole, divine gifts to the church, to be received with gratitude. Such versions should be preserved and bequeathed to our children, that they like us may hear the Word of God in language that is not only meaningful but magnificent.

A word of caution needs to be sounded in light of the above emphasis on the relation of beauty to truth. It is so easy, as Kierkegaard reminds us, to substitute the former for the latter. When we do so, we read the Bible for its purple passages. But no Protestant who is true to her heritage can ever forget that her basic interest in the Bible is religious, not literary. She sees in her Bible divine verities, not literary masterpieces. In *The Bible Designed to Be Read as Living Literature* (E. S. Bates, ed., New York: Simon and Schuster, 1936, p. 1236), we read: "As far as literary value is concerned, the King James Version . . . is unlikely ever to be superseded. Its position as a world classic seems to be secure as that of Homer, Dante, and Shakespeare; and it is the only translation in all literature of which that can be said." So the Bible is shelved along with Homer, Dante, and Shakespeare, never to be superseded as literature, which is a covert way of saying it is superseded as the Word of God.

Such a flight from reality cuts the very nerve of New Testament Christianity, which has as a fundamental ingredient decision for or against Jesus as the Christ. The whole message of the Bible is a call to men and women to come from the galleries of contemplation onto the stage of life where the drama is being played. The savoring of beauty for beauty's sake is but a manifestation of the theoretical mind that seeks to rest in the music of the invitation, "Come unto me, all ye who labor and are heavy laden," rather than in the One who gives the invitation. Delicious as the music of language is, we must be ever on our guard that we do not become intoxicated with its beauty, lest that which is good should become sin to us. To read the Bible as literature is to have the aesthetic mind; it is to be a citizen of Athens, not Jerusalem. It is to add one more idol to a city already full of idols. Amos Wilder warns of the inadequacies of a romantic version of Christianity and quotes W. H. Auden, who, in his Harvard Phi Beta Kappa poem, classifies reading the Bible for its prose with a variety of contemporary heresies:

> Thou shalt not be on friendly terms
> With guys in advertising firms,
> Nor speak with such
> As read the Bible for its prose,
> Nor, above all, make love to those
> Who wash too much.

(Wilder, *Theology and Modern Literature,* Cambridge: Harvard University Press, 1958, pp. 75-77.) As Christians, let us not forget that worship consists not only of a sense of awe before the mystery of God's being (which beauty serves to enhance), but also in a fellowship of mind between the worshipping community and the God who is worshipped. We must, then, keep our prayers, our hymns, our Bible, not only eloquent and beautiful, but up-to-date, reflecting a pattern of language that is intelligible as well as evocative.

C. THE UNITY OF SCRIPTURE

1. INTRODUCTION

One might wonder, in view of the freedom the Reformers evidenced in their approach to the canon, why the canonicity of various books of the Bible has seldom been debated in Protestant circles since the Reformation. The reason is implicit in the methodology that has come to prevail in the critical study of Scripture. Given such a methodology, the biblical documents have come increasingly to be investigated more as individual, historical sources than as documents together constituting a normative theological statement. When viewed as a whole, the so-called canonical writings are seen as containing diverse and contradicting perspectives that cannot possibly function as a norm for the faith and life of the church. The blood sacrifices, rituals, and taboos of Old Testament priestly religion are viewed as having nothing in common with the ethical imperatives of the reforming prophets; in the New Testament the gospel *of* Jesus, reconstructed from the traditions behind the gospels, is quite different from the gospel *about* Jesus, the supernatural Christ of the epistles, and the like. The Bible contains theologies—that of the Yahwist, of the Deuteronomist, of the Chronicler, of Paul, of John, of Peter; but it contains no theology in the traditional sense, a theology normative for the self-understanding and proclamation of the church.

This historicizing methodology has transposed the thought of a canon into such a different key that there need be no argument about "changing the canon" for the simple reason that there is no canon, in the traditional sense, to be changed. As a result of what has happened in the halls of academia, the "Holy Bible" functions in the pulpit and in the congregation simply as an ongoing symbol of the church's continuity with the past. Though it has great historical significance, it has no normative value. At the practical level the preacher, of course, needs a Sunday morning text from this "word of God"; but she is well advised to ignore its canonical context, preaching some "positive thoughts" on some contemporary theme.[28]

---

28. While many laypeople are only vaguely aware of these matters, the more discerning understand. "Unhappily enough," complains one such discerner, "many clergy and seminar-

Is there an approach to the question of the unity of Scripture that escapes the Scylla of fundamentalism (no higher criticism) and the Charybdis of liberalism (no single, unified canon)? In seeking an answer to this question we begin with the obvious. The unity of the Bible is seen in the fact that it is bound, circulated, and read by the church as a single volume. Yet its diversity is seen in that it is made up of two parts, the Old Testament and the New, and these two parts are themselves subdivided. The Old Testament is composed of the Law, the Prophets, and the Writings; the New of the gospels, the Acts, the epistles, and the Apocalypse. The Bible, then, is not a single book but a library of books whose literary genre differs markedly. Furthermore, in this Book, made up of many books, we are told, on the one hand, that "all is vanity" (Eccl. 1:2); on the other, that in the Lord our labor "is not in vain" (1 Cor. 15:58). Surely, then, if there is a unity of the Bible, it is a unity that can be found only "in, with, and under" its obvious diversity.

In light of the above, one can appreciate the popularity of the *Scofield Reference Bible* (1902-09, revised 1917, 1966), the most widely used study Bible ever published. One using this Bible is not only unencumbered by the problems of higher criticism, but also furnished with a key to understanding the unity-in-diversity with which the biblical material confronts the reader. That key, drawn from the writings of John Nelson Darby (1800-1882), an early leader of the English Plymouth Brethren, is known as *Dispensationalism*. Dispensationalism promises that one can see how the Bible harmonizes with itself theologically, by distinguishing seven dispensations in which God deals with the human family through various tests that follow chronologically upon one another and embrace the whole of human history. All these tests underscore the failure of every effort to obtain salvation by human endeavor. In his Introduction, Scofield, a devout layman, makes no mention of Darby or the Brethren, but quotes Augustine: "Distinguish the ages [dispensations] and the Scriptures harmonize" (Sec. 10). Augustine, however, was concerned with harmonizing Jesus' admonition to rebuke an offender privately (Mt. 18:15) with the pastoral instruction to rebuke sinners publicly (1 Tm. 5:2). Distinguish the times (circumstances), he says, and the Scripture agrees with itself— *Distribute tempora et concordat scriptura.* (*The Nicene and Post-Nicene Fathers,* New York: Christian Literature Co., 1888; 1st series, vol. VI, p. 360.)

---

ians, for all their apparent sophistication in academic theology, often are shockingly ignorant of the Bible. . . . Or so it appears, since they so seldom rely upon the Bible in preaching. Instead of the exposition of the Word of God in the Bible . . . , laymen are subjected to all manner of speeches, diatribes, commentaries, newscasts, patriotic declamations, poetic recitations, aphorisms, positive thoughts, social analysis, gimmicks, solicitations, sentimentalities and corn." William Stringfellow, *A Private and Public Faith* (Grand Rapids: Eerdmans, 1962), pp. 47-48.

2. UNITY-IN-DIVERSITY

a. One Covenant Differently Administered

As the institutional church became increasingly hierarchical, imposing a priestly class between God and the people after the analogy of the Old Testament; and as it increasingly embraced the hermeneutical principle of a manifold meaning of the text, it came more and more to read the Old Testament as it did the New and the New as it did the Old. Thus the diversity in Scripture gave place to a flat, undifferentiated unity. The Reformers, and those who came after them, having rejected both the institutional hierarchy and the allegorizing hermeneutic of the Roman Catholic Church, were compelled to face anew the problem of the diversity in the unity of Scripture. Just how is the "New in the Old concealed and the Old in the New revealed?"

In seeking to answer this question, the Reformers all agreed that the unity of the Bible is primary, its diversity secondary. They further agreed that this unity can be perceived only from the perspective of the New Testament witness to Christ. Christ, in other words, is the integrating center of all biblical revelation. He is, in Luther's words, "King and Lord of Scripture."[29] Thus Luther read the law in the light of the gospel. Calvin followed Luther in affirming this "law and gospel" approach to Scripture; but in elaborating it, he preferred to speak of old and new covenants. As both law and gospel revealed Christ in Luther's thought, so, for Calvin, Christ is revealed in both the old and the new covenants. In fact they are one covenant, the covenant of grace, first administered to Israel by promise and newly administered to the church by Christ who fulfills the promise. Thus the concept of *covenant* (בְּרִית) became, for Calvin, a leitmotif of biblical revelation. Through it he sought to preserve the unity of that revelation while at the same time acknowledging its diversity.[30] The God of Abraham and Sarah is the Father of our Lord Jesus Christ who is the angel of the old covenant as well as the mediator of the new one. The terms "old" and "new," therefore, should not be taken absolutely. The diversity is in the administration, not the substance, of the covenant. In the original, Old Testament administration of this one covenant, God condescended to human weakness by exhibiting the covenant promise for the contemplation of Israel under the figures of temporal and terrestrial blessings. Not that the covenant offered only earthly blessings; but the heavenly realities with

---

29. *Christus Rex et dominus Scripturae,* Weimarer Ausgabe 40.1.420.
30. See *Institutes,* II, 9, 10, 11.

which it was concerned were mirrored in these earthly blessings. In the Old Testament, then, the terrestrial blessings were a very real part of the promise: the land was a piece of geography; the seed, a literal offspring; even the promised blessing to all nations had its temporal side, as can be seen from the fact that Abraham restored to the petty kings of the Pentapolis the captives and goods he had recovered from the pillaging hand of Chedorlaomer (Gn. 14; also 13:14-15; 22:17).

But with the advent of Messiah—the promised Seed par excellence, and the Pentecostal effusion of the Spirit, the promise of salvation, foreshadowed in such earthly blessings to Israel, has been brought near. It is no longer on hope's horizon; it is an accomplished fact in history. Hence the temporal, earthly, typical elements of the Old Testament economy (including the "ceremonial laws," as Christians call them) have dropped away from the great house of salvation as scaffolding from a finished edifice. They are only shadows of what was to come; by contrast, the "body" (σῶμα, "substance," "reality") belongs to Christ (Col. 2:17), the mediator of a new and better covenant.[31]

b. Promise and Fulfillment

While some have emphasized one covenant differently administered, others have used the concepts of promise and fulfillment in seeking to relate the old covenant to the new. "It is in Hebrews," observes Schrenk, "that all is oriented in terms of fulfillment to such an extent that the Old Testament parables and institutions are understood typologically as shadows of the higher, future revelation in Christ." "Primitive Christianity no longer had any Scripture apart from Christ. It had a Scripture only insofar as the Christ event attains fulfillment *in its midst.*"[32]

This motif of promise and fulfillment does, indeed, pervade the New Testament. What Jesus says, according to the gospels (especially Matthew), fulfills what is written in the Old Testament. The same promise and fulfillment motif is prominent in the preaching of the apostles as recorded in Acts. (See Acts 2; 17:2; 28:23.) Further, Paul in his epistles makes it clear that

---

31. In the Reformed tradition, the covenant motif underlies what is called "federal theology," from the Latin *foedus,* "covenant." Prominent in the 17th century, federal theology sought to preserve the unity of Scripture not only by postulating one covenant differently administered, but also a "covenant of works" made with our first parents prior to the Fall. This covenant promised life upon continued obedience and threatened death upon disobedience. The breaking of this "covenant of works" (the Fall) occasioned the institution of the covenant of grace, administered to Israel under types that foreshadowed Christ.

32. "γραφή," *TWNT,* I, p. 760 (cf. TDNT, I, p. 760). Italics added.

whatever was written in the Old Testament Scriptures was written for our benefit and learning. He really says nothing less than that the Old Testament has its final validity in the emergence of the Christian community.

c. The Allegorizing of the Old Testament in the New

To speak of one covenant differently administered or of promises fulfilled in Christ is to view the unity-in-diversity of Scripture in a linear way, as Otto Weber would say.[33] While perfectly acceptable, indeed unavoidable, the linear approach has its inadequacies, as can be sensed even in the Old Testament itself. We have in mind the fact that when Israel breaks the covenant and is thrust out of the land, this would seem to be the end of the line—to continue a "linear" way of speaking. But Yahweh graciously restores the faithful remnant, promising them a new covenant (Jer. 31:31ff.) that can never be broken. *This* covenant is inward and spiritual— the law is "written in their hearts," rather than on tables of stone. Interestingly enough, however, in the Old Testament prophetic literature the blessings of this new covenant are still thought of largely in terms of the old. Israel will be restored to the land, the desert will blossom as the rose, Jerusalem will become the head of the nations, and David (or the Branch that springs from his roots) will reign in triumph over a glorious kingdom. Thus, to a degree, the linear approach prevails. (See Ez. 37:19; Is. 40; 42:4, etc.)

There is no way, however, to harmonize such Old Testament prophecies, in their literal meaning, with the Jesus event viewed as the fulfillment of the Old Testament. Recognizing this fact, the writers of the New Testament say nothing of the restoration of Israel to a literal land, so prominent in the vision of the prophets, much less of the restoration of blood sacrifice in a rebuilt temple as envisioned in Ezekiel 40–48. Paul's silence about the land in Romans 9–11 is eloquent, while the author of Hebrews explicitly declares that the blood sacrifices of the Old Testament are forever done away in Christ (Heb. 10). All such considerations bring us to the question of the allegorizing interpretation of the Old Testament found throughout the New. Apart from such an interpretation, the fundamental unity of Scripture could not have been maintained by the apostolic church; the diversity between the testaments would have become absolute and Marcion's "antitheses" would have prevailed.

---

33. See Otto Weber's *Foundations of Dogmatics,* vol. I (Grand Rapids: Eerdmans, 1981), esp. pp. 291-304.

Allegorizing, understandably, has had a bad press ever since the Reformers rejected the medieval allegorizings of the Roman Catholic Church and insisted that the text be interpreted according to its plain intent. "Allegorizings," fumed Luther, "are awkward, absurd, invented, obsolete rags" (as quoted by F. W. Farrar, *History of Interpretation*, New York: Dutton, 1886, p. 338). But there are not only bad but also good allegorizings. (Protestants have tacitly acknowledged as much when they have recognized the validity of the "typological" or "spiritual" interpretation of the Old Testament. Theologically speaking, there is no difference between an allegorizing and a typologizing of a text.) When the author of Hebrews, for example, speaks of the original tabernacle as a "copy" and "shadow" of the heavenly sanctuary (8:5), or when the apostle declares that the rock from which Israel drank in the wilderness was Christ (1 Cor. 10:4), both are doing what the apostle does expressly when he allegorizes the story of Sarah and Hagar in Galatians 4:21ff. The problem is not with allegorizing as such, but with allegorizing that rests on no true analogy between the original meaning of the text and the new meaning given the text. It was for want of such analogy that the early church could not follow Philo in allegorizing the Old Testament in terms of Greek philosophy. There was no univocal element between the two, that is, between the original meaning of the Old Testament text and the allegorical meaning imposed on it to make it harmonize with Greek philosophy.

Allegorical (typological, spiritual) interpretation may be defined as *the interpretation of one thing in terms of another.* To be legitimate, such interpretation must, as we have said, rest on analogy, an analogy between the original meaning of the text and that in terms of which it is interpreted. There must, in other words, be some univocal element of meaning between the two. Paul's allegorizing of the conflict between Hagar and Sarah (Gal. 4:21-31) in terms of the conflict between law and grace is an example of legitimate allegorizing, for it rests on a genuine analogy. The univocal element in the analogy can be clearly stated. As Ishmael was born of human effort, so the Judaizers are seeking righteousness by human effort. And as Isaac's birth was the result of God's gracious act in fulfilling his promise, so it is with the people of God. Being born of the Spirit, they become, by God's grace, children of the promise, members of Christ's body, and citizens of the Jerusalem which is above.

Paul equates Hagar with Sinai because the law, by which the Judaizers were seeking righteousness, was given at Sinai. Of course, Paul did not endorse such a legalistic understanding of the law, for it would have made the law work against the promise and so destroy the unity of revelation (Gal. 3:17-18). Nor should we suppose that when, in other places, he sharply contrasts the new covenant with the old, which he calls the "written code that kills," a "dispensation of death" (2 Cor. 3:6f.), that such polarity means he has abandoned the unity of Scripture altogether. He speaks rather, in all these passages, in terms of a Jewish misunderstanding of Scripture;

his argument is ad hominem. When they read the law with a veil over their minds (2 Cor. 3:14-15), Sinai becomes for unbelieving Jews (and Gentiles as well) a ministration of death. From such a misunderstanding of the law Paul had been delivered by the grace of God through faith in Christ. Thus Christ had become for him the "end of the law"; the end of the law, that is, as a means of justification before God (Rom. 10:4).

The Sarah/Hagar allegory is a striking instance of the way in which the New Testament interprets the Old. When the church accepted the Christian Scriptures by adding them to, rather than substituting them for, the Jewish Scriptures, it related the two by analogy. Thus the teachers of the church came, first in the Alexandrian school and then elsewhere, to speak of the "analogy of faith," meaning that the faith taught by the apostles is analogous to that taught in the Old Testament. This is the thought implicit in Augustine's cryptic remark, already cited, "The New is in the Old concealed, the Old is in the New revealed." The univocal element in the analogy is God's unique and gracious act of saving his people. As he came in grace to Israel of old, making a covenant promise to them, so he comes in grace to all, Jew and Gentile alike, fulfilling that promise in the Jesus event. In this event, anticipated in the Old Testament and proclaimed in the New, God himself, in the person of Christ, secures the benefits of the covenant for all the covenantees through his obedience, death, and resurrection. God's act of saving grace, then, is the univocal element in the analogy that justifies the New Testament interpretation of the Old in terms of something else, namely, the Jesus event. Of course, such an approach to the unity-in-diversity of Scripture is an act of faith. Yet it is not a faith that defies all reason, but only the autonomous reason that will accept no truth it cannot discover for itself apart from revelation.

Concerning this New Testament interpretation of the Old, the following may be said by way of conclusion. It acknowledges that everything in the Old Testament, for all its variety, centers in the relationship of Yahweh to Israel, a relationship secured by a covenant made in his goodness (grace) and freedom (election). While a legal understanding of the law is possible from within the Old Testament itself (as in Orthodox Judaism), such an understanding is no longer possible once one has encountered Jesus Christ, as did Paul on the Damascus road. Then a new interpretation, to which the Old Testament is open as a possibility, becomes for faith a necessity and a certainty. Seen, therefore, in the light of the Jesus event, the church does not discard the Old Testament but accepts it as newly understood in Christ.

All the human family, like Israel, has rebelled against God and broken covenant. The law then can only make the world—Jew and Gentile alike— guilty before God (Rom. 3:19). But in the person of his Son, God has taken the consequences of this disobedience upon himself and so, by his obedience, shown the law to be holy, just, and good (Rom. 7:12). Hence the gospel can never be heard apart from the law rightly understood. The choice is not a choice of law *or* gospel, but of law *and* gospel, a choice that the church has made in its acceptance of one Bible in two parts. In other words, as Christians we hear the voice of God in the Old Testament the way we have heard it in Jesus Christ.

D. THE AUTHORITY OF SCRIPTURE

1. INTRODUCTION

Scripture, we have argued, finds its unity as the rule of faith in the Jesus event. This event, we have further argued, is interpreted in the New Testament as fulfilling the Old, not literally but analogically. For this reason the Christian Scriptures do not take the place of the Jewish Scriptures but are added to them, added not as more of the same but as the "new" distinguished from the "old." This statement of the case brings us back to the fundamental question: How do we know that the church was justified in accepting the Jewish Scriptures, newly interpreted, together with the Christian Scriptures containing that interpretation, as normative revelation? To this question we have answered that only God can authenticate his word. This he has done by the inner testimony of his Spirit. As the Spirit speaks by and with the Scripture in our hearts, we perceive its divine origin and hear it as though the words were pronounced by God himself. The principal proof, therefore, of the divine authority of Scripture is derived not from a reasoned demonstration but from the character of the divine Speaker whose word it is.[34]

However, though the church cannot rationally demonstrate that the Bible is God's Word, it must in any case say what it means when it makes such a claim. At this point the church teaches that to say the Bible is God's word means that it is uniquely inspired by the Spirit of God. The same Spirit who confirms its truth in our hearts is the Spirit who guided the human authors of Scripture in what they wrote. In other words, the Spirit who inspired the prophets in their anticipation of the Messiah and the apostles in their witness to Jesus as the Messiah also inspired the written form of that prophetic and apostolic witness as it is preserved in the Scriptures of the old and new covenants. What early Christians said of the

---

34. Calvin, *Institutes*, I, 7, passim.

Jewish Scriptures (that they are "God-breathed" [θεόπνευστος], 2 Tm. 3:16), the church came to say of the New Testament Scriptures as well. Though in the form of human words, the Scripture is God's word in the form of human words. This is why the church has acknowledged the Scriptures to be normative for its self-understanding and for the ongoing proclamation of its message.

2. THE INSPIRATION OF SCRIPTURE

a. Introduction

Though the doctrine of inspiration is of paramount importance since it is the ground of the Scripture's authority as the word of God, no definition of the doctrine has ever commanded a general consensus in the church. There is, however, considerable unanimity on the subject, which we shall attempt to summarize at the beginning of our discussion in the form of a definition of our own: *Inspiration is that guidance, that influence, that superintendence of God's Spirit which enabled the authors of Scripture to speak the truth God would have them speak for his glory and our salvation, faith, and life.*

There can be little doubt that the authors of Scripture were aware of such divine influence, even though they do not use the word "inspiration" to describe it explicitly. The Spirit's message to a prophet is sometimes compared to a "burden" from which he can find no rest till delivered of it.[35] It is like a fire that consumes or a hammer that breaks rocks in pieces (Jer. 23:29). Paul protests that necessity is laid upon him; he simply must preach the gospel (1 Cor. 9:16). Through a variety of human experiences, whether it be the trance of a Peter (Acts 10:9-10) or the painstaking research of the historian Luke (Lk. 1:3), divine truth is disclosed to the human agent. As a result, the message in human words—often *very* human words—is ultimately not merely a human word but the word of the Lord. Hence, Paul thanked God that when the Thessalonians received the word they "accepted it not as a human word, but as what it really is, God's word [καθώς ἐστιν ἀληθῶς λόγον θεοῦ], which is also at work in you believers" (1 Thes. 2:13 NRSV). This human word is really a divine word because it conveys a message imparted in "words not taught by human wisdom but taught by

---

35. Translated idiomatically as "oracle," the Hebrew משָּׂא, from the verb "to carry," is rendered in the KJV as "burden," "load," something that camels and donkeys carry. See Isaiah 13:1; 15:1; 17:1; 19:1; 21:1; 23:1.

the Spirit" (1 Cor. 2:13). Therefore, we do well to give heed to such a word, for it has not come by human impulse, but, as Peter reminds us, "men and women moved by the Holy Spirit spoke from God" (2 Pt. 1:21 NRSV). To translate literally, they were "borne along," "carried onward" by the Spirit (ὑπὸ πνεύματος ἁγίου φερόμενοι) as a ship is borne by the wind over the sea. The most cited and discussed of all passages bearing on this matter is 2 Timothy 3:16: "All Scripture is inspired by God and profitable for teaching, for reproof, for correction, and for training in righteousness." The key term, *theopneustos* (θεόπνευστος), does not occur in classical, but only in Hellenistic Greek, and is found in this text and in no other in the New Testament. Translated idiomatically "inspired by God," it literally means "God-breathed" and clearly refers to the working of the Spirit (πνεῦμα, "breath" of God) in those who wrote Scripture.[36]

b. Concerning Dictation and Inerrancy

Mystery which can never be fully illumined surrounds the question of biblical inspiration. Early in its history, however, the church began to speak of inspiration, following the example of the Jewish rabbis, in terms so exclusively divine that the human element was reduced to a virtual passivity. The biblical writers became simply God's "hands," "quills," "amanuenses," "secretaries," even his "musical instruments." Athenagoras observed that their reason fell into abeyance, the Spirit making use of them as a flutist her flute. Reducing the human to the vanishing point, the Fathers often use the word "dictated" when speaking of the Spirit's work and viewed the resultant text as inerrant. Any apparent contradiction could be overcome by faith or resolved by a spiritual (allegorical) interpretation of the text.[37]

The frequency and regularity, through the centuries, with which the theologians came to speak of a dictated, inerrant Scripture can be easily documented by those who consult the sources. To be sure, the usage was not as common in some writers as in others; nor is it to be taken literally in every instance of its occurrence. (Calvin, for example, was fond of

---

36. While 2 Timothy 3:16 refers to the Old Testament, the church, as we noted, attributed the same God-breathed character to its own Scripture. Hence the blessing on those who hear the reading ("reading aloud") of the book of Revelation is due to the fact that such folk are listening to what the Spirit is saying to the churches as the book is publicly read to the congregation (Rv. 1:3; 3:6).

37. See Jaroslav Pelikan, *The Christian Tradition* (Chicago: University of Chicago Press, 1971), vol. I, pp. 60, 137; vol. II, pp. 40-41, 222-23, 251, with sources. Also any standard history of doctrine.

speaking of the writers of Scripture as "amanuenses of the Spirit," though his work as an exegete makes it obvious that he did not use the phrase in a strictly literal sense.) But howsoever such language may be understood in a given author, there can be no question that it is common currency in the Christian tradition, both Catholic and Protestant.

As late as 1920, in his encyclical letter *Spiritus Paraclitus,* Pope Benedict XV commends Jerome for teaching "received Catholic doctrine" when he affirms that the authors of Scripture placed themselves at the service of the "divine dictation." Benedict goes on to condemn the modern tendency to limit inerrancy to the "religious" element in the text. (See *Christian Faith: Doctrinal Documents in Catholic Faith,* Dupuis Neuner, pp. 77-78.) Protestants have preferred the word "infallible" to "inerrant," though an increasing number, especially in America, have not only used the latter term but given it special emphasis. Yet even these protagonists of the inerrancy of Scripture "in the whole and in the part" have protested that they do not espouse dictation. This championing of inerrancy, and repudiation of dictation, is a relatively recent development in the history of doctrine. Louis Gaussen, in his *Theopneustia,* published as late as 1880 and widely read in an English translation (Chicago: Bible Institute Colportage Press, n.d.) well into the present century, uses the term "dictation" freely. Moreover, he explains all the difficulties some have felt with the doctrine in such a way that these very difficulties, when properly explained, become "proofs" rather than "problems" for his thesis that the Bible is dictated by the Spirit and inerrant in all that it says.

The traditional association of dictation and inerrancy is wholly consistent, for if the Spirit dictated to his "secretaries," the resultant text would, surely, be without error, since God knows whereof he speaks. What is not as evident is how this partnership came to be dissolved so that one may reject dictation while insisting on inerrancy. Due to the critical, historical study of Scripture, it would seem that the differences of style among the various writers of Scripture have become so indubitably clear that it is no longer possible to speak of a dictated Bible. Hence, the term has been dropped and its long association with inerrancy has ended in a quiet divorce.

When, for example, one turns to Warfield's *Revelation and Inspiration,* one finds an emphatic denial of dictation along with an equally emphatic affirmation of inerrancy.[38] He argues—correctly, we think—that the phrases "it says," "Scripture says," and "God says" are synonymous for all theological purposes. As a result, the church has always accepted the New Testament writers as trustworthy teachers of doctrine. Therefore, what

---

38. Benjamin B. Warfield, *Revelation and Inspiration* (New York: Oxford, 1927), passim.

they say respecting the inspiration of Scripture is trustworthy doctrine in particular. We cannot, however, accept the conclusion Warfield draws from such considerations. Assuming that when these trustworthy teachers teach the *inspiration* of Scripture, they are teaching the *inerrancy* of Scripture, he concludes that if one rejects inerrancy, one calls into question the apostles' trustworthiness as teachers of doctrine.

Unlike Gaussen, Warfield admits that some of the difficulties in the text cannot be adequately explained, given our present state of knowledge; but, he insists, we cannot allow detailed difficulties to decide such a major doctrinal question as inerrancy. While "difficulties" are present, "errors" have never been proven. So, to affirm that the Bible is the churches' infallible rule of faith and practice means that it is inerrant in all that it teaches. But Warfield never tells us how he can hold this traditional view of an inerrant Bible while rejecting the traditional view of a dictated Bible. He claims that the matter has been fully explained in a paper written by himself and A. A. Hodge entitled "Inspiration."[39] But this is hardly the case; in fact, the paper even defends dictation, though the term is deemed applicable only to parts of the Scripture.[40] As for the rest of Scripture, according to Hodge and Warfield, what the biblical writers wrote was "for the most part the product of their own mental and spiritual activities." If this is so, however, we can no longer think of dictation as providing the best conceptual model of inspiration, since what secretaries write is not the product of *their* mental activities but of the one who does the dictating. But then, by the same token, we can no longer think of inerrant autographs as the best conceptual model to describe the end product of such inspiration. Yet modern-day inerrantists, like Warfield before them, have affirmed inerrancy, even insisting that it is a watershed of all sound theology, while at the same time they have repudiated dictation. Like him, however, they have failed to show how they can put asunder what the tradition of centuries has joined together and still insist that their position represents the classical doctrine of the church, believed everywhere, always, and by all (*ubique, semper, et ab omnibus*). Like their mentor, they have altered the argument in a subtle but significant way. The thesis "inspiration by dictation entails inerrancy" has been changed to "inspiration *without* dictation entails inerrancy." It is this latter argument that we cannot accept.[41]

---

39. This paper has been reprinted with an introduction by Roger Nicole (Grand Rapids: Baker, 1979).

40. Ibid., p. 12.

41. Inerrantists at this juncture sometimes attempt to explain what inerrancy means and what it does not mean until the term dies of a thousand qualifications. See, for example, the

c. The Divine/Human Character of Scripture

1) The Position of the Protestant Reformers

Obviously, what is needed is a statement of the doctrine of inspiration that will both preserve the divine character of the Bible as the word of God and do justice to its human character as the word of the various authors who wrote it. It is a divine/human book that the church recognizes as the written revelation of God. Theologians have traditionally (and rightly) thought of this revelation primarily in terms of its divine authorship; it is the inspired word of God. This emphasis, however, has led them too often to discount or at least ignore the agency of the human authors in the writing of the several documents that constitute the canon of Scripture. In seeking a more balanced doctrine, we need to recall certain aspects of the past experience of the church. Two things especially have happened in the course of the history of the church that together have compelled its teachers to seek a more balanced view of the inspiration and authority of Scripture—balanced, that is, in terms of its divine and human qualities.

We have in mind, in the first instance, the Reformers' rejection of the claims of the Roman Catholic Church. The authority of Scripture rests, they insisted, not on the authority of the church but on its own intrinsic character as the inspired word of God. In the second instance, we have in mind the rise of the science of higher criticism, which is concerned with the human and historical character of the documents constituting the Scriptures. While these two approaches—which emphasize the divine and the human in the Scriptures, respectively—are often at odds with each other, they need not be. Indeed, the historical approach to Scripture was anticipated in the work of both Luther and Calvin. Luther's comments in this regard are freer than Calvin's; yet Calvin also reflects an awareness of the historical character of the documents with which he worked as an exegete.[42] He knew Greek and Hebrew well and was the founder of what has been called the grammatico-historical method of biblical interpretation. He abandoned the scholastic fourfold sense of the text; he did not try to harmonize the evangelists but wrote a separate commentary on John; and he showed no concern to treat the New Testament as "Holy Ghost Greek." Indeed, he recognized the grammatical infelicities of New Testament Greek for what

---

nineteen articles in "The Chicago Statement on Biblical Inerrancy," issued in 1978 by the International Council on Biblical Inerrancy. We have not thought it worthwhile to pursue these "explanations."

42. As Luther was the prince of translators, so Calvin was the prince of commentators. His commentaries, after four hundred years, are still being published!

they were, recalling that the treasure of the gospel was contained in earthen vessels.

Though both Luther and Calvin were profoundly convinced of the authority of the Bible, one wonders if they would be welcomed in certain evangelical circles today. When, for example, Paul affirms that the Old Testament law concerning the ox that treads out the corn (Dt. 25:4) is given for our sakes *altogether* (πάντως, 1 Cor. 9:9-10), Luther rejoins: "my dear brother Paul, this argument won't stick." (See Schaff, *History of the Christian Church*, vol. VII, pp. 36-37.) Calvin, commenting on Matthew 27:9, says: "How the name of Jeremiah crept in, I do not know, nor am I seriously troubled about it. That the name of Jeremiah has been put for Zechariah by an error the fact itself shows, because there is no such statement in Jeremiah" (*Commentary, in loc.* See also his comments on the number [75] of Joseph's kindred who went down to Egypt, Acts 7:14). Contemporary inerrantists, by contrast, find it difficult to say they are not troubled by such matters, as is evident from the efforts they make to resolve all discrepancies. In citing such data from Luther and Calvin, we are not concerned to argue the merits of their conclusions in each particular, but to illustrate their candor and freedom in recognizing the humanity of the biblical witness to Christ. Only as we emulate the Reformers' example in this regard can we hope to frame a doctrine of inspiration free from the finespun redundancies and hermeneutical games some have played with the biblical text.

2) The Position of the Protestant Scholastics

As time went on, the relative freedom shown by the Reformers in their approach to Scripture began to suffer retrenchment. By the seventeenth century, both Lutheran and Reformed divines were basing the authority of Scripture on a rigorous, even mechanical, view of inspiration. No longer was dictation a striking metaphor and inerrancy a matter to be maintained with the help of fanciful allegorizing. They were rather the essential components of a carefully wrought definition of the doctrine of inspiration.

Thus was ushered in the period of Protestant Scholasticism, in which a theologian like the Lutheran Quenstedt could affirm that every text of Scripture was free even from "the tiniest of errors" so that "each and every thing contained in it is altogether true, be it dogmatic or moral or historical, chronological, topographical or onomastic."[43] Others declared that since the Scriptures were dictated, the will of the human authors was *utterly passive* in the writing of it.[44] Johann Gerhard, perhaps the leading Lutheran theologian of his day, spoke in this way in his influential *Loci*. In the

---

43. As cited in Jaroslav Pelikan, *The Christian Tradition*, vol. IV, pp. 343-44.
44. Ibid., p. 344.

Reformed community the scholastic view even found symbolic expression in the *Formula Consensus Helvetica,* authored in 1675 by Heidegger with the assistance of Gernler and Turretin. Composed 111 years after Calvin's death, this statement not only assumed that the Greek of the New Testament was dictated by the Holy Spirit but also declared that the Hebrew vowel points in the Old Testament were originally inspired and providentially preserved.[45] Therefore not a jot or tittle of the law could pass away till all was fulfilled (Mt. 5:18).[46]

While it would be easy simply to dismiss the views of these scholastic theologians, it would be unjust to do so, for they were learned scholars, often excelling their later detractors. Though their doctrine of inspiration was flawed in certain respects, they had no way in their day of reconstructing the critical history of the text of Scripture. Knowing that the Greek of the New Testament was neither classical nor modern, and having no knowledge of Hellenistic Greek, it was natural enough that they should have supposed that this Greek, being dictated by the Spirit, was sui generis. The same is true of their understanding of Old Testament Hebrew. They simply could not have known what we know of the history of the Masoretic text. Furthermore, they had inherited the controversy between the Reformers and the Roman Catholic Church over authority. As Catholic theologians in the Counter-Reformation honed their doctrine of the infallible authority of the Church till it pyramided in the doctrine of an infallible pope (1872), the Protestants naturally responded by defining the authority of Scripture as precisely as possible. Further still, within their own ranks there were the *Schwärmerei,* the enthusiastic, fanatical fringe that claimed the immediate inspiration of the Spirit, thus compelling Protestant theologians to stress the unique and final inspiration of Scripture. Thus the doctrine of inspiration

---

45. When Louis Cappel, a 17th-century Huguenot biblical scholar, came to realize that the Hebrew system of vocalization was late, he was advised to keep his knowledge to himself. As a result, his work (Lyden, 1624) appeared anonymously and, as expected, came under severe attack as a threat to the orthodox doctrine of inspiration.

46. Matthew 5:18, where Jesus affirms that neither "jot" nor "tittle" (the consonantal spines and horns, not the vowel points) shall pass away from the law, and John 10:35, where he affirms that Scripture "cannot be broken" (λυθῆναι, i.e., "nullified," "set aside," "rendered futile"), are sometimes cited to prove that our Lord taught inerrancy. True, both passages underscore Jesus' respect for the law and for the Scripture as a whole, even in the smallest detail. But the conviction of the early church, reflected in these logia, that Jesus came not to destroy but to fulfill the law, and the current debate over inerrancy, are such different agendas as to render the use inerrantists sometimes make of these texts doubtful. Whether reverence for Scripture as the only infallible rule of faith and practice requires one to view such texts as teaching inerrancy depends on the assumptions one brings to them concerning the nature of Scripture as a whole.

came to be rigorously spelled out in terms of divine dictation that guaranteed the church an inerrant Bible in the original autographs. Finally, we must not forget that, for all their faulty craftsmanship, the Protestant scholastics were preserving the great Reformation principle of Scripture *(sola Scriptura)* so essential to the church's faith and life. By doing so they have put the church forever in their debt.

While 17th- and 18th-century Protestantism preserved the doctrine of *sola Scriptura,* so basic in an evangelical theology, it left a more doubtful legacy. The problem is subtle and needs careful statement. Spurgeon (quoted on the flyleaf of Gaussen's *Theopneustia*) calls the doctrine of Scripture the "Thermopylae of Christendom." He asks: "If the foundations be removed, what can the righteous do?" and concludes that the loss of an infallible standard of truth is a foundation loss of the worst kind. This is a telling comment that reminds one of the words in the familiar hymn:

> How firm a *foundation,* you saints of the Lord,
> *Is laid for your faith in his excellent word!*
> What more can he say than to you he has said,
> To you who for refuge to Jesus have fled? (Rippon)

We must remember, however, that while it is in Scripture that the foundation is laid, Scripture is not itself the foundation. The foundation is Christ, to whom Scripture bears witness. "For no other foundation can any one lay than that which is laid, which is Jesus Christ" (1 Cor. 3:11). It is because of what God has said to us in Scripture concerning Jesus that we have fled to him, not to Scripture, for refuge. The church does well to sing of Scripture as

> . . . the golden casket
> Where gems of truth are stored;

but the reason is that Scripture is

> . . . the heav'n-drawn picture
> Of Christ, the living Word. (How)

The difficulty with making the inspiration of Scripture the *foundation* doctrine is that it then becomes axiomatic, a self-evident truth beyond dispute. Other doctrines may be altered, even rejected, in the light of Scripture; but the doctrine of the inspiration of Scripture is itself beyond criticism. The tendency in American evangelical circles to place the article on Scripture first in a statement of faith is not a faulty order in systematics (like Schleiermacher's remanding the doctrine of the Trinity to an appendix in his *The Christian Faith*), but it is symptomatic of a mentality that views the inerrancy of Scripture as a doctrine beyond debate, the first domino that, should it fall, would make the whole doctrinal row tumble. We can only observe (with Barth) that the first commandment, not the inspiration of Scripture, is theological axiom. We should not, therefore, regard the inspiration of Scripture as a theological a priori after the analogy of Euclid's axioms.

Speaking of the domino mentality, it is sometimes argued that were one error found in the Bible the whole biblical witness would be invalidated. Such reasoning is like arguing that one grain of sand in the marble of the Parthenon—to use Hodge's illustration—would threaten the collapse of the entire edifice. Obviously we do not read any other book by such a rule. Though Aristotle erred in postulating the infinite velocity of light, one does not doubt everything else he had to say for that reason. Why then should Stephen's (or Luke's) mistakenly attributing to Abraham the purchase of a field in Shechem cast doubt on the inspired character of his defense before the Sanhedrin? (See Acts 7:16, which confuses Gn. 50:13 with Gn. 33:19).

Before we suggest our own doctrine of the inspiration and authority of Scripture, we must, in the interest of clarity, make a few preliminary remarks. While we opt for the Protestant principle of Scripture, we are also convinced—obviously—that an adequate doctrine of its inspiration and authority must take into account the results of biblical criticism. Though at the time of Protestant origins such a science was virtually unknown, yet its methodological roots are in the Reformation. Hence, while many have claimed to do so, it is quite impossible, in our judgment, to approach Scripture as did the Reformers and at the same time hold to an inerrant original text. Such an approach spawns an endless effort to harmonize the data in ways that exhibit the "contortions of the sibyl without the inspiration."

Witness, for example, Harold Lindsell's attempt to harmonize the evangelists' accounts of Peter's denial of Jesus by postulating six different denials.[47] This is but a recent instance in a long series of sorry arguments that include such notions as that Hebrew was the original language spoken by Adam and Eve and therefore the basis of comparative philology; that God created the fossils in the rocks; that there were kangaroos from Australia in the ark; that the Sermon on the Mount (Mt. 5–7) was delivered verbatim on a mountainside even though such a view requires Jesus to have come down from the mount before he went up; that if two demoniacs were exorcised in the country of the Gadarenes (Mt. 8:28), then one was (Lk. 8:27), since where there are two there must be one; that blind Bartimaeus was healed when Jesus was going *out* of Jericho (Mt. 20:29; Mk. 10:46) and also when he was going *into* Jericho (Lk. 18:35), because there was an old city and a new city and Jesus performed his healing miracle while leaving one and entering the other, and so on.[48]

47. *The Battle for the Bible* (Grand Rapids: Zondervan, 1976), pp. 174-76. This is the mindset that forced Galileo on June 28, 1663, contrary to the plain evidence, to "objure, curse and detest the error of the earth's movement."

48. Sometimes it is argued that to admit an error in Scripture is to place reason above Scripture, so making it the judge of Scripture. But is it not just as much a rational judgment

As we see it, none of the problems posed by a critical reading of Scripture necessarily threatens the Protestant principle of scriptural authority. Yet they do warrant an honest acknowledgment of their existence and a humble admission that whereas we may resolve some of them, we will never resolve all of them, not for want of time and erudition, but because of their intractable nature. Of the many such problems that might be cited by way of example, none is more concrete and objective than that of the numbers in the Pentateuch. Whatever view one may have of the composition of the Pentateuch, the numbers seem to have undergone epic inflation. Leaving aside the account of the longevity of the antediluvians, in the more obviously historical portions of the Pentateuch the question of numbers clearly emerges. We are told, for example, that at the time of the Exodus and the conquest, Israel's army numbered over 600,000 men (Num. 1:45-46; 26:51). True, God promised Abraham and Sarah abundant seed, like the stars of heaven (Gn. 15:5); and Malthus has made us aware of the biological possibilities, given the number who went down into Egypt with Jacob and the length of time their offspring sojourned there. But how can we relate an army in excess of half a million to the Bible's own account of the conquest of Canaan, a conquest that was really not fully accomplished until David conquered the coastal Philistines? If Alexander the Great overthrew the Persian empire with an army in the neighborhood of 35,000, surely it should not have taken Israel (with Yahweh's help) 250 years (the exact time involved varies with the dating of the Exodus) to subdue Canaan with an army of 600,000. In the *Decline and Fall of the Roman Empire* (Chicago: Encyclopedia Britannica, 1952, vol. II, p. 32), Gibbon estimates that the "regular force of the empire had once amounted to 645,000 men." This was the largest army any emperor had ever put on the field. For the most part, Rome held sway over her vast domains, building a ring of steel around the Mediterranean and preserving the *Pax Romana,* with an army of considerably more modest proportions. (For a discussion of the "numbers in Numbers," see *Old Testament Survey,* W. S. LaSor, D. A. Hubbard, and F. W. Bush, Grand Rapids: Eerdmans, 1982, pp. 166ff. On the relation of the tradition that the conquest was prolonged till David's day to the tradition that it was completed in Joshua's day, see B. S. Childs, *Introduction to the Old Testament as Scripture,* Philadelphia: Fortress Press, 1979, pp. 247ff.)

As for the New Testament, other problems no less objective and obvious abound if one assumes an inerrantist position. One has only to reflect, for example, on the fourfold Gospel tradition. Because of the central significance of Jesus for the Christian faith, no portion of Scripture has been more intensely studied than the gospels. This critical study has brought to light many differences even in the Markan, Matthean, and Lukan traditions. But these differences in the Synoptics pale in significance when one turns to John. Whether one ponders the overall chronological structure of Jesus' public ministry as reported in the fourth Gospel, the prolonged discourses on the night of the Passover, the day of the crucifixion, or the locale of the resurrection appearances, there

---

to declare that Scripture is without error as it is to recognize the contrary? In fact, the harmonizing efforts of the inerrantists of the sort we have just cited appear to us to reflect a need to secure faith's acceptance of Scripture as divine revelation by grounding it on a rationalistic premise.

are a host of details in John that cannot be harmonized with the Synoptic tradition as it now stands, since we are so far removed from the events. This is not to say that we view the Bible as a compendium of errors and contradictions. On the contrary, we find that in all matters essential to faith and life Scripture manifests a unity so remarkable as to evidence itself to be the one word of the one, true, and living God. We do not, however, find this unity susceptible of the rigid alignment required by the scholastic view of inspiration. Such a view denies the genuine historical character of biblical revelation in all its rich and manifold variety; at least, so it seems to us.

3) Inspiration as Verbal and Plenary

How does one frame a doctrine of the inspiration of Scripture that does justice both to its divinity and its humanity? To circumvent this question by simply speaking of the Bible as the book to which we listen for a word from God in the existential moment is hardly adequate. The church acknowledges the authority of the Bible, not because it is inspiring but because it is inspired. True, God speaks to the church today in and through the words of the Bible. But this is because he spoke to no others—Dante, Shakespeare, Milton—as he spoke to the writers of Scripture, disclosing to them "words by which [we] shall be saved" (Acts 11:14 — author's trans.). In other words, the authority of Scripture presupposes its inspiration. God may speak when and where he will—through mundane events, great books, masterpieces of music and art—but were the church to read from a Kant, a Tolstoy, or even a Martin Luther King in lieu of an Isaiah or a Paul, it would cease to be the church because there can be no church without a word from God, a "thus says the LORD."

In our previous argument we have said that God reveals himself in nature as the Creator and in grace as our Creator and Redeemer. This special revelation culminates in Jesus Christ, to whom both prophets and apostles bore witness as the Spirit gave them utterance. This Spirit, the Spirit of the risen Christ, also inspired the written form of that witness contained in the Scripture. That is to say, the "inspiration" of the Spirit, which we have spoken of as the Spirit's superintendence or guidance of those who wrote the Scripture, is the basis of the churches' acceptance of the Scripture as the word of God.

We understand this inspiration to be both "verbal" and "plenary." When we speak of verbal inspiration, we mean that inspiration reaches even to the words in which Scripture is written. It is of Scripture as a book written in human words that we predicate inspiration. To qualify inspiration as verbal, therefore, is to give the *intensive* definition of the doctrine. When we speak of plenary inspiration (from the Latin *plenus,* "full"), we mean that the whole Bible, not just its purple passages, is inspired. To qualify inspiration as plenary, therefore, is to give the *extensive* definition of the doctrine.

As for verbal inspiration, problems arise, as we have seen, when theologians try to say exactly how the Spirit guided the writers of Scripture by speaking of that guidance as dictation. Dictation is a theory that has proven far too precise and mechanical in view of the evidence. It is unfortunate, however, that many have abandoned all thought of a verbally inspired Bible because they equate verbal inspiration with dictation. Verbal inspiration does not entail dictation. What it does entail is the thought that the writers of Scripture were quite different from so many geniuses, gifted with religious insight, who simply expressed their thoughts in their own words as best they could— "concept revelation," as it is sometimes called. Verbal inspiration means that the writers of Scripture were "taught by the Spirit" in the words they used to convey their message. "And we impart this [the message of God's grace] in words *not* taught by human wisdom but taught by the Spirit" (1 Cor. 2:13). Therefore we cannot have and hear the divine word apart from human words, specifically these human words which are found in the Bible. The truth God would have us know is not some universal truth we discover when we peel away, like an onion skin, the human words that are the temporal, historical, cultural medium in which the universal truth is hidden. This is not to say that any particular pattern of words as such is divine. God did not reveal himself to Israel in Hebrew because he spoke Hebrew (as Allah speaks Arabic), but because they spoke Hebrew. And the same is true of the church. When God would establish a universal Israel, he revealed himself in a universal language, not because he spoke Greek but because people did. Yet he did reveal himself in words, specifically these words which are Hebrew words and Greek words.

That the Bible is in Hebrew and Greek is a cultural accident, to be sure. Had God made covenant with the Mayan Indians and had that covenant subsequently been offered to a world in which the lingua franca was Chinese, then the Bible would have been written in Mayan and Chinese. The heart of the matter of verbal inspiration is not that the Bible is written in this or that particular language, but that it is written in human language. As the Word condescended to become flesh and dwell among us, so the Spirit has condescended to bear witness to that Word in human words in order that the gospel might be heard among us. Because of this condescending work of the Spirit, which the church calls the inspiration of Scripture, human words have become the special locale of divine revelation. A sacramental relation, as it were, has been established between the divine word and human words. It is, then, in and through the medium of the human words of Scripture that the divine word comes to us. God may speak to us through music, like that of Bach; but music is not, Beethoven notwithstanding, a higher form of revelation than word revelation.[49] Likewise, God may speak to us through the painting of some great master. But one cannot paint what God has to say to us in the same direct and primary way one can express it in words. Grand as the message of a Michelangelo may be, it is a message inspired, in the first instance, by words. The church was born not when some master painted a picture of Christ on the cross or carved a pietà or composed an oratorio, but when a fisherman from Galilee stood up and bore witness to the resurrection of Jesus with the words: "Let all of the house of Israel therefore know assuredly that God has made him both Lord and Christ, this Jesus whom you crucified" (Acts 2:36).

In other words, Christianity does not rest upon an aesthetic experience but upon a message preserved for the church in inspired words. Of course, divine revelation is more than words even as a painting is more than pigments; but as there is no masterpiece without pigments, so there is no saving revelation without words. God reveals his love to us in the death of his Son; but this revelation cannot be severed from words, namely, the words of the inspired apostle that God "put forward [Jesus Christ] as a propitiation by his blood, to be received by faith" (Rom. 3:25). For this reason we qualify inspiration as *verbal* inspiration.

"Plenary" inspiration, as we have said, means that all Scripture is inspired. When we say the Bible is the word of God, we speak of the Bible as a whole.[50] To speak in terms of our previous discussion of the canon, plenary inspiration means that the canon does not have fluid edges. The church, in other words, does not have the option of accepting a part of the Bible in lieu of the whole. It cannot—honesty compels us to say it ought not—proclaim the message of the reforming prophets while rejecting the priestly religion of Israel as primitive and even repugnant because it sanctions blood sacrifice. Nor should the church proclaim salvation by the blood of Christ and fail to give the cup of cold water in his name. Part of the message of the church is: "Let justice roll down like waters, and righteousness like an ever-flowing stream" (Am. 5:24). Another part of its message is that "without the shedding of blood there is no forgiveness of

---

49. Beethoven actually compares music not to biblical revelation but to "philosophy," the former being the supreme expression of truth, in his judgment. Otto Klemperer, a great interpreter of Beethoven's symphonies, contends, however, that even Beethoven put words above music when he ended his ninth symphony with a chorus.

50. Verbal inspiration conceived as dictation makes plenary inspiration mean not that the whole Bible is inspired, but that the Bible is as inspired as it can be. This too is an unfortunate view, in our judgment. It turns the Bible into a book that fell from heaven rather than a book that, like other books, is the result of historical process.

sins" (Heb. 9:22). To use another illustration, because biblical inspiration is plenary the church does not have the option of proclaiming the Jesus of the gospels, whose life is the supreme paradigm of love, while rejecting the supernatural Christ of the epistles as unacceptable in an enlightened scientific age. Rather, the church should proclaim both because it confesses the whole Bible to be the word of God.

Because plenary inspiration, the inspiration of the whole Bible, relates to the question of a canon-within-a-canon, we must pause to say a word about this approach. We take no exception to this concept insofar as it affirms that the fixed center of the canon is the witness of Scripture to Jesus Christ. But we do have problems with the thought that as one moves out from this center, the edges of the canon become indeterminate. Having opted for the traditional view that the canon is a library of books that can be listed, we do not subscribe to the thought that a document like Martin Luther King's classic, "Letter from a Birmingham Jail," is more canonical for the contemporary American church than, say, Jude, with its reference to a personal devil who disputed with the archangel Michael over the body of Moses (v. 9). Pressed to its logical conclusion, such a view would lead to a redefining of the canon in terms of whatever worldview was prevailing at the time.

Rather than thinking of the canon of Scripture in terms of concentric circles moving out from a firm center to a soft edge, we prefer the figure of a mountain range with peaks and valleys. There are materials more relevant to the church (peaks) and some less so (valleys), depending on the times and circumstances in which the church finds itself. The Everest will always be the biblical witness to Christ who died, was buried, and was raised on the third day (1 Cor. 15:3-4). Yet we must not so emphasize the peaks as to overlook the valleys altogether. It may, indeed, seem odd to one not acquainted with the nature of biblical revelation that the most read book in the Bible (Matthew) should begin with a long list of unpronounceable names. However, the genealogical materials in Scripture reveal the all-important truth that history, specifically Jewish history, is the medium of divine revelation. Salvation comes not through the union of the soul with the eternal Ideas but through the unfolding of the holy generations of Israel. When at last the seed of the woman (Gn. 3:15; Lk. 3:23-38), who is the seed of Abraham and Sarah par excellence (Gal. 3:16), appears, then the promise of salvation is brought near. To be sure, the genealogy with which the New Testament begins (Mt. 1:1-17) is the last in the Bible; and the all-important name in that genealogy is the last name, Jesus "who is called Christ" (Mt. 1:16). But every name in that genealogy, no matter how unpronounceable, is a part of the witness of Scripture to the Word that was made flesh.

d. Conclusion

In our discussion of the nature of Scripture as inspired revelation, the norm of the church's understanding of itself and its message, we have opted for a divine/human model. To say that the Bible is a divine word, to affirm that in Scripture the church (and the individual) hears the word of God himself, is not to ascribe too much to Scripture. The scholastic doctrine of a dictated Bible is nearer the truth than the liberal view that the biblical authors were simply geniuses whose writings are a significant part of our Western religious heritage.[51] However, the nature of Scripture as a divine revelation is not well served by setting aside its historicity, its genuine humanity. Scripture is made up of historical documents and those documents are made up of words of which it must be said, as it is of all words, that these

> Words strain,
> Crash and sometimes break under the burden;
> Under the tension, slip, slide and perish,
> Decay with imprecision, will not stay in place,
> Will not stay still. (Eliot, "Burt Norton V," *Four Quartets*)

The miracle of Scripture, then, lies not in the fact that by divine inspiration it escapes its humanity, but rather that it is inspired in words so human that one cannot doubt its humanity. The human authors were, indeed, "moved by the Holy Spirit" (2 Pt. 1:21); but the phenomena of Scripture suggest a broad spectrum of models for conceptualizing this "movement" of the Spirit. It is perhaps in the prophetic literature that the divine side of Scripture appears most in evidence. Amos, a shepherd who moonlighted by pruning sycamore trees, was driven by the Spirit of Yahweh all the way from Tekoa to the royal shrine in Bethel where the divine word of judgment, given through the words he spoke, incurred the wrath of Amaziah, the priest in residence (Am. 7:10-13). In the same way we would understand the tendency of the prophets to lapse into the first person when delivering their oracles. The spirit of the prophet merges, as it were, with the Spirit of the Lord, so that a "thus says an Isaiah or a Jeremiah" becomes a "thus says the LORD." Hence the expression "God foretold by the mouth of all the prophets" (Acts 3:18) sounded natural enough to early Jewish Christian ears. By the same token, like the prophets of old, the apostle Paul knew something of this irresistible domination by the Spirit. He knew that his words mediated a divine word; hence his message was one of which he must deliver himself, for "necessity" (ἀνάγκη) was laid on him (1 Cor. 9:16-18).

On the other hand, the human side of Scripture appears most in evidence in the Hagiographa. In fact, in the Jewish tradition the difference between these documents and the Torah occasioned much comment. In the latter we have instruction in the form of divine commandments; in the former, by contrast, we find pithy aphorisms and poignant complaints that

---

51. Here see the powerful essay of Kierkegaard, "On the Difference Between a Genius and an Apostle," in Søren Kierkegaard, *The Present Age* (Oxford: University Press, 1940).

are quite human in every way. This is true especially in the Psalms, consisting of hymns of praise and songs of lamentation, of individual complaints and thanksgivings. (Note how the Psalter has been used in the hymnbook—even *as* the hymnbook—in the worship of the church. But the hymnbook expresses the human response of the worshipping community to the divine word, in distinction to the Bible, which is read and heard as the divine word which evokes the response.)[52] Like the Old, the New Testament also includes passages containing such personal, human experience. Consider, for example, Paul's self-defense before the Corinthians (2 Cor. 11). How is such Scripture "the word of God" when God is not the One speaking but the One spoken to, sometimes in struggle, doubt, and even despair?

When we seek the answer to such a question we should not forget that the Spirit can move and speak even through the most human complaints. Those Scriptures which make up the confessions and petitions of the saints bear witness not only to the need, distress, and perplexity of those who cry "out of the depths" *(de profundis),* but also to the One who will "vindicate his elect, who cry to him day and night" (Lk. 18:7).[53] The Bible, then, is the word of God, but not in a way that excludes the human answer to that word. Rather, the human answer is taken up into the divine word and thus the true humanity of the divine word is further underscored.[54]

We may sum up matters concerning the divine/human nature of Scripture by saying, first of all, what has often been said: because it is inspired, the Bible is divine, the book that we celebrate in song.

> Holy Bible, book divine,
> Precious treasure, thou art mine;
> Mine to tell me whence I came
> Mine to teach me who I am. (Burton)

52. It was this problem with the Hagiographa that apparently led the synagogue to view the Psalms and the other Writings as the work of the prophets. Hence the Old Testament is sometimes spoken of simply as "the law and the prophets" (Lk. 24:27; Acts 2:30).

53. We must not forget that not only do we as sinners need to hear a saving word from God, but also that he should enable us to respond *to* this saving word. Why? Because only thus does his word become a genuinely *saving* word. Note the disciples' request, "Lord, teach us to pray" (Lk. 11:1).

54. In the Preface to his *Commentary on the Psalms,* Calvin observes that the Psalms are "an anatomy of all the parts of the soul; for there is not an emotion of which any one can be conscious that is not here represented as in a mirror. Or, rather, the Holy Spirit has here drawn to the life the griefs, the sorrows, the fears, the doubts, the hopes, the cares, the perplexities, in short, all the distracting emotions with which the minds of men are wont to be agitated." As cited in Philip Schaff, *History of the Christian Church* (Grand Rapids: Eerdmans, 1910), vol. VIII, p. 526.

Yet at the same time we must also say what has not so often been said: in its inspiration the Bible is fully human. It is God's self-witness in historical, human form. Because of this divine/human character of the biblical word, we can hear God's word aright neither when we treat the Bible as a purely historical document, nor when we ignore the human and historical form of the Bible in order to insure its supernatural, divine character as the word of God. The fact that we cannot separate the divine and the human in Scripture—it is a seamless garment, all divine, all human—does not mean that we cannot distinguish between them, even though in details such a distinction will be variously perceived in differing cultures and historical eras. The task, in other words, of relating the divine revelation of Scripture to the human form in which it is given will always remain an ongoing challenge to the church. The past experience of the church will help to clarify the task, though never completely; for the future will introduce new questions calling for new answers. Looking back, we can understand why the church initially was so shaken by the abandoning of a geocentric universe; it seemed to threaten the uniqueness of the Incarnation. If the Incarnation is center stage in the divine purpose (Eph. 1), then must not the stage on which the drama is played out (earth) be center stage in the physical universe? This surely seems to be the perspective from which the first creation narrative was written. Many similar illustrations could be given of problems raised and answers ventured, problems by which we no longer feel threatened and answers with which we no longer feel satisfied.[55]

Our task, then, in understanding Scripture as God's word in human words is an ongoing one. It is a task illumined by the past, but concerned with the present, as the church moves toward the future.

This means that the resolution of the question of how the humanity of Scripture is related to its divinity is not one that can be achieved in every particular, but only in principle. To be sure, many particular problems can and have been resolved; but others have not. Meanwhile, new ones emerge. As for a resolution in principle, we need say no more (or less) than this: the inspiration of the Spirit never bypasses the humanity of the authors of Scripture; on the other hand, their humanity never expresses itself independently of the Spirit's guidance, which secures to the church the sure word of God.

---

55. We can follow Luther's argument, for example, that if Copernicus was correct, then it was the earth, not the sun that stood still. But Joshua says that the sun stood still (Jos. 10:12); therefore, good-bye Copernicus. Luther was right; this is what the original Hebrew says. Yet few today would follow Luther in his conclusion. We live in another time and face other questions.

Meanwhile, going back to the Reformers, we would affirm that the authority of Scripture as inspired revelation cannot be grounded, in the last analysis, in any criterion outside itself, whether it be the claims of an infallible (inerrant) church or a reasoned argument that the original text of Scripture is without error. Both arguments (which are really nuances of the same argument) are contradicted by the evidence. Neither the church nor the autographs of Scripture (the original Bible X, which the church has never possessed) can be shown to be inerrant. The evidence just does not warrant the claims made in either case. Not only is Scripture not inerrant in every matter that concerns science, history, geography, and the like, but even the confession that one accepts Scripture as the "infallible rule of faith and life" is just that—a confession of faith, not a logical conclusion reached at the end of a syllogism.

Such a confession is, for many, possible to make, indeed impossible not to make, because of the inner testimony of the Spirit to the Scriptures as the word of God. When we introduce the testimony of the Spirit, we put our finger on the basic issue. The authority of the word of God as God's word can rest on no other ground than the authority of God himself, whose word it is. *Revelation can be recognized only through revelation, not through that which is not revelation.* It is God's authority that secures our human certainty that the Bible is his word. This, as we have said, is why the Westminster Divines closed the famous first chapter of their *Confession* with the words: "The supreme Judge, by whom all controversies of religion [not controversies about the age of the earth or the origin of fossils] are to be determined . . . and in whose sentence we are to rest, can be no other but the Holy Spirit speaking in the Scriptures."

Addendum: Continuing Problems and Possible Resolutions

Though we are not convinced of an inerrant church nor able to frame a theology of an inerrant Bible, we can make suggestions that bear on the problem of Scripture and present-day criticism. In our discussion of theological method we spoke of the principle of contiguity in dealing with matters of faith and science.[56] The more the conclusions of science impact the personal center of revelation—the biblical witness to Jesus Christ— the more they concern faith; the less they impact that center, the less they concern faith. Faith, to cite an example, can be relatively indifferent to geological conclusions about the age of the earth as those conclusions bear

---

56. See above, Unit One, II, Theological Method, pp. 17ff. "Contiguity" translates Brunner's *Beziehungsnähe*.

on the creation narratives of Genesis. On the other hand, faith can by no means be indifferent to the conclusions of Freudian psychology about the nature of sin as those conclusions bear on the Pauline indictment of human nature in his Epistle to the Romans.

But there are many problems raised by the critical study of the Bible to which the principle of contiguity does not apply. Much of what the Old Testament teaches, for example, about slavery, women, marriage, divorce, and the like is obviously less than Christian. One may see in the Year of Jubilee the amelioration of the abuse of slavery; yet surely a release granted only to one's fellow Israelites (Lv. 25:39-46) falls short of a Christian view of justice. One may also see in the "cities of refuge" (Nm. 35) the inchoate beginnings of the idea of "sanctuary"; and such an institution obviously did ameliorate Israel's Semitic heritage by curtailing the abuses of blood revenge. Yet even so, the *lex talionis* falls short of a Christian view of justice.

Our point is that matters of justice are central, not peripheral, to faith's understanding of the biblical witness. Such matters, therefore, cannot be resolved by adjudicating the relation of reason to faith, as in matters pertaining to the natural sciences. Rather, in such instances one must recognize the progressive character of revelation, which is due to the historical nature of the biblical witness, a circumstance clearly disclosed by the critical, historical study of the Bible. All history is in process, including biblical history, a fact illustrated in Jesus' use of the "but I say to you" formula in the Sermon on the Mount (Mt. 5:31-32). To affirm that revelation is progressive is not a clandestine way of judging Scripture by imposing upon it the criteria of autonomous reason and critical history. It is rather to say that because revelation is historical, Scripture judges itself, refines its own focus of the truth, as it were. This is why we must interpret Scripture in the light of Scripture, especially the Old Testament in the light of the New. Of course we will never reach unanimity in all matters. While the majority of Christians worship on the Lord's Day, some, to give an example, observe the Sabbath on the seventh day, as they believe them-selves enjoined to do by the fourth commandment (Ex. 20:8-9). So it is with other questions also.

What is more difficult is the implication of the progressive character of revelation for our understanding of the New Testament. If the Old is fulfilled in the New, if God has spoken a final word in Jesus Christ, does this imply that the Scriptures of the New Covenant transcend all historical conditioning? This is the way divines and preachers in antebellum America often read passages about slaves obeying their masters (Col. 3:22). And it is the way many still read passages about wives being in submission to their husbands (Eph. 5:22-25). But the recognition of the historical character of revelation applies not only to the Old Testament but also to the New; the latter is historical as well as the former. We live in the age of "fulfillment," not of "consummation." We have, therefore, not only to read the Old Testament in the light of the New, but the New in the light of itself, a light that is centered in Jesus Christ.[57]

Many questions still remain, of course. When the theologian accepts the historical character of revelation and thereby acknowledges the full humanity of the Bible, everything, from Bishop Ussher's dating of the creation at 4004 B.C. to the historicity of Jesus, falls within her purview as she seeks to frame a doctrine of the inspiration and authority of the Bible. The vast range of the questions concerned precludes the possibility that a systematician should control the data in a detailed way. But there is one area, namely, the Gospel narratives, that even the systematician cannot ignore, for, as we have noted, the Jesus event is the unifying center of all revelation. The questions, therefore, that have concerned New Testament scholars—such as the "quest" for the "historical Jesus" (Schweitzer) and the "demythologizing" of the gospel (Bultmann)—are not just problems in critical New Testament studies. They are ultimate, and therefore dogmatic, in nature. How one answers these questions determines one's view of Christianity as a whole. At this point, however, we can do little more than shoot arrows in the direction in which we judge some of the answers to lie. And we must do this without the help that the German language affords in providing two words for history, *"Geschichte"* and *"Historie."*

We begin with the commonplace that the gospels are not biography. The very arrangement of the materials makes this evident in a most conspicuous way. To report virtually nothing of the first thirty years of the life of one who lived thirty-three years and to concentrate on the last week of a public ministry of three years is surely no way to write a biography. Here, obviously, we have selective historical reporting based on theological interpretation. The historical character of the gospel story is a sine qua non, to be sure. Yet the story is much more than history; it gives us a portrait, not a photograph, of Jesus. Because this is so, the contemporary distinction between the "Jesus of history" and the "Christ of the kerygma" is helpful. It must be used, however, with great care. Sometimes it is used to validate the Christ encountered in the existential moment of faith, while remanding the historical Jesus to the shadows of the unknown. In this case, the historical basis of revelation is threatened. At other times it is used to affirm

---

57. For the use of this approach *in extenso,* see our *Man as Male and Female* (Grand Rapids: Eerdmans, 1975).

the "historical" Jesus while viewing the kerygmatic Christ as the mythological creation of the early church. When this is done, all succumbs to the
law of historicism; Jesus becomes a first-century Palestinian Jew and
nothing more. He may well have been a religious genius, but he has little
to do with the apotheosized Jesus whom the apostles preached as a divine
Christ.

In this whole matter it helps to remember that it was Jesus' primary
task to be the Messiah, not to proclaim that he was the Messiah. Such
proclamation was the later task of the apostles. Therefore, we should not
expect that the gospels would describe Jesus in the words of Philippians
2:5-11. In other words, though the gospels give us an interpretive portrait
of Jesus, there is, naturally, a significant difference between the portrait
of the Jesus of history drawn by the evangelists and the full-blown
theological portrait of the exalted Christ found in the apostolic kerygma.
Not that the two are ultimately incompatible; the Jesus of the gospels *is*
the Christ of the epistles. This is why his title "Christ" soon became a
part of his name. In this regard, one can sense a basic movement in the
New Testament from "Jesus" (gospels) to "Jesus the Christ" (Acts) to
"Jesus Christ" (epistles). But this movement was most natural and easy
for the New Testament community of faith because the early Christians
knew only a Jesus who both died and rose from the dead. The Jesus who
preached beside the Sea of Galilee (Mk. 4:1) and the risen Christ whom
they worshipped as their Lord (Jn. 20:28) was one and the same person,
the Lord Jesus Christ.

This personal identity of the Crucified One with the Risen One may
bear on the so-called "Johannine problem." It is often alleged that the
portrait of Jesus found in the Synoptics is so different from that found in
John that one must reject the latter as a late theological construct without
basis in historical fact. While we do not concur in such a judgment, we do
find it puzzling that the fourth evangelist, having adopted the form of a
Gospel narrative, yet deals with his materials in such a different way from
the Synoptics, both as to form and content. That is to say, the Jesus of John
seems to be a historical person, yet a much more transcendent one than
the Jesus of the Synoptics. In any event, of the many efforts to solve the
riddle of the fourth Gospel, as plausible to us as any is the thought that the
primitive Christian community made no fundamental distinction between
what Jesus said to his disciples while in the flesh and what he said, by his
Spirit, to the church, as the risen Lord of the church. Such an observation
also bears on the never-ending, always-changing, quest for the "authentic"
logia of Jesus. The authenticity of the dominical sayings is not a matter of
tape-recorded historical precision but of theological integrity, that is, an

integrity resting on the entire New Testament witness to Jesus as the Lord Jesus Christ.[58]

E. THE INTERPRETATION AND UNDERSTANDING OF SCRIPTURE

1. THE PERSPICUITY OF SCRIPTURE

Since Latin had become a dead language, the Protestant Reformers' decision to translate the Bible into the vernacular restored the Scriptures to the common people. They justified this bold decision by the divine example. God had initially revealed himself in a language (Hebrew) understood by those to whom the revelation came; and in the miracle of Pentecost his Spirit overcame all barriers of language in order that devout Jews "from every nation under heaven" might hear the apostles "telling in [their] own tongues the mighty works of God" (Acts 2:5, 11). This decision of the Reformers also assumed that the Bible, as a revelation of God's word, is intrinsically clear in the essentials of salvation, a property of Scripture traditionally called its perspicuity. It is appropriate, then, that we begin our discussion of the interpretation and understanding of Scripture with a comment on the *perspicuitas Scripturae*.

Because the Bible is clear in the essentials, anyone, whether trained or not, may read it and learn those things necessary to salvation. While the Roman Catholic Church feared that making Scripture directly available to the laity would fracture the church—a fear not altogether unjustified in the light of the proliferation of Protestant denominations—the Reformers remained committed to their decision because of their view of Scripture. To have placed the teaching office of the church between the Scriptures and the common people would have been to put more trust in the church than in the revelation God had given to the church, a revelation they deemed basic to all that the church teaches. Hence the risk of dividing the church, due to multiple interpretations of Scripture, was preferred by the Reformers over the preservation of the unity of the church by imposing on the people of God a single, official interpretation of Scripture that could not be ques-

---

58. Obviously, then, we do not judge the logia question as one that can be resolved by New Testament scholars getting together and dropping their little beads—red, pink, gray, or black—into a box as they vote on the probable "authenticity" of Jesus' sayings as recorded in the gospels. See the *Los Angeles Times*, 11 Nov. 1985, p. 17.

tioned. While the former might lead to schism, the latter, in the Reformers' experience, threatened the loss of the gospel itself.[59]

Though essential to the Protestant view, the doctrine of the perspicuity of Scripture runs the risk of fostering an exegetical methodology that conceals a latent rationalism. It may be assumed that because of its intrinsic clarity, Scripture can be understood by anyone possessed of native intelligence. At one level, of course, this is true. One can know Scripture, since it is a human book, "from a human point of view," even as one can know Christ "from a human point of view" (2 Cor. 5:16). But though it is fully human, Scripture is not merely human. It rather bears witness to the divine majesty of him who addresses us in it, which is to say that its meaning is not simply at the disposal of our native intelligence. While a literary, historical exegesis contributes to the understanding of Scripture at a surface level, it misses the essential message of Scripture altogether. This is because one discerns the essential message of Scripture only in the act of believing it. "We are not," as Weber reminds us,

> isolated readers facing a voiceless text, which is passively, patiently waiting there for us, but rather we are those who are addressed by the text and thus those who have been placed before a decision.[60]

Of course, to affirm that Scripture not only informs the reader but addresses her in a way that demands a response is not to affirm that it is our human response that makes the word of God efficacious. Scripture is in itself efficacious; it is "living and active, sharper than any two-edged sword" (Heb. 4:12). Such efficacy is intrinsic to the word of God because it is God's word. In other words, the efficacy of Scripture is wrought by the Spirit, who not only inspired the original authors but so illumines the minds of those who hear their message that their hearing becomes the hearing of faith, their understanding a saving understanding. "Faith comes from what is heard, and what is heard comes by the preaching of Christ" (Rom. 10:17).

---

59. For the official response of Rome to the Reformers on this score, see *Canons and Decrees of the Council of Trent,* Fourth Session, April 8, 1546. Pius IX went so far as to condemn Bible societies, which circulate Scripture without comment, in *The Papal Syllabus of Errors,* IV, 1864. Fortunately our Catholic brothers and sisters have since come to agree that the Bible should, indeed, be accessible to all the people of God in their own tongue. See above, this Unit, p. 109, note 17.

60. *Foundations of Dogmatics,* vol. I, p. 284.

2. THE COMPLEXITY OF THE HERMENEUTICAL TASK

a. *Introduction*

While we affirm the perspicuity of Scripture, we must at the same time confess, paradoxically, that the task of interpreting Scripture is exceedingly difficult. Hence, in framing a doctrine of Scripture we cannot avoid the question: How ought Scripture to be interpreted? This question is of prime importance, since it confronts the church anew in every age. The initial answer to this question, given by the teachers of the ancient church, takes us back to the New Testament itself and to the way the authors of the Christian Scriptures interpreted the Jewish Scriptures. As we have noted, they often allegorized the Old Testament, interpreting it not in terms of itself, but in terms of the Jesus event. The Levitical law, to cite a familiar case, is interpreted in Hebrews as a type fulfilled in the death of Christ; thus the priestly, cultic worship of Israel is given a meaning far beyond its original, literal meaning. Influenced by such New Testament examples, as well as by such non-Christian writers as Philo of Alexandria, theologians of the Old Catholic Church began to postulate various "levels" of meaning in Scripture. As they did so, they increasingly devalued the literal meaning, stressing the typical or allegorical meaning, especially when they found the "earthly" meaning impossible to accept.[61] Origen, who wrote the first major treatise on Christian hermeneutics, distinguished a threefold sense, which evolved, in the hands of those who followed him, into a fourfold sense: the literal, the allegorical, the moral, and the anagogical.[62]

While Thomas stressed the literal meaning as basic, in the writings of many of the Scholastics this axiom was more heeded in the breach of it than in the observance of it. As a result, the interpreter's imagination was given full play and the system ran out of control. In this way Scripture became a sealed book that only the church could interpret. (How, for example, could the uninitiated ever know that "thou didst break the heads

---

61. To cite a familiar case, to the Fathers it seemed that the law of leprosy (Lv. 13) contained an obvious contradiction at the literal level. If one is unclean when the disease breaks out in one spot, how can one be clean when the disease covers all the skin from head to foot (vv. 12-13)? Such passages were ripe for allegorizing, not only to get beyond the text to its deeper meaning, but away from the text in its literal meaning.

62. "Anagogical," from ἀνά and ἄγω, a leading up, referring to the elevation of the mind to celestial mysteries. Hence, to give an example, the word "Jerusalem" stood for a city (literal sense), the church on earth (allegorical sense), the faithful Christian (moral sense), and the church triumphant (anagogical sense). These several meanings constituted, for the Scholastics, the *sensus plenior* of the text.

of the dragons on the waters" [Ps. 74:13] referred to the exorcising of demons through baptism?) Thus, the church became the doorkeeper of Scripture, and by its theory of a mystical, fourfold sense it turned the perspicuity of Scripture into the obscurity of Scripture.

b. The Reformers' Position

Since both Catholics and Protestants had basically the same Bible and since both accepted its authority as revelation, the response of the Reformers to the hermeneutical question was of paramount importance. It was in their interpretation of Scripture that the issue of authority (Scripture vs. the church) was brought into clearest focus. As we all know, the Reformers rejected the fourfold sense of the text and insisted that, if the church is to hear God's word as revealed in Scripture, a new approach to the hermeneutical task must be found. They concluded that it is the task of the interpreter to discover the true and natural sense of the text and to make that sense meaningful to those who read the Scripture and sit under its preaching.[63]

We have used the term "natural," rather than "literal," to describe the sense sought by the Reformers, first of all because "literal" is opposed to "figurative"; and the Reformers recognized that oftentimes the natural meaning of the text is not literal but figurative. The devil does not literally go about "like a roaring lion" seeking someone to devour (1 Pt. 5:8). The natural meaning, then, is just the meaning as it is there in the text. It is arrived at by respecting the possibilities of the language in which the text is written and heeding the historical context of the document of which it is a part. The Reformers insisted, in other words, on what has been called the "grammatico-historical" method.

However—and this brings us to the second reason for speaking of the Reformers' effort as one in which they sought the natural rather than the literal meaning of Scripture—the Reformers did not limit the meaning of Scripture to the possibilities of grammar and history. While they pegged their interpretation to the grammatico-historical method and excoriated the

---

63. From the beginning, the interpretation of Scripture and its public exposition were closely associated by the Reformers. The first chapter of the *Second Helvetic Confession* contains a lengthy defense of the proposition: "The preaching of the word of God *is* the word of God." The association of preaching with hermeneutics arises out of the conviction that the text, though it is the product of the past, is the authoritative word of God for the present. Therefore the Protestant church has always viewed the Bible as the "text to be preached," the text that directly concerns the people of God in every age. Hence, preaching took the place of the Mass as central to congregational worship.

popular allegorizing of the medieval church, they did not abandon the allegorical method altogether. They rather condemned those allegorizings that were "fabricated by one's own intellect and ingenuity and which were without the authority of Scripture."[64] Another way of putting the Reformers' position is to say that the meaning of a text, over and beyond its grammatical, historical possibilities as such, is its meaning in salvation history. Salvation history is the context of a given text viewed as a part of the canon of Scripture. Salvation history, in other words, is the text's theological context. When therefore the apostle Paul alludes to the wilderness experience of the Israelites in drinking water from the rock as a drinking from Christ, such an allegorical understanding of Numbers 20:2ff. was in every way acceptable to the Reformers. They found such a meaning of the Old Testament text to be a "natural meaning," because, like Paul, they read the Old Testament in the light of the Jesus event. In fact, in their judgment, not to have done so would have been to break the analogy of faith.

A comment on the analogy of faith *(analogia fidei)* is called for at this point. Appearing in the Vulgate as the translation of ἀναλογίαν τῆς πίστεως in Romans 12:6, the word "faith" *(fidei)* in this phrase is to be understood objectively. It is the body of truth contained in Scripture as interpreted by the church and preserved in its tradition. (Modern translators generally construe Romans 12:6 subjectively, of one's personal faith; but this is immaterial to our discussion.) When it is said that one should observe the analogy of faith, the thought is that the interpreter should recognize the likeness-in-difference (analogy) between the Old and the New Testaments, as acknowledged in the church's general understanding of Scripture, when seeking the meaning of any given text in particular. It was the principle of analogy that enabled the church to claim that the Old and New Testaments together constitute the one norm of its teaching and life; they are the church's rule of faith *(regula fidei)*.

The new meaning that the apostles gave the Old Testament, in the light of the Jesus event, is therefore not a new meaning absolutely. Had the apostles construed the Jesus event as an absolutely new revelation of a new God, the church would have been compelled to follow Marcion's example, establishing its own canon de novo. But the church was not compelled to do that because the apostles understood the Scriptures of the Old Covenant in a way that made God's original revelation to Israel analogous to his new revelation in Christ. Even James, after much debate at the Jerusalem Council, could declare that the Spirit's work among the Gentiles, whereby they were made heirs of the covenant with Israel apart from circumcision, was according to the analogy of

---

64. Luther, "Concerning Allegories," in his late Genesis lectures (American edition, II, 150ff.), as cited in Weber, *Foundations of Dogmatics,* vol. I, p. 323, n. 305. As the above citation indicates, Luther, with the passage of time, became more restrained in his condemnation of allegorizing. Though Calvin consistently rejected the method of the medieval allegorists, he too drew exegetical conclusions that went beyond the strict limitations of the grammar and history of the text.

faith. He concluded, therefore, that the calling of the Gentiles fulfilled the Old Testament promise found in Amos 9:11-12:

> After this I will return,
> and I will rebuild the dwelling of David, which has fallen; . . .
> that the rest of men may seek the Lord,
> and all the Gentiles who are called by my name . . . (Acts 15:15-18).

*   *   *   *   *

Another way of looking at the "analogy of faith" is to say that Scripture interprets Scripture, a principle applied when obscure passages are interpreted in the light of plain ones. Closely related to this thought, in turn, is the argument that the entailment of Scripture is Scripture. The doctrine of the Trinity, the outstanding instance of such entailment, has been accepted by the church as the teaching of Scripture. Though the term "trinity" nowhere occurs in Scripture, the doctrine is recognized by the church to be analogous to what the Scriptures, especially the New Testament Scriptures, say about the nature of God.

For the Reformers, the discovery of the natural meaning of the text begins with exegesis. Only the objective meaning yielded by careful exegesis can preserve the church from the vagaries of allegorizing. But the meaning of the text is not limited to strict exegesis, for the text is not simply the word of a given author—an Isaiah, an Ezekiel, a Paul—in a given historical context. It is rather a text whose ultimate context is canonical Scripture as a whole; and since Scripture is the word of God, the text is to be interpreted as the word of God. Hence the Reformers, unlike many moderns, did their exegetical work as dogmaticians. They recognized that the task of interpretation is to insure that the word that the church hears in a given text of Scripture is heard not only in the complete seriousness of its specific historicity, but also as the canonical word of God.

To illustrate what we are saying, we offer the following on the interpretation of Ecclesiastes, reflecting the approach of Brevard Childs in his *Introduction to the Old Testament As Scripture,* pp. 580-89. Ecclesiastes may be understood as giving a corrective balance to Israel's wisdom tradition. The book had status in that tradition as associated with Solomon, whose name had become a part of the common memory of the covenant community. The epilogue of the book, editorial in nature, indicates the canonical shaping of the work. In this context, the sayings of "Koheleth" (the word probably refers to an office having to do with the study of wisdom in Israel) are to be understood not simply as private expressions of pessimism, but as canonical Scripture. In other words, they are to be understood as a part of Israel's corporate wisdom, in which the judgment of God's hidden understanding penetrates all human secrets, distinguishes good from evil, and relativizes all human effort. The author is reacting to the tendency to understand the traditional wisdom literature of Israel in a way that placed too much confidence in human understanding. As part of the canon, Koheleth is related to this literature somewhat as the Epistle of James is related to the Pauline corpus in the New Testament. As James corrects the tendency to understand Paul's view of faith and works in an antinomian way, so Koheleth corrects the tendency to suppose that human wisdom can "make sense" out of human history in a rationalistic way.

c. Statement of a Protestant and Evangelical Hermeneutic

1) Introduction

For us, a Protestant and evangelical hermeneutic is simply the hermeneutic of the Reformers, who defined the task of the interpreter to be the ascertaining of the meaning of the text as originally given and as found in the larger context of Scripture. But the Reformers were not interested, as we have noted, in the interpretation of Scripture as an exercise in itself. The end of all interpretation is to ensure that the church shall hear Scripture as the word of God, normative for its message and mission. That is to say, the original meaning of the text is indissolubly bound up with its meaningfulness in the present. Meaningfulness for whom? For all who, in any given time and place, read the text and hear it as the text preached. We must now explore further this distinction between what the text itself means and what it means *to us*. Such a distinction opens up large questions on which there are differences of opinion. The fact is obvious that there is always a text that says something, and that this "something" is said to "someone." Hence *hermeneutics*, defined as the science of the interpretation of Scripture, must be concerned with both the something said and the someone to whom it is said. Otherwise, the hermeneutical debate would be like arguing about the sound of a falling tree when there is no one to hear it.

Many have claimed to do hermeneutics (especially in the form of exegesis) with complete historical objectivity; and at a surface level this is quite possible. When we read that Joseph and Mary came and dwelt in Galilee (Mt. 2:23), such a text has the same meaning for everyone. But, as Ebeling has observed, it is possible to understand all the individual words in a text and still not grasp its message (*The Nature of Faith*, p. 16, as cited in A. C. Thiselton, *The Two Horizons*, p. 117). It is as when a doctoral candidate translates (with the help of a dictionary) every German word into a good English equivalent; yet the total result makes it obvious that she did not grasp the meaning of the passage as a whole.

This is what happened in the Enlightenment, when history was relativized and so lost the possibility of mediating truth in a normative way. As a result, the accidental truths of history could stand only in contrast to the absolute truths of reason. From this perspective, Scripture became the source of historical knowledge to be evaluated in the light of reason. Given such an approach, the Bible can confront the interpreter with nothing really new, since the Bible is a part of history and history simply discloses manifold variations on the common theme of human, historical possibility. Such human, historical possibility was defined in terms of the historian's present experience as falling within the limits of reason alone. Thus the alleged objectivity of the critical, historical method became a subjectivity of the most blatant sort. As a result, the Bible was no longer the word of God in the Reformers' sense at all. It did not confront the church with a "thus says the LORD," but simply informed the interpreter about the life and thought of those who lived long ago. Such an Enlightenment approach closed the gap between the "then" of the text (the something said) and the "now" of the interpreter (the someone to whom something is said) by simply imposing the historical consciousness of the interpreter on the text. In this way the text was brought into the present, but it was a present in which all that happens has a causal, rational, this-worldly explanation. The key to such a handling of the text, avers Thiselton, "is a historical methodology which approaches its subject matter on the assumption 'that all past events form a single interconnected web and that no event occurs without this-worldly causation of some sort.' " (Ibid., p. 72, quoting D. E. Nineham, *New Testament Interpretation,* p. 18).

But if we cannot limit the hermeneutical task to the question of what the text meant when it was written; if we must go on and ask what it means now when it is preached, how do we get from the "then" to the "now"? How do we get from the Scripture's past to our present, the two being so different from each other? As interpreters, we should not follow the Enlightenment and try to close the gap by simply making the text over in our image.[65] Yet we cannot get outside ourselves; we always bring to our understanding of the text our own context, our *Sitz im Leben.* This is what the early believers did when they read the Old Testament in the light of their new context as Christians who had come to worship Jesus of Nazareth as the risen Messiah.

We need, of course, to be cautious in using this illustration, since we have acknowledged that the apostolic reading of the Old Testament as preserved in the New is uniquely inspired of the Spirit and therefore normative. Yet we cannot ignore the Spirit's ongoing work in our present situation also. The Spirit who guided, that is, inspired the apostles in their

---

65. For examples of such, see H. J. Cadbury, *The Peril of Modernizing Jesus,* as cited in A. C. Thiselton, *The Two Horizons* (Grand Rapids: Eerdmans, 1984), pp. 60-61. Cadbury notes instances in which Jesus is made an "advertising expert," since he was a good mixer who established a quick rapport with his prospect—such as the Samaritan woman. Because he rose early, he was a "go-getter," a trait of character essential to a successful career. He had the makings of a businessman: "wist ye not that I must be about my Father's *business?*" Such examples, drawn from the discredited lives-of-Jesus literature, are matched today, we might add, by portraying Jesus as a potentially great athlete, a he-man who could have led any team to victory in the Super Bowl. Did he not single-handedly drive the money changers out of the temple; and did he not run safely through his opponents at Nazareth (Mk. 11:15; Lk. 4:30)?

new and definitive understanding of the Jewish Scriptures is the same Spirit who enlightens the church today in its ongoing understanding of Scripture.

> Come, Holy Ghost, for moved by thee
> The prophets wrote and spoke;
> Unlock the truth, thyself the key,
> Unseal the sacred book. (Wesley)

This unlocking the truth of the Scriptural text we call "illumination." In making a distinction between "inspiration" and "illumination," while attributing both to the same Spirit, we are following the traditional view, which says that it is always God's own work to reveal himself; it is he who finds us rather than we who find him.[66]

The reason that word and Spirit are always united in the thought of the Reformers is that the Spirit, and the Spirit only, guides into all truth (Jn. 16:13). "The believer has thus [by the Spirit] the consolation that God really gives one the true understanding of Scripture and that the true knowledge of the word will be maintained forever on the earth by God's gracious care."[67]

The doctrine of the illumination of the Spirit is simply an elaboration of what Paul says in 1 Corinthians 2:14, where he observes that the unspiritual person does not receive those things that pertain to the Spirit of God, for they seem to her so much foolishness. In fact, such a person is unable to receive them because they are spiritually discerned (ψυχικὸς δὲ ἄνθρωπος οὐ δέχεται τὰ τοῦ πνεύματος τοῦ θεοῦ, μωρία γὰρ αὐτῷ ἐστιν, καὶ οὐ δύναται γνῶναι, ὅτι πνευματικῶς ἀνακρίνεται·). Such a strong statement, obviously offensive to an Enlightenment mentality, implies that the gap between text and interpreter is, in the last analysis, not a historical but an ethical one. As a sinner the interpreter is incapable, apart from the illumination of the Spirit, of fusing the two horizons of divine wisdom and human wisdom; for human wisdom judges the divine wisdom, revealed in Scripture, to be folly and thus rejects the biblical witness to Christ.[68]

---

66. A "Prayer for Illumination" before the public reading of Scripture, in *Pilgrim Hymnal* (Boston: Pilgrim Press, 1959), p. 504, with sources. "O Lord God, who has left to us your holy word to be a lamp unto our feet and a light unto our path, give to us all your Holy Spirit, we humbly pray, that out of the same word we may learn what is your blessed will, and frame our lives in all holy obedience to the same, to your honor and glory and the increase of our faith, through Jesus Christ our Lord. Amen."

67. Heinrich Ursin, *Loci*, 1562, as cited by Heppe, *Reformed Dogmatics,* trans. G. T. Thomson (London: Allen & Unwin, 1950), p. 39. This joining of Spirit and word means, of course, that the neglect of commentaries and the rigorous academic study of the Scriptures is not a trusting of the Spirit but a subtle form of hubris.

68. The expression "fusion of horizons" is Gadamer's. See Thiselton, *The Two Horizons,* p. 15. Such an expression is analogous to the thought that the Bible both "is" and "becomes"

In the so-called "new hermeneutic" a congeniality between the original text and the expositor, often referred to as "pre-understanding," is affirmed as essential. Bultmann, for example, argues that the human awareness of God makes the understanding of Scripture possible. With this we agree in the broad sense that all humans, made in God's image, retain some knowledge of him and his will.[69] But this natural knowledge, essential though it be, must be radically transformed if one is to understand Scripture for what it is—the word of God. To be in Christ is to be a new creation (2 Cor. 5:17); and this includes a radical remaking of the pre-understanding with which we come to the text that bears witness to him. While it is true that we never get outside ourselves, the Spirit can so change us that we are no more our old selves but new selves, and therefore no longer have need to get outside ourselves.

This mystery, which the theologians speak of as the "new birth," wrought by the Spirit in effectual calling, is better illustrated than elaborated. The stories down through the centuries of those whose eyes have been opened amply afford such illustration. Young Luther, for example, as a strict Augustinian monk, struggled mightily over the meaning of the text that speaks of the "righteousness of God" (Rom. 1:17), a righteousness that Paul described as revealed through faith, for faith (ἀποκαλύπτεται ἐκ πίστεως εἰς πίστιν). Luther initially understood this text to speak of God's own righteousness (justice), which compelled him to punish sinners. But in due course he came to see that the apostle was speaking of a righteousness perfected by Christ which God freely reckons to sinners like himself, through faith. In this judicial act God acquits the sinner of all guilt for her sin and clothes her in the righteousness of Christ as a gift, on the sole condition of faith. This insight, Luther tells us, was like a revelation to him. He now read the Bible in a new light; it became to him a book of life and comfort. The two horizons, that of Paul, a first-century Hellenistic Jew writing to Christians in Rome, and that of Luther, a distraught German monk reading fifteen hundred years later what this Jew had written, were fused, and, to use the Reformer's own words, he walked through the gates of Paradise. The burden of his sin rolled off his back as it later rolled off the back of Bunyan's Pilgrim.

The traditional doctrine of the illumination of the Spirit does not deny that the interpreter comes to the text with a pre-understanding. But it does say that, at the deepest level, this pre-understanding is not simply corrected,

---

the word of God. Not that it becomes what it is not, but, for a given hearer, the Bible becomes, in the moment of faith, what it is in itself, the word of God.

69. See above, this Unit, I, pp. 68ff. for our discussion of natural revelation.

much less confirmed, by the text. It is rather shattered by the text. As a result, the interpreter gains a new understanding of the text, and this new understanding of the text brings with it a new self-understanding on the part of the interpreter. Such an approach deprives ordinary methodology of its security, since it is an approach derived, not from the worldview of the interpreter, but from the text; or better, from the One who reveals himself in the text. Being able to comprehend the mystery of God in Christ, as revealed in Scripture, requires that one be enabled by the work of the Spirit to receive that revelation. Not that the Spirit bypasses human reason, but he makes reason a reason that perceives the truth rather than one that defines the truth. No longer does the interpreter read Scripture for what she wants to find; rather, she listens to Scripture for what she was once afraid to hear.

2) Irreducible Differences of Interpretation: The Place of Faith and Reason in the Understanding of Scripture

While we do well to emphasize the understanding of the Bible not simply as a historical document but as the word of God, such understanding by no means validates all "believing" interpretation of Scripture. There remains a great deal of difference in the way Scripture is interpreted even when one approaches it as the word of God. Though one may argue (as we would) that there is a substantive core of biblical truth confessed by the church, truth secured by the objective form of the written text and the subjective illumination of the Spirit, there is a diversity of interpretation, even within the fellowship of faith, sufficient to compel comment by the theologian. How may one be guided amid the differing, sometimes stridently differing, interpretations of Scripture set forth in the Christian community?

As we seek to answer this question, we must admit that accepting the Bible as divine revelation does not enable one to set out rules that can be "objectively" applied so as to reach uniform results.[70] We must rather satisfy ourselves with a consideration of what appears to us to be the basic issue—namely, how should the faith of one who receives the Scripture as the word of God be related to one's reason in the task of understanding Scripture? Here, again, it is helpful to think of circles moving out from the center of biblical revelation (God's self-disclosure in Jesus Christ) to matters that are relatively impersonal and objective. Both faith and reason are

---

70. Many books containing such rules for interpreting the Bible—a parable has one basic meaning, etc.—have been written. We would not deny that such books can be very helpful in given situations, as when one is leading a group Bible study. Our concern is more general.

always present in the church's interpretation of Scripture. Faith, however, plays a more prominent role in understanding those texts at the center of the biblical message, while reason tends to be sufficient for understanding the texts that are secondary to that message. The sentence "Since all have sinned and fall short of the glory of God, they are justified by his grace . . . through the redemption which is in Christ Jesus" (Rom. 3:23-24) is not rationally incoherent. It can, therefore, be understood by reason apart from faith. But such a text has a deeper meaning that will never be accessible to reason alone. In fact, autonomous reason will find such a judgment against the human family offensive and the supposed divine solution, so central to the biblical message, a kind of foolishness. But as we move from the heart of biblical revelation to the periphery, though faith may be present, it will add little, if anything, to reason's grasp of the text. "And Gideon . . . was buried . . . at Ophrah of the Abiezrites" (Jgs. 8:32) is a sentence where critical, archaeological knowledge will tell the interpreter all that faith will need to know.[71]

Our reference to a "deeper meaning" of the text suggests, along with the mathematical figure of concentric circles, the geological figure of layers of depth to illustrate the relation of reason and faith in understanding Scripture. All the sentences in the Bible are written in ordinary language and according to the received rules of grammar. Their surface meaning, therefore, is accessible to reason. Though one who does not have the Spirit does not understand the things of the Spirit, she understands, at the lexical, grammatical level, the sentences in which spiritual things are set forth. Indeed, it is at this surface level that rational, critical scholarship has made its greatest contribution to the understanding of Scripture. No one, for example, can overestimate what the discovery of the papyri and the nature of Hellenistic Greek has done for our understanding of the New Testament. Adolf Deissmann's *Light from the Ancient East* is well named. On the other hand, at its in-depth level of meaning, Scripture demands a response to the One whose word it is. Only a positive response of faith brings a saving understanding of the text, in contrast to that understanding accessible to reason alone. Other levels of meaning nearer the surface require no such response.

---

71. In the above use of the figure of a circle, we are not thinking of what has been called (since Schleiermacher) the "hermeneutical circle." So far as the hermeneutical circle is concerned, it should be remembered that all understanding is circular. While a child's first word is something of a miracle, when, subsequently, she learns the meaning of new words, she does so in terms of the words she already knows. This is true of adults as well, as is evident from the fact that all the entries in a dictionary are defined in terms of each other. (Hence a dictionary in a wholly unknown tongue is useless.) The fact that the most exhaustive dictionary is, in a way, a big circle reminds us that *all* our knowledge is a big circle.

One can indeed declare this meaning, open to reason, to be the only meaning there is and so eliminate Christianity from the start. Then all Scripture, since there is only one level of meaning, can be interpreted "within the [Kantian] limits of reason alone." The Exodus can be construed as simply an instance of the migration of peoples; the exile, a political event that frequently occurs when small nations find themselves in the path of larger nations bent on conquest. Such interpretations are not only plausible but correct at the surface level. Even the death of Jesus can be understood solely in terms of the political and social forces which obviously enter into the Gospel accounts of that event. Jesus' death then becomes a tragedy, and such an interpretation makes "sense," for there are surely enough tragedies in history to which it may be likened by way of analogy.

To talk of levels of meaning in Scripture might seem to bring us full circle and leave us with the problem from which the Reformers sought to deliver the church, the problem of the natural meaning of the text over against a deeper, allegorical meaning. Actually this is not the case, for at no time does the in-depth perception of the meaning of the text allow one to ignore or contradict its surface meaning. When we understand a text at its deeper level as the word of the living God that engages us, we are not denying its surface meaning. Were that the case, we would be interpreting the text in terms of something alien to it. But the word of God that addresses us is never alien to the text of Scripture; rather, it is essential to it, for this is what the text of Scripture ultimately is, the word of God. When, therefore, we are interpreting the text as the word of God, we are interpreting it in terms of what it is in itself.[72]

As an aside, we might note that the problem of reading the text in terms of something else that is alien to it is present in some (not all) forms of Feminist Theology. Goddess worship, to cite an example, tends to lead away from the text. Matters are not so difficult for Black Theology. When one reads the Bible in terms of the black experience, it is easier to draw out of the biblical text what is already there than it is when one reads it in terms of the feminist experience. Perhaps this is due to the way the classic paradigm of the Exodus and deliverance from slavery permeates Scripture. We do not mean to suggest that framing a biblical, feminist theology is unnecessary, but just that it is more difficult to achieve, given an evangelical view of scriptural authority, because of the patriarchal setting of the documents that comprise Scripture.

72. Hence the concept of *sensus plenior* may be used (as it sometimes is) to describe the inclusion of the "existential" understanding of the text. Such a usage is not to resurrect all the old problems involved in the scholastic fourfold meaning of the text. It is rather to acknowledge that the Spirit speaks by and with the Scripture to me in my here and now as he did to Augustine in the garden of Milan, to Luther in his tower room, and to Wesley at Aldersgate.

In this whole matter of faith, reason, and the understanding of the text, nothing is more significant than the distinction between a reason that accepts and a reason that will not accept what the text is saying. The issue is subtle because understanding what the text says and accepting what it says can never be separated in a black-and-white way. It is rather a question of proportionality. Insofar as the text concerns surface matters, understanding is largely a function of reason alone; but as the text concerns the deeper matters at the heart of the biblical message, the will of the interpreter is engaged. The text evokes faith (or unbelief), a decision to say "yes" or "no" to its message. In other words, though we rightly distinguish between reason and will, the reason and will that we distinguish are never faculties in the abstract. They are rather faculties integrated in the personal self in such a way that they become components of a single response to the text on the part of the interpreter.

In this regard it is helpful to return once more to Paul's statement in 1 Corinthians 2:14. According to the apostle, the natural man or woman (i.e., one who does not have the Spirit of God) does not receive (δέχεται) the things of the Spirit of God. To "receive" or "not receive" is the language of will and choice. Yet the apostle goes on immediately to say why a natural person does not receive the things of the Spirit. It is because such things, to such a person, are so much foolishness (μωρία). But to speak of foolishness is to use the language not of volition but of reason. This movement from the language of volition to that of reason in one and the same sentence indicates how difficult it is to say where one leaves off and the other begins. When it comes to understanding Scripture as the church has always understood it, namely, as the word of God, the volition and reason of the interpreter are inextricably bound together. Of course one's will, either to believe or disbelieve, cannot make a text mean other than what it says. But the will may have a great deal to do with one's understanding of what the text means by what it says.

What William James called the "will to believe" makes many a text say what the interpreter wants to hear. Hence, to give an example, the affirmation "You are Peter, and on this rock I will build my church" (Mt. 16:18) will never mean the same thing to an ultramontane Catholic and a Pentecostal Protestant. But if there is a will to believe, there is also a will not to believe. Here an example comes to mind from E. D. Burton's *Commentary on Galatians,* Edinburgh: T. & T. Clark, in the 1921 edition of the *ICC* series. The relevant material begins with Burton's comments on Galatians 3:10. According to Burton's interpretation of Paul, the crucifixion redeems us from the curse of the law in that it makes it evident that God does not act toward humankind on the basis of any consideration of moral qualities. Hence the cross is the place where Christ suffered to make it evident that God blesses men and women apart from any necessity for an expiation of their sins!

ADDENDUM: CONCERNING PREACHING AND THE HEARING (APPLICATION) OF SCRIPTURE

We have said that the task of a Reformed and evangelical hermeneutic is to ascertain (*a*) the meaning of the text in its original context and (*b*) the meaning of the text for those who read and hear it preached as God's word to them, in their contemporary context. Another way to put matters is to say that a Reformed and evangelical hermeneutic seeks the convergence of two horizons, that of the text in its original setting and that of those who hear the text today in their contemporary setting. For such a convergence to take place, there must be the creation of a new horizon on the part of those who hear the text today. Understanding the text adequately is not a matter of combining the best insights to be found in our self-understanding (as men and women of the twentieth century) with the insights of an author in the fifth century B.C. or the first century A.D. To get from the author's past to the hearer's present, to bring together what the text meant and what it means, requires, in the last analysis, a hearing of the text as God's word that speaks the truth in that it addresses the hearer as a sinner and demands a response of repentance and faith.

At the human level, the primary bridge whereby God's word has been brought out of the past into our present has been preaching. To say as much is to imply that preaching itself participates in the revelatory process that begins with the text of Scripture.[73] Preaching is not simply an explanation of the text, as though the text were all-important and the explanation incidental. For the Protestant and evangelical, to be sure, Scripture alone is the norm of preaching, and that is why we began our treatment of written revelation with a discussion of the Scripture as canon. We do not, however, read that it has pleased God "through the inspiration of the Bible," but rather "through the foolishness of preaching," to save those who believe (εὐδόκησεν ὁ θεὸς διὰ τῆς μωρίας τοῦ κηρύγματος σῶσαι τοῦς πιστεύοντας, 1 Cor. 1:21). This preaching includes not simply the original, apostolic, heralding of the gospel but also, for all its failure and brokenness, the ongoing heralding of the gospel by the church. In the *viva vox ecclesiae* the gospel continues to be heard. Therefore, Christian people have every right to speak of preaching as "a proclaiming of God's word"; and while they may err in specific cases, they also have the right to complain when the preacher does not "preach the word."

When Paul says to those who demand a sign and ask for wisdom: "We

---

73. In this regard it should be remembered that while it is the ongoing norm of preaching, at the same time Scripture itself rests upon preaching, namely, the inspired oracles of the prophets (Old Testament) and the kerygma of the apostles (New Testament).

preach Christ crucified" (1 Cor. 1:23), he does not mean that the Jesus event is simply an event in the past that he describes in vivid detail to all who will listen. Christ's crucifixion is not like Hannibal's crossing the Alps or Caesar's crossing the Rubicon. It is a past event, to be sure, but not simply a past event. *Rather, it is an event in and as it is proclaimed in the present.* Of course, the event that is proclaimed can be researched in a neutral, objective way and thus certified to have happened. Then it becomes "true" in the sense of a correspondence between the event and the mind that hears of the event *(adequaetio rei et intellectus).* But the concern of preaching is not simply to inform the hearer concerning the past; it aims primarily at encounter with the crucified One in the present. Anyone can understand (as information) the text: "And when they came to the place which is called The Skull, there they crucified him" (Lk. 23:33). But one does not understand this text, in the Christian sense of understanding, until she responds: "We are convinced that one has died for all; therefore all have died. And he died for all, that those who live might live no longer for themselves but for him who for their sake died and was raised" (2 Cor. 5:14-15).

What we speak of has traditionally been called the application of the text. In former times, especially in Puritan circles, sermons were not only outlined, but the outline consisted of two main parts, exposition and application. While such a distinction may be a bit too neat, since exposition involves application and vice versa, it does have its place. It tends to foster engagement with the text on the part of those who hear it expounded. And such engagement tends both to overcome the distance between the hearer and the text and to correct the preunderstanding with which the hearer comes to the text, insofar as that preunderstanding impedes one's hearing the Spirit who speaks through the text. It is in such engagement that one not only understands the words of the text but understands the word through the words of the text. Thus the Spirit of God makes "the preaching of the word an effectual means of convincing and converting sinners and of building them up in holiness and comfort through faith unto salvation."[74]

Our stress on public proclamation not only serves to underscore the

---

74. *Westminster Shorter Catechism,* Q. 89. The traditional vocabulary to describe the several aspects of the Spirit's work vis-à-vis the Scriptures is worth noting, now that we are drawing our discussion of Scripture to a close. The Spirit "inspires" (uniquely guides) the writers of Scripture; the Spirit "testifies to" (gives inner assurance to) those who hear and read the Bible that it is God's word; the Spirit "illumines" (gives insight to) those who study the Scripture in prayer, seeking his help; the Spirit enables the sincere expositor to preach with "unction," that is, as anointed and taught by the Spirit. (Not to be confused with "unctuousness," i.e., suave, smug, sentimental, pretentious, ingratiating, spiritual drivel.) Finally, the Spirit "edifies" believers, that is, "builds them up in holiness and comfort" as they hear the word preached.

church's ongoing task of preaching but also reminds us that the saving understanding of the text, to which the individual hearer is brought, is not a private affair. The meaning of the text is not simply a meaning to which I come as a solitary individual, a meaning "for me"; it is rather a meaning "for us." My salvation, indeed, is my salvation; but my salvation is embedded in and draws its meaning from the larger context of the salvation history of God's people, the church, in all ages. Not simply what has happened to me, but what has happened to all the people of God, at Calvary, on Easter Sunday, on the day of Pentecost; in fact, all that happened leading up to these events—the Exodus under Moses, the restoration under Ezra and Nehemiah—all are the larger context that gives meaning to the sentence "I am redeemed." So, in response to the question with which we began, How is the Bible best interpreted? we come at last to a twofold answer. The Bible is best interpreted when we practice a hermeneutic that is both objective and subjective, both scientific and existential. Such a hermeneutic begins by understanding the text in its own context and ends by understanding it in the hearer's context.

A Book with a Difference

*A Sermon Preached by Marguerite Shuster
at Knox Presbyterian Church, Pasadena, California,
Lord's Day, October 30, 1988*

*For the word of God is living and active, sharper than any two-edged
sword, piercing to the division of soul and spirit, of joints and marrow, and
discerning the thoughts and intentions of the heart. And before him no
creature is hidden, but all are open and laid bare to the eyes of him with
whom we have to do.*

Hebrews 4:12-13 (RSV)

Four hundred and eighty years ago, a German monk, tormented by a sense
of his sin, sat in his lonely cell and pored day and night over the Scriptures,
particularly over Romans 1:17, which speaks of the righteousness of God—
a righteousness that this man believed referred to God's fully justified
punishment of sinners like him. He studied for years, consumed by his own
need, till at last, in his famous "tower experience," the text suddenly came
alive to him and changed the way he read the Bible as a whole. God spoke
a new word through the familiar words the monk knew so well. His new
understanding revolutionized his life—and changed the course of history.

Twenty-two years ago, a college student sat on the bottom bunk of a
bed at her university's overseas campus in France, poring over the reading
assignments for a philosophy class, one of which happened to be the Old
Testament story of Abraham and Isaac. Despite her parents' earnest efforts
during her childhood, she knew nothing of substance of Scripture—not

even where to find the story—and came to her task without the slightest existential concern. Or, I should say, she came without any particular concern about *God*. She was plenty concerned about doing well in her class. So she read the biblical story over and over, with the same diligence, and the same bad attitude, that she read everything else. About the third time through the story (bad attitude still intact, you understand!), it began to dawn on her that there was something different about reading the Bible than reading any of the other first-rate literature she had been assigned. Just exactly what, she couldn't say—not the beauty of the prose, or the intellectual profundity of the ideas, or the skillfulness with which the plot was developed, or anything else one could define according to the usual categories; but the biblical story simply grabbed her in a way that even her pagan, grade-oriented mindset could not deny. Something was *different* about that Book. Never since has she been able to escape it.

The monk, of course, was Martin Luther, who spearheaded the Protestant Reformation, which we celebrate today. The student, of course, was me. What has the world of a sin-tormented German monk to do with that of a grade-obsessed American university student? What has the sixteenth century to do with the twentieth or, for that matter, with the first century and even earlier centuries than that? What has an epistle of Paul to do with a story in Genesis? How can one Book pull all of these together?

Pushing the questions still further, why is it that you in this congregation would have every right to complain mightily if, on a Sunday morning, I started expounding from this pulpit the latest insights of psychology or philosophy or biology, or if I told you entrancing stories out of the world's great literature? Why is it that for personal devotional reading or Christian group study, no other book, however worthy, can completely supplant the Bible or can bear the constant scrutiny and rereading that we give to the Bible? Why is it that Christians in lands where Christian believers are persecuted or where Bibles are not readily available will treasure and copy and pass on even fragments and scraps of Scripture? Why is it that in the early days of the church its foes were so interested in destroying the Bible—in getting Christians, under threat of torture and death, to hand over the sacred texts? Why is it that even today, translators labor to make Scripture available in the languages of all peoples, and Bible societies distribute millions of copies of this Book without any felt need for explanation or comment?

If to all of these questions you respond, "Well, obviously, because this book, from Genesis to Revelation, is the word of God," you have spoken truly, but perhaps too quickly. Too quickly, because one can easily enough imagine a word from God that would be limited in its relevance to a particular time and people; or one that would be so complicated that only a trained elite could understand and interpret it; or one that might be true and yet make no particular difference to the way that we live our lives; or one that might come in multitudinous different ways and be found in many different places, all having equal authority; or one that we might not even recognize as God's word to us. Such a word, if we succeeded in identifying it at all, we might admire like a fine gem in a museum case; but for such a word we would hardly lay down our life or even significantly change our direction.

No, for it to make any *difference* that this is God's word, it must be, as my text says, "living and active, sharper than any two-edged sword, piercing to the division of soul and spirit, of joints and marrow, and discerning the thoughts and intentions of the heart." It must be the word of a God before whom "no creature is hidden, but all are open and laid bare to the eyes of him with whom we have to do." It must be a word that comes to us with absolute intrinsic authority and a word that is somehow adequate to our most essential needs.

To be fair to the setting of my text, I must acknowledge that in the first instance, Hebrews 4:12 does refer primarily to the word of God as spoken in the living voices of the prophets who addressed God's people Israel. We do not distort the text by applying it to Scripture, though; for to speak of God's word as "living" is precisely to affirm that it does not die when those die to whom it was first spoken, but it continues to speak with the same authority to all who hear it.[1] Obviously, the spoken word of God's revelation had to be committed to writing in order to preserve it: Scripture secures the word of God for the people. And the books that comprise the Bible, written over hundreds of years, became part of the Bible precisely because in these books, as in no others, the voice of the one God could be, and still can be, recognized.

If one asks how this can be, only one answer can be given: the same Spirit who inspired those who wrote the words of Scripture continues to work in our hearts to confirm those words.

> The Spirit breathes upon the word,
>   And brings the truth to sight;
> Precepts and promises afford
>   A sanctifying light. (Cowper)

Only God can authenticate his word. We can try, of course. We can develop all sorts of theories of inspiration and devise all sorts of proofs of

---

1. J. Fergusson and D. Dickson, *The Epistles of Paul and Hebrews* (Carlisle, Pa.: Banner of Truth Trust, 1978 [1635]).

why the Bible must be true and hold all sorts of rallies in supposed "defense" of the Bible. These may make us feel more secure when we already believe, but they have not been notably successful in persuading the unconvinced. If the word of God, in its original spoken or later written form, does not come with intrinsic authority, nothing else will finally suffice.

Consider the case of the call of Abraham, to leave home and go—just go. Rationally speaking, he should have responded indignantly, "Go? Go where? And why? And what for? And who are you, anyway? And what makes you think I should listen to you?" But, since the call was God's call, God's own word, and came with his full authority, Abraham simply got up and went. No alternatives presented themselves. Or consider the discouraged disciples after the crucifixion, joined on the road to Emmaus by a stranger who interpreted the Scriptures to them. After they recognized the stranger as Jesus himself, and he disappeared from their sight, they commented on how their hearts had burned within them as he had opened the Scriptures. Even in their despair and ignorance something about the word of God impressed itself upon them. Consider the overwrought monk in his cell and the college student on her bunk. Something about the word of God . . . the God who spoke, still speaks. We must simply testify to these things. We *point* to the active power of God's word; we do not *prove* it. Its power is a part of what it is, just as dynamite would not be dynamite without its explosive force.

To speak as if the power of Scripture were an external force like dynamite, though, would be misleading. Seldom indeed does God impose his will upon us from the outside, dragging us kicking and screaming where we don't want to go. Certainly that is not the way my text speaks. Rather, it speaks of a sharp, piercing word that gets to the very deepest part of us, searching out our inmost motives and ideas, touching the heartspring of our desires and actions and not being satisfied with labeling their outer manifestation. That word does not begin by answering all our questions about God and the world and ourselves. It begins by questioning us, by uncovering who we are, by revealing how desperately short we fall of what we were created to be. It calls us to account: the phrase referring to the God "with whom we have to do" is not a mere rhetorical flourish, but it reminds us of our responsibility to God as Judge.[2]

We know that, right? When we are being bluntly honest with ourselves, we know that what makes us most resist dealing seriously with Scripture is not fundamentally the Bible's pre-scientific worldview or its historical

2. *TDNT,* IV, p. 104.

obscurities. It's the way it fingers all too accurately where we fall short here and now. What troubles us is not what is not clear, but what is. As Mark Twain put it, "Many people are bothered by what they don't understand in the Bible. I, however, am greatly disturbed by what I *do* understand." And W. C. Fields said, "I have spent a lot of time searching through the Bible for loopholes."[3] By contrast, to affirm the biblical story in all its discomfiting clarity is to say with Karl Barth,

> Every verse in the Bible is virtually a concrete faith-event in my own life. . . . I have been personally present and have shared in the crossing of Israel through the Red Sea but also in the adoration of the golden calf, in the baptism of Jesus but also in the denial of Peter and the treachery of Judas. . . . And we shall have to answer this question and this question alone: whether, after the Word of God has sought to provide us with this movement and meaning, we have perhaps evaded it?[4]

This threat of judgment may scare us. But if we have not sought finally to evade God's word and by that very evasion brought its judgment upon us, we will find at last that its mightiest power is power to heal rather than to hurt. The sword we feared would destroy us becomes a surgeon's knife wielded to bring life. The word penetrates us not to wipe out our personal story but to reveal it to be part of a much larger story, one written by God himself.

The biblical story, then, as I have emphasized so many times before and as Barth said so graphically, is our own story. We may trust what it reveals to be adequate for our needs because that's why God gave it to us: he before whom nothing is hidden, he who knows all his creatures so well that nothing essential to their well-being escapes him, gave us exactly this collection of books. Oh, it won't tell us what stocks to buy or what career to pursue or even how long our quiet time should be. But it will challenge the thoughts and intents of our heart that underlie such questions. It will ask us about greed and envy, and whether we are using our God-given gifts in a way that glorifies God, and whether we have let the idol of a crowded agenda usurp God's place in our life. It will ask us where we are placing our hope and our trust, whether we are acting justly, whom we are called to serve as neighbor. It will meddle with everything basic to our salvation and faith and life. It will disturb and probe and insist, "Something is wrong here, and here, and here, too." And then, when we are stripped of defenses

---

3. Quoted in *Context*, 15 February 1985, p. 1.
4. *Church Dogmatics*, I/2 (Edinburgh: T. & T. Clark, 1956), p. 709.

and excuses, it will speak words of comfort and mercy with the same irresistible authority that it speaks judgment.

That's what happened to Martin Luther. He knew about God's righteous judgment. He knew about sin, his own sin. He knew he was guilty. He knew the standard Scripture set; he knew the law. Every time he came to the Bible, he found what he already knew was there, the righteousness of a just God that spelled certain doom for a sinner like one Martin Luther. Every time he came to the Bible, he found what he already knew was there—until one day the living word, the active word, the word empowered by the Holy Spirit, started to force its way out of the cage in which he had confined it for so long. "The righteousness of God": "For I am not ashamed of the gospel," says Romans 1:16-17: "it is the power of God for salvation to every one who has faith. . . . For in it the righteousness of God is revealed through faith for faith; as it is written, 'He who through faith is righteous shall live.' "

Could it be that this talk about righteousness was not a sentence of doom but was rather good news of a free gift of righteousness, given by God to all who trust in Christ? Could it be that not the law and exertion and merit but rather faith is the way that we are relieved of our guilt? Suddenly the Bible became a new book for Luther, a book full of comfort and life. It filled him with joy and peace and opened, as it were, the very gates of heaven.[5]

Although he never dreamed such a thing at the time, this intensely personal experience eventually led Luther on the course that culminated in the Protestant Reformation—a movement capsulated by the phrases "grace alone, faith alone, Scripture alone." Grace may come first; but it is through Scripture, in which God still speaks, that we know about grace. We cannot manage without Scripture. Thus Luther eventually translated the whole Bible into German, the common language of his land, knowing from his own experience the living power of God's word and wanting that power to be available to ordinary people, not just to priests who knew Latin or to scholars practiced in Hebrew and Greek. If we say that there are now so many Bibles in so many languages because there are Christians, that is no more true, and a good deal less important, than to say that there are Christians because of the Bible.[6]

So today evangelical Protestants insist upon their pastors' preaching from the Bible because in no other book do they hear God's word as they

---

5. P. Schaff, *History of the Christian Church*, vol. VII (Grand Rapids: Eerdmans, 1980 [1910]), pp. 122-25.

6. E. Brunner, *Our Faith* (New York: Scribner's, 1954), p. 7.

hear it in this one. Individuals and study groups read the Bible devotionally and probe it together because they know it is a living word that speaks to their condition today, telling them everything they need to know for their salvation and faith and life, even as it ferrets out their failings. Bible societies continue to translate and distribute it without comment because they know it is an active word, with the intrinsic power to make God's will and ways known. All of these, like Martin Luther himself, would resonate with the truth of the famous comment of Charles Spurgeon when he was disagreeing with those terribly concerned about "defending" the Bible. He said, "The way you defend the Bible is the same way you defend a lion. You just let it loose."[7]

7. Source unknown.

UNIT THREE

WHO GOD IS: THE DIVINE NATURE

In the year of Grace, 1654,
On Monday, 23d of November, Feast of St. Clement, Pope and
Martyr, and of others in the Martyrology.
  Vigil of Saint Chrysogonus, Martyr, and others,
  From about half past ten in the evening until about half
  past twelve.

FIRE

God of Abraham, God of Isaac, God of Jacob, not of the
philosophers and scholars.
Certitude. Certitude. Feeling. Joy. Peace.
God of Jesus Christ
Deum meum et Deum vestrum.
"Thy God shall be my God."
Forgetfulness of the world and of everything, except God.
He is to be found only by the ways taught in the Gospel.

                                        Pascal's *Memorial*

I. God Is Personal Being

A. GOD AND THE PHILOSOPHIC ABSOLUTE

Of the fifty "ideas" listed in the Synopticon of the *Great Books of the Western World,* ideas that have "given Western civilization its life and light," there is no entry allotted more space than that of "God." Virtually all the authors of the 443 works in the series have something to say on the subject, for it is a theme profoundly affecting our understanding of the universe as a whole and human life in particular. The last author to speak, Sigmund Freud, harbingers the present when he dismisses the idea of "God" as an illusion, a cosmic projection of the human father who serves to satisfy humanity's infantile dependence. While perhaps less crass in their conclusions, many thinkers since Freud have agreed with him, though they often have lamented this loss of a transcendent deity. "God is silent," says Sartre, "that I cannot deny—yet everything in myself calls for a God and that I cannot forget."[1] The "silence" of God" (Sartre), the "absence of God" (Jaspers), the "eclipse of God" (Buber), even the "death of God" (Hamilton)—these themes, which turn up again and again in the literature, indicate that although many religious thinkers may no longer be very sure of God, as were our forebears, neither are they very sure that the world is better off without him.

This modern *Götterdämerung* has proven less devastating for theology than might be feared, since theology, insofar as it is done Christianly, rests not on an abstract "idea" of God, which modernity compels one to abandon, but on the self-disclosure of the living God who addresses us in Christ as

1. As quoted in Wilfred Desan, *The Tragic Finale: An Essay on the Philosophy of Jean-Paul Sartre* (New York: Doubleday, 1960), p. 179.

sovereign Lord. God, in other words, is not an Idea; he is personal Spirit (Jn. 4:24). To be sure, "spirit" (πνεῦμα) translates the Hebrew (רוּחַ), which literally means "wind," an impersonal manifestation of energy. But it is clear that when Israel spoke this way of God, they spoke of him not as an impersonal force, but as the living Subject who, in his essential nature, is the invisible Power (Energy) behind all that is, the creative Breath that animates all living things. In its most fundamental meaning, this Energy is just God's will to be who he is. He is who he is by his own act. That is simply another way of saying that God's being is personal being, being that can be understood only as a self-determined "Self," an "I."[2]

By contrast, the gods of the Greeks were, in the last analysis, the impersonal, unchanging Forms of reality, whether one thinks in terms of the unifying Principles of Ionian physics or the eternal Ideas of the philosophers.[3] The Greeks could say: Love is God, but never God is love (1 Jn. 4:16). This exchanging of the personal Subject for its impersonal predicate expresses the difference between Greek philosophy and Christian theology. For the philosophical mind it is no help, in this regard, to say of God that though he is personal Being he is infinite personal Being. An infinite personal Being is a contradiction in terms since infinite Being is without limitation and hence not susceptible to that definiteness and uniqueness belonging to personal being, to One who is an "I." Therefore philosophy, concerned as it is with infinite Being (the Absolute), rejects the God of revelation, the "I am" who is the subject of Christian theology.[4]

Above all others, it was Pseudo-Dionysius who infected medieval theology with the impersonal approach to God. Dionysius, an unknown Christian Neoplatonist of the late fifth or early sixth century, started with the Neoplatonic concept of the metaphysical One who is the Source and

2. By the same token, the general term for God in Hebrew, El (אֵל), a primal word in Semitic vocabulary, designates that Power that transcends all human power. But this Power is never conceived in the Old Testament as though Power were God. Power is not God nor is God Power, but the powerful One, the Lord who is God Almighty. The personal character of God is an axiom of biblical revelation, never argued because it is everywhere assumed. (See G. Quell, "θεός: "El and Elohim in the OT," *TDNT*, III, pp. 79-89.)

3. See H. Kleinknecht, "θεός: The Greek Concept of God," *TDNT*, III, p. 68. For the Greeks, to change was to pass away. Hence, in the concept of "true Being," "Being as such," they found the fixed center of the universe. See Gunter Höwe, *Mensch und Physik* (Witten/Berlin: Eckhart-Verlag, 1963), p. 15.

4. Some have sought to resolve this problem by postulating a personal but *finite* God. See W. James, *Pragmatism* (New York: Longmans, Green and Co., 1931); E. Brightman, *A Philosophy of Religion* (New York: Prentice-Hall, 1940). The arguments for a finite God have had little appeal to common people who do not propose to take their problems to a God who has problems of his own. They respond, rather, to the God of the Negro spiritual who's "got the whole world in his hands."

Ground of all. He described God as the Being who transcends all Being, the Unknowable, the Nameless, the Inexpressible (Pierre Van Passen's "Great Anonymous of the Burning Bush"), yet giving names to all; the ultimate Unity causing variety in all.[5]

Many theologians in more recent times have turned away from this impersonal approach to God. Rejecting German Idealism and using the insights of biblical theology with its emphasis upon the God who speaks and acts, they have reaffirmed the truth that God is a personal self. In so doing they have restored to dogmatics its proper subject. The subject of theology is not the God who is the "Unmoved Mover," *"Prima Causa,"* "Ground of Being," "Source of Human Ideals," "Vital Urge in the Evolutionary Process," "Ultimate Integrating Principle," etc., but the personal, loving God who speaks to us and who says: "I am the LORD your God" (Ex. 20). The God of Scripture is not a god defined by abstract thought but the God who defines himself as he discloses himself in personal encounter. *This affirmation is theological axiom.*

Not only in medieval but also in Protestant Scholasticism one finds a tendency toward an abstract view of the divine nature. God is "perfect Being," the "highest Good." Barth complains that such an approach made it easy for Enlightenment theology to reduce God to the "Eternal truth of the theoretical-practical-aesthetic Idea of human reason" and correspondingly difficult for the theologian to escape Feuerbach's dictum, "All theology is anthropology" (*K.D.,* II/1, pp. 322f.; cf. *C.D.,* II/1, sec. 28.2).

"That the word 'person' has a certain fitness in statements about God may be suspected," observes Thielicke, "from the fact that some theologians are so emphatic in banishing it from the field" (*The Evangelical Faith,* vol. II, Grand Rapids: Eerdmans, 1974, p. 103). Thielicke cites, as examples from the nineteenth century, A. E. Biedermann and D. F. Strauss. "Personal being," declares Biedermann, "[in contrast to the Divine] is the specific subsistence form of the *human* spirit as *finite*" (as quoted by Emil Brunner, *Dogmatik,* vol. I, Zurich: Zwingli-Verlag, 1960, p. 142). In this century the most influential theologian to take exception to the language of the personal, when speaking of God, is Paul Tillich. Observing Brunner's profound dislike for the theology of Schleiermacher, whose trans-personal, mystical categories, when applied to our knowledge of God, contradict Brunner's own personalistic emphasis, Tillich asks him "whether it is possible to establish the divinity of the divine in merely personalistic

---

5. See the several treatises that make up the *Areopagitica,* treatises which greatly influenced theologians like Hugo of St. Victor, Peter Lombard, Albertus Magnus, Thomas Aquinas, et al. The concept of an anonymous, nameless God is known as "apophatic" theology (from ἀπό and φημί, literally "to speak away," "to deny"). One may properly speak of God by way of negation only — not to be confused with "apathetic" theology (from "ἀ," the alpha privative, and πάθει, "to feel"). Apathetic theology denies to God all feeling, emotion, or passion. On apophatic theology see below, this Unit, II, C, Addendum: Concerning Apophatic Theology, pp. 218-19. On apathetic theology see below, Unit Four, V, A, Excursus: A Historical Note, pp. 398ff.

terms, and whether both classical medieval and classical German philosophy of religion were not right in combining biblical personalism . . . with the basic ontological categories like being, life, spirit, and so on. I think they *were* right" ("Questions on Brunner's Epistemology," *The Christian Century,* 24 Oct. 1962, 1284). For this author they were not right. Indeed, they could hardly have been more wrong. The God of classical German philosophy of religion is not the God of Abraham, Isaac, and Jacob or of Sarah, Rebecca, and Rachel.

As for the "trans-personal, mystical" categories used by Schleiermacher to describe our knowledge of God, their corollary is the affirmation that the important thing in religion is mystical feeling. G. Ernest Wright quotes Schleiermacher's familiar dictum, "God is immanent in the human soul as it rises into perfect self consciousness," and goes on to reflect that he was

> so indoctrinated with this point of view in his younger years, that even now he does not feel that he has worshipped unless his emotions have been stirred up and his eyes become watery. God, in such an experience, is an indescribable Something, a great Blur, hazily perceived through dripping eyelids, the experience of whom, nevertheless, causes one to feel deeply. But to feel what? That is something which cannot be described (*The Challenge of Israel's Faith,* Chicago: University of Chicago Press, 1944, p. 50).

The God of Scripture, by contrast, is not an "indescribable Something," but a Someone who describes himself in that he names himself and thereby discloses himself to us.

B. THE NAME OF GOD

1. THE OLD TESTAMENT DATA

In the Old Testament, the name of a person is not simply a designation of convenience; rather, as one is named so is she. What is true at the human level is preeminently true of God; his name is himself, manifest in his word and works. Wherever God is known as a personal Presence, there his name is. Hence the phrase "we are called by your name" (Jer. 14:9 NRSV) is simply another way of saying: "You are in the midst of us."[6] The familiar Aaronic benediction pronouncing a triple blessing on Israel is said to be a putting of God's name on Israel (Nm. 6:24-27).

H. Braun, who rejected the dimension of the personal as inadequate to express a proper view of God, once thought to embarrass L. Goppelt in a radio broadcast by asking him to translate the word "person" into Hebrew.

6. See G. F. Oehler, *The Theology of the Old Testament* (New York: Funk and Wagnalls, 1883), pp. 126-27.

Without hesitating, Goppelt suggested the Hebrew word "name" (שֵׁם).[7] Properly speaking, only persons have names and one's name expresses one's personal identity, an identity that cannot be defined in terms of anything else because each person's identity is unique.[8] This is supremely true of God as the personal God. If we are to know who he is, he must speak to us, must identify himself, tell us his name. This he has done. In an overwhelming theophany, God revealed his glory to Moses, saying: "I will make my goodness pass before you, and will proclaim before you my name, 'The LORD'" (יַהְוֶה, Yahweh, Ex. 33:19).

God's name, in other words, is interchangeable with himself. For this reason, to seek, to love, to honor, to thank, to praise—as well as to desecrate, to despise, and to blaspheme—the name of God is to do all these to God himself. By the same token, God's name is a refuge. "A mighty fortress is our God," sang Luther; "the *name* of the LORD is a strong tower," declares the Old Testament proverb (Prv. 18:10).

For the Israelites, not only the divine name but human names as well were believed to have some special significance. For example, the prophet Isaiah was told to name his son Maher-shalal-hash-baz ("the spoil speeds, the prey hastens") in anticipation of the imminent ruin of Damascus and Samaria by the Assyrians. In an effort, more curious than convincing, to emulate such scriptural precedents, the Puritans' zeal knew no bounds. Some of the biblical names of which they were fond ("Hope," "Faith," "Grace") are still with us. It was especially between 1580 and 1640 that they turned biblical watchwords and even whole theological phrases into Christian sobriquets. "A jury impaneled in 1658 included such worthies as Faint-not Hewitt, Redeemed Compton, Becourteous Cole, Search-the-Scriptures Moreton, Kill-sin Pimple, Fight-the-good-fight-of-faith White, Weep-not Billing and Steadfast-on-high Stringer" (W. F. Moulton, *The History of the English Bible,* London: Kelly, 1911, p. 285). The most celebrated worthy in this class was Praise-God Barebone. Two of his brothers are said to have been called, respectively, Jesus-Christ-came-into-this-world-to-save Barebone and If-Christ-had-not-died-for-thee-thou-hadst-been-damned Barebone. Since the morals of the latter were not above reproach and since his acquaintances were wearied with the length of his name, we are told that they abbreviated it to the more curt than courteous, Damned Barebone. (See C. W. Bardsley, *Curiosities of Puritan Nomenclature,* London: Chatto and Windus, 1880.)

In modern America, black Baptist congregations have shown an arresting originality in naming their churches. Along with such stalwarts as Second Baptist and Trinity Baptist, the following names appear in the Church Service Section of the *Church and Community News,* Feb. 15, 1981, for Los Angeles, California: St. Peter's Rock Missionary Baptist Church, All Nations Bibleway Missionary Baptist Church, 1 Timothy Missionary Baptist Church, Echoes of Heaven Missionary Baptist Church. The term "star," the symbol of the

7. According to Helmut Thielicke, *Evangelical Faith,* vol. II, p. 107.
8. See James Baldwin's *Nobody Knows My Name* (Garden City: Doubleday, 1961).

light of truth and the sign in the heavens of Jesus' advent, seems especially popular. As of this writing, there is a Morning Star, a Rising Star, an Evening Star, a New Star, and a Greater Bright Star Missionary Baptist Church in Los Angeles.

2. THE NEW TESTAMENT DATA

As the equivalent of his person and work, the name of God remains central in the New Testament as it is in the Old. In the New Testament, however, that name is bound up with the name Jesus Christ. Jesus' mission as the Christ was to make God's name known (Jn. 17:26); and because he was faithful in this mission, God has given him a name that is above every name. Indeed, the name that he is given is the name by which God himself is known in the Old Testament, that is, "Lord" (κύριος). "Therefore," we read, "God has highly exalted him and bestowed on him the name which is above every name, that at the name of Jesus every knee should bow . . . and every tongue confess that Jesus Christ is *Lord* . . ." (Phil. 2:9-11).

As the early Aramaic confession behind the text in Philippians 2 implies, the risen Christ was worshipped from the beginning as the Lord Jesus (note Stephen's prayer, Acts 7:59). So he is not only the One who reveals God, but is himself revealed as God.[9] Hence his name is hypostatized, as was God's name in the Old Testament. The disciples leave the Jewish Sanhedrin rejoicing that they have been counted worthy to suffer dishonor for the name (Acts 5:41). Salvation is believing in the name; and without such faith one stands condemned (Jn. 3:18), "for there is no other name under heaven, . . . whereby we must be saved" (Acts 4:12). For this reason, Christians are people who do all that they do in the name of the Lord Jesus (Col. 3:17).[10]

9. Otto Weber notes *(Grundlagen der Dogmatik,* Neukirchener-Vluyn: Neukirchener, 1955), vol. I, p. 462, that Jesus is never called the Son of Yahweh or the Son of the Lord, but just the Lord.

10. The New Testament, of course, unites the Lord Jesus, as the Son, with the Father and the Spirit in a single name, the trinitarian name into which Christians are baptized (Mt. 28:19). As "Lord" is God's primary and personal name, so "Father, Son, and Holy Spirit" is his full and final name. Lord is the name of the God of Israel who in Christ has become the God of the Christians also. Hence one may regard God's trinitarian name, "Father, Son and Holy Spirit," as the final exposition of his personal name, "Lord." See Barth, *K.D.,* I/1, p. 311. The desire of some to escape the sexist overtones of "Lord" by substituting "Sovereign" is understandable. The problems, however, with all such substitutes are not easily resolved. Hence our decision to remain with the traditional translation of יהוה as "LORD" and to use the classic name "Father, Son, and Holy Spirit" in our exposition of the Trinity. See above, Unit One, III, D, First Addendum: A Comment on Sexist Language in Theological Discourse, pp. 44ff.

3. THE NAME יהוה / κύριος / Lord

The Greek κύριος ("Lord") renders the Hebrew יהוה ("Yahweh"), the personal name of the God of Israel.[11] The name "Lord" conveys the essential thought that in naming himself, God relates to us not as an equal but as he who is sovereign over all his creatures. By his will we live, move, and have our being; and by his word we are to order our lives. Even in human relationships, one who is "lord" exercises authority as master and one who has a master acknowledges that authority as servant. In the case of God and humankind, the relationship is grounded in God's mighty acts of creation (Gn. 1) and redemption (Ex. 20:1-3). To confess that God is our Maker and Redeemer is to acknowledge that he is our Lord, to whom we willingly submit in all of life. Of course, his authority is not tyrannical power, nor our submission abject resignation; it is rather that freedom of which Augustine spoke when he said, "The essence of liberty is bondage to your will, O God."

Hence "Lord" is the name by which Christians know and confess not God in general, but their God in particular, the God who has revealed himself through Moses and the prophets and finally in the person of Jesus Christ.[12] Hence also in the New Testament, as in the Old, "Lord" is the name of him who is Maker of heaven and earth (Acts 4:24) and at the same time, and in the most concrete and specific sense, the name of him who is our Savior, the Lord Jesus Christ. In him the personal God, who spoke by the prophets, has spoken his final word; indeed, in him the personal God, whose name is Yahweh, the "I AM WHO I AM" (Ex. 3:14), is present in a personal way, present in this person Jesus, who is Immanuel, God with us.

4. CONCERNING THE TETRAGRAMMATON

As we have seen, it was in the disclosure of his name, Yahweh/LORD, that God revealed himself to Israel. Indeed, God's name became so identified

---

11. "Yahweh" is a scholarly conjecture based on the usage of the early Fathers. The original vocalization of יהוה is unknown. "Jehovah" is little used—except by Jehovah's Witnesses—resting as it does on the deliberate mispointing by the Masoretes of יהוה, a name deemed too sacred to be pronounced in the synagogical reading of Scripture. Since the LXX translated יהוה into Greek as κυριος (LORD) and since the Masoretes pointed יהוה with the vowels of אדון (Lord), the Tetragrammaton is commonly translated into English as LORD. We have followed this usage. But we refer to Jesus as the Lord Jesus Christ.

12. For a contrasting position, see John Hick, *God Has Many Names* (London: Macmillan, 1980).

with himself that it was, so to speak, "a double of his being" (Von Rad) and therefore most sacred (Ex. 20:7; Mt. 6:9), a name never to be taken in vain. Because the memorial name of the God of Israel has become the name of the God of Christians as well, the question, What does it mean? has always interested theologians. To answer this question, they have turned to the account of Moses' call at the burning bush. When Moses asks God's name, God says, "I AM WHO I AM," an enigmatic phrase taken to be an elaboration of the Tetragrammaton, the four-letter יהוה, commonly translated "LORD." Unfortunately, theologians speculating about the abstract being of God have sometimes given the Tetragrammaton a connotation more philosophic than biblical.[13] Yet, to avoid this error, one need not abandon the traditional translation of Exodus 3:14. The fundamental thought implied in the phrase "I AM WHO I AM" is God's abiding faithfulness to his needy people. To keep covenant with his people in the threatening circumstances that had overtaken them in Egypt, he must both transcend their past history and at the same time act in their present history.[14]

The meaning of the Tetragrammaton is that God is truly who he is: the one who really exists, though he may have seemed to the oppressed Israelites to have been eclipsed by the brutal, tangible reality of the slavemaster's whip. God is the God who is present to Moses and his people in the time of their extremity, as he was to their forebears with whom he first made covenant. He and he alone is their hope and salvation, and in Jesus Christ he has become our hope and salvation too. Hence, as Christians we sing,

> The God of Abram praise,
> Who reigns enthroned above;
> Ancient of everlasting days,
> And God of love:
> Jehovah! Great I AM!
> By earth and heav'n confessed;
> We bow and bless the Sacred Name,
> Forever blest. (Olivers)

---

13. From early times, the Tetragrammaton was understood as meaning "That Which Is." And since God transcends all created beings, "That Which Is" is "Being" in the ultimate sense, the *summum esse* of the Neoplatonists. According to Augustine, *City of God*, VIII, 2, in Exodus 3:14 Moses says the same thing as Plato!

14. For this reason we prefer the traditional reading of אֶהְיֶה as a Qal of the verb rather than a Hiphil. The emphasis is on who God *is*, not on what he *does*, though he is revealed to be who he is by what he does.

C. SOME BASIC AFFIRMATIONS

1. GOD IS THE LIVING GOD

In the light of the revelation of God's name at the burning bush, we may appropriately turn from a discussion of the *nomen ineffabile* itself to a brief comment on those theological affirmations that theologians have associated with that name, affirmations with which we shall fill out and conclude our discussion of the personal nature of God.

Our first affirmation is that God, as personal, is the living God, the God who is aware of himself as a self, a subject—indeed, the Subject who calls worlds into being by the breath of his mouth. "'As I live,' says the Lord," is the typical form of the oath whereby God swears by himself since he can swear by none greater. Though we often use anthropomorphic expressions in speaking about him, the affirmation that God is a living self, an "I," not an "it," is no anthropomorphism but the truth that grounds the anthropomorphisms we use. As the living God, furthermore, he has so endowed humankind with life that is like his that we too are subjects, related to him and to one another as persons. In other words, he creates us in his image.

Hence, to speak of God as the living God, a personal self, is not to turn all theology into anthropology, as though Christians were like the cattle of whom Xenophanes spoke, which, could they have drawn, would have pictured their gods as cows. God is not a living self because we humans have projected our human mode of existence on him. Rather, it is the other way around; as the living God, the source of all life, he has given us life in his likeness, made us, as the psalmist says, "little less than God" (Ps. 8:5). He is all that we are as living persons, and more. The deficit is on our side, not on his. We are the ones who, as living persons, are yet less than living persons. We are the ones who are objects as well as subjects, having bodies that remind us at all times that we are in the process of passing away, that we shall at last succumb to death. By contrast, God, as the living God, is the Father who has life in himself, who gives to the Son to have life in himself (Jn. 5:26), and who is confessed (in the Nicene Creed) as the Spirit "who makes alive."

Hence our doctrine of God begins with revelation; and revelation begins with the affirmation, "I am the LORD your God" (Ex. 20:2). It has been said that a thousand sentences in the Bible contain the divine "I am." The essential matter, then, is not that God "is" or that he "exists," true as it may be that he is and therefore does exist; it is rather that God is who he says he is, the "I AM WHO I AM." To depart from this ground is to reduce the living God to an "it," a "neuter," an "object" of thought, the first fateful step on the way to turning theology into philosophy.

2. GOD IS UNIQUE

Our second affirmation is that God is unique as personal. To have a name implies uniqueness, and to have the name "Yahweh" as God has it, implies absolute uniqueness. The God with whom we have to do in Christian theology is he who declares, "I am God, and there is no other; I am God, and there is none like me" (Is. 46:9). Thus we see that God is not only unqualifiedly who he is, but consciously aware that he—and he only—is who he is. "I am the LORD, and there is no other, beside me there is no God" (Is. 45:5). God then is not to be thought of as an exemplar of divinity, a species of the genus Deity. He and he only is who he is. Nothing in the created realm is absolutely unique, for all created reality is tied together by the thread of analogy. Though individual difference is awesomely displayed in the created order—no two snowflakes are identical—yet every individual participates in a larger universal. This is true even of human beings, the most unique of all God's creatures known to us. Though each has her own face, each her own name, none is absolutely unique, for each participates in a common humanity. But God is not like anything or anyone.

> For who in the skies can be compared to the LORD?
> Who among the heavenly beings is like the LORD,
> A God feared in the counsel of the holy ones,
> Great and terrible above all that are round about him? (Ps. 89:6-7)

3. GOD IS FREE

Our third affirmation is that God as personal is underived and self-determined, that is, he is free in the ultimate meaning of the term. He is not free to be other than he is (he cannot deny himself, 2 Tm. 2:13), but he is free to be who he is. His being is his own being. We must disassociate from our thought about God any notion that he has become who he is. Rather, God has his existence in and of himself and is wholly sufficient unto himself. Our existence is determined by him, but his is determined by no one outside himself. This is the implication of his memorial name, I AM WHO I AM. We are who we are by his decision and choice to give us our being; but he is who he is by his own decision and choice. Classic theology speaks in this regard of God's *aseity*.[15] He and he only is without beginning of life or end of days; he and he only has immortality (1 Tm. 6:16); he and he only can declare the end from the beginning (Is. 46:10) because he is free from all contingency. No one has been his counselor; no one has first given to him that it might be given to him in return. Rather, of him and through him and to him are all things (Rom. 11:34-36); but he himself is of none, through none, and to none. That is to say, he is of, through, and to none other than himself alone. Hence he and he only can say without qualification, "I AM WHO I AM."

D. CONCLUSION

If God is indeed the personal God who addresses us saying, "I am the LORD your God," then he is the God with whom we have to do. We are who we are because of our unique relationship to him who gives us our very being in this relationship. His address grounds our own being as responsible persons. Because we are human persons, we must not only think about God, but respond to him.[16] We cannot escape the decision and choice that Elijah put before Israel: "How long will you go limping with two different opinions? If the LORD is God, follow him; but if Baal, then follow him" (1 Kgs. 18:21).

And if we do resolve to follow him, then all our affirmations about him arise out of our faith in him and our desire to obey him. Rather than being truths discovered by reason (as in the philosophy of religion), or pronouncements about our religious experience (as in the psychology of religion), our theological affirmations about God are basically secondary forms of our worship of his name. Hence the language of theology is not the language of philosophy or psychology, but the language that derives from doxology and worship; the language not only of reflection upon, but response to, revelation. To speak of worship brings us to our next major affirmation about God, namely, that he is the Holy One whose very Being evokes reverence and awe.

15. God differs, that is, from the creature in possessing his existence *a se* (in himself).
16. This necessity of our response, grounded in the personal character of God, is the possibility of prayer. One may contemplate the Ground of Being but one cannot pray to It. Having made the personal character of God basic to our exposition of the doctrine of the divine nature, we shall consequently give a large place to prayer in our exposition of the doctrine of the Christian life.

ADDENDUM: CONCERNING IDOLATRY

Idolatry, according to Scripture, is a cardinal sin just because it is the denial of the fundamental truths we have affirmed, namely, that God is the living God who affirms that he, and he only, is God. In its crassest manifestation the craftsman cuts a tree, using half of it to bake his bread and half to make an idol (Is. 44:14-17). Such idols cannot be God, for they neither see, hear, nor speak; they never even move! "Woe to him who says to a wooden thing, Awake; to a dumb stone, Arise! Can this give revelation" (Hb. 2:19)?

Surrounded as they were by idols, the early Christians, no less than the Old Testament prophets, abhorred idolatry. Though the original church in Jerusalem granted the Gentiles full liberty in Christ, they admonished them, expressly, to abstain from the pollution of idols (Acts 15:20). They did not—as we should not—dismiss the warning that God is a jealous God (Ex. 34:14) by appealing to the fact that God is love; for the same New Testament Scripture that says "God is love" (1 Jn. 4:8) also says that he is a "consuming fire" (Heb. 12:29), and that "it is a fearful thing to fall into the hands of the living God" (Heb. 10:31). Nor should we presume that because we are not guilty of the gross idolatry that bows down to wood and stone, therefore we can never be guilty of idolatry. Cowper was right in teaching the church to sing,

> The dearest idol I have known,
> Whate'er that idol be,
> Help me to tear it from thy throne,
> And worship only thee.

Mammon is the god of many in our modern capitalist world, and many have said to mammon: "Deliver me, for you are my god!" Yet mammon cannot say, as God said to Abram: "Fear not, I am your shield" (Gn. 15:1).

> The church today is trying to serve both God and mammon, and the attempt has divided our loyalties. In a world where most people are poor, a rich church is living testimony of idol worship. . . . We did not become affluent by sharing with the poor, but only through accumulation. . . . Our accumulation has put us in servitude to mammon. . . . God's people have forgotten who they are, forgotten to whom they belong, forgotten what it means to worship the Lord.[17]

The iconoclastic controversies of the ancient church broke out afresh at the time of the Reformation. For the Reformers, especially Calvin, the matter of idolatry was of prime

17. Jim Wallis, *A Call to Conversion* (New York: Harper & Row, 1981), pp. 71-72.

importance. The eleventh chapter of Book I of the *Institutes* is entitled "The Unlaw-fulness of Ascribing to God a Visible Form: All Idolatry a Defection from the True God." Locked in controversy with the Roman Catholic Church of his day, which regarded images and pictures as the books of the illiterate, Calvin cites the prophets to the intent that when the One who is incorporeal is likened to the corporeal, the One who is invisible to a visible image, the One who is Spirit to inanimate matter, then the Deity is supremely dishonored (*Institutes,* I, 11, 2). He concludes that "the Divine Majesty, which is far above the reach of human sight, ought not to be corrupted by unseemly figures" (ibid., I, 11, 12). Calvin does admit (ibid., I, 11, 2), however, the validity of sculpture and painting as art, though he would limit it to the world of nature, recalling the word of John: "Little children, keep yourselves from idols" (1 Jn. 5:21). There were no Sistine Chapels with frescoed ceilings in Geneva! The *Second Helvetic Confession* goes so far as to proscribe pictures even of the incarnate Christ (Chap. 4, "Of Idols or Images of God, Christ, and the Saints"). The *Westminster Larger Catechism* (Q. 109) teaches that the second commandment forbids even the making of a repre-sentation of God "inwardly in our minds."

While the heat of the argument has cooled with time, there is a permanent validity in the ancient protest of the iconoclasts. We should not seek to bring God within our world of material forms. God is not an object in any sense, but pure Subject, pure Spirit. Hence Israel is expressly forbidden to make "any likeness of anything that is in heaven above, or that is in the earth beneath, or that is in the water under the earth," or to "bow down to them or serve them" (Ex. 20:4-5). To speak positively, "God is spirit, and those who worship him must worship in spirit and truth" (Jn. 4:24). But if the God who reveals himself in Scripture is personal Spirit, and if, therefore, we stress the divine invisibility with its corollary that God is incorporeal—that is, without bodily parts—what do we make of the fact that Scripture frequently speaks of God in bodily terms? His "hand," "arm," "ears," "nostrils," "mouth," "lips," "tongue," "feet," and "face" are all mentioned.

So far as the Old Testament is concerned, such descriptions of God are not limited to the older and therefore (supposedly) more primitive strands of revelation. On the contrary, they increase in the later sources! (See Boman, *Das hebraische Denken im Vergleich mit dem Griechischen,* Göttingen: Vandenhoeck & Ruprecht, 1959, p. 85.) Boman observes, for example, that the ancient Song of Deborah (Jgs. 5) describes Yahweh's wrath and power without so much as mentioning bodily parts, whereas the latter part of Isaiah is replete with illusions to the bodily parts of God. (See also G. E. Wright, *The Challenge of Israel's Faith,* pp. 65f.) As for the New Testament, even though such usage is not as frequent and graphic as it is in the Old, it is present in a way that reflects how natural such a manner of speaking sounded in the ears of the early Christians. The coming of the Christ Child is God's showing "strength with his arm" (Lk. 1:51); having been raised from the dead, Christ sits at God's right hand (Col. 3:1). Christians are admonished to seek peace and pursue it, "for the eyes of the Lord are upon the righteous, and his ears are open to their prayer" (1 Pt. 3:11-12). The hymnal reflects similar usage: God is the "Eternal Father, strong to save/ Whose arm doth bind the restless wave"—Whiting.

The traditional explanation that such biblical usage is anthropomorphic has been criticized as reflecting the theologians' penchant for reading the biblical text in terms of the categories of Greek thought. The problem, as we see it, however, is not that theologians understand such statements anthropomorphically. It is rather the conclusion they sometimes draw, that because such statements are anthropomorphic, they are nonessential to a Christian doctrine of God. The better way is to recognize that these anthropomorphisms, auditory as well as visual, are, in their dynamic thrust, apt descriptions of God's personhood. They reveal not God's literal appearance (which would, indeed, sanction idols), but his essential nature as personal. Even at the human level, it is recognized that the language of the physical often describes personal and spiritual realities. To say, for example, that one's *"feet* are swift to shed blood" (Rom. 3:15) describes the spiritual nature of a murderer. This is so self-evident that it would be utterly ridiculous to use such a statement literally to describe the predatory instincts of the cheetah or the young lion stalking its prey. Some of the anthropomorphic statements of Scripture may be culturally different from ones we would use, but that is theologically inconsequential. When the Lord was angry, the psalmist tells us, "smoke went up from his nostrils, and devouring fire from his mouth" (Ps. 18:8). But does it really matter that Scripture speaks thus rather than saying that in his anger the Lord "knit his brow and his eyes became hard as steel?"

When we understand these affirmations of Scripture that attribute bodily parts to God as revelatory of his personal self as the living God rather than of his physical appearance, they are all in harmony with the perfections and attributes theologians have traditionally ascribed to him. His "hand" and his "arm" speak of his power and strength, whether it be in creation (Ps. 95:5; 119:73) or salvation (Is. 52:10); his "eye" and his "ear" speak of his knowledge, understanding, and wisdom (Ps. 139:16; 17:6). And his "face" is just himself, his personal presence, as he stoops to disclose himself to us. Hence, what theologians have called the "beatific vision," that is, knowing God in that new order beyond death and the grave, is, in the language of Scripture, knowing him "face to face" (1 Cor. 13:12).

By the same token, such an anthropomorphic understanding of these statements explains how the Lord God could breathe into our nostrils the breath of life without lungs (Gn. 2:7), speak to our first parents without a mouth (Gn. 2:15-16); cause his voice to be heard without a tongue (Gn. 3:9), walk without feet (Gn. 3:8), and make clothes without hands (Gn. 3:21). The lack of any mention of bodily parts in these opening narratives of the Old Testament sets the tone for the emphasis on the dynamic, the auditory, the action-oriented perspective of all subsequent biblical revelation. Such a perspective contrasts with the visual approach reflected in the idol worship of those cultures out of which both Israel and the early church were called. It also explains why Christians can sing,

> Whate'er I do, where'er I be,
> Still 'tis God's hand that leadeth me. (Gilmore)

while at the same time they address this God, who leads them by his hand, as

> Immortal, invisible, God only wise,
> In light inaccessible, hid from our eyes. (Smith)

Go, and the Holy One
Of Israel be thy guide
To what may serve his glory best, and spread his name
Great among the heathen round;
Send thee the angel of thy birth, to stand
Fast by thy side, who from thy father's field
Rode up in flames after his message told
Of thy conception, and be now a shield
Of fire; that Spirit that first rushed on thee
In the camp of Dan
Be efficacious in thee now at need.

Milton, *Samson Agonistes*

II. God Is the Holy One

A. INTRODUCTION

As the personal God, God identifies himself by name: "I," he declares, "am the LORD your God" (Ex. 20:2). In disclosing himself to us as Lord, he reveals himself to be the God who transcends our creaturely existence. To use the language of Scripture, he is the Holy One whose majesty is over all his works. This holy God has given us our being as humans in order that we might serve and glorify him. In this creative act, he has endowed us with his own image that we might have fellowship with him and "enjoy him forever." And so he reveals not only his holiness as the Lord who transcends creation, but also his love as the God who has made us in and for fellowship with himself. Believing that he is who he has revealed himself to be, the church has taught that God is the God whose very nature is Holy Love.[1]

To say that God is in himself Holy Love anticipates our doctrine of the Trinity. The fellowship God has established with us in creation (and renewed in redemption) points beyond itself to a mysterious and transcendent fellowship in God himself. As our human existence is grounded in the unique relationship we have with him, so God's existence is grounded in the unique relationship that he has with himself. The God who is the Holy One is the Father who loves the Son in the Spirit from all eternity. When, therefore, we have said what it means to affirm "God is the Holy

---

1. This twofold description of the divine nature corresponds to the twofold response that the knowledge of God evokes in those to whom he reveals himself. As Calvin beautifully observes: Such knowledge as God gives to us of himself "invites us first to fear God, then to trust in him," that we may learn to honor him with perfect innocence of life and sincere obedience to his will and to place all our confidence in his goodness (*Institutes,* I, 10, 2).

189

One" and "God is Love," we shall conclude our discussion of the divine nature with an exposition of the mystery of the trinitarian mode of God's existence.

Theologians, who agree that holiness and love together describe the nature of God, differ as to the order in which they should be discussed. Some have argued that since God's last word is spoken in Christ, we should begin with the good news of the gospel: God is Love. Others have argued that while God is Love, this love is the love of the sovereign Lord. It is as Lord that God freely gives himself to the creature in love. In fact, only the God who transcends our finitude, the God who is sufficient unto himself and in need of none, can love freely and without a cause. She who loves out of need to enrich herself loves not as God loves, for God's love is the sovereign, outgoing love of agape, not the acquisitive love of eros. Hence, the affirmation that God is the Holy One takes precedence over the affirmation that God is Love.

The essential matter, it seems to us, is to maintain the unity (not identity) of the divine holiness and love. Whatever the order followed in dogmatics, unity is the key to a correct doctrine of the divine nature. Holiness underscores the difference between God and the creature, and love his fellowship with the creature. As the Holy One, he is the Lord over all, claiming the whole creation for himself; as the God who is Love, he is the Lord *serving* all, giving himself without reserve to his creation. In our own case, we shall follow the order of biblical revelation, speaking first of God as the Holy One, yet doing so in the light of the ultimate revelation that the Holy One is in our midst as Love. Our primary concern is not so much order as balance of treatment, a treatment that preserves the inner unity of the divine nature.

As we turn to the exposition of the doctrine of the divine holiness, we would note that no work dealing with the subject has been more widely read in the twentieth century than Rudolf Otto's *Das Heilige (The Idea of the Holy).*[2] For many of the heirs of German liberalism, Otto's treatise contributed to the rediscovery of nothing less than the deity of God. Holiness, Otto argues, is the primal category of biblical thought used to describe the nature of God. As such it is not, in its fundamental meaning, an ethical term. Rather, God's holiness is the corollary of his lordship. To know God as the Lord is to relate to him as the Holy One. As Brunner has observed,

On the basis of revelation, the first thing to be said about God is that he is the Lord. With this first affirmation, however, a second is so

---

2. Rudolph Otto, *Das Heilige* (Munich: C. H. Beck'sche Verlagsbuchhandlung, 30th ed., 1936). The significant difference between Otto's methodology and our own can be seen in the fact that he speaks of the *Idea* of the holy (*Das* Heilige) whereas we speak of the Holy *One* (*Der* Heilige). In spite of his comparative religions approach, Otto's analysis reflects a profound grasp of certain aspects of the biblical data that puts the theologian forever in his debt.

closely bound up that one may ask whether or not it should have been spoken first: God is the Holy One.[3]

God's holiness is that quality of being which distinguishes him from all beings of a creaturely sort. To say that God is holy or that his name, his word, his Spirit, are holy, is just to say that in the perfection of his being God is the One who is above and beyond all creaturely existence. The creature can never, by reasoned argument, build a bridge that leads to the Creator. The holiness of God is not a universal category of the mind, a category in which, along with his creatures, God participates as one among many. Rather, God's holiness is that which belongs to him alone, that which is his exclusively. One may, therefore, describe the divine holiness as just the divine way of being, the way of being that pertains to God alone. "I am God and no mortal, the Holy One in your midst" (Hos. 11:9 NRSV).

B. THE BIBLICAL DATA

The theme of the divine holiness, which dominates the Old Testament, is movingly enunciated in the writings of the prophet Isaiah.

> For Isaiah, the concept of holiness is the central point of his whole theology. The Trisagion (Holy, holy, holy) heard in the vision of his call (Is. 6:3) remains normative for his conception of God. In a way it shows that the Lord of Hosts is holy to the third degree. . . . God's holiness designates his inmost hidden being. The terrifying nature of the holy God, the *numen tremendum,* comes to inimitable expression in the sacred awe of Isaiah. His trembling accompanies the shaking of the ground on which he is standing at the entrance to the temple and in the appearance of the divine he feels the deadly contrast to his own nature since he is "unclean and believes he must die."[4]

This God of the Old Testament, at whose presence the very foundations of the temple shake, is also the God of the New. The great throne scene of the Apocalypse (Rv. 4–5) is but an enlarged edition of the vision of Isaiah. Only now, unlike that of the prophet, the vision of John discloses a God who is triune. Summoned to "come up hither," he beholds the Father upon

---

3. Emil Brunner, *Dogmatik* (Zurich: Zwingli-Verlag, 1960), vol. I, p. 160.

4. D. Procksch, "ἅγιος," *TWNT,* I, p. 93 (cf. *TDNT,* I, p. 93). The title "the Holy One of Israel" (קְדוֹשׁ יִשְׂרָאֵל) is used to describe God no less than twenty-four times in Isaiah alone.

his throne surrounded by twenty-four elders while the four living creatures, like the seraphim of old, intone: "Holy, holy, holy." Before the throne are seven spirits representing the Spirit of God in the perfection of his being and plenitude of his gifts. Standing between the throne and the living creatures is the Son, as a Lamb who had been slain, who alone is worthy to open the seven-sealed scroll of the divine purpose. As he does so, the elders fall down in adoration before the throne, being joined by myriads of angels. Finally, the circle of worshipers enlarges to embrace the entire creation, as in a deafening diapason of sound the curtain falls.

This prostration in awe and boundless adoration on the part of the creature goes far beyond the commitment to some moral ideal. It reflects the awareness of what Otto has called the *mysterium tremendum*—the awesome strangeness, the fearsome otherness, the dreadful majesty of God; in short, his holiness, which makes him distinct from all others and comparable to no earthly being.[5] For this reason, though he speaks with God as a man with his friend, Moses covers his face at the burning bush for fear of looking upon the Holy One (Ex. 3:6); and so terrifying is the sight at Sinai that he trembles as in the presence of the Other, the Unearthly, and shakes with fear (Heb. 12:21). In like manner Job, acknowledging that he cannot contend with the Almighty, despises himself, repenting in dust and ashes (Jb. 42:6). So also the seraphim, though intimately associated with the most High as nearest the throne, cover their faces with their wings (Is. 6:2) as they intone praise of him who is thrice holy.

Even when this transcendent and mysterious God condescends to become one with us, he yet remains the One whose presence invokes reverence and awe. The more intimate the disciples became with Jesus, the less they understood him. In wonder they ask what manner of man he is (Mk. 4:41). Though among the inner circle of Jesus' confidants, even Peter falls down on his knees before him and like Isaiah of old confesses his utter unworthiness (Lk. 5:8). The fear that first filled the women at the empty tomb (Mk. 16:8) overwhelms the disciples when it dawns on them that he who is standing on the shore of Galilee is none other than the risen Lord himself (Jn. 21:12).

This sense of the divine as otherness is paramount in worship. Worship, indeed, is fellowship with God, the God who has drawn near to us in Christ. But it is fellowship informed by reverence and awe. Christians address God in prayer as "Our Father," a term of endearing familiarity; but he is always our Father "who art in heaven." The first of all petitions is "Hal-

---

5. Note how the deity is addressed in the eighth stanza of the *Dies irae: Rex tremendae majestatis* (King of Majesty tremendous), that is, of a majesty provoking trembling (Thomas of Celano, 13th century, tr. W. Irons).

lowed be thy name." Thus, when we worship we take, as it were, the shoes from our feet; in the presence of God we are always on sacred ground. Hence worship differs from theologizing. Worship is fellowship with God in which one experiences God as the Holy One; theology is an effort to frame a doctrine about God who is the Holy One. And because theology talks about God's holiness in rational categories, it tends to lose the sense of the more than rational that pertains to the numinous. It is, therefore, in the hymns that the poets have given to the worshipping community, rather than in the treatises of the theologians, that the doctrine of the divine holiness finds its noblest expression.

> Lo! God is here: let us adore,
> And own how dreadful is this place;
> Let all within us feel his power,
> And humbly bow before his face.[6]

Though the presence of the holy God moves the worshipper with awe and dread, it also moves her with a desire and yearning that is beyond all expression. "Whom have I in heaven but you," exclaims the psalmist, "and there is nothing on earth that I desire other than you" (Ps. 73:25 NRSV). Though the place where God is is "awesome"—as Jacob Inferred when he awoke from his dream of the ladder reaching to heaven (Gn. 28:10ff.)—it is the place of supreme beatitude, the place where we see what no eye has seen, hear what no ear has heard, and perceive what has never entered into the heart of humankind (1 Cor. 2:9). Like Moses at the burning bush, we cover our faces because we are afraid to look on God; for none can see his face and live (Ex. 3:6; 33:20). Yet we long to see him not only through the dark glass of this present life, but face to face (1 Cor. 13:12), that we may enjoy him forever.

Reflecting on this "contrast/harmony" of the *numinosen,* Otto uses the word *fascinans* to describe this fixation with the Holy One.[7] To know God as the holy God not only inspires one with awe but grips one with a spell of irresistible charm. No one, it may be, ever expressed this "fascination" of the beatific vision more movingly than Faber in the lines:

> Father of Jesus, love's reward,
>   What rapture will it be
> Prostrate before thy throne to lie,
>   And gaze and gaze on Thee.

---

6. Gerhard Tersteegen, 1729, as translated by John Wesley, 1739. It was Wesley who got Watts's paraphrase of Psalm 100 off to such a magnificent start with the lines: "Before Jehovah's *awful* (awe inspiring) throne, / You nations bow with sacred joy."

7. Otto, *Das Heilige,* p. 10.

Clustering around the concept of God's holiness is a congeries of biblical terms—"honor," "majesty," "greatness," "might"—that give it richness and color. Whereas the theologians have tended to use the word "transcendence" when speaking of the holiness of God, the biblical word most redolent of everything that these ancillary terms affirm is "glory."[8] The "glory of God" often refers to praise and homage rendered to him. But to speak of God's glory in this sense is to speak of it in a secondary way, that is, as the divinely awakened response in the creature to the disclosure of the divine glory. Glory in this sense is the jubilation of the creature that echoes God's joy in himself. The ultimate reality that evokes this response is just God himself, the all-glorious One. God not only receives glory, his is the glory (ᾧ ἐστιν ἡ δόξα, 1 Pt. 4:11). God's glory is the sum of all the divine perfections so manifested that they cannot be denied with impunity by the creature.[9] His glory is just his living presence, authenticated by no higher instance because God's being is above and beyond all other being. We say "above and beyond," not "remote from," for the glory of God has been revealed in our very midst in the face of Jesus Christ (2 Cor. 4:6).[10] He is the very radiance of God's glory (ἀπαύγασμα τῆς δόξης), as the writer of Hebrews says (Heb. 1:3); indeed, his name is "the Lord of glory" (1 Cor. 2:8; Jas. 2:1).[11]

8. No less than twenty-five Hebrew words, the most common being כָּבוֹד, are rendered in the LXX by δόξα, meaning "brightness," "splendor," "excellence," "renown," etc. For the striking departure from Hellenistic usage that this represents, see G. Kittel's remarks, "δόξα," *TDNT*, II, pp. 233-37. The term "Shekinah" came to be used to describe the glory of God manifested in the form of a cloud that hovered first over the summit of Sinai, then over the tabernacle, and later over the temple. This usage, initially developed by Jewish theologians in the targums, midrash, and Talmud, has become a part of the Christian theologian's vocabulary.

9. This statement of the case points to the strong eschatological component in the concept of the divine glory. In this present age, the sinful creature not only can but does deny God's glory, for "all have sinned and come short of the *glory* of God" (Rom. 3:23). This is the impossible possibility that dumbfounded the prophet Jeremiah. "Has a nation changed its gods, even though they are no gods? But my people have exchanged their Glory for worthless idols (Jer. 2:11 NIV). When God's purpose in Christ shall have been fulfilled and the Son of Man comes again, he will come with great power and glory (Mk. 13:26). Then he will judge those who do not obey the gospel, excluding them "from the presence of the Lord and from the glory of his might" (2 Thes. 1:8-9).

10. In the transfiguration scene (Mt. 17:1ff.), note the shining of his face like the sun, the garments white as light, the brightness of the theophanic cloud, and the response of the disciples, who "fell on their faces and were filled with awe." This scene is later described as Jesus' receiving glory from God the Father when the voice was borne to him by the Majestic Glory "when we were with him on the holy mountain" (2 Pt. 1:17-18).

11. See B. B. Warfield's study entitled *The Lord of Glory* (London: Hodder and Stoughton, 1907). Otto identifies, as an element of the *tremendum*, the "energy" of the *numinosen*,

When we read that God will never give his glory to another (Is. 42:8), this is just to say that he insists upon his honor. He chides Israel with the question: "If then I am a father, where is my honor?" (Mal. 1:6). God's honor is his worth, dignity, and virtue. He wills his honor in the sense that he wills that all should acknowledge him to be who he is, the all-glorious and holy God. God takes himself seriously, and so must we, for he is the God with whom we have to do, the God who is not mocked (Gal. 6:7).[12] When we do acknowledge God to be who he is, the Holy One, the all-glorious God, we acknowledge his greatness. "Great is the LORD," says the psalmist, "and greatly to be praised, and his greatness is unsearchable" (Ps. 145:3). God, the Holy One, is the utter opposite of all that is mean, lowly, despicable, and of no account. Because this is so, the proper reflex in the creature is to exalt his name, to magnify him, in the sense of extolling his greatness, acclaiming his goodness, acknowledging his power, and praising his grace. "My soul," says Mary, "magnifies the Lord, and my spirit rejoices in God my Savior" (Lk. 1:46-47). The ultimate meaning and motivating purpose of all that Paul did was to magnify Christ in his body, whether by life or by death (Phil. 1:20).

Thus to magnify the Lord is to acknowledge that he is clothed with honor and majesty (Ps. 104:1) and to celebrate "the glorious splendor of his majesty" (Ps. 145:5). God's majesty is all that wherein he is incomparable and unapproachable; all that whereby the creature is overpowered and constrained to acknowledge his own nothingness, exclaiming with the psalmist: "Praise the name of the LORD, for his name alone is exalted; his glory is above earth and heaven" (Ps. 148:13). Hence the appropriateness of the doxology with which the Lord's Prayer ends: "For thine is the kingdom and the power and the glory forever, Amen."[13]

---

expressed in such terms as "passion," "power," "action," "force," "arousement." (Note the way in which the soldiers who apprehended Jesus "drew back and fell to the ground" (Jn. 18:6) when they heard the 'Εγώ εἰμι, the "I am" of Jesus.) Whenever this factor has been introduced by theologians as an element in their God concept, it has carried with it the strongest protest against the contemplated God of philosophic speculation. According to Otto, this protest was the nub of Luther's controversy with Erasmus. "Luther's *'omnipotentia Dei'* in his *De servo arbitrio* is nothing else than the union of majesty, as the absolutely transcendent, with this 'energy' as the forceful, active, compelling, living One, ever tense and never at rest." *Das Heilige,* pp. 27-28.

12. When God's covenant is broken and his commandments transgressed, his honor is impaired. Hence the salvation of sinners cannot be accomplished apart from the question of the divine honor, as Anselm has argued in his *Cur Deus Homo.* Anselm was not simply a child of his (feudalistic) times in his understanding of the atonement.

13. The same note is struck in one of the most widely used hymns of the church, the *Te Deum laudamus.*

EXCURSUS: FURTHER COMMENTS ON MATTERS RELATED TO THE AFFIRMATION: GOD IS THE HOLY ONE

1. The Twofold Meaning of the Term "Holiness" as Used of God

When theologians say, "God is the Holy One," and when they say, "God is holy," they are not saying the same thing in different ways. The former way of speaking describes God in his essential being as qualitatively other than the creature: mysterious, majestic, awesome. The latter way of speaking, though it implies otherness, means that God, unlike the fallen creature, is in no way morally compromised. To say that God is holy, or a holy God, is to use a predicate (attribute) that is ethical in connotation and therefore virtually a synonym for his justice or righteousness. We shall discuss the divine holiness in this ethical sense when we treat of the attributes.

2. The Wrath of God

Where, in a systematic presentation, does one properly discuss the wrath of God? Protestant theology has often looked upon the divine wrath as the implication of God's moral character and therefore treated it exclusively as a manifestation of God's justice. Because God is just he must punish sinners. When speaking of the ethical attribute of justice, then, one should also speak of the divine wrath, an instance of retributive justice. (So Charles Hodge, *Systematic Theology,* vol. I, New York: Scribner, 1871, pp. 421ff.) In view of what we have just affirmed about the twofold meaning of God's holiness, this is not bad theology. Yet obviously something more needs to be said in the light of the biblical data. Especially in the Old Testament, but also in the New, wrath is a quality of the divine Being. Otto comments on the trembling evoked by the presence of the *numen.* Such trembling, he observes, is a response to a manifestation of the transcendent that is riddle-like and defies a completely rational analysis. It "burns"; it is similar to a "mysterious natural force"; it is like stored-up electricity that breaks forth against one who comes too close. (Otto has in mind such passages as 2 Samuel 6:6-11, where Uzzah is struck down for touching the ark.)

We praise you, O God, we acknowledge you to be the Lord . . .
To you cherubim and seraphim continually do cry,
Holy, holy, holy, Lord God of Sabaoth;
Heaven and earth are full of the *majesty* of your *glory.*

Anonymous, A.D. 400-450, as translated in the 1549 *Book of Common Prayer.* So also Jonathan Edwards: "Thus we see that the great end of God's works, which is so variously expressed in Scripture, is indeed but one; and this one end is most properly and comprehensively called, the glory of God." "Dissertation Concerning the End for Which God Created the World," *The Works of President Edwards* (New York: Leavitt, Trow, and Co., 1844), vol. II, p. 254.

To one who is accustomed to think of the Deity only in terms of the rational attributes, this [burning quality of the divine Being] must appear as caprice and arbitrary passion. Those who lived under the Old Covenant would surely have rejected such a thesis emphatically; for it appeared to them as in no way a cheapening of God's holiness but rather as a natural expression and essential element of that holiness that cannot be dispensed with. And rightly so. . . . Without doubt Christianity also has something to teach about the "wrath of God," Schleiermacher and Ritschl to the contrary notwithstanding. (*Das Heilige*, p. 20)

A concept like the wrath of God cannot but disturb those who will acknowledge in the divine character only such qualities as have to do with a paternal concern for the world, qualities like gentleness, goodness, and love. Since the Enlightenment, therefore, the tendency has been to dismiss all biblical statements about the "kindling of the Lord's anger" as crude anthropopathisms of an unenlightened age. Such a tendency, however, reflects assumptions quite alien to Scripture. True, God is a God of love. But a love that can know no wrath is sentimentalism. One cannot, then, speak of the divine holiness with no thought of the divine wrath. On the other hand, we can by no means relate the divine wrath simply to the divine holiness. It can be treated here only in an introductory way, since the wrath of God is an expression not only of his holiness but also of his love. God's wrath is the wrath of One who is Holy Love. His wrath is the expression of a love that cannot be spurned with impunity. We shall, therefore, have more to say on the subject when we elaborate the thesis that God is Love. (See below, this unit, III, D, 3, God's Love as Wrath, pp. 246-51.)

3. The Beauty of God

To speak of God's beauty has seemed easier to the Greek Orthodox and Roman Catholics, with their cathedrals and vestments, than to Protestants, especially those in the Reformed tradition. Given the latter's iconoclastic inheritance and Kierkegaardian fear of the substitution of aesthetic contemplation for existential decision, most Reformed theologians have preferred to say that God creates beauty rather than that he is beautiful. The heavens, which are themselves beautiful, declare the glory, not the beauty, of God (Ps. 19:1). While God has given us the capacity to create and enjoy the beautiful, this beauty is not a reflection of God's beauty but an ambiguous, earthbound parable of his glory.

Hymn writers likewise have been reserved. The so-called "Crusader's Hymn," *Schönster Herr Jesu,* which cannot be traced earlier than 1677 (Julian), is the exception that proves the rule. "Fairest Lord Jesus," by an unknown translator, is very popular in many American circles, Reformed as well as others. However, the translation *"Beautiful Savior! King of Creation,"* by J. A. Seiss, is seldom used.

The association of the beautiful with the holy has been justified by noting the arresting brilliance, the sheer radiance of that which is beautiful, setting it apart from the ordinary and mundane ("Gloire," *Vocabulaire de Théologie Biblique,* Paris: Les Éditions du Cerf, 1962, col. 413). Clerical vestments, however, and fine Sunday clothes have had mixed reviews, especially in the Puritan tradition. Are they instances of the "beauty of holiness" with which we are to worship the Lord (Ps. 29:2)? Or are they elegant ostentation, the "gold ring and fine apparel," of which James warns us, that alienate "the poor in shabby clothes" (Jas. 2:2)?

Karl Barth focuses on the joy evoked by the contemplation of the divine perfections as indicative of beauty in God, who is the object of joy. God, as the psalmist says, is he in whose presence there is exceeding joy (Ps. 16:11). Of course, such beauty is not perceived by all. In Christ there is no form or comeliness that we should desire him (Is. 53:2). The beauty of our Savior, rather, is in what he does, a beauty perceived only by those whose eyes have been opened and whose hearts have been filled with the joy of the Lord.

As a lover sees beauty in the countenance of the beloved (not always evident to the neutral observer), so a theologian sees beauty even in the science whose subject is God. To answer the question, What does it mean to say God is beautiful? would require a review of the whole of dogmatics. This is just to say, as every theologian knows from the joy of her work, that theology is not simply a utilitarian endeavor, a matter of instruction and information. Theology is a beautiful science — indeed, declares Barth, the most beautiful of all the sciences (*K.D.*, II/1, pp. 738ff. cf. *C.D.*, II/1, sec. 31.3). The study of theology is the earnest of the hope that we may dwell in the house of the Lord all the days of our life, "to behold the *beauty* of the LORD, and to inquire in his temple" (Ps. 27:4).

C. THE DIVINE TRANSCENDENCE

1. INTRODUCTION

When theologians say that God is transcendent, they mean that he is related to the world as prior to it, apart from it, and exalted above it. God is not "prior to" the world at a point on some time line extended into an infinite past; the thought is, rather, that he does not have a first moment as does the creation. Nor is he apart from the world in a deistic sense, unconcerned with the creature and absorbed, like Aristotle's Unmoved Mover, in thinking about thought. Rather, he is apart from the world in that he is not to be identified with the sum total of created reality (pantheism) nor with any creature in the world (idolatry).

As for the thought that God is "exalted above" the world, it is here that things have proven most difficult for modern thinkers. This is so because such language, commonly used in Scripture and the worshipping community, has spatial overtones. While theologians have spoken of God's "otherness," of the "infinite qualitative difference" (Kierkegaard) between God and the creature, there can be no doubt that this "otherness," this "difference," has been traditionally understood in a spatial way. God is the "high and lofty One who inhabits eternity, whose name is Holy" (Is. 57:15) and

> to him enthroned above all height
> the hosts of heaven their anthems raise. (Tersteegen)

Even when the Lord comes down to confirm the covenant with his people, Moses must go up to the top of Mt. Sinai to receive the tables of the law. Surely the thunder, lightning, and thick clouds that shake the mountain convey more than the thought that Yahweh is a storm God. These meteorological pyrotechnics have revelatory significance in such a context because they transpire in the region of the heavens which is over the earth. Speaking of God's lightnings that illumine the world and cause the earth to tremble, the so-called thunder psalm (97) goes on to celebrate his righteousness with the words, ". . . for you, O LORD, are most high over all the earth; you are exalted far above all gods."

Because of their height and mystery, mountains have always symbolized the point where earth and heaven meet. (The Aramaeans erred, not in calling God the God of the hills, but in excluding him from the valleys [1 Kgs. 20:23, 28]). Beautiful for elevation, the joy of all the earth, Mt. Zion is God's holy mountain, and the city of the great King (Ps. 48:2). Of course the truth greater than the symbolism is that neither on this mountain nor in Jerusalem is God worshipped (Jn. 4:21). Yet in Matthew's Gospel, Jesus, as the new Moses, enunciates the laws of the kingdom in a sermon delivered on a mount (chaps. 5–7). It is while in prayer with Peter, James, and John "on a high mountain apart" that he is transfigured before them (Mt. 17:1-2; Lk. 9:28ff.); and from the Mount of Olives he ascends as he is lifted up and a cloud receives him out of their sight (Acts 1:9ff.). (Bonatti, the great alpinist, observed that one must reverence a mountain if one is to master it. After a seventy-nine hour direct conquest of the north face of the Matterhorn (deemed an impossible feat), he commented: "While preparing for the Matterhorn climb, I lived as if I were in a state of grace" (*The Reader's Digest,* Sept. 1965, pp. 102ff.). The Herculean efforts—and sometimes tragic failures—that mark such human assaults on earth's puny heights foil the proud boasts of the king of Babylon as insane: "I will ascend above the heights of the clouds, I will make myself like the Most High" (Is. 14:14).

In classic Greek Idealism there were two vastly different worlds; one the immediate world of appearance and the other the suprasensible world of "true reality." Given the language of height in Scripture, one can readily understand how the early theologians, most of whom were Greek in their philosophic orientation, assumed this dualistic approach to reality when they thought of God as the Holy One. While the first Christian thinkers did not depreciate the sensible world as mere appearance and deception as did some of the Greeks, they wove the dualism of Greek metaphysics into their doctrine of the divine transcendence. God's proper abode, which is the world beyond this seen world, is a realm far above the mundane realm of everyday experience. For a thousand years (the "age of faith," as the Middle Ages has been called), God ruled and overruled in the mundane realm of everyday life from his lofty empyrean above the skies. And since God was in his heaven, all was well with the world.

But then things began to happen that sent tremors through the entire theological edifice. With Copernicus, the sun took the place of the earth as the center of the universe. In the ensuing defense and elaboration of this Copernican system, Galileo enormously enlarged the size of the universe and removed the earth even further from center stage. But it was Giordano Bruno who "first with audacious fist knocked the roof off the world and disclosed the limitless bounds of space."[14] Thus began what John A. T. Robinson has called the "reluctant revolution."[15]

At first the impact of the change was muted, because in place of the God who was "literally up there," Christians substituted the God who was "spiritually out there." But in our day, in the judgment of many thinkers, it has become impossible to postulate even a God "out there." This more radical step seems to threaten the very existence of God; for such moderns the sky has become empty. Christians, when they pray "Thy will be done, on earth as it is in heaven," have always presupposed that empirical reality is the image of a different Reality that is behind what they see, as real people are behind the images on the television screen. But now it seems that the picture on the screen is all that there is. As the heroic acts of a television drama can be viewed as no more than dots of light on a silver screen, so God can be viewed as no more than an idea imprinted, through cultural evolution, on the minds of the earthbound creatures who call upon him. This is why there are now even more "cultured despisers of Christianity" than there were when Schleiermacher first addressed them.

To understand why this is so, one must realize that the challenge to a Christian view of a transcendent deity, a challenge that began with the natural sciences, has been reinforced by the human sciences.[16] Critical

---

14. K. Heim, *Glaube und Denken* (Hamburg: Furche-Verlag, 1937), p. 33.

15. John A. T. Robinson, *Honest to God* (Philadelphia: Westminster, 1963), chap. 1.

16. It has also been reinforced by unspeakable manifestations of moral evil in human history. This is true particularly for the Jewish community living this side of the Holocaust. "Where was God at Auschwitz?" ask Rubenstein, Wiel, et al. Since we will treat the question of theodicy and moral evil in another place (the Fall and original sin), here we have chosen to limit the discussion of the doctrine of God's transcendence to those theoretical (cognitive) problems which have been emerged since Copernicus.

history, for example, tends to reduce Scripture to a merely human product. Likewise, psychology since Freud has appeared to many to show that the God who is "up there" or "out there" is really a projection of the human psyche and that this projection is grounded not in objective reality, but in human need and desire. This challenge of psychology has been intensified finally by sociology, because the latter throws light on the social dynamics that shape our theological conclusions.[17]

The sociology of knowledge indicates that our views of reality remain credible to us only to the degree that they find social support. This is especially true of our religious affirmations, since these are incapable of verification by direct sense experience and therefore lack the kind of "obvious" confirmation afforded the "truths of science." By substituting explanation of these truths for verification of them, sociology removes the last vestiges of mystery from the world of the theologian. The theological view of the world, like all others, has been constructed by human beings and hence it is simply one worldview among many. As history posits relativity as a fact of the human condition, the sociology of knowledge posits its necessity.[18] The only absolute left is John Dewey's "absolutely no absolutes." God has become simply a cosmic human being (Feuerbach).

This loss of the transcendent God threatens the entire universe of the theologian (and the universe of everyone else for that matter) with irrelevance. Many theologians have failed to realize the scope of the problem and have assayed to resolve it simply by transposing the traditional statement of the Christian faith into a secular key. Such efforts are doomed to failure, for even though the language of otherworldliness is retained, it is transferred to this-worldly referents. In other words, when the theologian plays the game by the cognitive rules of the opponent, what appears to be gained by her "being relevant" is really lost by the profound erosion of the traditional meaning of the terms she employs. Thus, in the end she finds herself talking not only to secularists but as a secularist. As Huston Smith has observed:

> Itself occupying no more than a single ontological plane, science challenged by implication the notion that other planes exist. As its challenge was not effectively met, it swept the field and gave the modern world its soul. For this is the final definition of modernity: an outlook in which

17. It also throws light on our praxis. Peter Berger, alluding to Bras's study of Catholic practice in France, cites his ". . . well-known statement that a certain railway station in Paris appears to have a magical quality, for rural migrants seem to be changed from practicing Catholics the very moment they set foot on it." Peter Berger, *A Rumor of Angels* (Garden City: Doubleday, 1970), p. 48.

18. Ibid., pp. 50ff.

this world, this ontological plane, is the only one that is genuinely countenanced and affirmed. In religion modernity demythologizes tradition to accommodate it to its one-story universe; if "God" in principle requires more exalted quarters, the nonexistence of such quarters entails his nonexistence as well; hence Death-of-God theologians. Existentialism does its best to give man purchase in a world built for the examination of things, but subjective truth is no match for objective, so in the main philosophy, too, accepts the working premises of science.[19]

But this secular paradise regained by science, for all its fair blandishments, has not satisfied the human spirit. If it has given the theologian a case of vertigo, it has left the common person with a sense of disenchantment. The erosion of mystery means the loss of ideals, standards, and values. Such loss has turned the world into a realm of cold measurement, boring statistics, and bland calculations. Such a world is one that has no angels, no heavenly hosts even at Christmas, but only a host of scientific specialists, not a few of whom appear as technically trained ignoramuses, the pundits of technology without the wisdom we need to live humanly. Laplace may have believed that he had no need of the "God-hypothesis," but many have not felt the exhilaration of his achievement even when they have felt the force of his argument. Hence they have sought to cauterize the sense of loss by embracing a philosophy of "unyielding despair." No one ever expressed this Sisyphian hopelessness with more Promethean eloquence than Bertrand Russell.

That mankind is the product of causes which had no prevision of the end they were achieving, that its origin, growth, hopes, fears, loves, beliefs are but the outcome of the accidental collocation of atoms; that there is no fire, no heroism, no intensity of thought and feeling which can preserve the individual life beyond the grave; that all the labor of the ages, all the devotion, all the inspiration, all the noonday brightness of the human race are destined to extinction in the vast death of the solar system; that the whole temple of man's achievement must inevitably be buried beneath the debris of a universe in ruins— all these things, if not quite beyond dispute, are yet so nearly so that no philosophy which rejects them can hope to stand. Only within the

19. Huston Smith, *Forgotten Truth* (New York: Harper, 1976), pp. 6-7. Smith goes on to observe: "That the scientific outlook should, in Carl Becker's words, have 'ravished' the modern mind is completely understandable. . . . There was the sheer noetic majesty of the house pure science erected, and above all there was method. By enabling men to agree on the truth because it could be demonstrated, this method produced a knowledge that was cumulative and could advance. It did not occur because scientists were imperialists but because their achievements were so impressive, their marching orders so exhilarating, that thinkers jostled to join their ranks" (p. 7).

scaffolding of these truths, only on the firm foundation of unyielding despair can the soul's habitation henceforth be safely built.[20]

Smith, as quoted above, alludes to Death-of-God theologians. The experience of God's absence, the complaint that we are the pawns of fate, is as old as the book of Job. But the thought that God is dead is another matter. This strident slogan is first found in Nietzsche's parable of the madman who is looking for God with a lantern in broad daylight. Accusing those who mock him of having murdered God, he runs into a church to intone a requiem to the deceased deity. (See his *Fröhliche Wissenschaft,* ed. K. Schlechta, vol. II, pp. 126ff.) Thus Nietzsche put the axe to the whole tree of Western civilization.

> The position Nietzsche was affirming is viewed too narrowly if we think he is proclaiming only the death of the Christian God. He is attacking the whole Western tradition, whose metaphysics has been characterized, since Plato, by a distinction between the sensory and the super-sensory world. (H. Thielicke, *The Evangelical Faith,* vol. I, p. 25)

There have been those who have called for the brave acceptance of this ultimate finitude even in the name of theology, even in the name of Christian theology. Theologians of the death of God (see Paul van Buren, *The Secular Meaning of the Gospel,* New York: Macmillan, 1963; T. J. J. Altizer and W. Hamilton, *Radical Theology and the Death of God,* Indianapolis: Bobbs-Merrill, 1966) try to say that God's death is an "event," not just a contemporary change of attitude. Yet somehow (just how depends on who is talking) Jesus as the Christ is center stage and those who become his disciples can live with direction and hope, freely affirming their humanity and celebrating life without the stultifying tradition of a transcendent Deity, a tradition that has outlived its usefulness! But, as Kenneth Hamilton has observed (*God is Dead, The Anatomy of a Slogan,* Grand Rapids: Eerdmans, 1966, p. 71), to be human is to have a memory and the loss of what has always been remembered is the loss of the self. The death of God, therefore, is the death of the God-expert, the theologian, as well.

It is not, then, to be wondered at that the effort to do without God and yet do Christian theology proved an ephemeral enterprise. Nonetheless, the fundamental question of the divine transcendence remains at the heart of the ongoing theological discussion. Feuerbach's "all theology is anthropology" is the theological "black hole" theologians eschew lest faith become not belief in something or somebody but—in the words of Simone Weil—"fidelity to the Void." Returning from a trip to Italy, Ralph Wood observes,

> Nowhere have I ever sensed the death of God so strongly as I did at an early evening mass in the cathedral of St. Mark in Venice. Tourists were milling about in the twilight, looking up at the mosaics and then down at their guidebooks. Only a handful of nuns and elderly women were gathered in the pews, appearing more like Greek fates than worshippers of the Risen Lord.

---

20. Bertrand Russell, "A Free Man's Worship," *Mysticism and Logic* (London: Longmans, Green and Co., 1950), p. 47. In this passage Russell writes the epitaph of the human race.

A chanter of the litany had a remarkably untuneful voice and was badly out of synchronization with the organ. And a heavy jowled priest was gabbling through the mass without any apparent feeling for the mystery he was enacting. ("'Innocents Abroad' No Longer," *The Christian Century,* July 5-12, 1978, p. 677)

One is reminded of Kierkegaard's terrible warning: "Christianity may be taken away from Europe as the one way of convincing people of its truth." Wood goes on to note that such sepulchral Christianity can be found in American Protestant churches as well as European cathedrals. Before we in the West criticize the Soviets for forcibly turning their churches into museums, we should consider whether we are not doing the same thing of our own accord. (As an antidote to Death-of-God theology, one should listen to Gertrude Behanna's *God Isn't Dead!* a recording [W-3179-LP] issued by Word Records Inc., 1965, in which she tells the story of her conversion.)

2. RADICAL RESTATEMENTS OF THE DOCTRINE

The literature on God's relation to the world is large and diverse. Often in this literature it is affirmed that however transcendence may be recovered, Christian theology cannot return to the traditional dualism. To do so would be to escape into otherworldliness. In 1941 Rudolf Bultmann issued a manifesto entitled "The New Testament and Mythology."[21] In this essay he argues that to make the New Testament message relevant to moderns, we must demythologize it—that is, we must abandon the myth of a transcendent order whence God invades this present world in a supernatural and miraculous way. The language of miraculous intervention from without, of descent and ascent, with which the Jesus event is described in the New Testament, is unintelligible to modern men and women. Bultmann's point was not lost on Dietrich Bonhoeffer. Writing from his prison cell, he began to call for a "this-worldly" transcendence and a "religionless Christianity."[22] Such striking paradoxes expressed his fear that if one persists in the traditional way of thinking she makes God an irrelevant hypothesis in the modern world. For the most part, the world that has "come of age" gets on well enough without the help of such a God. In other words, the traditional God has become the God of the gaps in the world's self-understanding, a deus ex machina. The more these gaps are closed by the advance of secular understanding, the more God is forced out of the

---

21. See Rudolf Bultmann, *Kerygma and Myth,* ed. H. W. Bartsch (New York: Harper and Row, 1961), vol. I, pp. 1-44.

22. See his *Letters and Papers from Prison* (London: SCM Press, 1971), pp. 279-86.

marketplace of life into the realm of individual need and aspiration, which is the private sphere of "religion."

Bonhoeffer himself never had the opportunity to think through the implications of his position.[23] His seminal remarks, however, have inspired many efforts at a theological restatement of transcendence that, broadly speaking, may be subsumed under the category of the "theology of the secular." Such secular theology does not intend to be God-denying and materialistic; yet it does want to affirm, even to "celebrate," the demise of the so-called "Sacral Age" and to make the gospel "relevant" to the urbanized, technocratic world in which we live.

In response to this effort to do "theology from below" rather than "from above," it should be noted that it has been much easier to state the problem than to find the solution. If to speak of God as "up there" or "out there" is to use the outmoded categories of Greek dualistic thought, are the categories of modern thought necessarily more satisfactory? Bultmann prefers the thought categories of modern existentialism over what he considers to be the prescientific categories of Greek dualism. Could it be, however, that this preference really stems from his radical, historical conclusions as a New Testament critic? In any case, his historical skepticism and his resultant distrust of the gospel tradition surely seem in some measure to have contributed to his oversimplifying the problem. We say "oversimplifying" because, to give an example, it is easier to reject the account of the Ascension—"he was lifted up, and a cloud took him out of their sight" (Acts 1:9)—as making Jesus a space traveler, than it is to say how one should speak of the Ascension once it has been demythologized. Hence Bultmann is best known for his negative contribution, his *de*mythologizing program. His disciples have inherited the struggle to find a way to re-mythologize (to add another jargon word to the English language), that is, to restate the gospel message in contemporary language without losing the message altogether.

While Bultmann and others have sought to resolve the problem of transcendence existentially, Tillich has urged the substitution of the ontological language of depth for that of height when speaking of God. In his widely read book, *Honest to God,* J. A. T. Robinson, having stated the problem of transcendence with the help of Bultmann and Bonhoeffer, seeks to resolve it by appeal to this Tillichian approach. God is not "up there"

---

23. The same may be said of Teilhard de Chardin, who tried to think of the "above" in terms of the "ahead" in the "upward" evolutionary movement of history toward Omega Point. See his essay "The Heart of the Problem," Teilhard de Chardin, *The Future of Man* (New York: Harper, 1964), pp. 260-69.

or "out there"; rather, he is the "Ground of Being." Such a way of speaking is supposed to assure us, without postulating the dualism of a heaven above and an earth beneath, that Reality is not shallow. Transcendence, from such a perspective, is concerned not with another world above this world, but with the way in which this world points beyond itself as the conditioned to the Unconditioned.[24]

But, it may be asked, is the language of depth different from the language of height? Are not both spatial metaphors? If God is not "up there" beyond the range of our telescopes, is he "down there" beyond the range of our microscopes? If astrophysics has knocked the roof off the geocentric universe, has not atomic physics knocked the foundations out from under it? Unless one is willing to settle for some form of pantheism or panentheism,[25] to say that the world points "beyond" itself, as the conditioned to the Unconditioned, is to imply some sort of duality. Is then the problem with the traditional doctrine that such an approach was supposed to overcome, really overcome? Are we not back at square one?

In any case, the primary difficulty for us with "Ground of Being" as a substitute for the God who is "out there" is that it threatens the fundamental affirmation that God is personal Subject, the "I AM WHO I AM." Given a Tillichian approach, God is not a personal God who relates to a human subject as an I to a thou. Rather, God is personal only in the sense that Reality, at the deepest level, has a personal quality. Such a radical break with the traditional view of God makes prayer impossible in any traditional sense. If we update the formula "Our Father who art in heaven," with which Jesus taught his disciples to pray, by substituting "Ground of Being," we have eliminated not only the Lord's Prayer but every other traditional Christian prayer as well.[26]

24. Robinson, *Honest to God,* pp. 47, 55.

25. Panentheism, from the Greek meaning everything is *in* God, as distinct from pantheism, everything *is* God. The term was coined by C. F. Krause (1781-1832) to describe his own philosophy. Barth rejects panentheism as worse than pantheism, which it is supposed to mollify (*K.D.,* II/1, p. 351; cf. *C.D.,* II/1, sec. 28.3). For a more favorable reading see Moltmann, *The Trinity and the Kingdom,* passim. We shall return to the question of the divine immanence when treating of the doctrine of providence.

26. Robinson, in his *Honest to God,* has a chapter on "Worldly Holiness" in which he seeks to understand prayer in terms of "penetration through the world to God rather than withdrawal from the world to God." One meets the divine Thou in and through one's unconditional engagement with one's neighbor, the other human thou. The I-thou encounter at the human level *is* prayer, when the encounter is informed by love and ultimate concern (ibid., pp. 97ff.).

3. MODERATE RESTATEMENTS OF THE DOCTRINE: TRANSCENDENCE AS PERSONAL ENCOUNTER

a. Introduction

But inasmuch as Christians still do address God as "Our Father who art in heaven," inasmuch as they still do confess that they believe that Jesus Christ "ascended into heaven, . . . from thence he shall come to judge the living and the dead," how do they understand this language of transcendence and how do theologians justify its continued use?

As we seek to frame an answer to these questions, we do so with diffidence. As a translator may garble a text through a faulty translation, much more may a theologian garble the Christian message through a faulty restatement. This will surely happen if one seeks to move from the biblical message to modernity by accommodation without confrontation. In the writer's judgment, this is the problem with the various "radical" and "secular" theologies to which we have already alluded; such theologies are long on accommodation, short on confrontation. The improper balance between these two is a problem as old as Schleiermacher's *Address on Religion to Its Cultured Despisers* (1799), and as new as Harvey Cox's *The Secular City* (1965). In the cognitive trade-off with the current Weltanschauung, too often more is lost than is gained, with the result that a compromise turns out to be a capitulation. Faith becomes so reasonable that it cannot be distinguished from reason; revelation so relevant and up-to-date that it cannot be distinguished from human insight. When this happens, Christianity is turned into a new Gnosticism.

Yet the task of restatement, for all its pitfalls, cannot be avoided. It only remains to decide how best to go about it. Many theologians today seek to illumine biblical statements about God as the Holy One by appeal to "intimations" of transcendence in our human existence, intimations that point beyond the objective world of the natural sciences. Given (it is argued) that we can no longer talk about God as literally "in heaven" as we are literally "on earth," it does not follow—linguistic analysts to the contrary notwithstanding—that such speech is meaningless. To be sure, there is no experiential referent to the term "God" in the sense that there are referents for the terms scientists use when speaking of objects in the world. The theologian can point to nothing in the world when she uses the term "God," because God by definition transcends the world; he is other than the world.

Indeed, were the theologian to identify God with someone or something in the world she would be an idolater.[27]

Nonetheless, many theologians would contend, there is in the world that which in some sense transcends the world in that it looks beyond the world. Such pointers are "intimations" of an ultimate transcendence.[28] According to many, especially the realm of the personal constitutes a concrete experiential locus of meaning that transcends the world of objects with which science is concerned. Persons, unlike things, must reveal themselves in order to be known. The "thou" who stands over against "me" is always a subject beyond the reach of my observation and analysis until she speaks and so discloses herself. Here then is a reality that is truly analogical to the divine Reality, a finite experience of transcendence that models the ultimate transcendence with which the theologian is concerned.[29]

In other words, the knowledge of persons is different from the knowledge of objects, for knowledge of persons depends on what the person does who is the one known. Even if the person hides herself with misleading information, the difference between scientific and personal knowledge still prevails, since the former, unlike the latter, presupposes that things are as they appear to be and that they behave according to the objective laws of nature. But the being who can appear to be other than she really is can never be known by this scientific method. If she is to be known at all, she must declare herself; she must say who she is. Thus she who speaks discloses herself to the other, and so the other encounters her in that she hears what is spoken. This experience of encounter with another "thou" is an experience of transcendence that is not unlike the "divine/human encounter" whereby the One who is transcendent in a more ultimate way makes us aware of himself by disclosing himself to us as the divine Thou.[30]

27. Note the lead editorial, "What's Revolutionary About Idolatry?" *The Christian Century,* 6 Oct. 1965, 1211, critiquing a "contemporary" liturgy used at the Metropolitan Cathedral of Secular Issues in Chicago during the biennial General Synod of the United Church of Christ.

28. We do not have in mind the voguish fascination with astrology and various data of parapsychology—psychokinesis, ESP, precognition, séances, and the like. If, indeed, such phenomena do constitute an opening to the "beyond," it is hardly evident that one encounters through such phenomena the God who is revealed in Jesus Christ.

29. One may, of course, by observation know a great deal about another self as an object in the world. But the doctor in the emergency room who knows my sex, race, approximate age, and, with the help of medical techniques, even more about me than I know about myself, does not know *me* until I speak to her and tell her my name, that is, tell her who *I* am.

30. See Gordon Kaufman, "On the Meaning of 'God': Transcendence Without My-

b. The Position of Karl Heim

The suggestion that in the experience of human I-thou encounters we have an "intimation" of transcendence ("intramundane transcendence," as some have called it) has been probed in a suggestive way by Karl Heim.[31] Heim's analysis is especially interesting since it has to do with questions of both personal and spatial reality. Thus it focuses on the two matters central to the Christian doctrine of divine transcendence: that God is personal ("our Father"), and that he is not part of our time-space world ("our Father who art in heaven").[32]

As for the personal dimension, says Heim, it has generally been ignored by the natural sciences in the name of objectivity. The concern of science is the world that confronts the researcher with an immense panorama of objects, from subatomic particles and waves to the galactic systems that wheel in their illimitable expanse over hundreds of millions of light-years. That this objective world should hold an intense interest for science is understandable, since it bombards us constantly with an overwhelming plenitude of sense impressions. By numbering, measuring, analyzing, and classifying the objects of this natural order, science has given us an enormous body of knowledge that is controlled, objective, and precise. But what the scientist should not forget is that the entire scientific enterprise begins with the personal self, the researcher, who is there before she observes the galaxies in her telescope or the patterns of genes and chromosomes in her microscope.

As for this personal self, this "I," it is not the body with all of its complex physiology and chemistry, for the body also belongs to the objective world that can be observed and measured. I see and know my body as I see and know other "things." But I cannot see myself anymore than

---

thology," in *Transcendence*, eds. H. W. Richardson and D. R. Cutler (Boston: Beacon Press, 1969), pp. 114ff.

31. In the following summary (with our own commentary), we are principally dependent on his *Der christliche Gottesglaube und der Naturwissenschaft* (Hamburg: Furche Verlag, 1953), which has been translated as *Christian Faith and Natural Science* (New York: Harper, 1953) in the Harper Torchbook series. See also his *God Transcendent: Foundations of a Christian Metaphysics* (New York: Scribner's, 1936).

32. Heim's discussion of the divine transcendence also includes time, that is, the difference between the neutral time of space (measured objectively by seconds, minutes, etc.) and the existential time of the personal self—the "now" *(Augenblick)* of moral choice and decision that is laden with eternity. However, since the contemporary problem of the divine transcendence is concerned primarily with space, we shall take up the discussion of God's relation to time when dealing with the attribute of the divine eternity. See below, Unit Four, VI, B: God and Time, pp. 422ff.

the eye can see itself.[33] In the physical realm everything that I see (for example, a book) must be kept at a distance from the eye. So it is with the personal "I" in relation to the objective world as a whole. This objective world, which I come to know by the probing analysis of research, is a world other than me; it is ever at a distance from me. Yet at the same time I know myself, whom I cannot observe, better than I know any object "out there" that I can observe. It is true that I constantly use the language of space when speaking of myself, my ego. I may speak of myself, for example, as standing on the left side of the table since I indwell the body that is on the left side of the table. But such spatial language is not really accurate. Strictly speaking I am not on the left side of the table as my body is on the left side of the table, for I do not "dwell in" my body as a bird dwells in a cage (Plato). No surgeon's scalpel, no scanning X-ray camera, will ever locate "me" (the self, the soul) in the pineal gland (Descartes) or anywhere else "in the body."

Of course I have a unique relationship to the objective world, indeed, to a very specific part of the objective world, namely, my body. This is my destiny, and because the relationship is irrevocable, whatever happens to my body happens to me. I can never be a neutral spectator in this instance as I am when I observe what is happening to another's body. Thus I am "here" and cannot alter the fact that I am "here." I am "cast on my here" (Heidegger). That is to say, though I cannot objectify myself (for I am a person, not an object), yet I can never completely transcend the objective world. But the link that I have with the visible world leads back from that world to an invisible center, which, though not lost in the mists of the unknown (mysticism), is nonetheless beyond the reach of science. This center is the self, which is not a part of the three-dimensional world of space but rather is "outside" it, that is, prior to the experience of such a spatial world and making the experience of such a world possible.

Besides the experience of this "I-it" relation, I also experience an "I-thou" relation. Even as I am not an object, so I am not you. To be an "I" excludes me from occupying the place of the other, "the ever strange thou" (Griesbach). Unlike the classic Idealists, we have come to see (with the help of Ebner, Buber, and others) that the "I" not only stands over against the objective world of things, but she also coexists with another self, the "thou"— indeed, with many other selves. This relationship to other selves further confirms the truth of a transcendent reality beyond the objective world of three-dimensional space and therefore beyond the realm of natural science.

---

33. "I cannot *see* myself; I can only *be* myself." Heim, *God Transcendent*, p. 80. His italics.

It might be objected — contra Heim — that this is not the case, for the Transcendent must always be in the singular. If the ego is not sole, if it has number, if there are many egos (selves), then the ego loses its uniqueness and becomes like all other entities having number, susceptible of generic description and behaving according to the inviolable laws of the objective world.

In response, we would admit that at one level this objection is true. That is why we may speak of psychology and sociology as the human sciences. They are human sciences because they are concerned with human beings, and human beings are not wholly transcendent but exist objectively in the world. As I am tied to the objective world by my body, so I am limited in the personal realm by my neighbor who exists objectively over against me. Yet the "intimation of transcendence," the "otherness" of the personal dimension remains, even though such objective selves are many and not one. This can be seen from the fact that no psychological or social determinist can predict future human behavior as astronomers can predict eclipses. (Indeed, when appearing in court, psychiatrists and sociologists cannot even agree on the explanation of past human behavior that is fixed and definite.) But this is not because they are faulty scientists; rather, it is because the "objects" of their science are more than "objects" and hence their science cannot be wholly "objective" and therefore wholly "scientific."

As the relation of the self to the objective world is mysterious, so also is the relation of the self to other selves. In the former instance, I am "cast on my here" in that I have a body. In the latter instance I am bounded by the existence of the other. I can never place the world as I experience it alongside the world as you experience it, as I might place two pictures alongside each other to decide which is more beautiful. Nor are my world and your world adjacent as two rooms in a house so that I (and you) may pass from one to the other at will to determine similarities and differences. I am the person that I am even as you are the person you are, and therefore your world is closed to me even as mine is to you. My world is a self-contained, unbroken continuum—as is yours. It embraces all that is in the objective world of three-dimensional space from galaxies to quarks—as does yours. But we can never say that we see the same world without adding, "from different perspectives."

There is, then, no wall of partition where your world ceases and mine begins. We are talking about the same world so far as objects in space are concerned. Yet we are talking about different worlds so far as the nonobjectifiable realm of the personal observer is concerned. This difference is expressed by the term "will," which has no objective referent in the world of things. Yet, though the will be nonobjectifiable, it is more directly known than all its objective effects in the "real" world. The will is the particular form of the ego "beyond" the realm of objects; the will is "where" the I encounters the thou. The struggle of the I with the thou in the effort to shape the molten present before it becomes the frozen past is the manifestation of will. So the cognitive-volitional self, the I, stands not only over against the objective world of things but also over against the personal world of the cognitive-volitional thou. Thus I remain forever in my world as you remain in yours. For the self, then, the world of the other is unapproachably "far off" and at the same time "near at hand."

Such paradoxical language (how can a world be both "far off" and "near at hand" at one and the same time?) shows that we need other terms when distinguishing between the personal worlds of the I and the thou than those we use when distinguishing objects within the spatial world of the scientist. But what might those other terms be? What word or words might we use? The term that Heim uses is Griesbach's "dimension" or "dimensional boundary." To speak of a dimensional boundary between the personal world of the I and the impersonal world of the object, or between the personal world of the I and the personal world of the thou, reflects a radical change in the way of perceiving reality. It is to perceive that there are fundamentally different modes of being than that of the three-dimensional, spatial reality with which science is concerned.

Naturally, because we are mysteriously bound to the objective world through our bodies—I am "here" and you are "there" — and because this objective world bombards us on every side through the senses, it is easier for us to recognize those differences which are differences of spatial content (two chairs in a room) than those differences which are differences of dimensional polarity (two selves "in" a room).[34] Yet the ease with which we recognize the differences of spatial content does not imply that our perception of dimensional differences is an illusion. If such perception is not illusory, then we ought, along with the language we have traditionally used, to be open to other language that will help clarify the meaning behind our traditional language.

As for traditional language, since in one and the same space there are many objects, from the furniture in the room to the stars in the sky, and all these objects are distinguished from each other by their location in space, we can understand why, traditionally, theologians have spoken, and laypersons have thought, of the divine realm spatially. But when we speak of this transcendent realm of the divine reality in this spatial way, we speak as though we were describing something contained in one and the same space with objects in the world. That is why for many moderns our pre-Copernican vocabulary has become largely unintelligible. We need, therefore, to clarify the spatial-sound-

34. Of course, "polarity" is also a term drawn from the objective world. It designates the condition inherent in bodies that attract each other while exhibiting opposite or contrasting properties. Heim obviously uses it, in this discussion, analogically.

ing prepositions we use—"above," "over," "beyond," "outside" — when we use them of the realm (dimension) of the divine transcendence.

Up to now about all we could do was use this language as a serviceable metaphor and try to convey its new meaning by raising it to infinity.[35] But though we magnify the difference between God and ourselves to the utmost we are still in the same plane that marks one object as distinct from another. This interchange of essentially noninterchangeable kinds of relationships, this speaking of realities that are dimensionally different as though they were spatially related, is the origin of the symbolical imagery in human language with all its limitations and inadequacies. Furthermore, literally to conceive the doctrine of the divine transcendence in such spatial categories, as though God were occupying the upper story of a single cosmic space, would entail a Deistic denial of the divine immanence.[36]

But if there is an I-thou space (dimension) that cannot be reduced to the three-dimensional space of objects, why should there not be a space (dimension) of the divine Reality that cannot be reduced to our personal space as human? (Heim often uses the term "space" as a synonym for "dimension" in an effort to speak the language of science.) Such space might be called "suprapolar" space. The qualifying adjective "suprapolar," when used of such space, conveys the thought that God's "space" contrasts with our space in that God is not subject to the limitations (the polarities) of our space; that is, he is not limited to a "here" in contrast to a "there."

Further to clarify his argument, Heim uses illustrations drawn from the world of modern physics and mathematics. Contemporary physics has undergone a far-reaching transformation in its conception of space. Traditionally it was assumed, following Euclid, that the shortest distance between two points is a straight line. Such an axiom was considered to be true, a priori; Kant even argued that it was a part of the structure of the mind, something we bring to the data of sense perception. Now, however, it appears that space is curved, though this curvature is measurable only over vast distances. If this is so, then geometry is an experimental science, in which case there can be more than one kind of geometry, each of which is valid in its own space. The appropriate geometry depends upon the kind of space one is working with. If one is working with

---

35. Heim has in mind not only such traditional phrases as "highest heaven" but also "absolute qualitative difference" (Kierkegaard); "perpendicular from above" (Barth); "parabola tangent at a point," that is, at the point of the Jesus event (Brunner), etc. Such metaphors, Heim concedes, are not wholly misleading, for they do describe a distinction, whether literally between objects in the ordinary world or figuratively between God and the world. The difficulty is that this latter distinction is really another kind of distinction: it is not a spatial distinction but a dimensional one.

36. This can be seen from the obvious fact that if God is far from us in a spatial sense—in a high and holy place literally—then he cannot be near to us in one and the same spatial sense—with us literally as we gather in a given place to worship.

curved space, then the shortest distance between two points is not a straight line but the straightest possible line, which is the arc of a circle. So we are confronted with a concept of space that is much more comprehensive than Euclid's axioms allow. In fact, it is now possible to conceive many spaces of which Euclid's three-dimensional space is only one particular type. Of course, we cannot visualize such spaces, but our inability to "picture in our minds" such spaces does not mean that they do not exist.

At this juncture Heim appeals to a novel, *Flatland, a Romance of Many Dimensions* (1884; 4th ed., Oxford, 1932), written by the Englishman Edwin Abbott under a pseudonym (A. Square) and published thirty years before Einstein advocated his theory of relativity. Mathematicians like Abbott anticipated developments in physics. Riemannian geometry, for example, was ready at hand when Einstein needed it, an astounding coincidence, to say the least. In his novel the author likens us earth dwellers, as we try to imagine spaces having more than Euclid's three dimensions, to the inhabitants of a fictional world called Flatland. Flatlanders can picture how points become lines when they are moved straight ahead and how the lines become squares when, in turn, they are moved sideways. Thus they can easily get from Pointland to Lineland to their own Flatland; the more complex reality includes the simpler. But the thought that a square can become a cube by moving points upward is just too much for Flatlanders to visualize. They therefore reject it as heresy. To picture such a figure in the mind one needs to dwell in Spaceland—as we do.

But there is no logical (mathematical) reason that we Spacelanders should feel so superior as to assume that our Land represents the end of all spatial possibilities. If beyond Pointland there is Lineland, and beyond Lineland Flatland, and beyond Flatland Spaceland, then there may well be other lands beyond Spaceland, and indeed mathematics and modern physics indicate that there are such lands. Hence, we have another "intimation" of transcendence, an opening to a reality beyond the reality we ordinarily perceive as we observe the world of objects in three-dimensional space. If there are spaces (i.e., "dimensions") beyond our three-dimensional space, then who is to say that there can be no structures of reality other than those accessible to the empirical sciences? May it not be that even as one who dwells in three-dimensional space does not know the limitations of a Flatlander, so there is a God who does not know the limitations of a Spacelander? The modern secularist, for whom all reality is the objective reality of three-dimensional space as seen in the telescope and microscope, is like a Flatlander; she lives in a shallow world and identifies all Reality with her own reality. At bottom, according to Heim, there are only two views of reality: one is the view of a consistent and mature secularism (naturalism and materialism); the other, belief in the living, personal God, Creator of heaven and earth. These two views cannot be brought together by any compromise or synthesis. They confront one with the ultimate either/or.

> Secularism, to be consistent, must necessarily attack the belief in suprapolar space as being purely illusory. It must therefore entirely reject all such words as God, eternity, conscience, ethics, . . . guilt, responsibility, repentance, forgiveness and atonement, as inadmissible borrowings from a view of the world opposed to its own. It must strike such words out of its vocabulary, as foreign bodies stemming from a different general picture of reality in which alone they possess a meaning. For as soon as even one of these words is

uttered, we find ourselves in the midst of suprapolar space, so that all the relations in which we live and think are brought into a new light and all these fundamental words which pertain to the space of God come into force simultaneously all along the line. . . . This is in itself sufficient to explain why, in a nation in which the controlling authorities live in polar space, people whose lives are grounded in theism can be treated as criminals and traitors. (Heim, *Christian Faith and Natural Science*, pp. 231-32)

This last remark had definite "existential" meaning for Heim and his initial readers, who had lived as confessing Christians in a Nazi state.

To say that God dwells in another space (dimension) from our three-dimensional space is not to say that he is far removed from our space, transcendent in a deistic sense. God is not separated *from* the world as two objects are separated *in* the world. God and the world are not separated as, for example, a ship is separated from the remote stars that guide its navigator. All such objects, though separated from each other, are really separated in the world. But God is not in the world; therefore he is not near to some objects in the world and far from others. Though he is distinct from all his creation, he is near to all, for all spaces (dimensions) interpenetrate one another.[37]

True, we cannot visualize how the divine dimension (suprapolar space) interpenetrates the structures of our spatial reality as we can visualize the interpenetration of two-dimensional space by three-dimensional space when perpendicular planes intersect each other. But neither can we visually represent the way in which the "I" dimension ("consciousness space") interpenetrates the "it" dimension of three-dimensional space, even though we cannot doubt the interpenetration, since our own bodies are in such space. Nothing is nearer to me than my own hands and feet (except God), yet for all this proximity I cannot be reduced to an "it." While "I" am limited by the three-dimensional, objective world—and God is not—I cannot be reduced to that world, for I am not an object but a person. (I remain I even though I lose my hands and feet.) In this respect my intramundane (limited) transcendence as a personal self is analogous to God's supramundane (unlimited) transcendence as the Personal Self, the "I AM" who creates and upholds all other selves and all other objects, whatever the structures of their reality may be.

---

37. Here Heim uses the verbs *durchdringen* and *hindurchgehen*. He also speaks of suprapolar space as "embracing" *(übergreifend)* all other spaces. See his *Glaube und Denken*, pp. 92-93. Of course such language, in its literal meaning, is that of three-dimensional space. But see above, Unit One, III, Speaking of God, pp. 25ff.

The question naturally arises: If it is true that our human creaturely reality—our dimension, our space—is interpenetrated by the divine Reality, so that in fact "we live and move and have our being" in God (Acts 17:28), how do we become aware of this truth? Is there any key at hand whereby we may be delivered from the prison of three-dimensional space in which the secularist mind would incarcerate us? Few theologians would find this key in some sort of reasoned demonstration. Indeed, God would not be truly transcendent if we could grasp him at the end of a syllogism, any more than he would be if we could see him beyond the farthest galaxy. Rather, as it is at the human level so it is here: the human "I" can know the divine "Thou" only when the latter speaks and so discloses himself. Of course, at the human level the conversation may begin with either party, for both alike are human persons. But in the case of the divine, the conversation must begin with God; he must speak the first word, for we live, move, and have our being in him, not he in us. To use the language of Heim, God's "space" interpenetrates ours, not ours his. As Flatlanders can know of those who dwell in three-dimensional space only when Spacelanders disclose themselves to them, so we who are Spacelanders can know of him who dwells in suprapolar space only when he discloses himself to us.

While it is true that there are "intimations" of the divine transcendence in our human reality, only God himself can so speak, so testify to himself, that all our doubt is overcome in certainty. The path to God may be disclosed to us in those "intimations" of a Reality that is other than the reality of time and space, yet only God can give us the assurance to walk down that path. But when one does walk down that path, a new light falls on all reality. It is as when one studies Manet's famous *Bridge over the Thames*. At first it appears as a two-dimensional surface splashed over with color.

> Then suddenly part of the surface retreats into the haze and there stands out in the foreground the arch of a bridge lighted up by the morning sun and passing over it in the early light men and women, horses and carriages. The change from two dimensions to three does not take place through any change in the lines and colors. In both cases the colors and figures are the same. The change takes place because we ourselves begin to see the same colors and figures in three, instead of two, dimensions.[38]

It is the divine inbreaking into one's consciousness (the "new birth") that accounts for this all-transforming, in-depth change in one's perception. Such a change can never be brought about by rational argument or empirical

38. Heim, *God Transcendent,* p. 74.

observation. If it could, then it could also be explained by such a rational and empirical approach and so reduced to one of the many possibilities of self-understanding open to us apart from the "God hypothesis." Furthermore, when this change takes place, one looks no longer "to the things that are seen [in three-dimensional space] but to the things that are unseen; for the things that are seen are transient [even stars die], but the things that are unseen are eternal" (2 Cor. 4:18). And what (or who) are these unseen realities? The straightforward answer is: God and those in his heavenly court, the "cherubim and seraphim who continually do cry, Holy, Holy, Holy, . . . the glorious company of the apostles, . . . the goodly fellowship of the prophets, . . . the noble army of martyrs," . . . and all his "saints in glory everlasting," of which the church has sung in the *Te Deum* down through the ages.

It was this vision of ultimate Reality that enabled Moses to endure "as seeing him who is invisible" (Heb. 11:27). The biblical writers did not have the conceptual tools to work out the implications of their thought about God and his relation to the world in terms of personal and impersonal dimensions with different spatial structures. Yet they speak of God in a way that is consonant with such an approach. Even as far back as the dedication of the original temple, God is addressed as the God who said of the house that Solomon built, "My name [i.e., I myself] shall be there" (1 Kgs. 8:29). Yet the prayer of dedication opens with the rhetorical question, "Will God indeed dwell on the earth?" Of course not! Hence, the very prayer addressed to the God who dwells "there" (in the temple) includes the repeated request, "Hear from heaven your dwelling place" (vv. 30, 32, 34, 36, 39, 43, 45, 49). Yet God is not even in heaven as we are on earth. The same prayer, therefore, solemnly acknowledges, "Behold, heaven and the highest heaven cannot contain thee; how much less this house which I have built" (v. 27). So God is both "there" in his temple and also "in heaven," though contained in neither an earthly house nor the highest heaven.

It is evident, then, that the authors of Scripture do not speak of God as dwelling "on Mt. Zion" or "in heaven" in the same sense that Homer spoke of Zeus and the lesser gods as dwelling on Mt. Olympus. If they had, Yahweh and his hosts long since would have suffered the fate of the Titans and Olympiads. Rather, God, who is our Father, is worshipped neither on Mt. Gerizim nor Mt. Zion but in spirit and truth (Jn. 4:20-21).[39] In other words,

---

39. Because the biblical writers think of God as present in all spaces (dimensions) yet limited by none, we can understand why they could use the language of three-dimensional space and speak of Christ as having ascended "into heaven" (Acts 1:9-11), as having sat down "at the right hand of the Majesty on High" (Heb. 1:3); and at the same time reject as superstition the Greek notion that God dwells in temples made with human hands (Acts 17:22ff.), a fact that John A. T. Robinson finds "remarkable." See his *Honest to God,* p. 11.

God is not limited, as we Spacelanders are, by the polarity of here *or* there. Hence, he can be here searching "out my path and my lying down"; and there, even "if I ascend to heaven" or "make my bed in Sheol" (Ps. 139). He is the Holy One and therefore he can say, "I dwell in the high and holy place and also with him who is of a contrite and humble spirit" (Is. 57:15). This "and also" is the crucial matter. It tells us that God's space is suprapolar—to use the language of our discussion. His is a "space" that knows the limits neither of the objective space of inanimate objects nor of the personal space of human subjects. God's presence is not a here or a there, but a here (with the contrite) and a there (in a high and lofty place).

Hence, the authors of Scripture are not in the least troubled by the paradox throughout their writings that God is the God who is distinguished from all creation by an infinite, qualitative difference, yet never remote from that creation but everywhere present to it. The God of Scripture is both the "God at hand" and also the God who is "afar off" (Jer. 23:23-24). He is the God who "fills heaven and earth," yet who is not contained in heaven or earth. He is the Holy (transcendent) One. *Every sentence in the Bible and in dogmatics assumes this divine transcendence. At the same time he is "the Holy One in our midst." Every sentence in the Bible and in dogmatics assumes this divine immanence.* Were he not in our midst as the *Holy One* he would one day cease to be in our midst, for what is seen is temporal, but he who is unseen is eternal. Were he not the Holy One who is in our midst, he would be the Unknown God whom the Athenians ignorantly worshipped (Acts 17:22-23).

ADDENDUM: CONCERNING APOPHATIC THEOLOGY

Pseudo-Dionysius, in his influential treatise *De divinis nominibus (On the Divine Names),* turned the thought that God transcends our being as creatures into the thought that he transcends our understanding as human. As a result, we can say nothing of God as he is in himself. Hence, the best we can do is to speak of God in negatives, though he is really not only beyond affirmation but beyond negation as well. Our knowledge of God is but a "knowing ignorance." Silence thus becomes the fitting expression

---

It also helps to explain why persons like Sayers, Lewis, and Phillips have been so successful in presenting the Christian drama of salvation while using the spatial language of a God "up there" who "comes to earth" to redeem us. Robinson (*Honest to God,* p. 15) attributes this success to "a ready made public for whom this whole frame of reference still presents no difficulties . . ." even though it is a picture of God ". . . coming to earth like some visitor from outer space. . . ." But it is no such picture. The God who comes from outer space is already in space, that is, in our three-dimensional space.

of our relation to him, for he cannot be comprehended; he can only be contemplated in the mystic vision that is beyond all rational affirmation. Of course theologians, including Dionysius, have continued to talk about God. Dionysius himself spoke not only of the *via negationis,* which denies of God all the limitations of the creature, but also of the *via eminentiae,* which ascribes to God all the perfections found in the creature, heightened to an infinite degree. Though it has been influential in both Catholic and Protestant scholasticism, many theologians in more recent times have deplored this method of negating and at the same time heightening human qualities when speaking of God. Such an approach, it is alleged, leaves us with a God who in himself is a bare essence, and such a view is a denial of the God revealed in Jesus Christ. Deriving its impetus from Neoplatonism rather than biblical revelation, such an approach results in a metaphysic of being rather than in a biblical theology. Instead of confronting us with the God of creation and salvation, it makes God the coordinate of our experienced reality. Thus we end up with a theology of the "nameless God," whereas the name of God is a basic theme of the biblical revelation on which that theology is supposedly based!

*   *   *   *   *

Speaking of the "nameless God," in the vision of the mystic the divine transcendence is often experienced as Overwhelming Power whose reflex is the feeling of sinking into nothingness, of becoming dust and ashes. Such an experience leads to the assimilation of the self into the Other and the exaltation of the Transcendent as the sole, all-encompassing Reality. Such a Reality, like the nameless God of Dionysius, is beyond words. As Faust said to Margaret,

> Fill up your heart with it, great though it is,
> And when you're wholly in the feeling, in its bliss,
> Name it then as you will,
> Name it Happiness! Heart! Love! God!
> I have no name for that!
> Feeling is all in all;
> Name is but sound and smoke
> Beclouding Heaven's glow.[40]

In Christian theology, on the other hand, "name" is everything, for there is no other name under heaven . . . by which we must be saved (Acts 4:12).

---

40. Goethe, *Faust,* Great Books, vol. 47, ed. R. M. Hutchins (Chicago: Britannica, 1952), p. 84.

A Fire and a Name

A Sermon Preached by Marguerite Shuster
at Arcadia Presbyterian Church, Arcadia, California,
Lord's Day, November 30, 1986

And the angel of the LORD *appeared to him in a flame of fire out of the midst of a bush; and he looked, and lo, the bush was burning, yet it was not consumed. And Moses said, "I will turn aside and see this great sight, why the bush is not burnt." When the* LORD *saw that he turned aside to see, God called to him out of the bush, "Moses, Moses!" And he said, "Here am I." Then he said, "Do not come near; put off your shoes from your feet, for the place on which you are standing is holy ground." . . . Moses said to God, "If I come to the people of Israel and say to them, 'The God of your fathers has sent me to you,' and they ask me, 'What is his name?' what shall I say to them?" God said to Moses, "I AM WHO I AM." And he said, "Say this to the people of Israel, 'I AM has sent me to you.'" God also said to Moses, "Say to the Israelites, 'The* LORD, *the God of your fathers, the God of Abraham, the God of Isaac and the God of Jacob, has sent me to you': this is my name forever, and thus I am to be remembered throughout all generations."*

Exodus 3:2-5, 13-15 (RSV)

November 30: the first Sunday in the Christian year, the first Sunday in the season of Advent, when we recall—and anticipate once again—God coming to be among us. God, among us. What in the world are we daring to say when we say that? On the face of it the whole idea is preposterous, like the cartoon I have in front of me. Dennis the Menace stands at his easel, diligently drawing away with his crayons. His mother stands in the background, throwing up her hands and inquiring, "How can you draw a picture of God? Nobody knows what he looks like." In the next frame Dennis replies confidently, "They will now."

Or perhaps you remember the story, no doubt apocryphal, that Dr. Ian Pitt-Watson told from this pulpit some five years ago about the six-year-old Scottish youngster from Aberdeen. One morning his Sunday school teacher was waxing particularly eloquent on the theme that God is everywhere (a theme hard enough for adults, much less six-year-olds, to conceive). The boy came home and began querying his mother, asking first if God were in Scotland. Now, if you know Scottish Presbyterians, you will perceive that answering this question in the affirmative was easy, for however much Scots may seek to affirm the incredible reach of God's mercy to other lands and peoples, they are quite sure that he himself is a Scottish Calvinist. The boy went on, "Is God in Aberdeen?" "Yes," came the confident reply. "Is God in this house?" "Yes, indeed." "Is he in this very room?" "Yes, he is." Looking around, the boy saw a hinged, wooden box on the coffee table and pressed his inquiry. Picking up the box, its top open, he asked, "Is God in this box?" Unwilling to go against logic, his mother affirmed, "Yes, he is." Immediately the boy snapped the lid shut, and said with delight, "I've got him!"

We laugh at these stories precisely because, if we know anything at all about God, we know that we cannot neatly capture him, in boxes or pictures or concepts (or, for that matter, in sermons!). We know that if God is God, he is *transcendent,* somehow above and beyond the limits of our world and our ideas. Since it is by definition beyond us, transcendence is a pretty difficult thing to talk about, so difficult that sometimes people argue that it can only be described negatively, that is, by saying that God is not visible (despite Dennis's drawing), not changeable, not limited by space or time, and so forth. Those things are true enough, of course. Today, however, I want to talk about transcendence positively and about God as the Holy One.

First a caution. In our day and age, when we hear the word "holy" we tend to think in moral or ethical terms. To be holy in the ethical sense is to be good and pure and righteous. When we speak of God as holy in that sense, we mean that he is not compromised by sin, as we are. Speaking that way is perfectly proper, as we can see, for instance, from Leviticus 11:45, where we read, "You shall be holy, for I am holy." We more or less understand that verse, even if we cannot fulfill its demand. We know that we should be better than we are. The duty may be beyond our power to accomplish, but it isn't wholly mysterious. If we tremble at this verse, we tremble more because of our sin than because of our ignorance or finitude. We know what the word "holy" means.

Or do we? Turn to verse 5 of my text, where God says to Moses from out of the burning bush, "Do not come near; put off your shoes from your feet, for the place on which you are standing is *holy* ground." Holy *ground?* How can ground be holy? And why the warning to keep one's distance? Something funny is going on here, something quite different from our nice, tame, everyday ideas about holiness, something that leaves us uneasy and even a little afraid.

The feeling of uneasiness, of awe, is fully justified, for the ethical meaning of the term "holy" is derivative and secondary. A quite different meaning is more fundamental. The holy in its primary sense is the mysterious sphere of the divine power, which can easily be perceived as not only superior, but also threatening and urgent and wholly incalculable. The divine power is a transcendent power, and the holy God is a transcendent God, marked by majesty, glory, sovereignty, and unfathomable mystery, by an absolute difference from the whole created order. To the presumption that would seek to approach him he says, "Do not get too close." Anything so much as associated with the holy God, even the ground, becomes holy, not because of some quality in itself, but simply by its relationship to him. And thus we have the roots of the separation of the sacred and the profane or secular realms.

The point here, however, is not the fact that religious practices themselves have their root in attempts to separate the holy from the profane, to prevent the holy from being polluted by the profane. That is true enough, but our current purpose is rather to point out the experience of inexplicable awe that leads to the sense of holiness in the first place. That awe cannot be known by the mere spectator, observing from a safe distance, or the philosopher or theologian interested only in the theory of holiness. It is known, rather, by direct involvement and confrontation with what is beyond one. Short of personal experience, we get our best "feel" for holiness in its primary meaning from literature.

Take this example from *The Wind in the Willows:*

> Rat and Mole were looking for Portly, a baby otter who had gotten lost. They were transfixed by the unearthly music of the "piper at the gates of dawn," the animal's god Pan. They made their way toward the source of the music.
>
> "Then suddenly Mole felt a great Awe fall upon him, an awe that turned his muscles to water, bowed his head, and rooted his feet to the ground. It was no panic terror—indeed he felt wonderfully at peace and happy—but it was an awe that smote and held him and,

without seeing, he knew that it could only mean that some august Presence was very, very near."

Finally the Mole dared to look up, and found himself in the presence of "the Friend and Helper," with whom, safe and content, was the baby otter.

"Rat!" he found breath to whisper, shaking. "Are you afraid?"

"Afraid?" murmured the Rat, his eyes shining with unutterable love.

"Afraid of *Him?* O, never never! And yet—and yet—O Mole, I am afraid."[1]

The description is of a "pagan" experience, but it well conveys the tone of the experience of the holiness of the biblical God.

Similarly, the familiar passage from C. S. Lewis's *The Lion, the Witch and the Wardrobe,* where Mrs. Beaver speaks about the story's Christ-figure Aslan. She says,

"If there's anyone who can appear before Aslan without their knees knocking, they're either braver than most or else just silly."

"Then he isn't safe?" said Lucy.

"Safe?" said Mr. Beaver. "Don't you hear what Mrs. Beaver tells you? Who said anything about safe? 'Course he isn't safe. But he's good. He's the King, I tell you." (Pp. 75-76)

He's the *King.* One feels fear and one's knees knock. Safe? Of course not. The transcendent God will not be tamed and made safe by us. He is the Holy One to whom no one approaches too closely. So we come back to my text. "Do not come near," says God from the bush; "And Moses hid his face, for he was afraid to look at God."

Note, too, the significance of the fact that the voice of the transcendent God comes from a *burning* bush. Throughout Scripture, fire is a symbol of holiness. The appearances of God, for instance on Mt. Sinai, where "the LORD descended . . . in fire" (Ex. 19:18), characteristically have fire as a central element. Similarly in Habakkuk (3:4): "His brightness was like the light, rays flashed from his hand, and there he veiled his power." The manifestation of God's judgment is also in fire, as we see in Zephaniah's (1:18) description of the Day of the Lord: "In the fire of his jealous wrath, all the earth shall be consumed." The seraphim, whose name means "fiery ones," are they who sing "holy, holy, holy"

---

1. As quoted by Robert McAfee Brown, *The Bible Speaks to You* (Philadelphia: Westminster Press, 1955), p. 54.

before Yahweh's throne in Isaiah, and one touches the prophet's lips with a burning coal. And the author of the letter to the Hebrews says, "Our God is a consuming fire." These examples are a mere sampling of those that could be provided.[2]

In a sense, fire is a perfectly natural symbol for God's holiness. We think of our fascination with fire, its mysteriousness, the fear we have of its power. We can describe with chemical formulas what happens during combustion, but the formulas leave untouched the hold that dancing flames have upon us. Fire warms us from its place in our fireplace; it terrifies us when it sweeps across a brush-laden hillside toward our homes. It is used for refining and purifying—here we see the ethical meaning of holiness developing naturally with the symbol—but we don't necessarily want to lose everything it burns away. Both of these elements have to do with fire as a natural phenomenon in our world, elements that make it a meaningful pointer to something beyond itself.

However, God isn't satisfied with meaningful natural pointers. The fire in Exodus 3 is also a supernatural pointer. Everybody knows that fire burns, and consumes, bushes. That's obvious, and though it's sometimes frightening, it is not news. So we label it "natural" and pretend we've explained it. But what do we say about a fire that burns a bush and does not consume it? Here God breaks through the limits of our human experience and refuses to be bound either by the natural order itself or even by a splendid natural symbol. He will not stay neatly confined in any of our little boxes.

When we call him the Holy One, the transcendent God, we mean to say that our categories fail to capture him and our symbols fail to encompass him. If we use fire to point to holiness, he shows himself in a fire that doesn't quite behave properly. If we use the metaphor of height to suggest that he is "above" us in the heavens, we yet know of a certainty that we are no closer to him in a spacecraft than Jonah was while residing in the great fish. We have to use our language and the elements of our world to talk about God; there is no alternative other than remaining silent. But as soon as we slip into thinking our language is adequate to God's reality, we are quite simply worshipping an idol.

Well then, what next? If there is no way we can search out God by our efforts; if God himself warns us to back off if we get too presumptuously buddy-buddy with him—and incidentally, I do think the modern idea

---

2. On the symbolism of fire, see below, this Unit, III, Addendum: The Divine Wrath and the Symbolism of Fire, pp. 252ff.

of our being God's "partners" is presumptuous—what then? Do we *hide* our faces with Moses, or what *do* we do?

That is the wrong question. The right question, the one that my text answers, is not "What do *we* do?" but "What does *God* do?" And the answer is, he gives us his name. We cannot reach up into the sphere of the transcendent God, but he can reach down into our sphere, just as a plane, a two-dimensional figure, will not contain a cube; but every cube, a three-dimensional figure, has two-dimensional components.

What does it mean that God gives us his name? Well, for one thing, it makes clear that he is a personal God, not a cosmic force or abstract principle like "progress." His transcendence is not so much like that of a mindless power bigger and stronger than we are as it is like the transcendence of another person. Even on our human level, we get to know one another only as we give ourselves to one another and share the mystery of what is inside us. You may draw some conclusions about me by watching what I do and how I do it, but you don't really know me unless I tell you about myself. And even when I do, a part of me—like a part of each of you—remains hidden and inaccessible. Well, God's transcendence is as much greater than yours or mine as the fire of the burning bush was greater than ordinary fire; but it is a personal, not an impersonal, transcendence.

Second, in giving his name God gives us a sort of power with respect to himself. In Scripture, God's name is used almost as a double of his being. The second commandment says we shall not take God's name in vain. In the Lord's Prayer we pray, "Hallowed [or holy] be thy name." In giving his name God gives himself, as he later does supremely in the person of Jesus Christ, who, in turn, is given "the name which is above every name, that at the name of Jesus every knee should bow, in heaven and on earth and under the earth" (Phil. 2:9-10). He is the King.

But again, we can find an analogy from our human experience of the linkage of our name and our person. If some stranger's name is shouted over the loudspeaker at the airport, we can seldom so much as recognize what name was spoken. But if it is our name, it takes hold of us and commands our attention, almost against our will. Similarly, the remarks of Frederick Buechner—a man with a strangely spelled and oddly pronounced handle—about his name:

> If somebody mispronounces it in some foolish way, I have the feeling
> that what's foolish is me. If somebody forgets it, I feel that it's I who
> am forgotten. . . . I can't imagine myself with any other name—Held,
> say, or Merrill, or Hlavacek. If my name were different, I would be
> different. When I tell somebody my name, I have given him a hold

over me that he didn't have before. If he calls it out, I stop, look, and listen whether I want to or not.

In the Book of Exodus, God tells Moses that his name is Yahweh, and God hasn't had a peaceful moment since.[3]

A name in its own meaning also often says something about the person named. Jacob means "Usurper." Isaac means "Laughter." Yahweh means— what? The divine name is often enigmatically translated "I AM WHO I AM," as it is in the version before you. And certainly we get the picture from the context that while God is answering Moses' inquiry, he is not exactly fully satisfying his curiosity. He certainly is not putting himself unqualifiedly in Moses' power, to be used for Moses' plans. It is Yahweh's plans for Moses that are really at issue, not the reverse. And in that context, the real thrust of the divine name is most probably something like, "I will be there for you." Yahweh says, "I have seen the affliction of my people . . . I know their sufferings. . . . I have seen the oppression (vv. 7ff.)." So in commissioning Moses to deliver the people, he won't abandon Moses to his own devices, but rather he will be there for him and his people. God declines to give mere information about himself, to give Moses—or us— the illusion that we understand him. Instead, his self-disclosure is combined with a call for commitment; his invitation to trust him and obey him is combined with a promise of his presence.

Who is it, again, who gives himself? It is the King. It is he before whom we tremble and are afraid. It is he whose mystery we cannot penetrate and whose power we cannot fathom. It is the transcendent God, the Holy One. He of the fire—an unearthly fire that burns but does not consume— he of the fire gives us his name—and, later, his Son, the truth we celebrate as we gather around his table set before us at the beginning of this Advent season.

---

3. *Wishful Thinking* (New York: Harper & Row, 1973), p. 12.

Who knows not love, let him assay
And taste that juice which, on the cross a pike
Did set again abroach; then let him say
If ever he did taste the like.
Love is that liquor sweet
and most divine,
Which my God feels as blood,
but I as wine.

George Herbert, *The Agonie*

III. God Is Love

A. INTRODUCTION

The God who is the Holy One is the God who is in our midst as Love. We must now probe the meaning of the apostle John's remarkable statement: God *is* Love (1 Jn. 4:8). The paradox in our doctrine of the divine nature becomes evident at once. Holiness speaks of God's transcendence, his otherness, his remoteness from us; love, of his immanence, his giving of himself to us. The one affirmation is distance-making, the other distance-breaking. Yet the authors of Scripture never think of God's holiness and love as mutually exclusive; they rather view them as mutually inclusive. Not that God's holiness and love are ultimately synonymous; to say that God is the Holy One and that he is Love is not to speak in tautologies. But his holiness and love encompass each other, contain and comprise each other in a mysterious embrace. Hence for the prophet Isaiah, the divine purpose in Israel's judgment is salvation! It is as the Holy One who judges Israel that God becomes Israel's Redeemer and Savior (Is. 41:14; 43:3; 47:4).

What is true for Isaiah is true for the prophets in general. This is especially the case with the prophet Hosea. The text we have so often quoted when speaking of divine transcendence—"I am God and no mortal, the Holy One in your midst" (Hos. 11:9 NRSV)—is a text whose larger context is the love of God. It was Hosea who saw more clearly than most that the love of God was the fundamental reality in God's dealings with his people. What but the divine love could explain the abiding relationship of a holy God with a sinful people like Israel? Living in a time when the whole structure of official religion had collapsed, the prophet realized that only the power of God's incomparable love kept Israel in existence. Having loved Israel from childhood, having called her out of Egypt, having taught Ephraim to walk, having led her with the bands of love, he loves her still. Though she remain bent on turning away from him, though she sacrifice to the Baals and burn incense to idols, he cannot give her up, he cannot hand her over, he cannot make her like Admah nor treat her like Zeboiim. His heart recoils within him at the very prospect; his compassion grows warm and tender. Therefore he will not execute his fierce anger nor destroy Ephraim (Hos. 11:1-9).

Here we behold the marvel of an agonizing deity, a God who can destroy—for he is God—yet will not because his love is a godlike love, the love of him who is the Holy One. It is, then, not for Israel's sake, but for his own name's sake that he defers his anger; it is for the sake of his own praise that he restrains his wrath and does not cut his people off (Is. 48:9). Therefore the covenant remains in force because the God of the covenant remains true to himself. His fellowship with his people will be restored because he is the God who wills that it shall be, and who can bring his counsel to naught? He is God and not a human that he should repent (1 Sm. 15:29). He is the Holy One in the midst of his people—as Love. Therefore Israel shall not be destroyed.[1]

Eventually this invincible, godlike love, this "love divine all loves excelling" (Wesley) was revealed in the gift of God's Son (Jn. 3:16). Naturally, the early Christians first thought of God's love in terms of this love for the sinner revealed in the cross and shed abroad in their hearts by the Spirit (Rom. 5:8; 8:11). But given this disclosure of redeeming love and convinced that God in himself is who he has revealed himself to be, in due time the church drew the inference that God in himself is a fellowship of Love from all eternity. Hence the statement of the apostle John that God is Love (ὁ θεὸς ἀγάπη ἐστίν, 1 Jn. 4:8, 16) means more than simply that he is loving as he is powerful, wise, and just. Here is a sentence of the same order of meaning as "God is Spirit" or "God is the Holy One." That is, the God who speaks as personal Subject (Spirit); the God who says, I am the *Holy One* in your midst, is *so* in our midst—as the crucified God—that he must be, in the mystery of his own, eternal being, Love itself.

---

1. "That the infinitely distant One is near at hand, that the Holy One is sheer Goodness, that the *Majesty* makes himself the One who can be trusted; this contrast/harmony is the soul of Luther's Religion." Otto, *Das Heilige* (Munich: C. H. Beck'sche Verlagsbuchhandlung, 30th ed., 1936), p. 123. Note also the juxtaposition of majesty and pity in the eighth stanza of the *Dies irae;* the God who is the "King of majesty tremendous" is the God who hears the suppliants' prayer, "Fount of pity, then befriend us!"

Thy nature, gracious Lord, impart;
  Come quickly from above,
Write thy new name upon my heart,
  Thy new best name is — Love. (Wesley)

As T. F. Torrance has noted:

In this statement [God is love] the "is" is determined by the nature
of its subject "God," and is only therefore the kind of "is" that God
is. When it is said that "God is love" the love in question is thus not
any kind of love but divine love, love that issues from God and is in
accordance with the nature of God. . . .[2]

B. AGAPE AND EROS

For contemporary theologians, the biblical understanding of love has come
to revolve around two Greek words that make up the title of a pioneering
study of Anders Nygren: *Agape and Eros.*[3]

That agape should have become the exclusive Greek word used in Scripture for God's
love is indeed noteworthy. Such a striking choice is undoubtedly due to the Septuagintal
translators' perception that the love of God for Israel is different from the acquisitive
love of eros. (This would be true whether one were speaking of אָהֵב, God's "electing
love," or his חֶסֶד, "covenant love." The former grounds the covenant, the latter is the
means of its continuance. See N. Snaith, *The Distinctive Ideas of the Old Testament,*
London: The Epworth Press, 1944, pp. 139ff.) The New Testament writers simply took
over the usage of the Septuagint, and with reason. They were persuaded that God had
commended his love to us in that Christ died for us while we were yet sinners (Rom.
5:8). This is surely not the love of eros! In prebiblical Greek, "to love" is (*a*) ἐρᾶν, the
passion that desires the other for oneself, glorified in the erotic cults and sublimated in
Plato's "heavenly eros" to denote the soul's aspiration after the suprasensible world of
the Ideas; (*b*) φιλεῖν, the affection that is concerned for the other; (*c*) ἀγαπᾶν, a word
of unknown etymology whose meaning is pale and vacillating, often a stylistic substitute
for either of the above two words. (See E. Stauffer's comments, "ἀγαπάω," *TDNT,* I,
pp. 35-38.)

2. T. F. Torrance *Theological Science* (London: Oxford University Press, 1969), pp.
233-34.
3. Anders Nygren, *Agape and Eros* (Philadelphia: Westminster, 1953). For an overview
of the lexical data relating to the biblical concept of "love" see B. B. Warfield, "The
Terminology of Love in the New Testament," *Biblical Doctrines* (New York: Oxford, 1929),
pp. 511ff.

Nygren does not write in terms of theological loci but of fundamental thought motifs. But inasmuch as such thought motifs are the enduring response to those basic issues that have ever engaged the human mind, his analysis makes a significant contribution in answering our question: Who is God? To this question, as Nygren points out, Christianity gives a unique answer: God is Agape.[4] To appreciate the significance of this affirmation, one must, according to Nygren, have some knowledge of the eros piety that dominated the Greek world into which Christianity came. Eros has its roots in the sensual love of men and women, the mutual desire and attraction of the sexes. But it is in the sublimated form of the longing of the soul for salvation that Eros stands over against Agape and confronts us with a fundamental choice that bears on our understanding of the very nature of God. First in the Mysteries, then supremely in Plato's *Dialogues,* the sublimated form of Eros is elaborated as the attraction of the soul for the higher world of the Ideas.

Characteristic of Plato's thought is a dualism distinguishing the sensual world from the ideal world. Since humankind is a part of both worlds, one's salvation consists in delivering one's soul from the sensual world that it may ascend to its proper element, the celestial realm of the Ideas. This is possible by virtue of Eros, the power that informs the soul and moves it with longing for the pure world of the Good, the True, and the Beautiful. Awakened by the light of things beautiful, nourished by the recollection *(anamnēsis)* of its pretemporal existence, the soul ascends, as it were, on the ladder of heavenly Eros from things earthly to things eternal. Hence Eros is an acquisitive love, a love evoked by worth in its object. It is also an egocentric love, for it seeks its own. And it is an aspiring love, the upward quest of the human for the divine.[5]

The New Testament, says Nygren, is wholly at variance with this view of love as Eros. According to the Christian vision, love is not Eros but Agape. Agape love is spontaneous and unmotivated in the sense that its ground is found in God himself, not in some extrinsic value in the

4. Here a disclaimer, not unlike the one made concerning the methodology of Otto, is in order. The approach of motif-analysis betrays Nygren, in our judgment, into the error of making the sentence, God is Love, reversible. Nygren refers to 1 John 4:8 as the supreme, formal statement of the primitive Christian Agape motif. "Nothing greater can be said than this: *God is love, and love, Agape, is God." Agape and Eros,* p. 147 — his italics. It was to avoid this error of turning the sentence, "God is Love," into the sentence, "Love is God," that we began our discussion of the doctrine of God with the affirmation that God is the personal God who names himself: I am the LORD. A "motif" does not name itself.

5. See Nygren, *Agape and Eros,* "The Platonic Idea of Eros," pp. 166ff. with sources from Plato's *Republic, Phaedrus,* and *Symposium.* Nygren refers to the stages of the soul's ascent as sketched in *Symposium* as the *"ordo salutis* of Eros."

object or person loved. To say that God loves humankind does not tell us about humankind but about God; it tells us not who we are but who God is. The distinction between the worthy and the unworthy, the righteous and the sinner, sets no bounds to this divine love. Rather, God's love is a love that stoops to the creature apart from all considerations of worth and value. Agape does not recognize value, it creates value. And this is the meaning of Agape: it is the love that imparts value by loving.[6] Thus, fellowship with the creature is initiated by an act of condescending love on the part of the Creator. Christianity teaches not that we can ascend to God (heavenly Eros) but that God has come down to us ("incarnational Agape").

While we are on the subject, we should note that in Process Theology God is defined as the Primary Lure of the creature who draws the creature forward toward ever new and creative possibilities. Such a view of God is obviously at variance with the meaning of the biblical affirmation that God is Agape. To speak of the God who lures the creature to himself is to speak in terms of eros, not agape. The love of God revealed in Scripture does not lure the creature to God but rather, if we might so speak, lures God to the creature. He is the God who, in a love that is outgoing, stoops to embrace the sinner. The difference between these two views of God is one that confronts us with a choice having large consequences for theology. Is the biblical message about a God for whom the human spirit yearns with devout longing? Or is it the God who comes to us in an act of infinite condescension, the God who is found by those who did not seek him (Rom. 10:20)?

C. THE BIBLICAL DATA

Hosea, as we have said, was among the first to grasp the nature of the divine love in a profound way. The word Hosea uses to describe God's love for Israel (חֶסֶד) had taken on a special significance for the prophet because of his own domestic life. As he had remained faithful to his wife

---

6. Ibid., pp. 75ff. Here Nygren pauses to challenge Harnack's affirmation of the "infinite value of the human soul," a thesis that turns the divine agape into eros, since God forgives in the sense that he disregards human failings and reckons only with the imperishable *value* that belongs to our humanity as such. Cf. Harnack's *What is Christianity?* (New York: G. P. Putnam's Sons, 1901), pp. 63ff. To the same effect Kenneth Hamilton tellingly challenges Tillich's plea for an ontological interpretation of love in terms of the unity of being, which means that "God loves himself—for what else is there to love or be loved except being-itself and the structure of being which God is?" Hamilton, *The System and the Gospel* (Grand Rapids: Eerdmans, 1963), p. 104.

Gomer with a steadfast commitment that even her infidelities could not destroy, so the Lord had remained faithful to his people Israel in spite of their worship of alien gods.[7]

Pursuing the figure of married love, Hosea likens the time of Israel's wilderness wandering to courtship (2:15, 17). But the honeymoon is over now; Israel has turned aside to new loves (the Baals of Canaan). Yet through it all God's love is unfailing and sure. By likening God's love for Israel to the love of a marriage partner for an unfaithful spouse, Hosea underscores the truth that it takes two not only to make but also to break a covenant. And when one of the covenant partners is the Holy One of Israel, who can annul the covenant if he has proposed to keep it? So the Lord will make love again to Israel, for his love is steadfast and unswerving.[8] This is the reason for the wondrous struggle to which we have already alluded, a struggle within God himself in which his love triumphs over his justice so that he will not destroy his people. His is an undying love that will not let Israel go (11:8ff.). Jeremiah, like Hosea, proclaimed the steadfast character of God's love. Even though carried away into exile, God's people will be brought back (chaps. 31–33, passim), for he will not, indeed cannot, forsake them utterly.

Of course, all the prophets were certain that the sins of the people would meet with divine retribution. Thus they were compelled to ask: How is the justice of God (his מִשְׁפָּט) related to his love? The final answer to this question—the Christian doctrine of the atonement—was, naturally, far beyond their ken; they saw the promise only from afar (Heb. 11:13). Yet in their vision the answer began to take shape. They believed that God would make a new start, establishing a new covenant with a faithful remnant. In doing so he would solve the problem of the old covenant,

---

7. In keeping with the patriarchal culture of the Old Testament, the woman (Gomer) symbolizes the sinful creature, the man (Hosea) the chastising, forgiving God (Hos. 1–3)—one more reminder of the inadequacies of patriarchalism. See below, p. 237, for further comment.

8. Note the fifth stanza of Johann Heermann's *Herzliebster Jesu*, as translated by poet laureate Robert Bridges:

> Therefore, kind Jesus, since I cannot pay you,
> I do adore you, and will ever pray you:
> Think on your pity and your love *unswerving*,
> Not my deserving.

This "love unswerving" is the exact meaning of חֶסֶד, translated "steadfast love" in the RSV. (The KJV often uses "lovingkindness," one of the most beautiful words in the English language.) This love is steadfast because it is determined by God's covenant faithfulness. Hence the propriety of likening it to a spouse's faithfulness in marriage, a relationship that is covenantal in nature.

which was the hardness of Israel's heart. To that end the new covenant would guarantee that the law should be written not on tablets of stone but on the fleshly tablets of the heart. "I," says the Lord, "will put my law within them, and I will write it upon their hearts" (Jer. 31:31ff.; Ez. 36:26).

Thus the prophets perceived that just because God is the Holy One, his justice is not some impersonal norm above him to which he must conform regardless of his love. The "I will" of the promise of a new heart is the word of him who is the Lord and whose love, therefore, will have its way. The manifestation of such love is the expression of his very nature. It is a sovereign love, a love that will create a new situation consonant with his justice. Because it is a sovereign love, it is not conditioned by the merit of those on whom it is bestowed. The answer, then, to the question, How can a holy God continue to love his sinful people? is, in the last analysis, the same answer as is given to the question, How could God have loved Israel in the first place? In both instances it is found in the freedom of God's love, not in Israel's worth or merit. It is not their righteousness but the word which the Lord swore to their forebears that secures Israel in his favor (Dt. 9:4-5). God has set his love on Israel, choosing them not because they were more in number than any other people, but simply because he loved them (Dt. 7:6-8).

The thought, "I love you because I love you," is surely no explanation as we commonly think of explanations. But it does tell us that, unlike Greek eros, the divine agape is a love that is without cause in the one loved. It is a love whose cause is past finding out, for it depends solely on the will of the Lover, who is God himself. Hence, it is "for his own sake" (a recurring phrase in the Psalms and prophets) that the Lord loves Israel.

This wondrous, divine love of which the Old Testament speaks, a love that embraces the unlovely, is given its clearest definition in the life and death of Jesus, the "man for others," to whom the New Testament Scriptures bear witness. The teaching of Jesus, with which these Scriptures begin, reflects the love of God as a dominant theme. In the finest of his parables, the Prodigal Son (Lk. 15:11-32), Jesus likens God to a father who bestows unconditional love on a wayward son. Parables have been defined as earthly stories with a heavenly meaning. In the case of this parable, the heavenly meaning is obviously the overriding consideration. Had it been a mere earthly story about a mere earthly father, it is most likely that the wayward son, who returned with nothing but good intentions, would have been put on probation until he had made at least some token amends. This was, indeed, the son's intention; but the words "Make me as one of your hired servants" never even escaped his lips as he was caught up in the loving embrace of his father. Such a parable does not teach us a truth about God that is self-evident and that can be taken for granted. Rather, it teaches that the Holy One loves the sinner in a way that is anything but self-evident, in a way, indeed, that baffles all reasonable calculation. It is a love that can be inferred from no a priori, a love that is unmotivated, spontaneous, and free.

For the apostle Paul, this love was given its fullest expression in the cross of Christ. The meaning of the cross and the meaning of agape (love that "does not insist on its own way," 1 Cor. 13:5) are indissolubly bound together. Without the love of God there would have been no cross; but without the cross we could never have taken the full measure of that love. A pivotal passage is Romans 5:6-11. In this passage Paul tells us that God shows us what his love really is in that while we were yet sinners Christ died for us. Were one to die for a godly person, there would be at least some rhyme and reason to the act. But Christ died for the ungodly. Surely, then, such love is not evoked by any merit in those loved. Love of this sort, in which the Lover sacrifices himself for unlovely sinners, discloses to us the true meaning of love. "By this," the apostle John says, "we know love, that he laid down his life for us" (1 Jn. 3:16).

The final implication of this *theologia crucis* is drawn by John when he declares twice over (1 Jn. 4:8 and 16) that God is love. Nygren calls this affirmation the "coping stone, so to speak, on the edifice of the primitive Christian conception of Agape."[9] God reveals himself as the God of love because in himself he is Love. At this point the biblical data we have reviewed impinge most directly on the theological question before us, which is this: How should we understand the statement "God is Love"? How does it bear on the doctrine of the nature of God? To this question we must give our attention — after a brief comment on married love.

ADDENDUM: EROTIC LOVE AS THE SYMBOL OF AGAPE

In the above discussion we have followed the distinction commonly made since Nygren's day between agape and eros. Unlike the spontaneous, unmotivated, outgoing, divine love of agape, eros, we have argued, is the acquisitive love evoked by worth in its object. This is the love exemplified in the sexual attraction between man and woman, an attraction expressed in the relationship of marriage. But if marriage is an expression of erotic love, how is it that the writers of Scripture see marriage as adumbrative of

9. A. Nygren, *Agape and Eros*, p. 148.

the divine, agape love? (Israel is the bride of Yahweh, and the church is the bride of Christ. Therefore the eschatological union of Christ and the church is characterized as a marriage feast, a celebration of the nuptials of the Lamb and his bride, who is arrayed in fine linen, clean and white [Rv. 19:7-9]). Why do the Scriptures speak this way? Is agape, after all, somehow like eros?

In response to this question, it should be noted that even though one understands eros and agape as having quite different meanings, it does not follow that married love cannot illumine God's covenant love for his people. True, married love includes erotic attraction as a significant component.[10] But it is a gross oversimplification to suppose that married love involves nothing other than erotic attraction. Such an oversimplification may be acceptable in Hollywood, where marriages, completely erotic in character, have a way of beginning passionately and ending precipitously. But marriage, according to Scripture, is a lifetime commitment not to be entered into lightly. While it may (and should) be entered into romantically, it is a commitment that goes far beyond erotic attraction as such. This can be seen in Hosea's marriage to Gomer. It can also be seen in the Christian marriage vow that promises "to have and to hold, for better or for worse, . . . till death do us part." Sensual passion and romantic attraction, for all their ecstatic power, are not sufficient to sustain such long-term commitment and sacrifice. But it is the fidelity, the lasting commitment, even when such commitment is costly, that makes married love a fitting symbol of the divine love. "I have loved you," says the Lord, "with an everlasting love" (Jer. 31:3); "Jesus . . . having loved his own . . . loved them to the end" (Jn. 13:1).

In fact, the great poets of eros have instinctively recognized this truth. In a group of sonnets intended only for the eyes of her lover, Elizabeth Barrett speaks the words of eros in what Louis Untermeyer has called "one of the most eloquent love poems in the language." Ruminating on the passionate desire of their love, she can only plead that the love Robert Browning has confessed for her may rise above such desire. In so doing, even if unwittingly, she sings of a love that is the earthly exemplar of a heavenly agape, a love that goes far beyond self-interest, a love that is "for love's sake only," a love "enduring through love's eternity."

> If thou must love me, let it be for naught,
> Except for love's sake only. Do not say,
> "I love her for her smile—her looks—her way
> Of speaking gently — for a trick of thought

---

10. The Bible, especially the Song of Solomon, speaks of such erotic love in a way that cannot be mistaken.

That falls in well with me, and certes brought
A sense of pleasant ease on such a day"—
For these things, in themselves, Beloved, may
Be changed, or change for thee—and love, so wrought,
May be unwrought so. Neither love me for
Thine own dear pity's wiping my cheeks dry—
A creature might forget to weep, who bore
Thy comfort long, and lose thy love thereby!
But love me for love's sake, that evermore
Thou may'st love on, through love's eternity.[11]

Of course not every marriage is as happy as that of Elizabeth Barrett and Robert Browning. Hosea's marriage to Gomer, to which we have referred as adumbrative of Yahweh's unswerving love to unfaithful Israel, sends a mixed message to those many women who suffer violence at the hands of dominating men.

> . . . They say that this language of Hosea's relationship with Gomer is actually metaphorical, as though they had said something illuminating, as though the whole issue of whether this language is metaphorical is indeed the issue. That the language is metaphorical is where our inquiry begins, not where it ends. . . .
>
> Is there really sexually violent language in Hosea? Read with me Hosea 2. . . . You tell me, is there sexually violent language in Hosea? . . . The story of Hosea and Gomer, in my mind, can be deceptively noble or, in other minds, nobly deceptive. . . .
>
> To the extent that we argue that divine retribution is theologically acceptable, and to the extent that we image God as a husband and the people as his [unfaithful] wife, the image of a husband beating his wife becomes unavoidable. . . . This is the risk of metaphor, a risk that the church must be sensitive to and vigilant about protecting itself against. . . . [Such] violence is too prevalent in our land and culture and world for us to take [it] lightly as theologians.
>
> But you say, the real thrust of the story is not about violence but about God's love—God's unceasing love for Israel. Yes, I will admit that you are right, but in the case of Hosea and Gomer it is a love which is preceded by violence. This we see so often in our society. . . . Whereas Hosea is able to use the marriage metaphor to talk about the intimacy and the love, it is perhaps the father and son image in chapter 11 that will shed more light on the whole issue of chastisement and retribution. (Renita Weems, "An Unfaithful Wife But a Violent Husband," Seventh Annual Women's Lectureship Series, Fuller Seminary, 1987)

---

11. *Sonnets from the Portuguese,* No. 14. See Louis Untermeyer, *A Treasury of Great Poems* (New York: Simon and Schuster, 1955), pp. 800-801. Was ever a man more fortunate than Robert Browning?

D. THEOLOGICAL ANALYSIS

1. INTRODUCTION

In answering the question, What bearing does the statement "God is Love" have on our understanding of the divine nature? we must obviously keep in mind what has already been said about God as personal Subject. We are not concerned with love in the abstract but with the One who says: "I have loved you with an everlasting love." "God's love is, for the authors of Old Testament, a correlate of his personal nature."[12] However, it is not simply the thought that God is a personal God, but that this personal God is a Trinity of persons, which constitutes the final and uniquely Christian answer to the question: What does it mean to say, God is love? As C. S. Lewis observes, God's love of the world is "gift-love," because in God there is no need that must be filled in and through his love of the creature. He creates freely, not of necessity. "To be sovereign of the universe is no great matter to God. In himself, at home in 'the land of the Trinity,' he is sovereign of a far greater realm."[13]

Some are not altogether convinced by this line of reasoning. Nygren, for example, speaks of John's "metaphysic of agape" (1 Jn. 3:16) and cites the Johannine statements about the Father loving the Son eternally (Jn. 3:35; 5:20; 17:24) with misgivings. For would not God's love lose its agape character as love of the unworthy if it finds its supreme expression in the love of the Father for the Son? Surely the Son is not an unworthy, but a most worthy, object of the Father's love. Thus agape, in its highest expression, is compromised by eros.

This consideration forces Nygren to the implausible conclusion that in bringing agape to its ultimate expression John weakened it. It is Paul, then, rather than John, who understands agape in its true depth. Knowing that God loved him when he was his enemy, and proclaiming that love even to estranged Gentiles, Paul could write in unmatched eloquence of God's love as the love of the unworthy. So far from illuminating the character of such love of the unworthy, the doctrine of the Trinity has changed it, for Nygren, into love of the worthy, which is eros. The unceasing desire of the creature, the yearning of the earthly for the blessedness of the heavenly, finally

---

12. G. Quell, "ἀγαπάω: Die Liebe im AT," *TWNT*, I, p. 22 (cf. *TDNT*, I, p. 23).

13. C. S. Lewis, *The Four Loves* (New York: Harcourt Brace, 1960), p. 175. The affirmation that God is love implies that he loves himself. The doctrine of the Trinity, which states that God is a fellowship of persons, helps us understand how this divine self-love is not that of the original Narcissus.

comes to rest in God in an eternal returning upon itself. Thus God is, in Augustine's phrase, the *summum bonum,* the ultimate object of all devout desire. Given such a trinitarian approach, the statement "God is love" means that his is a love that centers on itself in a blessed enjoyment of his own perfection, a love that gathers all loves, aspiring heavenward, into itself. Since love can rise no higher than God himself, "the divine being revolves within itself in self-love," which is the love of eros.[14]

This picture of a universal urge heavenward (heavenly Eros) that in the highest Being, God, becomes an eternal circle (the trinitarian *perichoresis*) is the strangest part of Nygren's thesis, in our judgment, especially in view of his own admission that John's statement "God is love" is the "coping stone" of the edifice of Christian agape. It is certainly true that this agape love is most clearly revealed in Christ's death for unworthy sinners. But this does not mean that the divine love can be a love of the unworthy only. In fact, the essence of this love is the giving of the self to the other freely and without reserve. Though the love that eternally unites the members of the Godhead is not a love for the sinful other, a love that gives itself to the unworthy other, it is a love that gives itself freely to the other in an ongoing and outgoing spontaneity.

Such a God, Brunner suggests, who is in himself active, outgoing love, may be likened in his self-communicating activity and fellowship to radium, the element that by definition streams outward.[15] To speak of God's love in this way does not make the act of creation necessary nor does it imply that the creature is the indispensable object of the Creator's outgoing love. Rather, God's creative act wherein he freely gives the creature being, and especially his redemptive act wherein he freely restores the sinner's being, reveals his eternal being as Holy Love. This is the mystery of the Trinity and the reason (in part) for the Christian confession that God's full and final name is Father, Son, and Holy Spirit.[16]

---

14. See *Agape and Eros,* esp. pp. 150-53, 739, 740, 753ff.

15. E. Brunner, *Dogmatik* (Zurich: Zwingli-Verlag, 1960), vol. I, pp. 195ff. God is *"geistige Ausstrahlungsenergie."*

16. "If there had been no creation would Love have practiced love? And would Love have had an adequate object to love? Nicaea answered, Yes. It confirmed beyond all creation, in the incomprehensible Alone, the cry of *Felicitas:* 'Another is in Me? The Godhead itself was in Coinherence.'" Charles Williams, *The Descent of the Dove,* as quoted by Mary Shideler, *The Theology of Romantic Love* (New York: Harper, 1962), p. 79. It is, then, human sin, not the divine love per se, which makes that love, in the creature's case, not only outgoing but sacrificial. For our exposition of the doctrine of the Trinity as a fellowship of love, see below, this Unit, IV, D, 3, c, The Mutual Indwelling of the Persons of the Godhead, pp. 297ff.

2. GOD'S LOVE AS GRACE

As God's love is eternally a giving of himself to the Other in the fellowship of the Godhead, so it is historically a giving of himself to the other in the fellowship of creation and redemption. The freedom, the spontaneity, and the costly character of this love is most sharply focused in the sinner's redemption because in redemption the Lover condescends to love the unworthy even to the point of giving his very life for the one loved. "Herein is love, not that we loved God, but that he loved us and sent his Son to be the propitiation for our sins" (1 Jn. 4:10 KJV). This is love indeed, not the selfish love of eros, nor even the general humanitarian love of *philia*, but the steadfast love of agape.

> O Love, how deep, how broad, how high,
> O great and wondrous mystery,
> That God, the Son of God, should take
> Our mortal frame for mortals' sake! (Thomas à Kempis)

This divine love which "seeks not its own" but rather "endures all things," this love which "never fails" (1 Cor. 13), viewed from the perspective of those who are its unworthy beneficiaries is called grace. "Grace," declares Robert McAfee Brown, "is the most important word in the Protestant vocabulary."[17] Furthermore, when Christians use the word "grace," they are speaking concretely and particularly of the grace of the Lord Jesus Christ. It is through him that grace and truth have come to us (Jn. 1:17). Indeed, grace is personified in him in that he has come to us in an act of incomparable condescension and thus revealed God's love toward us. "You know the grace of our Lord Jesus Christ," says Paul, "that though he was rich, yet for your sake he became poor, so that by his poverty you might become rich" (2 Cor. 8:9).

Like other basic theological words, "grace" is a term with so many overtones of meaning that systematicians are hard-pressed to classify the materials in a satisfying way. They have, in fact, written whole books on "the doctrine of grace," treating it as a major component of dogmatic thought.[18] And in these books the exposition of grace embraces a host of other doctrines. The most important of these "other" doctrines is the In-

---

17. Robert A. Brown, *The Spirit of Protestantism* (New York: Oxford, 1961), pp. 53f.

18. Cf. Rudolph Otto, *Das Heilige* (Munich: C. H. Beck'sche Verlagsbuchhandlung, 30th ed., 1936), p. 43, on the surpassing wonder and mystery of that which has been designated by the term "grace." Our own understanding of such standard theological phrases as "nature and grace," "means of grace," "state of grace," etc., will be elaborated in the various relevant loci.

carnation, which teaches that God himself has come down to us and become, in the person of Jesus Christ, one of us.

> Love came down at Christmas,
> Love all lovely, Love divine. (Rossetti)

Christ is not one with us as the "Ideal Man," the high point in the evolution of the religious consciousness of the human race. Nor is he the one among us who most perfectly actualizes the aspirations of the human spirit for God. Such a view would turn agape into eros, grace into works, and Christianity into Greek philosophy. Rather, he is himself the God who has condescended to our lowly estate, taken our humanity upon himself that he might have fellowship with us.[19] Not only has God come to us in Christ, but he has really come all the way *to* us. Christ was not God masquerading for a time as a man; he was and is the God who became a man.[20] Furthermore, in this coming to us he took upon himself the form of a servant. Here is a surprise, for we have said that God is the Lord, and lords *have* servants. But he who is Lord of lords has *become* a servant. Here, supremely, we see the downward movement of the divine love. Such condescending love, a love that stoops to the sinner, is the meaning of grace.

> Love caused your Incarnation,
>> Love brought you down to me;
> Your thirst for my salvation
>> Procured my liberty.
>
> Oh love beyond all telling,
>> That led you to embrace,
> In love all loves excelling,
>> Our lost and fallen race. (Gerhardt)

In fact, the thought that God stoops to us in our sin is so central to the Christian faith that even Origen—whose exposition of that faith left much to be desired—was compelled to defend it against the barbs of Celsus, who found the whole idea of a God who descends absurd, especially one who descends to identify with sinners.

The absurdity of the thought that the grace of God has come to us in Jesus Christ is likewise felt by the rational mind when it comes to the effects of grace in the lives of sinners. Those who are not only in the world but of it understand life in a fundamentally

---

19. We speak thus because we regard Christ's act as God's act, for only God can save us. This is why Athanasius asserted that the Son is *homoousious* with the Father.

20. This is why the church has insisted that the Son as incarnate is *homoousios* with us.

different way from those who have been "called in the grace of Christ" (Gal. 1:6). The latter are called to have the mind that was also in Christ Jesus, who condescended to take the form of a servant (Phil. 2:5-7). In other words, truly to lead a Christian life is to find that the room is at the bottom, not at the top; we climb down the ladder to success, not up. We save our lives by losing them (Mk. 8:35). Reflecting on our success-oriented society, on the drive for upward mobility in which becoming number one is the goal of life, Henri Nouwen observes: "The spiritual life is the life of the Spirit of Christ in us, a life that sets us free to be strong while weak, to be free while captive, to be joyful while in pain, to be rich while poor, to be on the downward way of salvation while being in the midst of an upwardly mobile society." ("The Selfless Way of Christ: Downward Mobility as Christian Vocation," *Sojourners,* June 1981)

The marvel of God's grace is not just that he became poor, but that he became poor for our sakes, that through his poverty we—who are unworthy sinners—might be made rich. As Paul says, we are saved by grace and not by works (Eph. 2:5, 9). Obviously, as we have said, the reason for such love, since it is the love of the unlovely, cannot be in those who are loved but only in the resolute purpose of the Lover.

> "Wherefore should any set thee love apart?
> Seeing none but I make much of nought" (He said),
> "And human love needs human meriting:
>   How hast thou merited—
> Of all man's clotted clay the dingiest clot?
>   Alack, thou knowest not
> How little worthy of any love thou art!
> Whom wilt thou find to love ignoble thee
>   Save Me, save only Me?"[21]

We should not be surprised, then, that Scripture frequently grounds the grace of God not in human decision and choice but in the divine will and purpose. "God," we are told in 2 Timothy 1:9, "[has] saved us and called us not in virtue of our works but in virtue of his own purpose and the grace which he gave us in Christ Jesus ages ago." Such grace, bestowed according to the divine purpose, is electing grace, the grace which has been bestowed on those who have been chosen "in Christ before the foundation of the world" and "destined . . . for adoption as his children . . . to the praise of his glorious grace." We have obtained "the forgiveness of our trespasses, according to the riches of his grace" (Eph. 1:4-6 NRSV).[22]

---

21. Francis Thompson, "The Hound of Heaven." See Untermeyer, *A Treasury of Great Poems,* p. 1002.

22. Following Paul, Augustine was the first to associate the doctrines of grace and

For reasons we shall consider in due course, "grace" is a more pleasant word to many than "election." But really the two go together, for they are alike essential to the biblical doctrine of God.[23] God is love; and, as we have said, his love is sovereign and free, grounded in his purpose rather than in our merit. Hence, there is no better way to describe how this divine love is manifest to sinners and how sinners are aware of this love than to speak of God's "electing grace."

Some human relationships are based on merit: a baseball club employs a player because he can hit .340 or is exceptionally adept with a glove. Some relationships are based on need: I get acquainted with a garage mechanic because he can fix my broken carburetor, or I get acquainted with a banker because he can help me stay solvent. Some relationships are based on appeal: a man does not love a woman because she can fix his carburetor or help him stay solvent, but because he finds her beautiful, or appealing, or exciting to be with. (He may even be so swept off his feet by her that he ends his sentences with prepositions.)

The relationship based on grace is unlike the relationship based on merit or need or appeal. God does not enter into personal relationship with his children because they are "good." They are not. Nor does he do so because he "needs" them. He does not. He is not gracious to them because they are "appealing." They are not. Quite the contrary. The Bible is emphatic in asserting that God's relationship to man is not based on the fact that man offers something to God, but on the fact that God offers everything to man. . . .

The sovereign God whom we meet in the Bible is the electing God. The Bible is quite straightforward about this. God "elects," God chooses, and he elects a special group of people, the Jews. They are chosen, we recall, because it is God's good pleasure to choose them. . . .

Christians who dislike the notion of the "chosen people" are not only making a judgment on the Jewish community, but on the Christian community as well. They are repudiating what they themselves have been called to be. . . . Christians are those who are "called out" by God into the new fellowship of the church in which the covenant promises have come true.

The minute we realize that *we* have been elected, we understand afresh that election is an act of sheer grace. No one, looking at oneself, can assert that one deserves this election. No one, looking at the church, can assert that Christians deserve this election. No one deserves it, and yet it is given anyhow.

---

election in a profound way, and this association has continued down to the present, though with many modifications.

23. See Norman Snaith's helpful comments on the Old Testament meaning of the divine love as agape. Snaith observes that the exclusiveness in God's love—he fixed his love on Israel to the exclusion of other nations—is a part of "the offense of the gospel." God's choosing and electing are ideas so firmly embedded in both Old and New Testaments, he avers, that if we reject them we must hold to a doctrine of God's love that is other than biblical. N. Snaith, *The Distinctive Ideas of the Old Testament* (London: Epworth Press, 1944), p. 139.

That is why it is an election of grace.[24]

This mystery of electing grace is quite beyond rational analysis. We can never show, by any compelling argument, why, of all the nations in the ancient Near East, God should choose Israel (Am. 3:2); why he should have "many people" in the city of Corinth in Paul's day (Acts 18:10), but none, so far as we know, in Tenochtitlán, the capital of the Aztec empire, in the reign of Montezuma I. God is in heaven and we on earth; therefore his thoughts are not our thoughts. Yet to affirm the election of grace is to confess that his thoughts are thoughts about us. Even when he is not in our thoughts we are in his, for he loves us with an everlasting love (Jer. 31:3).

3. GOD'S LOVE AS WRATH

Some have associated God's holiness and love in a nonreciprocal way. As a result, they think of the divine wrath as a manifestation of God's holiness, but not of his love.[25] When combined with the view that God's power is absolute, such an approach turns the concept of the divine wrath into arbitrary tyranny. This is the problem that the double predestinarians have never been able to put to rest.

Luther, to cite a well-known example, sometimes speaks of the hidden God *(Deus absconditus)* and the revealed God *(Deus revelatus)* in such a way that the distinction threatens to become a difference in God himself. There is a God revealed in Christ and a God apart from Christ. The latter is a God of absolute power and naked majesty. As one who had had his salvation taken completely out of his own hands, Luther sometimes spoke as though others had had their condemnation taken completely out of their own hands. It is especially in his *Bondage of the Will* that, as a double predestinarian, he so speaks. Luther never speaks of two Gods, to be sure, but he does speak of God's two wills wherein he desires that sinners should live (Ez. 33:11) but secretly determines that some shall die. The latter he identifies as the "vessels of his wrath" spoken of in Romans 9:22. (For numerous citations from Luther's works, see Paul Althaus, *The Theology of Martin Luther,* Philadelphia: Fortress Press, 1966, pp. 166ff., 274ff. Althaus criticizes this strand of Luther's thought as going against the reformer's own theology and taking the dangerous path that leads to the ultimate dualism of two Gods.)
    In the best of Luther, however, this dualistic threat in his doctrine of God is overcome in a profound way so that the God who is the Holy One is none other than the God who is Love. God's love, in the last analysis, is related to his wrath in such a way that love uses wrath to its own service and end. Wrath is God's alien work, but

24. Robert McAfee Brown, *The Spirit of Protestantism* (New York: Oxford U. Press, 1961), pp. 55, 84, 85.
    25. See above, this Unit, II, B, Excursus 2, The Wrath of God, pp. 196-97.

love is his proper work. (For details, see the definitive monograph of Theodosius Harnack, *Luther's Theologie mit besonderer Beziehung auf seine Versöhnungs- und Erlösungslehre*, Erlangen: Blaseing, 1862, pp. 438ff.)

Though he tends to speak more in terms of God's power and justice than of his wrath and love, Calvin, like Luther, subordinates God's wrath to his love. Early in the *Institutes* (I, 10, 2) he cites Exodus 34:6—"The LORD, the LORD, a God merciful and gracious, slow to anger and abounding in steadfast love . . . but who will by no means clear the guilty"—and calls this text a description of God's "genuine countenance" in which Moses "certainly appears to have intended a brief comprehension of all that is possible for men to know concerning him." That God's wrath is subservient to his love is implied in those Scriptures that describe God as slow to anger and abounding in steadfast love (Ex. 34:6; Ps. 103:8); as deferring his anger for his own name's sake (Is. 48:9); and as hiding his face from Israel in the wrath of the moment, but having compassion on them with a love that is everlasting (Is. 54:8).

In reacting to the vengeful Deity of naked majesty, others have gone to the opposite extreme. They also have spoken of God's holiness and love in a nonreciprocal way, but in a way that leaves no room for his wrath. In the view of such thinkers, the place given to the divine wrath in traditional theology reflects a faulty understanding of God drawn from the Old Testament with its emphasis on the divine holiness. Ritschl, for example, affirms that the Old Testament has been superseded by the revelation of God in the New Testament as the God who is "loving Will." "There is," he assures us,

> no other conception of equal worth besides this [that God is loving Will] which needs to be taken into account. This is especially true of the conception of divine holiness, which, in its Old Testament sense, is for various reasons not valid in Christianity.[26]

We are simply not persuaded by this Ritschlian approach. Love is not the only conception worthy of God. Indeed, to speak of the divine love apart from the divine holiness sentimentalizes that love in a way that subverts the doctrine of God and thereby the Christian faith as a whole.[27] While it is true that where there is no love there is no God, it is also true that where there is no wrath there is no love. We are told that it is because God loved us that he sent his Son to be the propitiation for our sins (1 Jn. 4:10). Thus the Scripture interprets an act that appeases the divine wrath as an act that reveals the divine love!

---

26. *The Christian Doctrine of Justification and Reconciliation* (New York: Scribner's, 1900), pp. 273-74.

27. As an example, one may cite the rejection of the orthodox doctrine of the atonement as superfluous, even offensive, in Ritschlianism. See James Orr, *The Ritschlian Theology and the Evangelical Faith* (London: Hodder and Stoughton, 1897), especially chap. VIII.

To be sure, when we speak of the divine wrath as essential to the biblical doctrine of God, we are not saying that God is by nature wrath. Though the statement "God is a consuming fire" (Heb. 12:29) is grammatically identical with the statement "God is love" (1 Jn. 4:16), were we to give the verb "is" the same meaning in both instances we would make God a schizophrenic and threaten the doctrine of God with a rational contradiction of the sort alleged by Ritschl and his followers. In and of himself the holy God is a triune fellowship of Love, not of wrath.[28] Wrath, then, has no place in God's being as such. Wrath describes not God as he is in himself, but rather as he is related to the sinner who spurns his love and dishonors his name.

God's wrath is just his resolve to vindicate his claims against the creature who will not acknowledge them. It is his passionate opposition to all who are evil, all who would "burst his bonds asunder and cast his cords from them." It is his holy laughter, scorn, and derision; it is the fury with which he declares that, for all the opposition of "the kings of the earth," he has set his king on his holy hill of Zion (Ps. 2:1-6). As Lord of all, he will get himself glory — if not through the creature, then over the creature.[29]

But we must never forget that this burning anger of a judge is the fury of an injured lover.

> Here lies the deepest root of the concept of the divine wrath and from this perspective the overwhelming force of the [prophetic] message becomes comprehensible: it is *Yahweh's injured love, his holy love* which awakens his wrath. The wrath of God is the correlative of his קֹדֶשׁ [holiness] and his חֶסֶד [steadfast love], the turning of Yahweh toward Israel, which constitutes the foundation of the covenant relationship.[30]

There is, then, no magical way open to the sinner to escape the Lord's anger. There is only the plea that in wrath he should remember mercy (Hb.

---

28. The only trinity of wrath known to the writers of the New Testament is the counterfeit trinity of hell—the dragon, the beast, and the false prophet—set forth in the apocalyptic visions of Satan's kingdom in the book of Revelation. Thrown out of heaven, the devil comes down to earth "in great wrath" and empowers the beast out of the sea and the lesser beast out of the earth to deceive the nations that they should worship the dragon, receive his mark, and thus identify with him in his revolt against heaven (Rv. 12:1–13:18).

29. Note Pascal's claim in the eleventh *Provincial Letter* that the divine comment, "Behold, humankind has become as one of us!—*Ecce Adam quasi unus ex nobis!*" (Gn. 3:22) is a taunt of derision, "a grievous and cutting piece of irony" in which God, in his wrath, stung our first parents to the quick.

30. J. Fichtner, "ὀργή," *TWNT*, V, p. 404 (cf. *TDNT*, V, p. 403). Italics his. It will be recalled that Jonathan Edwards, who preached "Sinners in the Hand of an Angry God," in another sermon, entitled "Ruth's Resolution," spoke of that same God as an "abyss of love."

3:2); only the sigh of the fainting spirit, "Has his steadfast love forever ceased? Are his promises at an end for all time?" (Ps. 77:8). God's final answer to such plaintive questions is Jesus Christ. He is the King whom the Lord has set upon his holy hill in spite of the rage of the nations; and this King whom the Lord has established is "the King of Love, whose goodness faileth never" (Baker).

But this unfailing love of God, revealed in Christ, is a love that stands ever in dialectical relationship to his holiness, in the New Testament as well as the Old. In every strand of the New Testament witness to Jesus as the Christ, not only the love but also the wrath of God is prominent. Indeed, in Jesus' personal presence it is supremely manifest. As an infant in Simeon's arms, Jesus is the child "set for the fall . . . of many in Israel" (Lk. 2:34); his winnowing fork is in his hand, warns John the Baptist, and he will cleanse his threshing floor, burning the chaff with unquenchable fire (Mt. 3:12); he is the Stone which, if it falls on one, will crush her (Lk. 20:18). Though he is the Son sent into the world, not to condemn the world but that through him the world might be saved (Jn. 3:17), yet by him all humanity is divided into believers and unbelievers, those who are not condemned and those who are (Jn. 3:18).

Jesus' personal wrath is a specific instance of this wrath that condemns. It will not do to see in our Lord's "righteous indignation," as it has traditionally been called, simply the frailty of his humanity. When he looks "around at them with anger" who watch him in the synagogue to see if he will heal on the Sabbath day, his wrath is the wrath of him who is himself the Lord of the Sabbath, whose majesty is injured by such unbelief so that he can only grieve at their hardness of heart (Mk. 3:5).

Warning his hearers that they will perish if they do not repent (Lk. 13:5), he tells the parable of a barren fig tree (Lk. 13:6-9), a parable that he acts out on another occasion as he curses a fig tree without fruit (Mk. 11:14). In such warnings and parabolic acts (consider the casting out of the money changers in the temple, Mt. 21:12), the present merges with the future, which is to say that his anger not only anticipates the divine wrath that will be revealed in the day of judgment, but, in a sense, his anger is that eschatological wrath. Jesus is himself the Master who in the last day will cast the unprofitable servant into outer darkness (Mt. 25:14-30). He is the King who will slay his enemies that would not have him rule over them (Lk. 19:11-27). Such parables show how aware Jesus was that the wrath that he manifested in history grounded the judgment that will take place at the end of history. Hence the solemn warning at the close of the Sermon on the Mount: "On that day many will say to me, 'Lord, Lord' . . . and then will I declare to them, 'I never knew you; depart from me, you evildoers' " (Mt. 7:22-23).

In warning of the "wrath to come," Jesus follows in the footsteps of the Old Testament prophets and especially John the Baptist (Mt. 3:7). However, unlike them he does not simply warn of that coming wrath, but identifies himself as having a central role to play in its execution. That the early Christians so understood him is made indubitably clear by their acceptance of the Apocalypse of John as a canonical description of the denouement of holy history. A fundamental motif of this book, which closes the Christian Scriptures, emerges when the wicked call upon the rocks and mountains to fall on them and hide them "from the face of him who is seated on the throne, and from the wrath of the Lamb; for the great day of their wrath has come, and who can stand before it?" (Rv. 6:16-17).

This motif of the divine wrath is elaborated in the breaking of the seals (6:1–8:5), the sounding of the trumpets (8:6–11:19), and the pouring out of the bowls (15:1–16:21). It reaches its apogee in the vision of the catastrophic fall of Babylon. Anticipated by the taunting dirge of the great angel (18:1-3), echoing Isaiah 21:9 and Jeremiah 50:39, and followed by the hymn of triumph—a hallelujah chorus in a context of judgment—this vision closes with a grand, antiphonal "Amen" intoned by the twenty-four elders (19:1-4). Thus the curtain falls on the drama of holy history, a drama not only of salvation but of judgment.

Closely related to the biblical notion of God's wrath is his hatred (from the verbs שָׂנֵא/μισέω), meaning his detestation, his abhorrence of that which is evil. The worship of false gods provokes him to anger and he pleads with his people, "Oh, do not do this abominable thing that I hate" (Jer. 44:2-4). "I hate, I despise your feasts, and I take no delight in your solemn assemblies" (Am. 5:21).

The most difficult texts of all have to do not with practices but with people, as when we read, "Jacob I loved, but Esau I hated" (Rom. 9:13 quoting Mal. 1:2-3). Over and beyond abominable practices, does God also hate those who do them? Even when we try to purge the word of its overtones of malevolent rancor, ill will, and the spite which poison human relationships, how can the God who is Love be said to "hate" the creature whom he has made? Obviously he cannot, if the word is used in the sense of all that is antithetical to love. So to speak of the God who is Love as the God who hates would be like speaking of darkness as the essence of light.

A clue to how the difficulty may be resolved is found in the different ways in which Jesus speaks of love and hate when describing human relations. On one occasion he clearly bids his disciples not to hate their enemies, but rather to love them (Lk. 6:27). On another he bids them, if they would truly be his disciples, to hate even the members of their own family (Lk. 14:26). Obviously, in such usage, love and hate are not mutually exclusive and antithetical, as though his disciples should love their enemies but not the members of their immediate family! To hate one's father and mother, even one's own self, in order to be a worthy disciple must refer to one's conscious renunciation of anyone whose claims would compromise the ultimate claims that he, Jesus, makes as

Lord. So, in an analogous sense, God may be said to "hate," that is, to renounce, the sinner who will not acknowledge his claims as Lord and God. He declares: "I am the Lord your God," and this claim is, if we might so speak, God's first priority; he will not give his glory to another.

E. CONCLUSION

When doing dogmatics, a mistake in one's doctrine of God can have far-reaching consequences. One with an instinct for the discipline will sense that the question of the divine wrath is a critical instance of this truth; here one can easily take a wrong turn that has large implications for one's theology as a whole. One is reminded, at this juncture, of the observation once made by H. R. Niebuhr concerning 19th-century American liberalism: "A God without wrath brought men without sin into a kingdom without judgment through the ministrations of a Christ without a cross."[31] We have expressed the confidence that by treating the wrath of God in the light of both his holiness and his love, the theologian can escape this complacent God of liberalism, on the one hand, without, on the other, making God a capricious tyrant who creates men and women to be damned. As we draw our discussion to a close, we shall seek to show how this is so by a few brief reflections on the meaning of the cross.

It is a commonplace that the Scriptures interpret the cross as both an act of divine love and of divine wrath. It is in the cross that God's alien work as the angry God comes to its full expression. Here God's wrath against the sin of the creature is clearly manifested. At the same time, it is also in the cross that the inner nature of the divine wrath is perceived. In the cross God reveals his wrath in an act of love; in the cross the love of God breaks through his wrath. Thus the God of wrath is seen to be, in his true self, an "abyss of love" (Edwards) and this love, revealed in his wrath, is his proper work. It was this perception that led Watts, speaking of "the sweet wonders" of the cross, to sing,

> Here I behold God's inmost heart
> Where grace and vengeance strangely join,
> Here his whole name appears complete,
> His wrath, his wisdom and his love.[32]

31. H. R. Niebuhr, *The Kingdom of God in America* (New York: Harper, 1959), p. 193.
32. From the hymn "Nature With Open Volume Stands." Erik Routley calls this hymn ". . . the greatest of all hymns on the atonement" yet "one that is hardly known outside of one or two branches of English Dissent." E. Routley, *Hymns Today and Tomorrow* (New

Of course the natural man and woman—for whom the cross is no revelation because they turn their backs on the God whose love is revealed in that cross—will know God only in his alien work as the angry God. Just because God takes his love, that is, himself, seriously, he can do no other than respond in anger when his love is spurned. His anger, then, is not in contradiction to his love, for God is not a God in contradiction to himself. Rather, his anger is the response of his love to those who, as sinners, live in contradiction to themselves and to their Creator. But when through the work of the Spirit sinners perceive "the sweet wonders of the cross," then they discern how the work of God's left hand (to speak with Luther) has as its ultimate intent the gracious work of his right hand. Then the cross, which is itself a slaying, the work of the angry God, becomes God's most genuine work of love and so reveals his "inmost heart." Thus the cross of Christ becomes the final answer to the question of how the wrath of God is related to his love; of how there can be a work of God that is alien to his nature as Love which yet serves the ultimate intent of that Love.

A word of comment—sadly enough—is called for here, due to the deplorable anti-Semitism that has compromised the heart of the Christian message. We have affirmed that the cross is the place where God's "grace and vengeance strangely join," where God reveals that the inner motive of his wrath is his love. But contrary to this proper *theologia crucis,* Christians, including Christian theologians like Luther, for whom a right theology of the cross was central, have often spoken as though the grace (love) revealed in the cross is reserved for those who are Gentiles, while God's vengeance (wrath) is for the Jews. The God who relates to the Gentiles in mercy relates to the Jews in judgment. Thus, the mysterious dialectic of reciprocity is taken out of the relationship between God's wrath and his love. As a result, the relationship is quite rational and, in this case, cruelly so.

Commenting on the way in which Christians have ordinarily interpreted the cross in terms of God's unmerited love for sinners, Isaac Rottenberg (executive director of the National Christian Leadership Conference for Israel) asks,

> But what happened when it came to Christians' encounters with Jews? In that case, in a spirit of incredible self-righteousness and cruel malice, the cross was frequently turned into a crusader's sword, a curse against the people who were called "Christ-killers," an instrument for scapegoating that has set the stage for persecutions, pogroms, and holocausts. ("The Holocaust and Belief in a God of Holy Love," *The Reformed Journal,* May 1982, p. 23)

York: Abingdon Press, 1964), pp. 68ff. In her familiar hymn "Beneath the Cross of Jesus," Elizabeth Clephane—in an oft-omitted stanza—speaks of the cross as "A safe and happy shelter / A refuge tried and sweet / A trysting-place where heaven's *love* / and heaven's *justice* meet!" Why would a hymnal committee ever omit such a marvelous stanza?

Little wonder, then, that while Christians sing, "In the cross of Christ I glory," Jews have had an utterly different response. "One evening several years ago," observes Father Flannery,

> I walked north on Park Avenue in New York City in the company of a young Jewish couple. Behind us shone the huge illuminated cross the Grand Central Station displays each year at Christmas time. Glancing over her shoulder, the young lady—ordinarily well disposed toward Christians—declared, "That cross makes me shudder. It is like an evil presence." (*The Anguish of the Jews,* New York: Macmillan, 1965, Introduction, p. xi)

Unbelievable, but true. Yet which is more unbelievable, the revulsion of the Jewish people at the sign of the cross, or the unspeakable presumption of those who claim the name of Christian that has brought on this tragic response? As though God were angry with those who do not acknowledge his love in Christ, but not with those who pervert it even while they profess to experience it. Jesus had a word for those who take away the key of knowledge, those who do not enter themselves and hinder those who would (Lk. 11:52).

The answer, then, to the question, How shall we understand the wrath of God in the light of the ultimacy of his Love? is not an answer found at the end of a syllogism or verified by sense observation. Rather, it is found in an historical event, as that event is interpreted in the New Testament. Given the eye of faith, the cross of Christ becomes the linchpin that brings and holds together the seeming disparate truths that the angry God is the loving God and that in knowing the one we know the other. It is, of course, easier to set the law over against the gospel, God's wrath over against his love, the majesty of his hiddenness over against the graciousness of his revealedness, even as it is easier to interpret the Old Testament apart from the New and the New as superseding the Old. But the theological price of such undialectical simplicity is distortion of the truth. The law, whose demands in themselves will slay the sinner, is contained in the ark of the covenant and therefore under the blood that sprinkles the mercy seat.[33]

---

33. See Barth, *K.D.,* I/1, p. 407 (cf. *C.D.,* I/1, sec. 10.1). To say that one must be "given the eye of faith" to see the cross as it is interpreted in the New Testament is just to say that the paradox of subjective revelation corresponds to that of objective revelation. God must wound that he may heal, slay that he may make alive. Only when the old Adam has died and one has become a new creature in Christ does the foolishness of the cross become the wisdom of God that is wiser than all human wisdom (1 Cor. 1:23-25). Otherwise we "pass that cross unheeding . . . though we see him wounded, bleeding" (Savonarola).

ADDENDUM: THE DIVINE WRATH AND THE SYMBOLISM OF FIRE

In Scripture fire is one of the basic symbols of the divine being and presence. (In Pascal's *Memorial,* one will recall, the operative word is— fire.) In the awesome theophany at Sinai, the mountain is wrapped in smoke because the Lord descends upon it in fire (Ex. 19:18; Heb. 12:18). In the vision associated with Ezekiel's call, the gleaming likeness of a human form upon the throne is as the appearance of fire (Ez. 1:26-27). Sometimes the emphasis of the symbolism is on illumination, as when the pillar of fire guides the children of Israel through the awful wilderness (Ex. 13:21- 22). But generally the divine presence as fire denotes God's wrath. In his wrath a fire is kindled (Jer. 15:14), and when he is angry smoke goes up from his nostrils and devouring fire from his mouth (Ps. 18:7-8).

In view of our emphasis on the interconnectedness of God's holiness and love, and in view of our thesis that the divine wrath is God's injured love, it is instructive to note that fire, as a basic scriptural symbol of the divine wrath, has a double meaning: it is both purgative and punitive. As purgative, it cleanses the sinner of all that defiles, as dross is consumed in the fire. When he shall come, who is the messenger of the covenant, he will be "like a refiner's fire. . . ; he will sit as a refiner and purifier of silver, and he will purify the sons of Levi and refine them like gold and silver, till they present right offerings to the Lord" (Mal. 3:3). This word of the Jewish prophet is like that of the Christian apostle when he warns that those who build poorly upon the one foundation, which is Christ, shall be saved in the day of judgment, yet so as by fire (1 Cor. 3:15).

But in that day, when the Lord Jesus is revealed from heaven in flaming fire, he will also take vengeance upon those who know not God and obey not the gospel (2 Thes. 1:8). His eyes burning like fire, his name the Word of God, he shall smite the nations with the sword of his mouth and tread the winepress of the fury of the wrath of God Almighty (Rv. 19:12ff.). Hence the writer of Hebrews warns that to spurn the Son of God and outrage the Spirit of grace is to invite the fearsome prospect of judgment and the fury of fire that shall consume the adversary (Heb. 10:26-27). Thus in the symbolism, as in the reality, when we have to do with God, the God who is Holy Love, we have to do with fire.

> The dove descending breaks the air
> With flame of incandescent terror
> Of which the tongues declare
> The one discharge from sin and error.

The only hope, or else despair,
    Lies in the choice of pyre or pyre—
    To be redeemed from fire by fire.

Who then devised the torment? Love.
    Love is the unfamiliar Name
Behind the hands that wove
The intolerable shirt of flame
Which human power cannot remove.
    We only live, only suspire
    Consumed by either fire or fire. (T. S. Eliot, *Four Quartets,*
"Little Gidding IV")[34]

34. Though the death of Christ is frequently interpreted in the New Testament as a sacrifice, it is in Hebrews, especially, that the whole burnt offering, involving the immolation of the sacrificial victim, is construed as a type of Christ's death.

Love's Resolve

*A Sermon Preached by Marguerite Shuster
at Knox Presbyterian Church, Pasadena, California,
Lord's Day, October 18, 1987*

*Then she started with her daughters-in-law to return from the country of Moab, for she had heard in the country of Moab that the L*ORD* had visited his people and given them food. . . . But Naomi said to her two daughters-in-law, "Go, return each of you to her mother's house. May the L*ORD* deal kindly with you, as you have dealt with the dead and with me. . . . Then they lifted up their voices and wept again; and Orpah kissed her mother-in-law, but Ruth clung to her.*

*And she said, "See, your sister-in-law has gone back to her people and to her gods; return after your sister-in-law." But Ruth said, "Entreat me not to leave you or to return from following you; for where you go I will go, and where you lodge I will lodge; your people shall be my people, and your God my God; where you die I will die, and there will I be buried. May the L*ORD* do so to me and more also if even death parts me from you."*

Ruth 1:6, 8, 14-17 (RSV)

Every once in a while—not very often, perhaps, but every once in a while—something in our all-too-ordinary daily lives gives us an insight, a flash of understanding, of the nature of God. And if we pay attention, if we receive and believe that insight, our lives will be changed. I can recall as if it were yesterday an event of that sort in my own life some fifteen years ago. I was in seminary, and a former university professor of mine was coming to lecture. Nothing so astounding about that; but it just so

254

happened that this particular professor was the one person in whom I had confided, by letter, for the preceding five years. He knew more than any other human being about my doubts and fears and struggles. And I hadn't seen him in five years. To say that I was scared doesn't quite say it. An indication of my courageous approach to this situation is the manner in which I sneaked away to class after the first lecture without so much as saying hello. But he was scheduled to have lunch with students, and for that event I arrived early. I still get a little shaky when I think of seeing him walk through the conference room door with his cafeteria tray in hand. Glancing around the room, he saw me half hiding on the other side. He is a shy man, but he abandoned the tray, rushed over, threw his arms around me, and said only, but repeatedly, how glad he was to see me. And for the first time in my life I knew experientially what grace—God's grace—was like. No questions about whether I'd managed yet to gather the pieces of my life together. No list of suggestions for improvement. Just an abundant welcome that covered my faults and failures with its own warm acceptance. I sort of "floated" around town for weeks!

A second example. More recently, in a group setting, we were discussing how people experience God's love; and I abruptly asked a friend how she knew God loved her—a set-up, right, when a pastor asks the question? My friend, a very solid, experienced Christian, came out with a very proper and theologically correct set of answers. Being in one of my frequent contrary moods, I brushed aside these perfectly legitimate and important responses and kept pushing, saying, "No, what makes God's love *real* to you? How do you know what it's *like?*" She looked confused and hesitated and then responded a little sheepishly, as if she feared what she was saying was foolish, "Well, I guess my husband really loves me." Exactly. Someone who really knows her—all sides of her—and has known her for a long time, really loves her and isn't going to abandon her the moment he discovers what she is "really like."

It's hard, terribly hard, for those who have never experienced deep human love and grace to catch a glimpse of God's love and grace. In fact, just a couple of days ago I was talking to a person who was afraid she would die soon and was profoundly suspicious of the whole idea of heaven. Given her devastating experience in this world, she was fearful that heaven itself would have some snare, some wrinkle, some catch, that would make it hell for her. Such persons may understand intellectually and believe that God is a loving and merciful God who welcomes them, which certainly is sufficient for salvation—that isn't the question. But at least here on this earth our human experience matters too; and that experience is heavily dependent on the actions and attitudes of other people.

Well, every once in a while, as I was saying, something in our daily lives may give us a deep insight into God; and I'm making this point because the story of Ruth is like that. In many ways it is a perfectly ordinary, though beautifully told, story. God is surely at work; but he is, as it were, at work "behind the scenes," through ordinary events and human motivation.[1] In this story he does not intervene dramatically to forestall famine, or to prevent the death of Naomi's husband, or to lengthen the lives of her two sons. He doesn't miraculously provide supplies for the journey or food and lodging upon arrival. And yet . . . and yet . . . we know he's there.

You recall how the beginning of the story goes. There was a famine in Bethlehem, so a family went to live in Moab, to the east. The husband Elimelech died, leaving his wife Naomi and her two sons. The sons married Moabite women, Orpah and Ruth, but in ten short years the young men died too, leaving the three women with nothing. Word arrived that the famine was over in Bethlehem, so naturally enough Naomi started for home. The daughters-in-law started off with her, but Naomi encouraged them to return to their own people, since she had nothing now, and no prospects for the future to offer them. Eventually Orpah was persuaded, but Ruth refused with the memorable words, "Entreat me not to leave you or to return from following you; for where you go I will go, and where you lodge I will lodge; your people shall be my people, and your God my God; where you die I will die, and there will I be buried. May the LORD do so to me and more also if even death parts me from you"—words of the highest sort of human love and loyalty.

Note that there are no villains in this story. There is no indication that famine and death hit this family as a judgment against them. Orpah's return home was in no way wrong—indeed, Orpah went only at Naomi's urging. And the same is true if we read the story to the end: we find no villains. What any of the various people do is in no meaningful sense bad. That's part of the dynamic of the story, part of what shows off to such fine advantage extraordinary, uncalled-for goodness. To do no wrong is fine in itself, but greater possibilities remain. Through its demonstration of extraordinary goodness we learn something from this story of the character of God.

The key to the story comes in verse 8: "Naomi said to her two daughters-in-law, '. . . May the LORD deal kindly with you, as you have dealt with the dead and with me. . . .'" "May the LORD deal kindly with you, as you have dealt": *their* kindness is like God's kindness, a kindness

---

1. W. S. LaSor, D. A. Hubbard, and F. W. Bush, *Old Testament Survey* (Grand Rapids: Eerdmans, 1982), in loc.

that finds its deeper expression in Ruth's eventual refusal to leave her mother-in-law. You see, that term, often translated in the KJV with the beautiful word "lovingkindness," is regularly linked, when used of God, to his faithfulness, and includes the ideas of his goodness and grace. It's a word that designates not just an attitude, but the act that emerges from the attitude—an act that preserves or promotes life. It's a word that can connote the very essence of God, that can even stand for God himself.[2] Ruth's human loyalty points beyond itself to help make real for us this steadfast love of God. Let's see what it looks like.

First of all, it is not based on obligation, or duty, or the worth of the person loved, or on what one can expect to get out of the deal; no, it has an element of spontaneous freedom about it. Ruth had evidently fulfilled, and more than fulfilled, every duty owed to her dead husband. It was the obligation of sons, not of daughters-in-law, to care for aging parents: in that culture daughters-in-law had scant resources for such a task. No moral pressure and no dictate of common sense could lead Ruth to believe that she had to link herself to Naomi at all costs. And costs there seemed certain to be. Naomi had nothing to offer Ruth—no home, no money, and worst of all, no husband. Naomi was past child-bearing age, and even if she weren't, how could Ruth wait for an infant yet to be born to mature to a man? Naomi couldn't even offer her the security of a familiar community. What would be the prospects in a strange town of a foreign widow who wasn't getting any younger? Not too splendid, surely. No, there's no way of supposing Ruth hoped to "get something" out of this relationship. She loved Naomi because, well, because she loved her. And that was that. But note how we tend to assume that Naomi must have been a fine person if Ruth loved her so much: self-giving love confers value on a person by its very nature, no matter what the actual characteristics of the person. The very fact that she is loved makes her more valuable than she was before.

Note how it works in our own lives. If someone we admire loves someone, we assume that the loved person has some fine qualities, even if we can't see them. We also know that the love itself may create or bring out those qualities. When someone loves us, we generally hope that there are some specific qualities they like, lest the love be based on sheer blindness or patronizing condescension; but we hope they won't run out of love when we run out of attractive qualities. We will have trouble believing it is really we who are loved if we don't know that sometimes we are loved in spite of ourselves—that is, in spite of our less agreeable

2. H.-J. Zobel, *"hesed,"* in G. J. Botterweck and H. Ringgren, *Theological Dictionary of the Old Testament* (Grand Rapids: Eerdmans, 1986), vol. V, pp. 44ff.

attributes. At its best, even at the human level, love *creates* worth as much as *responds* to worth. It is an act of grace. Hence, Ruth's love for Naomi shows us something of the *gracious* character of God's love.

Second, this love lasts. It isn't here today and gone tomorrow, dependent on whim or a change in the weather. It would be so much easier to be loving if we could just sort of do it and get it over with. We might even manage to love very unlovely people if we didn't have to keep on doing it day after day, or we might love in trying circumstances if only we had a reasonable assurance the circumstances would change. Ruth had no such assurance. Her commitment to Naomi was like a blank check covering the whole of their earthly future, all the way from "where you go I will go" to "where you die I will die, and there will I be buried." She holds on to nothing of her own, not even a sentimental wish to be buried among her own people. We see no chance that an alteration in circumstances will lead Ruth to say, "Well, obviously, *this* is a bit more than I bargained for. Of course I didn't mean my vow to you to hold under *these* conditions." We see no chance that she will "outgrow" her commitment, like a child outgrows his devotion to a beloved stuffed animal. As long as the child loves it, that animal is valuable, no matter how ratty-looking; but no one expects the value conferred to endure forever. Heaven forbid the sight of a fifty-year-old businessman carrying around a ratty-looking stuffed animal. Not all value-giving loves lasts, or even should last. But some, like Ruth's, do.

By contrast, I'm reminded of the story told by the owner of a photographic studio. A college boy came in with a framed picture of his girlfriend. He wanted the photo duplicated, so it had to be removed from the frame. In doing so, the studio owner noticed the inscription on the back of the picture: "My dearest Tommy: I love you with all my heart—I love you more and more each day—I will love you forever and ever. I am yours for all eternity." It was signed "Dianne" and contained a postscript: "If we should ever break up I want this picture back."[3] Under those circumstances, the postscript absolutely contradicts the message, as surely as if Ruth had added a P.S. to her vow, to the effect that if Bethlehem didn't measure up to her expectations, she wanted guaranteed passage home. No, certain sorts of commitments must be "for keeps" if they are valid in the first place. Ruth's love for Naomi shows us something of the *steadfastness* of God's love for us.

Finally, this love freely *sacrifices* itself. We can perhaps imagine a love that graciously confers value and that lasts without involving self-sacrifice, but all we can do is imagine such a love. In a world like ours, there is no

3. *Parables*, March 1987, p. 6.

real love without cost to the lover. That is not to say that the lover is supremely conscious of sacrificing herself: one could say that being conscious of self-sacrifice is failing deeply and truly to love.[4] We would not consider it loving if Ruth made a detailed list of all the things she was going to give up for Naomi's sake and presented it to Naomi as proof of her affection. No, a greater demonstration of affection is the degree to which thought of making the list never occurs.

Nonetheless, the fact that love does not figure out the cost ahead of time does not mean that there is no cost. There is. There always is. But in C. S. Lewis's words,

> Christ did not teach and suffer that we might become, even in the natural loves, more careful of our own happiness. If a [person] is not uncalculating towards the earthly beloveds whom he has seen, he is none the more likely to be so towards God whom he has not. We shall draw nearer to God, not by trying to avoid the sufferings inherent in all loves, but by accepting them and offering them to Him; throwing away all defensive armour. If our hearts need to be broken, and if He chooses this as the way in which they should break, so be it.[5]

We may suppose that after already having her heart broken by the death of her husband, Ruth did not try to protect herself either by refusing to love again or by trying to find safe circumstances in which to love. She laid herself, her own life, on the line for Naomi, freely and willingly. Love gives itself away for the other—an essential quality of God's love.

"When Naomi saw that [Ruth] was determined to go with her, she said no more. So the two of them went on until they came to Bethlehem." And so, every once in a while—not often; not often enough, but every once in a while—something in our mundane human lives shows us something of the nature of God. Hundreds and hundreds of years before the birth of Christ, the human loyalty of his ancestor Ruth — for she was, of course, the human ancestor of Jesus—gives us a glimpse of the divine love, a love that graciously bestows infinite value on God's children, that is from everlasting to everlasting, that gives itself even over to death that we might live. The story of Ruth, written in ordinary human terms, can open our eyes, and perhaps our hearts. And the story of Ruth also challenges us, challenges us to seek, by grace, to be ourselves the sorts of people that make it easier rather than harder for others to believe in the steadfast love of God.

4. See Dorothy Sayers, *The Mind of the Maker* (New York: Meridian Books, 1956), p. 130.

5. *The Four Loves* (San Diego: Harcourt Brace Jovanovich, 1960), p. 170.

If Christianity were something we were making up, of course we could make it easier. But it is not. We cannot compete in simplicity with people who are inventing religions. How could we? We are dealing with Fact. Of course anyone can be simple if he has no facts to bother about.

C. S. Lewis, *Mere Christianity*

IV. God Is a Trinity of Holy Love

A. INTRODUCTION

The first Christians were Jews for whom the truth about God was summed up in the familiar words of the Shema: "Hear, O Israel: the LORD our God is one LORD" (Dt. 6:4). As they bore witness to their faith, these early Jewish Christians were joined by Gentiles who turned from their many idols to serve this one, true, and living God (1 Thes. 1:9). By such behavior they witnessed to a profound change in their understanding of God. But these early Gentile Christians were not the only ones whose understanding of God had undergone a radical transformation. The same was true, in a different way, for the Jewish Christians as well. The hallmark of their faith was no longer simply that God is one; as the first Christians, they had not merely made proselytes of the Gentiles to Jewish monotheism. Rather, they bore witness to the fundamental conviction that the one, true God whom their forbears had worshipped had personally revealed himself in Jesus of Nazareth whom they confessed to be their Messiah, the Son of the living God (Mt. 16:16). These early convictions about God and Jesus and Jesus' unique relationship to God are reflected, in one way or another, in all the documents of the New Testament. Paul, in a very striking passage, affirms that in Jesus "the whole fullness of deity dwells bodily" (Col. 2:9). God, then, had not simply revealed himself through this man as he had in the past through the prophets; rather, he was fully present in this man. Where Jesus is, *God* is.

The generation of Christians who came after the apostles, for all their differences, were one in this conviction. When, therefore, they confessed Jesus as Lord, they meant the Lord of heaven and earth. The title "Lord" (κύριος) that they ascribed to him had the same fundamental meaning for these early Christians that it had always had for the Jews when they affirmed: The LORD our God is *one* LORD. The oldest Christian sermon outside the New Testament begins with the words: "Brothers [and sisters,] we ought so to think of Jesus Christ as of God." The oldest record of Christian martyrdom outside the New Testament contains the declaration: "It will be impossible for us to forsake Christ . . . or to worship any other." The oldest pagan report about Christians describes them as gathering on a stated day to sing "a hymn to Christ as to a God." And the oldest surviving liturgical prayer is addressed to Christ: "Our Lord, come!"[1] In other words, in confessing Jesus as Lord, the early Christians were confessing that, in some sense, he was their God.

Obviously, then, these early Christians had no problem, at the level of piety and worship, with the confession ascribed to Thomas when he encountered the risen Christ and addressed him as "my Lord and my God" (Jn. 20:28). In fact, when it came to worship, even the Arians, who insisted that Christ was a creature, continued to pray to him as to a God and to baptize into the threefold name of the Father, the Son, and the Spirit, a liturgical posture that was obviously inconsistent with their doctrinal principles, as their more orthodox opponents were quick to remind them.

But though ready to point out the inconsistencies of the Arians, the Orthodox were not without their own problems in this matter. Early on, they found that engaging in worship was one thing; teaching and defending the faith in which they worshipped was another. Not that their worship could finally be separated from their doctrine, but the consensus enjoyed in the former proved exceedingly difficult to achieve in the latter. The quest for agreement, at the conceptual level, between the confession, "Jesus is Lord," and the confession, "the LORD our God is one LORD," convulsed the entire church in controversy over a period of centuries. The end result of this prolonged, intense, and sometimes acrimonious debate, as we now know, was the doctrine of the Trinity, a doctrine to which the church finally came not by accident but of necessity. Being inchoate trinitarians from the start, Christians became conscious trinitarians in the end. Confessing with the prophets of Israel that the Lord their God was one, and with the apostles of Christ that Jesus was Lord, they eventually came to unite these truths, so fundamental to their faith, in the doctrine that God is the triune God,

---

1. See J. Pelikan, *The Christian Tradition* (Chicago: University of Chicago Press, 1971), vol. I, p. 173, with sources. Of course the confession of Jesus as Lord reflected not only the early Christians' acceptance of the usage of the Old Testament in which יהוה (LORD) is the name of the God of Israel, but also their rejection of the decision of the Roman senate by which the title κύριος (Lord) was given to the emperor.

Father, Son, and Holy Spirit. And all Christians since that day have had a similar experience: they have become trinitarians because they are Christians, not Christians because they are trinitarians. The time has come to elaborate this basic Christian doctrine in detail. Before we take up this difficult task, however, we need to say a preliminary word about several matters bearing on the doctrine in a general way.

B. THE SIGNIFICANCE OF THE DOCTRINE AND ITS LOCATION IN THE STRUCTURE OF SYSTEMATICS

The doctrine of the Trinity has been called the *archē,* that is, the first principle, of Christian theology. There is much, it would seem, to corroborate this judgment. It dominated the doctrinal development of the ancient church; it found general acceptance in the medieval church; and it was defended by the Reformers and their followers until the rise of Protestant liberalism. The liberal "declaration of independence" from the doctrine, which began with Schleiermacher, only illustrates the adage that every heresy is, at bottom, a heresy about God. Often, indeed, the protest is raised that defense of the doctrine, in its traditional form, simply reflects an undue reverence for the thought forms of the past that have become so discontinuous with our own that we can no longer work with them. However, the efforts to restate the doctrine in contemporary thought forms are little more than restatements of ancient heresies. And, like ancient heresies, these efforts are so discontinuous with the content of Scripture that one cannot recognize in them the God who reveals himself in Jesus Christ. The "new map," in other words, is harder to read than the old. Of course, given the Protestant doctrine of *sola Scriptura,* one must admit the possibility that in framing the doctrine of the Trinity the ancient church misunderstood the Bible. One should, however, if one rejects the traditional doctrine, candidly admit that one is saying the ancient church, in this all-important question, was heretical. It misunderstood its own Scripture in a fundamental way. But is this likely?[2]

Furthermore, the doctrine of the Trinity is of elemental significance when viewed from the vantage point of the structure of systematics. Surely

---

2. See Barth, *K.D.,* I/1, pp. 397-98 (cf. *C.D.,* I/1, sec. 9.4). "These three names, Father, Son and Holy Spirit, are in their unity and difference, the content and meaning of the New Testament. The early Christian community lived by the reality that the Father was theirs through the Son and that they were united to Father and Son through the Holy Spirit." See also E. Brunner, *Dogmatik* (Zurich: Zwingli-Verlag, 1960), vol. I, p. 210.

it is no accident that the Apostles' Creed consists of three articles, so that this oldest ecumenical confession of the Christian faith is a confession of God as Father, Son, and Holy Spirit. In our day, to be sure, it may be more popular to speak of the so-called monotheism that unites us with Jews and Moslems than to dwell on the trinitarianism that distinguishes us as Christians. But as soon as one begins to elaborate one's faith as a Christian, one is confronted with the fact that the doctrine of God is the doctrine which is basic to all others, and that the doctrine of the Trinity is basic to the doctrine of God.

One may argue that the gospel consists of good news about God's reconciling act in Christ, not orthodox doctrine about the essential oneness of the Father and the Son; that the New Testament does not teach us to say, "I believe that the Holy Spirit eternally proceeds from the Father and the Son," but rather asks us the existential question, "Have you received the Spirit?" But the very act of proclaiming the message of Scripture, with the existential questions such a message entails, involves the interpretation of that message. Hence, as God has, so to speak, interpreted himself to us in revelation, so the church has interpreted this revelation in the doctrine of the Trinity.

But to speak of a trinitarian interpretation of revelation is to imply a trinitarian understanding of the Christian faith in all its doctrinal elaboration. Not only such obvious questions as those discussed when speaking of the divine nature—what does it mean to say God is one? God is three?— are answered in terms of the Trinity, but questions concerning Christ, the Spirit, and salvation as well. To be trinitarian means that one not only rejects a unitarian view of the Father, but also an Arian view of the Son and a Pelagian view of the Spirit. For a trinitarian, God is not simply our Creator, as in natural theology; nor is Jesus simply the supreme instance of God-consciousness, as in liberal theology; nor is the Spirit simply the potential of the human spirit to achieve the good, as in ethical Idealism. Rather, salvation is wholly God's work, the God who adopts us as his children in Christ, through the Spirit, who enables us to cry, "Abba, Father!" (Rom. 8:15). In fact, it was the conviction that only God could save us that led the early Fathers to insist on the full deity of the Son and eventually of the Spirit also.

Finally, the fundamental character of the doctrine of the Trinity is seen in worship. How often a service of public worship begins with a choral procession singing, "Holy, holy, holy. . . . God in three Persons, blessed Trinity" continues with the congregation responding to the word read with, "Glory be to the Father and to the Son and to the Holy Ghost," and it concludes with a benediction, "The grace of our Lord Jesus Christ, the love of God, and the fellowship of the Holy Spirit be with you all." Furthermore, in their private as in their public worship, Christians pray to the God who is their Father, in the name of Christ who is their Savior, through the Spirit whose inner witness assures them they are God's children. And so trinitarian doctrine is rooted in Christian worship in a fundamental way. Just as the individual Christian who has no formal knowledge of the doctrine is a trinitarian when she kneels by her bed in prayer, so the early church, before there was any formal promulgation of the doctrine, was trinitarian when gathered as a congregation to worship. The doctrine of the Trinity, then, is not some procrustean bed into which Christian devotion is forced to lie; on the contrary, it structures Christian devotion, even as it undergirds Christian doctrine. There is, in other words, a fundamental congruity between what we say when we talk to God in worship and when we talk about him in our theologizing. In both instances we speak as trinitarians and thus we see that the Trinity is indeed the *archē*, the first principle of Christian theology.

> *The doctrine of the Trinity is the immediate implication and therefore the presupposition of the worship of the God who has revealed himself to us in Christ. The gospel can be neither truly stated, nor the Word truly proclaimed nor God truly worshipped, without our affirming what is made explicit in the doctrine of the Trinity.*[3]

As for the location of the doctrine of the Trinity in systematics, it is instructive to note that Calvin, a master systematician, spent twenty-five years (and twelve editions) in resolving the order of the materials in the *Institutes*. In the end, he settled for the so-called trinitarian order. (Bks. I, II, and III deal with the Father, the Son, and the Spirit respectively.) Thus it appears that the question of the location of the doctrine in systematics is not unrelated to that of its significance. In fact, it is hardly too much to say that the location of the Trinity in the table of contents tells the discerning student more about a treatise on systematics than anything else short of reading the book itself. In the Preface (VIII) of *The Christian Faith*,

---

3. Claude Welch, *The Trinity in Contemporary Theology* (New York: Scribner's, 1952), p. 290. Italics his. In speaking as we have above, we do not mean to say that historically the movement is wholly from worship to dogma. That it was the other way also can be seen from the effects of the anti-Arian motif on the development of the liturgy after Nicaea. It is, for example, no doubt true that this anti-Arianism secured the coordinated form of the doxology — "Glory be to the Father *and* to the Son *and* to the Holy Ghost" — over the ancient usage that ascribed glory to the Father *through* (διά) the Son and *in* (ἐν) the Holy Ghost. The coordinated form made it clear that Christ was not simply the mediator and the Spirit the medium of worship; both, rather, are proper recipients of worship along with the Father.

Schleiermacher disarmingly protests that he has invented nothing new
". . . except my order of topics and here and there a descriptive phrase."
But how new his order is can be seen from the fact that he places the
doctrine of the Trinity at the very end of his exposition, something never
done before in a treatise on Christian theology. It constitutes a kind of
appendix to his system because, as he says, "it is not directly a statement
about our Christian consciousness at all."[4] Obviously then, Schleiermacher's *The Christian Faith* involves more than a new order in presenting
the materials. It marks a turning point in the understanding of Christianity
that has earned for its author the title "the father of modernism."[5]

The traditional order of first treating the divine nature and attributes and then the Trinity,
was, according to Rahner, established by the triumph of Thomas's *Summa* over Lombard's *Sentences*. The sequence that Thomas adopts, beginning with the treatises *De
Deo uno* (concerning the Oneness of God), followed by *De Deo trino* (concerning the
Threeness of God), Rahner regards as "didactic rather than fundamental." He warns,
however, of the danger of speaking first of God "as though there were no Trinity at
all" (*A Rahner Reader,* ed. G. A. McCoal, New York: Seabury, 1978, pp. 133-34). Weber
has deeper reservations about such an order. To begin with a general doctrine of God
(nature and attributes), he claims, means that when one comes to the Trinity, one must
ascribe attributes to the Son and the Spirit that have already been defined *apart* from
the Son and the Spirit.

As for the order of biblical theology, beginning with the Old Testament emphasis
on the oneness of God and proceeding to the New Testament consciousness of distinctions in God, this does not imply, in our judgment, that systematic theology should first
speak of God's oneness and then of his threeness in separate treatises. After all,
systematics rests on Christian revelation, and while it affirms that this revelation begins
with the Old Testament, it also affirms that it is consummated in the New, which contains
the Spirit's witness that Jesus is the Son of God. Hence the question of who reveals
himself (God) cannot be separated from the question of how he reveals himself (as
Father, Son, and Spirit).

*   *   *   *   *

Related to the question of the location of the Trinity in the exposition of the doctrine
of God is the question of whether the doctrine of the Trinity is the direct, or only the

---

4. Ibid., p. 750.
5. By the same token, one can easily see the pedigree of Tillich's theology when he
complains that Barth in his *Church Dogmatics* made the doctrine of the Trinity *pro*legomenon
when he should have made it *post*legomenon. See "Part 4, Life and the Spirit," in his
Systematic Theology (Chicago: University of Chicago Press, 1976), vol. III, p. 285. Barth
may have overreacted to his liberal theological training when he located the doctrine of the
Trinity in his prolegomenon, still, such a placing of the doctrine tells us something of the
enormous difference between his and Schleiermacher's understanding of the Christian faith.

indirect, implication of New Testament revelation. Those who argue the latter complain that to reverse the traditional dogmatic order and treat the Trinity before the attributes is to ignore the difference between the proclamation of revelation and the intellectual reflection arising out of that proclamation. The doctrine of the Trinity is not the gospel contained in the kerygma. It is admittedly a doctrine that is necessary to keep the proclamation of the church from error, but it is not per se the content of that proclamation. It is rather *Schutzlehre,* to use Brunner's term. It secures that which is central to Christian preaching, namely, that God has revealed himself as Father in the Son and sealed to us this revelation by the Spirit of adoption. The doctrine of God, therefore, should conclude, not begin, with the Trinity.

On the other side it has been argued that this doctrine of the Trinity is not simply a synthesis but an analysis of the fundamental data of revelation on which the kerygma rests. Hence it is not a secondary, but the primary and immediate implication of revelation, essentially identical with the content of that revelation. (See Welch, *The Trinity in Contemporary Theology,* pp. 161ff.) Not that the dogma of the Trinity is explicitly worked out in the New Testament. But it is implicitly there in a way that makes the dogma the direct implication of the Christian Scriptures. This is why the doctrine of the Trinity was the first dogmatic decision of the church concerning God. It is also why the systematician can "make sense" of the other doctrines of the Christian faith only in the light of this doctrine.

Whatever the merits of this debate, in the present writer's judgment the lengthened shadow of Schleiermacher—which creates a situation the Reformers did not face— warrants the treatment of the Trinity prior to the divine attributes. We also find specious the argument that the traditional doctrine of the Trinity can have only a secondary place in one's understanding of God because of its speculative character. Schleiermacher and his followers, who ground Christian theology in religious experience, are the truly speculative theologians. As Weber once noted,

> The widespread objection that the doctrine of the Trinity is "speculative" and therefore, in order to preserve dogmatics from speculation, it should not be placed at the beginning [of one's exposition of the doctrine of God], is an utterly fallacious argument. It is precisely the doctrine of the Trinity that can help preserve dogmatics from speculation. (*Dogmatik,* vol. I, p. 389)

*   *   *   *   *

It is disconcerting to see how even evangelicals, though far removed from the theology of Schleiermacher, sometimes give the Trinity little more than honorable mention in their treatises. Donald Bloesch, for example, in his *Essentials of Evangelical Theology,* vol. 1, San Francisco: Harper & Row, p. 357, subsumes the doctrine under the general heading, "The Sovereignty of God." Thus the Trinity is included among God's attributes. His specific treatment of the Trinity opens with the sentence, "God is sovereign but not solitary," which is little more than homiletical alliteration. In this regard it is also disconcerting to note that the doctrine of the Trinity was not even listed among the fundamentals of the faith discussed and defended in the celebrated series of four volumes, *The Fundamentals,* published by the Bible Institute of Los Angeles in 1917.

C. THE BIBLICAL BASIS OF THE DOCTRINE

The perennial objection to the doctrine of the Trinity, that the term itself is not found in Scripture, cannot simply be ignored.[6] Not only does the word "trinity" never occur in any biblical text, but the thought behind it is not immediately evident even to many who are familiar with Scripture. This can be seen from the difficulty that beginning students of theology feel when they first encounter the doctrine. It can also be seen from the protracted controversy in the early church which preceded the acceptance of the doctrine. The fact that the learned and devout, who read and believed the same Scriptures, wrestled for 200 years before they reached agreement on such a fundamental article of the faith, advises us that the biblical materials, while too pervasive to be ignored, are too complex to yield easy answers. For this reason, we shall preface our exposition of the doctrine with a brief review of the data of biblical revelation, data that have compelled the church to confess that the one God is a Trinity of persons— Father, Son, and Holy Spirit — a mystery whose confession distinguishes Christianity from all other faiths.

The emphasis in the Old Testament upon the oneness of God is well known: "Hear, O Israel, the LORD our God is one LORD" (Dt. 6:4); "I am the LORD and there is no other" (Is. 45:5-6). This emphasis is found in the New Testament as well. Jesus cited the Shema ("the LORD our God is one LORD") when he identified the commandment of love as the first and greatest of all (Mk. 12:29). And his followers who authored the New Testament—most of them Jews—evidently felt no incongruity between their view of God as Christians and the emphasis on the oneness of God found in the Jewish Scriptures. They continued to confess one God and rejected all the heathen idols around them as nothing because "there is no God but one" (1 Cor. 8:4). As their ancestors before them had forsaken the many gods of the Canaanites, so they now forsook the many gods of the Greeks and Romans.

Yet at the same time, when they spoke of this one God, these first Christians spoke out of an implicit, yet obvious, trinitarian consciousness. They confidently proclaimed that the God whom they worshipped so loved the world that he had given his only Son that whosoever believes in him should not perish but have everlasting life (Jn. 3:16). And they were firmly

---

6. "Trinity" translates the Latin *trinitas,* a term generally attributed to Tertullian (ca. A.D. 220), though it may have been coined by an earlier author. Before "trinity" became current usage, the Fathers often spoke of the divine "Triad," from the Greek τριάς, a usage occurring as early as Theophilus of Antioch, ca. A.D. 180.

convinced that through this Son they had received the indwelling Spirit of God by whose power they were enabled to put to death the deeds of the body (Rom. 8:13). There can be no doubt about the fact that the two events, the sending of the Son (the Christmas miracle) and the giving of the Spirit (the Pentecostal miracle), were accepted by the writers of the New Testament as revelatory of the one true God of Israel. It was through these events that God had fulfilled the covenant promises made to his people Israel. These pivotal events in salvation history, which occurred after the writing of the Old Testament and before the writing of the New, constitute that "revelation in the middle" in the light of which the apostles, as founders of the Christian church, both read the Old Testament and wrote the New.

This placed before the early interpreters of Scripture the exacting task of reading the Old Testament in the light of the New without reading the New back into the Old. In this task they often failed. No theologian today would prooftext the doctrine of the Trinity by citing Old Testament passages dealing with three of this and three of that, as did the early apologists. Yet the church has always believed that the God who reveals himself in Christ is the God who revealed himself to Israel. The Bible may be in two parts, but it does not reveal two Gods. Hence, there must be data in the Old Testament concerning God that are at least amenable to the Christian understanding of God.

Given this assumption, theologians have noted, for example, that the Hebrew word for God, *Elohim*, is a plural form. This form is, in view of the pervasive monotheism of the Old Testament, a striking stylistic usage, to say the least.[7] When it occurs in the first creation narrative together with the use of plural pronouns—"Let us make humankind in our image, according to our likeness; and let them have dominion" (Gn. 1:26 NRSV)—surely it is an intimation that God is not a solitary monad, especially since the creature, who is like him, is a fellowship of male and female.

Pointing in the same direction is the way in which Moses is instructed to place God's name upon Israel in blessing by repeating that name three times: "The LORD bless you, . . . the LORD make his face to shine upon you, . . . the LORD lift up his countenance upon you . . ." (Nm. 6:24-26). Such a threefold form of expression is so natural to Christians that they

7. Some look upon it as reflecting a "common Semitic view which perceives the Divine as a 'plurality of forces'" (*Vocabulaire de Théologie Biblique*, col. 217). It is frequently regarded as a "plural of majesty" by which God is included among the heavenly beings of his court (so Von Rad). Thorleif Boman cites this "plural of majesty" as an instance of how the Hebrew mind, in contrast to the Greek mind, tended to use the plural ending *"im"* not only to denote plurality but also intensity. *Das Hebraische Denken im Vergleich mit dem Griechischen* (Göttingen: Vandenhoeck & Ruprecht, 1954), p. 145.

frequently use this Old Testament benediction liturgically, interchanging it with the specifically Christian benediction of Paul: "The grace of the Lord Jesus Christ and the love of God and the fellowship of the Holy Spirit be with you all" (2 Cor. 13:14).[8] As Israel heard the name of God pronounced upon them three times in blessing, so the prophet Isaiah heard the seraphim ascribe a threefold holiness to the same God: ". . . and one cried to another saying, Holy, holy, holy is the Lord of hosts . . ." (Is. 6:3). This latter usage (in the original context probably a superlative attained by repetition) is every way congruous with the triple ascription of holiness in the great throne scene of the Apocalypse where the context is markedly trinitarian. There is One who sits upon the throne; and before the throne are the seven Spirits of God, while in the midst of the throne stands the Lamb. And around this throne are living creatures who, like the seraphim of old, never cease to intone the solemn "Holy, holy, holy, is the Lord God Almighty, who was and is and is to come" (Rv. 4:2-8).[9]

Theologians have also noted the way in which the wisdom of God is personified in the Old Testament as God's Architect and Counselor in creation, the Instructor of the wise who bestows the divine Spirit upon all who seek understanding (Prv. 8). It is this usage that the writers of the New Testament reflect in their view of Jesus as the Logos (Word/Wisdom) who was in the beginning with God and by whom all things were made (Jn. 1:2-3). There is also the striking Old Testament phenomenon of the angel of the Lord, the mysterious messenger of the covenant (Gn. 16:2-13; 22:11, 16; 31:11, 13; 48:15-16; Ex. 3:2, 4-5; Jgs. 13:20-22). Here is One whose title and task distinguish him from God, yet whose presence evokes a response at the human level appropriate only when one is in the presence of God.

Of course, the so-called messianic strand of Old Testament revelation was understood by the writers of the New Testament as anticipating, in some way, the distinction in God that they postulated when they worshipped

8. Thus to interchange an Old and a New Testament benediction is also natural to the Christian because the three names mentioned in the latter—Jesus Christ, God, Holy Spirit—are all called Lord (κύριος) in various texts of the New Testament (Jas. 3:9; 2 Cor. 3:17-18). Furthermore, κύριος is simply the Greek translation for Yahweh, the name used in the threefold Aaronic benediction.

9. This biblical usage, common to both Old and New Testaments, is the basis of the *Tersanctus,* a part of nearly all Eastern and Western rites, as well as the *Trisagion,* a short hymn of response used in the Eastern Church. It also inspired the familiar "Holy, Holy, Holy" by Reginald Heber (1827), which many consider the finest Protestant hymn on the Trinity. The author will not soon forget the moving rendition of this hymn on a Sunday morning by an overflow congregation in Shanghai, China, where most, for want of hymnals, sang the entire hymn from memory.

him both as the Father and as Jesus the Messiah. (See, for example, the use, in Matthew 22:41-45, of the distinction in Psalm 110:1 between "the LORD" [Yahweh] and "my Lord" [Adonai] to imply that Messiah is not just David's son, but also his Lord.) The author of Hebrews argues in an analogous way, quoting Psalm 45:6-7 as an instance of God addressing God. Such a way of speaking implies a distinction in God that warrants the Christians' worship not only of God, but of Jesus as the Son exalted above the angels (Heb. 1:5-9).

Here, then, are intimations contained in the Old Testament, the original revelation of God to his people, that help us understand how the first Christians, who were devout Jews, could continue to read their own Scriptures and at the same time do so in the light of their confession that Jesus is Lord. Indeed, they were convinced that this confession was made in and by the power of the Spirit who had originally inspired those Scriptures. As B. B. Warfield aptly observes,

> The Old Testament may be likened to a chamber richly furnished, but dimly lighted; the introduction of light brings into it nothing which was not in it before; but it brings out into clear view much of what is in it but was only dimly or even not at all perceived before. The mystery of the Trinity is not revealed in the Old Testament; but the mystery of the Trinity underlies the Old Testament revelation. . . .[10]

As for the revelation of God in the New Testament, we have already alluded to the inchoate trinitarian consciousness that pervades the Christian Scriptures. The New Testament story begins with the birth of Jesus. In the annunciation to his mother, she is told (1) that the Holy Spirit shall come upon her, (2) that the power of the Most High shall overshadow her, and (3) that he who is born of her shall be called the Son of God (Lk. 1:35). When Jesus enters upon his public ministry and is baptized, the Spirit descends upon him in the visible form of a dove and a voice from heaven acknowledges him to be the Son in whom God is well pleased (Mt. 3:16-17, par.). In the course of his public ministry, Jesus frequently speaks of God as his Father in a way that implies that he is God's Son in a unique sense. (See especially Lk. 10:22.) And he not only claims to be uniquely related to the Father, but also to the Spirit of God by whose power he does his works. (See Mt. 12:28.)

It is especially in John, where the theological interpretation of Jesus' life is most pronounced, that an implicit trinitarianism is evident. Jesus and the

---

10. B. B. Warfield, "The Biblical Doctrine of the Trinity," *Biblical Doctrines* (New York: Oxford U. Press, 1929), pp. 141-42.

Father are one in such a mysterious way that he who has seen Jesus has seen the Father (Jn. 14:9). Jesus is the One who came from God, a God with whom he had fellowship before the world began (Jn. 16:30; 17:5). As his ministry draws to a close, reference is made to another Paraclete who will come to take his place. This other One, who comes from the Father at the request of the Son, is identified as the Spirit of truth (Jn. 15:26). As Jesus' discourse about the coming Spirit unfolds, both distinction and oneness are assumed in his relationship to the Father and the Son. When this other One comes, even though he comes in Jesus' stead, at the same time his coming is the coming of Jesus and the Father as well (Jn. 16:6-26).

After his resurrection, Jesus appeared to his disciples and commissioned them, according to Matthew's Gospel, to baptize their converts "into the name of the Father and of the Son and of the Holy Spirit" (Mt. 28:19). The trinitarian structure of this passage is so obvious that many have doubted its historicity, though it is clearly a part of the earliest available Matthean text. In any event, it is a most remarkable statement. Jesus' followers are to be baptized into one name, not three; yet this one name is threefold; it is the name of the Father and of the Son and of the Holy Spirit. Remembering that God's name in the Old Testament is virtually a synonym for God himself, the early Christians must have understood this baptismal formula to imply that he who had formally made himself known as the LORD (Yahweh) had now made himself known as Father, Son, and Spirit. Though the risen Lord was not supplanting the God of Israel with a new God, he was telling his disciples that the one, true God, whom they had known as the LORD (Yahweh), they should know henceforth as the Father, Son, and Holy Spirit.

The same trinitarian consciousness can be felt everywhere in the New Testament. Paul, writing early in the second half of the first century, greets his readers in the name (note the singular) of "God our Father and the Lord Jesus Christ" (Rom. 1:7). The Spirit of God, he says, is related to God as the spirit of an individual human self is related to that self (1 Cor. 2:11). Thus, all in whom the Spirit of God dwells are really indwelt by God; they are the temples of God (1 Cor. 3:16). Hence Paul constantly associates the Lord Jesus Christ, God the Father, and the Holy Spirit as together the common source of salvation. "Through him [Christ] we both have access in one Spirit to the Father" (Eph. 2:18-22).

As Paul speaks, so do the other New Testament authors. Peter, for example, refers to the foreknowledge of God the Father according to which his readers were elect in sanctification of the Spirit unto obedience and the sprinkling of the blood of Jesus Christ (1 Pt. 1:2). Jude exhorts his readers to pray in the Holy Spirit, keeping themselves in the love of God and looking for the mercy of our Lord Jesus Christ unto eternal life (Jude

20-21). The last book of the Bible, the Apocalypse, opens with a greeting so beautiful in form and so trinitarian in nuance that it is sometimes used liturgically to begin a formal service of worship in lieu of a call to worship: "Grace to you and peace from him who is and who was and who is to come, and from the seven spirits who are [sevenfold Spirit who is] before his throne, and from Jesus Christ the faithful witness, the firstborn of the dead, and the ruler of kings on earth" (Rv. 1:4-5).

So throughout the New Testament we have this trinitarian way of speaking about God, the author of peace in the Christian community and the source of divine grace in the Christian life. It is a language clear, unstudied, and natural, yet at the same time so mysterious and profound that we know we shall never fathom its depths even with our most careful definitions. But then, the church did not define the doctrine of the Trinity in order to resolve the mystery of the divine nature but rather to preserve it.

EXCURSUS: CONCERNING THE *VESTIGIA*

Before we turn our attention to the exposition of the doctrine, a word is in order about the "pictures" of the Trinity that theologians have seen in nature. Obviously the thought of one God, undivided and indivisible, who in his essential being is yet distinguished as Father, Son, and Holy Spirit, is anything but self-evident. It is not surprising, then, that many have sought analogies from the created realm to aid the understanding, likening the Trinity to something in the world of everyday experience that exhibits oneness and threeness. Early on, Basil, Gregory of Nyssa, and others argued that as the root, stem, and fruit are one tree, so the Father, Son, and Spirit are one God. Many and ingenious have been those who have followed in their steps. Examples are drawn from nature (solid, liquid, gas); culture (grammar, dialectic, rhetoric); history (the Old Testament age, the New Testament age, the present church age); religion (the soul's subjective states of knowledge, meditation, contemplation); the ancient mysteries (triads of deities like Osiris, Isis, Horus); and human psychology (memory, intelligence, will). This last was a favorite with Augustine, who also related this threefold structure of the human psyche to the *imago Dei*. (Augustine devotes three books [IX-XI] of his treatise *De Trinitate* to the *vestigia*, thus assuring them a permanent place in the ongoing theological discussion.) These and other examples can be found in theological disquisitions stemming from ancient, medieval, and modern times.

Yet many theologians have had reservations about these so-called "vestiges" of the Trinity in the created order, and with reason. For one thing, such analogies are often farfetched, more ingenious than substantive. Furthermore, even the most plausible and seemingly correct are sometimes more illustrative of heresy than of orthodoxy. Depending upon the circumstances, water does, indeed, occur in the threefold form of a solid, a liquid, and a vapor. In like manner, the Sabellians argued, God, depending on the circumstances, appears in the form of the Father, the Son, and the Spirit. So our illustration ends up in Modalism. To be sure, there are triads of deities in the mystery religions. But if the Father, the Son, and the Spirit are said to be like them, our illustration ends up in tritheism. Unfortunately, such faulty illustrations are common in preaching—and often the only part of the sermon that is remembered!

Not only is the ground slippery under our feet when we say the Trinity is like this or that, but there is a real danger that we will unwittingly move beyond the effort to illustrate the Trinity and seek to establish the doctrine on the basis of such arguments. When this happens, we are well on our way to reducing the truth of biblical revelation to that immanental knowledge that regards the Trinity as an instance of our self-understanding, that is, as religious myth. This possibility was in Barth's mind when he asked if the concept of the *vestigia trinitatis* might not be a Trojan horse that we have too readily allowed into our theological citadel. (For his sympathetic yet rigorous critique of the *vestigia*, see *K.D.*, I/1, pp. 352-67; cf. *C.D.*, I/1, sec. 8.3.)

In any case, surely we must be very clear about the fact that the doctrine of the Trinity is grounded in revelation and has no other ground whatever. We believe and confess God to be the triune God—Father, Son and Holy Spirit—because he has so disclosed himself to us in the Incarnation and at Pentecost. We must not bring revealed truth into captivity to the world, but the world into captivity to revealed truth; otherwise, we stand in violation of the second commandment. For one whose mind and heart are already illumined by the truth revealed, such illustrations are no more than illustrations, edifying pointers in the direction of the truth.

In a memorable book, *The Mind of the Maker* (New York: Harper, 1941), Dorothy Sayers lays out an analogy between "the mind of the maker" (the human agent) and the Mind of the maker's Maker (the triune God). She elaborates her argument in terms of her own art as a creative writer. First there is the book as thought—the Idea in the writer's mind. Secondly, there is the book as written—the Energy or the Word incarnated, the express image of the Idea. Third, there is the book as read—the Power of its effect in the mind of the responsive reader. All of this is true because the archetype and pattern of the creative artist's own personhood is the threefold Personhood in whose image she is made.

This argument is forceful, not only because it is put with erudition and consummate skill, but because it rests upon a likeness between God and the one creature on earth who, in the Christian vision, is indeed made in the divine image. It therefore escapes both the superficiality (one and three for their own sake) and the distorting profundity (as in the Hegelian dialectic of thesis, antithesis, and synthesis) that so often make efforts of this sort less than satisfying. Sayers's argument may well be the most successful defense of the *vestigia* yet achieved.

D. THE EXPOSITION OF THE DOCTRINE

1. THE TRINITY OF BEING: THE ONENESS OF GOD

a. Introduction

As we have already noted, the first Christians were Jews, and the God whom they worshipped was the God of the Jews, the one, only, true, and living God whose name was Yahweh/LORD. As Christians, they continued to believe that "there is no God but one" (1 Cor. 8:4) and to identify this one God with the God whom their forebears worshipped. In this conviction they never wavered. When Gentile converts joined their ranks, they too were said to have turned from idols to serve this one God (1 Thes. 1:9). At the same time, they confessed Jesus as Lord, making him the object of their worship. But how could this be? How could these early Christians both believe in the one God whose name was Yahweh/LORD and at the same time confess that *Jesus* was Lord?

The answer to this question, achieved only after a long and difficult debate, was the doctrine that affirms both that God is one, yet that he is also three-in-one: the Father, the Son, and the Holy Spirit. As they worked through the problem, Christian theologians began with the assumption that God is one. Recognizing the inheritance of the church in Israel, they never doubted the divine unity. Yet in the end they concluded that this oneness of God is not a oneness of undifferentiated identity (as in Islam), but rather a oneness-in-fellowship. To describe this new teaching, they coined a new word: "trinity." This doctrine of the Trinity, as finally developed, affirms that *God is one in his essential being; but in this one, essential being there subsist eternally three distinct Persons: the Father, the Son, and the Holy Spirit. The Father is of none, neither begotten nor proceeding; the Son is eternally begotten of the Father; and the Spirit eternally proceeds from the Father and the Son.* We must ask and seek to answer the question: What do Christians mean and what does the church teach that they mean when they confess this doctrine of the Trinity? Before we do so, however, we pause to summarize the story of how the church came to believe and declare that God is a Trinity.

Excursus: A Historical Note

In the trinitarian controversy, all the gamut of bitter passion and the prejudice of fanatical zeal were exhibited in an argument that engaged everyone from the emperor in the imperial court to the slave in the marketplace. The contestants were firmly convinced that they were enunciating a theology that it would be "impious to doubt and fatal to mistake" (Gibbons). But for all this display of human frailty, in and through the din of party strife, the Spirit of God led the church into the truth, as is evidenced by the fact that the doctrine of the Trinity is confessed by all major branches of the Christian church down to the present day.

The early teachers of the church approached the problem from one of two directions. Some, especially in the East, began with the man Jesus of Nazareth, and attributed divine sonship to him by virtue of his "adoption" into the Godhead (hence the name Adoptionists). Through the bestowal of God's Spirit at his baptism, the divine Logos came to dwell in the man Jesus (Paul of Samosata, et al.). This early effort preserved the oneness of God by postulating a radical distinction between the Father (God in the primary sense) and the Son (God in a secondary, i.e., honorary, sense). Others approached the problem from the opposite perspective, making no significant difference between the Father and the Son. In this view, the oneness of God was preserved by saying that the one God revealed himself in the Old Testament as the Father of Israel and in the New Testament as Jesus. God is not the Father and the Son, but the Father or the Son according to the mode and time of his appearing. (Hence the name Modalism or Sabellianism, from Sabellius, the most celebrated teacher of Modalism in the West.)

Meanwhile, with the appearance on the scene of Arius, a presbyter of Alexandria, the issue became ever more agitated. According to Arius, Jesus was more than an exalted man. He was a preexistent creature, indeed the first of all God's creation. Citing Proverbs 8:22-31, which hypostatizes God's "Wisdom" that he "created for the sake of his other works," Arius and his followers identified this Wisdom of God with the "Logos" and "Son" of God. These titles described the divine in Christ, who was the "only begotten" in the sense that he alone was immediately created by God and all other creatures were created through him. Thus, in Arian thought Christ was uniquely related to both God and humankind but identical with neither. The Arians also appealed to Colossians 1:15, where Christ is called the firstborn (πρωτότοκος) of all creation. But though he is thus unique as the first and best of creatures, he is a creature still. Since God is one, the Son cannot also be God in the ultimate sense of the word. That would be a contradiction that can be relieved only when we affirm that though he was created before all worlds, there was a time when even he was not. The opponents of Arius, on the other hand, understood the πρωτότοκος of Colossians 1:15 to refer to the priority of dignity granted the risen Christ as "head over all things for the church" (Eph. 1:22). They also pointed out that the verses immediately following Colossians 1:15 do not say that "in him all *other* things were created" and that "he is before all *other* things." They rather say that "in him *all* things were created" and that he is before *all* things.

As the controversy heated up, the whole church was transformed into a theological battleground through the importance of the subject and the zeal of the protagonists. Emperor Constantine, a Christian catechumen (and a shrewd politician), perceived this threat to the unity of the church as a threat to the unity of the empire that he was determined to restore. When it became apparent that he could not reconcile the warring parties through the channels of diplomacy, he followed the advice of his aging mentor, Bishop Hosius of Spain, and called the first ecumenical council of the church. It met at Nicaea in 325 to resolve the burning question of the relation of the Son to the Father. The council was officially convened by Constantine himself (a fateful commingling of church and state that marks the birth of what many have called "Christendom"), in the central building of the royal palace. The assembled bishops, some of whom bore in their bodies the scars of the Diocletian persecution, rose from their seats to greet the emperor, who admonished them to put away all strife and loosen the knots of discord.

Arius and his followers were opposed by the Orthodox, who insisted on the full deity of the Son. Their most able spokesman was Athanasius, a youthful archdeacon who, like Arius, was from Alexandria. The initial statement offered by the Arians having been rejected, the mediating party offered a statement which acknowledged that Christ was divine but avoided saying that he was *homoousios*—that is, of the same essential being—with the Father. Wishing a creed to which no true Arian would subscribe, the Orthodox for their part insisted on using the term *homoousios,* since the Arians despised it as unscriptural and Sabellian. As a result, a statement was introduced by Bishop Hosius in which the full deity of Christ was secured by the affirmation that he is "the Son of God, begotten of the Father, only begotten—that is, of the *ousia* (essence) of the Father—God from God, light from light, true God from true God, begotten not made, *homoousios* with the Father." Virtually all the bishops signed this orthodox formula. Arius, however, refused to do so, surely an act of courage as well as integrity under the circumstances. In fact, some feel Arius's firm stand forced the church to greater precision of thought and so contributed in the end to the cause of orthodoxy.

After the council, the controversy became more acrimonious than ever due to a commingling of politics and theology. This was especially so during the reign of Constantius, a fanatical Arian partisan, who inherited his father Constantine's throne. Athanasius, who had emerged at Nicaea as the leading spokesman for the Orthodox and who was made bishop of Alexandria in 338, was especially marked for ruin. Being driven on one occasion from the cathedral in Alexandria by 5,000 armed soldiers during a service of divine worship, he was in and out of office five times during his tenure. In all, he spent twenty years either in exile or as a fugitive! Above all others, his name has been associated with the doctrine of the Trinity, and rightly so, for he devoted all his time and energies to its elaboration and defense. Eventually, due to his labors, and due also to the internecine controversies within the ranks of the Arian party and to the long and powerful reign of Theodosius I, a champion of the Nicene Creed, orthodoxy prevailed.

Theodosius called the second ecumenical council at Constantinople in 381 to restore the unity of the church. No new statement was formulated, but the article on the Spirit in the original Nicene Creed was considerably enlarged to read: "and [we believe] in the Holy Spirit, who is the Lord and Giver of life, who proceeds from the Father, who with the Father and the Son together is worshiped and glorified, who spoke by the prophets." In this Creed, now known technically as the Niceno-Constantinopolitan, we have the essentials of the orthodox confession of the Trinity. Since the Niceno-Constantinopolitan eventually displaced the original Nicene Creed (except among certain sects of the Eastern church), it is now often referred to simply as the Nicene Creed. A later creed, whose origin is obscure, dating from the middle of the fifth century, spread from Gaul throughout the West and eventually came to be accepted also in the East. This document, called the Athanasian Creed, which teaches the procession of the Spirit from the Son (*filioque*) as well as from the Father, marks the final form of the development of the orthodox doctrine of the Trinity. (The Eastern version of the Creed omits the *filioque.*) Sometimes referred to as the *Quicumque Vult,* from the first two words of the original Latin text, it is a masterly statement: clear, rigorous, and precise, though marred by anathemas (characteristic of the age) against any who dared demur at any article of the trinitarian faith.

b. God's Oneness: A Oneness of Essential Being

We shall begin our exposition of the doctrine of the Trinity where our definition begins, that is, with the oneness of God. In what sense are Father, Son, and Spirit *one* God? What do Christians mean, and what does the church teach that they mean, when they make such a confession? As we have noted, this question initially confronted the church as it sought to understand how Jesus, the Son of God, is related to the God whom he called his Father. The breakthrough finally came with the consensus that the Son is one with the Father in his essential being as divine. Once this consensus was reached, the church went on to agree that the Spirit is likewise one, both with the Father and the Son; hence he also, in his essential being, is divine. And so the three are one God; that is to say, the members of the Godhead are one in their divine nature or essence, one in their deity or Godhead.[11]

The technical term used by the Fathers for the being of God was the Greek οὐσία; Latin *essentia, natura, substantia;* English "essence," "nature," "substance." At Nicaea, Jesus the Son was declared to be ὁμοούσιος with the Father — that is, of the same substance, consubstantial, with the Father. This formula (dear to the orthodox) offended the Arians, who viewed Jesus as a creature and would say no more than that he was ὁμοιούσιος, of *like* substance with the Father.[12] In our day this term "consubstantial" is sometimes criticized, even by those who are not opposed to trinitarian doctrine as such, on the score that "substance" describes an object, whereas the God of the Bible is a personal God, a subject, indeed the absolute Subject. Thus Brunner, for example, observes: "That this fatal concept [*substantia*] came into the *Credo* was a genuine misfortune."[13] Such concern for the personal dimension as ultimate in our thought about God is, indeed, commendable. And it does require that one take into careful account the way in which the term "substance" was used in ancient and

11. The theological term "Godhead" translates the Greek θεότης (Col. 2:9) or θειότης (Rom. 1:20). The two terms are virtual synonyms and refer to all that makes God God and grounds his claim to the exclusive worship of the creature.

12. The difference between these terms of one Greek letter (iota) has provoked the derision of many since the days of Gibbon.

13. Emil Brunner, *Dogmatik* (Zurich: Zwingli-Verlag, 1960), vol. I, p. 243.

medieval theology. When we do so and thus come to understand the meaning of "substance" (οὐσία) in classic theological usage, our present-day emphasis on the dimension of the personal will be seen to complement rather than contradict the traditional way of speaking of God.

In the Middle Ages, the term "substance" had a different meaning from that of "matter." Substance referred to the form in which matter is organized; matter was the stuff that is organized by the form. On the lowest end of the scale were inanimate objects whose form makes them one thing in distinction from another. (Thus a book is distinguished from the chair in which I am sitting when I read it.) At the other end of the scale were immaterial substances, pure forms, such as angels. They are real beings, but not material beings. Between these two extremes, we have animate substances ranging from plants to humans. Each is made of matter that is given form by its soul. At death, when the soul departs, the matter, having no form in itself, lapses back into its original disorganized state. A living cat that eats, sleeps, purrs, and catches mice is *substantially* a cat. A dead cat is simply matter in the process of losing its organized cat shape through decay.

> We remain nearer to the scholastic use [of the term "substance"] when we say: "Give me the substance of that document"—meaning by that, neither the material ink and paper, nor yet the "accidental" form of the words, but the underlying (substantial) sense which makes the document what it essentially is—a greeting, a transfer of property, a proposal of marriage, a dog license or what not.[14]

As for the fact that "substance" often means, in our day, the same thing as "matter," it should be remembered that in modern physics even matter is not as "substantive" as it once was. Though everyday usage may not have changed significantly, those who work on the frontiers of the physical sciences speak of the world of material substance as an illusion. In this regard, it is interesting to recall Sir Arthur Eddington's introduction to his Gifford lectures, *The Nature of the Physical World,* where he talks about the two tables on which he is writing. Table number one is a commonplace object in the world.

> It has extension; . . . above all it is *substantial.* . . . I mean that it is constituted of "substance" and by that word I am trying to convey to you some conception of its intrinsic nature. . . . There is nothing substantial about my second table. It is nearly all empty space—space pervaded, it is true, by fields of force, but these are assigned to the category of "influences," not of "things." Even in the minute part which is not empty we must not transfer the old notion of

---

14. Dorothy L. Sayers, trans., *The Divine Comedy,* II: *Purgatory* (Baltimore: Penguin Books, 1959), p. 212. The above comments are taken from her illuminating discussion of this matter, to which we are indebted.

substance. In dissecting matter into electric charges we have travelled far from that picture of it which first gave rise to the conception of substance, and the meaning of that conception—if it ever had any—has been lost by the way. . . . The external world of physics has thus become a world of shadows. In removing our illusions we have removed the substance, for indeed, we have seen that substance is one of the greatest of all illusions. (*The Nature of the Physical World*, New York: Macmillan, 1929, pp. ix–xi, xiv)

If then our usage were *truly* contemporary, the term "substance" might be almost—though for other reasons—as nonmaterial in its meaning for us as it was for the theologians of the Middle Ages. (See Heim's remarks on the theological implications for religious materialism of the abandonment, this side of Planck's quantum theory, of the absolute material object of physics. *The Transformation of the Scientific World View*, London: SCM, 1953, chap. 2.)

Be that as it may, there is value in retaining the classic "metaphysical" language used to speak of God, along with the contemporary language of the personal. Such traditional language preserves the doctrine of the Trinity from being reduced to subjective, psychological categories that do not describe God as he has revealed himself to be, but rather in the way in which we *experience* him.[15] Given the classic doctrine in which the Father, Son, and Spirit subsist eternally in one Being (οὐσία), there can be no doubt that there is a real Trinity transcending the realms of changing, subjective human experience.

When all is said and done, of course, it must be admitted that such terms as "being," "substance," and "ultimate reality" are not used in Scripture to describe God. Even "godness" (θειότης) and "godhood" (θεότης) occur rarely in the New Testament. The Bible does not speak of God as one in "essence" or "being" but as one Lord (Dt. 6:4). But the Bible does use the verb "to be" of God; and theology has the task of elaborating the meaning of the biblical text, including the text "God *is*. . . ." We do not believe, therefore, that the doctrine of the Trinity, as traditionally expounded, loses sight of the text when it elaborates the oneness of God in terms of his being or essence. We agree with Barth when he says,

We can equate the concept of God's *lordship*, the concept to which we found the entire notion of biblical revelation to be related in our former discussion, with what was called, in the language of the ancient

15. Treatments of the doctrine of the Trinity since Schleiermacher are often not so much studies in theology as in the psychology of religious experience. The Trinity is construed functionally, phenomenologically, immanently, but never ontologically. Ontologically, God is simply absolute *Geist*. See, as an example of such, H. P. Van Dusen's *Spirit, Son and Father* (New York: Scribner's, 1958).

church, the essential being of God, the Deity or Divinity, the divine *ousia,* essence, nature, or substance. The essential reality of God is the being of God as *divine* Being. The essential reality of God is just the *Godhood* [*Gottheit*] of God.[16]

When we refer, therefore, to God's "essence," we refer to that whereby he, who reveals himself as Lord, is who he is, the "I AM WHO I AM" (Ex. 3:14). The ultimate difficulty, as we shall see, is not in saying that the Father, Son, and Spirit are one God, consubstantial as well as coeternal, but in saying how they can be thus. How is God at the same time essentially one and yet personally three in such a way that we must say that he is one-in-three and three-in-one? This difficulty will become more sharply focused as our discussion unfolds.

ADDENDUM: THE TRINITY IN PROCESS THEOLOGY

In our day some object to speaking of God in the traditional language of "being" (οὐσία), at least in an unqualified way, for ultimate philosophic reasons. We have in mind the theologians of Process. Here we face an issue of profound significance for the Christian doctrine of God. (In what follows we shall reflect primarily the thought of Norman Pittenger as found in his *The Divine Triunity,* Philadelphia: United Church Press, 1977, one of the clearest specific statements on the doctrine of the Trinity by a Process thinker.) Because they are themselves seeking to restate the faith in terms drawn from the philosophy of Whitehead and his disciples, Process thinkers are not inclined (as are those who do biblical theology) to condemn the early Fathers of the church for using terms drawn from the Greek philosophy of their day. In fact, the Fathers (in the sometimes condescending appraisal of Process thinkers) did the best they could, given the thought categories of Neoplatonism that they had available to them. But approval of what they did in their day does not mean that we can accept it in ours.

Anyone who has even a cursory acquaintance with Process thought will hardly be surprised at this judgment. Process thought represents a type of philosophic conceptuality in which the ultimate reality is "becoming," not "being"; "process," not "substance." Hence, to describe the unity of God as Father, Son, and Holy Spirit in terms of substance/essence/being

16. *K.D.,* I/1, p. 369 (cf. *C.D.,* I/1, sec. 9.1). His italics. The dictionary definition of οὐσία, as used by the ancient Fathers in the trinitarian debate, is simply "a particular entity regarded as the subject of qualities." See J. N. D. Kelly, *Early Christian Creeds* (London: Longman, 1972), pp. 243-44.

is unthinkable for Process theologians. We now see the world through the glasses of evolution and quantum theory. Such a perspective gives us a wholly different picture of reality from that of antiquity, including the picture of the divine Reality. Consequently, even the common terms "Trinity" and "trinitarian" are unacceptable to a Process theologian like Pittenger, who speaks always of the "Triunity" and of the "triunitarian" pattern of human experience rather than the Trinity and the trinitarian nature of God.

> A simple example here [of the difference between traditional and contemporary ways of thinking] is the common acceptance in the Patristic Age of the concept of substance (οὐσία in Greek) as the basic reality in all that is known and experienced. We today are much more likely to accept the concept of activity, energy, happening, or event as the fundamental reality in the world. (Ibid., pp. 35-36)

Hence, the difficulty with traditional theology (orthodoxy) is that it makes the concept of "being" the key to understanding the divine Reality. In contrast to this traditional approach we now perceive that a thing is what it does and this means that God is his activity. This divine activity is principally the inspiration of worship, the "lure which God offers and the sheer attraction of his goodness in action" (ibid., p. 106). Furthermore, this divine activity is given human statement in Jesus, a statement that impels a response so pervasive that the first Christians understood it as the presence of God's Spirit. Thus God is ever operative alongside and upon nature, history, and human lives. This divine action with and through nature and history occurs both in an incarnational way—as Logos—and in an immanent way—as Spirit. We must not, however, confine the working of God as Logos to Jesus as known in the Christian community, for it is not possible to identify Jesus as the unique Son of God. And the same is true for the New Testament account of Pentecost. To construe such an event as unique would confine the working of God, as Spirit, in an intolerable way. Hence Pittenger and other Process theologians can find no place for the orthodox doctrine of the Trinity in their understanding of the term "God."[17]

Hendrikus Berkhof, who offers no treatment as such of the doctrine of the Trinity in his *Christian Faith*, ends his discussion of Christology with a section entitled "The Covenant as Tri-(u)nity." Here he observes that the three names "Father-Son-Spirit, or, with equal validity, of Father-Spirit-Son, proves to be the summarizing description of the covenantal event, both as to its historical and its existential aspect. . . . With the term

17. For a lucid and sensitive critique of Process Theology and the Trinity, see John J. O'Donnell, *Trinity and Temporality* (New York: Oxford U. Press, 1983).

'Trinity' we point to a continuing and open event, directed
event in which we participate as we are conformed to the image
through the Spirit. Thus we see how God has "made himself c\
Together with us he is involved in a process, which also does something
to him because as Father it enriches him with sons and daughters."[18] Thus
in Berkhof's theology the triune God of the Creed becomes a triune event;
rather than ruling over history, God is enriched by history. His name is not
"I AM WHO I AM," but "I am becoming who I hope to be."

Barth's thought that God's being is "being as event" reflects, we might
note, an entirely different agenda from that of Process thought. Barth is
interested in the contrast between Aristotle's Unmoved Mover and the
Christian God. The latter, he argues, is a trinitarian fellowship and this
fellowship is an event, internal to himself, an event that is the ontological
ground of the external event of historical revelation. (See also E. Jüngel,
The Doctrine of the Trinity, Grand Rapids: Eerdmans, 1976.) Along the
same lines Brunner observes that while God, in contrast to the Platonic
deity, hears prayer and so enters into the human event, such an accom-
panying *(mitgehen)* of our temporal order does not mean that God is subject
to that order.

> His accompanying a temporal event by no means signifies that
> favored notion of moderns: the *becoming* God. The concept of a
> becoming God is a mythological game. Were God himself one who
> becomes, all would sink in the morass of relativism. . . . A changing
> God is no God to whom we can pray, but a mythical being who
> provokes our sympathy. (*Dogmatik,* I, p. 275)[19]

2. THE TRINITY OF BEING: THE THREENESS OF GOD

a. Introduction

Having considered how God is one, we must now consider how he is three.
Obviously it would be foolishness, not only to Greeks but also to Christians,
to say that God is three in the same sense that he is one. So the church
used a new and different term to describe the distinctions in God. While
God is one in his being (οὐσία) as God, there subsists eternally in this one

---

18. Hendrikus Berkhof, *Christian Faith: An Introduction to the Study of the Faith,* rev.
ed. (Grand Rapids: Eerdmans, 1986), pp. 335-37.
19. Emil Brunner, *Dogmatik,* vol. I, p. 275.

being three distinct persons (Greek ὑπόστασις; Latin *persona*)—the Father, the Son, and the Spirit.

ὑπόστασις, the technical term used in the East from the time of Origen to designate the distinctions in God, was problematical for the ancient Fathers. For many of them, it was basically synonymous with *ousía*, so that to speak of Father, Son, and Spirit as "hypostases" seemed to suggest they were three distinct beings in a way that verged on tritheism. This was somewhat true even in the West, where Jerome darkly warned that there was poison in the word "hypostasis." Adding to the difficulty was the fact that in the Western church, the Latin term "persona" (person) used to translate ὑπόστασις was more nearly the equivalent of πρόσωπον, meaning "face" or "countenance." The Easterners shied away from this term because it could mean "mask," that is, the "face" with which an actor appears in a play. This suggested the Sabellian notion that Father, Son, and Spirit were not ultimate distinctions in God but simply modes of his appearance. The one God assumes different faces, depending on the times and circumstances.

A further complication was that in the later christological controversies, this trinitarian usage was reversed. While in the Godhead there are three persons in one nature, in Christ there are two natures in one person. As Pelikan observes,

> In the Trinity, "nature" and "ousia" referred to that which was one, "hypostasis" or "person" to that which was more than one; in the person of Christ "nature" or "ousia" referred to that which is more than one, "hypostasis" or "person" to that which was one.[20]

Finally, the use of "person" to describe the distinctions in God has been criticized in modern times because, at the human level, it designates individual selves and thus makes the trinitarian distinctions too radical. Father, Son, and Spirit become three individuals like the three musketeers in Dumas's novel.

For all of these semantical problems, however, the term "person" has prevailed for want of a better one. Hence we shall use it, trying in the ensuing discussion to make the sense in which we use it as plain as possible. One term, however, we shall never use when speaking of God, and that is "personality." Personality, viewed as the distinctive character traits manifested by an individual in a social context, has become so completely the domain of psychology that we prefer not to use it in theology. What with "personality conflicts" and the like, it only confuses matters to use the term when speaking of God. There are multiple persons in the Godhead, but not "multiple personalities." Even the incarnate Son, though fully human, is not treated by the evangelists in terms of the traits of his "personality." Fortunately, the Jesus of the gospels cannot be made the subject of psychological analysis any more than he can be made the protagonist of contemporary social and political theories or the product of religious evolution.

As has often been observed, the Christian affirmation that God is one is intended to say that God alone is God, to the exclusion of all other gods,

---

20. J. Pelikan, *The Christian Tradition,* vol. II, p. 81.

not that God is alone in the sense of monistic singularity and solitude. According to the Christian confession, so far from being a lonely, solitary God, the true God is really an eternal fellowship of persons: the Father, the Son, and the Holy Spirit. These designations describe personal distinctions in the very being of God himself. But what does "person" mean in this trinitarian context? What is the common thought that makes the term equally applicable to all three—Father, Son, and Spirit?

So difficult is this question that it was certainly no mock humility that led the medieval theologians to refer to the plurality in God as ineffable. Approaching the question negatively, all agreed that the *ineffabilis pluralitas* is not a matter of properties or qualities of the divine essence. The three persons are not three attributes of God—though some modern theologians have actually subsumed the Trinity under the divine attributes. God the Father is not the wrath of God, nor are the Son and the Spirit respectively the mercy and love of God. Nor is the principle that is common to the three persons the one divine being (essence) in the sense that the three persons were three parts of the one God. The divine persons are not distinctions *of* God's being — as though each made up a third part of God — but distinctions *in* his being. In our definition of the Trinity, it will be recalled, we did not say that in God's one, essential being there eternally exist three distinct persons, but rather, in the one, essential being there eternally *subsist* three distinct persons. This distinction between "existence" and "subsistence" is important because, as we shall see, it bears upon the meaning of the term "person" in trinitarian usage.

b. God's Threeness: A Threeness of Personal Subsistence

As for the thought that the three divine persons "subsist in" the essential being of God rather than "exist as" three divine persons alongside one another, it is not difficult to see that the former way of speaking helps to avoid the impression that the three persons in the Godhead are three separate persons. To "subsist" is to be in a certain manner, form, or state, as white "subsists" in snow. As snow would not be snow apart from whiteness, so this particular whiteness of which we speak when we say that snow is white would not be whiteness apart from snow. So it is with the divine persons; they do not exist independently, but rather subsist mutually, in the Godhead. As God would not be God—could not be God— save as Father, Son, and Spirit, so the Father, Son, and Spirit would not, indeed *could not*, be Father, Son, and Spirit save as God.

It is for this reason that theologians have seen in "subsistence" a concept that points in the direction of an answer to the difficult question:

What does "person" mean when used of the members of the Godhead? Thomas defines a divine person (in contrast to a human person) "as an incommunicable subsistence in the divine essence." By using the term "subsistence" rather than "substance," he sought to avoid the substantive definition of person (Boethius) that would imply that the Father, the Son, and the Spirit are three substantive beings, that is, three Gods after the likeness of three individual beings at the human level. By qualifying each subsistence as "incommunicable," Thomas affirms that the members of the Godhead are distinct one from the other; their mode of subsistence involves properties unique and unshareable. This unique subsistence is what the persons do not have in common in contrast to their essential deity, which they do have in common as the one God.

What might these incommunicable properties be whereby each person is distinguished from the other? Thomas finds the answer to this question in their relations one to another. These relations have to do with the origins of the several persons; the Father is of none, the Son is of the Father, and the Spirit is of the Father and the Son. The divine persons, in other words, are to be understood relationally. As Thomas says, ". . . a divine Person signifies a *relation* as subsisting."[21] In this understanding of the term, Thomas was followed by Calvin. Early in his exposition of the Trinity, Calvin offers the following definition of a trinitarian person: "What I call a Person is a subsistence in the divine essence, which is related to the others, yet distinguished from them by an incommunicable property."[22] This thought, that the key to understanding the term "person," in an intertrinitarian sense, is the relationship which the members of the Godhead have one to another, pervades the history of the doctrine of the Trinity.[23]

---

21. See his *Summa Theologica,* Q. 29, The Divine Persons (in Four Articles), especially Art. 4. Also Q. 30, Art. 1.

22. *Institutes,* I, 13, 6. The term "property" in Calvin's definition translates ἰδιότης/*proprietas,* first used by Basil, et al., to denote that particularizing characteristic or identifying peculiarity which distinguishes each member of the Godhead. Thus the term is technically distinct from "attribute," which denotes those characteristics that are common to all the persons, such as mercy, justice, and the like. In this place, Calvin goes on to justify the distinction between subsistence and essence with the observation, ". . . if the Word were simply God and had no peculiar property, John would have been guilty of impropriety in saying that he was always *with* God. When he immediately adds that the *Word* also *was* God, he reminds us of the unity of the essence."

23. See Barth, *K.D.,* I/1, pp. 384-85 (cf. *C.D.,* I/1, sec. 9.3), who cites the sources of the *Relationenlehre* beginning with Tertullian and going on to the Cappadocians, Augustine, Anselm, Thomas, Luther, and Calvin. It was given official, dogmatic definition at the Council of Florence, "The Decree for the Jacobites" (1442). Barth complains that Melanchthon

c. The Relational Meaning of the Trinitarian Name: Father, Son, and Holy Spirit

In elaborating the meaning of the trinitarian name into which Christians are baptized, theologians have, as we noted, emphasized the concept of origins; the Father is of none, the Son is of the Father, and the Spirit is of the Father and the Son. It is this approach that accounts for the order whereby the Father is called the first person, the Son the second person, and the Spirit the third person of the Godhead. As we have seen, when reviewing the biblical data, this order is not reflected in New Testament usage, though it is implied in the flow of redemptive history. God is the Father of Israel, who in the fullness of time sends the Son to save his people. The Son, in turn, pours out the Spirit on the gathered community at Pentecost. However, it is not salvation history but the eternal relations of the members of the Godhead that account for the universally recognized order in the doctrine of the Trinity. This order is an order of propriety arising out of the mysterious relationship that the members of the Godhead have one to another. And, we might add, we speak of it as an order of "propriety" because it is not an order of dignity: all three persons are alike God, coequal and consubstantial.

Our question, then, is this: What are these unique and mysterious relationships whereby one member of the Godhead is the Father as distinct from the Son and Spirit; another is the Son as distinct from the Father and the Spirit; and still another is the Spirit as distinct from the Father and the Son? What is the "incommunicable property," to use Calvin's phrase, whereby one is eternally the Father, one eternally the Son, and one eternally the Spirit? Classically, the answer has been given that the first person is uniquely the Father in that he, and he only, is begotten of none and proceeds from none; the second person is uniquely the Son in that he, and he only, is begotten of the Father; the third person is uniquely the Spirit in that he, and he only, proceeds from the Father and the Son.

Elaborating on this general statement, theologians have affirmed that when we identify the distinctive property of the first person to be that he is "of none, neither begotten nor proceeding," this carries with it the thought that he is the first principle of the Trinity. Therefore, as we speak of him as "Father" in a secondary way, because he is the source of all created reality ("I believe in God the Father almighty, Maker of heaven and earth"),

---

weakened Lutheran Orthodoxy by failing to include the doctrine of the *relationes* in his definition of the term "person" to designate the members of the Godhead.

so we speak of him as Father, in a primary way, because he is the source of those eternal distinctions in the divine Reality which we call the Son and the Spirit. To be of none, then, is his incommunicable property.[24]

Likewise, the second person is called the "Son" because he is begotten of the Father. Filiation is his incommunicable property. The reason theologians have spent so much time on this aspect of the doctrine is that the question of Jesus' essential deity as the Son of God was the question with which the whole discussion began. It was because the church worshipped Jesus as divine that it ultimately came to confess the doctrine of the Trinity. "We believe," says the Creed, that Jesus Christ is "the only begotten Son of God, begotten of the Father before all worlds."[25] The expression "before all worlds" should not be taken as a barren abstraction. In speaking thus, the Creed is affirming that the Son did not become the Son in the Incarnation; rather, he who became incarnate as Jesus of Nazareth was the Son begotten of the Father from all eternity. The Incarnation was the act of an eternal Subject.[26]

In speaking of the Son as "begotten of the Father," the preposition "of" (literally, "out of") is important. The Son is "of" the Father in the sense that he has his very being, as Son, from the Father. This obviously implies that there is an eternal difference between them, a distinction of Father and Son in the one God. Hence the Creed goes on to say that the Son is true God of true God (θεὸν ἀληθινὸν ἐκ θεοῦ ἀληθινοῦ). Both Father and Son are the one, true God, yet not in an undifferentiated way. The one is God, the other is also God; yet the other is not just God, but the God who is "out of" God, the God who is distinct from God—not distinct as God, for there are not two distinct Gods—but distinct as God the Son from God the Father.

In describing the mysterious relationship wherein God is the Father and God is the Son, theologians have used the terms "begetting" and "begotten," which are terms of generation. By so doing, they repudiate the Arian doctrine that denies the full deity of the Son by regarding him as a

---

24. Here it should be noted that we are not saying that the Father begets the Son as God, but as the *Son*. Nor are we saying that the Spirit proceeds as God, but as the *Spirit*. Father, Son, and Spirit are distinctions *in* God, not *between* Gods. See below, pp. 315ff., on economic subordinationism.

25. In the ensuing discussion, "the Creed" refers to the *Symbolum Niceno-Constantinopolitanum*, ratified at the Council of Constantinople, A.D. 381. This is the creed, as Barth observes, which says clearly what Protestant liberalism cannot bear to hear and for this very reason is crucial to all evangelical dogmatics. *K.D.*, I/1, p. 445.

26. The order on which we are here insisting—first he *was* the Son, then he became incarnate *as* the Son—is the theological explanation of the historical fact that Nicaea (A.D. 325) preceded Chalcedon (A.D. 451). The ancient church, to speak in contemporary terms, did its Christology "from above."

creature. Though we cannot fathom the mystery of the eternal begetting of the divine Son (indeed, we cannot fathom the mystery of the temporal begetting of a human son or daughter), by such language the church has been preserved from the teaching of the Arians. On this score, therefore, the Creed is very express. He who is the Son of God and God the Son is "begotten not made" (γεννηθέντα, οὐ ποιηθέντα). Here we see the essential truth that is preserved in the inadequate language of the dogma. As C. S. Lewis observes,

> We don't use the words *begetting* or *begotten* much in modern English, but everyone still knows what they mean. To beget is to become the father of: to create is to make. And the difference is this. When you beget, you beget something of the same kind as yourself. A man begets human babies, a beaver begets little beavers and a bird begets eggs which turn into little birds. But when you make, you make something of a different kind from yourself. A bird makes a nest, a beaver builds a dam, a man makes a wireless set.[27]

We must, Lewis goes on to observe, be very clear about this distinction between begetting and creating. What God creates is not God, even as what humans make is not human. But what humans beget or bear is human just as what God begets is God. Of course, what a human begets comes after him in time; a human father lives before his son. But he does not live as a father before his son lives as a son. He becomes a father only when he begets a son, just as a son becomes a son only when he is begotten of a father. Even in the created realm of time, then, the essential matter is not the temporal sequence, but the relationship whereby one is a father and another a son. Hence the analogy, wherein we speak of the first person as the eternal Father who begets, and the second person as the eternal Son who is begotten, is by no means misleading. There is an element of univocacy between the divine begetting and the human begetting, even though the latter is temporal and the former eternal.

The Christian God is not only the Father and the Son, but also the Spirit. He too subsists eternally as a distinct person in the Godhead. The doctrine of the Spirit was the last to be defined, due to the historical fact, already noted, that the primal Christian confession, "Jesus is Lord," focused the attention of the church, initially, on the Son rather than the Spirit. But there were other considerations at work as well. For one, in Scripture the Father and Son are more clearly distinguished from each other than from the Spirit. For another, the very term "spirit" has an indefiniteness about

27. C. S. Lewis, *Mere Christianity* (New York: Macmillan, 1952), p. 138.

it, since it is a general designation of God ("God is Spirit," Jn. 4:24) as well as a specifically trinitarian one. Even when we qualify "spirit" with the adjective "holy," we are using a term that also applies to God generally. One could confess, therefore—as did the ancient Fathers—that God is present where his Spirit is manifest and that to believe in God is to believe in the Holy Spirit, without answering the question: In what sense is the Spirit divine and how is he related to the Father and the Son?[28]

There is, finally, the more subtle consideration that the Spirit is uniquely concerned with the saving response of the sinner to the divine word. If this response is never possible apart from the work of the Spirit, what of the creature, whose response it is? To acknowledge the full deity of the Spirit, in other words, seemed to threaten the creature with less than her due, if one accepts the doctrine of human freedom current in the Eastern Church at the time of the early trinitarian debate. If he who works salvation in the heart is as fully God as he who accomplished it at Calvary, then the sinner is no longer in her own right a partner with God in accomplishing her salvation. To confess the deity of the Spirit compels one to acknowledge that salvation is God's work, not only in its initiation (the Father gives the Son, Jn. 3:16), not only in its accomplishment (the Son makes purification for our sins, Heb. 1:3), but also in its efficacy (the Spirit enables the sinner to call Jesus Lord, 1 Cor. 12:3). Once, therefore, the trinitarian doctrine of the Spirit had been worked out, the debate between Augustine and Pelagius over sin and grace became inevitable. For this reason, liberal Protestantism, with its Pelagian view of salvation by character ("education," to use Lessing's term), is really a return to the pre-Nicene ambiguity concerning the Spirit.[29]

The trinitarian doctrine of the Spirit affirms of the Spirit all that is said of the Father and the Son. As the Father is eternally the Father and the Son eternally the Son, so the Spirit is eternally the Spirit. To confess God the Holy Spirit is not simply to confess that God is Spirit, but rather that in the fellowship of the Godhead there subsists eternally one who is called

28. Hendrikus Berkhof, in his Warfield lectures on the Spirit, observes that we have "reason to say farewell to the person-concept in pneumatology," since New Testament studies have made it clear the term "spirit" simply designates the exalted Christ at work in the world. *The Doctrine of the Holy Spirit* (Atlanta: John Knox Press, 1964), p. 115. The New Testament data, in our judgment, point in a significantly different direction, which explains why the Christian confession is trinitarian rather than binitarian. Even 2 Corinthians 3:17: "the Lord is the Spirit" (ὁ δὲ κύριος τὸ πνεῦμά ἐστιν) does not identify Jesus with the Spirit—as though Pentecost were in some way a repetition of Christmas. This text rather affirms that to the Spirit belongs the Godhood of the Lord that was the subject of the preceding verse. See Barth, *K.D.*, I/1, p. 473; cf. *C.D.*, I/1, sec. 12.1.

29. See Barth, *K.D.*, I/1 (cf. *C.D.*, I/1, sec. 12.2), p. 491.

the Holy Spirit. As the Son did not become the Son at Bethlehem (nor in his baptism, nor on the morning of Easter), so the Spirit did not become the Spirit at Pentecost. Rather, he who is eternally the Holy Spirit came at Pentecost as the promised Paraclete. And because he who *is* the Holy Spirit is so in eternal distinction from the Father and the Son, the historical distinction between Christmas and Pentecost is, by the same token, a genuine theological distinction. Though the one God is revealed in both events, it is the one God who, as Father, gives his Son and, as Son, bestows his Spirit on the church.

"Procession" has been traditionally recognized as the best term to describe the relation between the Spirit and the other members of the Godhead. The Spirit's "eternal procession" is the "incommunicable property" whereby he is distinguished from the Father and the Son. But what does it mean to affirm the "procession" of the Spirit? In its negative connotation, at least, the answer to this question is clear. The affirmation that the Spirit proceeds from the Father (and the Son) means that he is not a creature. (Creation is not a procession or emanation out of God. It is rather an act of God that grounds that reality which is both dependent upon him and essentially different from him.) As the Son is not made but "begotten," so the Spirit is not made but "proceeds." Thus, as in the case of the Son, the doctrine of the church secures the full deity of the Spirit in terms of his unique relationship to the other persons in the Godhead.

But what does it mean, positively, to speak of the eternal procession of the Spirit? Here matters become more difficult, for as the trinitarian name "Spirit" is less definite than that of "Son," so the relationship of "procession" is less definite than that of "generation." One can appreciate why Barth says that to be faithful to revelation we must affirm the difference between the *processio Spiritus* and the *generatio Filii*; yet at the same time, when we seek to explain that difference, we face a difficulty that seems insuperable.[30]

By way of elucidation, if not explanation, theologians have suggested (we can hardly use a stronger term) that "procession" is a divine "breathing" (Latin *spiratio*). The Father (and Son) eternally "spirate" the Spirit, whose very name means "breath" or "wind."

> Breathe on me Breath of God,
> Fill me with life anew,

---

30. *K.D.,* I/1, p. 498 (cf. *C.D.,* I/1, sec. 12.2). The Cappadocians (especially Basil) distinguished the mode of the Spirit's origin (procession) from that of the Son (generation) to escape the Arian jibe that the *homoousios* of the Spirit meant that the Father had two Sons.

That I may love what thou doest love,
And do what thou wouldst do. (Hatch)[31]

Because the Spirit is, from all eternity, the life-giving breath of God, he is revealed as the *Creator Spiritus* whose presence renews the face of the ground (Ps. 104:30). By the same token, it is he who works through the waters of baptism to bring forth new life in the minds and hearts of the heirs of salvation. (To see the kingdom, our Lord said, one must be born of water and the Spirit; Jn. 3:5.) Again, because the Spirit is the very breath of God, the Scriptures that he inspired are aptly described as "God-breathed" *(theopneustos),* as we read in 2 Timothy 3:16. More examples need not be given at this time inasmuch as we shall return to the ways in which the eternal God is revealed as Spirit (as well as Father and Son) when we speak of the Trinity of revelation.[32] Thus all that is taught and affirmed of the Father and the Son is also taught and affirmed of the Spirit. The three are one God, coequal and consubstantial, yet eternally distinct as the Father who begets, the Son who is begotten, and the Spirit who proceeds.

Concerning "Monogeneis," "Procession," and the "Filioque"

The above discussion on the threeness of God involves, as we have seen, some simple and some complex distinctions that we have tried to state not only precisely, but as clearly as possible. This concern has led us to omit certain parts of the discussion that are nonetheless worthy of consideration for the benefit of those whose interest leads them to pursue the more technical aspects of the trinitarian question.

First of all, the use of the language of generation to describe the relation of the Father to the Son requires a comment on the meaning of *monogeneis* (μονογενής) in John 3:16 and 18. The consensus of contemporary scholarship would regard the primary meaning of this term, in the Hellenistic period, to be "only," as when Jesus raises the "only" son of his mother (Lk. 7:12). (Here *monogeneis* can hardly mean "only begotten" since mothers do not beget.) To speak of Jesus, then, as the *monogeneis* of the Father is to affirm that he is related to God as his "only" Son, a phrase having virtually the same meaning as Paul's designation of him as God's "own Son" (Rom. 8:3, 32). Jesus then, in contrast to believers, who are also God's sons and daughters, is uniquely the Son to the exclusion of all others. He has no true siblings. In the same vein is the Johannine statement that Jesus claimed God was his own (ἴδιον) Father, thus making himself equal with God (Jn. 5:18).

On the other hand, the dogma of the Trinity not only underscores the uniqueness

---

31. The impalpable nature of "breath" relates also to the archaic use of "ghost" to designate the third person of the Godhead, a usage still retained in the "Gloria Patri" and the familiar doxology of Bishop Ken.

32. See below, this Unit, IV, D, 4, e, pp. 311-15.

of the Son's relationship to the Father, but also spells out that relationship in terms of generation. The only Son is said to be the "only begotten" Son. In view of the fact, observed above, that in Hellenistic usage *monogeneis* accents the "only" rather than the "begotten," what is to be said of the traditional use the church has made of this term as the exegetical basis of its doctrine at this point? Surely this much: to say Jesus is God's only son and that God is his own Father, who shared his glory with his Son before the world was (Jn. 17:5), implies a relationship that may be described as an eternal "begetting." Such a conclusion is consonant not only with the teaching of Scripture in general, but also with the specific statement that the Son is "he who is begotten" (γεγεννημένος, 1 Jn. 5:18) of God. Hence the traditional understanding of *monogeneis* as meaning "only begotten" when used of the Son remains a theologically correct inference from the New Testament (see F. Büchsel, "μονογενής," *TDNT,* IV, pp. 737-41).

The term "procession," as used in the doctrine of the Trinity, is taken from John 15:26, which speaks of the Paraclete whom "I will send (ἐγὼ πέμψω) to you from the Father, even the Spirit of truth, who proceeds from the Father" (ὃ παρὰ τοῦ πατρὸς ἐκπορεύεται). The traditional understanding of this text presupposes that the distinction made in it is of genuine theological significance. The One who will be sent (future tense) by the Son as the other Paraclete is identified as the Spirit who proceeds (present tense) from the Father. The sending obviously refers to Pentecost and describes the One who will come at that time in his role as the Paraclete. The "proceeding," by contrast, identifies who this coming One is: he is the eternal Spirit who "proceeds" from the Father. As the Son is uniquely qualified to become the Christ because he is the eternal Son who is begotten of the Father (Jn. 3:16), so the Spirit is uniquely qualified to become the Paraclete because he is the eternal Spirit who proceeds from the Father. Hence God is equally present in the persons of the Son and of the Spirit, though in a manner that is distinct and unique. The Son is not the Spirit who proceeds from the Father, nor is the Spirit the Son who is begotten of the Father.

The traditional understanding of John 15:26 is often dismissed by contemporary New Testament commentators as a "habit of the theologians" reflecting "a fourth-century debate." Such a judgment against the traditional view tends to reduce the text to a tautology, since the sending of the Spirit (by the Son) and the proceeding of the Spirit (from the Father) are then made to refer to one and the same historical event, namely, Pentecost. But the text does not say that the Paraclete is One whom the Father will send to you. Furthermore, no fourth-century debate concerning the trinitarian interpretation of John 15:26 ever occurred. The debate—which is still unresolved—concerned another question to which we must now give consideration—namely, Does the Spirit proceed not only from the Father but also from the Son?

The doctrine of the Trinity, as subscribed to in the Western Church, affirms the procession of the Spirit from both the Father and the Son. The phrase "and the Son" *(filioque)* is not, of course, expressly contained in the text of John 15:26. On the other hand, neither the text of John's Gospel nor the Eastern form of the Creed says (or even implies) that the Spirit does not proceed from the Son. Indeed, the intent of the Creed, as subscribed in the Eastern Church, is to secure the full deity of the Spirit along with the deity of the Son in order that (as the Creed goes on to say) the Spirit might be worshipped and glorified as God together with the Father and the Son.

Furthermore, if the doctrine of the Trinity is (as we have argued) the necessary implication of revelation; if God is, in himself, the same God he has revealed himself to be, then surely the Spirit is the Spirit of the Son even as he is the Spirit of the Father. It is as the risen and glorified Christ that the Son received from the Father the promise of the Spirit and poured out the Spirit on his gathered disciples (Acts 2:33). Hence, all those who belong to Christ are said to have his Spirit. Indeed, they cannot belong to Christ unless they have the Spirit of Christ (Rom. 8:9-10). But if the Spirit by whom we are renewed is the Spirit of Christ, the Son of God, how can the Spirit be, eternally in himself, the Spirit of the Father alone? The Western Church has, therefore, argued that the Spirit comes to us in revelation as the Spirit of Christ because he is, eternally, the Spirit who proceeds not only from the Father, but also from the Son. To be sure, the Eastern usage whereby the Spirit is said to proceed from (ἐκ) the Father through (διά) the Son is also found in early Western usage. As the schism between East and West hardened, however, the East construed the phrase "from the Father" to mean "from the Father only," and this is the thought the Western church has rejected.

The *Filioque* was established in Western theology through the influence of Augustine. It appears to have been used liturgically in Spain as early as the sixth century, though it did not become an official part of the Roman Mass until A.D. 1014. (The Eastern Churches still reject the *Filioque,* confessing only that the Spirit proceeds from the Father.) Some Eastern Orthodox spokesmen have darkly blamed the *Filioque* for everything wrong in the West from the claim of papal infallibility to Kantianism and the Enlightenment concept of progress. Moltmann (*The Trinity and the Kingdom,* New York: Harper, 1981, pp. 178-87), in the interest of healing the breach between East and West, suggests the following restatement of the Creed: "[We believe in] the Holy Spirit, who proceeds from the Father of the Son, and who receives his form from the Father and the Son."

3. THE TRINITY OF BEING: GOD'S ONENESS-IN-THREENESS AND HIS THREENESS-IN-ONENESS

a. Introduction

We have spoken of how God is one in his essential being yet three in the personal mode of his being, the God whose name is Father, Son, and Holy Spirit. The time has now come to review various efforts theologians have made to illumine this mystery of a God who is one, yet whose oneness is a oneness-in-threeness and a threeness-in-oneness. As we have seen, from the beginning Christians confessed that God is one, and they held firmly to this confession even when they finally came to affirm the full deity of the Son and the Spirit along with the Father. As members of the Godhead, Father, Son, and Holy Spirit are consubstantial, that is, of one and the same essence. This affirmation was made not only against the Arians within, but also against the polytheists without. The many gods of the Greeks and Romans were, for the early Christians, false gods in contrast to the true God, who is one, not many. This is the truth that the church sought to preserve in affirming the oneness of God's essential being. While there are many who are called gods, there is only one who really is God (1 Cor. 8:4-6).[33]

b. God's Oneness Viewed as Numeric Identity

In the Eastern Church, following Nicaea, the term "consubstantial," meaning "oneness of essential being," was often interpreted (in the interests of peace and harmony) a bit loosely to mean that the Father and Son share the same divine nature. But as time went on the ambiguity was more and more removed from the phrase "same nature," as the church came to teach that the unity of the Godhead should be construed as a numeric and not simply a generic oneness. Father, Son, and Spirit do not share a common divine nature as Peter, Paul, and Mary share a common human nature. They are not three individual Gods as Peter, Paul, and Mary are three individual humans. This tendency toward a numeric, rather than a generic, understanding of the divine oneness was given a fillip by the widespread conviction—more Greek than biblical—that the divine essence was simple and therefore indivisible.

To be sure, some of the theologians of antiquity, especially the Cappadocians, suggested an analogy between the oneness of the members of the Godhead and the universals of philosophy, but even they recognized that such an approach was problematic. In the end, the numeric understanding of God's oneness prevailed, being reinforced by the obvious fact that in revelation, God always discloses himself as "I" (*I* AM WHO *I* AM), never as "we." In the words of the Fourth Lateran (1215), the unity of the divine persons is "a unity of identity of nature." At this council the view of Joachim was condemned because it construed the oneness of Father, Son, and Spirit collectively as the many faithful are one Church. When Jesus prays (Jn. 17:22) that his disciples may be one even as he and the Father are one, "the word 'one' as applied to the disciples is, according to the Council, to be taken in the sense of the union of charity in grace; but in the case of the divine Persons, in the sense of the unity of identity of nature."

---

33. Of course, for the early Christians the falseness of the many gods of the empire was not simply in their numbers but also in their manners. Especially among the ancient Greeks, who were most deeply interested in humanity, not divinity, the gods were cast in an anthropomorphic mold. See Werner Wilhelm or W. W. Jaeger, *Paideia* (New York: Oxford, 1945), vol. I, p. xxiii. It was these all-too-human gods, guilty of every human vice, that evoked the scathing contempt of Augustine in *The City of God,* Book VI.

As cited in Dupuis Neuner, *The Christian Faith* (Westminster, Md.: Christian Classics, 1975), pp. 103-05.

The view enunciated at the Lateran Council, which construed the *homoousios* of the creed as teaching a numeric oneness, was permanently established in the ongoing theological discussion with the supplanting of the *Sentences* of Lombard by the *Summa* of Thomas. According to Rahner, at this time a truly momentous distinction was introduced into the doctrine of God. It was a distinction reflected in Thomas's tractates *De Deo uno* and *De Deo triuno*. The reason Thomas made this distinction and adopted this order was apologetic. It enabled him as a theologian to begin with the existence of one God, a proposition he believed could be demonstrated by the natural light of reason. Given such a demonstration, he could then move on from this base in natural theology to discuss the trinitarian nature of God's being with the aid of the supernatural light of revelation. Such an approach easily lent itself to making the oneness of the divine nature, in the numeric sense, the fundamental affirmation concerning God. (See Moltmann, *The Crucified God,* New York: Harper, 1974, who cites Rahner's historical observation and is critical of the theological result.)

The understanding of the unity of the persons in the Godhead as a "unity of identity of nature" was taken over by the Reformers. Of course they were not interested in basing revealed theology on natural theology; but they did assume the numeric view of the divine unity.[34] This view was reinforced, in turn, by the fact that the discussion of the Trinity came increasingly to be located by the dogmaticians after the treatment of the attributes, as though the attributes were predicates descriptive of the one nature rather than the three persons.

Speaking of the understanding of the divine unity as a numeric oneness, in modern times Barth has come down emphatically on this side of the theological universe. Fearing that the term "persons" conveys the thought of discrete individuals, he prefers the term "unique ways of existence" *(eigentümliche Seinsweise)* to describe the distinctions in God. While he admits that the threefold distinction in God is ultimate and cannot be reduced, blurred, or eliminated, yet his view that the concept of numerical identity of essence is the only way to construe the unity of the members of the Godhead compels him to use language in a unique way to express how God is not only One but Three-in-One. God, he says, manifests himself "in a three-fold recapitulation"; God "distinguishes himself from himself"; God posits himself "in another way a second (and a third) time"; in God there is a "repetition of eternity in eternity" (*K.D.,* I/1, sec. 9, pp. 367ff.). He even goes so far as to alter the meaning of Article I of the *Augsburg Confession.* Whereas classic doctrine says that the three persons properly subsist in the one essential being of God, Barth says it is not the persons as such who properly subsist,

---

34. Hence the complaint of Hodgeson that even Calvin retains the thought that the Father is the *principium* of the Godhead, a notion that he defended with "verbal sophistries" because he understood the divine oneness as *simplex unitas,* that is, as a simple, numeric unity. *The Doctrine of the Trinity* (London: Nisbet, 1943), pp. 104ff.; 171ff.

"but *God* in three Persons, or rather: God as threefold, proper subsistence" (*K.D.,* I/1, p. 380).

For Barth, God is *a* person who subsists essentially in a threefold way. This is a significant departure from the traditional view that God is a fellowship of three persons who subsist in one essence. Not only is it a departure from the tradition, but it does not fit the data of the New Testament in many instances. In Acts 22:8-10, for example, the risen Christ identifies himself, saying, "*I* am Jesus of Nazareth whom you are persecuting"; and Paul responds, "What shall I do, Lord?" Is it not forced interpretation of the text to say that the title "Lord" and the personal pronoun "you" on the lips of Paul refer to God as the personal subject who, on this occasion, reveals himself "in the unique way of being" called the Son, incarnate as Jesus of Nazareth? Is it not more natural (and scriptural) to say that "Lord" and "you" refer to the second person of the Godhead who, as the eternal Son, became incarnate as Jesus of Nazareth? Such a way of speaking is not, as Barth implies, to read the Trinity of persons off the data of experience, but rather to acknowledge that our awareness of God as a Trinity of persons rests on the data of revelation. Barth never does untie this knot in his exposition of the doctrine, but fortunately he ignores it, for the most part.

c. The Mutual Indwelling of the Persons of the Godhead

Significant strands of theological reflection show that the numeric conception of the divine unity is not the final word on the subject. Christians, as a matter of fact, never have believed that God is one in an unqualified way. They believe in a divine unity, but it is a unity-in-diversity. Christians do not believe that God is one as Allah is one; Christians are not monotheists in a Unitarian sense. Their confession that God is one is not the primary and fundamental confession to which they add, as an afterthought, that he is also three. For Christians, the threeness of God is just as ultimate as his oneness.[35] The one God they worship as the Lord is the God whom they address as their Father, through the merits of Christ their Savior, having received the Spirit of adoption who teaches them how to pray. Strictly speaking, then, Christians are not monotheists, but trinitarians. Their God is not a single Monad, solitary and alone, anymore than he is a celestial committee of three Gods. Rather, he is the God who is One-in-Three and Three-in-One, a fellowship of holy love. It is disturbing to note how often, in the modern dialogue with other religions, those who speak for the church view the Christian understanding of God as

---

35. God, to be sure, disclosed himself to Israel as *one,* long before he disclosed himself as three-in-one by sending his Son and giving his Spirit. This temporal sequence, however, does not imply that the divine unity is primary, and the diversity in that unity secondary. Since redemptive revelation begins with Israel, a people surrounded by and called out of a polytheistic culture, it also begins, naturally enough, by emphasizing God's oneness in contrast to the many gods of Canaan. But this is a propaedeutic matter.

an instance of a general philosophic theism and tacitly deny the church's trinitarian confession. One can surely empathize with such bridge-building efforts, especially with the Jewish community. But those who are Christians must confess that the God they worship is not only the God of Abraham and Sarah, whose name is Yahweh/Lord, but also the God of the apostles, whose name is the Lord Jesus Christ. The doctrine of the Trinity, in other words, has two foci: the essential unity of God and the personal distinctions in God. Both are integral to the Christian understanding of God. Though it is no easy matter to do justice to both, such balance is essential to the integrity of the Christian message.

If we do not construe the unity of the Godhead as a numeric unity, how ought we to speak of the relationship that the members of the Godhead have with one another as the one God? Obviously it is a relationship that involves an intimacy of being far beyond any that we can know at the human level. Taking their cue from Scripture, theologians have spoken of this relationship as a mutual indwelling of the divine persons, an eternal *coinherence*. When Philip asked to see the Father, according to John 14:8-11, Jesus responded with surprise in words that are indeed mysterious: "Have I been with you so long, and yet you do not know me, Philip? He who has seen me has seen the Father. . . . Do you not believe that I am in the Father and the Father in me? . . . the Father who dwells in me does his works." (See also Jn. 1:18, which speaks of the Son who is "in the bosom of the Father," and Jn. 10:38: "the Father is in me and I am in the Father.")[36]

Theologians have inferred from such Scripture that the divine persons—Father, Son, and Spirit—are not eternally "with," that is, alongside, one another, but eternally "in" one another.[37] From John of Damascus comes the classic term to describe this eternal inhabitation of the persons of the Godhead: "perichoresis" or "circumincession."[38] Obviously, such a mutual indwelling is beyond all human experience and reality. God is, in

---

36. This language of mutual interpenetration is also used in the New Testament to describe the work of Christ and the Spirit in the economy of redemption. To be indwelt by the Spirit of God is to be indwelt by the Spirit of Christ. By the same token, to be indwelt by the Spirit of Christ is to be indwelt by Christ himself (Rom. 8:9-10).

37. In modern times Brunner especially has deplored a sequential *(nebeneinander)* view of the Trinity, as though God were three persons standing in a line. *Dogmatik,* vol. I, pp. 220ff.

38. From the Greek περιχώρησις, a "circulating," "going about," rendered by the Latin *circumincessio.* For some, we here touch a mystery worthy of all reverence: "Who can look upon . . . the incomprehensible circumincession . . . reserved for angels' eyes?" Dingby, *Natural Bodies,* 1657, p. 143. For others, it is a speculation provoking only contempt—"the deepest and darkest corner of the whole theological abyss." Gibbon, *Decline and Fall of the Roman Empire,* vol. 1, chap. XXI.

the phrase of C. S. Lewis, "super-personal." Lewis goes on to observe that in a one-dimensional world we have straight lines; in a two-dimensional world, squares; in a three-dimensional world, cubes. But as we advance to higher levels, we do not leave behind the things we found in the simpler levels; we rather combine them in new ways. The Christian view of God involves the same principle. At the human level matters are relatively simple; one person is one being and two persons are two beings and three persons are three beings. But at the divine level persons are combined in new ways that we, who do not live on that level, can hardly imagine. In God's dimension we find a Being who is three persons while remaining one Being, as a cube is six squares while remaining one cube. While we cannot fully conceive a Being like that, we can get a faint notion of it.[39]

St. Augustine, perhaps the greatest theologian of them all, spent his life reflecting on the Trinity (the subject remanded by Schleiermacher to an appendix). In the year 419, his *De Trinitate,* an extensive treatise on which he had worked for twenty years, appeared. Its most original (some would say speculative) contribution was his understanding of the divine mystery of the circumincession in terms of the Spirit as the bond of love (*vinculum caritas*) between the Father and the Son. Because the Spirit proceeds from both Father and Son—that is, because he is related to both alike—he may, Augustine argued, be regarded as the bond between them. When we are admonished to "maintain the unity of the Spirit in the bond of peace" (manifest in the one body which is the church [Eph. 4:3]), we are being admonished in our Christian communal life to imitate the communal life of God himself. And what is the nature of this bond that unites us in one body? It is love, the very same love of God which is shed abroad in our hearts by the Holy Spirit (Rom. 5:5). We have such love as a gift, but God is such love by nature. Therefore, Augustine reasoned, the Spirit may be said to be the bond of love uniting Father and Son in an eternal fellowship of love.

Thus Augustine sought to probe the mystery behind the love that God has revealed toward us. Beyond the love of John 3:16 is the eternal love that God is in himself. Before all worlds he is the Father who loves the Son (Jn. 3:35) and the Son who loves the Father—in the Spirit. God, then, from all eternity, is the One-who-is-for-Others in himself; that is, he is a Trinity of holy love. And as such he reveals himself. In creation he becomes the One-who-is-for-others-outside-himself, namely, his creatures. In redemption he becomes the One-who-is-for-sinful-others, namely, his people whom he restores to fellowship with himself. Thus the eternal fellowship

39. *Mere Christianity,* book IV, "Beyond Personality: or First Steps in the Doctrine of the Trinity," p. 142.

of the divine, trinitarian life grounds God's fellowship with us to whom he gives himself in love as our Maker and Redeemer.

d. The Individual (Psychological) and the Social Analogies of the Trinity

When theologians speak of God as One-in-three and Three-in-one, when they say that his unity is a unity in tri-unity, they are not simply engaging in verbal sophistries and irrational absurdities (Harnack). Such language has its roots in the biblical data itself. Assuming (against Marcion) that the God of the Old Testament is the God of the New, the very data of revelation compel the church to understand the oneness of God in terms of the distinctions in God and the distinctions in God in terms of his oneness.

Before the Incarnation and Pentecost this was not the case. To suppose that God was one without distinction was a plausible reading of the data so far as the Jewish Scriptures are concerned. God disclosed himself to Israel as the Lord, the "I AM WHO I AM." But in the New Testament things became more complex. The New Testament, to be sure, like the Old continues to speak of God in the singular. Even the trinitarian name of God is a single name. Christians are baptized into the name, not into the names, of the Father and of the Son and of the Holy Spirit (Mt. 28:19). Furthermore, Christians always address God in prayer using the singular pronoun "thou" ("you") even when addressing God as three persons.[40]

There can be little doubt, then, that he is one after the analogy of an individual person at the human level. Understandably, therefore, many theologians not only accept the individual analogy as an appropriate way to speak of God, but insist that it is the only way to speak of him. God is more like one person than three persons. Granted, God is One-in-three, yet he is *One*-in-three.

> "I and the Father are *one*"—I *and* the Father; only in this separateness is the "one" valid—yet "*one*"; only in this oneness is there the "I and the *Father*."[41]

40. See, for example, the beautiful prayer of Lancelot Andrews, *The Private Devotions of Lancelot Andrews* (New York: World Publishing Co., 1956), pp. 199-200. The "you" that modern usage increasingly favors over "thou" is, of course, both singular and plural. But this has no bearing on the theological question. The "you" of Christian prayer is always a singular. "Religious worship," says the *Westminister Confession*, XXIII, 2, "is to be given to God, the Father, Son, and Holy Ghost; and to *him* alone. . . ." Italics added. See also the Toledo Symbol (A.D. 675) with its insistence that while the Trinity "is not without number; yet it is not comprised by number. . . ." Neuner, *The Christian Faith*, p. 101.

41. Barth, *K.D.*, I/1, p. 462 (cf. *C.D.*, I/1, sec. 11.2). His italics.

However, when Christians do theology they must take into account the revelatory events of Bethlehem and Pentecost as well as that of the burning bush. They must reckon with the fact that the "I AM" who spoke to Moses has spoken to us in these last days in a Son (Heb. 1:2) who speaks of himself as "I" and his Father as "Thou" (Jn. 17); they must reckon, too, with the fact that there is the Spirit who is the "other" Paraclete (Jn. 14:16). That is to say, the theological affirmations of Christians must reflect these new data that they propose to interpret. Theologians, in this respect, may be likened to scientists. When faced with new data, scientists learn to think in new ways about the universe and to speak of "curved" space and the "indeterminate" behavior of particles. For theologians, Incarnation and Pentecost are the "new data." In fact, in the light of such data, some theologians have insisted that the social analogy is the only proper analogy to use when speaking of God. God is more like three human persons than one. Appealing to the New Testament and working out from the center of revelation, God's self-disclosure in Christ, these theologians highlight the mysterious fact that God is in fellowship with God; a divine "I" over against a divine "Thou." "The crucial issue," avers William Hasker,

> is just this: Is the relationship between Jesus and the Father, as depicted in the Gospels, only the relationship of a man with his God, similar to that enjoyed by other men, only perhaps on a higher spiritual plane? Or, is Jesus also "God, the Son of God," and was his relationship with the Father not only the relationship between a man and God—though it was that—but also the relationship, lived out on earth, between the eternal Son and his eternal Father—a relationship, in fact, between *God and God?* This is the question of all questions for the Trinity.[42]

Interestingly, the emergence of liberation theology has given a genuine boost to the social analogy as the preferred way to think about the triune nature of the Godhead. Migliore notes that

> the "social analogy" of the Trinity is needed to correct and comple-ment the psychological [individual] analogy. . . . The social analogy looks to the phenomenon of persons in relationship for a clue to the mystery of the divine life. . . . It is on the basis of a trinitarian understanding of God that Juan Luis Segundo criticizes the image of God that is reflected in the oppressive social and economic structures of the affluent nations of the world. For Segundo, trinitarian theology

42. "Tri-Unity," *The Journal of Religion* 50 (1) : 6.

speaks of God as a community of love; this idea of God is liberating because it stands in radical opposition to existing society. Thus the trinitarian definition of God is an impetus to implement new and more humane social initiatives that go far beyond the existing order.[43]

Jürgen Moltmann, to whom South American liberation theologians have frequently appealed, rejects the individual analogy out of hand as making God the "absolute Subject" corresponding to the bourgeois cult of personality. Speaking of Barth's view of the Trinity as a *repetitio aeternitatis in aeternitate,* a triple repetition of one and the same God who is Lord, Moltmann calls it empty and futile. Such a view, he complains, conceives God in terms of power over his property (he is "Lord over the world") rather than in terms of personal relationship. By contrast, the proper doctrine of the triune God represents and expresses the inexhaustible life that the three persons have in common as they are present with one another. What has been called the "perichoresis" was understood by patristic theologians as the sociality of the divine persons. Hence, the doctrine of the Trinity provides the intellectual means, according to Moltmann, to overcome the antithesis between the individual and the social, so that the rights of the individual and of society do not fall apart. Such a convergence of the two in the direction of a truly "humane" society is a vital necessity in our day.[44]

As we ponder these things, we can only conclude that for ourselves we must use both analogies, the individual and the social, when speaking of God as a Trinity. On the one hand, everyone finds it necessary at times to speak of God as we would of an individual. Even for the most avid defenders of the social analogy, God is "he," not "they." Yet "he" is also "they" even for the most avid defenders of the individual analogy. We have quoted Barth to the effect that God is ever the same Subject, never two Subjects. But three pages after he says this, he affirms that the right understanding of revelation requires us to say that the Father, as well as the Son, is the Subject of the event of reconciliation (spoken of in the second article of the Apostles' Creed) and that the Son is *also* the Subject, as well as the Father, of the event of creation (spoken of in the first article).[45] And so one Subject becomes two Subjects, and that in the space of a very

---

43. Daniel L. Migliore, *Called to Freedom* (Philadelphia: Westminster, 1980), pp. 173-75.

44. Jürgen Moltmann, *The Trinity and the Kingdom* (New York: Harper & Row, 1981), pp. 139-42.

45. *K.D.,* I/1, see p. 462 (cf. *C.D.,* I/1, sec. 11.2), in distinction to p. 465. Note also the "we" of John 14:23. ". . . we [the Father and I] will come to him and make our home with him."

few pages. This does not mean that the author is a careless or hasty workman. It rather means that matters are difficult when the theologian seeks to be faithful to Scripture and not reduce the antinomies of biblical revelation to a self-evident, rational consistency.

We must, then, go on using our broken analogies until faith becomes sight; but we should not chafe under such limitations, for it is common to the human situation. If the physical reality of which we are a part proves mysterious at the end of telescope and microscope, is it to be wondered at that the high and lofty One who inhabits eternity (Is. 45:22) should prove to be mysterious to us? *Indeed, the dogma of the Trinity is not intended to eliminate the divine mystery but to preserve it.* And so we use analogies: but we worship a God who is beyond all our analogies: the one God, who is Father, Son, and Holy Spirit.

ADDENDUM: CONCERNING THE LOGOS

The term "logos" (λόγος, literally "word") was used by the Greek philosophers, particularly the Stoics, to designate the Rational Principle immanent in all reality and the one giving it meaning. Philo, the Jewish philosopher of Alexandria (20 B.C.–A.D. 54), conceived of the Logos as the biblical equivalent of the Platonic Ideas in the mind of God. By the Logos, then, in the act of creation matter is formed into a rational and ordered cosmos.

The prologue of John's Gospel opens with the familiar: "In the beginning was the Logos, and the Logos was with God, and the Logos was God" (Jn. 1:1). There can be no doubt that in this passage John is using a current philosophic term, Logos, to describe the man Jesus, whose words and deeds are the subject of his Gospel. Hence there also can be no doubt that while he is using a philosophic term familiar to his readers, he is using it in a new sense by identifying the Logos with Jesus, who gives ultimate meaning to the world as the Creator and Redeemer of humankind. Because of this Johannine usage, the term has come to have a significant place in Christology and so impinges on the doctrine of the Trinity.

For John, Jesus was the Word of God, not only in the sense that the words that he spoke (as reported in the lengthy discourses of John's Gospel) are the words of God, but also in the sense that he is himself the Word of God in person. Just as he brings light because he is the Light (Jn. 1:9), gives life because he is the Life (Jn. 14:6), speaks the truth because he is the Truth (Jn. 14:6), so he proclaims the word because he is the Word (Jn. 1:1). The word of God, then, as the apostolic kerygma, is not simply a repetition of what Jesus said and did, but is a proclamation of who Jesus is. And who is he? According to John, he is the One who was with God in the beginning (Jn. 1:2). We cannot reverse this affirmation and say, God was with the Word in the beginning. John does not say, "God was with the Word" (θεὸς ἦν πρὸς τὸν λόγον) but just, "the Word was God" (θεὸς ἦν ὁ λόγος). Obviously, then, he who is the Word who became flesh (Jn. 1:14) is identical in John's thinking with the Son of God, given that we might have everlasting life (Jn. 3:16).[46] The designation "Word," when used of Jesus, is for all theological purposes the equivalent of "Son." Jesus is the Word, that is, the Son of God.[47] So the designation "Word of God," though infrequent in the New Testament, points, like the designation "Son of God," beyond Jesus' earthly life to a preexistence with and as God. In fact, John's use of the terms "with God" and "was God" ("the Word was with God and the Word was God") obviously reflects the same identity-with-distinction found in the doctrine of the Trinity as it was subsequently developed: the Word is identified with God as God, and yet is distinguished from God as the Word who is with God. One could then speak of the Trinity as "Father," "Word," and "Spirit," though this is not the usage that has prevailed in the church due to the frequent New Testament references to "Father" and "Son."[48]

As on the human level the "word" that one speaks is a revelation of oneself, that which makes visible the invisible self ("speak," said Ben Johnson, "that I may see thee"), so God's Word is God in his self-revelation. The Word, then, is not created, but spoken. And how is this uncreated Word spoken? By becoming flesh and dwelling among us. In this incarnate Word, God discloses himself to us and enters into conversation with us, even as he is in himself the God who is eternally in conversation with himself. As conversation implies fellowship, it is natural to infer that this God, who is eternally in conversation with himself, is an eternal fellowship. And such is the meaning of the doctrine of the Trinity: God is an eternal fellowship of Holy Love.[49]

---

46. Therefore it is also obvious, given this biblical usage, that the term "Word" belongs to the vocabulary of the ontological Trinity. Scripture does not say that the Son became the Word but that the Word became flesh (Jn. 1:14). Note, in this regard, the title of Athanasius's work, *De Incarnatione Verbi Dei*, where "Word of God" is the theological equivalent of "Son of God."

47. It should be noted that John describes the Word who became flesh as the *monogeneis* of God (Jn. 1:14), the same term he uses in John 3:16 of the Son.

48. See Tertullian's tract *Against Praxeas*. Also Thomas, *Summa*, Q. 34, "The Person of the Son" (in three Articles), where he argues, following Augustine, that the "Word" is a personal, not an essential, designation in God and therefore is properly used of the Person of the Son.

49. For a provocative discussion of the use of Logos to overcome the sexual imagery

4. THE TRINITY OF REVELATION

a. Introduction

Having discussed the Trinity of being, we shall conclude our exposition of the doctrine with remarks on the Trinity of revelation. The exposition of this aspect of the doctrine is, fortunately, less demanding since we will be working more directly with the prima facie data of revelation.

What we have called the Trinity of being is sometimes referred to as the "ontological" or "essential" or "immanent" Trinity. In such a context, the word "immanent" is used not as the opposite of "transcendent" but in the sense of "belonging to the inmost nature or constitution of." Like "ontological" and "essential," the "immanent" Trinity refers to God's own self. To the question Who is God? the answer is given, God is an eternal Trinity of Holy Love. In distinction to this ontological Trinity, theologians have spoken of the "economic" Trinity. In traditional theological usage, "economy" is used of the order or realm of creation and of redemption, both of which concern the world. Hence, "economic" Trinity refers to the trinitarian way in which God relates to the world, the way he, who is eternally a Trinity, has revealed himself as our Maker and Redeemer. This economic Trinity, sometimes called the "revelational" or "functional" Trinity, is the subject now before us.

As our question has been, Who is God in and for himself? so it shall now be, Who is he for us? The discipline of systematics follows this order because the being of God grounds the revelational acts of God. God makes himself known as a Trinity because he is in himself a Trinity. It must be acknowledged that many would reject the questions we have sought to answer concerning the being of God as speculative abstractions. Theology, they would contend, should be concerned with the practical question of how God relates to us, not with the question of who God is in himself.[50] Such a practical approach would seem to simplify matters, yet the church has rejected it out of the profound conviction that God is in himself who he has revealed himself to be in his relationship to us. Obviously we cannot know God as the triune God apart from a personal encounter with him— Kaufman's "genuinely revelational relationism." But the genuineness of

---

in the traditional doctrine of the Trinity, see Patricia Wilson-Kastner, *Faith, Feminism and the Christ* (Philadelphia: Fortress, 1983), pp. 92ff.

50. "We must, then, reject any attempt to speak of the inter-trinitarian relations, God as he is in and for himself. . . . Karl Barth's attempt to resurrect medieval trinitarian speculations, appears to me a most unfortunate consequence of his substituting a rationalistic theological *objectivism* for a genuinely revelational relationism." Gordon Kaufman, *Systematic Theology* (New York: Scribner's, 1968), p. 251, n. 7. His italics. Rather grandiloquently final!

this revelational relation is grounded in God himself, not in the relationship as such. Hence we have made the doctrine of the ontological Trinity our first concern. From that primary concern we now turn to consider the various roles assumed by the members of the Godhead in the economies of creation and salvation. This is the doctrine of the economic Trinity, a doctrine that is concerned, one might say, to show how God's presence to us corresponds to his presence to himself; how he who is a fellowship of love in himself as Father, Son, and Spirit reveals himself to us in a fellow-ship of love as our Father, our Savior, and our Sanctifier. Having spoken of God (in the words of the hymn writer) as

> God the Father, God the Son,
> God the Spirit, Three in One,

we shall now go on to speak of him as the one to whom we pray, saying,

> Love that caused us first to be,
> Love that bled upon the tree,
> Love that draws us lovingly:
> We beseech you, hear us. (Pollock)

b. The Works of God Are One, Yet by Appropriation

We have affirmed that God is one and that this one God eternally subsists as a fellowship of three persons. The doctrine of the economic Trinity affirms that because God is one in his essential being, all his works in creation and redemption are the works of the one God. Yet, as this one God subsists as three distinct persons, so there are distinct roles or tasks appropriated by the members of the Godhead in carrying out the works of creation and redemption. As one is said, in common usage, to "appropriate" what one takes as one's own, so in theological usage one member of the Godhead is said to "appropriate" a certain task or role with which he is preeminently, though not exclusively, associated in Scripture.

Opera trinitatis ad extra indivisa sunt (Augustine) means literally "the outward works of the Trinity are indivisible." The qualifying phrase ad extra is used by theologians, over against the phrase ad intra, which designates the intertrinitarian acts of generation and procession. These are "divisible" works, that is, works divided among, rather than common to, the members of the Godhead. Only the Father begets, only the Son is begotten, only the Spirit proceeds. But the one God — Father, Son, and Spirit — creates, governs, and redeems the world he has made. These are his works ad extra, common to all the members of the Godhead. As for the thought, also taken from Augustine, that all God's works ad extra are by appropriation (per appropriationem) on the part of the several members of the Godhead, some theologians (Thomas, et al.) have distinguished between "appropriation" and "mission." Those who make such a distinction use it primarily of the Son. Salvation is said to be the work of the Son by "appropriation." His becoming incarnate that he might save us by his life, death, and resurrection is said to be his "mission" (*Summa,* Q. 43, in eight articles). Sometimes the principle of appropriation is loosely used of those attributes which are predicated of all the members of the Godhead, but which may be associated preeminently with one member. Witness, for example, the attributes in the hymn,

> Holy and blessed Three,
> Glorious Trinity,
> > Wisdom, Love, Might
> Boundless as ocean tide,
> Rolling in fullest pride,
> Through the world far and wide,
> > Let there be light! (Marriott)

Theologians have used differing terms to describe the tasks or roles appropriated by the several persons in the Godhead. Barth speaks of "Revealer," "Revelation," "Revealedness," or "Creator," "Reconciler," "Savior."[51] We shall follow Luther's catechetical usage, and speak of "Father," "Savior," and "Sanctifier."[52] Though using different terms, all who accept the traditional doctrine of economic appropriation have agreed on certain ground rules, so to speak. They are the following:

1. There should be a genuine analogy between the personal distinctions in the Godhead and the roles they are given by appropriation. To the Father, for example, may be assigned, by appropriation, the role of Creator because he is, in himself, as the first person in the Godhead, the origin and source of the eternal distinctions in God.

2. The doctrine of appropriation must never be pressed to such an extent as to violate the unity of God's works *ad extra*. As we should not speak of the persons in the Godhead as distinct individuals (three Gods), so we should not speak of their works as individual acts in isolation. Though the Son, for example, is by appropriation said to have redeemed us because he gave himself as a ransom for our sins in his death on the cross, redemption is the work not of the Son exclusively, but of the triune God: Father, Son, and Holy Spirit.

---

51. The last is, in our judgment, odd in the light of scriptural usage, which ordinarily uses the designation "savior" (σωτήρ) of Jesus, not the Spirit. (See *K.D.,* I/1, p. 470; cf. *C.D.,* I/1, sec. 12.1.)

52. "Sanctifier," Luther's economic name for the Spirit, is also reflected in the answer to the fifth question of the *Anglican Catechism* concerning what is learned from the Apostles' Creed: "First I learn to believe in God the Father who has made me. . . . Secondly, in God the Son who has redeemed me. . . . Thirdly, in God the Holy Spirit who *sanctifies* me. . . ."

3. The doctrine of appropriation should never be slighted so as to blur the distinctions in God. As the distinctions are real in the eternal Godhead, so they are real in God's works *ad extra*. As the Father is not the Son nor the Son the Spirit, so our Father is not our Savior Jesus Christ who was crucified, nor is our crucified Savior the sanctifying Spirit whom he sent.[53]

The doctrine of appropriation, it is sometimes said, is to the Trinity of revelation what the doctrine of perichoresis is to the Trinity of essential being. As God works *ad intra* in a fellowship of mutual love, so he works *ad extra* in a fellowship of complementary acts. We shall now turn to the biblical data concerned with these complementary acts, acts in which God reveals himself to us as our Father, our Savior, and our Sanctifier. Though our subject is still

> Jehovah—Father, Spirit, Son,
> Mysterious Godhead, Three in One,

we shall now be preeminently concerned with the

> Father of heav'n, whose love profound
> A ransom for our souls has found,

with the

> Almighty Son, incarnate Word,
> Our Prophet, Priest, Redeemer, Lord,

and with the

> Eternal Spirit, by whose breath
> The soul is raised from sin and death. (Cowper)

c. The *Father* Who Becomes *Our* Father

When discussing the doctrine of the ontological Trinity, we noted that we properly speak of the first person of the Godhead as the eternal Father because he is the source of the distinctions in God, the *fons trinitatis*. So, when we confess God to be our Father, we confess that he is the source of our being as the Creator (Ps. 100:3). When we thus bow the knee to him who is our Father, we also acknowledge him to be the Father of "whom every family in heaven and on earth is named" (Eph. 3:14-15). In other

---

53. This canon is violated when ministers and others, as they lead a congregation in prayer, address God as Father and then, as the prayer continues, thank him for dying on the cross for their sins.

words, we perceive and confess that he is the source not only of our being but the being of all the members of the human family; indeed, the source of the world as a whole. This is the ultimate truth about our human reality that Paul proclaimed to the Athenians as he stood before the Areopagus. He named for them, as it were, their unnamed God when he told them that this God was the Maker of heaven and earth and that they were his offspring (γένος), even though they did not know him (Acts 17:22ff.). This is the truth in the theological perspective of Protestant liberalism with its emphasis on the "Fatherhood of God and the brotherhood of man" (Harnack). God is indeed the Father of all, in that all men and women are his "offspring," his creation. He is the Father of lights, the Giver of every good endowment and every perfect gift (Jas. 1:17), who has given us our very being as those uniquely endorsed with his image.

Some have reasoned that since, in our finitude, we need a Cosmic Provider, and since God is the Creator who provides for the creature, therefore we may assume that the universal fatherhood of God as Creator is the biblical doctrine *simpliciter*. But, as a matter of fact, the biblical understanding of the fatherhood of God is not a truth inferred from the creation; rather, it is a truth revealed to us as sinners who are "in Christ." And to be in Christ is to be a new creation (2 Cor. 5:17). Hence, only as we die to our old self, only as we are crucified with Christ and raised up unto newness of life by the power of his Spirit, do we who are sinners have the right and confidence to call God our Father. When we come to him in this confidence, we are acknowledging that he who is the source of our being as our Maker is the source of our new being as our Redeemer. It is he who has given us his Son (Jn 3:16), that "inexpressible gift" (2 Cor. 9:15); and it is this Son, who only knows the Father, who has revealed him to us as our Father (Mt. 11:27). For those who are the beneficiaries of this revelation, the name "Father" is not a general name for God, common to the piety of all religions; rather, it is the name we take upon our lips as Christians who pray to the God whom the Son has made known to us.

There can, then, be no doubt that in the biblical vision God's fatherhood is understood primarily in a soteriological way; though God is our Father as Creator, he is preeminently so as our Redeemer in Christ. As sinners we know God as our Father because we have received the adoption of grace. Only when we are reconciled to God in Christ and assured of our adoption by the witness of his Spirit with our spirit do we have the liberty to address God as "Abba! Father!" (Rom. 8:15-16).[54] Given this liberty, which is ours

---

54. For this reason we shall treat the doctrine of adoption as an integral part of salvation (rather than creation) along with such themes as justification and sanctification.

as Christians, we approach God in the intimate way that Jesus taught us
to do when we pray the familiar prayer, "Our Father, who art in heaven
. . ." (Mt. 6:9ff.).

In keeping with our general discussion of the meaning of the term "Father" as an
economic distinction in God, we should always remember that the first person is not
alone the source of our being. We may properly speak of him as our Father in that he
is our Creator—"I believe in God the Father almighty, Maker of heaven and earth."
But the Son is also our Creator, for he is the Logos through whom all things were made
(Jn. 1:3). And the same is true of the Spirit who is the Creator Spirit. "When you send
forth your spirit, they are created; and you renew the face of the ground" (Ps. 104:30
NRSV). This is just to say, using the terms of dogmatics, that the eternal Father becomes
our Father by appropriation.

d. The Son Who Becomes Our Savior

As the eternal Father becomes our Father, so the eternal Son becomes our
Savior. ("You shall call his name Jesus, for he will save his people from
their sins," Mt. 1:21.) This is the heart of the gospel, the central theme of
the Christian faith. The very vocabulary of the New Testament—and of
theology—has been enlarged to encompass this all-important role that
belongs, by appropriation, to the Son. He is Emmanuel (Mt. 1:23), the
Christ (Acts 2:36), the Redeemer (Col. 1:14; Rv. 5:9), the Advocate (1 Jn.
2:1), the One who reconciles us to God (Rom. 5:10; 2 Cor. 5:18).

In the role that the Son assumes as our Savior, the trinitarian distinctions in God are most clearly revealed due to the nature of the Incarnation.
It is not the Father, nor the Spirit, but the Word that "became flesh and
dwelt among us" (Jn. 1:14). Hence, throughout the New Testament there
is a clear and inescapable distinction between One who sends and One who
is sent. In fact, as we have already noted, it was this distinction which
eventually led the church to confess the doctrine of the Trinity as the
necessary implication of Scripture. He who is eternally begotten of the
Father is, in the fullness of time, sent by the Father to accomplish our
redemption (Gal. 4:4-5). All the affirmations of the second article of the
Creed apply preeminently to God the Son, not to God the Father or God
the Spirit. It is the Son who was "conceived by the Holy Spirit, born of
the virgin Mary, suffered under Pontius Pilate, was crucified, dead, and
buried"; it is the Son who on "the third day rose again from the dead; he
ascended into heaven, and is seated at the right hand of God the Father
almighty; from there he shall come to judge the living and the dead." It is
this incarnate Son, and he only, who is the mediator between God and
humankind (1 Tm. 2:5; Heb. 12:24).

In this regard, the trinitarian distinctions in the Godhead are clearly reflected in the economic tasks appropriated by the Son. To deny the trinitarian character of these distinctions is to blur the distinction between our creation and our salvation, our finitude and our sinfulness. This is why they who conceive the oneness of God in a unitarian way conceive salvation in a human way, that is, as a human work. For such, salvation becomes the actualizing of the Creator's gifts in the spirit of the man from Nazareth rather than the penitent acceptance of the salvation offered by a crucified and risen Savior. Contrariwise, if we accept the economic distinction between the Father and the Son in a trinitarian way, then salvation is ultimately God's work, even as creation is his work. The Savior is God the Son, even as the Creator is God the Father. We no longer value Christ because of his benefits (Melanchthon/Ritschl), but rather we value his benefits because they are bestowed by him who is the great God and our Savior, Jesus Christ (Ti. 2:13).

e. The Spirit Who Becomes Our Sanctifier

In the case of the Son, who is God incarnate as Jesus, the Man-for-us, the difference between God as Father and as Son is relatively clear because the role that the Son appropriates in accomplishing our salvation is relatively distinct from that of the Father. By contrast, the difference between God as Son and as Spirit is less clear because the role that the Spirit appropriates in the work of salvation is relatively less distinct from that of the Son.[55] For example, to be "in Christ" is to be "in the Spirit"; to be "indwelt by Christ" is to be "indwelt by the Spirit"; to have Christ intercede for us is to have the Spirit intercede for us (Rom. 8:9, 10, 26; Heb. 7:25). Such scriptural usage, however, should come as no surprise; as we have already noted, certain strands of revelation tend to focus on the differences in God and in his works while others focus on his oneness as he is revealed in the manifoldness of these works. It is the doctrine of appropriation, we have argued, that gives us the flexibility needed properly to understand the Scriptures in such matters.

In his appropriative task, the Spirit has been given different titles, all of which describe his role and work as a member of the economic Trinity. He has been called our "Sustainer," our "Guide," our "Helper," our "Comforter," our "Counselor," our "Sanctifier." Such an array of terms does not

---

55. This fact is illustrated, to cite a well-known case, in the way Calvin departs from a trinitarian title in Book III of the *Institutes:* Book I, "On the knowledge of God the Creator"; Book II, "On the knowledge of God the Redeemer"; Book III, "On the Manner of Receiving the Grace of Christ." In this third book, however, Calvin expounds the Spirit's work as God the Sanctifier and so maintains the trinitarian structure of his material.

arise out of any obscurity in the reality of the Spirit's work. It is rather the sheer scope, the unparalleled breadth of that work, which makes matters so difficult. It is the Spirit who gives us not only a new past (in our effectual calling) and a new future (in our glorification), but also a new present (in our sanctification), being the seal of the promise and the "guarantee of our inheritance" (Eph. 1:13-14). Whatever one may call the Spirit, all theologians are agreed that the Spirit's role in the economy of redemption is to be expressed in the present tense. The doctrine of the Spirit is the doctrine of God as a present reality in the life of the world, the church, and the individual. Whereas the verbs in the second article are either in the past tense ("he was conceived, born, crucified, rose, ascended") or future ("shall come"), the Spirit is God at work in the here and now. "The theme that is before us," notes Brunner,

> is none other than that of the God who is present and who comes to be the God who is experienced. Whereas the first article of the Creed is concerned with God the Creator, that is, with the Eternal Ground of all being and the presupposition of all individual and universal history; and whereas the second article is concerned with the entering of God into history, the event of the once-for-all historical revelation; the third article (Holy Spirit) is concerned that the "then" becomes "today," that the "there" becomes "here," that what is "without" becomes what is "within," that the "Christ-for-us" becomes the "Christ-in-us." "Now we shall see," says Calvin, at the beginning of the third book of the *Institutes,* "in what way the blessings which the Father has promised to his only-begotten Son come to *us.* "[56]

The distinction between the economic roles or tasks assumed by the Son and those assumed by the Spirit is reflected in the movement of holy history from Incarnation to Pentecost. Such a distinction is not merely a matter of chronology; the Spirit who comes is not the Son coming back in a different mode suited to a different task—as Modalists have argued. Rather, the economic distinction between the task of "Savior" and that of "Sanctifier"/"Sustainer"/"Guide"/"Helper"/"Comforter"/"Counselor" rests upon and reveals the ontological distinction between the Son and the Spirit. This is why the Scripture says that the Spirit comes as the *other* Counselor (Paraclete); and this Counselor, who is the other Counselor, comes when and only when the Son, whom the disciples have acknowledged to be the Christ, has left them (Jn. 14:6; 15:7).

This is the theological reality that grounds the structure of the New Testament canon. The New Testament begins with "the gospel of Jesus Christ, the Son of God" (Mk. 1:1). It then goes on from the story of Jesus

---

56. Emil Brunner, *Von Werk des Heiligen Geistes* (Tübingen: Mohr, 1935), p. 5. His italics.

the Son to the proclamation of that story in the book of Acts and its interpretation in the epistles, a proclamation and interpretation given in the demonstration and power of the Spirit (1 Cor. 2:4). This distinction between the God who is first present in the person of Jesus the Suffering Servant, and then in the power of the sanctifying Spirit, is a trinitarian distinction of an "economic" sort. This economic, trinitarian distinction, in turn, reflects the ultimate, ontological distinction between the Son and the Spirit. Because God is the Spirit who proceeds eternally from the Father and the Son, he is the Spirit "sent" by the Father (Jn. 14:16) and the Son (Jn. 15:26) to teach the disciples all things (Jn. 14:26), and to convince the world of sin, righteousness, and judgment (Jn. 16:8).

While the Scriptures have much to say about the manifold work of the Spirit, we shall at this point offer only the briefest summary.

1. It was the Spirit who enabled the apostles so to speak to those to whom they were sent that their words were God's words. They spoke in the power and demonstration of the Spirit (1 Cor. 2:4). Thus their human words were taken up, as it were, into the constellation of revelation. As the divine Word became flesh, so the apostolic word became divine; it was a word heard "not as the word of men but as what it really is, the word of God" (1 Thes. 2:13). For this reason the church came to acknowledge those documents containing this apostolic kerygma to have the authority of revelation. As the Jewish Scriptures are "God-breathed" (2 Tm. 3:16), so these new Scriptures are inspired by the Spirit, the third person of the Godhead.

2. By the same Spirit, the inspired word becomes not only a word to us but also a word in us (effectual calling), as through the hearing and reading of that word we are brought to the obedience of faith. We who were at enmity with God and our neighbor thus experience the love of God shed abroad in our hearts by the Spirit (Rom. 5:5); and so we confess our faith, a faith that works by love (Gal. 5:6).

3. We who are thus renewed by the Spirit are, in an ongoing way, led by the same Spirit into the truth (Gal. 5:18; Rom. 8:14), for the Spirit is the Spirit of truth (Jn. 16:13). We are anointed by him that we might know all things (1 Jn. 2:20) and thus live in hope.

And so, to summarize our summary of the Spirit's role in the economy of redemption, the Spirit reveals himself as the Lord who frees us to know and do what we could never in ourselves have known and done, namely, to acknowledge Jesus as Savior and confess him as Lord, that we might be saved. Thus, by the power of God, present as the sanctifying Spirit, the humanly impossible becomes the divinely possible, as is so beautifully indited in the striking paradoxes of Wesley's lines:

> Hear him, you deaf, his praise you dumb,
>   Your loosened tongues employ;
> You blind, behold your Saviour come,
>   And leap, you lame, for joy!

So to frame the doctrine of the Spirit's work is to confess that salvation is God's work, his new creation. In other words, the distinction between accomplished salvation and experienced salvation is not basically a distinction between what God has done and what we must do (Pelagianism). Rather, it is a distinction between the Son and the Spirit, between what God has done as the Son, our Savior, and what he is now doing as the Spirit, our Sanctifier; it is a trinitarian distinction.

But as is always the case, when we so distinguish the work of the members of the Godhead, we do so not absolutely but by appropriation. The Spirit who reveals to us the Son is the Spirit of the Father (Acts 2:33); hence it is the Father who reveals the same Son, as Jesus assured Peter at Caesarea Philippi (Mt. 16:17). Again, when the Spirit comes, the disciples shall not be alone because Jesus comes (Jn. 14:16-18). Indeed, the Spirit, who is the Counselor, bears witness to another who has the same name, "Wonderful Counselor" (Is. 9:6), since he does the same work. It is he, the glorified Son, who counsels us to buy of him gold, raiment, and salve to anoint our eyes that we may see (Rv. 3:18). And so, in the coming of the Spirit both the Father and the Son come to us and make their abode with us according to the promise of our Lord as found in the fourth Gospel (Jn. 14:23). In all this we are again reminded that "though the three are spoken of as personally distinct, each by his presence and action involves the presence and action of all."[57]

The Meaning of "Paraclete"

As the biblical name for the Son in his economic role of Savior is "Christ," so the name of the Spirit in his economic role as Sanctifier is "Paraclete" (Jn. 14:16). While the former is common and easily understood (the "Anointed One"), the latter is more obscure. Since it means "advocate" when used of Jesus (1 Jn. 2:1), it would seem natural enough to give it a similar meaning when used of the "other One" whom Jesus promises to send in his place. The chief difficulty, however, with interpreting Paraclete as meaning "advocate" when applied to the Spirit is that the statements in John's Gospel about the sending and activity of the Spirit seem to move in a rather different direction. The Spirit is One who will "teach," "bear witness," "convict," but not One who will intercede for someone else. It would seem that "Paraclete," when applied to the Spirit, has less a forensic and more a kerygmatic meaning, that is, rather than interceding for the disciples, the Spirit inspires them as witnesses to Christ in their preaching.

57. Charles Gore, *Belief in Christ* (London: J. Murray, 1922), p. 239.

An effort has been made to illumine the meaning of Paraclete, as applied to the Holy Spirit, by the history-of-religions approach. (See J. Behm, "παράκλητος," *TDNT*, V, pp. 806-12.) Assuming such an approach, appeal is made to the figure of the "Celestial Helper" found in Gnosticism, particularly in the Mandaean literature. When one makes a close comparison, however, between the Mandaean figure of the "Helper" and the Johannine description of the "Paraclete," the analogy is hardly sufficient to suggest that the latter concept derives from the former.

The traditional translation "Comforter" has dominated not only the major versions of the Bible, but also the hymnody of the church. See, in the familiar "Come, You Disconsolate" by Thomas Moore, the stanza,

> Joy of the desolate, Light of the straying,
> Hope of the penitent, fadeless and pure,
> Here speaks the Comforter, tenderly saying,
> "Earth has no sorrow that heaven cannot cure."

Beautiful lines and true! But for all its illustrious pedigree—it appears from time to time in the Greek and Latin Fathers and was used by Luther and Wycliffe before the King James—"Comforter" is not the best term to use. While it is true that Jesus spoke of the Paraclete in a discourse aimed at comforting his disciples, saddened by the thought of his leaving (Jn. 14:18), when he describes the Spirit's ministry it is not in terms of comfort or consolation that he speaks but of witness and conviction.

If one wants to avoid the technical name "Paraclete," what is one to use in its place? This question has plagued translators for a long time. The American Revised Version retains the traditional "Comforter," footnoting "Advocate or Helper"; the Revised Standard uses "Counselor"; the New English, "Advocate"; the New American Standard, "Helper" with the marginal reading "Intercessor." Phillips cuts the Gordian knot with "Someone else to stand by you." Some such paraphrase is probably the best for the average reader. The student of theology, meanwhile, will continue to use "Paraclete" as the precise New Testament name for the Spirit in his unique role as the Sanctifier.

f. Economic Subordinationism

Subordinationism may be defined as any doctrine that supposes the Son and the Spirit are so related to the Father as to be dependent upon him and therefore subject to him. Faced with the difficult question of how Jesus is related to God, whom he called Father, the early Eastern theologians postulated a relationship of subordination. Some taught that Jesus was a holy man, whose life merited the unique gift of the Logos (Wisdom) of God. Thus he was enabled to perform those mighty deeds recorded in the gospels and live a life worthy of adoption into the Godhead. According to Arius, Jesus was much more than a divinely endowed man who at his baptism (or resurrection) became God's Son by adoption. He was rather a supernatural, preexistent creature, the firstborn of all creation (πρωτότοκος πάσης κτίσεως, Col. 1:15). But obviously, as a creature he was less than God. Therefore he must be subject to the Father, who is God in the proper sense.[58]

Subordinationism in this radical form was repudiated by the church with the acceptance of the *homoousios* doctrine that declares that the Son and the Spirit are coequal and consubstantial with the Father. Indeed, Nicene trinitarianism really makes all forms of subordinationism in the eternal Godhead to be heretical: "And in this Trinity none is before or after another: none is greater or less than another. But the whole three Persons are co-eternal together and co-equal, that in all things, as aforesaid, the Unity in Trinity and the Trinity in Unity is to be worshiped."[59]

Traces of a mild form of subordination, though not a part of the official teaching of the church, can be found in the thought of many post-Nicene theologians of orthodox persuasion as they expound and interpret trinitarian doctrine. The occasion of this mild but persistent subordinationism is the notion that the Father is the first principle of the Trinity. While this affirmation may mean no more than that the Father is the first person of the Godhead, a position accepted by all, theologians have often drawn inferences from it that compromised the homoousios doctrine. Since the first person is of none, neither begotten nor proceeding, it is easy to suppose that the Father is God in a more ultimate way than the Son and Spirit; and thus there is more and there is less of God in the Godhead.

Many theologians have pointed out that the Father has his essential being as God in and of himself. Some have even argued that while the Son is God himself, the Father is God *in* himself. They do not hesitate to say that the Father is "God preeminently." He is, properly speaking, the God (ὁ θεός), while the Son is just *God* (θεός)—shades of Jehovah's Witnesses! In giving such a designation exclusively to the Father, many have understood the begetting of the Son and the spiration of the Spirit to be an eternal communication of the divine essence. Thus the language of generation, used originally to preserve the full deity of the Son against the Arian doctrine of the Son's creation,

58. In due course, some who were influenced by Arianism taught that as the Son was the first creation of the Father, so the Spirit was the first creation of the Son. Those who entertained these radical subordinationist views of the Spirit were sometimes called Macedonians (from their leader Macedonius, himself a moderately Arian bishop); sometimes they were called Pneumatomachi (meaning "fighters against the Spirit"); and Tropici, probably because they taught that Scripture passages implying the deity of the Spirit were mere tropes, that is, figures of speech.

59. *Symbolum Quicumque,* as translated by Schaff, *History of the Christian Church* (Grand Rapids: Eerdmans, 1910), vol. III, p. 693. So also the Eleventh Council of Toledo, *Symbol of Faith:* "Hence, we confess and believe that each Person distinctly is fully God and the three Persons together are one God. Theirs is an undivided and equal Godhead, majesty and power, which is neither diminished in the single Person nor increased in the three." Neuner, *The Christian Faith,* p. 14. The editors of this compendium, interestingly, venture that the Toledo statement on the Trinity is the finest ever achieved.

came to be understood in a manner that threatens to reintroduce the thought of subordination which it was originally intended to guard against. Luther, for example, clearly speaks in terms of a communication of essence, though he draws no inference from it in favor of subordination. (See his *Von den letzten Worten Davids,* 1543, Weimarer Ausgabe 54, 58, 4, as quoted by Barth, *K.D.,* I/1, p. 385; cf. *C.D.,* I/1, sec. 9.2.) Ursinus, coauthor of the *Heidelberg Catechism,* in his *Commentary* on the same, repeatedly appeals to the notion of a communication of essence when elaborating the doctrine of the Trinity.

> The Son is the second Person, because the Deity is communicated to him of the Father by eternal generation. The Holy Ghost is the third Person, because the Deity is communicated to him from the Father and the Son by an eternal inspiration or procession. (*Commentary,* tr. by G. W. Willard, 3rd American ed., Cincinnati: T. P. Bucher, 1851, p. 135)

While Ursinus's intent is simply to explain the order in the Godhead, such an explanation, it would seem, is susceptible of a subordinationist interpretation.

Charles Hodge goes so far as to say that while the unity of God's being means that the Father, Son, and Spirit are equal, the Son is "subordinate" to the Father, and the Spirit to the Father and the Son, "[both] as to their mode of subsistence and operation. These are Scriptural facts to which the creeds in question add nothing; and it is in this sense they have been accepted by the church universal" (*Systematic Theology,* vol. I, p. 462). Such a statement is, to say the least, remarkable in its confusion. Subordination in "mode of subsistence" has never been "accepted by the church universal," nor is it a "fact" of Scripture. As for the Athanasian Creed, to which Hodge alludes as affirming this subordination, it is this symbol which, above all others, expressly condemns all subordinationism as heretical.

Deploring such subordinationism, which is still reflected in much of the traditional language of the church, B. B. Warfield comments on Calvin's position:

> In particular it fell to Calvin, in the interests of the true Deity of Christ—the constant motive of the whole body of trinitarian thought—to reassert and make good the absolute self-existence *(autotheotos)* of the Son. Thus Calvin takes his place, along side of Tertullian, Athanasius, and Augustine, as one of the chief contributors to the exact and vital statement of the Christian doctrine of the triune God. (*Biblical Doctrines,* p. 171)

Warfield also observes that though it would be natural to see in the very designations "Son" and "Spirit" some intimation of derivation of being and hence subordination, as a matter of fact the underlying concept behind such designations, in the language of Scripture, is just "likeness." Equality, then, rather than subordination, is the thrust of biblical usage. Therefore, when we speak of "Son" and "Spirit," as well as when we speak of "Father," we are speaking of "just God himself."

This conclusion is well taken, for it states the thought behind the oft-made observation that subordinationism compromises the very character of the revelation that is given in Christ. Why? Because if subordination is affirmed, the revelation of God in Christ is really no longer a revelation of God but of One who is like God. Otto Weber, reflecting on this issue, observes that the struggle in the ancient church over the Trinity concerned not some abstract theological reflection that had dislodged itself from preaching, but rather the very heart of all preaching that is the message of God's salvation. Therefore, subordinationism is the most acute form of that temptation which the church had to resist, the temptation to say that what appeared in Jesus Christ was something from God, something Godlike, but not just God (*Grundlagen der Dogmatik,* vol. I, pp. 408-09). The detailed exposition of those New Testament passages that have been traditionally understood to refer to Jesus as "just God" will concern us when we develop the doctrine of the Person of Christ.

While subordination in the eternal Godhead has been rejected in the creeds and confessions, the church has always acknowledged the subordination of the Son and the Spirit in the economy of redemption. In fulfilling their tasks as Savior and Sanctifier, tasks that they have voluntarily assumed, the Son submits himself to his Father's will in all things, becoming "obedient unto death, even death on a cross" (Phil. 2:8). So also the Spirit submits not only to the Father but also to the Son as he takes not of his own but of the things of Christ and reveals them to us (Jn. 16:15). This "economic subordination," clearly taught in the New Testament, was used by the Arians to defend their doctrine of the ontological subordination of the Son. By such appeal to Scripture they sought to enhance the plausibility of their position.

Since the church has rejected the Arian reading of the New Testament, how should the data to which they appealed be understood? How is the Lord Jesus Christ, who became our Savior, related to the One in whose name he came? This is the very question, of course, with which the entire trinitarian debate began. Having reviewed that debate and having defended the conclusions to which the church came concerning the eternal subsistence of the three persons in the one essence (*una substantia—tres personae*), it comes as no surprise that we view the subordination of the Son (and Spirit) to the Father not in terms of nature (οὐσία) but of tasks or roles. The Son enters our world to accomplish his Father's will as our Savior. Obviously, as the One who comes in another's name, as the One sent to accomplish a mission, he is subject to him who sent him. It is, then, in his work *ad extra,* in his mission as the incarnate Lord Jesus Christ, that we understand those passages to which the Arians have appealed, passages that teach that the Son is not only other than the Father, but less than the Father.

Perhaps the most striking materials are found in the Synoptics, where Jesus not only lives his life in obedient submission to the Father, but, as his ministry draws to a close, prays to the Father as the One who is able to save him from death (Mk. 14:36, par.). But even in John, where our Lord's ministry is interpreted much more overtly in the light of the Easter event, Jesus says, "The Father is greater than I" (Jn. 14:28). This Johannine

Jesus not only distinguishes himself from the One who sent him, but refers to him who sent him as "the only true God" (Jn. 17:3). Even when Jesus makes the stupendous claim—attributed by many to the later theologizing of the church—that no one comes to the Father but by him (Jn. 14:6), it is to the Father that they come, through him.

When we turn from the gospels to the epistles of Paul, it is obvious that the apostle tends, in his own way of speaking, to reserve the term "God" for the Father in distinction to the Lord Jesus Christ: "Grace to you and peace from God our Father and the Lord Jesus Christ" (1 Cor. 1:3). In fact, the Father is not only our God, but also the God of our Lord Jesus Christ (Eph. 1:17). For Christians, the apostle says, there is one God only, the Father, and one Lord, Jesus Christ (1 Cor. 8:6). We are of Christ as Christ is of God (1 Cor. 3:23). Even in the beautiful trinitarian benediction found in 2 Corinthians 13:14, he speaks not of the Father, but of God as distinct from Jesus and the Spirit: "the grace of the Lord Jesus Christ and the love of God, and the fellowship of the Holy Spirit be with you all."[60]

Looking at these data, the Arians argued that obviously the Father is truly God and Jesus is his Son—like him, but not one with him in his essential being. How could he who is himself God have died the agonizing death of one who is forsaken by God (Mk. 15:34)? And why should he who is himself God have uttered up his petitions and entreaties with loud cries and supplications to One who was able to save him from death (Heb. 5:7-8)? Why? Because, the church has answered, he spoke out of his messianic humiliation; that is, he spoke "in the days of his flesh," as the author of Hebrews would say.[61] That is why the *Quicumque vult* affirms (Art. 33) that he is "equal to the Father as touching his Godhead; inferior to the Father as touching his Humanity." And as he is inferior in his humanity, so he is subordinate in his mission.

He, then, is the One who made himself of no reputation, took upon himself the form of a servant, and was made in our likeness; and being found in fashion as a man, he humbled himself and became obedient unto death, even the death of the cross (Phil. 2:7ff.). Indeed, even in his subsequent exaltation "at the right hand of God" (Acts 2:32-33) he is subordinate to the One who sent him, whose will he obeys in all things. We do not read that having been raised from the dead he has highly exalted himself, but rather that "God has highly exalted him and bestowed on him

---

60. See also 1 Corinthians 12:4ff., where the apostle speaks of the same *Spirit*, the same *Lord*, and the same *God*—the last being he who works all things in all.

61. For our own reflections on a trinitarian understanding of what happened at Calvary, see below, Unit Four, V, B, 3, *Theologica Crucis:* A Comment, pp. 409ff.

the name which is above every name, that at the name of Jesus every knee should bow . . . and every tongue confess . . . to the glory of God the Father" (Phil. 2:9ff.). Hence, though his voice shall give life to the dead (Jn. 5:25), this unheard-of power beyond all human power—the power to destroy the last enemy, death—is a power given him by the Father ("For as the Father has life in himself, so he has granted the Son also to have life in himself" (Jn. 5:26). And when he shall have exercised this power, when he shall have reigned till all his enemies—including the last enemy, death—are put under his feet, then, as the anointed servant of the Lord, he shall give over the kingdom to God, even the Father, being in subjection to the One who subjected all things to him, that God may be all in all (1 Cor. 15:23-28).[62]

So the subordination of the Son is clear even in his messianic exaltation. But we must never forget that the subject of this subordination-in-exaltation is not one who has been humbled by a greater power, as was Pharaoh of Egypt. Unlike the king of Babylon, no dirge is taken up over him (Is. 14:12). Rather, he is the One who humbled himself, because he is the One who had no need to grasp equality with God. The sin of hubris could not be his, for he is the One who is by nature in the very form of God (ὃν ἐν μορφῇ θεοῦ ὑπάρχων, Phil. 2:6). *Hence, even his exaltation as the Messiah is his condescension as the eternal Son.* Therefore, theologians have spoken of him both as the eternal Son—one with the Father and the Spirit—and at the same time as the One who, like the members of the human family with whom he has identified, submits to his Father's will and so becomes the man for others.

What is true of the Son is true also of the Spirit. When we speak of the Trinity, we speak not only of the God who sends (Father) and who is sent (Son), but also of the God who gives (Father), who bestows (Son), and who is given and bestowed (Spirit). God is not only our Father who sends the Savior; he is not only our Savior who is sent by the Father; he is also our Sanctifier whom the Son receives from his Father and bestows on his people. Peter, in the first Christian sermon, declares: "Being therefore exalted at the right hand of God, and having received from the Father the promise of the Holy Spirit, he [the risen Christ] has poured out this which

---

62. The Incarnation is not a temporary but a permanent act of the Son, as can be seen from the fact that his resurrection is not a putting off of our humanity but a glorifying of it. Hence, it is generally assumed, as the above passages imply, that the messianic subordination of the Son is likewise permanent. Viewing the Corinthian text in this light, some have taken the final reference to God ("that God may be all in all") specifically of the Father (a frequent usage in the Pauline epistles). Others, however, have understood the reference generically of just the triune God. We are definitely inclined to the latter view.

you see and hear" (Acts 2:33). Such a text reflects the doctrine of the Spirit's twofold economic subordination. In his saving, sanctifying power, the Spirit comes both as the gift of the Father to the exalted Son and the gift of the Son to his waiting disciples.[63]

The same twofold subordination is reflected in the Johannine material concerning the Spirit. The Spirit whom Jesus promises to give (the "other Paraclete") is the Spirit of truth whom he requests of the Father (Jn. 14:16) and whom he sends from the Father (Jn. 15:26). Hence, the Spirit may be spoken of as the Spirit of God or of Christ, the two expressions being virtually synonymous (Rom. 8:9; Gal. 4:6). As the Spirit of God it is his task to glorify Christ and to reveal him to us. Indeed, the spirit that does not reveal Christ is not the Spirit of God. "By this you know the Spirit of God: Every Spirit which confesses that Jesus Christ is come in the flesh is of God, and every spirit which does not confess Jesus is not of God" (1 Jn. 4:2-3).

The Spirit's subordinate role in the economy of redemption must be borne in mind when one evaluates the contribution of Pentecostalism to the ongoing theological reflection of the church. The ministry of the Spirit has indeed been neglected in Protestant theology generally. On the other hand, the church is to "preach Christ and him crucified," not the Spirit and his unique gifts. The Son is the Savior, and it is his saving work that the Spirit is sent to accomplish. This he does by taking the things not of himself, but of Christ, and revealing them to us.

> More about Jesus let me learn,
> More of his holy will discern;
> Spirit of God my teacher be,
> Showing the things of Christ to me. (Hewitt)

A balanced approach neither ignores the Spirit's ministry nor gives it the central place that the church has traditionally given to the person and work of the Son.

*   *   *   *   *

Understanding the implications of the Spirit's subordinate role to the Son in the economy of redemption enables one to avoid a kind of Christianized mysticism. To the

---

63. Though it is customary to regard the event of Pentecost (and Luke's interpretation of it in Acts 2) as the primary paradigm for understanding the Spirit's role in the economy of redemption, we must not forget that the Spirit is revealed in this economic role long before Pentecost. He is the Spirit of Christ in the prophets (1 Pt. 1:11); and when the Christ comes, in fulfillment of the prophetic word, he is conceived by the Spirit (Lk. 1:35); when baptized by John, he is anointed by the Spirit (Lk. 3:22); when tempted in the wilderness, he is driven by the Spirit (Mk. 1:12); when sent from God to speak the word of God, he is endowed with the Spirit (Jn. 3:34).

thesis that the New Testament doctrine of the Spirit contains strands of mystical Hellenistic thought, it may be replied that in the teaching of the New Testament the Spirit never bears witness to himself but to Christ crucified and risen. The New Testament doctrine of the Spirit has little to do, then, with the immediacy of mystical experience. The direction of the Spirit's witness is not away from history into the depths of the human psyche; it is rather toward history, that is, the history of the Jesus event.

ADDENDUM: CONCERNING THE SUBORDINATION OF THE SON TO THE FATHER AND THE WOMAN TO THE MAN

Today, the case for sexual hierarchy is seldom reinforced by the traditional view of the woman's inferiority—though men often reflect such a view in the day-to-day relationships that make up life. However, while they affirm the equal worth of the woman, there are still those who defend sexual hierarchy on theological grounds. We bring up the matter at this juncture because it is sometimes argued that the creation ordinance on which such hierarchy supposedly rests is grounded ultimately in the trinitarian nature of the Creator himself. Because the Trinity is such an awesome mystery, this argument can be made to sound, if not awesome, at least impressive. As the Son is of the Father, so the woman is of the man (Gn. 2:22-23). Hence, as the Son submits to his Father, so the woman submits to the man; or at least she ought to, especially if she is a Christian. Thus, by divine intent her life is to reflect, at the creaturely level, the sacrificial love manifest in the life of God himself as that life is revealed in the Son, who submitted to his Father's will in all things.

The difficulty with this analogy is patent to anyone who understands the orthodox doctrine of the Trinity. Subordinationism, as we have argued in the foregoing discussion, is from one perspective biblical orthodoxy; from another, however, it is Arian heresy. To teach that the Son is subordinate to the Father by nature is heresy; to teach that he is subordinate by a free and voluntary choice is orthodoxy. Just as the Son is by nature fully God (*homoousios* with the Father, and therefore equal to him) so the woman is by nature fully human (*homoousios* with the man, and therefore equal to him). And as the Son is Son and the Father is Father by virtue of their relationship to each other, so the woman is woman and the man is man by virtue of their relationship to each other.

Obviously, a relationship between those who are of the same nature and equal to each other does not entail hierarchy. The hierarchy in the Trinity rests not upon nature but upon a free act of the Son, who humbled himself (Phil. 2:7). His submission to the Father arises not out of his being as such, but out of the freedom of his own choice, whereby he loved us and gave himself for us (Gal. 2:20). In the technical terms of the above discussion, the Son is not ontologically subordinate as the Son, but economically subordinate as the Savior. Those, therefore, who argue for the subordination of the woman—as woman—to the man have no right to ground such an argument in the doctrine of the Trinity as traditionally understood. When they do so, they are really making the same mistake in anthropology that the Arians made in theology. So far as the economic subordination of the Son is concerned—since it is his voluntary act of condescension and not a necessary condition of his nature—it is an example of self-giving love equally applicable to all, both men and women, as members of Christ's body, the church. When the apostle, therefore, exhorts his readers, "Have this mind among yourselves, which you have in Christ Jesus" (Phil. 2:5), he is not talking to women as such, but to Christians of both sexes; they should relate mutually one to another not in selfish vainglory, but in a voluntary and humble submission as the circumstances may warrant.

E. SEXIST LANGUAGE AND THE DOCTRINE OF THE TRINITY

We have already addressed the question of the analogical character of theological language, including the language used in the trinitarian name: Father, Son, and Holy Spirit. Now that we have finished our treatment of the nature of God and are about to turn to the question of the divine attributes, it is fitting that we make a few added comments on our speech about God, as that speech in its traditional form reflects a use of language that many regard as sexist. We say it is fitting because, at this juncture, we shall turn not only from the subject of the divine nature to the divine attributes, but also from the traditional male use of language about God to the use of female language. In speaking of the attributes, God will be likened not to a father (Ps. 103:13) but to a mother (Is. 66:13).[64]

Analogical language, to be meaningful, must of course rest upon some univocal element between the human reality from which it is taken and the divine reality to which it refers. In our exposition of the doctrine of the

---

64. For our initial remarks, see above, Unit One, III, First Addendum: A Comment on Sexist Language, pp. 44ff.

Trinity, so far as God's name—Father, Son, and Spirit—is concerned, we have identified the univocal element in the concept of origins. The second and third persons in the Godhead originate, as persons, with the first person, who is therefore called "Father." The Father "begets" the Son and "breathes" ("spirates") the Spirit. But obviously in using such terms as "begetting" and "breathing" to describe how the second and third persons of the Godhead have their origin in the first, we speak analogically, not univocally. And since this is so, feminine figures could as well be used without altering the substance of our thought about God. If the woman, like the man, is created in the image of God (Gn. 1:27) and is therefore as much like God as the man, then female imagery is just as capable as is male imagery of bearing the truth that God is a trinitarian fellowship of holy love. After all, women have as much to do with origins, at the human level, as men—unless one subscribes to the discredited biological theory that our essential humanity is carried from generation to generation by the sperm lodged in the womb.

If we describe the relationship between the first and second persons of the Godhead analogically as a "begetting" and a "being begotten," may we not as well, still speaking analogically, describe it as a "bearing" and a "being born"? Since God is like a woman as well as a man, may God not be likened to a mother who eternally bears a daughter as well as to a father who eternally begets a son? And may not a mother also breathe the Spirit as well as a father? Do not women have breath as well as men? Are they not alive? We are, it is granted, speaking in a purely hypothetical way, since, as a matter of fact, in the Incarnation God assumed male humanity. But there is nothing either in the concept of God, or in the concept of Incarnation, that leads by logical entailment to masculinity. Given the patriarchal society of Israel, the revelation of God naturally takes a patriarchal form. (We say "naturally" rather than "necessarily" because even in patriarchal cultures female gods were known and worshipped.) It is not surprising, then, that God reveals himself to Israel as the "Father" of "his" people. Being disclosed as the Father of Israel, it is likewise natural that God should send one called a "son," who naturally assumes male humanity. Here an element of necessity does come into the picture; but it is a necessity of a secondary sort. It is due not to the essential, masculine nature of God but to the sexual polarity in which the Creator has given us our humanity. As a result of the way in which we are given our individual humanity, we describe ourselves, not analogically but literally, as male or female. This is why God, in becoming one with us, must of necessity become a man or a woman. Neither the gospels, however, nor the Chalcedonian Christology of the church, lays any emphasis on the maleness of Jesus. In the Incarnation he who is *vere Dei* becomes *vere homo,* not *vere masculus.* Of course, once "the matchless deed's achieved, determined, dared, and done" (Smart), there is a kind of finality, though not ultimacy, in the form of God's self-disclosure that is normative for the church. Christ Jesus is the one mediator between God and humankind (1 Tm. 2:5), and this Christ Jesus is the *man* Christ Jesus.

Nonetheless, to speak of God as a mother who discloses herself to us in a daughter, though it is a hypothetical way of speaking, is not a heretical way of speaking. Given the realities of salvation history, we grant that it is a way of speaking with no prospects of being other than hypothetical. God the Creator, as we have observed, has given us our humanity in a sexual polarity and God the Savior has assumed that humanity as a male rather than a female. Yet the need to speak in this hypothetical way comes from the fact that women are justified in their complaint that the traditional understanding of our traditional language about God has made them second-class citizens both as members of the human race and as members of the family of God. It is to help men hear language about God as many women today hear the traditional language the church has used of God that we have chosen to use feminine language in our next unit, which is entitled What God Is Like: The Divine Attributes.

The dogmaticians' understanding of the traditional male language used of the Deity illustrates the way in which all male language has been understood by males. Such language is sometimes generic, sometimes specific; but the rules as to when it is one and when it is the other depend not on objective criteria so much as on the subjective inclination of the male who is using the language. Unfortunately, theologians are no exception to this *sic et non.* To give an example, when ruminating on the general nature of God talk in Unit One, III, pp. 25-28, we observed that theologians recognize the analogical character of theological speech in general. But in speaking of God, specifically, the rule does not hold; while we may call God a "mother," a "shepherd," a "laundress," etc., analogically, when we call God a "father" suddenly we are speaking literally. God is like a mother, but God *is* a father. John Baillie, in his otherwise excellent Gifford Lectures, *The Sense of the Presence of God,* notes with Barth that when we say God is a "father" we speak "properly" of him, not analogically. Fatherhood is not an attribute, but the property *(proprietas)* of the first person of the Godhead. (See p. 120, citing Barth, *Credo* and *K.D., I/1,* pp. 413ff. [cf. *C.D., I/1,* sec. 10.2]. See the latter also for Barth's understanding of Eph. 3:14-15: God is "the Father from whom every family in heaven and on earth is named.") This subtle non sequitur, drawn from the doctrine of the *proprietas,* says it all. (For our own treatment of the *proprietas* doctrine, see this Unit, IV, D, 2, c, The Relational Meaning of the Trinitarian Name, pp. 287ff.)

The Oldest Math

A Sermon Preached by Marguerite Shuster
at Knox Presbyterian Church, Pasadena, California,
Lord's Day, May 29, 1988

Now there was a man of the Pharisees, named Nicodemus, a ruler of the Jews. This man came to Jesus by night and said to him, "Rabbi, we know that you are a teacher come from God; for no one can do these signs that you do, unless God is with him." Jesus answered him, "Truly, truly, I say to you, unless one is born anew, he cannot see the kingdom of God." Nicodemus said to him, "How can a man be born when he is old? Can he enter a second time into his mother's womb and be born?" Jesus answered, "Truly, truly, I say to you, unless one is born of water and the Spirit, he cannot enter the kingdom of God. That which is born of the flesh is flesh, and that which is born of the Spirit is spirit. Do not marvel that I said to you, 'You must be born anew.' The wind blows where it wills, and you hear the sound of it, but you do not know whence it comes or whither it goes; so it is with every one who is born of the Spirit." Nicodemus said to him, "How can this be?" Jesus answered him, "Are you a teacher of Israel, and yet you do not understand this? Truly, truly, I say to you, we speak of what we know, and bear witness to what we have seen; but you do not receive our testimony. If I have told you earthly things and you do not believe, how can you believe if I tell you heavenly things? No one has ascended into heaven but he who descended from heaven, the Son of man. And as Moses lifted up the serpent in the wilderness, so must the Son of man be lifted up, that whoever believes in him may have eternal life."

For God so loved the world that he gave his only Son, that whoever believes in him should not perish but have eternal life. For God sent the Son into the world, not to condemn the world, but that the world might be saved through him.

John 3:1-17 (RSV)

You've heard of the new math, right? Where one plus one plus one equals what looks to the uninitiated like "10," if you're working in base three, and "11," if you're working in base two, and so on? It's enough to drive one quickly back to the old math, where one plus one plus one always equals a nice, tidy *three,* period. Life was simple in the good old days. Maybe. Because you may not have heard of the oldest math of all. In the oldest math of all, one plus one plus one equals—what? One. That's right, one. Before you or I existed, before any human being existed, before a world or a universe or a cloud of hot gasses existed, from all eternity, the Father, the Son, and the Holy Spirit were and are one God. One plus one plus one equals one.

It is a great mystery, of course—much more mysterious than the new math, which is straightforward enough when you understand it. It's a mystery we'll never solve by our own intellects. And hence there are those who consider the doctrine of the Trinity to be as irrelevant as it is baffling. Dorothy Sayers tries to capture the sentiments of those who feel that way in one of the questions and answers in a mock examination paper on the Christian faith:

Q: What is the doctrine of the Trinity?

A: "The Father incomprehensible, the Son incomprehensible, and the whole thing incomprehensible." Something put in by theologians to make it more difficult—nothing to do with daily life or ethics.[1]

Why, then, have Christians from ancient times believed that the one God is indeed a Trinity of three Persons: Father, Son, and Holy Spirit?

Since today is Trinity Sunday, let's take a look at that question by examining just one very familiar theme—that God is love, in the context of one very familiar passage, John 3:1-17, to see an example of how the roots of the doctrine are everywhere in Scripture. (We could, of course, have chosen to look at any number of other passages, but since the doctrine is complex, the simplest and most familiar settings are perhaps most help-

---

1. *The Whimsical Christian* (New York: Macmillan, 1978), p. 25.

ful.) I shall proceed by elaborating three affirmations: (1) God is love; (2) God loves us; and (3) God enables us to love him.

God is love: Scripture tells us so specifically in 1 John 4:16, and the fundamental theme of my text this morning is the greatness of God's love. Now, love itself is a very mysterious thing, but we do know a few things about it from our human experience, which, since it's the only experience we have, we must use as an analogy. We know, for one thing, that real love would be inconceivable if one lived all one's life in a glass bubble and never knew that such a thing as other creatures existed. Indeed, under such circumstances we could scarcely be considered persons; for without relationships—without community, sharing, fellowship of some sort—personal life simply does not exist. To be absolutely alone is to be neither loving nor persons.

Further, we know almost instinctively that there is something not quite complete about love directed toward something less than we are, like animals or objects. Most of us think something is wrong when an elderly woman wills her whole million-dollar fortune to her cats. We want people's love to spill over, so that they are kind to animals, but we pity those who pour out all their affection on pets; for however loyal and comforting pets may be, their capacity to respond is simply too limited. And, obviously, it's worse yet if a man lavishes all his passion on his yacht or his stamp collection, which cannot respond at all. True human love requires a suitable object: an object different from oneself, but fundamentally like—not less than—oneself. And when one is deeply in love, one tends to see one's lover as very, very much like oneself: one feels at one with him or her, and at the same time more truly oneself than one has ever been before. The Bible even speaks of a couple as becoming "one flesh." What in our human experience can be more alike, while at the same time being more different, than a man and a woman?

Now look at Genesis 1:26: "God created humankind in his own image, in the image of God he created him; male and female he created them." Remarkably enough, what images or mirrors God in his creation is not a single creature, all alone, but two equal yet differentiated creatures in relationship one to another. The point of the analogy here, which is of course only an analogy, is not to attribute sexual differentiation to the persons of the Trinity, but simply to point to a biblical clue that God should not be conceived as being in himself isolated and solitary, as being utterly alone before he created the world, as having no truly adequate object for his love. If he were in himself utterly alone, it would be impossible to conceive his being, in himself, before creation, both loving and personal—two of the most crucial affirmations Christians make about God.

God is, however, still one: the Christian God is not several individual persons in relationship, much less a committee. When we humans talk about love and "relationships," as often as not we are thinking about stresses and strains and pain, about others who are not wholly at one with us, much as we wish they were. We can only grope after the kind of unity for which we long. God has that unity absolutely. Thus the Scriptures speak of the persons of the Trinity "indwelling" one another. Jesus says, for instance, "I am in the Father and the Father in me" (Jn. 14:11). And again, when Philip asks that Jesus show him the Father, Jesus says, "He who has seen me has seen the Father" (Jn. 14:9). Such language is as close as we can come to understanding perfect relationship, perfect unity, perfect love.

Why, though, some of you may be asking, do we care what God is like in himself? Isn't it his relationship to us that really matters, as far as we are concerned? Yes and no. Yes, we are directly affected by his relationship to us. But if we think about it, don't we want to know that what he reveals to us of himself is what he is really like? Don't we want to know that God isn't just playing hide-and-seek with us, leaving certain clues that may prove to be misleading or dead wrong in the end? If God is not in himself a fellowship of love, how can we possibly trust his claim that he loves us?

But he is love, as a holy Trinity, and he does love us. In the words of my text, "God so loved the world that he gave his only Son, that whoever believes in him should not perish but have eternal life." God himself, at a specific point in history, chose to come to us in the person of the incarnate Son. He didn't come because he was lonely and needed us, like an elderly lady needs her cats. He came in the overflow of love that is his very nature. He came to make himself and his love known to us by dying to save us from our sins: "As Moses lifted up the serpent in the wilderness, so must the Son of man be lifted up. . . . For God sent the Son into the world, not to condemn the world, but that the world might be saved through him."

Note here that if Jesus Christ is not himself God, the whole thing fails. First of all, the revelation fails, for only God can adequately show us what God is like. If a goldfish were to say to her fellow goldfish that she proposed to show them what people are like, she ought not to be believed, however much she might think she knew about people. Goldfish are not and will never be people, even if they know a few things that are true about people, like their propensity to tap incoherently on a fish tank. But it is also true that real people cannot by any means communicate very effectively with goldfish. To communicate something of what people are like to goldfish, a person would have to become a goldfish—a thing that cannot be imagined. God did, however, become a human being—also a thing that cannot be imagined, but that actually happened. True, God in coming to us as a human being cannot reveal all there is to know of God, any more than a person incarnate as a goldfish could tell goldfish all there is to know of people. But if what Jesus does reveal is not true, then there has been no revelation at all. God must do the revealing; and what he reveals must in some meaningful sense correspond to what God is really like.

Second, if Jesus were not God, God's purpose to save us would fail, for the death of one more human being, however noble he might be, would just add to the sum of evil in the world and not accomplish something fundamental to defeat it. Only God can deal with sin in any ultimate sense. John 3 elaborates no theory about how God does it, but simply points to the death of Jesus.

All right, we've said that both revelation and atonement for sin rest absolutely upon the fact that Jesus is truly God, and not just a fine human being. That may be true logically speaking, but are there pointers in my text that suggest that the Son is God? Yes indeed, at least pointers. Verse 13: "No one has ascended into heaven but he who descended from heaven, the Son of man." Jesus' proper abode is not earth, but heaven, from whence he came. Verse 7: "You must be born anew." We must, but Jesus gives not the slightest indication that he must. Jesus needs no rebirth. And, pointing at the very least to the uniqueness of Jesus, verse 16: God gave his only Son—we are not sons and daughters of God in the same way that Jesus is the Son of God.

God loves us. He shows that by accomplishing our salvation by coming to us in the person of the incarnate Son. He establishes a relationship with us. And because what he does truly reveals who he is, the very fact that he establishes a loving relationship with us suggests that his very nature involves a loving fellowship of the persons of the Trinity.

God is love. God loves us. But how do we come to love God? Only as God enables us to do so; and he enables us by the power of the Spirit who is the third person of the Trinity. Jesus' example is not enough. His revelation is not enough. Even his dying for our sins is not enough, unless somehow we can be moved to see and receive what he has done for us and be empowered to follow him. And if that final step were left to us— to our own strength and piety—all the rest would be for naught. As every psychologist knows, all the knowledge and all the moral instruction in the world do not change people. Something has to get hold of a person's heart. If Jesus accomplishes our salvation, objectively speaking, by dying for us, it is the Holy Spirit who accomplishes our salvation, subjectively speaking, by enabling us to appropriate what Christ has done for us. 1 Corinthians 2:14: "The unspiritual person does not receive the gifts of the Spirit of

God, for they are folly to him, and he is not able to understand them because they are spiritually discerned." 1 Corinthians 12:3: "No one can say 'Jesus is Lord' except by the Holy Spirit." And in my text, John 3:5, 7: "Unless one is born of water and the Spirit, he cannot enter the kingdom of God. . . . You must be born anew."

Naturally enough, poor Nicodemus was quite baffled. Thoughtful Jews had expected fulfillment of their hope to come as a continuation of the old line of law and prophets. Nicodemus had come asking for help, for insight. Jesus insisted upon an entirely new beginning. Nicodemus thought it was all quite impossible as well as wholly incomprehensible: "How can a man be born when he is old? Can he enter a second time into his mother's womb and be born?" (Notice how many times the little word "can" appears in this passage: humanly speaking, the difficulties attending salvation are insuperable.) Jesus readily admits the mystery, but not the impossibility: "The wind blows where it wills, and you hear the sound of it, but you do not know whence it comes or whither it goes; so it is with every one who is born of the Spirit." Something radical and new must happen, something that is not in our control, any more than the wind is at our beck and call. And that "something" depends wholly upon the Spirit.

You see, then, what is happening in my text? Salvation in its entirety is the work of God alone. Only God can save us. We can in no way save ourselves. But who is this God? He is God the Father, who loves the world so much that he sends God the Son to make himself known. He is God the Son, Jesus Christ, who shows his love by dying for our sins and who sends to us his Spirit to guide us into all truth (Jn. 15:26; 16:7, 13). He is God the Holy Spirit, by whom we are reborn and so enabled rightly to see and believe in Jesus—by whom we are enabled to love God. This God is the one God—Father, Son, and Holy Spirit—whose very nature is love. Without referring to all three persons of the Trinity, this very familiar passage, John 3:1-17, could never have been written. And the doctrine of the Trinity is similarly implicit throughout Scripture. That, of course, is why theologians developed the doctrine—to make sense of what the Bible actually says, so that we might hear what God has done for our salvation.

The mathematics—how one plus one plus one really can equal one— will remain a mystery. The Trinity will remain incomprehensible in the sense that we will never succeed in encompassing God in the little circle of our own understanding. But the mystery itself gives us the clue we most need to the nature of God—that he truly is the God who is love—the God who (1) loves us, (2) gives himself for us, and (3) enables us to love him. We can trust him because he is who he reveals himself to be.

UNIT FOUR

WHAT GOD IS LIKE: THE DIVINE ATTRIBUTES

My God, how wonderful thou art,
Thy majesty how bright,
How beautiful thy mercy seat,
In depths of burning light!

How wonderful, how beautiful,
The sight of thee must be,
Thine endless wisdom, boundless power,
And awful purity!

Faber

"Great is thy faithfulness," O God my Father,
There is no shadow of turning with thee;
Thou changest not, thy compassions they fail not;
As thou hast been thou forever will be.

Chisholm

God is a God,
He don't never change;
God is a God
And he always will be God.

Negro Spiritual

I. Introduction

A. MAY ATTRIBUTES BE PREDICATED OF GOD?

As we turn to the subject of the divine attributes, the first question that confronts us—strange as it may seem to the uninitiated—is whether it is proper to ascribe attributes to God. Do they describe God as she really is?[1] Those who have followed our discussion thus far will recognize this question as simply a nuance of an ongoing problem with which we have struggled from the beginning. Both when speaking of God as personal being and especially when speaking of her as the Holy One, we lamented the profound but doubtful influence of Pseudo-Dionysius on medieval theology and the resultant affirmation of the divine transcendence in terms of a metaphysic of pure Being. Given such a view of transcendence, God tends to become a bare Essence rather than the living God revealed in salvation history, a God whom we cannot describe but only contemplate in mystical silence. We turn once again to this problem because it bears in a significant way on the ensuing discussion.[2]

Inevitably, as we have noted, theologians have used philosophical categories of thought in doing theology. Being Greek in their culture, the early theologians naturally used the categories of Greek thought in their interpretation of the Bible. However, this encounter between Greek and biblical thought

---

1. It will be recalled that in this unit we shall use the feminine pronoun of the divine Subject and the masculine pronoun of the human subject both in the text and in quoted matter. See above, Unit One, III, First Addendum: A Comment on Sexist Language, pp. 44ff.; also Unit Three, IV, E, Sexist Language and the Doctrine of the Trinity, pp. 323ff.

2. In this discussion we have found helpful the article "Gott, VII, Philosophisch," by J. Klein, *Die Religion in Geschichte und Gegenwart* (hereafter *RGG*), vol. II (Tübingen: Mohr, 1958), col. 1741ff.

forms, unavoidable though it was, spawned many a problem for the Christian church, especially in the working out of a doctrine of the divine attributes. Dazzled as they were by the Greek assumption that the highest dignity belongs to the "One," in contrast to the many particulars of the passing world of the senses, theologians saw this assumption as paralleling the biblical emphasis on the unchanging and essential oneness of God in contrast to the multiplicity and change in the created order. It was all but inevitable, therefore, that in their thinking about God, her many attributes should lose out to her essence, which is eternally one and the same.

This assimilation of biblical to Greek thought was unfortunate. While it is true that pagan Greek thinkers, who understood the manifold of created reality in terms of the Absolute, sometimes called this Absolute "God," this God was personified only in a figurative sense. "He" or "She" was in reality an "It," the final immanental Principle or the absolute Form of the material universe. This static, impassive God of metaphysics was quite other than the dynamic, living God of which the Scriptures speak. Hence, the theologians' tendency to identify the eternal God of the Scriptures with the primary Principle of the universe meant that the personal view of God as the living God gradually retreated before a static view of God as the unchanging One. As a result, God became the one who, properly speaking, is above all distinction, even above the distinction of the one and the many. When we speak of her, therefore, in terms of the one (she "is") and the many (she is "just," "merciful," "wise," etc.), in the latter instance we speak in a way that does not describe God as she really is. While we can know that God is (her *Dasein*), we can never truly know how she is (her *Wiesein*).

The trouble with all this is that the Bible does say something—in fact, a great deal—about how God is. Many and ingenious, therefore, have been the efforts of theologians to make similar statements about God and to explain how such statements can be construed as more than simply projections of the finite categories of the mind on the ineffable Infinite of metaphysics. In our judgment, such efforts are attempting the impossible because they begin, to borrow the language of Pascal's *Memorial*, not with the God of Abraham, Isaac, and Jacob, of Sarah, Rebecca, and Rachel, but with the God of the philosophers and metaphysicians, the God whose oneness is that of an absolute Simplicity.

Early in this century, Hermann Cremer felt it necessary to make the observation that the treatment of the divine attributes in the science of dogmatics has been one of the most sterile loci in the discipline.[3] He

---

3. Hermann Cremer, *Die christliche Lehre von den Eigenschaften Gottes* (Gütersloh: Bertelsmann, 1897).

marveled at the anomaly that from the time of the Greek Fathers through that of the Protestant Scholastics, theologians wrestled with the problem of whether or not attributes even belong to God, properly speaking. This they did (as we have seen) because they assumed that properties or qualities (attributes) denote definiteness, limitation, conditioning, multiplicity, all of which they deemed incompatible with the thought that God is the infinite, eternal, and unchanging One. According to Cremer, with whom we agree, the only resolution of this impasse is to consider God in herself to be who she has revealed herself to be in Christ. We must, in other words, renounce the dualism of Greek philosophical thought.[4] Such dualism tends to make God the Other, one who is, so far as the world is concerned, so wholly other that she can be thought of only in terms of the ultimate Unity and Harmony reflected in the world (Origen); a Unity that is beyond even the distinction of substance and accidents (being and attributes), a Simplicity that excludes all plurality, a Oneness that makes her a kind of celestial *Ding an sich.*

Cremer's desire to break with the past has not been easy to achieve. The theological issues involved are complex and the task correspondingly difficult. Before we turn to this task, however, we need to say a word about the long-standing debate between the Nominalists and the Realists, a debate bearing on our problem.

CONCERNING NOMINALISM AND REALISM

Theological Nominalism has its roots in a philosophical argument, going back to Greek antiquity, as to whether primary reality belongs to individuals or to universals. Some (the Nominalists) hold the former, others (the Realists) the latter. The Nominalists insist that universals are simply concepts (names) by which we describe the common features belonging to a given class of individuals and so organize the data of sense perception. Hence the idea (universal) of "chair" exists only in the mind; the real chair is this particular rocking chair in which I am sitting and thinking about the problem. But, say the Realists, this particular rocking chair, and all other particular chairs, come and go like Heraclitus's river, whereas the concept "chair" (the "universal") is not subject to such change. So it is more real after all.

In any case, theological Nominalism, represented by Occam, Biel, and others in the Middle Ages, holds that all predicates (attributes) ascribed to God are really no more than subjective distinctions in our minds, which have no corresponding reality in a God whose being is pure simplicity. Such distinctions are useful, some would even say necessary, for us, in order that we may organize the data of Scripture and so speak meaningfully about God. But when we so speak, we are not describing God as she

4. Ibid., pp. 7-19.

really is in herself. This extreme and consistent form of Nominalism obviously has all the problems we have complained of in our earlier rejection of apophatic theology. (See above, Unit Three, II, C, Addendum: Concerning Apophatic Theology, pp. 218-19.) Yet many theologians, in their effort to underscore the oneness of God, or the incomprehensibility of God, or the value of a practical over a theoretical knowledge of God, have spoken in ways that echo this nominalist mindset.

Other theologians have succumbed to what might be called a reductionist approach to the question. While they have not sided with the strict Nominalists and spoken of the being of God as a naked essence in contrast to the concepts in our minds, nonetheless they have sought to reduce the multiplicity of attributes found in Scripture to a single category. For some of the medieval Scholastics, "will" was the ultimate attribute. Later on, not a few Protestant theologians, following the Newtonian revolution in physics, tended to view God as a kind of celestial clock maker; hence, of all her attributes, the most fundamental was that of wisdom, in the sense of rational intellect. With the rise of critical history and the widespread adoption of Kantian epistemology, Protestant theology became increasingly anti-metaphysical. This rejection of metaphysics, however, by no means harbingered a return to a biblical view of God. So far as the doctrine of God was concerned, it rather meant that pronouncements about God (the traditional attributes) were understood as pronouncements about our religious experience. Understanding God in terms of ultimate "causality," Schleiermacher, for example, construed the attributes that we distinguish in God as describing the way in which we experience our utter dependence on the divine Causality. God's attributes are many in the sense that we have a manifold experience of the divine Causality in the varied circumstances of life and in the various stages of our religious development both as individuals and as a society. Ritschl, for example, and those who followed him (Hermann, Stephan, Troeltsch), understood the attributes as expressions of the ethical values of the kingdom manifested in human social progress.

In all such approaches, one is reminded of a favorite illustration of the ancient and medieval theologians, who likened the question of God and the attributes to the sun and its rays. As the rays of the sun produce diverse effects in nature, yet by means of one and the same solar energy, so God produces different effects in us, though she is one and the same in herself. Kantian and Neo-Kantian theologians, correspondingly, tended severely to limit their pronouncements about God and to understand those which they did make as descriptions of her effects in our experience. (Schlink, *"Gott,* VI, *Dogmatisch," RGG,* II, col. 1736, dubs this approach a "modalistic" view of the attributes, since they describe God not as she is in herself but as she is variously perceived in human experience.) Thus statements about God become statements about ourselves; theology is turned into anthropology.

One cannot deny, of course, the meaning and value that the divine attributes have for us in our human experience. But the fact that the attributes describe how God is related to us and we to her does not mean that they are not perfections of her own being apart from her relation to the creature. As Thomasius, in defense of theological Realism, said long ago,

If God stands only in relation to the world, then all her attributes are really only outward relations, revelations and effects . . . and such a view jeopardizes God's independence from the world. In that case she always becomes what she is, first through her relationship to the world. . . . In reality, however, there is a relationship of God with herself. . . . And this grounds the right to declare that there are immanent or essential attributes of God. (*Christi Person und Werk,* 1886, Bd. I, S. 38, as quoted by Barth, whose own theology is marked by a rigorous turning back to this orthodox [realistic] position on the attributes. See *K.D.,* II/1, p. 371; cf. *C.D.,* II/1, sec. 29.)

G. Ernest Wright, to cite a more contemporary source, is well taken when he says, "The proclamation of what God has done, whence it is inferred what she is, is the central concern of the Bible" (*God Who Acts,* p. 18). He goes on to endorse a theology that speaks of God as she *is* because such an approach contravenes the view that the gospel is simply a matter of teaching ethical values that have only a vague transcendental reference.

B. THE ANTHROPOMORPHIC/ANALOGICAL CHARACTER OF SUCH PREDICATION[5]

The effort to escape a dualism that separates being from attributes in one's doctrine of God is, as we have noted, difficult. One reason for this is that God is indeed other than her creation. She is the Holy One who transcends heaven and earth, of whom no creaturely likeness (image) is to be made. Therefore, even in her revelation she remains the hidden God. As a result, although our affirmations about her are taken from Scripture and are therefore true to Scripture, in making them we but touch the hem of her garment. To predicate attributes of God is, in other words, to speak anthropomorphically.[6] When we speak of God, who is other than the human creature in a way that is meaningful to the creature, we of necessity use terms that literally describe not God but the creature. Hence what we say about God, though not erroneous, is necessarily anthropomorphic. While the attributes describe what God is really like, they do not describe her fully. They describe her adequately for our needs in faith and life, but not

5. See above, Unit One, III, Speaking of God, pp. 25ff.

6. In our general discussion of theological language, we described such language as "analogical." What we here call "anthropomorphic" language is simply an instance of the language of "analogy." It is analogical language taken specifically from the human (anthropic) realm. Because all the attributes predicated of God are human qualities or the negation of them, theologians speak of such predication as "anthropomorphic." On the other hand, when speaking of the nature of theological language generally, they tend to use the less specific term "analogical."

adequately in the sense of a full and complete description of the divine mystery. They describe God as she is, but never altogether as she is.[7]

C. CONCERNING THE ATTRIBUTES AND THE DOXOLOGICAL STATEMENTS OF WORSHIP

Noting that the more the *Numen* is "incomprehensible" the more it "reveals" itself, Otto ruminates on this cryptic paradox by observing that

> "revealing oneself" does not at all mean simply to give oneself over to understandable conceptuality. Something can, in its profoundest essence, be known to feeling . . . for which every concept of the understanding fails. One can, through feeling, "understand" something in a deep and inward way without "grasping" it with the understanding, as, for example, music. What is grasped conceptually about music is not music itself.
>
> To "know" and to "understand conceptually" are not all one and the same; in fact, they are often mutually exclusive. . . . The *Deus absconditus et incomprehensibilis* [the hidden and incomprehensible God] is no *Deus ignotus* [unknown God]. Paul knew [her] only too well with all the fear and trembling of a timid spirit. And in like manner, Paul "knew" the peace of God that "passes all understanding"; otherwise he would not have spoken in its praise.[8]

While one may have emphatic reservations—as we do—about the way in which Otto tends to equate the "Divine" with the "Irrational" and the "understanding" of the Divine with "feeling," nonetheless the above observation reminds us that even as God is greater than our powers of thought so we are more than thinkers of thoughts when we relate to her. As a matter of fact, it is as we relate to her that we are able to say what we say about her. This is why theology originally emerged out of the faith

7. The natural scientist faces a situation somewhat similar to that of the theologian when he seeks to describe "objects" beyond the reach of telescope and microscope. Günter Ewald, *Wirklichkeit, Wissenschaft und Glaube* (Wuppertal: R. Brockhaus Verlag, n.d.), pp. 19ff. compares theological language to those scientific models which admittedly do not describe things as they really are, as, for example, Niels Bohr's model of the atom as a tiny planetary system. But the inadequacy of such a planetary model does not mean that one could just as well liken the atom to Don Quixote's windmills. For further comment on these matters, see above, Unit Two, II, Addendum: God Hidden in His Revelation, pp. 85ff.

8. Rudolph Otto, *Das Heilige* (Munich: C. H. Beck'sche Verlagsbuchhandlung, 30th ed., 1936), p. 163.

of the worshipping community, and if it is to remain true theology it must express the ongoing faith of that community.

Reflecting on the traditional "problem" of the attributes, Schlink (*RGG*, II, col. 1736ff.) observes that the theologians' tendency to give the question of God's being priority over that of her attributes meant that the doctrine of God was not primarily, but only secondarily, based on the revelation mediated through her redemptive acts in history. As a result, first God's existence was established by reason and then her attributes rationally deduced from her nature. Only then was special revelation brought into the picture in order to have a basis for the doctrine of the Trinity. This approach of natural theology was followed by many later Protestant scholastics with the result that the original meaning of the statements about God—found in Scripture and the early confessions—was obscured. These statements became general affirmations whose function was to unite in a rational overview what the church believed about God and the world, rather than confessional utterances of the sort used in worship, reflecting an encounter with the living God in her word. One is reminded of Thielicke's comment to beginning theological students: "Theology can be a coat of mail which crushes us and in which we freeze to death. It can also be—this is its purpose!—the conscience of the congregation of Christ, its compass and with it all a praise-song of ideas" (*A Little Exercise for Young Theologians*, p. 36).

The right understanding of the statements we make about God comes not from submitting those statements to rational analysis but rather from an understanding of the forms of faith's speech. Foremost among these forms is doxology. Doxological statements are not strictly statements about God, but rather utterances to God out of which statements about God (the attributes) arise. Hence it is the task of theology to serve the needs of the worshipping community by keeping faith, when it takes the form of confession and witness, within the bounds of revelation. To do this, the doctrine of God cannot be approached in the reductionist way of semi-nominalism. Rather, theology must use the rich manifold of statements by which God testifies to herself in biblical revelation as true in themselves because they are true of God in herself. The doctrine that God is one can be properly maintained, in other words, only by a realistic and not a nominalistic understanding of the attributes. The manifold of human pronouncements about God all testify not to an *ipsum esse* (Supreme Being) but to the one Name of the one true God, the trinitarian name into which we are baptized.

It is arguments such as the above that have led this writer to locate the discussion of the Trinity before rather than after the discussion of the attributes. While order in the arrangement of the materials in dogmatics is oftentimes indifferent, serving only the interests of clarity, in this instance, it would seem, more is involved. To discuss the nature and attributes of God before the doctrine of the Trinity, as has been traditionally done, leaves one open to a natural theology whose subject is just God in the general sense rather than the God who is the proper subject of all Christian theology—namely, the God who is revealed in Christ the Son through the Holy Spirit.

D. THE ULTIMATE UNITY OF THE DIVINE NATURE AND ATTRIBUTES

We have noted how the tendency to understand God's being in terms of undifferentiated unity has acted as a wedge between the nature of God and those perfections predicated of her in Scripture. God becomes essentially a God beyond all description; hence the attributes predicated of her have only a secondary, pragmatic significance. The only antidote to this dualism of a God-in-herself in contrast to the God-of-whom-we-speak is to acknowledge that God is in herself the God she has revealed herself to be in Christ. Only as we listen to how she has spoken about herself can we speak about God as she is in herself. God is indeed a unity, but a unity-in-multiplicity. The multiple perfections of God are not grounded in the nature of the creature's experience of the divine, but in God herself. God's act of revelation, then, is the basis of the assurance that our affirmations about her are objectively true and that theology is not just a game about the "Great Unknown."[9]

This is not to say that the distinction between nature and attributes has no place in elaborating a doctrine of God. There is a certain naturalness in differentiating the "who" from the "how" of God. But it is more a convenient, propaedeutic device than a matter of theological substance. Because of the convenience of such a distinction we have retained it in our outline and doubt not that it will continue to be used as long as efforts are made to set forth a doctrine of God in a systematic way. Yet when one probes beneath the surface, one soon becomes aware that the materials are just too complex to fit neatly into the classification of "nature" and "at-

9. Faith and worship know nothing of such an unknown God. Rather, the plurality of attributes predicated of God by the theologians describes the *living* God in the richness of her own inner life and being. The attributes, one might say, are the letters that spell the one word "God." When we speak of the nature of God, we say God *is* so and so; when we speak of the attributes, we say that God is *so and so* (Weber). See also Barth, *K.D.*, II/1, pp. 362ff. (cf. *C.D.*, II/1, sec. 29). Barth notes that the unity-in-distinction whereby we speak of God in terms of nature and attributes parallels that ultimate unity-in-distinction whereby we speak of her as a Trinity, a God in three persons. The medieval Nominalists, it will be recalled, were accused of being Unitarians and for this reason Nominalism was finally condemned.

tributes." The lines of distinction become blurred. As we turn, then, to the question of the divine attributes specifically, it will become evident that we are simply continuing what we have already begun. In discussing God's nature in the previous section we have said a great deal about what she is like. We have spoken of her holiness and love, her uniqueness, honor, majesty, glory, greatness, might, justice, righteousness, wrath, zeal, grace, and beauty. What more, one might ask, is left to be said? Well, as a matter of fact, a great deal more. Because she who is the Subject of our study is so great, so wonderful, so beyond all thought yet ever in our thoughts, one should not wonder at the length—though one might wonder at the content—of many treatises on theology.

We have yet to talk about God's "endless wisdom," her "boundless power," and many other perfections that help us to grasp something of her "awful majesty." And in so doing we shall draw out the implications of what we have already said. Having made four affirmations about God in Unit Three, so fundamental that apart from them we could not know who she is, we shall now turn to other affirmations that flow out of these basic four. Thus we shall complement and complete our treatment of the Christian doctrine of God—who is the thrice Holy One, an eternal fellowship of love.

FIRST ADDENDUM:
ON THE CLASSIFICATION OF THE ATTRIBUTES

The fact that it is quite impossible to draw a hard-and-fast line between "nature" and "attributes" when talking of God can be illustrated by comparing the table of contents of any standard treatises on dogmatics. What is "nature" for one theologian is "attribute" for another. Furthermore, the very multiplicity that marks the effort to classify the attributes is indicative of the fact that no particular scheme is sufficiently superior to have gained general acceptance. One reads of "negative" and "positive," "internal" and "external," "absolute" and "relative," "immanent" and "transcendent," "ethical" and "metaphysical," and, especially in the Reformed tradition, of "communicable" and "incommunicable" attributes. About all one can say is that a twofold structure of some sort has been generally accepted and this structure, in a very loose way, is related to the twofold character of God's nature as the Holy One who is Love.

For ourselves, we have simply paired the attributes, and the sequence of pairs we have chosen begins with God's will and power and ends with her omnipresence and eternity. This sequence is in keeping with our emphasis on the personal character of God. In a general way, then, through the sequence we have chosen, we have sought to emphasize the more personal (in traditional language, "ethical") attributes over the less personal ("metaphysical") attributes. This we have done in conscious awareness of, and opposition to, the order in which the attributes are often arranged that give the primary place to the metaphysical over the ethical. Such an order, in our judgment, is susceptible to an impersonal understanding of God. It does not do justice to the fact that the divine attributes are based on historical revelation rather than deduced from a metaphysical postulate.

In conclusion, we should note that as the line between "nature" and "attributes" is anything but sharp—since, whether we speak of the one or the other, we are always talking about God—so it is with the several attributes in particular. Not that the attributes should be fused into one, as though God's righteousness and mercy were ultimately the same. But neither are they to be separated, as though God were partly righteous, partly merciful, and partly something else. As Dorner observed in the last century, there is a sort of *perichoresis* of the attributes as well as of the persons in the Godhead. One will see this likeness-in-distinction illustrated especially in our treatment of God's justice and mercy.

* * * * *

Our preference for the historical and personal over the metaphysical in treating of the divine attributes invites a comment on the way in which Scripture oftentimes speaks of God. As readers of the Bible know, God is frequently described, especially in the Old Testament, by the use of all kinds of personal images, pictures, figures, and metaphors drawn from the historical life of Israel. "Yahweh's relationship to his people," says Eric Heaton in his book *His Servants the Prophets,* "is represented under the figures of a father, mother, nurse, brother, husband, friend, warrior, shepherd, farmer, metalworker, builder, potter, fuller, physician, judge, tradesman, king, fisherman and scribe—to mention, almost at random, only a few of the activities of the community."[10]

While these figures and images of God have not been given a prominent place in dogmatics, they have been freely used, not only in Scripture but

---

10. Eric Heaton, *His Servants the Prophets* (London: SCM, 1949), p. 71, as quoted in Ian Ramsey's *Words About God,* pp. 202-03. Ramsey cites various texts illustrative of these usages and adds a few of his own, such as "dairy maid" (Job 10:10), "laundress" (Is. 4:4; Mal. 3:3), and others.

also in the worship of the church. Both in preaching the word and in responding to it, the worshipping community has made them a familiar part of its vocabulary. All Christians join in singing "Come, Thou Almighty King" (Anon.); "Saviour, Like a Shepherd Lead Us" (Anon.); "Rock of Ages, Cleft for Me" (Toplady); "O Lamb of God, I Come" (Elliot); "Come, Holy Spirit, Heavenly Dove" (Watts); "No earthly father loves like thee, no mother half so mild" (Faber); "Star of the East, arise" (Laurentii); "Lead, Kindly Light, Amid the Encircling Gloom" (Newman); etc. There is no essential difference between the way in which the church uses these terms of God and the way in which dogmaticians use the traditional predicates or attributes of Deity. To say that God is "omniscient" is to say that she is a kindly "Light" who leads us in this dark world of sin; to say that she is "faithful" is to say that she is the good "Shepherd," the loving "Father," the caring "Mother."

The obvious usefulness of such terms, it would seem, is to give concrete expression to our thought about God, our understanding of "who" and "how" she is. Of course there must be some analogy between these terms which we use and the truth they disclose or they would not disclose the truth. It is true, however, that some of these images and figures will have more, and some less, viability, depending on when and where they are used and who is using them. The "star" figure (Rv. 22:16), for example, will mean more to a seaman than to a city dweller for whom the garish lights have forever dimmed the night sky. People like Horatius Bonar, who grew up in Scotland, where he could see shepherds and sheep any day, would experience more "transcendent disclosure" through the shepherd image than would an Eskimo. Hence he confesses,

> I was a wandering sheep,
> I would not be controlled,
> But now I love my Shepherd's voice,
> I love, I love the fold.

SECOND ADDENDUM: CONCERNING THE DIVINE SIMPLICITY

The doctrine of God's simplicity has often led to tangled arguments about God as "uncomposed" and "indivisible," arguments that threaten the doctrine of the divine attributes with which we are now concerned. When this happens, the affirmations we will make that God is "holy," "just," "merciful," "forebearing," and the like, ultimately mean the same thing, whatever the common denominator (will, power, causality) may be to which they are reduced. Given this view of the divine simplicity, the number one is absolutized (glorified?) in such a way that the theologian can no longer speak of God as God speaks of herself in the Bible. The statement "God is simple" is turned into the statement "the Simple is God." (An instance of such is Schleiermacher's view that God is the *ens summum prima causa.* Hodge justly complains that such an effort to reduce all the attributes to the single concept of causality reflects a view of the divine simplicity that leads to Pantheism.)[11] Correctly understood, the doctrine of the divine simplicity denies neither the personal distinctions in the Godhead nor the wealth of personal perfections (attributes) that we are about to predicate of the Godhead. God's simplicity refers rather to the thought that she is not compounded as are her creatures. Living things, including human persons, who are embodied spirits, are contained in spaces and divisible into parts. But God is indivisible—that is, simple, without bodily parts. As pure Spirit she is whole and entire in herself and in her presence to all things outside herself.

---

11. Charles Hodge, *Systematic Theology* (New York: Scribner, 1871), vol. I, pp. 391-95.

II. God's Will and Power

A. INTRODUCTION

Even the casual student of science is aware of the boundless and beautiful display of power nature affords; we literally live in an ocean of energy. This all-encompassing power, this "horrendous strength" of the physical universe, is often manifest in terrifying ways. Vesuvius erupts and a city that was centuries in the making lies in ruins. Mount St. Helens explodes, heaving 400 million tons of debris into the atmosphere and leveling primeval forests seventeen miles away. By such events we are reminded of the seething cauldron of energy over which we live. Not all of nature's displays of power are so devastatingly destructive, but they are no less awesome. Our sun pours out six trillion quadrillion (6 followed by 27 zeros) calories of heat per minute and each year this heat lifts a hundred thousand cubic miles of water from our lakes, rivers, and oceans to lubricate the mighty weather machine on which all life depends. It appears, indeed, that our entire universe was born in a titanic explosion in the remote past. Though Albert Einstein was unable to reduce all of these natural forces to a unified set of equations, his celebrated pronouncement that $E=mc^2$ makes the astonishing claim that all matter is energy; energy, to be sure, under invincible lock and key, but so immeasurably vast that could it be released—an event he deemed beyond human possibility—there would be enough in an ordinary railroad ticket to drive a high speed passenger train around the earth several times.[1]

Power—in this sense of the physical forces of nature, the sheer energy

1. See the Life Science Library volume *Energy,* by Mitchell Wilson and the editors of *Life* (New York: Time Incorporated, 1963), especially chap. 7.

that sustains us and our technological civilization—is, of course, not what the theologians have in mind when they speak of the power of God, at least not in a primary way. God's power is not impersonal force but just the divine freedom to do whatever she wills to do—the ability to bring to pass the divine good pleasure and to actualize the divine purpose in the Creator's own time and way. Yet the awesome power displayed in creation constitutes a parable at the physical level of the personal power belonging to the Creator.[2] In the Old Testament we have many illustrations of this truth, especially in the events (earthquakes, fire, and smoke) surrounding the Exodus and the meeting with God at Sinai (Ex. 19:16ff.). And inasmuch as God's people confess that the Creator who made heaven and earth is also their Redeemer, mighty to save, they have freely and joyously acknowledged God's power in their worship of the Deity.

The first article of the Creed begins appropriately with the words, "I believe in God the Mother Almighty." Little wonder, then, that theologians of all traditions have had much to say about God's power. "Power and might," observes Calvin, "are contained under the title *Elohim*."[3] But before we turn to what the theologians have said about the divine power, a brief review of the Scriptural data on the subject is in order.

B. THE BIBLICAL DATA

In reviewing the biblical data, it is important to note at the outset that in the Old Testament the divine power is not, as is often the case in classical Greek and Hellenistic thought, synonymous with the ultimate principle of the cosmos. Whether that principle be Number (Pythagoreanism) or the Efficient Cause of all appearances (Stoicism), the Old Testament is not concerned with such neutral forces of nature. God's power, according to the Old Testament, is not the immanent lawfulness of natural forces but the expression of her will as personal being.

---

2. Speaking of his boyhood in Connecticut, Jonathan Edwards comments: "I felt God, so to speak, at the first appearance of a thunderstorm; and used to take the opportunity, at such times, to fix myself in order to view the clouds and see the lightnings play, and hear the majestic and awful voice of God's thunder . . . leading me to sweet contemplations of my great and glorious God." *Personal Narrative,* as quoted in H. A. Redmond, *The Omnipotence of God* (Philadelphia: Westminster, 1964), p. 167.

3. *Institutes,* I, 10, 2. Responding to the high priest, Jesus says, "You will see the Son of man seated at the right hand of the Power" (τῆς δυνάμεως) — commonly translated, "the right hand of *God*" (Mt. 26:64).

The difference between Greek and Hebrew thought, then, is due to the Hebrew conception of God. Because God is a personal God, her power serves her will; by the exercise of her power she effects her will. She is not a nature god but the God of nature who rules the natural order, giving the wind its weight (Job 28:25) and the sea bounds that it cannot pass (Prv. 8:29). This means that the natural order is the theater of history, a history in which the Almighty works her sovereign purpose and so fulfills the eternal counsel of her will. Though she "speaks through earthquake, wind and fire," yet her "still, small voice of calm" (Whittier) is not contained in them (1 Kgs. 19:12). When the divine is defined in terms of the forces of nature, one ends up with a plethora of powerful spirits (polytheism); but when one thinks of the divine as personal Spirit, then God cannot be identified with any natural object or force but only worshipped as the Power who stands behind all nature and whose overruling will is manifested in it. As we have already observed, such transcendent Power is the meaning of the generic word for God (אֵל) in Hebrew. When El is combined with the epithet Shaddai (אֵל שַׁדַּי), it is commonly translated as "God Almighty," that is, the God who holds sway over all things, the ruler of all.

Even when God's power is displayed in judgment, even in the judgment of her own people, it is never a matter of the unpredictable forces of chaos, but rather the operation of personal will. And this will is the will of her who has entered into a covenant relationship with Israel, a relationship in which she keeps faith and in which she reveals herself as steadfast and true, ready to aid her people in every need.

Israel's trust in the sovereign God of history who keeps covenant with her people was grounded preeminently in the event of the Exodus. Had there been no deliverance at the Red Sea, no relief in the awful wilderness, no entrance into Canaan, there would have been no covenant, no worship of Yahweh—no Israel. Hence, the very existence of the people of Israel is a testimony to God's power, power to help and deliver those with whom she makes covenant, even though they are oppressed by an earthly power (Pharaoh) that is implacable. They are the people, small in number, who rely wholly on the power of One whose will shapes their history and determines their destiny. In the words of the Deuteronomist, "What god is there in heaven or on earth who can do such works and mighty acts as thine?" (Dt. 3:24). Thus the Lord God is Israel's sovereign ruler, enthroned above the ark of the covenant; and in her rule the people of Israel exult whenever they keep festival (Ex. 15:18; Dt. 33:5).

These mighty acts of God, so definite and concrete, constituting the tangible evidence of her power, are enshrined in the title Lord of Hosts (יְהֹוָה צְבָאוֹת). To speak of God as the Lord of Hosts (Sabaoth) is to speak of her in the figure of a monarch, surrounded by armies that are under her command to do her will. In many hymns of the psalter we have a view of God as a God of power and doer of wonders, a view that remains alive throughout Israel's history, reaching its highest level of intensity in the vivid and picturesque language of the prophets. ("For thus the LORD said to me, 'As a lion or a young lion growls over her prey, and when a band of shepherds is called forth against her she is not terrified by their shouting or daunted at their noise, so the LORD of Hosts will come down to fight upon Mount Zion and upon its hill,'" Is. 31:4).

The mighty power by which God delivered their forbears from Egypt and brought them into the land of promise eventually became the paradigm whereby the Israelites understood the regularities of nature as well. They perceived the power displayed in the Exodus and the conquest as manifested also in the courses of the stars and the returning of the seasons— seedtime and harvest. Thus God was revealed to Israel as Lord of the whole natural order, as the Creator as well as Redeemer. She was seen to be the God who not only kept covenant by delivering their forbears from bondage in Egypt, but the God who also created and preserves the whole world by her almighty word according to her sovereign will. And so not only history, but the world in which the drama of history unfolds displays God's power, a power that works infallibly to accomplish the will of her who is the God of the covenant community and, in a larger sense, of all the nations and peoples of earth.[4]

In the New Testament, the several strands of Old Testament revelation are taken up into the Jesus event and so qualified in a distinctive way. This is eminently true of the revelation of God's power. In the Jesus event God's creative power inaugurates a new age, an age that is eschatological in nature because it fulfills Old Testament history. This age is heralded by John the Baptist, who comes in the spirit and power of Elijah (Lk. 1:17). Jesus, of whom John bears witness, is anointed at his baptism with the Spirit of God (Mt. 3:16 par.) and so enters upon his ministry as "a prophet mighty in deed and word before God and all the people" (Lk. 24:19). The power displayed in his mighty words and miraculous deeds culminates in his resurrection. He is "designated Son of God in power . . . by his resurrection from the dead" (Rom. 1:4).

The power of his resurrection is not limited to that event as such. The risen Christ promises his disciples that they too shall receive power when

---

4. Even in the exile, as well as in the restoration of the remnant, God's power is displayed. Assyria is the rod of her anger (Is. 10:5), Nebuchadnezzar her servant (Jer. 25:9), and Cyrus her shepherd who fulfills her purpose (Is. 44:28).

the Holy Spirit has come upon them (Acts 1:8). Hence in Acts and the epistles we read again and again of the Spirit's dynamic presence and power displayed in the calling and sanctifying of the people of God. Thus the almighty Creator of heaven and earth fulfills her purposes in the new creation in Christ. Indeed, in the last analysis, Jesus' power as the power of the Christ is just the power of God. He it is who upholds all things by the word of his power (Heb. 1:3), and by this power subjects all things to himself (Phil. 3:21). Though at present it is only to those who are called that Christ is the power of God (1 Cor. 1:24), there will be a day when all the tribes of earth shall see him as he comes "with power and great glory" (Mt. 24:30 par.).

As an impersonal view of divine power leads to magic, ritual, and superstition, so a personal view leads to obedience, prayer, and doxology. One can sense throughout the New Testament the note of passionate joy with which the devout experience the power of God. In the *Magnificat*, for example, the virgin rejoices in God, for she "who is mighty has done great things for me" (Lk. 1:49). The early Christians, upon the first threat of persecution, lifted their voices in unison to God, whom they addressed as "sovereign Lord (Δέσποτα), who made the heaven and the earth, the sea and everything in them." Being confident that with signs and wonders she would enable them to proclaim the name of Jesus, they asked that she would grant them all boldness in their witness (Acts 4:24-31). Paul, among the boldest of those witnesses, prays that his converts may know "what is the immeasurable greatness of her power in us who believe" (Eph. 1:19). When they contemplated the final revelation of God's power at the end of history, these believers ascribed "to her who sits on the throne and to the Lamb . . . blessing and honor and glory and might for ever and ever!" (Rv. 5:13). And so the reign of God is consummated with a "hallelujah," for she who reigns is none other than "the Lord our God the Almighty" (ὁ θεὸς ἡμῶν ὁ παντοκράτωρ, Rv. 19:6).

The Scriptures cited above make it plain that unlike our self-determination, the will of the Creator knows no creaturely limitations; hers is the sovereign assurance of effectual action. She is the God who declares "the end from the beginning . . . saying, 'My counsel shall stand, and I will accomplish all my purpose'" (Is. 46:10). Many problems have beset the ongoing theological discussion of this affirmation of God's sovereign power, and we shall now touch briefly upon them as we ponder the staggering thought that the dominion of the Most High is an everlasting dominion and that ". . . she does what she wills with the host of heaven and the inhabitants of the earth; and there's no one who can stay her hand or say to her, 'What are you doing?'" (Dn. 4:35 NRSV).

C. SOME BASIC AFFIRMATIONS[5]

1. GOD DETERMINES THE MEANING OF HER POWER

First of all, we must remember that when we speak of God's power, we are not speaking of power in and of itself. Too often, in the elaboration of the divine attribute of power, theologians have dealt with the question abstractly, ruminating on the concept of absolute power as such. Such ruminations imply that God and power are interchangeable. But we are not making any such statement. We are not saying that God *is* power but that God *has* power.[6] Another way to make the point is to insist that in the sentence "God is omnipotent," we should never allow the predicate to define the subject. To define God in terms of the abstract concept of power is, as Barth warns, worse than defining her in terms of some abstract notion of simplicity, immutability, or infinity, because it threatens to turn God into a capricious despot.[7] From the time of Marcion to the present, such a distortion has aided and abetted those who reject the concept of God Almighty as a myth symbolizing a cruel tyranny over the hapless race of mortals.

The only way to avoid this problem is to remember that as basic as the affirmation is that God is all-powerful, more basic still is this affirmation: she is by nature the God who is holy love. Since she cannot deny herself (2 Tm. 2:13), we therefore should not deny her by drawing inferences from an abstract concept of power that are unworthy of the God who has revealed herself to us in Scripture as our loving Mother, Savior, and Sanctifier.

Furthermore, when we say that God cannot deny herself, that her being who she is determines the use of her power, we should not be concerned that some have objected that such a statement involves a contradiction. To say that God cannot become other than God is not to deny her omnipotence and thus to deny that God is God. Not what she can do but what she wills to do is the way to approach the doctrine of omnipotence. Not power as such, but God's power is the proper subject of theological discourse. Were God able to deny herself, that is, able to be untrue to herself, then she would be like the fallen sinful creature, only infinitely more so. Were God

---

5. For a more philosophic treatment of our subject, see "God, Freedom, and Evil" by Alvin Plantinga, in *The Power of God, Readings on Omnipotence and Evil*, eds. L. Urban and D. Walton (New York: Oxford, 1978), no. 32, pp. 223ff.

6. The affirmation in Scripture that nothing is impossible with God (Mt. 19:26; Lk. 1:37) does not mean that God can do everything conceivable. It is rather an affirmation of her transcendence. Not limited, as we are in our finitude, she can do the humanly impossible.

7. See *K.D.*, II/1, p. 589 (cf. *C.D.*, II/1, sec. 31.2).

able to sin as we are, it would be an evidence not of her omnipotence, but of her impotence. Surely it is no contradiction to omnipotence that it cannot become impotence, and no affront to God Almighty that she cannot become the devil.

By the same token, there is no contradiction in saying that God cannot make a triangle with four sides or a stick with one end. Were we to say that she can, we would be defining God's omnipotence not in terms of herself but in terms of something else, namely, an impersonal concept of absolute power. Given such a concept, God's omnipotence would mean her ability to do everything that can be imagined. So to understand God as she-who-can-do-everything-imaginable is to misconstrue the sentence "God is omnipotent." It is to read the sentence so as to define God by the predicate "omnipotence" (as though power were God), whereas one should define the predicate "omnipotence" by the subject "God," and say "God is powerful."

We say this knowing that St. Thomas, and many theologians influenced by him, would have reservations about such a conclusion. To them it would appear to rest on circular reasoning.

> If, however, we were to say that God is omnipotent because she can do all things that are possible to her power, that would be a vicious circle in explaining the nature of her power. For this would be saying nothing else but that God is omnipotent because she can do all that she can do.[8]

But should we—can we—say anything else? To say that we can define what God can do only in terms of herself is just to admit that we must let her define herself to us in her self-revelation. Not the principle of absolute possibility, but that possibility which has been divinely revealed, is the measure of the divine omnipotence. To say that God is omnipotent simply means that she defines her own possibilities and that there are no possibilities apart from her. Of course, faith believes that $2 + 2 = 4$ because God wills that it shall be, not because of some ultimate, autonomous structure of reality that, like an eternal platonic blueprint, is imposed on the Creator. But faith does not ask the question (though many theologians have): Could God have made $2 + 2$ equal to other than 4? And why does faith not ask this question? Because faith is not concerned with imagined possibilities, but trusts God in what she has done, trusts her in those possibilities she has actualized.[9]

8. *Summa,* I, Q. 25, Art. 3.
9. On this question see Descartes, *Objections Against the Meditations and Replies,*

As for the argument of the medieval scholastics over whether God could make the past not to have been (Peter Damian *pro,* Anselm *con*), the only reasonable answer is a negative one.[10] But such an answer is not, as Thomas reasoned, because God cannot do what is in and of itself inherently contradictory.[11] It is rather because God freely chose that the past should be unchanging by creating the temporal order. In other words, we are speaking of a limitation she has imposed on herself, not a limitation imposed upon her, when we speak of God's relationship to the created order of time. God is always free to determine her own possibilities, and this is what she did when she created a world that endures in time and therefore has a past that is fixed and unchangeable.

2. GOD'S POWER IS NOT NATURAL CAUSALITY

We should never think of God's power as simply the sum total of natural causes. It is true that Scripture, especially the Old Testament, speaks of God's "causing" something to happen, as when she "caused a deep sleep to fall upon the man" in order that she might make the woman (Gn. 2:21). But such scriptural usage denotes the personal agency of the sovereign God who is free to work when and as she will. By contrast, many theologians, having defined God's power in terms of omni-causality (following Schleiermacher), end up speaking not of the God of Scripture who is personal Subject, but of a realm of ordered Being. This ordered Being, in which the impersonal laws of cause and effect reign supreme, is, when viewed as a totality, what they mean by the divine omnipotence.

> The divine omnipotence can never in any way enter as a supplement (so to speak) to the natural causes in their sphere; for then it must, like them, work temporally and spatially; and at one time working so, and then again not so, it would not be self-identical and so would be neither eternal nor omnipresent. Rather, everything is and becomes altogether by means of the natural order, so that each takes place through all and all wholly through the divine omnipotence, so that all indivisibly exists through One.[12]

"Reply to the Sixth Set of Objections" (Chicago: Great Books, Britannica, 1952), vol. 31, pp. 228-29.

10. "But past who can recall, or done undo? / Not God omnipotent, nor Fate. . . ." Milton, *Paradise Lost,* IX, 926-27.

11. *Summa,* I, Q. 25, Art 4.

12. Schleiermacher, *The Christian Faith* (Edinburgh: T. & T. Clark, 1928), "Third Doctrine: God is Omnipotent," sec. 54, p. 212.

Such a view obviously excludes the miraculous; but what is not so obvious is that it does so by imprisoning God in her own universe. If there is no distinction between what God may do and what she does do through the "means of the natural order," then there is no distinction between the power of God and the impersonal power at work in the world. In the last analysis, such a view leads to the apotheosis of the "laws" of nature.

The biblical view, by contrast, is that God's power is over all her works. If God made heaven and earth by the word of her power (Ps. 33:6; Jn. 1:3), and if that word shall never lose its power though heaven and earth pass away (Mt. 24:35), then heaven and earth (the world seen through telescope and microscope) do not constitute the parameters of that power. While God's power is manifest in all that happens in the ordered realm of nature, it is not limited to that realm. As God is the Lord over her works, transcendent and free, so her power is a power that may work not only in and through, but also apart from, ordinary means.[13]

While the understanding of God's power in terms of causality has led some theologians to reduce her power to the cause/effect nexus of nature, it has led others to reduce human power (decision/choice) to the realm of the inconsequential, having only instrumental significance. Zwingli, for example, in his *De Providentia,* viewed God's power as the ultimate cause of all that happens in such a way that

> one and the same deed, therefore, adultery, namely, or murder, as far as it concerns God as author, mover and instigator, is an act, not a crime; as far as it concerns man, is a crime and wickedness. . . . David's adultery, so far as concerns God as the author of it, is no more a sin to God than where a steer covers and impregnates a whole herd. And even when she slays a man whom she kills by the hand of a robber or of an unjust judge, she sins no more than when she kills a wolf by a wolf or an elephant by means of a dragon. . . . And though she impels men to some deed which is a wickedness unto the instrument that performs it, yet it is not such unto herself. *For her movements are free.*[14]

To the same effect Luther, in his *De Servo Arbitrio,* speaks of the human will as a donkey that must go as the rider directs, whether the rider be God or the devil.

---

13. Such is the implication of the statement in Scripture that nothing is impossible with God. Though she did not, she could have raised up children to Abraham of the stones (Mt. 3:9; Lk. 3:8) and sent legions of angels to deliver her Son from death (Mt. 26:53).

14. "On the Providence of God," *Works of Zwingli,* ed. Henke (Philadelphia: Heidelberg Press, 1922), vol. II, chap. V, p. 182. Italics added.

We shall have more to say of these matters when we come to the doctrines of humankind and providence. At this time we wish simply to note that understanding God's power as causality is a faulty view that leads both to a faulty statement of how God's will is related to the created order and of how the will of the creature is related to that of the Creator. It is our concern so to understand God's power that she is free to do the mighty works (miracles) that belong to her as Creator and Redeemer, while at the same time we are free to do those works that belong to us as responsible creatures in her image. We must so understand the power of God that neither is she captive to those laws which are immanent in the world she has made nor does she, if we may so speak, hold us captive in the world in which she has placed us by her sovereign rule over us.[15]

3. GOD'S POWER IS HER PERSONAL WILL, WHICH IS SUPREME OVER ALL

When speaking of God's power, we must say not only that it is by her power that all things are (doctrine of creation) but also that they remain by her power what they are and become what they become (doctrine of providence). And if this power by which all things are created and sustained is the power of a personal God, then all things are created and sustained by her will, which is her free decision and choice. This is not to say that she approves all that is, yet it is to say that all things are according to her will in the sense that she calls into being, preserves, and rules her creatures and all their actions. "Thy hand in all things I behold, / And all things in thy hand" (Longfellow). Of course, she does not rule over the stars in their courses in the way that she rules over those who are free and responsible agents in her image. Yet, of her and through her and to her are all things (Rom. 11:36), whether they be things astronomical or personal, things pertaining to natural law, or human decision and choice.

---

15. The understanding of God's all-powerful will as the cause of all causes (*causa causarum*, as in Augustine, *De Trinitate,* III, 2; Thomas, *Summa,* I, Q. 19, Art. 4) has always run the risk of making God's will not only the *primal* cause but the *sole* cause of all things. Thus her power is conceived not simply as manifest in all that happens, but identical with all that happens. This position leads inevitably to one or the other extreme mentioned above. Either God and the creature become two sides of one and the same Reality or, as divine Agent, God is the *sole* agent and human agency is a chimera. In the former instance the way to pantheism is short. The almighty God becomes Almightiness, that is, the All-Conditioning-Power known to us as the lawfulness of nature. In the latter instance, the human agent becomes a puppet whose response to the divine string is not a response but simply an effect of a cause and therefore without moral quality.

Even the sinful acts of the wicked do not ultimately thwart her will. For she is the Lord who

> brings the counsel of the nations to nought;
> she frustrates the plans of the peoples.

By contrast

> the counsel of the LORD stands forever,
> the thoughts of her heart to all generations. (Ps. 33:10-11)

To her is the glory now and evermore—in all the realms of her creation.

To acknowledge God as the Lord God almighty is to acknowledge that there can be no will outside her own that in any way baffles, circumvents, or confounds her will. Though God may not will all things in the same way or in the same sense, yet all is by her will, and apart from her will it would not be what it is or even be at all. If we ask after the mystery of being; if we ask why there is anything and why it is what it is and as it is, the answer must finally be this: because God wills it. This is the way God is free to be God both in herself and for us. Hence we should never think of God and the world that she has made as related by some sort of mutual necessity. Heaven and earth are limited by God's will; there is no autonomy of the creature vis-à-vis God, only the would-be autonomy of the sinful creature. But heaven and earth can impose no limits on God. Hence

> through the right understanding of God's will, every form of dualistic thought is made impossible. Such a position is espoused when one exchanges the limitations of being which are due to the will of God for a limitation of God and her will as though in that limitation there stood over against her another divine will, the will of an evil God, a God against God, a sort of adversary, as it were, of God.[16]

Even that which is contrary to the will of God—that is, contrary to her precept and command—is not wholly apart from the will of her eternal purpose.

---

16. Barth, *K.D.*, II/I, pp. 633-34 (cf. *C.D.*, II/1, sec. 31.2).

4. GOD'S POWER REVEALED IN THE WEAKNESS OF THE CROSS

Finally, if it is true that the power of God is at the service of her will and if her will is and can be expressed only in terms of her essential nature as personal—if, that is, the Subject (God) defines the predicate (omnipotence)—then the power of God is not only manifest in the almighty word of the Creator who called the world into being, but also in the condescending act of the Son "who . . . did not count equality with God a thing to be grasped, but emptied himself, taking the form of a servant . . . and became obedient unto death, even death on a cross" (Phil. 2:5-8).

This seeming contradiction, that God's power is revealed in weakness, is not simply a Christian conceit dreamed up to harmonize the claim that God is almighty with the fact that her only Son succumbed to death on a Roman cross. Rather, it is deeply imbedded in biblical revelation, as careful reflection on the content of that revelation shows. Israel's knowledge of God's power, to be sure, began with their experience of the Exodus, when God came to liberate them from the hand of the invincible oppressor (Ex. 3:1-12). But this concrete demonstration of power, which overwhelmed Pharaoh and his hosts, was not a display of power for power's sake; it was rather a remembering of the covenant. Seeing the affliction of her people and moved with compassion for them, she came to deliver them according to her promise. And this promise is finally fulfilled in the coming of Jesus Christ, who liberates his people from the ultimate bondage, that is, a bondage to sin and death.

In this event of Incarnation, the almighty God with whom all things are possible does the impossible; the Maker of heaven and earth steps across the boundary between the Creator and the creature in order to become one with us. Here in the Jesus event the eternal Logos who is with God and who is God becomes flesh. And why does the Logos become flesh; why does the Logos stoop to partake of our nature—*Cur Deus Homo?* The answer is given in the Epistle to the Hebrews: "that through death he might destroy him who has the power of death, that is, the devil, and deliver all those who through fear of death were subject to a lifelong bondage." But how does he accomplish this mighty act; how does he deliver us from the fear of death and a lifelong bondage? Through death, his own death, we are told (Heb. 2:14-15). He bruised the serpent's head by being bruised himself (Gn. 3:15).

When, therefore, we speak of the power of God—when we speak of her invincible will, her inviolable counsel, her unchanging decree, her eternal purpose—if we would speak biblically, we must speak of the God who is revealed in Christ crucified! In him the divine omnipotence has its concrete center. "In the weakness of the historical Christ we recognize God's omnipotence as so absolutely superior to all other power that God is almighty, even in that which is the worldly antithesis to power."[17] Of course, this perception of Christ's death as a display of divine power-in-weakness came to the disciples this side of the resurrection. But they did not artificially separate these events as though the cross were a display of weakness and the resurrection a display of power. They confessed Jesus to be in his own person what he was shown to be in his resurrection, namely, the "Son of God in power according to the Spirit of holiness" (Rom. 1:4). In Jesus Christ they perceived God's power as personally present. Therefore it was not possible that he, like us, should be held by death.

To autonomous reason, the thought that the crucified Jesus should rise is an impossibility. (Hence the scoffing at Paul's preaching in Athens, Acts 17:32.) But to the disciples the real impossibility was that he should not rise, for he was the Lord, the Author of life itself (Acts 2:24; 3:15). How could the Author of life finally succumb to death? His was "the power of an indestructible (ἀκαταλύτου) life" (Heb. 7:16); how, then, could that life be vanquished in death? Since it is given to him, as the Son, to have life in himself (Jn. 5:26), how could that life be lost? The answer the New Testament gives to these questions is unequivocal. It is impossible that death should have triumphed over him. Indeed, his death is his own act and, paradoxical as it may seem, it is an act of power. "No one takes it [my life] from me, but I lay it down of my own accord. I have power to lay it down, and I have power to take it again" (Jn. 10:18).

Convinced as they were that Jesus was the One whom the prophet had named the "Mighty God" (Is. 9:6), the apostles saw his death as a further manifestation of that same power with which he had exorcised the unclean spirits during his earthly ministry (Col. 2:15). Of his mighty works, his death was the mightiest. In his death the principalities and powers of darkness were disarmed; they were made a public example and triumphed over by him who is "the head of all rule and authority" (Col. 2:10). Hence all that can be said of God's omnipotence is summed up in remembering that God is the God who, in the fullness of time, delivered us by the death of her Son from our adversary, Satan. The gospel of which the apostle Paul was not ashamed (Rom. 1:16) is the power (δύναμις) of God for salvation because it is the good news of the crucified One who is himself the power of God (1 Cor. 1:23-24).

That God's power should be revealed in the death of her Son is not,

17. Schlink, "Gott, VI, Dogmatisch," *RGG,* II, col. 1738.

we grant, a self-evident truth. In fact, it is a stumbling block to the Jews and folly to the Gentiles just because it is anything but self-evident. But to those who are called it is the foolishness of God that is wiser than human wisdom; it is the weakness of God that is stronger than human strength (1 Cor. 1:24-25). This strength, this power of God manifest in weakness, is revealed, Paul says, to those who are called. Here too, in the word of the call, God's power is manifest. Reason would say that he who is given over to his enemies to be mocked, reviled, and crucified can never be the revelation of God's power. But one who experiences God's call cannot doubt that it is so: to him nothing less than the wisdom and power of God are revealed in Christ crucified.

Here, then, is power, greater than all earthly power, a power that reconciles us to God, a power that makes peace by the blood of his cross (Col. 1:20). Can there be any greater power than this, the power that is the freedom of God that sets us free? Constrained but not coerced by the amazing love displayed at the cross, our pride is humbled, our fear overcome, and we taste not only the goodness of the word of God, but also of the powers of the world to come (Heb. 6:5). Thus God is revealed in Jesus Christ, the crucified, not only as the loving God, but also as the Almighty God.[18]

---

18. By the same token, the apostle Paul, knowing the grace that makes the divine power perfect in human weakness, boasted of his weakness in order that the power of Christ might rest upon him (2 Cor. 12:9).

A Strange Power

A Christmas Sermon Preached by Marguerite Shuster
at Arcadia Presbyterian Church, Arcadia, California,
Lord's Day, December 22, 1985[1]

In the sixth month the angel Gabriel was sent from God to a city of Galilee named Nazareth, to a virgin betrothed to a man whose name was Joseph, of the house of David; and the virgin's name was Mary. And he came to her and said, "Hail, O favored one, the Lord is with you!" But she was greatly troubled at the saying, and considered in her mind what sort of greeting this might be. And the angel said to her, "Do not be afraid, Mary, for you have found favor with God. And behold, you will conceive in your womb and bear a son, and you shall call his name Jesus.

He will be great, and will be called the Son of the Most High; and the Lord God will give to him the throne of his father David, and he will reign over the house of Jacob for ever; and of his kingdom there will be no end."

And Mary said to the angel, "How shall this be, since I have no husband?" And the angel said to her,

"The Holy Spirit will come upon you, and the power of the Most High will overshadow you; therefore the child to be born will be called holy, the Son of God.

And behold, your kinswoman Elizabeth in her old age has also conceived a son; and this is the sixth month with her who was called barren. For with God nothing will be impossible." And Mary said, "Behold, I am the handmaid of the Lord; let it be to me according to your word." And the angel departed from her.

Luke 1:26-38 (RSV)

1. When originally preached, the masculine pronoun of God was used in this sermon.

Looking back—a long way back, now—I can tell you for sure that it did not happen the way I would have expected—or the way any sensible person would have expected, for that matter. My mother told me the story first, I think; and her mother told her; and her mother. . . ; and so on, all the way back to when *his* mother told it first. It must have been she who told it: after all, she was the only one who knew for sure what happened (and even she must have doubted sometimes). Joseph did not know—not really. All he knew was what he had to do with it—or rather, that he did not have anything to do with it. No, it must have been Mary who told the story first, even if, later, Joseph might have repeated it, trying very hard to believe that it could, just possibly, be true.

But the fact of the matter was, to be quite frank, it was not exactly plausible. Joseph as a carpenter surely was not so far removed from real life as to be confused about where babies came from. And Mary's story—well, as I said, it just was not very plausible. That part was bad enough—you know, embarrassing and all that. But the other part—the other part was even worse. Maybe Joseph was spared thinking about the other part. Maybe in his day people never said it as bluntly as they said it later. Maybe he never even dared frame the idea. How could he? How could he see that helpless baby as God? God? Become a *baby?* It is hard enough to imagine God as an adult human being, but as the most helpless and vulnerable of all humans? Preposterous. Everybody *knows* God is not like *that*. God is—well, among other things, God is *powerful* — almighty, omnipotent — you know all those five-dollar words. Yes, yes, babies can be powerful too, as anyone who has been around one knows, but not powerful the way *God* is powerful. The whole thing, from beginning to end, just does not make sense: "Almighty God decides to come into the world as a baby born to a virgin peasant girl." Even the *National Enquirer* would not promote a story like that. Nobody would buy it.

But Mary insisted that is the way it was. And that is more or less the way I heard it, and more or less the way you heard it too, I suppose; though by now we have heard it so often that it scarcely seems strange any more. We may by now believe it without noticing that it does take some believing. If you think about it, though, it is pretty queer all around. Makes you wonder. Makes you wonder, in particular, whether the power of God is somehow different than we thought, different than the power of the very, very richest, strongest, smartest (and so forth) being we can imagine. Because why would that sort of being become a baby? And become a baby under unreasonable, if not to say dubious, circumstances. And become a mere peasant baby in apparent fulfillment of old prophecies of a glorious Messiah who would finally deliver the Israelites. Not likely. Something funny is going on here.

We might as well start with the prophecies. People back then were expecting something; and what is more, they had been expecting it a long time—hundreds and hundreds of years. That should count for a long wait by almost any standards, especially when the wait was for help. When I need help, I start getting impatient in minutes, if not sooner. But I digress. They were expecting something. A messiah. Help. But the prophecies were a bit ambiguous, so expectations differed. A first-century Gallup Poll would have gone something like this:

First Man (very matter-of-factly):
Me? I'm looking for a descendant of David, to come and rule the way King David did. Those were the days! We had land, food, prestige, and a great king. Someday God will send another David who will rule over us. Then we'll have peace and justice, and the enemy will be destroyed. I only hope he comes soon.

Second Man (with a snarl):
I don't know just how we'll recognize the Messiah, but I can tell you this. He'll be a great warrior. He'll push those blasted Romans back into the sea, and we'll have our own land once again, without a bunch of foreigners ruling us, taking all our money in taxes and keeping us poor. I'll join up with his army first thing, and we'll hatch a revolution that will smash the Romans to bits.

Third Man (rather wild-eyed):
No, it won't be as easy as that. We're in too deep for any mere man to deliver us. Our only hope lies in a heavenly creature, sent down from the clouds of heaven, with legions of angels. The sort of thing The Book of Daniel talks about. One who'll smite the oppressive Romans and deliver us from them, and then set up a heavenly Kingdom right here in Palestine. That's the only thing that can save us.[2]

Power. Various sorts of power. If you did not already know how the story came out, you could by reading the prophecies pretty well see where these folk got their ideas: "Behold, the days are coming, says the LORD, when I will raise up for David a righteous Branch, and he shall reign as king and deal wisely, and shall execute justice and righteousness in the land. In his days Judah will be saved, and Israel will dwell securely" (Jer. 23:5-6). "And I will set up over them one shepherd, my servant David, and he shall feed them: he shall feed them and be their shepherd" (Ez. 34:23). "Rejoice greatly, O daughter of Zion! . . . Lo, your king comes to you; triumphant and victorious is he, humble and riding on an ass, on a colt the foal of an ass. I will cut off the chariot from Ephraim and the war horse from Jerusalem; and the battle bow shall be cut off, and he shall command peace to the nations; his dominion shall be from sea to sea" (Zec.

2. Robert McAfee Brown, *The Bible Speaks to You* (Philadelphia: Westminster, 1955), p. 91.

9:9-10). "But you, O Bethlehem Ephrathah, who are little to be among the clans of Judah, from you shall come forth for me one who is to be ruler in Israel. . . . And they shall dwell secure, for now he shall be great to the ends of the earth. And this shall be peace, when the Assyrian comes into our land and treads upon our soil, that we will raise against him seven shepherds and eight princes of men; they shall rule the land of Assyria with the sword" (Mi. 5:2, 4-6a). "The people who walked in darkness have seen a great light; those who dwelt in a land of deep darkness, on them has light shined. . . . For to us a child is born, to us a son is given; and the government will be upon his shoulder, and his name will be called 'Wonderful Counselor, Mighty God, Everlasting Father, Prince of Peace' " (Is. 9:2, 6). "A young woman shall conceive and bear a son, and shall call his name Immanuel" (Is. 7:14). "Behold, with the clouds of heaven there came one like a son of man. . . . And to him was given dominion and glory and kingdom, that all peoples, nations, and languages should serve him; his dominion is an everlasting dominion, which shall not pass away, and his kingdom one that shall not be destroyed" (Dn. 7:13-14). Jeremiah, Ezekiel, Zechariah, Micah, Isaiah, Daniel. Everybody drew conclusions from what these prophets wrote. We now think they were quite wrong conclusions, but not because they were dumb. No, they just thought about God and power the way most of us do, when we stop to think about them at all.

We Christians recognize the clues the way we recognize clues in a mystery novel if we cheat and read the last chapter first. "Bethlehem," "Son of David," "Immanuel"—these are what catch our ear today. But that is not the main point just now. The point is what the prophecies teach us about this business of God's power. That it shows itself in unexpected ways, obviously. But there is more.

The prophecies, like the whole history of Israel of which they are an expression, can teach us that God's power is never raw, arbitrary power, but is always an expression of a larger purpose. They tell us God is up to something, but they do not let us be too sure how it will be accomplished, as if God had to do it the way we would. Sometimes, as in the Exodus, God's purpose to deliver her people is expressed mightily. Sometimes, as in the time of waiting surrounding the prophecies, God's intention seems largely hidden. Sometimes, as in the birth of Jesus, what God does is so surprising that only afterward can we see how it fits what she has promised. But the important thing is that God's purpose and power are all of a piece. What she does and what she promises do fit together. What God does accomplishes her ends.

God's power expresses her purpose. God's omnipotence—almightiness—must be defined in terms of her ability to accomplish her purpose. To know God's power, we must know her purpose. You know where we see that purpose best? Right there in that baby, and, of course, in the man he became, and in that man's death. What we learn in looking at that baby is that God is a personal God, and that she keeps her promises, and that her promises are that she will save her people. Did you ever notice that the only attribute of God mentioned in the Apostles' Creed is that she is almighty? Well, look again, and notice that that affirmation of her power is hooked right up with her personal character and her love: she is the *Mother* Almighty. You cannot tear the two apart. The power of God without her personal, saving love would indeed be raw, arbitrary, destructive power, not God's power.

That is why it is meaningless to ask whether God, if she is *really* all-powerful, could make a stick with one end, or make a rock so big she could not lift it, or make 2 + 2 = 5, or tell a lie. Doing any of those things would work against what we can understand both of God's purpose in her creation and of her character. Because it would work against her purpose, doing such things would make God less powerful, not more powerful. That does not mean, though, that God is somehow the slave of the natural laws she instituted in the world she created. It does not mean that God, once she set this world in motion, can no longer do anything significant about it. The laws of cause and effect, for instance, generally hold because God has determined that they should, not because she is determined by them. A couple of details of our story should make that plain enough.

To begin with, take the angels. Like the rest of the story, they are so familiar to us now that we just sort of assume their presence. They create a nice, heavenly sort of atmosphere, suitable for Christmas. Today, since this is the day we lit the angels' candle, we have maybe thought a little of them and sung about them and generally found them pleasant. But that is not just exactly the way Mary experienced the angel that came to her, or the way the shepherds experienced the angel that came to them. Angels were not any more a part of their daily lives than they are of ours. These people did not get up in the morning, greet the local angel, and proceed to go about their business, any more than we do. That is clear enough from the way the story is told. For another, take the virgin birth. All kinds of arguments have gone on about that, as everyone knows. One side insists that affirming the virgin birth is important to our rightly understanding who Jesus is, both God and human being. The other side considers it an affront to modern scientific intelligence and to the orderliness of our world. But that is just it: a virgin birth was not any more likely 2,000 years ago than it is today. It is not "modern" scientific understandings that are at stake, but common human understandings of what ordinarily happens. The poet Auden has some wonderful lines in his Christmas oratorio, the part on the temptation of Joseph, where the chorus speaks the thoughts that must have been haunting him:

> Joseph, you have heard
> What Mary says occurred;
> Yes, it is may be so.

Is it likely? No.
. . . .
Mary may be pure,
But, Joseph, are you sure?
How is one to tell?
Suppose, for instance
. . . Well . . .
. . . .
Maybe, maybe not.
But, Joseph, you know what
Your world, of course, will say
About you anyway.

Joseph responds,

All I ask is one
Important and elegant proof
That what my Love had done
Was really at your will
And that your will is Love.
. . . .

And the angel Gabriel replies,

No, you must believe.
Be silent, and sit still.[3]

"One important and elegant proof"—that is what we shall not have, for such supposed proofs come out of those laws of nature and reason we presume to understand. But God transcends nature and reason. "My thoughts are not your thoughts, neither are your ways my ways, says the LORD. For as the heavens are higher than the earth, so are my ways higher than your ways and my thoughts than your thoughts. . . . My word . . that goes forth from my mouth . . . shall not return to me empty, but it shall accomplish that which I purpose, and prosper in the thing for which I sent it" (Is. 55:8-9, 11). Nature and reason are God's servants, not her masters. God can freely do miracles when miracles suit her purpose. Not only can she, but sometimes she does. And that baby is a miracle.

A miracle, and also a baby, a baby born to a powerless couple of young people in a rather threatening world. And that, too, says something very important about God's power. God manifests her power in weakness. At

---

3. *Collected Poems*, ed. Edward Mendelson (New York: Random House, 1976), pp. 280-82.

Christmas, as the theologians would say, "the almighty God, with whom all things are possible, does the impossible; the Maker of heaven and earth steps across the boundary between the Creator and the creature in order to become one with us." What that means is that God becomes the God who is tempted, and suffers, and dies. The Sunday school child who was hearing the story of the crucifixion for the first time in a way understood the "impossibility" of the whole thing better than we usually do. He responded to Jesus' death by exclaiming indignantly, "If Superman had been there, they wouldn't have gotten away with it!"[4] But again, that is just it: God's power is not like the power of Superman, who solves everything by sheer force. God has chosen another way; she accomplishes her will through what the world calls weakness.

Clues of this, too, may be found in the prophets of the Old Testament. Even that the Messiah should come from Bethlehem, and not Jerusalem, the City of David, "presupposes that the family of David, out of which [the Messiah] is to spring, will have lost the throne, and have fallen into poverty. This could only arise from the giving up of Israel into the power of its enemies."[5] God has been known to do that sort of thing with her people— but to get involved in it herself? No. A suffering, dying Messiah was unknown in Judaism. Yet that is what we have. Power in weakness.

"We have not a high priest who is unable to sympathize with our weaknesses, but one who in every respect has been tempted as we are. . . . Let us then with confidence draw near to the throne of grace" (Heb. 4:15-16). "For the foolishness of God is wiser than humankind, and the weakness of God is stronger than humankind. For consider your call, brothers and sisters; not many of you were wise according to worldly standards, not many were powerful, not many were of noble birth; but God chose what is foolish in the world to shame the wise, God chose what is weak in the world to shame the strong, God chose what is low and despised in the world, even things that are not, to bring to nothing things that are" (1 Cor. 1:25-28).

What God has chosen, she has not hesitated to become: a baby, a baby born under unlikely circumstances, a baby born to powerless parents, a baby born to die—for us. A strange power indeed. But the power of God for salvation to all who believe. Well, that is the story. Not, for sure, what anyone would have expected. But we are here today because we, like thousands upon thousands of others before us, have believed it is true. Amen, and Merry Christmas in the name of our Incarnate Lord.

4. Dick Van Dyke, *Faith, Hope and Hilarity* (Garden City, NY: Doubleday, 1970), p. 80.
    5. C. F. Keil and F. Delitzsch, *Commentary on the Old Testament*, vol. X (Grand Rapids: Eerdmans, 1978), p. 483.

III. God's Wisdom and Knowledge

A. INTRODUCTION

The theologian comes to the subject of the divine wisdom and knowledge with a sense of unease, aware, as he is, of the tension between the academy and the church, the philosopher and the Christian. He understands only too well what Tertullian had in mind when he asked what Athens had to do with Jerusalem. Yet every theologian is the pupil of Hellas as well as of heaven. He knows that "to think well is to serve God in the inner court."[1] The Christ who, for Tertullian, is against culture is in the last analysis not a different Christ from that of the astronomer Kepler who as a scientist devoutly sought to "think God's thoughts after him." We say this because the Christ revealed in Scripture is the Logos who was in the beginning with God, the Wisdom through whom all things were made (Jn. 1:1-3). He is the Light of the world, a world that includes Athens, the "violet crowned city of light" (Pindar) as well as Jerusalem, that "City of God" of which "glorious things are spoken" (Newton).

Though Tertullian's Christ-against-culture approach is too severe (see H. R. Niebuhr, *Christ and Culture*, New York: Harper, 1951), yet all who read the Bible as revelation will perceive that the relationship between Athens and Jerusalem is somewhat less than happy. While sometimes overdrawn, especially by those "biblical theologians" who contrast "Greek" and "Hebrew" thought, the differences are not wholly inconsequential. Unlike Israel, the Greeks extolled reason in the objective form of logic and mathematics ("In reason [λόγος] humanity finds a physician for its grief"—Neander).

Of course, such abstract, impersonal knowledge is essential to the life of the human

---

1. Thomas Traherne as quoted by Alexander Miller, *Faith and Learning* (New York: Association Press, 1960), title page.

spirit (and the life of God). Were we unable to use the laws of logic and mathematics, we could not make change in the grocery store, much less theologize. But large ranges of truth cannot be grasped in such a narrow way; life has its dynamic aspect, and thought its creative activity. We understand not only by reason but by insight born of action.

Obviously biblical thought especially is open to this latter approach to truth. For the Israelites, to know and to do were so closely related as to be, in some instances, virtually synonymous: "Now Adam 'knew' (יָדַע) Eve his wife, and she conceived . . ." (Gn. 4:1). Yet the Greeks too loved knowledge, not simply for itself, but for its bearing on life. They not only invented philosophy (from φίλος and σοφία, "the love of wisdom"), but the philosopher king was seeking meaning in life that he might know and teach others how to live.

Still there are nuances of difference; Israel did not pursue theory as did the Greeks; there are no mathematicians, astronomers, or system builders in the Bible. However, since the writers of Scripture obviously viewed God as the ultimate source of all wisdom, they surely believed that, in some sense, she is the God of Homer, Sappho, and Euripides as well as of Abraham, Isaac, and Jacob. Hence Paul could preach before the Areopagus in Athens that there is one, true God who will judge Greek and Jew alike by Jesus Christ (Acts 17:18-33). Though they laughed at his message, which the Jews never did, yet the fact that the apostle preached to Greeks at all assumes his conviction that the God who is the God of all wisdom is not far even from the wise and understanding of Athens; that, indeed, they also are her offspring (Acts 17:28).

B. THE BIBLICAL DATA

Due in part to contact with other nations, especially Egypt, Israel came to cultivate an ever greater interest in the subject of wisdom as it had to do with the practical affairs and skills of life. Wisdom in this mundane sense, extolled especially in the Hagiographa, becomes Israel's link with its neighbors, enabling it to appreciate the presence of truth in other cultures while remaining deeply persuaded of the unique character of the truth revealed in the Law and the Prophets. This they could do because they became convinced that the Lord, who made covenant with their forebears at Sinai and whose fear is the beginning of wisdom (Ps. 111:10), was the source of all wisdom, even the wisdom found in other nations.

Scholars differ in their reconstruction of the historical process by which Israel arrived at this conviction, but they tend to agree that as Israel came to appreciate the transcendent ground of human wisdom, the word of the seer, as well as that of Moses and the prophets, was understood as the word of the Spirit of Yahweh. Wisdom was God's call to humankind, the teacher of nations, the mediator of revelation, the principle of reason behind the world, going back to the very beginning of creation. Hence the world is not simply the product of God's will and power but also of her wisdom. "O LORD, how manifold are your works! In wisdom you have made them all" (Ps. 104:24 NRSV).

Thus wisdom was understood as a basic attribute of God. This wisdom (understanding, knowledge) by which God created the world was personified in Proverbs 8 as God's intimate companion when the heavens were established and the foundations of the earth were laid. In fact, creation is a kind of sporting, a cheerful recreation for God's premundane wisdom. In a striking figure, we are told that God creates because she enjoys doing so; and she does so in and by her Wisdom. Wisdom is her creative, arranging, energizing thought which finds cheerful diversion in making the world and all that is in it. This figure of playfulness, of course, does not lessen the insight that the world displays a wisdom that is wondrously profound. The divine wisdom is ever God's secret, which encloses the world even as her glory encompasses it.

To affirm that God is wise is to make a statement not only about her relation to the world in general but also about her relation to Israel in particular. She who made the world in her wisdom and who rules over it, orders the affairs of human history with a view to the salvation of her people. To this end, she who "determines the number of the stars and gives to all of them their names" also declares "her word to Jacob, her statutes and ordinances to Israel" (Ps. 147, passim).

In the New Testament this salvific wisdom is given marked preeminence over the wisdom first manifest in creation. Marvelous as is the latter, more marvelous still is the purpose to bring salvation both to Israel and to all the nations through Jesus Christ. In this "mystery hidden for ages in God who created all things," Paul sees a wisdom that is indeed manifold (Eph. 3:9). God's wisdom, then, is supremely revealed in Jesus. As the divine Wisdom invites all to her banquet (Prv. 9:1-4), so Jesus invites all who are weary and heavy laden to come to him (Mt. 11:28). So to compare the two was natural to the early Christians because they were convinced that in the person of Jesus one who was wiser than Solomon was in their midst (Mt. 12:42). In fact, all the treasures of wisdom and knowledge are hid in him (Col. 2:1-3).

> O come, thou Wisdom from on high,
> And order all things far and nigh;
> To us the path of knowledge show,
> And cause us in her ways to go. (Latin Antiphons/Neal)

Hence those who in faith embrace him for salvation know a wisdom not of this present age, which is doomed to pass away, but the hidden wisdom of God, decreed before the ages for our glorification (1 Cor. 2:1-7).

C. SOME BASIC AFFIRMATIONS

1. GOD'S WISDOM AND KNOWLEDGE ARE ULTIMATELY ONE

As when we speak of God's will and power, so when we speak of her wisdom and knowledge, we speak of those perfections of being that arise out of her very nature as personal. God is the all-wise, all-knowing Subject who not only displays her wisdom in creation but knows her creation exhaustively even as she knows herself. Of course, it is not the mystery of the divine self-knowledge but the knowledge God has of the creation that has primarily engaged the theologians. In speaking of this knowledge, they have assumed that it is analogous to that of the creature endowed with her image. In so doing, they have simply followed the example of Scripture, which refers to God's wisdom and knowledge (Rom. 11:33), understanding (Ps. 147:5), discernment (Heb. 4:12); to her taking counsel (Ps. 33:11), thinking (Ps. 33:11), numbering (Mt. 10:30), naming (Is. 8:3), and the like. In speaking thus, Scripture not only speaks of God after the analogy of the creature, but also represents her as intimately involved with her creation. She is no mere spectator; much less is she like Aristotle's Unmoved Mover of whom the philosopher concluded: "Therefore it must be that the Divine Thought thinks of itself (since it is the most excellent of things) and its thinking is a thinking about thinking."[2] Rather, God thinks about *us;* she is the God who knows the thoughts she has toward us and puts our tears in her bottle (Ps. 56:8)!

Yet God's knowledge differs from ours in the way in which it is related to her will. God does not know something because it is, but she knows it because she wills it to be what it is. God, in contrast to the creature, not only knows what she wills, but wills what she knows. This is just to say that hers is a sovereign knowledge, the knowledge of the Almighty. Hence her knowledge is never a posteriori but always a priori. Whereas the world would not be known to us unless it already existed, to God it would not exist unless it were already known. Thomas, in the eighth Article on the divine knowledge, asks "whether the knowledge of God is the cause of all things?" He answers in the affirmative, citing Augustine's dictum: "Not because they are, does God know all creatures, . . . but because she knows them therefore they are."[3]

Because of the a priori character of the divine knowledge, theologians have not understood those statements of Scripture literally which speak of God's knowledge as learned

---

2. *Metaphysics,* XII, 9.
3. *Summa,* I, Q. 14, citing *De Trinitate,* XV.

from experience. The questions addressed to our first parents—Where are you? Who told you you were naked? Have you eaten of the tree? (Gn. 3:9-11)—are rhetorical. When Scripture tells us that "the LORD came down to see the city and the tower, which the sons of men had built" (Gn. 11:5), that she came to verify the cry she had heard against the plain cities of Sodom and Gomorrah (Gn. 18:20-21), we are taught that God's knowledge is firsthand rather than based on hearsay. Of course, many would dismiss such scriptural statements as simply primitive ways of thinking about God. They tell us more about human ignorance of the divine than about divine knowledge of the human. Such post-enlightenment rejection of the anthropomorphisms of Scripture, however, presuppose a quite different view of God from that found in the Bible and confessed in the church.

The a priori character of the divine knowledge, whereby God is able to declare "the end from the beginning" and call things which are not as though they were (Is. 46:10; Rom. 4:17), is what makes God's knowledge all one with her wisdom. The wisdom of God consists in her knowing both what she wills and why she wills it. She knows the why and the wherefore of all her creation because all creation unfolds according to her plan and purpose. Hence, in a dark hour, Gerhardt was able to sing,

> Leave to God's sovereign sway
> To choose and to command;
> So shall you, wondering, own her way,
> How wise, how strong her hand. (tr. J. Wesley)[4]

2. GOD'S KNOWLEDGE IS BOTH COMPREHENSIVE AND INTENSIVE

To many, to affirm that God knows all things simply conveys the thought that she is possessed of infinite information. If she chose, she could write an encyclopedia that would never need a supplement. While this is true, there are other nuances of biblical thought implied in the doctrine of the divine omniscience. For one, God's knowledge is both analytic and synthetic. That is to say, she knows not only each tree but the forest as a whole. As humans, we quickly come to the "x" that marks the limits of our knowledge, whether as philosophers we seek to frame a system or as

---

4. Because our knowledge, unlike God's, in so many ways is a posteriori, the distinction between knowledge and wisdom in our case is often very pronounced. To perceive that this is so one has only to ponder the knowledge we possess to unleash the energy of the atom and the wisdom we lack in knowing how to use it. Knowledge gives power, but only wisdom guarantees the right use of power.

cosmologists we try to piece together the baffling data of the physical universe.[5] But with God it is not so. Her knowledge penetrates to the final depth and embraces the ultimate whole. Whereas from our limited perspective there are surds and riddles as we see through the dark glass of human frailty and finitude, from her "no creature is hidden, but all are open and laid bare to the eyes of her with whom we have to do" (Heb. 4:13). She understands Tennyson's "flower in the crannied wall . . ." not only as we do but "root and all, and all in all."[6]

To say this is to imply that whatever wisdom, knowledge, and understanding we have comes ultimately from God. Warning against that wisdom that is "earthly, unspiritual, devilish," James admonishes his readers to seek rather the wisdom that is "from above" (3:15-17), a wisdom God gives to all who ask (1:5).[7] In fact, theologians have drawn the conclusion that all human wisdom and knowledge, insofar as they are not flawed by pride, are of God, whether or not those who possess such gifts acknowledge the One who gives them. We see light only in her light. Even the formal truths of logic and mathematics witness to the "light of God that lightens everyone coming into the world" (Jn. 1:9, author's translation). Were not a rational conclusion on earth rational in heaven, it would not be rational on earth either. The laws of natural science have the same transcendent ground. Creation is susceptible to rational understanding just because it is the work of mind, that is, of an intelligent Creator. Even the Greeks, who did not begin with the Hebrew doctrine of creation, came to perceive the universe not as random chaos, but as a cosmos.[8] In other words, to say that God is

---

5. "I do not know," observed Newton, toward the close of his life, "what I may appear to the world; but to myself I seem to have been only like a boy playing on the seashore and diverting myself in now and then finding a smoother pebble or a prettier shell than ordinary, whilst the great ocean of truth lay all undiscovered before me." Quoted in *Great Books,* vol. 34 (Chicago: Britannica, 1952), p. x.

6 See Louis Untermeyer, *A Treasury of Great Psalms* (New York: Simon and Schuster, 1955), p. 837; also Barth, *K.D.,* II/1, pp. 624-25 (cf. *C.D.,* II/1, sec. 31.2).

7. The Greek Idealists also believed that wisdom had a transcendent ground. For Plato wisdom had its content and being in the eternal Ideas. Therefore wisdom "belongs to the gods." And the human yearning (eros) for this heavenly wisdom is that love of wisdom (φιλοσοφία), that aspiration, which overcomes all. In this latter regard, biblical thought differs from Greek thought in that this heavenly wisdom is the *gift* of God. We do not aspire to it; it comes down to us—in Christ.

8. See Emil Brunner, *Dogmatik* (Zurich: Zwingli-Verlag, 1960), vol. I, pp. 289-90. The transcendent character of the truths accessible to reason explains not only their universal acceptance but also their objective character. To understand a mathematical proof involves the subjectivity of the student, to be sure. Yet this subjectivity does not ground the proof. That the interior angles of a Euclidean triangle are equal to two right angles would be true even though none of the students in the classroom were carried by Euclid's reasoning. See Thorleif Boman, *Das Hebraische Denken,* pp. 170ff.

all-knowing in the intensive sense is to imply that all knowledge is grounded in her knowledge. But it is a Christian act of faith to confess that this is so and to seek wisdom from her who is "the only wise God" (Rom. 16:27).

As for the thought that God actually knows everything, while the affirmation is commonly made, the implications are staggering. (Bavinck cites Jerome's protest that God does not know "how many bugs, fleas, and flies there are in the world."[9]) Yet such is the plain implication of many Scriptures. She who as the Spirit knows the deep things of God (1 Cor. 2:10) is the God who is greater than our hearts and knows all things (1 Jn. 3:20). She is the God who does not forget one sparrow who falls to the ground and even numbers the hairs of our head (Mt. 10:29-30; Lk. 12:6-7). The locus classicus for the doctrine that God's knowledge is comprehensive is Psalm 139: God knows us in the womb and before we are born she has written our days in her book.[10] She sees us in the darkness as though it were the noonday light, and leads us in the remotest parts of the sea. The psalmist frankly confesses that such knowledge is too wonderful for him, too high for his reach, and exults,

> How precious to me are your thoughts, O God!
> How vast is the sum of them!

Such exhaustive knowledge, of course, assumes the divine transcendence over space and time. (Jesus, it will be recalled, told an overly confident Peter the details of his denial before the events occurred. See Mk. 14:30 par.) The thought of God's knowledge as transcending space and time, especially time, has raised many difficult questions. To these we must now give our attention.

3. GOD INFALLIBLY KNOWS THE FUTURE

In the many disquisitions on God's foreknowledge—here we use the term in the sense of "prescience"—one frequently reads that the creature's knowledge

---

9. Herman Bavinck, *The Doctrine of God*, ed. and trans. William Hendriksen (Grand Rapids: Eerdmans, 1951), p. 188. One wonders what dear Jerome would have said had he known that each bug, flea, and fly is made up of cells that are made up of molecules that are made up of atoms that are made up of particles that are made up of quarks and gluons, and that God knows how many in each case!

10. "In the depths of the earth" (בְּתַחְתִּיּוֹת אָרֶץ) (Ps. 139:15) is simply a Hebrew idiom for "in the womb."

is "discursive" while God's is "intuitive."[11] The intent of theologians in making such a distinction is to say that the creature thinks in time, that is, successively, one thought after another, whereas God's thought is not involved in the stream of time and hence not limited to past and present.

Thomas, quoting Augustine to this effect, goes on to comment that our knowledge is also discursive in the sense that we always proceed from the known to the unknown. But such is not true of God. Citing Romans 4:17, where the apostle says that God calls the things that are not as though they were, Thomas affirms that God comprehends, over all of time, all that exists in any given time, as present to her.[12] This includes even those things that are evil, since evil things are involved in the good—as, for example, in the crucifixion.[13] It also includes things future that are contingent to us. Granting "that human works are contingent, being subject to free will, yet they are known to God. For while they are future in relation to their own causes [and therefore uncertain to us] they are present to her sight since, as the psalmist says, 'She who fashions the hearts of all observes all their deeds.' "[14]

Ultimately the how of the divine foreknowledge escapes us. (Heppe cites Heidegger, "Here we are certainly as blind as bats.")[15] In this matter, as in others, we are driven back to Paul's statement—which is doxological in nature, not theoretical: "O the depth of the riches and wisdom and knowledge of God! How unsearchable are her judgments and how inscrutable her ways" (Rom. 11:33). Our knowledge, by contrast, is limited by the continuum of time and space.[16] True, within limits we also can transcend time and predict the future, yet such "foreknowledge" of future events is tied to our knowledge of causal relationships. Under such circumstances, the future that we "fore-know" is really an inchoate present, as, for example, an eclipse of the sun.

---

11. Literally speaking, "discursive" thought is reasoning from a premise to a conclusion or from particulars to a generalization. "Intuitive" thought, by contrast, is thought without the use of such inference, thought that is directly apprehended, as when Archimedes exclaimed "eureka!" or when—if we can believe Voltaire's account—the apple struck Newton's head. Such "aha" moments are very brief in duration, "flashes" of insight. Of course all human thought, whether discursive or intuitive, takes time. But since the former takes much more than the latter, theologians have used such terms by way of analogy to contrast divine and human knowledge.

12. *Summa*, I, Q. 14, Art. 7. In other words, we know the beginning and *then* the end. God, by contrast, knows the end *from* the beginning (Is. 46:10).

13. Ibid., I, Q. 14, Art. 9, 10.

14. Ibid., I, Q. 14, Art. 13, quoting Psalm 33:11, Vulgate.

15. H. Heppe, *Reformed Dogmatics* (London: Allen & Unwin, 1950), p. 76.

16. This is certainly the case, in the final analysis, whatever one may say about certain phenomena in parapsychology.

When it comes to the freedom of the "other," the future choice of a true "thou," we face a contingency that we can never overcome. Here the only "foreknowledge" that we have is the knowledge of our ignorance; the only certainty, our uncertainty.[17] But God's knowledge is perfectly clear, absolutely certain, and unfettered by any future contingency.

Hence the authors of Scripture, taught by the Spirit, clearly affirm God's foreknowledge of all that shall come to pass. Yet they avoid those overweening speculations that have tempted theologians; their concern is rather practical than theoretical. They assure us that since God foreknows all things, we can face our own contingent (and therefore anxiety-provoking) future in the confidence that she will be with us; that her care, concern, and love will go before us. For us, there is always a discontinuity between our knowledge and future reality, between our thought and final being. But for God there is no such discontinuity; the uncertainties with which the future threatens us are fully known to her. Hence they have lost their terror for us. Because she knows the future, we may put our hand in hers and walk by faith into the future; she knows the way we take.

According to Augustine, the "faith of piety" confesses both human freedom and divine foreknowledge. From the efficacy of the divine will it does not follow, as Cicero infers, that nothing depends on the exercise of our free will, "for our wills themselves are included in that order of causes which is certain to God and embraced in her foreknowledge" (*The City of God*, V, 9, 10). This is really as far as we should go. In reacting to the Reformers' use of Augustine's thought at this point, the Spanish Jesuit Molina (1535-1600) postulated a middle knowledge *(scientia media)* conditioned by the human response to grace. God's foreknowledge of the free choices of the creature is, according to the Molinists, really her reaction to the creature's action. The human choice to cooperate with grace is determined wholly from within the human self. Barth expresses shock that seventeenth-century Protestant theology, especially Lutheran theology, was so cordial to this Jesuit view. "The creature who conditions God is no longer God's creature and the God who is conditioned by the creature is no longer the creature's God" (*K.D.*, II/1, p. 645; cf. *C.D.*, II/1, sec. 31.2). God, in other words, is not subject to the ticker tape of history.

*   *   *   *   *

While Reformed theologians have rejected the doctrine of a *scientia media*, they have spent considerable time discussing the divine foreknowledge of the contingent. In the words of the *Westminster Confession*, Chap. III, Sec. 2, "God knows whatsoever may

---

17. Herbert Hoover, a few months before the crash of 1929, affirmed, "We in America are nearer to the final triumph over poverty than ever before in the history of our land." F. D. Roosevelt predicted at the end of World War II that in the future U.S. problems would principally center in South America. See *The Christian Century*, 18 July 1984, p. 109.

or can come to pass upon all supposed conditions." While it is intriguing to speculate about the answers to certain questions (what would have happened had Napoleon known of the fateful ditch at Waterloo? what if King Edward VIII had not met Wally Simpson?), we all know that it is futile. And it is equally futile to speculate on the content of the divine mind concerning such hypothetical possibilities—that God knew what the inhabitants of Keilah would do if David remained with them (1 Sam. 23:11-12) implies only that she knew the thoughts of their hearts. When our Lord tells his hearers (Mt. 11:21, 23) that if the mighty works done in their midst had been done in Tyre and Sidon they would have repented, he is not disclosing his knowledge of hypothetical cases, but delivering a stinging rebuke to the citizens of Chorazin and Bethsaida by comparing them unfavorably with notorious sinners of whose unbelief they were all too aware. We must remember that God's omniscience does not mean that she can know everything conceivable any more than her omnipotence means that she can do everything conceivable. As God defines the meaning of her omnipotence, so she defines the meaning of her omniscience. She knows whatever she wills, and she wills whatever she pleases. But it is what she who cannot deny herself pleases, that she knows, not every contingency and possibility that can be imagined in the games theologians sometimes play.

D. CONCLUDING OBSERVATIONS

1. GOD'S OMNISCIENCE AND THE QUALITY OF HUMAN LIFE

Because God is the all-knowing One, we live always *coram Deo*. "The eyes of the LORD are in every place, keeping watch on the evil and the good" (Prv. 15:3). Hence the prayer,

> Thou, whose all-pervading eye
> Nought escapes, without, within,
> Pardon each infirmity,
> Open fault and secret sin. (Doane)

This is the truth expressed in the ancient symbol of the Trinity that pictures God as a triangle enclosing a large eye. Because all is naked and laid open before God's eyes (Heb. 4:13), the devout Christian, like the devout Israelite of old, should never say, "My way is hid from the LORD, and my right is disregarded by my God" (Is. 40:27). Rather, the Christian should take comfort, as did the Babylonian exiles, in this assurance: "I know the plans I have for you, plans for welfare and not for evil, to give you a future and a hope" (Jer. 29:11). That God is the all-knowing One is not only a comfort to the godly, but a warning to the ungodly. Those who slay the widow and stranger in the confidence that "the LORD will not see, neither will the God of Jacob regard it," are dullards without understanding who will never learn wisdom. To refute such fools, it is sufficient to pose the question, "She who planted the ear, does she not hear? She who formed the eye, does she not see" (Ps. 94:9)?

Both the comfort and the threat of the divine knowledge are reflected in the story of the Fall in Genesis 3. Our first parents hid themselves from God's face—and with reason—yet the Lord God sought them out. She will not allow even fallen humanity to fall out of her thoughts altogether! This practical orientation of the doctrine of the divine wisdom and knowledge remains prominent throughout the Bible. God's keeping track of sparrows and her numbering the hairs of our head are not exercises in erudition. They are rather words that give solace in the hour of trial and inspire awe in the presence of One who knows our thoughts before they are our own!

Perhaps the most familiar symbol in Scripture for the divine wisdom and knowledge is light. Hence Christians sing of God as

> Immortal, invisible, God only wise,
> In light inaccessible, hid from our eyes. (Smith)

In fact, the Scriptures say not only that God dwells in light (1 Tm. 6:16), but that God is light (1 Jn. 1:5). God's first recorded word in the Bible is, "Let there be light" (Gn. 1:3). Thus begins the work of creation of which the psalmist exclaims, "O LORD, how manifold are your works! In wisdom you have made them all" (Ps. 104:24 NRSV). And when Simeon holds the infant Jesus in his arms, he describes him as "a light to lighten the Gentiles and the glory of your people Israel" (Lk. 2:32). In Jesus' coming, the early Christians saw the fulfillment of the comforting word of Isaiah, "Arise, shine, for your light has come" (60:1). Hence, there is every propriety in the claim of the Johannine Christ, "I am the light of the world" (Jn. 8:12). Hence, also, there is propriety of the words in the Nicene Creed describing Jesus, the Son, in relation to the One who sent him, as "Light (out) of Light, true God (out) of true God" (φῶς ἐκ φωτός, θεὸν ἀληθινὸν ἐκ θεοῦ ἀληθινοῦ). Jesus Christ is not simply illumined by the light of divine wisdom to an unprecedented degree; he *is* that Light.

The radicalness of the departure from Nicene Christology on the part of many contemporary theologians is seen in the analysis of this phrase in the Creed by John Macquarrie in his provocative study, *God-Talk* (pp. 208-22). Observing that "light" for moderns is no longer a mysterious effluence, he suggests that "light" as a symbol translates existentially into "openness." To say "God is light" is to say "openness is constitutive of Being." Jesus is "Light (out) of Light," as the Creed says, in the sense that

> Jesus was the man fundamentally open to the Father; . . . we can think of Christ as the God-man because he moves out to fill the openness that is potential in all human existence. . . . This thought of Christ's openness,

moreover, gives us a clue to the mystery of what we mean by "incarnation." A human life that has gone out in complete openness is the manifestation in the flesh of the openness of God.

One wonders how this "existential translation" of the biblical symbol of "light" into "openness as constitutive of Being" would work in the prayer of John Henry Newman, which thousands have prayed after him:

> Lead kindly Light, amid the encircling gloom,
>   Lead thou me on;
> The night is dark, and I am far from home,
>   Lead thou me on.
> Keep thou my feet; I do not ask to see
> The distant scene,—one step enough for me.

2. GOD'S WISDOM REVEALED IN THE FOOLISHNESS OF THE CROSS

Reflecting on the young Augustine's struggle with Greek thought in the light of biblical thought, Günter Howe observes that the most crucial issue with which Augustine had to wrestle was the cyclical view of history versus the uniqueness of the event of the Incarnation. With his conversion to Christianity and his embracing the central doctrine of Incarnation, "philosophy discovered time."[18] This is not to say that history is intrinsically rational (Hegelianism), but rather that history is the means by which God achieves her ultimate purpose, a purpose revealed in the coming of Jesus Christ to redeem us from our sins. It is, then, from the perspective of the cross, which is the foolishness of God that is wiser than human wisdom (1 Cor. 1:25), that the Christian sees all other history. The wisdom that illumines the Christian understanding of history is not "the wisdom of this age or of the rulers of this age, doomed to pass away." It is rather "a secret and hidden wisdom of God, which God decreed before the ages for our glorification" (1 Cor. 2:6-7).[19]

In speaking of God's power and will, we noted that God's power is manifest in weakness. The same paradox confronts us here. In fact, the argument of Paul in 1 Corinthians 1–2 intertwines the double paradox of power-in-weakness and wisdom-in-foolishness in a most profound way. Because it has pleased God, in her wisdom, to save through the foolishness of preaching those who believe, the apostle does not preach the gospel in

---

18. Günther Howe, *Mensch und Physik* (Witten/Berlin: Eckhart-Verlag, 1963), p. 21.

19. In other words, the Christian understands the meaning of history *sub specie contraria*, that is, from the aspect of an event that appears in itself meaningless.

the eloquent words of human wisdom, "lest the cross of Christ be emptied of its power" (1 Cor. 1:17). Instead, he tells the Corinthians that, as an apostle of the divine wisdom, if this wisdom is to be "justified in her children," he can neither dance as the world pipes nor weep as the world mourns. The gospel, which is the power of God to salvation (Rom. 1:16), is an expression of the divine wisdom that is self-authenticating. Here is a wisdom not discovered by human reasoning, but revealed by the Spirit who probes the deep things of God, a wisdom that no eye has seen nor ear heard nor heart conceived (1 Cor. 2:9), a wisdom hid from the wise and revealed to babes (Mt. 11:25), a wisdom perceived by those who become fools that they may be wise (1 Cor. 3:18). Hence it is a wisdom that enables Christians to walk by faith, to "give to the winds their fears," and to "hope and be undismayed" (Gerhardt).

IV. God's Justice / Righteousness and Mercy

A. INTRODUCTION

From the time of classical Greek thought to the present, the question "What is justice?" has been answered in two fundamentally different ways. Some have said that might makes right and therefore justice is a matter of expediency. Our modern world, with its economic exploitation and political totalitarianism, affords many illustrations of such a positivistic, anti-metaphysical approach to the subject. Given such a view, the strong do whatever they please and the weak suffer whatever they must. On the other hand, others say that justice is not a mere formal concept whose material content is relative because it is historically determined. While injustice may call itself "just" in the name of racial superiority, property rights, or the will of the state, as a matter of fact might does not make right unless it is rightly used. Justice is not a matter of might but of right, the right being viewed as a norm that is transcendent and ultimate rather than pragmatic and relative. This eternal and absolute right pertains to all people at all times. As the American Declaration of Independence affirms, there are certain "inalienable rights" that belong to all by virtue of their humanity; and human governments are instituted not to determine but to secure these rights. What the state cannot create it ought not to destroy; its task is not to define but to preserve and guarantee justice.

This transcendent idea of the right (*jus natural*) behind civil codes of justice is essentially rational; it gives everyone his due; it treats all equitably. It is also impartial; as she holds the scales, Dame Justice's eyes are blindfolded.[1] Of course, this like treatment of all is a formal equality given

---

1. The Roman goddess *Justitia*.

material content only as one considers the actual differences in a given situation. Aristotle, pondering this question of material justice, speaks of simple justice that treats everyone alike as "equalizing" justice. When the inequalities or differences inherent in many situations are taken into account, justice becomes "distributive" ("proportional") justice.[2]

B. JUSTICE AND THE DIVINE WILL

Christian thinkers, of course, have sided with those who affirm a transcendent ground of justice. That transcendent ground is just the will of God the Holy One. God, having implanted the knowledge of the right in the human heart (conscience), has revealed her justice to us in her provision for our needs and the needs of all her creatures, and in rendering to us what we deserve as obedient (or disobedient) to her will. Justice, then, belongs to the very nature of God. To say that God is just is to say that she is the God who approves in herself, and works in her creation, that which is according to her holy will. This divine justice gives structure, order, and meaning to the life of the creature who is made in her image. Whatsoever one sows, therefore, one shall reap, whether it be from the flesh corruption, or from the Spirit eternal life, for God is not mocked (Gal. 6:7).

Theologians have often spoken of this justice as a divine attribute in and of itself, especially when treating the concept of civil justice common to all cultures, including those apart from any contact with biblical revelation.[3] We, however, have chosen to speak of the divine justice only in conjunction with the divine mercy. Of course, we have treated all the attributes as complementary pairs—will and power, wisdom and knowledge, etc. But in no other instance is the complementarity more essential

2. *Nicomachean Ethics*, Book V. Aristotle also speaks of "corrective" justice designed to rectify errors of distribution. Such "corrective" justice is similar in certain ways to "retributive" justice, according to which punishment is administered to offenders who have transgressed against the rights of their fellow citizens.

3. So Brunner, in his *Gerechtigkeit* (Zurich: Zwingli-Verlag, 1943), where he is concerned with the basic laws of the social order. Here he appeals to the "ordinances of creation" *(Schöpfungsordnungen)*, thus grounding justice in natural revelation in conscious rejection of the effort of Barth, et al., to ground all ethics christologically. There is a fine line between Brunner's approach and the traditional view of "natural law." The natural-law approach, of course, risks the danger of ending up with the Stoics, who grounded natural rights in the *Ratio* viewed as endemic to humanity as such. This Stoic view is reflected in the conclusion of the natives of Miletus when they observed a deadly viper on Paul's hand. He was undoubtedly a murderer, they reasoned, whom justice would not allow to live (Acts 28:4).

to a right understanding than in the case of the divine justice and mercy. As a matter of fact, in Scripture the meaning of the divine justice is so bound up with that of the divine mercy (goodness, forbearance, kindness, compassion) that in the New Testament the classical term for justice (ἡ δίκη) recedes before the term "righteousness" (δικαιοσύνη) which takes on nuances of meaning unique to biblical revelation. This is due ultimately to the fact, we believe, that God in herself is a triune fellowship of holy love. Holiness without love is severe; love without holiness is sentimental. But God is neither an implacable tyrant nor a doting sentimentalist. Her justice, therefore, is a justice "seasoned with mercy."

That the justice of the God-revealed-in-Christ cannot be understood apart from her mercy does not mean that her justice is not distributive in the strict sense. Even the Old Testament concept of an eye for an eye and a tooth for a tooth (Lv. 24:19-20) expresses a fundamental principle of biblical revelation. For all its inadequacy, behind the *lex talionis* there is a rightness, namely, the need to restore the order established in the creation by the Creator and violated by the sinful creature. This is the function, therefore, of a human judge insofar as his judgments are just. Of course, such justice (as Aristotle observes) is easier to obtain when concerned with goods than with persons. For this reason Christians would all agree that "a false balance is an abomination to the LORD, but a just weight is her delight" (Prv. 11:1). By the same token, they would agree that an adequate wage for honest labor pleases God, for she is a just God who hears the cry of the laborers when their wages are kept back by fraud (Jas. 5:4). In the realm of the personal, however, such simple justice is not always possible. Often when one has perpetrated, and another suffered, a wrong, only a substitutionary restitution can be made. Rather than a literal "eye for an eye," justice imposes the payment of a fine or the loss of freedom by incarceration.

Such retributive justice is a manifestation of that justice which God would have "roll down like waters," a justice more acceptable to her than the hypocritical observance of feast days and solemn assemblies (Am. 5:21-24). Even capital punishment for a capital offense cannot be faulted as a miscarriage of justice per se unless, with Ritschl and others, one understands God's character solely in terms of her love to the exclusion of her holiness. The reason capital punishment ought to be abolished is not that it is "cruel and unnatural." While it has surely been administered in many very cruel and unnatural ways, the problem with capital punishment is that it will inevitably be administered, in a sinful society, in an inequitable way. The statistics on the number of black Americans in proportion to white Americans who receive capital sentences is enough to establish this point for any theologian whose critical powers of thought are not overcome by the color of his skin. While inequity prevails in the administration of all human justice, no other form of justice is so final and irremediable. Such punishment, therefore, belongs to God, whose judgment is infallible, the God who at Calvary—if we may so speak—inflicted capital punishment on her own Son for a sinful people.

Again, unless one understands God's nature in terms of love apart from holiness one will not argue that retribution is a perversion of justice. It is, indeed, a perversion of justice to take matters into one's own hands out of a spirit of revenge. (As an error in one's doctrine of God, revenge is the opposite extreme of the error of sentimentalism.) A vengeful person is one who acts as though the holy God were a God of hate rather than love. Readers of *Moby Dick* will remember what Ahab's attempted vengeance on the white whale did to him and his crew. Some are offended when Paul (Rom. 12:19), quoting the Old Testament proscription of vengeance (Lv. 19:18), goes on to appeal to the vengeance (ἐκδίκησις) of the Lord, citing Deuteronomy 32:35. The word "vengeance" is, indeed, easily misunderstood. What is meant by the "vengeance" of God is not an act of vindictiveness, but a judgment against an incorrigible sinner. We are to be subject to governors for the Lord's sake because the governor is sent by her to punish those who do wrong and to praise those who do right. Simon Wiesenthal's efforts, therefore, to bring the perpetrators of the Holocaust to punishment is no less just than the efforts to persuade the Soviets to release Raoul Wallenberg, the Swedish diplomat whose courage in World War II saved thousands of Hungarian Jews from annihilation.

Close to the thought of the divine vengeance is the thought that God avenges, in the sense of vindicates, those who are the victims of injustice. When God is likened, in a parable of Jesus, to an unjust judge it is not because she is unjust but rather because she will "vindicate her elect, who cry to her day and night" as the judge finally vindicated the widow against her adversary (Lk. 18:1-7). That is, God will make things right for them, especially and finally when the Lord Jesus is revealed from heaven (2 Thes. 1:7-8).

C. THE DIVINE MERCY

1. INTRODUCTION

Turning to consider God's justice as it is "seasoned with mercy" and her mercy as it is revealed in her justice, we shall seek to answer the question: How can the Lord be a God merciful and gracious, forgiving iniquity and transgression (Ex. 34:6-7), while at the same time being the One who will by no means clear the guilty but will visit their iniquity upon them (Nm. 14:18)? We shall begin by reflecting on the meaning of certain basic terms.

The Hebrew root for justice (צדק) means "to be straight." God's justice, one might say, is her being and doing what is straight, that is, right. It is her being and doing what corresponds to her holy will that is the norm of justice for the creature in her image.[4] It might seem that while God's justice

---

4. In such a context, God's justice and her holiness are virtually synonymous. Holiness becomes, like justice, a moral attribute of God; it refers not to God's transcendence of being but to her ethical integrity. As God is *essentially* other than the creature (the Holy One), so she is *morally* other than the *sinful* creature — that is, she is the God who is holy and undefiled. See above, Unit Three, II, God Is the Holy One, pp. 189ff.

corresponds to her holiness, it contrasts with her mercy. But this is not the case. Though God's mercy and justice are not synonymous, neither are they antithetical. God not only does what is right because she is the Holy One, but loves what is right because she is the God who is Love. To perceive that this is so helps one understand why there is something unique about the justice of God revealed in Christ and why her justice can be understood only in the light of her mercy. It also explains why we shall give precedence to the word "righteousness" over that of "justice" as our discussion unfolds, conscripting the English language to give us help, small as it may be, in this exacting task. But first we must say a word about the way Scripture speaks of God's mercy as such.

2. DIVINE MERCY FROM THE BIBLICAL PERSPECTIVE

"Mercy" is one of the happiest words in the Bible; it encompasses many other divine qualities—"gentleness," "graciousness," "long-suffering," "forbearance," "patience," "goodness," "lovingkindness"—in its large embrace. We have already discussed the nature of God as Love, but love is a "many-splendored thing," some of whose splendors we must now consider as we unwrap the divine attribute of mercy, the *misericordia Dei*. Because of its breadth of meaning, "mercy" as a divine attribute cannot be exactly defined but only looked at from various perspectives. If grace is the love of God as that love is experienced by undeserving sinners who repent, then mercy is the grace of God as that grace is experienced in the ongoing life of repentant sinners. Mercy is grace that is ever renewed in God's covenant faithfulness. As we read in the "Magnificat," God's mercy "is on those who fear her from generation to generation" (Lk. 1:50).

God's mercy is seen not only in her faithfulness but also in her gentleness (ἐπιείκεια, "clemency," "graciousness"). This divine gentleness should not be confused with weakness. When Paul entreats the Corinthians by the "gentleness" of Christ (2 Cor. 10:1), it must be remembered that this is the same Jesus Christ who has been highly exalted, at whose name "every knee should bow . . . and every tongue confess" (Phil. 2:9-10). The gentleness of Christ, then, is the gentleness of One possessed of power, the power by which heaven and earth were created, the power by which Jesus is exalted as the Messiah to manifest God's forgiving love; the power displayed by the Spirit who bears effectual witness in our hearts that, for all our unworthiness, God is our gentle Mother.

God's mercy is also her "goodness" (χρηστότης), her "lovingkindness" (φιλανθρωπία) by virtue of which she has saved us (Ti. 3:4). When, by her grace, we take Jesus' "easy" ("kind," χρηστός) yoke upon us (Mt. 11:30), then we know the kindness of the Lord; then we taste and see that the Lord is good (Ps. 34:8). And so, as we look at Scripture, we perceive that God's mercy, like the light of the spectrum, has many hues and tones. We perceive that

> There's a wideness in God's mercy,
> Like the wideness of the sea;
> There's a kindness in her justice,
> That is more than liberty.
>
> For the love of God is broader,
> Than the measure of our mind,
> And the heart of the Eternal
> Is most wonderfully kind. (Faber)

There are two words in Scripture, especially, that add to our understanding of this "wideness" in the divine mercy. They are μακροθυμία, meaning "longsuffering," "forbearance," "patience"; and σπλάγχνον, meaning "compassion," "sympathy," "pity."

As for the divine patience, it is God's mercy viewed as the "space" between the two poles of her grace and her wrath. As such it involves time, time for the sinner to repent. It is not the uncertainty of hesitation, dallying indecision, or doting indulgence; but it is the willingness to wait a while—a long while, if need be—for the sinner's repentance toward her who is "The LORD, the LORD . . . merciful and gracious" (Ex. 34:6).[5] The divine patience is the affirmative answer to Wesley's existential question,

> Depth of mercy! Can there be
> Mercy still reserved for me?
> Can my God her wrath forbear,
> Me the chief of sinners spare?

The divine patience reveals a God who "spreads out [her] hands all the day to a rebellious people" (Is. 65:2; Rom. 10:21), a God who is longsuffering toward us, not willing that any should perish (2 Pt. 3:9). This factor of time is strikingly illustrated in the account of the Lord's patience with Israel in the days of the judges (Jgs. 2:11-22), and in the remark of the author of 1 Peter that those who perished in the flood were those who

---

5. Just because the divine patience is not vacillation but God's "lordship over her anger" (Barth), it leads either to the sinner's repentance or to his judgment (Rom. 2:4-5).

persisted in their disobedience "when God's patience waited in the days of Noah, during the building of the ark" (1 Pt. 3:20).[6]

So far as the individual is concerned, the time God allots the sinner to repent means that her mercy respects the integrity of the creature. The independence implied in her creating one who is in her image is not violated in the encounter with her grace. In ways that we cannot fathom, God, who is supremely free, freely works her sovereign will in and through the freedom she has given the creature. Her mercy does not violate human freedom; rather, it transforms that freedom from a freedom to rebel into a freedom to live unto righteousness (Phil. 2:12).[7]

The perfections that cluster about the quality of the divine mercy are analogous to those human virtues that should adorn the lives of the godly. To forgive an offending brother or sister, not seven times but seventy times seven (Mt. 18:21-22), calls for a goodly measure of forbearance and patience, a showing mercy of the sort we have received in Christ. The writers of the New Testament appeal to the virtue of patience, especially as the antidote to the vexing problem of the suffering of Christians in this evil world and the seeming delay of the parousia. Admonishing his readers to be patient until the coming of the Lord, James reminds them of the prophets who endured affliction and rejection in their day. And the writer of Hebrews tells his or her readers that they need patience in order that, as they do the will of God, they may obtain the promise (Heb. 10:36-37).

On the larger canvas of dogmatics, the time God allots sinners to repent is time that makes human history, as a whole, possible. We say this because our history is the history of a fallen race, a race that is alienated from its Maker. Reflecting on the constitutive character of the element of time in the concept of the divine patience, Brunner observes that the concept appears, for this very reason, wholly irrational to the critical mind and is dismissed as so much anthropomorphism.

> In reality [however] it has nothing whatsoever to do with anthropomorphism; it rather affirms that God is ceaselessly involved in the events of time. The patience of God is nothing less than the possibility of history. . . . If there is to be an end, if one day the book of history is to be closed and the hour of judgment is to strike—then why not already, why not long ago? To this question there is no other answer than this, that God's mercy provided this reprieve to the sinful race

6. See this theme of repenting-while-there-is-time powerfully developed in "Noah Built the Ark," James W. Johnson, *God's Trombones, Some Negro Sermons in Verse* (New York: Viking Press, 1957), pp. 34-35.

7. For this reason the traditional adjective "irresistible," used to describe the efficacious grace of God revealed in Christ and sealed by the Spirit, is unfortunate and misleading.

. . . to give them the possibility of converting, the possibility of repentance.[8]

Though the element of time may be essential to the concept of the divine patience, in the end God's patience is not simply an exercise in self-restraint. It becomes virtually synonymous with her grace viewed as the gift of salvation. In Jesus' parable of the forgiven and unforgiving servant (Mt. 18:23-25), the huge debt—10,000 talents—owed the master, not only contrasts with the insignificant debt—100 denarii—owed the servant; its sheer enormity underscores the impossibility that the debtor should ever repay, no matter how long an elapsed time. The parable really moves, then, in the same theological universe of discourse as Paul's constant emphasis on the impossibility of salvation by human effort and the need for justification by grace apart from the law. No one was ever more conscious of this truth as a reality in his own life than this apostle. Though he was the chief of sinners, though he had persecuted the church of God, he had received mercy in order that in him Christ Jesus might show forth his "perfect patience" (τὴν ἅπασαν μακροθυμίαν) as an example to future believers (1 Tm. 1:16).

Along with patience, the other pregnant, biblical term that helps us grasp the scope of the divine mercy is σπλάγχνον, meaning "compassion," "affection," "tenderness," "pity." To continue our spatial figure, if God's patience discloses the wideness in her mercy, her compassion discloses the depth of that mercy. As the "love of God is broader than the measure of our mind," so "the heart of the Eternal is most wonderfully kind." This we know because the Scriptures tell us of God's tender affection, or her compassion for the oppressed, the poor, the disinherited, the lost.

What is God's compassion but her mercy welling out of a heart of love?[9] This can be seen from three familiar parables that Jesus told his

---

8. *Dogmatik* (Zurich: Zwingli-Verlag, 1960), I, p. 281. Here one should recall the sequel to the story of the flood, cast in terms of a universal covenant with nature whose sign is the bow in the clouds (Gn. 8:21-22). The rainbow, one might say, is the sacrament of the divine patience with the human race in its ongoing sinfulness and rebellion.

9. It is interesting to note that the Greek σπλάγχνα literally refers to the viscera, particularly the bowels or intestines, viewed by the Hebrews as the seat of the most gripping and moving affections. (We, of course, use the word "heart" in this way; but compare our slang expression, "to feel something in our guts," that is, to feel it with gripping vigor.) The Hebrew equivalent of σπλάγχνα is רַחֲמִים ("compassion"), from רֶחֶם ("womb"), and means literally "motherly feeling," one more hint that "the heart of the Eternal," which "is most wonderfully kind," is as much like the heart of a woman as that of a man.

disciples in which everything turns on the verb "to have compassion" (σπλάγχνίζομαι). The first we have already referred to—it is the story of the unforgiving servant on whom the master "had compassion" ("had pity," RSV; Mt. 18:23-35). The second is the greatest of all our Lord's parables, that of the Prodigal. We read that when the son returned a penitent, his father saw him afar off and "moved with compassion" (Lk. 15:20) ran to welcome him with a kiss. The third is the familiar story of the good Samaritan that climaxes with the words, "But a Samaritan . . . came to where he [the man who had fallen among thieves] was; and when he saw him, he had compassion" (Lk. 10:33).[10]

Jesus not only talked about compassion in his parables, but frequently exemplified it in his life. Note his attitude toward the multitudes (Mk. 6:34; 8:2), toward two blind men who cried for mercy (Mt. 20:30), and toward a widow whose only son had died (Lk. 7:13). Most scholars are of the opinion that, in the Synoptic tradition, the word "compassion" is used as a messianic attribute. It characterizes Jesus as the Christ in whom the divine mercy is actively present. H. Köster notes that the term is always used of Jesus' conduct in such a way as to underscore the essential divinity of his acts.[11] As a result of this early Christian usage, compassion becomes so intimately associated with the divine character as to color the meaning, not only of God's mercy, but also of her justice, that attribute we have associated with mercy in this section. Don Quixote assured Sancho that while all God's attributes are equal, surely her mercy is more pleasing to contemplate than her justice. This would be true were the last word on the subject of divine justice that narrow justice with which our discussion began. But it is not. The last word concerns a justice in which there is kindness, a divine justice. Of this divine justice— which we will call "righteousness"—we must now speak.

Before we turn to the subject of the divine righteousness, a special word on God's "goodness" is called for. One of many concepts we have associated with God's mercy, goodness designates, in the Old Testament primarily, Yahweh's readiness to help her people in need, as, for example, in the Exodus. One of the most sung of all the psalms, Psalm 100, celebrates this goodness. It closes with the admonition to enter the Lord's gates with thanksgiving and her courts with praise. Why so?

> Because the Lord our God is good,
>   Her mercy is forever sure;
> Her truth at all times firmly stood,
>   And shall from age to age endure. (Geneva Psalter)

10. For an arresting contemporary version of the parable of the good Samaritan, see Robert McAfee Brown, *Unexpected News* (Philadelphia: Westminster Press, 1984), p. 108.
11. *TDNT,* vol. VII, p. 553.

In the theological tradition of the church, this concept of God's goodness has often been equated with her benevolence. And her benevolence, in turn, has been understood as a broad category that embraces her general love and concern for all creation (common grace). At the same time, following the Old Testament usage, God's goodness has also been understood to include her covenant love for her people. Both in medieval and Protestant Scholasticism, this covenant love *(agape)* is viewed as flowing out of the divine benevolence. This explains why, in the *Westminister Shorter Catechism* definition of God, there is no mention of her love but only her goodness (Q. 4). In our own handling of the materials, we have given the divine love a much more prominent place, making the affirmation God is Love one of four fundamental affirmations concerning God's essential nature. (See above, Unit Three, III, God Is Love, pp. 228ff.)

D. THE DIVINE RIGHTEOUSNESS AND THE CROSS

There is a consensus among theologians that God's mercy is never at the expense of her justice, even when that justice is understood in the strict sense of retribution. Justice is an essential perfection of the divine character. In fact, God's justice is so central in the Old Testament that it marks her relationship not only with Israel, but also with the whole human family. God determines what is just and right not only for Israel, but for all her creatures. And as a just God she binds herself to do what is just and right in relating to them. This is the truth to which the psalmist clung even when he was moved with envy at the prosperity of the wicked. He comes to himself, as a devout Israelite, when he enters God's sanctuary and contemplates their end. Those who are far from the Lord shall surely perish (Ps. 73). Such retribution is essentially right; it is as things ought to be. To justice, then, belongs the place of highest honor; indeed, justice and judgment are the very foundation of God's throne (Ps. 89:14). The same is true of the New Testament view of God. Jesus warns that when the Son of Man comes, he "will repay every one for what has been done" (Mt. 16:27). Paul also speaks of the day when the righteous judgment of God shall be revealed, a day when "she will render to every one according to his works" (Rom. 2:5-6).

But if God is evenhanded in her treatment of sinners, if she is no respecter of persons (Rom. 2:11) but renders to everyone his due, how can she be at the same time a merciful and forgiving God? Justice punishes, it does not forgive.[12] Mercy forgives, to be sure; yet a mercy that forgives at the expense of

---

12. For a sobering comment on unbending justice, see Prosper Merimee's "Mateo Falcone" in his *Mosaique,* translated in various collections of short stories.

justice is compromised; it is a mercy in which there is no truth. This is why God requires of us both to do justice and to love mercy (Mi. 6:8); and she requires both of us because she is herself the God who so does and so loves. But how? How do her justice and her steadfast love meet; how, in the words of the psalmist, do her "righteousness and peace kiss each other" (Ps. 85:10)? Reason can never discover the answer to this question because the answer is not an abstract, rational one.[13] It is rather a historical one, given in the ongoing covenant relationship between God and her people.

This historical answer is anticipated in the Old Testament in that God regards the law, which is the norm of her impartial justice, as essentially fulfilled in acts of love for God and neighbor.[14] But the disclosure of how God's justice is related to her love is finally given only in the event of the cross. Only when we perceive that event Christianly, only when we embrace the interpretation of the death of Christ found in the New Testament, do we perceive how God can be just (δίκαιος) and at the same time justify the sinner. When we understand the meaning of what happened at Calvary, we can understand how Scripture can approve both Solomon's prayer to a God who condemns the guilty "by bringing his conduct upon his own head" (1 Kgs. 8:32), and Paul's affirmation that God—the same God—is the God "who justifies the ungodly" (Rom. 4:5).

Though this is not the place to elaborate a detailed theory of the atonement, yet we cannot ignore the significance of the cross altogether if we would understand the meaning of the divine justice. As the cross of Christ reveals God's power in weakness, as it reveals God's wisdom in foolishness, so also it reveals God's justice in mercy. Hence, especially in Paul, the profound interpreter of the cross, the term δίκαιος ("justice") undergoes a definite modification when used of God. God's justice is her righteousness; it is a justice "seasoned with mercy." That is to say, the "righteousness of God" (δικαιοσύνη τοῦ θεοῦ) is no longer the simple

13. As an example of a rational approach to the question, consider Schleiermacher's definition of the divine justice: "The justice of God is that divine causality through which, in the state of universal sinfulness, there is ordained a connection between evil and actual sin." *The Christian Faith* (Edinburgh: T. & T. Clark, 1928), sec. 84, p. 345. Little wonder that he should treat the *mercy* of God in an appendix, introduced with the affirmation, "To attribute mercy to God is more appropriate to the language of preaching and poetry than to that of dogmatic theology." Ibid., sec. 85, p. 353. The dualism that thus distinguishes the language of theology from that of preaching is a sure sign that theology is in trouble!

14. See Deuteronomy 6:4-5; also John 22:5 and especially Mark 12:30-31 and Matthew 22:37-40 where our Lord affirms that on the two commandments—love of God and love of neighbor—hang all the law (with its demand for justice) and the prophets (with their plea for justice).

equivalent of the forensic justice (δίκη) of the law; it is rather a justice revealed "apart from the law" (χωρὶς νόμου, Rom. 3:21). Not that God simply ignores her law. Since it is her law, were she to ignore it she could not be righteousness, for she would be, as it were, ignoring herself. Yet since it is her law, she is the Lord of the law. Therefore, she has the freedom in her lordship sovereignly to set aside the claims of the law on the sinner by suffering herself the sanctions of the law in the sinner's place.

> Then God beheld my wretched state
> 　　With deep commiseration;
> She thought upon her mercy great,
> 　　And willed my soul's salvation.
> She turned to me a Mother's heart;
> Not small the cost! to heal my smart
> 　　She gave her best and dearest. (Luther)

Hence we find the paradox in Scripture that the righteousness of God is revealed in the forgiveness of the sinner. What, after all, is the end of all righteousness? Is it not that God should come into her right as Lord? And where is her right as Lord over all more clearly revealed than in her forgiving the sinner who has faith in Christ? Here, at Calvary, God sovereignly exercises what may be called her "grace option." In doing so, she comes to her right and so reveals herself to be the righteous God. Therefore, paradoxical as it may sound, the *justitia Dei*, biblically speaking, is supremely revealed in the justification not of the righteous, but of the unrighteous! This justification of the unrighteous, according to Paul—in a passage that has been happily called the "Acropolis of the Gospel" (Rom. 3:21-26)—is through him whom God put forward to be a propitiatory sacrifice (ἱλαστήριον), through faith in his blood. This she did to declare her righteousness on account of the remission of sins that are past, in the forbearance of God, in order to prove her righteousness at the present time, that she might be righteous and the justifier of the one who has faith in Jesus (πρὸς τὴν ἔνδειξιν τῆς δικαιοσύνης αὐτοῦ ἐν τῷ νῦν καιρῷ, εἰς τὸ εἶναι αὐτὸν δίκαιον καὶ δικαιοῦντα τὸν ἐκ πίστεως Ἰησοῦ).

To perceive the divine righteousness in the light of God's grace option at Calvary helps us to relate the "strict" justice of the state, which is God's ordinance (her διάταξις, Rom. 13:2), to the "kind" justice of her kingdom. It was not to illustrate some laissez-faire economic theory of capitalistic justice, but this "kind" justice, this divine righteousness that prevails in the kingdom of heaven, that Jesus told the parable of the laborers in the vineyard (Mt. 20:1-16). We must remember that the parable begins, not with the words "the free enterprise system is like," but with "the kingdom of heaven is like. . . ." The kingdom of heaven is a kingdom in which those who are called to serve (work in the vineyard) in the eleventh hour of life are the beneficiaries of that same kind justice (righteousness) which those enjoy who are called early in the morning of life. At the foot of the cross the ground is level; the first are as the last and the last as the first. This righteousness that prevails in the kingdom of heaven is, in contrast to the kingdoms of this world, as we have noted, anticipated in the Old Testament. The psalmist, for example, declares, "The LORD is just in all her ways" and then goes on to parallel this affirmation with a second, "and kind in all her doings" (Ps. 145:17). Because this righteous God is kind in all her works, she displays her righteousness in forgiving, in helping, in saving her people. She hears the prayer,

> In thee, O LORD, do I seek refuge;
> let me never be put to shame;
> in thy righteousness deliver me! (Ps. 31:1)

While we might have expected the psalmist to say, "In thy mercy deliver me," we perceive, in the light of the cross, no need to amend the text. Furthermore, the word of the psalmist in the Old Testament is confirmed in the apostle's word in the New. It is the assuring word, so often heard in Christian worship—"If we confess our sins, [God] is faithful and just [i.e., righteous, δίχαιος], and will forgive our sins and cleanse us from all unrighteousness [ἀδιχία, 1 Jn. 1:9]." When we as Christians speak of God's justice, we speak of a justice that forgives! But it is not a justice that forgives cheaply; it is rather a justice revealed in the death of Christ. We have called it God's "righteousness," and, we might note, he whose death reveals this righteousness is appropriately called the "Holy and Righteous One" (Acts 3:14).

Finally, this divine righteousness that does not forgive cheaply also does not forgive indiscriminately. While those who believe in this Righteous One are not condemned, those "who do not believe are condemned already, because they do not believe in the name of the only Son of God" (Jn. 3:18). Such condemnation, of course, stands only so long as one remains willfully outside the circle of faith. But though this condemnation is reversed through faith in Christ, such a statement reminds us that God is not only a Savior but a Judge, the Ritschlians to the contrary notwithstanding. While it is true that at Calvary we are saved not from the hand of God but by the hand of God, as Barth reminds us, we must also remember that "it is a fearful thing to fall into the hands of the living God" (Heb. 10:31). The cross reveals not only the kindness in God's justice but also the severity in her kindness. The grace revealed in the cross is not a cheap grace, a blanket amnesty for sinners. God's patience never turns into procrastination, even as her mercy never impairs her majesty. The proper use of her forbearance, therefore, is to repent (Rom. 2:4), to "seek the LORD while she may be found, call upon her while she is near" (Is. 55:6). And she has come near to us in Jesus. Jesus is our city of refuge (Nm. 35:6), our "strong tower" (Ps. 61:3), for it is through faith in his name that we have salvation.

In dogmatics, the concerns of liberation theology are reflected primarily in the loci of anthropology and soteriology. However, such concerns impinge, in one way or another, on one's doctrine of God. Our treatment of the divine attributes of justice and mercy should make this obvious. One frequently hears the argument that the God revealed in Christ is concerned with those who are spiritually lost, oppressed, and disinherited, and that we should not "politicize" this biblical message by applying it to social and economic issues that pertain to the kingdoms of this world. It is true beyond all doubt that the ultimate reference of the biblical message is spiritual and otherworldly. But such an argument becomes a broken reed when used to avoid the issues of social justice. It is specious to argue, for example, that black theology is primarily race-oriented, feminist theology sex oriented, and South American liberation theology class-oriented, whereas true biblical and evangelical theology is Christ-oriented. The Christ with whom evangelical theology is concerned is the Logos who in the beginning was with God and was God (Jn. 1:1), the God in whose image all races are created (Gn. 1:26), the Christ in whom there is no male and female (Gal. 3:28), the One anointed with the Spirit to proclaim release to the captives and to set at liberty those who are oppressed (Lk. 4:18). Hence, if we consider ourselves to be citizens of the kingdom of God, the God who is just and merciful, we must be concerned with the injustice manifested in the kingdoms of this sinful world and do whatever we can to further justice and mercy in this world, even as we pray "Thy kingdom come, thy will be done."

V. God's Faithfulness and Suffering

A. INTRODUCTION: CONCERNING THE DIVINE IMMUTABILITY / IMPASSIBILITY[1]

Both the Ideas (Forms) of Plato and the Prime Mover of Aristotle are immutable in the sense of an eternally fixed and unchanging Being. Virtually all of the early Fathers of the church came to a similar conclusion concerning the being of God, convinced as they were that since she is not bound by time, she is not subject to change. Though they were really not concerned with the philosophic Absolute but with the true and living God, yet in their theologizing they tended to think of God as the "Ever Fixed Eternity" (Augustine). As a result, immutability, in the sense of an existence that is the opposite of all movement and change, became a primary attribute of God, a kind of undisputed axiom underlying the understanding of all the other attributes. The Fathers were fond of citing such texts as Numbers 23:19, "God is not a human being, that she should lie, or a mortal, that she should change her mind" (NRSV). They reminded their opponents that God had declared, "I the LORD do not change" (Mal. 3:6); and that God is the source of light "with whom there is no variation or shadow due to change" (Jas. 1:17). But then there were other texts that gave them difficulty, texts that say that God does change. She repents (Gn. 6:6; Jn. 3:10); she is a God who can affirm, "So will I satisfy my fury on you. . . , [then] I will

---

1. Immutability (the quality of being incapable of change or alteration) and impassibility (the quality of being incapable of feeling or suffering) have, as divine attributes, been closely associated by theologians. This is because it is assumed that God cannot change and, at the same time, that feeling, emotion, and suffering involve change. Hence the conclusion that God's immutability entails his impassibility. Due to this close association we have separated them, in the above heading, with the diagonal rather than the conjunctive.

be calm, and will no more be angry" (Ez. 16:42). In other words, when it comes to the divine unchangeableness, there are texts, and then there are texts.[2]

As a result, though the Fathers assumed the divine immutability as unquestioned, they ended up discussing it at great lengths, not only because of the many texts that spoke of change in God, but because at a deeper level the God of whom they predicated immutability is anything but an unmoved Mover or the eternal Form of the visible world. She is rather the living God who acts in history—indeed, who enters into and becomes a part of our history as Immanuel, God with us.

Since the Incarnation is at the heart of the Christian faith and since the Fathers understood the Incarnation to entail the union of the divine with the human in the one person *(unio hypostatica)* of the Mediator, they were hard put to answer the Arian contention that their understanding of the Incarnation contradicted their understanding of the divine immutability. They could (and did) argue, to be sure, that the Incarnation was the assumption of the human by the divine, not the changing into the human of the divine; thus the sufferings of the God who became a man, like the nature that he assumed, concerned his humanity, not his divinity. And in all of this they were not missing the mark altogether. They were surely right in their conviction that one cannot infer that all that is true of God as incarnate is true of God per se. In Jesus' case, no doubt his "seeing" involved physiological changes such as photons impacting the retina of his eyes, which set off chemical reactions in the rods and cones, which in turn triggered electrical impulses that traveled along the nerve cells to his brain. But it does not follow that all this is true of God as such when she "looks down from heaven . . . to see if there are any that are wise" (Ps. 53:2). Since God does not have bodily parts, her "seeing" the city and the tower that humankind had built (Gn. 11:5), her beholding the evil and the good that is in every place (Prv. 15:3), does not involve chemical reactions and electrical impulses of some celestial sort. So also her being angry (Ps. 79:5), her showing pity (Ps. 103:13), and her expression of ardent love (Jer. 31:3) do not involve glandular secretions, a literal flushing of the face and beads of perspiration. God's love is quite apart from any "cold sweat in propinquity." Likewise, though we may grieve the Spirit (Eph. 4:30), we cannot measure the salt content of her tears.

---

2. The Hebrew root (נחם), "to be sorry," "to be moved to pity" for others, or "to rue," "to repent of" what one has done, is used some thirty-five times of God in the Old Testament. Twenty-eight instances are positive (God may or does show pity and repent), while seven are negative (God does not or cannot repent).

If this were all that is meant when the theologians speak of the divine immutability/impassibility, when the creeds say that God is "without bodily parts or passions, immutable,"[3] there could be little debate. But matters are not that simple. Not just the human, physiological basis of feelings and emotions, but all feelings and emotions as such have been denied to God as unworthy of her who is immutable. Such a view raises the basic question: Is there more reason to deny emotion to God because she is without glandular secretions than there is to deny thought to her because she is without brain waves? If God is a God who "thinks" and "purposes" as the living God, the God who is Spirit, Self, Subject, the "I AM," why should she not also be the God who is "angry," the God whose "anger" is "appeased," the God who "repents," who "grieves" and "rejoices?"

EXCURSUS: A HISTORICAL NOTE

As is the case in many difficult matters of theology, a knowledge of how the church in other times sought to resolve the issues may prove helpful in this instance. (In the ensuing historical survey we are primarily relying on the researches of J. K. Mozley, *The Impassibility of God,* Cambridge: The University Press, 1924.). So far as the divine impassibility is concerned, virtually all of the Fathers recognized that in the Incarnation, to use the words of Irenaeus, not only was the invisible made visible and the incomprehensible comprehensible, but also the impassible was made passible (*Adversus Haereses,* III, 17, 6). Yet not all the Fathers were consistent in their meaning, and their efforts to illumine these antinomies led to many devices. While they did not make shipwreck of the faith, many of them sailed perilously close to the rocks of Docetism.

Clement of Alexandria (*Stromateis,* VII, 3), for example, affirms that Scripture, when it speaks of God's anger and threatenings, has no intention of ascribing affections to God, for she is without passion and desire. This is true even of God incarnate. Even the most mundane, bodily passions and desires were unknown to our Lord. Jesus never felt the pangs of hunger. He "took food only to prevent those who were with him from falling into docetic error which came in at a later date" (ibid., VI, 9).

This thought that the incarnate Son even in his humanity was impassible is found in the early Western church as well. Hilary of Poitiers says that when Jesus was struck with blows, he felt the force of suffering, yet without pain. He had a body that could suffer, but not a nature that could feel pain. Hilary goes on to point out that the gospels never say that our Lord ate or drank or wept when he was hungry or thirsty or sorrowful. From this he concludes that he did these things to confirm the reality of his body, out of concession to our habits rather than his own necessity (*De Trinitate,* X, 23, 24). Suffering undertaken without pain, however, is not the suffering that has drawn men

---

3. *Westminster Confession,* chap. II, sec. 1.

and women to the cross of Christ. Rather, in our suffering we "take óur hope and encouragement in God only," because we perceive that

> What you, my Lord, have suffered
> Was all for sinners' gain:
> Mine, mine was the transgression,
> But yours the deadly pain.
> Lo, here I fall, my Savior!
> 'Tis I deserve your place;
> Look on me with your favor,
> Vouchsafe to me your grace. (Bernard of Clairvaux)

Standing at the beginning of the great scholastic period of theological reflection, Anselm both asked and answered a question that came to mark the entire theology of the Middle Ages in this regard. "How [O God] are you compassionate and at the same time passionless?" He answers that God is compassionate in terms of our experience but not in terms of her own experience.

> For when you behold us in our wretchedness, we experience the effect of compassion, but you do not experience the feeling. Therefore you are both compassionate, because you save the wretched . . . and not compassionate, because you are afflicted by no sympathy for wretchedness. (*Proslogium,* chap. VIII, tr. S. N. Dean, LaSalle: Open Court, 1962, pp. 13f.)

While such scholastic subtleties may leave us quite unmoved, it must be remembered that the early theologians, who set the stage for these later refinements, were reacting to the monstrous anthropopathisms of pagan mythology. The gross passions ascribed to the Olympians were viewed, and with reason, as corrupting the very essence of those divinities who were the victims of them. (See Augustine, *The City of God,* VII, 26.) Hence, in their perception it would compromise the blessedness and perfection of the true God were one to allow even the possibility of such ungodlike frailty to be ascribed to her.

Yet the Bible speaks plainly of God's experience of pity, compassion, grief, anger, and the like. The effort to be faithful to Scripture in this regard, while affirming that God transcends all those passions that have led both gods and humans astray, explains why some of the Fathers tried to escape the treacherous shoals of *apatheia* (the view that God is without passion) by distinguishing "feelings," which were good, from "passions," which were evil. The former express our nature, the latter our corruption and depravity. Such a distinction goes back at least to Tertullian, who used it in his conflict with Marcion. There are "divine feelings" that the Marcionites deny to God, such as gentleness and especially goodness, "the very womb of them all," which must be attributed to the Deity (*Adversus Marcionem,* II, 16).

Even Tertullian, however, worked with the assumption that God is ultimately impassible. Hence, in the Incarnation the One who sent the Son could not have suffered with him, for to suffer with another is to be passible. "She does not suffer, but gives the Son the power to suffer" (*Adversus Praxeam,* 29). And the same is true of the Spirit. Because of the assistance she renders the Son in his suffering, the Spirit may be said to suffer in the Son. Of course the suffering of the Son himself cannot be in his divine nature but only in his humanity, for the divine nature is beyond affliction. Gregory of

Nyssa argued that the Son sustained all his bodily passions, not as we who are human, but by the power of his will (*Adversus Eunomium*, IV, 1). But this notion of Gregory and others—that Christ suffers as we do, yet only in that he wills to suffer—leaves us with this question, which none of the Fathers could answer satisfactorily: How could our Savior will to suffer, as human, when suffering is contrary to his nature as divine?

For all the problems with the traditional view that the Reformers inherited, their doctrine reflects no basic change in the understanding of the divine immutability and impassibility. Luther, indeed, because of his stress on the communication of the divine and human attributes (*communicatio idiomatum*) in the person of Christ, believed that we may say that "the right, true God" suffered and died. Yet he also affirmed that suffering and death are alien to the divine nature per se and cannot be attributed directly to it. Calvin also, for all his differences with Luther over the interpretation of the *communicatio,* assures us that the many statements of Scripture that speak of God as sorrowing or rejoicing are really accommodations made by the Spirit to our capacity of understanding. In a similar vein the Lutheran divine Johann Gerhard, when speaking of those Scriptures which ascribe to God the feelings of regret, happiness, grief, anger, and the like, approves the standard scholastic statement, "Affections in God describe effects in us" (*Loci Theologici,* 2, chap. 8, sec. 5).

We may, then, sum up the historical situation by saying, first of all, that traditionally the church has affirmed the divine immutability/ impassibility almost without dissent. Yet the teaching that the Son became a man, and suffered even unto death for our salvation, is so central to Scripture and the Christian faith, that all docetic teaching has also been condemned almost without dissent. Second, however one may understand the general teaching of Scripture about God's "pity," "sorrow," "anger," "joy," and the like, the specific teaching that the Son suffered death did not mean, according to the Fathers, that in his essential deity he experienced corruption, diminution, change, or distinction. (In keeping with this view, the statements in Acts 2:27 and 31—"you will not let your Holy One experience corruption"; "nor did his flesh experience corruption"—were often understood literally of Jesus' body even in the tomb!) Finally, it must be noted that since the turn of the century the traditional doctrine has come under increasing attack. Even those who have had nothing in common with Process thought have complained of the "Passionless Potentate" of the theologians and sought to frame a doctrine of the "suffering God" to take the place of the "Infinite Iceberg of Metaphysics" set forth in traditional dogmatics. (Orthodoxy, we might observe, immobilizes Satan in ice, not God. See Dante, *The Divine Comedy,* I: Hell, Canto xxxiv.)

This revolt against the tradition has by no means been unanimous. Indeed, few have found comfort in the doctrine of a changing God. However, if God is subject to change, as the creature is subject to change, then she is also subject to death, and so we are no better off.

> Change and decay in all around I see;
> O thou who changest not, abide with me

is a prayer that the Christian will not lightly abandon. On the other hand, if the divine immutability, pressed to extremes, turns God into a celestial sphinx, then God might as well be dead. Barth, in fact, has admitted that "if the pure immobile is God, then death is *God*" (*K.D.,* II/1, p. 555; cf. *C.D.,* II/1, sec. 31.2). What we shall attempt, then, is a restatement of the doctrine of the *immutabilitas Dei* that will both preserve the transcendence of the Holy One and at the same time reckon with the truth that this Holy One is the God who acts in history, the God who has, in fact, entered into our history in an act of sacrificial love.

B. A RESTATEMENT OF THE DOCTRINE OF IMMUTABILITY

1. INTRODUCTION

In our exposition of the doctrine of the divine nature, we began with the affirmation that God is personal being.[4] At that time we argued that any statement about the nature of God must do full justice to the truth that God reveals herself in Scripture as the living God, the "I AM WHO I AM." This God, we further argued, is the transcendent One.[5] Though she is the living God, she does not live her life as we who are carried down the stream of time. This latter truth is equally essential to an adequate view of the divine nature. We recall these affirmations because they bear on the doctrine of the divine immutability now before us, and lead us to say certain things about that doctrine at the outset of our discussion.

First of all, the concept of the divine immutability should not be stated in terms of the truths of philosophy (important as they may be), for such universal truths cannot "react" to what happens in time, much less "enter into time." Nor should we think of the divine immutability in terms of the truths of science, as though God's immutability were all one with the reliability of the fundamental mechanisms of nature. While science is rightly concerned with the discovery and formulation of the "laws of nature," the theologian is concerned with the faithfulness of the living God. To be sure, the faithfulness of God is reflected— for the eye of faith—in the impersonal regularities of nature.

> Summer and winter, and springtime and harvest,
>   Sun, moon, and stars in their courses above,
> Join with all nature in manifold witness,
>   To your great faithfulness, mercy, and love. (Chisholm)

Yet there is a dimensional difference between the impersonal regularities of natural law and the faithfulness of a personal God. Nature is not the

4. See above, Unit Three, I, God Is Personal Being, pp. 174ff.
5. See above, Unit Three, II, God Is the Holy One, pp. 189ff.

measure of God; rather, God is the sustainer of nature—in other words, not the celestial equivalent of a unified field theory, but the God who is ever faithful is the God revealed in Scripture, the God with whom the theologians have to do. This is why we shall opt for such terms as "unchangeableness" (to use the negative), "steadfastness," "constancy," or "faithfulness" (to use the positive) as best reflecting the biblical truth expressed in the classic doctrine of the divine immutability. In any case, were one to prefer the traditional affirmation—God is immutable—one must ever remember that when one so speaks, God is the subject of the sentence and immutability the predicate, not vice versa. To say that the Immutable is God is to come into hopeless conflict with the data of revelation. Why? Because the God of Scripture not only acts; this God also reacts to the creature's act.

> God is concerned with the act of the human agent; she conducts herself accordingly. There is a *personal correspondence;* God's conduct is altered in accordance with that of humankind. Precisely therein is she the living God in contrast to the Deity of abstract thought.[6]

This "personal correspondence," this entering into creaturely events, is just as much a part of revelation as the affirmation that God transcends all creaturely events as sovereign Lord over history. All that the doctrine of immutability, therefore, should say is that God remains who she is in all her changing relationships with her creatures. She is the God who is without alteration, diminution, deviation, or discontinuity; in the words of Scripture, she is without "variation or shadow due to change" (Jas. 1:17). She does not repent as the creature who makes a wrong choice repents, for she is not a creature who makes wrong choices and therefore needs to repent (Nm. 23:19). Nevertheless, as the "living" God she is the God of will, movement, decision, action. While never free to be other than herself, she is ever free to respond to the human situation in a way in which she is true to herself.

This divine constancy—"you are the same, and your years have no end"—may seem, indeed, to contradict the affirmation, I will repent of the evil that I thought to do unto them (Ex. 32:14). But it is not necessarily so. It is not as though Scripture reveals a God with two faces—one sphinx-like and unmoved, the other fickle and changing. It is rather that she is of such a nature—the God of holy love, the God whose gifts and calling are without repentance (Rom. 11:29)—that she must show herself as the repenting God when the creature shows himself as the penitent sinner

---

6. E. Brunner, *Dogmatik* (Zurich: Zwingli-Verlag, 1960), I, pp. 274-75. Italics added.

(Jon. 3:5-10). Yet she cannot repent of being who she is. Hence, in all her varied relationships with humankind, she remains the God who is who she is, the great "I AM." Hers is not the continuity of a static Absolute but a continuity in life, a life of holiness and love. Therefore, God rejoices and mourns, laughs and complains, is well pleased with one and moved to anger toward another. And she is all this and does all this in conformity with herself as the living God. In the words of the psalmist, she shows herself merciful with the merciful, upright with the upright, pure with the pure, and froward with the froward (Ps. 18:25-26).[7]

As we turn to our task of restating the doctrine of the divine immutability, we pause to note that back in 1856 Dorner published his essay "Correct Statement of the Dogmatic Concept of God's Immutability" (*Gesammelte Schriften,* Berlin, 1883, pp. 188-377). Dorner rejects neither the doctrine of the divine immutability nor its correlate, the divine transcendence. But he insists that these must be related to what he calls the divine "livingness" *(Lebhaftigkeit).* The questions raised by the traditional statement of the doctrine must be resolved not in a theoretical, but in an historical way because the God whom Christians worship is incarnate in the historical Jesus. Jesus Christ is the union of the "immutability" and the "livingness" that we seek in our understanding of God. He is the Jesus Christ who is "the same yesterday and today and forever" (Heb. 13:8), and at the same time the Jesus Christ who can say, "I am the first and the last, and the living one" (Rv. 1:17-18). In Christ, therefore, is disclosed the way to unfetter God so as to affirm her livingness without prejudicing her true immutability and thus threatening her divine transcendence. But to accomplish this, we must walk a fine line between the metaphysical view of the divine nature, which has dominated the tradition, and the ethical view revealed in the Incarnation.

The ethical conception of the divine nature—God is holy love—leaves room for "livingness," "movement," even "alteration" in God, if only we preserve her self-identity as an ethical Subject, which is the true meaning of the divine immutability. Of course, God's response to the human situation is always the same because it is always commensurate with her nature. She is the Holy One who cannot abide evil and at the same time the Loving One who is ever ready for reconciliation. But for this very reason one is able to postulate change not only in the human situation, but also in God herself.

This view, which Dorner calls "ethical identity" or "biblical realism," explains why God in her self-identity does not always behave in the same way in relating to the creature. She may repent that she has made humankind and resolve to destroy them in a flood (Gn. 6:6ff.); she may determine to judge idolatrous Israel in her wrath and renounce this intent at Moses' intercession (Ex. 32:7-14); again, she may spare the Ninevites who repented at the preaching of Jonah (Jon. 3:9-10; 4:2), etc. But it is

---

7. Here we must reject the translation (RSV) of this text, "With the crooked thou dost show thyself perverse." The root פָּתַל means "twisted." Brown, Driver, and Briggs translate: "With the twisted thou dost deal tortuously" (תִּתְפַּתָּל). Were Yahweh to show herself "perverse," she would deny herself; she would reveal herself to be other than she is.

especially in the coming of Christ that the divine immutability is indissolubly united with her livingness in a way that has far-reaching implications for our doctrine of God. In the Jesus event, not only is the relation of the world to God changed, but also God's relation to the world. Christ's appearance, though a part of God's eternal purpose, is a new activity in God, a new deed of God. What was once a potency of decree is now an actuality of history. God is reconciled to the sinner through the death of her Son.

Dorner concludes with a brief allusion to the Holy Spirit, whose coming and presence exemplify the divine immutability in a manner similar to that of the coming of the Son. Christian participation in the work of the Spirit is not through moral resolution, self-reproduction, contagion, or the act of the will of the community as a whole. Rather, it is by a new act of God who sends her Spirit into our hearts (Gal. 4:6) as she sent her Son into our history. For this reason, the new birth of the individual is described in Scripture (Jn. 3:5) as an act of the Spirit; that is, as an act of God in our individual inner experience and time (Rom. 5:5). Because of this act of the Spirit, worship is seen to be not only an act of the creature but an actual ingredient in the historical life of God. Worship, indeed, supposes the divine transcendence and immutability of the One who is worshipped; otherwise there would be no worship. But neither would there be worship if it were only our devotion to God informed by that reverence which her transcendence inspires. There must also be the actual, temporal ingredient of God's devotion to the worshipping community, in which she imparts herself, as it were, to the community; and this she has done by uniting herself in the Spirit with that community. (See the apostle Paul's description of the experience of unbelievers when they enter a Christian assembly. Falling on their faces they declare that "God is really among you" [1 Cor. 14:25].)

Finally, it is this act of God reciprocating the act of the worshipper that is essential to the life of prayer. To affirm that God hears and answers prayer is to affirm an instance of what Dorner calls "biblical realism." Prayer, as communion with God, presupposes a reciprocal relationship between the one who prays and the living God who answers prayer (Lk. 18:1-8). Prayer, to be sure, is submission to God's will, but it is not mere submission, much less resignation to that which is written in the stars. Rather, in prayer God in her sovereign majesty yields to the entreaty of her children. Not that God hands over the reins of government to her people. But she is the God who shares with her friends the knowledge of what she intends to do (Gn. 18:17ff.), and deals with them in a historico-temporal way as the instruments of her purpose and counsel. Thus Dorner would hold the divine immutability in tandem with the divine mobility, as he sees this divine mobility taught in Scripture. In other words, the divine immutability is not an idealized concept with which we come to Scripture to critique what it says about God, but rather a concept whose meaning is learned from Scripture as we listen to what it says about God.

2. SALVATION, AN ACT OF SUFFERING LOVE

a. Old Testament Anticipation

God's act of salvation presupposes, of course, her act of creation. As for creation and the doctrine of the divine immutability, theologians following

Augustine have been exercised to show that in becoming Creator God does not become other than she is from eternity. Though dependent on her, creation is distinct from her and does not in any way alter her essential being. This is so because in her own self there is distinction and diversity (Trinity) prior to the distinction and diversity manifest in the created order; in her own self there is life and movement prior to the life and movement manifest in the world; in her own self there is wisdom and power prior to the wisdom and power manifest in creating the world. Creation, then, is God's free act in which she reveals herself. But just because she reveals herself as who she is, she remains who she is, was, and is to be, "the one eternal God/Ere ought that now appears."

When one moves from the doctrine of creation to salvation, however, matters become more difficult. In creation God calls the world of time and space into being, but in response to the sin of the creature (according to Christian teaching) she actually enters this world, becoming a member of the human family with all its mutability and passibility.

The problem posed by the Incarnation for one's doctrine of God is anticipated in the Old Testament, which is no surprise, since God's saving act in Jesus Christ is the fulfillment of the covenant first made with Israel.[8] On the one hand, God simply declares that she will multiply the seed of Abraham and Sarah, making them a blessing to all the earth. As the unchanging God, this is her resolute purpose, which no contingencies can frustrate. Such a view of the covenant—reflecting the paradigm of a "royal grant"—obviously stresses the divine constancy; the emphasis is on God's transcendent, unchanging character. On the other hand, the covenant as promulgated at Sinai, the most memorable instance of covenant-making in the Old Testament, gives prominence to the necessity for Israel's obedience and threatens sanctions against all disobedience—reflecting the paradigm of a "suzerainty treaty." God requires obedience of her people as a lord of a vassal. How do these two paradigms, the one unconditional, the other conditional, relate to each other?

Though we are dealing with two distinct paradigms of the covenant, it does not follow that we are dealing with two covenants. The covenant made with Abraham and Sarah implies an obedient response on their part—a tacit conditionality. (They are to leave Ur and go to a land they have never seen.) By the same token, the covenant made at Sinai is really a remembering of the

---

8. In the following summary, I am indebted to the careful work of Dennis Johnson in his unpublished doctoral thesis, *Immutability and Incarnation* (Fuller Theological Seminary, 1983), chap. 5. For sources in Mendenhall, Von Rad, Eichrodt, et al., the interested reader should consult the above-mentioned thesis.

Abrahamic covenant (Ex. 2:24). It therefore rests upon God's unswerving love and resolute purpose—a tacit unconditionality. We are reinforced in this conclusion that the covenant is essentially one by the way in which Paul reasoned with the Galatians early in the Christian era. It was, no doubt, the pronounced emphasis on obedience—"keeping the law"—in the Sinaitic form of the covenant that led the Judaizers to the position they took in Galatia. Paul, it will be recalled, sought to refute this position by affirming the essential unity of the covenant made with Abraham and Sarah, on the one hand, and their descendants at Sinai, on the other: ". . . the law, which came 430 years afterward, does not annul a covenant previously ratified by God, so as to make the promise void" (Gal. 3:17).

But how are these two aspects of the covenant—the conditional and the unconditional—to be brought together? Well, in the Old Testament they never really are. As Israel's history unfolds, catastrophe overtakes Israel as a disobedient and covenant-breaking people. Through their unfaithfulness they forfeit their land, king, temple, priesthood, and, especially in the northern kingdom, their very identity as God's people. Though God may once have known and acknowledged them as her own, she does so no more. Their covenant is abrogated because they have failed to keep it; they have not met the condition of obedience.

On the other hand, a faithful remnant never abandons hope. In spite of the loss of the blessing of the covenant, they remain convinced that the bond of the covenant must somehow transcend Israel's unfaithfulness. But how? Here the prophets, and the faithful remnant who listened to them, "take their hope and encouragement in God only." Though they cannot say how it will be accomplished, yet because they are persuaded that the God of the covenant is the unchanging God, they likewise believe her covenant promise inviolable. The Lord will not, indeed cannot, break the oath she swore to their forebears. Hence the present reversals suffered by the covenant community are temporary, for the Lord will not hide herself forever (Ps. 89). Though Israel by her sin has proven unworthy of those promises, the Lord's steadfast love will go beyond the faithfulness of any earthly suzerain in keeping her covenant engagement.

For this reason, her love merges in the prophets with her mercy. (See Hos. 2:19.) In place of the broken covenant, the Lord will make another covenant with Israel that cannot be broken. When in her mercy this covenant is fulfilled, the time of Israel's judgment will seem as but a moment beside the everlasting compassion God will show toward her people (Is. 54:7ff.). Intimations of this eschatological resolution are contained even in the Old Testament itself. In the vision of the latter prophets we learn that the condition of the covenant — obedience — will not be simply waived. Rather, in making a new, everlasting covenant, the Lord will renew the hearts of the covenantees so that the condition of obedience will be willingly met by all. "A new heart I will give you, and a new spirit I will put within you; I will take out of your flesh the heart of stone and give you a heart of flesh. And I will put my spirit within you, and cause you to walk in my statutes and be careful to observe my ordinances" (Ez. 36:26-27). Jeremiah speaks of this covenant as a new covenant in which the law is no longer written outwardly on stony tables as at Sinai, but inwardly on the fleshly tables of the heart (Jer. 31:31-32).

Along with this promise of the inner renewal of the covenantees by the Spirit, Isaiah speaks of the Servant of the Lord on whom the Spirit will rest in a unique way (Is. 42ff.). This Servant is himself the Covenant of the Lord with her people and the light that will lighten the nations as well (Is. 42:6; 49:6). In fact, he will so identify with God's people in their transgressions as to undergo the covenant curse for them ("he was cut off out of the land of the living, stricken for the transgression of my people," Is. 53:8). Here we have the clearest intimation found in the Old Testament of how the Lord will both satisfy the sanctions and secure the blessings of the covenant. As for the sanctions, her Servant will take upon himself the consequences of the covenantees' sins; as for the blessings that she has promised with an oath, these she will secure by the renewing work of her Spirit.

So we see how, in the prophetic vision, God will show herself to be the unchanging God whose gifts and calling are irrevocable (Rom. 11:29). At the same time, we also see how her immutability is not that of an unmoved Absolute, but of the God who acts (and reacts) in history. Hence the answer to the question of how we should understand God's immutability is not a theoretical but a historical one.[9] Such a historical answer is compatible with the fundamental truth that God is the personal, living God who acts in and through history to reveal and fulfill her purpose. To see how this is so brings us directly to the eschatological fulfillment of the vision of the prophets in the Incarnation and in Pentecost. Because of their unique bearing on the subject of the divine immutability, we shall at this juncture give our attention particularly to Christ's passion and death. For it is not only in Christ, the seed of Abraham and Sarah par excellence (Gal. 3:16), but particularly in his cross, that the suzerain's promise and the servant's obedience meet in a true fulfillment of the eternal purpose of an unchanging God.

9. See Dorner's remarks above, pp. 403-04.

b. New Testament Fulfillment

When one makes the Incarnation the primary paradigm for understanding what God is like, obviously the doctrine that God is immutable must be understood concretely and historically; it cannot be deduced from the idea of the divine as such. Specifically, one must reckon with the life, death, and resurrection of Jesus of Nazareth, for it is in him that God is revealed in person. The story of Jesus' life is recorded and interpreted in the gospels. It tells us of one who, as the Word, was in the beginning with God and was God (Jn. 1:1-2). At the same time it tells us that this one who was the Word became flesh and dwelt among us (Jn. 1:14). While dwelling among us, he "rejoiced" (Lk. 10:21), "wept" (Lk. 19:41), and was moved with "indignation" (Jn. 2:17) and deep "compassion" (Mk. 6:34). That God is immutably this God, revealed in Jesus Christ and none other, is a thesis that dominates the entire New Testament.

The paradoxical truths such a thesis holds in tandem are most clearly focused in Hebrews. The author of Hebrews is concerned with one who bears the very stamp of the divine nature; one who upholds the universe with his power; one who, in contrast to heaven and earth, will never change (Heb. 1:1-12; 13:8). Yet in the days of his flesh this unchanging one "offered up prayers and supplications, with loud cries and tears" and so was "made perfect" by learning obedience through the things he suffered (Heb. 5:7-10). The author of Hebrews makes no effort to reduce this paradox, no effort to explain how one who transcends the change that marks the created order could at the same time so become a part of that order as to learn through suffering. The author's concern is not theoretical but practical. In Jesus Christ we have one whose priesthood is permanent, since it does not rest on human descent but on the power of an indestructible life. Yet here is a priest who is capable of sympathy and compassion because he was made like us in every respect, apart from sin (Heb. 2:17-18; 4:15; 5:2).

Though Scripture emphasizes the practical, theologians have naturally probed the more theoretical implications of revelation at this point. Unfortunately, in doing so, they have too often simply assumed from the start that in her essential being God is incapable of suffering.[10] Hence they have divided the human from the divine in the person of the Redeemer, limiting his suffering to his humanity. Fortunately, in its worship and devotion the

---

10. Here again we are confronted with the doctrine of apatheia. William Temple complained that Aristotle's "apathetic God" is so enthroned in the human mind that no idol has been found harder to destroy." *Christus Veritas,* p. 260, as noted by John K. Mozley, *The Impassibility of God* (Cambridge, Eng.: University Press, 1926), p. 163. So also Moltmann, *The Trinity and the Kingdom* (New York: Harper & Row, 1981), p. 22.

church has never felt the hesitancy of the theologians nor held that, being God, the Son knows our suffering in his human nature only. Rather, as a personal self he suffered as do we who are personal selves. No subject more dominates the song of the church than the labor, toil, pain, sorrow, agony, and despair suffered by him who is our Savior.

> For me, kind Jesus, was your Incarnation,
> Your mortal sorrow, and your life's oblation;
> Your death of anguish and your bitter passion,
> For my salvation. (Heermann)

> See, from his head, his hands, his feet,
> Sorrow and love flow mingled down;
> Did e'er such love and sorrow meet,
> Or thorns compose so rich a crown? (Watts)

Because they have believed that he suffered thus for them, the people of God have also believed that

> Evermore for human failure
>   By his passion we can plead;
> God has borne all mortal anguish,
>   Surely she will know our need. (Simpson)

And if God has borne our mortal anguish as the Son, then the One who sent him and the Spirit who was sent by him have also suffered in his anguish, for the three are one God. True, God is master of the grief and pain that is the price of loving the sinner, as we see when the suffering of Calvary is turned into the triumph of Easter. Yet at Calvary God is revealed as the suffering Lover who is moved (affected) with compassion, even as at Easter God is revealed as the master of suffering, the transcendent, unchanging God who triumphs over death as the Lord of life.

3. *THEOLOGIA CRUCIS:* A COMMENT

When speaking of the divine love for Israel, we noted that more than any before him, Hosea realized what that love had cost the Lord in suffering and anguish.[11] Though her fierce anger was kindled against her unfaithful people, her heart recoiled at the thought of giving them up forever and her compassion grew warm and tender (Hos. 11:1-8). This inner divine

---

11. See above, Unit Three, III, A, Introduction, pp. 228-29.

struggle, this wrestling with herself, was not inimical of her unchanging character; indeed, it rather confirmed it. It was just because she was God, the Holy One in their midst, that she did not destroy them (Hos. 11:9). Yet, this godlike resolve is costly; it reveals an agonizing Deity. And as holy history unfolds, it becomes clear that this divine agonizing entails suffering beyond anything that even the prophet Hosea could have imagined. It is the beginning of the *via dolorosa* that leads ultimately to Calvary.

The meaning of the cross has traditionally been discussed as part of the doctrine of Christ and salvation, and naturally so. It was Christ Jesus who, though he was equal with God still humbled himself, took the form of a servant, and, for our salvation, became obedient unto death, even the death of the cross (Phil. 2:5-8). Yet in a deeper sense, since the act of the atonement is God's act, the subject in the event, which took place on Calvary's cross, is just God. In other words, the cross must be understood not only in terms of the person and work of Christ but in terms of the God who is revealed in Christ, namely, the God who is a Trinity-in-Unity. While it is essential to view what happened at Calvary in terms of the Son who became incarnate, it is also essential to understand what happened there in terms of all the members of the Godhead. The cross is not simply the suffering and death of the divine Son who assumed our humanity; it is the suffering of God herself in the Son. God is revealed at Calvary not only as the Son who obeys, but also as the Father who is obeyed and the Spirit through whom this obedience is accomplished. Our consciences are purified, as the writer to the Hebrews reminds us, by "the blood of Christ, who through the eternal Spirit offered himself without blemish to God" (Heb. 9:14).[12]

In his provocative study *Der Gegreuzigte Gott (The Crucified God)*, Moltmann argues that the traditional understanding of the cross, for all its

---

12. The assumption that the event of the cross should be interpreted solely in terms of the second person, in distinction to the other members of the Godhead, explains why many exegetes have understood the phrase "through the eternal Spirit" (διὰ πνεύματος αἰωνίου) in Hebrews 9:14 to refer to Christ's spiritual nature as the eternal Son, rather than to the Holy Spirit. Given such a view, the text means that, in contrast to the sacrificial animals in the Old Testament who had no will, no πνεῦμα that could make their sacrifice their own act, Christ through his eternal divine nature (his πνεῦμα) acquiesced in the purpose of the One who sent him and offered himself freely. Thus his own spirit as a divine person is the agent in his sacrifice, acting through and penetrating his humanity that was sacrificed. Given the trinitarian view, for which we are here opting, the phrase "through the eternal Spirit" refers rather to the Holy Spirit by whom Jesus was conceived (Lk. 1:35), by whom he was anointed at his baptism (Lk. 3:22; 4:1), and through whose power he did his mighty works (Mt. 12:28; Mk. 3:28-30) and accomplished at last the supreme work of his atoning death. In other words, he offered up himself to God through the Holy Spirit.

merit, has not been radical enough. We must ask the question, What does the cross of Jesus mean for God? We must look upon the death of Jesus as a statement about God herself.[13] As we do so, Moltmann affirms, we perceive that the answer to the problem of how God both did and did not die at Calvary is not just a Christological, but a theological one. Rather than seeking to resolve the problem simply in terms of the two natures of Christ, we are led by it into the mystery of the intertrinitarian relationships. And in the light of these intertrinitarian relationships, we perceive that the material principle of the Trinity is the cross, even as the formal principle of the cross is the Trinity.[14]

What really happened, then, at the cross, so far as God is concerned, is that God delivered over (παρέδωκεν) her Son to death (Rom. 8:32); Jesus was abandoned by the very God who was uniquely his God. The Son is betrayed, cast out, forsaken by the one who sent him (Mt. 27:46; Mk. 15:34). Thus the one who sent him does what Abraham did not have to do to Isaac. In this act of forsaking Jesus, the God who sent him is afflicted with him in his death. Hers is the unspeakable grief that she suffers by the loss of her own beloved Son.[15] Thus, all suffering in the creation, all forsakenness, all sinking into nothingness, is taken up into God herself. Because this is true, eternal salvation is nothing else than community with this God who is the suffering God, a God who knows the pain of a love betrayed by sinners whom she created in and for fellowship with herself.[16]

And so although God does not suffer out of constraint or necessity, as the creature does, she does suffer. In her freedom as the sovereign Lord

13. Jürgen Moltmann, *Der Gegreuzigte Gott* (Munchen: Kaiser Verlag, 1973), p. 201. Here Moltmann cites Rahner to the effect that Christ's death not only "affects" God, but "expresses" God; also Hans Urs von Balthasar, who "traces the self-surrender, the grief, and the death of the crucified Christ back to the inner mystery of God in herself and finds in this death of Jesus the fullness of the trinitarian relationship of God *herself.*" Ibid., p. 202, with sources.

14. Ibid., p. 241. Here Moltmann quotes Steffen (*Das Dogma vom Kreuz: Beitrag zu einer staurozentrischen Theologie,* 1920, p. 152) to the effect that "the shortest expression of the Trinity is the divine act of the cross" in which the first person of the Godhead "allows the Son to sacrifice himself through the Spirit."

15. Though Moltmann accepts the conformity of will and the essential consubstantiality (*homoousia*) of the persons in the Godhead, he is, understandably, strongly inclined to the "social" analogy of the Trinity. "Eschatological faith in the cross of Jesus Christ must acknowledge the theological trial between God and God. The cross of the Son divides God from God to the utmost degree of enmity and distinction." Ibid., p. 152.

16. Ibid., p. 246. In the above summary we have sought to avoid those aspects of Moltmann's concept of a "crucified God" to which well-taken objections have been expressed by Klaus Runia in his *The Present-Day Christological Debate* (Leicester: InterVarsity Press, 1984), pp. 42ff.

God willingly gives herself over to suffer on behalf of sinners. This godlike suffering finds its supreme expression in the cross, the yardstick, as we have seen, of all the divine attributes. A suffering God, not an apathetic God, is the God in whom Christians hope. It adds to the richness of our understanding of God to perceive that she is not only the Almighty who hears the groaning of her suffering people and humbles Pharaoh (a basic paradigm of black theology), but also a God who suffers with them and for them, which is the basic paradigm of all theology.[17]

17. In an article, "The Divine Suffering in Contemporary Theology," *Scottish Journal of Theology* 33 (1980): 35-53, Warren McWilliams cites, among others, the work of a leading Japanese theologian, Kazoh Kitamori, entitled *The Theology of the Pain of God.* Doing theology in a land where the atom bomb was dropped, Kitamori argues that the pain of God is at the heart of the gospel since God's love is rooted, as well as expressed, in pain. God's pain is not a distanced empathy for human misery but a pain caused by her embracing the sinner in forgiving love, a costly love revealed in the giving of her only Son to suffer and die for the sinners' redemption (Jn. 3:16).

VI. God's Omnipresence and Eternity

A. GOD AND SPACE[1]

1. INTRODUCTION

The God revealed in Scripture is not only transcendent but immanent, the God who is not only "up there" but "down here" as well. As the hymn writer confesses,

> Within thy circling power I stand,
> On every side I find thy hand;
> Awake, asleep, at home, abroad,
> I am surrounded still with God. (Watts)

But how is God related to our space; how is she "down here"? "Do the heavens and the earth," asks Augustine,

> contain you, since you fill them? . . . But you who fill all things, do you fill them with your whole self? Or since all things cannot contain you wholly, do they contain part of you? And all at once the same part; or each its own part, the greater more, the smaller less? And is, then, one part of you greater, another less? Or are you wholly every-where, while nothing contains you wholly?[2]

Space, like time, is both obvious and mysterious. In ordinary affairs the location of objects in space is accepted as beyond doubt. But though we assume the reality of space

---

1. See above, Unit Three, II, C, The Divine Transcendence, pp. 198ff. Our comments in this prior section on transcendence are presupposed in the ensuing discussion.
2. *Confessions,* I, 3.

in everyday life, its ultimate nature has eluded the greatest minds. Is space a receptacle into which objects are placed? Or is it simply a measure of relationships—feet, miles, light-years—which are not antecedent to objects, though inseparable from them as thought is from mind? Further questions (Is space an a priori structure of the mind [Kant] or simply an impression from without [James]? How can objects act on each other—gravitationally, magnetically, electrically—when at a distance from each other? Is the "geometry" of space disturbed by matter?) are all fascinating indeed, but they are not questions with which the theologian is concerned. Rather, he is concerned with the God who is both the Lord of space as the transcendent Creator and at the same time immanent "in" space as the providential Sustainer of all that she has made.

To answer the question of how God is related to our space, theologians have used the term "omnipresence," which means that God is present— wholly present—in (to) all places in the created order. To Augustine's question, "Are you wholly everywhere, while nothing contains you wholly?" they have answered, "Yes." God is not only "afar off" but "at hand" (Jer. 23:23-24); though heaven is her throne, earth is her footstool (Is. 66:1). She encounters the runaway slave girl Hagar in the wilderness (Gn. 16:7), and dwells in the midst of her people Israel (Ex. 25:8; Ps. 135:21). Indeed, she is present to all nations, having determined their allotted times and the boundaries of their habitation (Acts 17:26).[3] As the Bible begins with the God who walks in the garden where she had placed the man and the woman (Gn. 3:8), so it ends with the God who dwells with her people in the new Jerusalem where there shall be no more tears (Rv. 21:3-4). Heaven is heaven because God is there with the redeemed from every nation and people (Rv. 14:6).

Reflecting on these and similar passages of Scripture, theologians have found it easier to say how God is not present in (to) every space and place than how she is. Surely she is not extended throughout space as a spiritual ether, nor is she present by way of identity with all that is.[4] The older theologians spoke of God's "immensity," by which they meant that God

3. We may smile at the doctrine of the divine omnipresence expressed by the Syrians when they were defeated by Israel: "The LORD is a god of the hills . . . but . . . not of the valleys" (1 Kgs. 20:28). But we moderns show the same mindset when we limit God to a day (Sunday), a place (church), a realm (the sacred), etc.

4. Theologians have eschewed all such pantheistic options. Christian mystics, on the other hand, have freely used language capable of pantheistic interpretation to express some very Christian thoughts. The ever-present danger with the mystical vision is that it threatens the distance, the "space" between God and the creature, and so undercuts human responsibility. We must have "space" between ourselves and God, both if we are to rebel against her and if we are to "draw near" to her that she may "draw near" to us (Jas. 4:8).

is present to all space yet is not contained in a particular space; unlike the creature, she does not have a "here" over against a "there."[5]

2. THE JESUS EVENT AS PARADIGM

If God is not spatially circumscribed, if she is not even "in heaven" as we are "on earth," then what do we mean when we speak of God as being "somewhere"? If she is not "in" the wilderness, as was Hagar (Gn. 16:7ff.); not "in" Jerusalem, as were Solomon and the temple he dedicated (1 Kgs. 8:22ff.); then is she really "anywhere"?[6]

Here, as in all our theologizing, the answer to our question can come only from God herself, for she is the Lord of space.[7] If she tells us that she is present in (to) our space—and the Bible is filled with such affirmations—then we can know the "how" of it only as we accept her word in faith. And this revelation, which we embrace by faith, comes to us supremely in the person of Christ. He is Immanuel, "God with us." Hence Christians have always confessed that God was uniquely present in our world in the man Jesus Christ. We use the word "uniquely" because the presence of which Christians speak when they affirm that God is present in the person of Jesus is not simply a figure of speech to denote Jesus' openness to God's will. The thought is not that a potential we all have (openness to the divine will) was supremely actualized in the life of Jesus. Rather, God is present in Jesus in the sense that "in him the whole fullness of deity dwells bodily" (ἐν αὐτῷ κατοικεῖ πᾶν τὸ πλήρωμα τῆς θεότητος σωματικῶς, Col. 2:9; see also 1:19). Here, in the person of Jesus, the Word becomes flesh (Jn. 1:3, 14); here the Word, by and through whom all things were created, takes upon him our space and place in the most literal, tangible, and objective sense. In Jesus, God is present in a place that can be located on a map. He is in Bethlehem, Nazareth, Capernaum, and

---

5. Traditionally the two terms "immensity" (*immensitas*) and "eternity" (*aeternitas*) have been subsumed under the single concept of infinity (*infinitas*). God's infinity vis-à-vis space is her immensity vis-à-vis time, her eternity. Here one is reminded of Bavinck's remark that God's infinity is not a matter of magnitude, for she is incorporeal; nor of multitude, for she is one. H. Bavinck, *Doctrine of God* (Grand Rapids: Eerdmans, 1951), p. 152.

6. Here it seems of little help to play on the terms "everywhere" (*ubique*) and "nowhere" (*nusquam*) and to say that since God is everywhere she is really nowhere because she is not limited to some particular "where." Such an approach tends to reduce the notion of the divine omnipresence to an empty concept. While it is true that there is nowhere where God is not, she is not nowhere. There is a doctrine of God's omnipresence, but not of her omniabsence.

7. To say that God is the Lord of space means that her will is the reason and ground of space as a property of her creation. Therefore, she is not subject to any particular space, as the creature is.

finally Jerusalem. Christians confess not only that God was crucified, but also where it happened (see Heb. 13:12).

> There is a green hill far away,
>   Without a city wall,
> Where the dear Lord was crucified,
>   Who died to save us all. (Alexander)

This presence of God in a unique and primary way in the person of Jesus grounds the confidence of the Christian that in former times God was also present with Moses at the burning bush, with the devout in the temple at Jerusalem, and that he will be present wherever two or three are gathered together in Christ's name (Mt. 18:20), even to the end of the age.

> And so one sees that the reality of the particular presence of God in *other* places rests upon its relationship to *this* place [the Jesus event]. In this relationship also lies the difference between God's presence in those other places and her presence in this one place. Those other places could not be places of her presence without this *real* place, just as the circumference of a circle could not exist without a center. God is really present in those other places—indeed, is really present everywhere—but she is really present here, there and everywhere because she is *here*. . . . God is present *here* in a primary way, *there* and *everywhere* in a secondary way.[8]

As for God's secondary presence in (to) her creation, the manner of it varies according to the nature of the creature. God is present with the stars as to power, with the wicked as to justice, with the redeemed as to grace, and with all things as to glory. This is not to say that God simply exercises power, exacts justice, shows grace, and gets glory in all that happens in the world of space, while remaining herself the spaceless One. To speak of God as the spaceless One requires one to pursue the question of the divine omnipresence philosophically rather than historically and biblically. (For example, consider Schleiermacher's discussion of "the absolute spaceless causality of God, which conditions not only all that is spatial, but space itself as well"; *The Christian Faith*, sec. 53; see also Biedermann's treatment in *Dogmatik*, Berlin: Fussli, 1869, pp. 627-28, of the "pure, non-temporal, non-spatial, eternal essence of the Absolute Ground of the world.") God is not the spaceless One, according to Scripture; rather, she has freely entered our spatial world in the person of her Son Jesus Christ, who was born in Bethlehem, reared in Nazareth, and crucified in Jerusalem.

To distinguish this primary presence of God in Jesus Christ from her secondary presence in the created order generally is definitely more faithful to Scripture than to

---

8. Barth, *K.D.*, II/1, p. 545 (cf. *C.D.*, II/1, sec. 31.1). His italics.

dismiss the Old Testament as superseded by the New because the former involves a supposedly primitive view of Yahweh's literal presence with Israel, while the latter sets forth a spiritual view of the divine presence of God with the followers of Jesus. Even the book of Hebrews does not so contrast the Old and the New. Though the author surely does affirm the superiority of the antitype to the type, yet in both instances he or she speaks spatially, whether of sacrifices offered every year in the tabernacle or of a sacrifice offered once and for all outside the walls of Jerusalem. Furthermore, this latter sacrifice (the crucifixion) is made effective by Christ's "entering into" the heavenly holy of holies, a most concrete, spatial, Old Testament way of speaking (Heb. 9:11-12). So God reveals herself in both the Old and the New Testaments in a spatial way; that is, in a way that shows her to be free in space rather than free from space. Hence Jesus is not other than, but greater than, the earthly temple in the Old Testament (Mt. 12:6).

Speaking of the Old Testament, the term "theophany" (from the Greek θεός and φανέω) has traditionally been used to designate special manifestations of God's presence prior to the Incarnation. While the emphasis in the theophanies falls on the senses, especially sight and sound, we should not overlook the fact that a theophany always involves a place. Note the visitation to Abraham and Sarah "by the oaks of Mamre" (Gn. 18), the awesome appearance to Moses "at Sinai" (Ex. 19), and the dazzling vision of the glory of the Lord that Ezekiel experienced "by the river Chebar" (Ez. 1). From the perspective of the Old Testament, theophanies constitute signs of the divine omnipresence—"surely the LORD is in this place; and I did not know it" (Gn. 28:10-17). As such, they anticipate the Incarnation. But once Immanuel has come as the "Word made flesh," the Incarnation constitutes the final paradigm for understanding the relationship of God to space. We have chosen, therefore, to work from the center of revelation (the Jesus event) outward, rather than from the beginning of revelation (the Old Testament theophanies) onward in an exposition of the doctrine of divine omnipresence.

Because we now view the Incarnation as the proper paradigm for understanding the biblical doctrine of God's omnipresence, we must remember that the Jesus event is a personal event. Here God is present in our space in person; here we meet God, as it were, face to face so that one who has seen Jesus has seen the One who sent him (Jn. 14:9). This is why the "personal dimension" affords a scriptural and rewarding way of conceptualizing the divine presence in and to the created order.

In other words, when speaking of the divine omnipresence the question of space, objectively considered, is the shell around the essential matter of personal fellowship. In the Old Testament, to be sure, emphasis is laid on objective space as the locale of the divine presence. The covenant promise involves a holy land (Canaan) geographically separate from other lands; in this land is a holy city (Jerusalem), and in this city a holy mountain (Zion), and on this mountain a holy building (the temple), and in this temple a holy place (the "Holy of Holies"), where God dwells above the cherubim. Yet the Old Testament also speaks of God as the One who dwells with those of a humble and contrite heart (Is. 57:15), an eloquent expression of the divine presence, not in terms of a particular space, but in terms of an intimate, personal fellowship.[9] Witness is borne to this same truth in a negative way when the prophets protest against Israel's "magical" understanding of God's presence in their midst. Such a "magical" view, based on an impersonal, objective concept of space, provokes Jeremiah to warn, "Do not trust in these deceptive words: 'This is the temple of the LORD, the temple of the LORD, the temple of the LORD'" (Jer. 7:4). Woe to those, says Isaiah, who "confess the God of Israel, but not in truth or right. For they call themselves after the holy city" (Is. 48:1-2).

Yet on the other hand we cannot simply limit the question of the divine omnipresence to "personal" space in contrast to "objective" space. As the Incarnation involves an objective, bodily presence, so God's ongoing, personal presence with her people involves her relating to us as objects in space. Indeed, our very existence, including our objective, bodily existence, is as real for her as it is for us, for she gives us our existence, not only as subjects but also as objects, that is, as persons with bodies. When two or three are gathered in Christ's name, they are not two or three spirits, but embodied selves in a given place; and it is "in" this place where they are gathered that the resurrected Christ is present in their midst (Mt. 18:20). Of course, as our quotation marks indicate, Christ is not, like them, limited to this place and space, for he is, at one and the same time, in the midst of his people in the many places where they meet. In brief, the divine omnipresence is not a spaceless presence, but a presence in space; yet it is a presence that is not restricted to this space in contrast to that space. Though the ultimate nature of this presence escapes us, we have in our primary paradigm (the Jesus event) pointers that help us understand the mystery of this divine omnipresence in an elementary way. To a consideration of these pointers we now turn.[10]

---

9. It is certainly correct to say that the divine omnipresence involves God's presence with Hagar in that wilderness space between Kadesh and Bered where there was a spring of water (Gn. 16:7-14). Yet obviously the ultimate concern of the text is not place and space. Rather, it is God's *personal* presence there with a word of comfort and admonition to the surprised Egyptian slave girl. Weber, *Grundlagen der Dogmatik* (Neukirchen-Vluyn: Neukirchener, 1955), I, p. 497 notes that the great number of holy places preserved in the Old Testament tradition are always associated with personal, revelational encounters. This teaches us never to think of God's *Allgegenwart* (omnipresence) apart from her *Gegenwart als du Sein* (presence as personal being).

10. We deliberately avoid, at this time, the complex question of the nature of Christ's presence in the Lord's Supper. For us, that discussion belongs in another place. In any case, even those who accept the dogma of transubstantiation would not simply equate this "eucharistic presence of Christ," spatially located on the altar, with his presence in the midst of two or three who gather in his name.

3. CONCERNING "EASTER SPACE"[11]

The Jesus event includes not only our Lord's life and death but also his resurrection. While the resurrection was not a spatial event as were his life and death, it was by no means a spaceless event. The tomb was empty not simply in the minds of the "distraught women" (Renan), but empty as any tomb is empty when the body is gone. While the empty tomb does not establish the resurrection, it is a sign of the fact that Jesus' resurrection was a bodily resurrection, an event having, therefore, objective continuity with his life. Though the postresurrection appearances are not spatial, as was his crucifixion at "a place called Golgotha" (Mt. 27:33), the fourfold gospel tradition unanimously gives these appearances spatial reference. The resurrected Lord appeared to Mary weeping "outside the tomb" (Jn. 20:11ff.), and to certain disciples going to Emmaus, "about seven miles from Jerusalem" (Lk. 24:13). He stands in the midst of his disciples gathered in a room in Jerusalem, showing his hands and feet that they might know he was not present with them as a spirit but as having flesh and bones (Lk. 24:36ff.). In such instances, we have to do with what may be called "Easter space," for while manifest in our space, after the resurrection our Lord obviously transcends it. In the Passion narratives, the evangelists tell us in detail where Jesus was during the days and nights of the last week of his life. In the resurrection narratives, by contrast, when he leaves the disciples in Emmaus, having blessed the bread at table, they do not tell us where he went. We are simply told that later that evening he was in a house in Jerusalem with the disciples, though "the doors were shut" (Jn. 20:26). So he is in space, but in space as the Lord of space.

The ascension also, like the resurrection, is not a spatial event—Jesus is no space traveler—yet at the same time it is a spatial event. Jesus led them (the disciples) as far as Bethany, blessed them there, and departed from them (Lk. 24:51). Luke later tells us that "they returned to Jerusalem from the mount called Olivet" (Acts 1:12). The risen Lord ascended, then, not from Olympus, nor even from Sinai, but from Olivet, a place "near Jerusalem a sabbath day's journey away" (Acts 1:12). So, even to the end he was with his disciples in a place on the map, yet not with them as they were with one another, for he left them to go where they could not come (Jn. 13:33). *There* he will prepare a *place* for us. Hence we live in hope that the Lord of space will keep his promise, come again, and take us to himself, that where he is there we may be also. But

---

11. "Easter space" and "Easter time"—the expressions are Barth's.

this "there" is not a part of Einstein's universe; it is not curved space filled with the light of distant stars. It is, rather, Easter space.[12]

4. THE PENTECOSTAL EVENT AS PARADIGM

Because God is a personal God who has revealed herself supremely in a person, to us who are persons in her image, the question of God and space is essentially a matter of "personal" space. To be "near" to God or "far" from her is to be in or out of personal fellowship with her. (We do not, as some, dismiss an expression like "enjoying personal fellowship with Christ" as the language of devotion rather than theological analysis.) When we transpose the question of God and space into the key of personal fellowship, it must be remembered that our basic paradigm is not the Jesus event in isolation, but the Jesus event viewed in conjunction with the Pentecostal event. The God who came to us in Jesus, who is the Christ, is the God that comes to us in the Spirit who is the Spirit of the risen Christ. Hence, when we say that the only place to flee from an angry God is to the reconciled God, we are indeed confessing the biblical doctrine of the divine omnipresence; but we are confessing it in terms of a relationship wrought by the Spirit. It is because God is omnipresent as the Spirit that we can flee from her only by fear, not by physical separation; and that we can draw near to her only by penitence, not by pilgrimage. As Augustine and many others after him have observed, it is not by a change of place that we draw near to God but by a change of heart—that is, by cultivating pure desires.[13]

To be sure, such an inward, personal "drawing near" to God occurs in our geographical space. For Paul, that space was a road to Damascus; for Augustine, a garden in Milan; for Wesley, a meetinghouse at Aldersgate. But the matter of geographical space, indispensable as it is for us who are creatures of time and space, is but the outer shell around the essential matter. The essential matter is that God is the God who is with us as Immanuel and in us

---

12. Though the Lord for about thirty-three years lived in our space as we live in it, our space was never for him, as for us, an absolute given. Unlike the creature, he entered it freely. Consider the episode (Mk. 6:45ff.; Mt. 14:22ff.) where he sends his disciples across the sea while he retires to pray. Not only does he "see that they are distressed in rowing," but he comes to them, while the boat was "many furlongs distant from land," without the help of helicopter or hydrofoil. And when they received him, according to the Johannine account, "immediately the boat was at the land to which they were going" (Jn. 6:21). Little wonder people who had seen him on the other side of the sea should ask, "Rabbi, when did you come here?" (Jn. 6:25).

13. *Christian Doctrine*, I, chap. 10.

as the Paraclete. The elaboration of these things falls, for the systematician, in the locus of salvation as the work of Christ and the Spirit. In the saving work of Christ we are redeemed by his life, death and resurrection. In the saving work of the Spirit we are made contemporaneous with Christ in his life, death, and resurrection and so become, by God's grace, a new creation in Christ (Gal. 2:20; Rom. 6:4; 2 Cor. 5:17). Hence, we shall speak of these matters no further at this time save to note that our subsequent elaboration of the doctrine of salvation will presuppose our present exposition of the doctrine of God, including our understanding of the divine omnipresence.

When theologians transpose the spatial concept of omnipresence into the key of "personal correspondence," what they are doing may be illustrated by noting the way in which we speak, at the human level, of being "near" or "far" from others in terms of personal fellowship rather than physical proximity. We speak intimately by letter to those who are far removed from us in physical space because we are "nearer" to them, as kindred spirits, than to those living with us under the same roof or working with us in the same office.

> Blest be the tie that binds
> > Our hearts in Christian love.
> The fellowship of kindred minds
> > Is like to that above. (Fawcett)

Such a way of speaking also bears on our understanding of the familiar biblical expression that Christians are "indwelt" by the Spirit. Obviously the Spirit of God does not dwell within us as an unborn infant in its mother's womb. But the reality, described after the analogy of physical space, is nonetheless a reality for all of that. Indeed, the intimacy of personal fellowship assumed in Paul's question, "Do you not know that your body is a temple of the Holy Spirit within you?" (1 Cor. 6:19) makes the Spirit "nearer" than any mother and unborn child can ever be. Even an expectant mother simply "carries" her child for a time, but the Spirit of the omnipresent God lives in the heart of the godly always. Yet, if there is an analogy between a mother indwelt by her child and the Christian who is "indwelt by the Spirit"—and without such analogy the language of Scripture and devotion is meaningless—then we must remember that spatiality is involved in the latter thought. When Paul tells the Corinthians, "the Spirit is within you," he is speaking to persons in space; he is saying that the Spirit is within the Corinthians who were living as Christians in an ancient city called Corinth.

One final word. While it is true that God's presence with us as Immanuel in Galilee and Judea, and her presence in us as the indwelling Spirit are different modes of her presence, the latter should not be thought of as a mystical, but as an experiential, existential, and personal presence. It is not a presence in contrast to the historical, a presence that makes the historical indifferent, as does the mystical. It is rather the presence of the Spirit who bears witness to the Jesus Christ of history, the Jesus Christ who "suffered under Pontius Pilate" outside the walls of Jerusalem.

B. GOD AND TIME

1. INTRODUCTION

When we turn from a discussion of God's relation to space to that of her relation to time, our task becomes, if possible, even more difficult. Philosophers have probed the mysteries of time and poets accused it of tyranny; but the mystery and the tyranny remain. It is that "wingéd chariot hurrying near" that reduces both desire and its object to a common dust. It has not only closed Helen's eyes, but in due course will remand Homer's pages and all that is written on them to a like oblivion. Meanwhile, astronomers and physicists have boggled our minds with their measurements of time. They tell us that we live in a galaxy that has been wheeling on its axis for hundreds of millions of years in a universe that began, perhaps, twenty billion years ago. And in this cosmos of planets, stars, and quasars, there are also quarks and antiquarks in a subatomic realm where events last about one ten-trillionth of a trillionth of a second. So precise are scientists' measurements of this cosmic and microscopic time that they must add a "leap second" every year or so to their atomic clocks to align them with the crudities of solar motion. But what is this "something" that scientists measure so precisely, that we all experience so inevitably and resist so futilely? Philosophers have often linked it with space by suggesting that time is the measure of motion—motion, that is, of objects in space. Common people have likewise associated time with space by speaking of it in spatial ways. We all speak of the "time line" and refer to time as "behind" and "before" us. In more recent times, Einstein has spoken of "the four dimensional time-space continuum" of which time is the fourth coordinate. Thus time and space are not only associated, but hyphenated, in a mysterious unity that points to the mystery of all physical reality.

For all the mystery, philosophers have, for the most part, assumed the everyday distinction between past, present, and future. Yet they have been unable to agree as to whether the present is simply the division between past and future or whether it is the all-important center that draws past and future into itself. In any case, only the present is; the past is no longer and the future is not yet. By memory we can cheat the present by bringing from the past fond recollections; and by imagination we can cheat the future with plans and purposes that transcend the present. But we cannot escape the present, though we know not, theoretically, what it is. We can only existentially wait for it to pass and for the future to come. Yet, much as it may baffle and threaten us, without time we could not live. Were time literally to "stand still" we would all be dead, for where there is no time there is no movement, and where there is no movement there is no life. Since our nature consists of motion, "complete rest," as Pascal observed, "is death."[14]

To the theoretical question of the ultimate nature of time, Christian thinkers have been as short on answers as anyone else. They have viewed time existentially, rather than theoretically, regarding it as a gift of the Creator to be redeemed by diligent use. By such diligence, one may render a good account in the life to come. (Jeremy Taylor introduces his classic, *Holy Living,* with an entire section on "The Care of Our Time.") As those who live their "now" in the light of the future life, Christians have not been cowed by time's relentless pace.

> . . . glut thyself with what thy womb devours,
> Which is no more than what is false and vain,
> And merely mortal dross. . . .
>
> And last of all thy greedy self consumed
> Then long Eternity shall greet our bliss
> With an individual kiss. . . . (Milton)

2. THE AUGUSTINIAN LEGACY

Augustine, the first major theologian to reflect on the nature of time, concludes that it is part of God's creation. Before God created the world there was no "before"; time, like space, is a property of creation.[15] Time is not only duration, but movement: "All time past is driven on by time to come and all to come follows upon the past." Hence the present is ever in motion. It is in contrast to this movement of the creature's present that Augustine seeks to understand the Creator's eternity. God's eternity is, as

14. In this regard, see Poe's *The City in the Sea,* where "Death hath reared himself a throne in a wilderness of glass." Also Coleridge, "The Rime of the Ancient Mariner" (part II), where the mariner's vessel is becalmed in a silent sea, "As idle as a painted ship/upon a painted ocean." When he lost his sense of time, Bonivar, the last surviving prisoner of Chillon (Byron, *The Prisoner of Chillon*), could only lament:

> There were no stars—no earth—no *time*
> No check—no change—no good—no crime—
> But silence, and a stirless breath
> Which neither was of life nor death;
> A sea of stagnant idleness,
> Blind, boundless, mute and motionless.

15. *Confessions,* XI. Here (sec. 12-14) he raises the question of what God was doing before he made heaven and earth, and replies that he knows not. He repudiates the answer—often mistakenly ascribed to him—that "God was preparing hell for pryers into such mysteries." Such comment, he feels, makes sport of a profound question, substituting laughter for understanding.

it were, both a present that does not pass away and a present that embraces all coming years. It is, in other words, a present at rest. For us, the past is present as a memory, the present as sight, the future as expectation; but for God there is a present of things past, a present of things present, and a present of things to come. Her past, present, and future are an eternal now. "Your day is not daily, but Today . . . your Today is Eternity."[16] This is not to say that God does not distinguish past, present, and future. She most certainly does, for, as Augustine noted, time—past, present, and future— is her creation.[17] Hence she is conscious of time, though she is not herself in time; in contrast to the creature she "inhabits eternity" (Is. 57:15). She is the eternal God, our refuge (Dt. 33:27).

Yet God's eternity, like our time, is ultimately mysterious. Congruently, the best that a thinker of Augustine's rank can suggest is that with our quest for understanding we combine a prayer that confesses our ignorance. Appropriately, his own treatment of the time/eternity problem ends with a doxology to the One to whom all places are known and all times present.[18]

EXCURSUS: A COMMENT ON PROCESS THOUGHT

Whitehead (*Process and Reality,* New York: Macmillan, 1929, p. 520) once complained that "the church gave God the attributes which belonged exclusively to Caesar." That is to say, the church joined the monarchical elements in the Old Testament idea of the Deity with the Greek concept of ultimate Being in such a way that the God of the theologians became the immutable God of metaphysics, the impassible sovereign, untouched by time and what happens in time. To remedy this fault, Whitehead distinguished two aspects in the divine nature. The one he called God's "consequent" nature whereby she participates with the creature in the concrete process of history. God in this sense interacts with the creature, not from above but in real history. What happens in the world makes a difference not just to God but in God. She so participates in each moment of the world's becoming that we can no longer hold to the Augustinian-Thomistic ontology of the perfection of God—that is, the idea that

16. See also Boethius: "The now that flows away makes time, the now that stands still makes eternity"; *De Trinitate,* IV.

17. One should not suppose, then, that 2 Peter 3:8—"with the Lord one day is as a thousand years, and a thousand years as one day"—means that God does not know the difference! She, in fact, created the difference. The text obviously means that the lapse of time effects no change in her that would alter her ability to accomplish her purpose and fulfill her promise.

18. The above survey by no means does justice to this remarkable section of the *Confessions.* Weber, *Grundlagen,* vol. I, p. 505, n. 3, alludes to it as remaining through the centuries "the most vigorous discussion of the time problem *sub specie aeternitatis,* in all theological literature."

the temporal world adds nothing to God. Yet Whitehead also posits a "primordial" nature of God that does not change. God is the eternal Orderer of the world and, as such, possesses a perfect, timeless vision. If there is a world of time and process, then there must be an order that makes possible that world and sets the boundaries of possibility for that world. (Ibid., *passim.* See also Hartshorne, *The Divine Relativity,* New Haven: Yale University Press, 1948.)

Process theologians who work with Whiteheadian categories have followed their mentor in trying to have it both ways. (See Schubert Ogden, *Christ Without Myth,* New York: Harper, 1966; and Daniel Day Williams, *The Spirit and the Forms of Love,* New York: Harper, 1968, especially the section "A Metaphysical Alternative," pp. 162ff.) Though God's "becoming" is more ultimate than her "being," yet in process thought she is not related to time without qualification, as we are. In our judgment, this element of God's transcendent control of the process is the Achilles' heel of the process theologians' restatement of the doctrine of God. Even their God in some significant way is beyond change. Hence their doctrine seems to contribute little to resolving the problem allegedly posed by the traditional view of the divine eternity.

3. WHAT IT MEANS TO SAY "GOD IS ETERNAL"[19]

a. Introduction

Though we acknowledge the ultimate mystery, is there any penultimate light that the centuries of theological discussion can throw on the subject of the divine eternity? To begin with the obvious, the "now" of the present moment is a moment from which the creature can never escape. As the present moves along the stream of time, it carries us all irrevocably to our last moment (Ps. 90:5-6). This is true not only of the individual, particular creature, but of the creation as a whole. Even the universe had a first moment and is moving toward a last moment, a cold death.[20]

The fact that we plead in vain with any moment, "Tarry, you are so beautiful," is, according to Heidegger, the source of that *Angst* which is of the essence of human life. Nothing escapes the Heraclitean flux. Even matter *is* not; matter *happens* according to modern physics. The Idealist argument that the ego stands outside the stream of time, because it cannot be objectified in space, is a non sequitur. Rather, the human ego experiences presentness and becoming in a most emphatic way. For this reason, the famous boast of Fichte, "When the youngest of all the millions of suns now blazing above me has long ago sent out its last ray, even then shall I be still unscathed and unchanged, the very same that I now am" (quoted in Heim, *God Transcendent,* p. 118),

19. Here one should consult the previous section (V) of this Unit, "God's Faithfulness and Suffering," especially our comments on the divine impassibility, pp. 396ff.

20. We are here supposing the ultimacy of the second law of thermodynamics and rejecting pulsating models of the universe, matters discussed in Unit Five, IV, pp. 470ff.

is an idle boast. As Heim notes, the Hebrews cast the whole conjugation of the verb into the imperfect and the perfect; and Spengler believed that the tragedies of all cultures revolve around the fact that the line between the two worlds of the past and the future can never be moved back (*ibid.,* pp. 121ff.); yesterday's tragic decision is today's fait accompli. Einstein's slowing down of the clock, we might add, is of no comfort in this regard, though it can be the object of the most delightful and diverting tales. (See *Mr. Tompkins in Wonderland,* by the renowned cosmologist George Gamow, London: Cambridge University Press, 1941.)

In contrast to the creature, theologians have said, God the Creator knows no first moment nor will any moment be her last. To say that God is eternal, then, is to say that she is not carried down the stream of time as are we. The sands of time do not slip through her hourglass; she does not acquire rings as a sequoia. She is the God who is "from everlasting to everlasting" (Ps. 90:2); she does not have a beginning, she is "in the beginning" (Gn. 1:1); her name is Alpha and Omega (Rv. 1:8; 21:6; 22:13). Not only did she create heaven and earth in the beginning, but when they pass away she will be the same, for her years shall not fail (Ps. 102:25-28; Heb. 1:10-12). She and she only is "eternal."

But can we go beyond this *via negationis* in defining God's eternity? Can we say more than that God is not, as we, tied to a given moment that is borne down time's "ever-rolling stream"? Not really. Most theologians, following Augustine, however, have pursued the thought that when we define eternity in contrast to time we can at least say that eternity knows no succession, that it is simultaneity. Thomas, for example, contrasts eternity as "nonsequential simultaneity" with time, which he understands as the succession of "before" and "after." And since temporal succession entails movement, change, and alteration, eternity must entail an inviolable changelessness. God's name is never "I Was" or "I Will Be," but always "I AM." Therefore, as we apprehend time by the flow of the now, "so the apprehension of eternity is caused in us by our apprehending the now as standing still."[21] Thomas admits that the creature (humans, angels, demons) may be said to be "eternal" in the sense of never ceasing to exist. But such duration without end is eternity only in an "accidental" sense. (The same is true even of duration, that is, without beginning.) The "substantive" difference between time and eternity is the difference between succession and simultaneity; "eternity is the simultaneously whole" and belongs properly and truly to God alone.[22]

21. *Summa,* I, Q. 10, Art. 2.
22. Ibid., Arts. 3 and 4. Hence the ζωὴν αἰώνιον of John 3:16 is nicely rendered "everlasting life" in the KJV in contrast to the less precise rendering, "eternal life," of the RSV. The thought of everlasting life as succession without end is given poetic expression in Newton's familiar lines:

The traditional understanding of God's eternity as simultaneity, in contrast to succession, has not been accepted by all. In his widely read *Christus und die Zeit* (translated as *Christ and Time,* Philadelphia: Westminster, 1949), Oscar Cullmann stresses that the God of the Bible acts in time, and affirms that it is with historical revelation that we must begin when we frame an understanding of God's eternity. In doing so, we escape the Platonic idea of timelessness and perceive that God's eternity is "time stretching endlessly forward and backward." God is the One "who is and who was and who is to come" (Rv. 1:4). Of course, God is related to time differently than are we. As Lord of time, she fully knows, rules over, and controls endless time, being without beginning of days and end of life. In saying as much, Cullmann tacitly concedes the divine transcendence. And in so doing, he is left with all the problems Augustine originally faced. In the preface to the second edition of his work, he admits that he has not solved the many questions facing the systematician. Rather disarmingly, too disarmingly, he asks if the most valuable service New Testament scholarship can render dogmatics may not be to let stand those questions that are not resolved in the New Testament.

We would reply that biblical theology renders the best service to dogmatics when it sketches the scriptural parameters within which dogmatic answers must fall for one who reads the Bible as divine revelation. It cannot be doubted that the prima facie meaning of the temporal language in Scripture, when used of God, is, as Cullmann says, "time without limits," "time that is endless backward and forward." As the psalmist says, "From everlasting to everlasting you are God" (Ps. 90:2 NRSV). But the same is true of spatial language used of God in Scripture. Yet we can hardly forego all further comment on what the New Testament means when it says that God is "in heaven"; we must reflect on the implications of such language. And so it is with temporal language as well.

b. God's Eternity as "Easter Time"

Though most dogmaticians have found the suggestion that God's eternity is "time without limits" (Cullmann) less than satisfying, they have had reservations about construing eternity as the opposite of time. Rather than think of eternity, in contrast to time, as timelessness, they have sought to relate eternity to time with the help of the concept of the "present." Both God and the creature have a "now"; only, as we have observed, for us it is moving, while to God it is standing still, a *nunc aeternum.* This is a helpful approach; yet it is sufficiently close to the idea of "timelessness" that it has its pitfalls. An illustration of what we mean is the tendency of many theologians to construe God's eternity in terms of an abstract immutability. Granted, God is the One with whom there is "no variation or shadow due to change" (Jas. 1:17). But too often this changeless God has

---

When we've been there ten thousand years,
  Bright shining as the sun,
We've no less days to sing God's praise
  Than when we first begun.

become a timeless God, a celestial sphinx who is more like the Unmoved Mover of Aristotle than the living God who acts in history. Furthermore, when God, who is the supremely real Being (*ens realissimum*), is conceived as immutable, such an understanding threatens to give time and the changing events that occur in it a kind of unreal being, a mere appearance.[23]

Such a view is wholly incompatible with Scripture, which regards time as the theater of ethical decision. As such, time is not simply a sequence of moments, much less a mere appearance; it is rather *kairos,* that is, time laden with eternity. Not only does God regard the decisions that the creature makes in time as significant decisions, but she herself has actually entered our temporal reality and become one with us. This act, which we call Incarnation, makes it evident that God's eternity and our time are not completely disparate spheres. Therefore, as with the divine omnipresence, so with the divine eternity, we shall use the Incarnation as our paradigm in the quest for understanding, giving special attention to our Lord's resurrection and postresurrection ministry.

This ministry is surely not a timeless ministry. As our Lord was born under Caesar Augustus (Lk. 2) and crucified under Pontius Pilate (Mk. 15), so he was raised from the dead "on the third day" (1 Cor. 15:3-4) and showed himself alive to the apostles and others, "appearing to them during forty days" (Acts 1:3). We grant that the forty days were not forty days for the risen Lord as they were for the disciples. While we may say that Jesus was about thirty-three years old when he died, we surely would not say that he was forty days older when he ascended. Yet the postresurrection ministry occurred in a time span of forty days. And in this period of time our Lord is revealed neither as the timeless God nor as the time-bound creature. Rather, he is revealed as the God whose eternity is both freedom over our time and freedom for our time, that he may accomplish the divine purpose of salvation in our time.

It is in the light of this "Easter time" that the whole New Testament is written. It was Easter that enabled the disciples to perceive that the Jesus event as a whole was not just another event like the life of a Moses or a David. His was rather a life that revealed God's time "in the middle" between the promise (Old Testament) and the consummation (the age to come). His life was, in the words of the apostle, the "fullness of time" (Gal. 4:4 NRSV).

Such a view of time is at odds with the Greek Idealists' effort to lift the "ego" out of the flux of history into the realm of the eternal Ideas. It is also at odds with the critical Idealists' effort to argue that the ethical "now" transcends the stream of past

23. One will recall the Platonic depreciation of the temporal world of flux as contrasted with the eternal world of the Ideas.

and future. Such efforts are the expression of that unbelief which would be lord of its own time rather than bow before the Lord of the creature's time. For such unbelief, there is an unavoidable offense in preaching, since preaching is witness to the God who is revealed in Christ—that is, the God who is revealed as the God-in-time. Lessing found this offense to be the "nasty, wide ditch" *(garstiger, breiter Graben)* over which he could not pass. For how can "the accidental truths of history" ever constitute "the proof of the necessary truths of reason?" (See Weber, *Grundlagen*, I, p. 504, with sources to the same effect from Kant and Schleiermacher.)

In the Jesus event we have God's eternity revealed as that mysterious "other time" on which our time rests and in which it finds its true meaning and fulfillment. When the Eternal One enters our time, this unique event is "the fullness of [our] time," the event that gives meaning to our time. This is not to deny in the least that when he lived among us, Jesus' time was uniquely and individually his. Like all other men and women, Jesus as a man had a lifetime bounded on the time line by his birth and death. It is only as the man of his own times that he is Lord of all time. The gospel, then, is good news in the form of a story that begins: "Once upon a time. . . ." But there would be no such story, no gospel, no good news, had Jesus been the prisoner of time, had he not risen "on the third day."

But because he did rise, because time, that "ever rolling stream," did not bear him away, the apostles perceived that he was not simply the child of his own times. For this reason, the documents coming from the age of the apostles (the New Testament) are not simply concerned with the historical Jesus but with the Jesus whose history begins at that very time when the history of any other person would have ended. We refer to the "history" of the Jesus who is risen, ascended, and coming again. It is an utter misunderstanding of the New Testament to reduce this ongoing "history" of the risen Lord Jesus to an instance of the influence of great people's lives on subsequent generations. The writers of the New Testament are not interested in the impact of Jesus' life as ordinary historians are interested in the impact of Alexander's conquests or Caesar's Gallic wars on subsequent history. Rather, they proclaim that as by his birth he was revealed in "the form of a servant" (Phil. 2:7), so by his resurrection he was revealed as the One who, from the beginning, was "in the form of God" (Phil. 2:6), the One who ever existed as the eternal God.

When the Scriptures say that Jesus Christ is "the same yesterday and today and forever" (Heb. 13:8), they do not mean that he shares the immortality of fame that all great men and women of the past enjoy. Rather, they mean that he transcends the past, present, and future of our time in an eternal simultaneity. He is the contemporary of all who have lived, now live, or ever will live, because he is the eternal Son of God whose time is "Easter time," time that overcomes our past, present, and future. He is the One not only of whom it is said, but who himself says, "I am the Alpha and the Omega, the first and the last, the beginning and the end" (ἐγὼ τὸ Ἄλφα καὶ τὸ Ὦ, ὁ πρῶτος καὶ ὁ ἔσχατος, ἡ ἀρχὴ καὶ τὸ τέλος, Rv. 22:13). And because the risen Lord speaks this way, the church has "crowned him with many crowns," not only as the King of love but also as the Lord of time.

> Crown him the Lord of years,
>   The Potentate of time;
> Creator of the rolling spheres,
>   Ineffably sublime. (Bridges)

As with "Easter space" so with "Easter time," we must not sharply delimit the forty days of the postresurrection ministry from the rest of Jesus' ministry. Yet it is true that what happened in the postresurrection appearances revealed, in a way that the disciples could not doubt, that Jesus was not limited by time as we are. In his resurrection ministry it became apparent that he had not lived his life "as a tale that is told." Rather, as he had been present with them before his death, so he was now present with them after his death. As by his birth he could never again be the Messiah who had not yet come, so by his resurrection he could never again be the Messiah who had no longer come. By his resurrection he showed himself to be the One whose "present" could never be lost in the past nor threatened by the future. As the "Alpha and Omega, the first and the last, the beginning and the end," he is uniquely the One who is "the same yesterday and today and forever" (Heb. 13:8).

His "today," in other words, does not deny that he had a yesterday; it rather affirms that he did not succumb to that yesterday when he hung on a Roman cross, that his disciples need no longer say, "We had hoped that he was the one to redeem Israel" (Lk. 24:21). Nor does his "today" deny that he has a future or that he will come again. It rather affirms that he is not limited by that future; his disciples do not simply wait in hope. For he who will come is he who says, "Lo, I am with you always, to the close of the age" (Mt. 28:20).

How can one who lived two thousand years ago, one for whom we look in the future as we utter the prayer, "Come, Lord Jesus" (Rv. 22:20), be the one who is with us today and all our days? The answer is that he is with us always as the Lord of time, whose past and future are taken up in (cohere in) an abiding present. And so God is revealed in Christ as the God who is eternal even as she is the God who is omnipresent. As she is the Lord of space, so she is also of time. That is why the New Testament understands God's presence with us as an ongoing presence, a presence not only in all places but at all times.

This means, as we have already noted, that when we make the Jesus event the primary paradigm for our understanding of God's relation to space and time, we cannot do so apart from, but only in conjunction with, the Pentecostal event. Christians do not live "in the flesh" but "in the Spirit"; and, says the apostle, "anyone who does not have the Spirit of Christ does not belong to him." But "if Christ is in you"—which is the same as Jesus' promise, "Lo, I am with you always"—"your spirits are alive because of righteousness" (Rom. 8:9-10). The giving of the Spirit, then, is much more than a recollection of the "spirit" in which Jesus once lived, a recollection so vivid that it inspires us in our own day to live in the same spirit of openness to God and neighbor. There is, indeed, recollection of the past: "I delivered to you . . . what I also received," says Paul, "that Christ died for our sins . . . that he was buried, that he was raised . . ." (1 Cor. 15:3-4). But this recollection of the past is not the recollection of a past Christ but of the Christ whose Spirit dwells in us as an ongoing Presence. The God revealed in Christ, in other words, is the Eternal One, the One whom Watts calls our "help in ages past," our "hope for years to come," and also, now, in the present, our "shelter from the stormy blast." And because this God is the God of our past, our present, and our future, she is the God who is "our eternal home."

c. Conclusion

By way of summary and as a conclusion to our discussion we note the following:

(a) Time is not "first," God is; there is no god named Chronos prior to Yahweh. "I am the first and I am the last; besides me there is no god" (Is. 44:6). Time, in other words, is God's creation. Were there no eternal God there would be no temporal world. But the reverse is not true; were there no world there would yet be God, for God is the eternal One.

(b) Though the Scriptures speak of God's eternity as a time line of infinite extension in both directions—she is God "from everlasting to everlasting"—yet God's eternity is not endless time. Were we to understand God's eternity as the time line of our existence extended to infinity, God would simply enjoy an idealized form of our creaturely existence, her own allotted time, as it were. But God has no allotted time; she rather is the God who allots time, the God who writes our days in her book (Ps. 139:16).

(c) God's eternity is not timelessness. "The theological concept of eternity must be set free from the Babylonian captivity of an abstract opposite to time."[24] Greek Idealism ascribed eternity to the truth of propositions: 2 + 2 = 4 is indifferent to time and therefore, according to the Idealists, eternal. But the propositions of mathematics, according to the Christian understanding of the world, should not be considered as true in and of themselves but in and by God's will, for her will is the source and ground of all truth. And this God, the ground of all truth, is not herself an abstract proposition, an eternal idea, an impersonal absolute, but the One who declares, "I AM WHO I AM" (Ex. 3:14).

(d) Because God created time and is therefore the Lord of time, she knows—indeed, she brings about—the past and the present out of her future; but for her, past (before) and future (after) do not "fall apart" in the present as they do for us. "Before me no god was formed, nor shall there be any after me" (Is. 43:10). God, being eternal, does not know the past and the future as separation, as distancing, as dominated by succession. She rather knows all time after the analogy of the present. Inadequate though it be, we can only define God's eternity as "simultaneity," the coinherence of past, present, and future. As the living God, her "present" never slips by her into a fixed, unalterable past; nor does it come to her out of the womb of an unknown and contingent future. God's eternity, in the words of Boethius, "is her simultaneously whole-hearted and perfect possession of interminable life."[25]

We, as creatures in her image, in our own small way, know time as qualified by eternity when we are aware of our present as the moment laden with decision and choice, the *Augenblick* of Kierkegaard, the *kairos* of the New Testament. ("Behold, now is the acceptable time; behold, now is the day of salvation," 2 Cor. 6:2). But the eternal God lives not in a moment of decision but in an eternal decision. She is who she is by her own free decision, the triune God, begetting, begotten, and proceeding, yet not in succession but in simultaneity.

(e) Because God is eternal, when we refer to her as she who is, who was, and who is to come (Rv. 1:8), we must remember that her "was" and her "will be" are determined by her "is." She is who she is, the "I AM WHO I AM" (Ex. 3:14). This emphasis on the present, this understanding of God's eternity as her "eternal now," does not, however, warrant a stressing of the present of God's redeeming purpose at the expense of the past or the future. We should rather seek a balanced view of the divine

---

24. Barth, *K.D.,* II/1, p. 689 (cf. *C.D.,* II/1, sec. 31.3). His italics.
25. *De Consolatione Philosophiae,* V, as cited by Thomas, *Summa,* I, Q. 10, Art. 1, pt. 1.

eternity. Such a balanced view affirms that God's past creation is the basis of our existence, her present redemption the renewal of our existence, and her future coming the meaning of our existence.[26]

(f) Finally, to affirm God's eternity carries with it very practical implications. For one, since she knows no future contingencies, God is free to be constant, always who she is, never other than she is. Hence we can trust her to keep her word as we face our own uncertain future. Furthermore, we can be assured that in her eternal present she always hears the prayers of her people. Though offered by countless individuals and congregations in endless and overlapping succession, they are heard by her in a continued simultaneity. She is not confused by our myriad petitions and praises, but she hears them all as though we were the only ones speaking to her. Further, since she is the eternal God time does not have and hold her as it does us in its downward flood. Therefore, even though we may be "lost in following years" so far as this life is concerned, we shall never be lost to God. "Our times are in her hands." We can, therefore, trust her not only to redeem our guilty past and fulfill our empty present but also to secure our uncertain future according to the promise that she will never leave nor forsake us. It is in this confidence that we sing,

> Even down to old age all her people shall prove,
> Her sovereign, eternal, unchangeable love. (Rippon)

---

26. This balance in dogmatics does not, of course, preclude the doing of theology in terms of one's concrete present, as did the confessing church of Nazi Germany in subscribing the *Barmen Declaration*. The same is true of much that is being done today in black, feminist, and South American liberation theology.

UNIT FIVE

WHAT GOD HAS DONE: CREATION

Little lamb, who made thee?
Dost thou know who made thee;
Gave thee life and bid thee feed
By the stream and o'er the mead;
Gave thee clothing of delight,
Softest clothing, woolly, bright,
Gave thee such a tender voice
Making all the vales rejoice?
Little lamb, who made thee?
Dost thou know who made thee?

Little lamb, I'll tell thee,
Little lamb, I'll tell thee;
He is called by thy name,
For he calls himself a Lamb.
He is meek and he is mild;
He became a little child.
I a child and thou a lamb,
We are called by his name.
Little lamb, God bless thee.
Little lamb, God bless thee.

William Blake, *The Lamb*

I. Introduction

Having discussed who God is (Unit Three) and what God is like (Unit Four), we now turn to the question of what God has done. In this unit we shall defend and elaborate the thesis that God has created the heavens and the earth. As we begin our task, one may recall that we have said:

(a) that God's being is determined by no one outside himself; he is who he is by his own will and choice;

(b) that in his freedom, God has willed to bring this world into being with all that is in it;

(c) that this divine will should not be construed as impersonal Power or Force but as the freedom of the living God to do whatever he chooses to do; and

(d) that in bringing this world into being, God manifests not only his power but also his wisdom, namely, his creative, energizing thought that finds cheerful diversion in making all that is.[1] As we consider in more detail what it means to say that God has created the heavens and the earth, we should not allow our familiarity with the subject to dull our sense of reverence before the mystery of which we speak. "Towering majestically over all, inscrutable and inescapable," Banesh Hoffmann reminds us, "is the awful mystery of Existence itself, to confound the mind with an eternal

---

1. In the ensuing discussion, context will determine the meaning of the word "world." Sometimes it will mean planet earth and sometimes, as here, the universe as a whole. Since the word "universe" is a scientific rather than a biblical term, we shall use it, for the most part, when discussing scientific data that impinge on the work of the theologian in framing a doctrine of creation. The term "cosmos" will be used primarily when thinking of the ordered structure of creation as a whole, whether that order is viewed from the perspective of philosophical monism, scientific law, or the divine purpose.

enigma."[2] While those who confess the Christian doctrine of creation are not confounded by the "eternal enigma of Existence" (they do not even spell it with a capital "E"), yet they do stand in awe of the thought that "by the word of the LORD the heavens were made, and all their host by the breath of his mouth" (Ps. 33:6).

What evokes awe in some, however, evokes disdain in others. Fichte, for one, denounced the thought of creation as the fundamental error of all metaphysics and religion. Such a thought was, for him, simply inconceivable. The positing of a creation, he claimed, is the first criterion of the falsity of a religious vision and the rejection of creation the first criterion of its truth.[3] In speaking thus, Fichte was simply giving sharp expression to the general awareness of autonomous reason that the concept of creation threatens the continuity of human thought with an absolute discontinuity. Given the concept of creation, God stands over against the world and the world over against God. There is no necessary connection between them. To accept creation, then, requires one to acknowledge that the world cannot be understood, ultimately, in terms of itself but only in terms of that which is other than itself. Such a conclusion is simply unacceptable to that autonomous reason which is not open to truth given by revelation but shut up to the continuity of rational thought.[4]

Karl Marx recognized that humanity enjoys only a relative freedom over against nature and must ever strive to acquire new freedom by means of labor and work. He does not speak, therefore, of humanity's absolute freedom, as Fichte does. But he agrees with Fichte that nothing is more intolerable than to exist by, for, and through another. Hence he found human work, on the one hand, and the work of God the Creator, on the other, to be mutually exclusive. Only one who owes one's existence to oneself alone is really free. Hence freedom must be grounded in one's own work and one's own work alone. To base one's existence upon God's creative work makes one dependent, a condition that, for Marx, is by definition slavery. (See Miroslav Volf, *Das Marxsche Verständnis der Arbeit: eine theologische Wertung, aus Zagreb,* Jugoslawein: Volk, 1985, pp. 184-87).

2. Banesh Hoffman, *The Strange Story of the Quantum* (New York: Dover, 1959), p. 190.

3. See Otto Weber, *Grundlagen* (Neukirchen-Vluyn: Neukirchener, 1955), vol. I, p. 515, n. 1, quoting from Fichte's *Anweisung zum seligen Leben.*

4. One is here reminded of Robert Jastrow's comment that the implications of an expanding universe are, for many scientists, like a bad dream. But more of this presently. See below, pp. 473ff.

II. Rejected Options: Platonism, Gnostic Emanation, and Pantheism

The rejection of the Christian doctrine of creation, reflected in the thought of many contemporary philosophers and scientists, dates back to the time of the ancient Greeks. It was, some would argue, the abandoning of the myths of creation by the Ionians of the sixth century B.C. and the submitting of the question of origins to theoretical and causal inquiry that marks the "true origin of scientific thought."[1] Subsequently, to be sure, Plato returned to myth to explain the origin of the world as a whole. According to the *Timaeus*, the original production of all things is the work of the Demiurge fashioning primordial matter according to the patterns fixed by the eternal Ideas.[2] Yet Plato's view, for all its mythological form, would not offend a Fichte or a Marx. Nor would it be, like the Christian doctrine of creation, a bad dream to a present-day cosmologist. Plato's doctrine is perfectly congruous with the categories of rational thought. The Demiurge is not a transcendent Other, but a kind of celestial craftsman. He imposes order on preexistent materials—the elements of earth, air, fire, and water—as does a human craftsman. Not only is the matter with which he works eternal, but so are the intelligible patterns that generate the visible forms. Such a creator is conditioned by the world as

1. See Werner Jaeger, *Paideia* (New York: Oxford, 1945), vol. I, p. 156.
2. Timaeus even invokes the aid of the gods that he may answer Socrates in an intelligible way on this difficult question. See *Plato*, Great Books (Chicago: Britannica, 1952), p. 447. Brunner claims that Plato turned to myth when treating of creation because he could not take philosophical responsibility for such a concept. *Dogmatik*, vol. I, p. 150. Be that as it may, Plato's argument is plausible in the highest degree considering that he was a pioneer thinker working with reason and experience alone. The Demiurge brought the cosmos out of chaos as did Praxiteles his masterpieces out of raw marble.

440

well as is the world by the creator. He is not the Lord, who in his freedom calls all that is into being out of nothing.

Perceiving this fact, the early theologians of the church rejected Platonism. Tertullian argued that the eternity of matter was inconsistent with the freedom and sovereignty of God. Augustine noted that when God made heaven and earth he had nothing in his hands. For whence could he have had anything that he himself had not made? "For what is but because you are? Therefore you spoke and they were made."[3]

In stating and defending the Christian doctrine of creation, the first theologians had more to contend with than the teachings of a Plato. They had also to refute the views of the Gnostics, whose speculations about creation reflected not only Platonism but many strands of Eastern and even Christian thought as well. "Gnosticism," in the opinion of Schaff, "is the grandest and most comprehensive form of speculative, religious syncretism known to history."[4] Since the Gnostics believed that matter is evil, they expended much effort in seeking an answer to the question of how a good God could create this evil, material world. They assumed the validity of the dualism that such a question implies: on the one hand, God is good; on the other, the material world is evil. They resolved the problem by denying that God created the world, at least in any direct way. The immediate creator of the material world was the Demiurge, whom they distinguished from God in the truest and highest sense.

This distinction between the Demiurge and God was crucial for the Gnostics. Out of the being of the true God there emanates a series of Aeons, which are the unfolding powers of the divine nature. (Christ is the highest of these Aeons.) As the Aeons emanate from God—whether by self-limiting love or metaphysical necessity—the lower links of the chain come ever nearer the abyss until the lowest Aeon falls, as a spark of light, into the dark chaos of matter. Thus, where Spirit surrenders to matter and the Infinite enters into the finite, the germ of the divine life is imparted. This impregnating of matter with life sets the stage for the creation of the material world by the Demiurge. Often identified by the Gnostics with the God of the Old Testament, the Demiurge is the creation of the fallen Aeon. Standing thus, by nature, between God and matter, the

---

3. *Confessions,* XI [V], 7. Aristotle, like Plato, taught that matter is eternal (*Physics,* I, 10, 8). He was later defended by Thomas on the score that no rational arguments are conclusive against the eternity of the world. Creation is an article of faith and therefore not accessible to philosophy. See Pelikan, *The Christian Tradition* (Chicago: University of Chicago Press, 1978), vol. III, p. 290.

4. Philip Schaff, *History of the Christian Church* (New York: Scribner, 1910), vol. II, p. 448.

Demiurge makes this visible, material world, evil as it is, and rules over it.[5]

Irenaeus of Gaul, the first Christian theologian in the modern sense, opens his magnum opus, *Adversus Haereses*, with a refutation of the Gnostics. Like Tertullian in Africa, he taught that the God of the Old Testament, the God revealed in Jesus Christ, is the Creator of the world and all that is in it. By his will and word alone all things are made, apart from any intermediaries. Thus the will of God is the final reason of all existence, a view that excludes every form of emanation.[6] The creation, since it is the work of God who is good, is in its essential nature good. Evil is a corruption of the natural order and will be destroyed by God's redemptive power. The Gnostics, according to Irenaeus and other early theologians of the church, do not have a true doctrine of redemption because they do not have a biblical doctrine of creation.[7]

Along with Gnostic emanation, the church also rejected all forms of pantheism. While the word "pantheism" (from the Greek πᾶν, "all," and θεός, "God") is of relatively recent origin, the view that God and the world are in some way identical draws on sources already present in Hellenistic thought when Christianity came on the scene. If theories of Gnostic emanation err on the side of transcendence in an effort to keep God from defiling his hands by making this evil material world, Pantheism errs, the theologians have argued, on the side of immanence by merging God with the world and so divinizing it. Augustine, for example, protested that if God is the soul of the world and the world is the body of God, then "impious and irreligious consequences follow such as that whatever one may trample, one must trample a part of God."[8] What Augustine is here protesting is

5. Marcion, excommunicated by the church in Rome, embraced the dualist approach of the Gnostics and argued that a good, all-knowing, all-powerful God could not have created this evil world. Since bad fruit comes from a bad tree, the God of the Old Testament cannot be the good God revealed by Jesus. See Pelikan, *The Christian Tradition* (Chicago: University of Chicago Press, 1971), vol. I, pp. 73-74.

6. The world, observes Oden, does not seep or leak or flow from the being of God after the analogy of fragrance from flowers. See his *The Living God* (San Francisco: Harper, 1987), p. 233.

7. Gustaf Wingren argues that Irenaeus, in his battle against the Gnostics, is saying "yes" both to the doctrine of creation and to the Old Testament. An analysis of Irenaeus's reasoning shows that we have the Gnostics to thank for the fact that as early as the second century (when Gnosticism was at its height) the church received its two basic documents: a Bible with two Testaments and a creed with three articles, both beginning with the doctrine of creation. See his "The Doctrine of Creation: Not an Appendix but the First Article," *Word and World,* ed. A. J. Hultgren, vol. IV, no. 3, p. 365.

8. *City of God,* IV, 12. At a much later time, William Carey complained of the difficulties he faced in trying to make the gospel meaningful in India because the "Spiritual Essence,"

quite different from the thought that God may be seen in his works. Obviously it is one thing to say with Luther that all nature is God's mask, which faith sees through to God and his love. It is another to say with Alexander Pope,

> All are but parts of one stupendous Whole,
> Whose body nature is, and God the soul; . . .
>
> To him no high, no low, no great, no small;
> He fills, he bounds, connects and equals all![9]

The same pantheistic approach can be seen in the way many today speak of "nature" in personal terms and so avoid speaking about a personal Creator. All the evolving work of the landscape architect, we are told in the preface to a book on beautiful gardens, "had the cooperation of that greatest of landscape designers, Nature, with her unerring sense of color, her skillful manipulation of form . . . etc." (Paige Rense, foreword to *Gardens,* Los Angeles: Knapp, 1983). It is also interesting to note how an intelligence appropriate to a personal Creator is often attributed to animals. Popular books on nature speak, for example, of species of birds on the Seychelles Islands that have only one offspring because of the limited food supply while their African cousins have several. Such birds evidently manage their planned parenthood program better than the various nations of the human family!

Though rejected by theologians and though problematic for all who would confess the biblical doctrine of creation, pantheistic ways of speaking have appealed to Christian mystics (Gerson, Eckhart, Boehme, et al.) as expressing the union of the soul with God and assuring salvation through participation in the divine. But pantheism is as heretical in its doctrine of salvation as in its doctrine of creation. Nature, though it be deified, cannot convey grace, a truth to which Thompson eloquently testifies in his *The Hound of Heaven.*

> In vain my tears were wet on Heaven's gray cheek.
> For ah! we know not what each other says,
>   These things and I; in sound *I* speak—
> *Their* sound is but their stir, they speak by silences.

---

though it is a metaphysical abstraction, yet "pervades everything, it contains everything, nay, it is itself everything and everything is it. . . ." As quoted by C. L. Manschreck, *A History of Christianity* (Englewood Cliffs, N.J.: Prentice-Hall, 1964), p. 475.

9. As quoted in Manschreck, ibid., p. 235. "The writer was dining one day with Tholuck and five or six of his students, when he took up a knife from the table and asked, 'Is this knife of the substance of God?' and they all answered, 'Yes.'" Hodge, *Systematic Theology* (New York: Scribner, 1871), vol. I, p. 554, n. 3.

Nature, poor stepdame, cannot slake my drouth;
Let her, if she would ewe me,
Drop yon blue bosom-veil of sky, and show me
The breasts o' her tenderness;
Never did any milk of hers once bless
My thirsting mouth.

In contrast to both Gnosticism and pantheism, the doctrine of creation asserts that God has called into existence all that is other than himself by his own will and choice. Created reality, therefore, is neither to be condemned as unworthy of a holy God nor deified as somehow an expression of his being. The doctrine of creation postulates neither a contradiction between God and the world nor his identity with the world, but rather a qualitative difference between them. This qualitative difference not only preserves the transcendence of the Creator, but also implies "space," an over-againstness of the creature and the Creator, an independence of the creature vis-à-vis the Creator. This independence, to be sure, is not an ultimate, but a penultimate, one. Yet the "space" postulated by the Christian doctrine of creation preserves the freedom of the creature, made in the divine image, to respond to the Creator. Of this response, be it one of love or enmity, we shall have more to say at another time. Our present concern is simply to understand creation in a way that will insure a right understanding, in due course, of the sin and salvation of humankind, themes of central importance in biblical revelation.

ADDENDUM: CREATION AS "BIRTHING"?

In the burgeoning literature of feminist theology, the doctrine of creation is sometimes set forth in terms of a mother giving birth to a child. Virginia Mollenkott deems it likely that the very first image of God in the Bible (Gn. 1:2) is that of a mother eagle fluttering over the primal waters as she gives birth to the universe. Christian feminists, then, are only reclaiming their biblical heritage when they see the origin of all things "not in terms of masculine impregnation but rather in terms of feminine involvement in the birth and nurturing process. God is our eagle-mother."[10]

In the light of our rejection of all notions of emanation and pantheism, obviously we can only deplore such a suggestion as a serious departure

---

10. *The Divine Feminine: The Biblical Imagery of God as Female* (New York: Crossroads, 1983), pp. 89-90. For our own quite different interpretation of Genesis 1:2, see below, this Unit, III, D, First Addendum, pp. 462ff.

from the biblical doctrine of creation. Furthermore, to juxtapose "birthing" and "impregnation," as though there were a choice between them, is a strange way to proceed. Where does Scripture (or the church) ever speak of God's "begetting" the universe? Were one to do so, it would be plain heresy. The universe is not of God as a son or daughter is of a father and therefore essentially like a father. In fact, the universe is not essentially like God at all. Rather, it is essentially unlike God, having its origin in his free and voluntary decision to call the universe into being. That is why Scripture and the church, when speaking of the origin of the world, speak of God as "Creator" and his act in which the world originates as "creation," in contrast to both "begetting" and "bearing."[11]

It should be noted, on the other hand, that the use of feminine language about God does not necessarily entail a pantheistic, birthing concept of origins. Such a claim is often made, but it cannot be sustained. Elizabeth Achtemeier, for example, observing that it is typical of feminist theology to speak of a female deity, goes on to say, *"Indeed, when female terminology is used for God, the birthing image becomes inevitable."*[12] Such an argument is a plain non sequitur. The Creed, to be sure, uses male terminology of God. But obviously this does not make inevitable the image of begetting. Even though we begin our confession, "I believe in God the Father, Almighty," we do not go on to say, "Begetter of heaven and earth." Therefore, were we to begin our confession, "I believe in God the Mother, Almighty," we would not go on to say, "Bearer of heaven and earth." At least we should not do so, for God neither begets nor bears heaven and earth—God creates them. Many, it may be, oppose calling God "Mother" because they believe that while God may be likened to a mother, God *is* Father. Such a position, as we see it, is without warrant in the light of reason and the data of Scripture.[13]

---

11. As we noted, when speaking of the Trinity and the eternal generation of the Son, what God creates is not God even as what humans make is not human. But what humans beget or bear is human just as what God begets is God. See above, Unit Three, IV, D, 2, c, The Relational Meaning of the Trinitarian Name, pp. 287ff. To disregard the distinction between "creating" and "procreating" invites a pantheistic divinizing of the creature.

12. "Female Language for God: Should the Church Adopt It?" *The Hermeneutical Quest: Essays in Honor of James Luther May on his Sixty-Fifth Birthday,* ed. D. G. Muller (Allison Park: Pickwick Publications, 1986), p. 6. Her italics.

13. See above, Unit Three, IV, E, Sexist Language and the Doctrine of the Trinity, pp. 323ff. Also Unit One, III, First Addendum: A Comment on Sexist Language, pp. 44ff. As we note in these places, *all* theological language is analogical.

III. Who Is the Creator and What Has He Done?

A. CREATION IS THE WORK OF THE FATHER THROUGH THE SON AND THE SPIRIT

In reviewing those efforts to understand the origin of all things that the church has rejected—the imposing of form on eternal matter, emanation from the divine Essence—we have affirmed over against these options the Christian consensus that the world is and that it is what it is because God has willed that it shall be and that it shall be what it is. "There can be do doubt," says Brunner,

> that the created order has its origin solely and alone in the thought and will of God. The world is because God wills it; the world is as it is because God would have it so. Therefore it is the expression, manifestation, and revelation of his thought and will.[1]

When we thus ground creation in God's "effortless, self-conscious thought and will" (Eichrodt), we must remember, first of all, that as Christians we speak not of just any God but of the God revealed in his Son Jesus Christ. In our discussion of the divine nature we asked who this God is and answered that he is a trinitarian fellowship of holy love.[2] God is the Father, Son, and Holy Spirit. Obviously this is the God of whom the Creed speaks, for it not only begins with "God the Father almighty, Maker of heaven and earth" (Art. 1), but goes on to speak of "Jesus Christ, his only

---

1. E. Brunner, *Dogmatik* (Zurich: Zwingli-Verlag, 1960), vol. I, p. 311. The problems raised for such a view by the fact of evil, especially moral evil, will be discussed in due course. See below, this Unit, V, D, The Problem of Evil, pp. 496ff., for some preliminary remarks.
2. See above, Unit Three, IV, God Is a Trinity of Holy Love, pp. 261ff.

Son, our Lord" (Art. 2), and concludes with "and the Holy Spirit" (Art. 3). If creation is the first article of the Creed confessed by Christians, surely the Trinity is the fundamental article, for it gives structure to the whole.

But for this very reason the first article is in need of further comment at this juncture. If when Christians speak of God as the Maker of heaven and earth they mean the triune God—Father, Son, and Holy Spirit—why in the first article is the Father alone mentioned as the Creator? How should we understand the Creed in this point? Theologians have answered that creation is the work of the Father, not *simpliciter,* but by appropriation.[3] As we noted in our discussion of the Trinity, the first person is called "Father" because he is the the source or origin of the trinitarian distinctions in the Godhead (*fons Trinitatis*). Thus he is also called our Father because he is the source (origin) of our being, indeed, of all being, as the Creator. He is the Father "from whom every family in heaven and on earth is named" (Eph. 3:14-15).[4]

The Creed, then, speaks properly when it speaks of "God the Father Almighty" as the "Maker of heaven and earth," for creation is the Father's proper work. But it is not the intent of the first article to exclude the Son and the Spirit from the work of creation. While the Creed speaks properly, it does not speak exclusively, of the first person. It does not say, "I believe in God the Father almighty, who, apart from the Son and Spirit, is the Maker of heaven and earth." Though it is true that the Scripture says, "In the beginning God [the Father of Israel] created the heavens and the earth" (Gn. 1:1), it also says that in this same beginning there was the Word (λόγος) through whom all things were made (Jn. 1:3).[5] Obviously, for the author of the fourth Gospel, this Word, through whom the world was made (Jn. 1:10), is not some abstract Idea in the mind of God—the presupposition and possibility of a rational order (i.e., a cosmos). Rather, this Word is Jesus, the Word who is with God and is God; the God without whom "was not anything made that was made" (Jn. 1:3).

Hence, in the Christian understanding of creation, Genesis 1 is always interpreted in the light of John 1. And this association of the Son (Word)

3. The ensuing discussion presupposes what has been said of the economic Trinity, especially the section on economic appropriation. See above, Unit Three, IV, D, 4, b, The Works of God Are One, Yet by Appropriation, pp. 306-08.

4. We should not forget the implications of this aspect of trinitarian doctrine for our speech about God. In calling the first person "Father," the univocal element in the analogy with the human is the thought of source or origin, not the thought of maleness. Therefore both male and female language is appropriate to God since fathers and mothers are equally the source of their offspring.

5. See above, Unit Three, IV, D, 3, Addendum: Concerning the Logos, pp. 303-05.

with the Father in creation is a theme found not only in John but throughout the New Testament. It is the Son through whom (δι' οὗ) God created the world (Heb. 1:2) and who in the beginning founded the heavens (Heb. 1:10). "In him (ἐν αὐτῷ) all things were created, in heaven and on earth, visible and invisible. . . , all things were created through him and for him" (δι' αὐτοῦ καὶ εἰς αὐτόν, Col. 1:15-18). Given such a view, the early Christians naturally applied to Jesus, the risen Christ, the word of the psalmist, "In the beginning, LORD, you founded the earth, and the heavens are the work of your hands" (Heb. 1:10 NRSV; Ps. 102:25). For Christians, then, "there is one God, the Father, from whom are all things (ἐξ οὗ τὰ πάντα) and for whom we exist, and one Lord, Jesus Christ, through whom are all things (δι' οὗ τὰ πάντα) and through whom we exist" (1 Cor. 8:6).

While John's prologue obviously distinguishes God from the God who is with God, and while Paul distinguishes God, who is the Father, from the Lord Jesus Christ, the distinction is not a distinction between God and a Gnostic intermediary. The Son is not simply the instrumental cause of all things, the Father being the final cause.[6] Rather, to the Son, our Lord Jesus Christ, is ascribed the status, power, and dignity of Creator, a status, power, and dignity he shares with the Father. And the same is true of the Spirit. The Spirit is called the *Creator Spiritus* because, when he is sent forth, the face of the ground is renewed and the earth teems with the creatures that are created (Ps. 104:24-25, 30).

To affirm that creation is the work of the Father by appropriation, and therefore the work of the Son and the Spirit as well, is the way theologians have sought to deal with the data of biblical revelation. When the question is asked, Who is the Creator? the Christian answer is a trinitarian one of an economic sort. The Creator is properly God the Father, who, with the eternal Logos (Son) and the Spirit, brings the world into being by a personal act of will.

Speaking of the data of biblical revelation and the doctrine of creation, a further comment is called for. Systematics, as a discipline, seeks to order the data of revelation in a sequence that illumines the inner coherence of the Christian faith. It proceeds,

---

6. Though the preposition ἐν with the dative ("in," "by") and especially διά with the genitive ("by," "through") lend themselves to such a Gnostic and Arian construction, it should be noted that similar expressions may also be used of the Father. "God is faithful, by [through] (διά) whom you were called into the fellowship of his Son, Jesus Christ our Lord" (1 Cor. 1:9). To speak thus is simply to say: "God is faithful, who called you into the fellowship of his Son." No instrumentality is implied. Of course, the correctness of the church's understanding in this matter does not rest on the fine points of Greek grammar, but on the way in which the New Testament always places the Son on the side of the Creator in distinction to the creature.

therefore, from God's original work of creation to that of salvation and final consummation as from "a" to "b" to "c." Scripture, however, sometimes subsumes all three of these—creation, salvation, and consummation—under the single rubric of creation, distinguishing only between the original and the new creation. "In the beginning," we are told, "God created the heavens and the earth" (Gn. 1:1); and in the end, we are further told, the seer hears him who sits upon the throne say, "Behold, I make all things new" (Rv. 21:1, 5). This final, new creation has already begun in the here and now. "If anyone is in Christ," the apostle says, "he is a new creation" (2 Cor. 5:17). Both present salvation and the future consummation toward which it looks are God's work of creation. At the same time, this present salvation also looks back to the original work of creation. The God "who has shone in our hearts to give the light of the knowledge of the glory of God in the face of Christ" is the God who said in the beginning, "Let light shine out of darkness" (2 Cor. 4:6). Creation, then, in the usage of Scripture, describes all God's works *ad extra*—past, present, and future.

Such scriptural usage poses no problem for the insights of faith. In worship and devotion, the language of faith moves freely from the God who creates in the beginning to the God who creates anew both now and in the future. Christians confess that the Maker of heaven and earth is God the Father almighty; at the same time a little lamb is assured that she is made by a Lamb. (See Blake's poem introducing this unit.) Obviously the little lamb is a part of that heaven and earth which the Father made in the beginning; yet just as obviously the Lamb who made the little lamb is not the Father but the One by whose "precious blood . . like that of a lamb without blemish or spot" we have been redeemed (1 Pt. 1:18-19).

While it is not for the systematician to put asunder what biblical revelation thus joined together—for both creation and salvation are the one work of the one God— yet she does have the task of clarifying the relation between them. This relationship may be stated as follows: As Redeemer of the original order of creation, now fallen and alienated, God in Christ becomes the Creator of a new order. This new order is manifest especially in the church, which is the creation of Christ by the Spirit. "The church's one foundation is Jesus Christ her Lord / She is his new creation by water and the word"—Stone.) But Christ becomes the Creator of the new order because he is the Creator of the original order; he is the eternal Logos (Jn. 1:1-3) who in the beginning laid the foundations of the earth (Heb. 1:10). His messianic exaltation as head of the new creation is, indeed, the result of his messianic obedience. But it is an exaltation grounded in his essential nature as the One who from the beginning was in the form of God, though he did not think such equality with God a thing to be grasped (Phil. 2:6). In other words, the cosmic dimension of Christ's redeeming work—his being made head over all things to the church (Eph. 1:22) — rests ultimately on the fact that in and by him all things were originally created, things in heaven and things on earth (Col. 1:16). We will, of course, have much more to say at a later time about all aspects of Christ's redemptive work. For the present our concern is simply to state how that work relates to the original creation. To pursue the matter further at this time would lead us directly into the question of the telos of creation: Why did God decide to make the world in the first place? Was his intent to provide a theater for the drama of sin and salvation? Before we seek to answer this difficult question, however, we must say more about God's act of creation as such.

B. CREATION IS THE ACTUALIZING
OF THE DIVINE WILL

1. INTRODUCTION

As we have already noted, creation means that the world has its origin solely in the will of God—Father, Son, and Holy Spirit. Creation, therefore, is the actualizing, the setting, the positing of the divine will. It is God's giving objective existence to that which corresponds to his thought and purpose. "The Maker of the universe," as Basil tells us, "needed only the impulse of his will to bring the immensities of the visible world into being."[7]

God's will to create must, of course, be associated not only with his thought and purpose but also with his power. To bring into being by an act of will what one has thought, to achieve a correspondence between what is and what one wills to be by the exercise of that will alone, is surely a demonstration of unimaginable power. The God of Scripture is the God who brings to pass his good pleasure, the God who says, "As I have planned, so shall it be, and as I have purposed, so shall it stand" (Is. 14:24). It is, then, no accident that the first article speaks of the Creator as "God, the Father almighty." By the same token, it will be recalled, we began our discussion of the divine attributes by reflecting on God's will and power as corresponding, mutually conditioned, qualities of the divine nature. (See above, Unit Four, II, pp. 348ff.)

To declare that God's will is the supreme, unconditioned, all-conditioning, final reason for everything that is underscores what theologians have in mind when they emphasize God's freedom in creation. The mysterious, divine impulse whereby God becomes the Creator, an impulse to have and to hold fellowship with the creature, should not be construed as a necessity intrinsic to the nature of God as such. God is in himself an eternal fellowship, and in this fellowship he is sufficient unto himself. His will, therefore, to fellowship with those who are other than himself is his free decision and choice. As Creator he supplies our need; as creatures we do not supply his. The relationship between the Creator and the creature is not one of complementarity but of freedom on his part and dependency on ours.

In stressing the creature's dependency on God we are not saying what Schleiermacher says when he makes the "feeling of absolute dependency" rather than the question of origins the proper paradigm for understanding creation. Since we have only the aware-

---

7. See his "Sermon on Creation," as cited in Ray C. Petry, ed., *A History of Christianity* (Englewood Cliffs: Prentice Hall, 1962), p. 104.

ness of continuous, finite being and no consciousness of the beginning of being, the question of origins is raised, according to Schleiermacher, not in the interest of piety but of curiosity. Such a question properly belongs not to dogmatics but to natural science. It became a part of dogmatics, he contends, simply because Scripture was read in the ancient and medieval church as science. In more recent times, Schleiermacher's view has been reaffirmed by those in the liberal tradition, in the interest of a rapprochement between science and faith. (See below, this Unit, III, C, pp. 455ff.) Barth has criticized this position because it bases the doctrine of creation on human consciousness rather than divine revelation (*K.D.,* III/1, pp. 8ff.; cf. *C.D.,* III/1, sec. 40). Brunner complains, in a similar vein, that according to Schleiermacher, Ritschl, et al., Christian faith is simply not interested in the thought of creation (*Dogmatik,* vol. II, p. 47).

God is not only free to be, or not to be, the Creator, but also free as the Creator. In contrast to Greek thought, the Christian view of creation posits no primordial stuff, no recalcitrant clay antithetical to God that frustrates him in achieving his purpose or sets bounds to his creative powers.

When we say that naught can frustrate the free exercise of the Creator's power, it is granted that the writers of the Old Testament sometimes reflect the language of struggle and combat commonly found in the creation myths of the ancient Near East in general and of Babylon in particular. But the element of struggle itself is gone. There is no warfare in the Old Testament between God and an evil divinity, as between Marduk the god of Babylon and Tiamat whom he overcomes. Because God is all-powerful, deliberating only with himself in creation, the Old Testament writers feel free to use the mythological language of their neighbors without the threat of misunderstanding. Yahweh has crushed Rahab (a mythical, hypostasized opponent) "like a carcass" (Ps. 89:10), pierced the dragon (Is. 51:9), broken "the heads of the dragons on the waters" (Ps. 74:13), and "pierced the fleeing serpent" (Job 26:13). But these pictures of the Creator's relationship to the world in terms of combat with monsters are of no consequence for Israel's theological understanding of that relationship. Such ways of speaking no longer have a life of their own; they belong to the common treasure house of poetry, used—as Milton used the imagery of Greek and Latin mythology—to adorn the author's thoughts in rich apparel. (See W. Eichrodt, *Theologie des Alten Testaments,* Stuttgartiklotz, Teil II, pp. 72-73; also *Vocabulaire de Theologie Biblique,* pp. 172-73.)

2. CREATION AND THE DIVINE DECREE *(DECRETUM DEI)*

The doctrine that creation has its origin solely in God's will explains why many classic confessions and systematic treatises begin the treatment of the doctrine by speaking of the divine decree(s).[8] Indeed, some have

---

8. When used in the singular the term "decree" reflects the unity of the divine purpose.

elaborated the subject of God's decree (purpose, counsel) as an independent locus prior to the treatment of creation and providence. Such an order emphasizes that all that is and all that comes to pass is the unfolding of God's purpose. While we have not chosen to follow this order of treatment, obviously we concur with its fundamental intent. To trace the world back to the decree of God is to say that the world is not here by accident but by the resolve and purpose of an all-wise Creator. Yet our concurrence with "decretal theology" is not without reservation. The doctrine of the divine decree is easily stated in such a way that the relationship between God and the world becomes a static rather than a dynamic one. Such a static view threatens not only one's doctrine of creation, but also one's doctrine of providence, by undercutting the reality of human freedom, the seriousness of human responsibility, and the significance of human history.

The word "decree" is taken from the world of the oriental potentate, whose every whim had the cogency of law in his realm. The decrees of Ahasuerus stripped Queen Vashti of her royal prerogatives (Est. 1:19ff.), threatened the Jews with destruction (3:13ff.), and hanged Haman on the gallows he had prepared for Mordecai (7:9ff.). The decree of Nebuchadnezzar brought Shadrach, Meshach, and Abednego into the fiery furnace (Dn. 3:8ff.), and the decree of Caesar Augustus (the most powerful monarch that ever lived) brought Mary and Joseph to Bethlehem on the night of Jesus' birth (Lk. 2:1ff.).

Such a concept has its place in theological vocabulary as conveying the thought that God's purpose transcends the change and flux of history. The arbitrary connotation the word "decree" tends to have, as descriptive of the power of absolute despots, is overcome in the context of Christian faith by heeding the significant way in which the will and power of the Creator are in Scripture always united with his wisdom. The divine decree is carried out not only in a holy but also in a wise and loving exercise of power. Hence it should be understood not in terms of arbitrariness but in terms of God's sovereign constancy. It is, perhaps, because of the desire to avoid the connotation of arbitrariness that scriptural usage favors such terms as "counsel" or "purpose" rather than "decree" when speaking of God's eternal will and plan.

It is also worth noting that when the word "decree" is used in Scripture it sometimes refers to the creation ordinances of nature. God has "made a decree for the rain, and a way for the lightning of the thunder" (Job 28:26). The word "decree," then, seems especially appropriate to designate the will of the Creator vis-à-vis those creatures whose behavior is fixed and determined by the very nature he has given them.

> The earth with its store of wonders untold,
> Almighty, your power has founded of old;
> Has established it fast by a changeless decree,
> And round it has cast, like a mantle, the sea. (Grant)

When used in the plural, it reflects the rich and manifold character of the Creator's works by which his purpose is accomplished.

Other terms frequently used in Scripture to describe God's will as it relates to the freedom and choice of responsible creatures (προγινώσκω, "to foreknow," i.e., "to choose beforehand"; προορίζω, "foreordain," "predestine") will be discussed in due course.

3. CREATION AND CAUSALITY

Our reservations about using the term "decree" to describe the divine decision to create are felt even more strongly (though for other reasons) with the term "cause." To speak of God or of God's will as the cause of creation echoes, of course, the traditional vocabulary of dogmatics.[9] But with the impact of the natural sciences on the world of thought it has become increasingly difficult for the theologian to think of God's will in terms of causality.[10] Causality pertains to the realm of scientific explanation. Hence, to think of the origin of the world in terms of causality threatens to transpose the theological question of creation into the scientific question of cosmology. To the extent that the world can be causally explained, it carries its own immanent meaning. While the theologian is interested in such scientific meaning—as our subsequent discussion will show—such questions are not her primary concern. Her primary concern is not with the world's causal explanation but with its final explanation, which is the free decision and choice of a personal God.

To speak of God or his will as the "first cause" of all that is tends to make God a part of the cause-effect process. It also tends to substitute some sort of impersonal force for the God who is personal Subject. God is outside the causal order altogether, and that is why the writers of the Old Testament chose an entirely different concept to account for the origin of all things, namely, "creation."[11] Creation describes a miracle freely wrought by the transcendent will and power of the living God. It is a truth that can be known only through God's self-declaration: "I made the earth, and created humankind upon it; it was my hands that stretched out the heavens . . ." (Is. 45:11-12 NRSV). And since this is so, the doctrine is obviously an article

9. In the *Summa,* Thomas begins his "Treatise on the Creation" with Question 44: On the Procession of the Creatures from God, and of the First Cause *(Prima Causa)* of All Things.

10. We have already anticipated this problem in our discussion of the divine attributes. See above, Unit Four, II, C, 2, God's Power Is Not Natural Causality, pp. 355ff. Here we simply wish to focus on the implications of what we said there so far as the doctrine of creation is concerned.

11. See Heim, *Der christliche Gottesglaube und die Naturwissenschaft* (Hamburg: Furche Verlag, 1953), pp. 87-88.

of faith. It is "by faith we understand that the world was created by the word of God, so that what is seen was not made from things which appear" (εἰς τὸ μὴ ἐκ φαινομένων τὸ βλεπόμενον γεγονέναι, Heb. 11:3).

EXCURSUS: ON THE LOCATION OF CREATION IN THE CREED AS THE FIRST ARTICLE

While all Christians view creation as an article of faith rather than a scientific postulate, its location in the Creed as the first article calls for comment. We have in mind, particularly, Gustaf Wingren's criticism of Barth's so-called Christomonism or Christocentricity. In stating this criticism, Wingren makes much of the fact that creation is the first article of the Creed, not a "postscript" to Christology. Barth, according to Wingren, just does not like the order of the Creed; he wants the second article to be first. The Creed, on the other hand, simply follows the order of Scripture—it respects the structure of biblical revelation. (See his "The Doctrine of Creation: Not an Appendix but the First Article," *Word and World: Theology for Christian Ministry* [Fall 1984]: 353ff.)

We agree with Wingren that creation not only happens to be but ought to be the first article. This is the order that systematics requires. There is something to be said, however, on Barth's side of the argument. In the first place, whatever view of order a given systematician may take—and the systematician is never indifferent to the question of order—all would agree that to say, "the LORD made heaven and earth, the sea, and all that is in them" (Ex. 20:11) is to make a statement of faith. Barth (*K.D.*, III/1, p. 12; cf. *C.D.*, III/1, sec. 40) is as eloquent as any on this score. It is, he observes, only the twenty-four elders before the throne representing the confessing community of Israel and the church that can say: "You are worthy, our Lord and God, to receive glory and honor and power, for you created all things, and by your will they existed and were created" (Rv. 4:10-11 NRSV). Creation cannot be thought—in this Fichte was right—for it transcends thought; it can only be confessed. It is a truth that is reasonable only to that reason which is open to truth it cannot discover, reason that strives not simply to think its own thoughts after itself but God's thoughts after him. One is reminded of Bertocci's observation: "If there were anything a *created* mind could not be expected to understand, it would be its own creation!" (*Introduction to the Philosophy of Religion,* New York: Prentice-Hall, 1951, p. 451). To confess God as Creator, then, is an act of faith to which one is brought through the knowledge of God as Redeemer.

In the second place, the Creator who makes heaven and earth is, as we have noted, also the Redeemer who makes a new heaven and a new earth (Rv. 21:1). Hence, though the systematician treats first of creation and then of salvation, she would be ill-advised to separate the two, for both are the work of one and the same God. Furthermore, in the experience of the believing community the order of systematics is actually reversed. Israel's faith begins with the affirmation: "I am the LORD your God, who brought you out of the land of Egypt" (Ex. 20:2). This knowledge of God as Redeemer is gradually enlarged to include the knowledge of God the Creator who in the beginning created the heavens and the earth (Gn. 1:1). That is to say, in the faith of Israel Yahweh the

Redeemer becomes God the Creator. That Exodus follows Genesis in the canon reflects a logical, not an existential, order. The Israelites did not say "The Creator is Yahweh," but "Yahweh is the Creator."

We grant, of course, the antiquity of Israel's belief in creation in view of the ancient creation myths of her near neighbors. Such myths are found in Egypt, Mesopotamia, and in Akkadian texts reflecting the Sumerian tradition (*Vocabulaire,* p. 171). But it is her faith in God the Redeemer that gives Israel full insight into the meaning of creation. As W. Foerster observes (*TDNT,* III, p. 1001), the whence *(Woher)* question is really a "boundary question" for the people of Israel, a question whose answer derives from their understanding of the "what" *(Was)* and the "whereto" *(Wohin)* of their own existence. As the time of the exile approached, the questions of "what" and "whereto" were deeply probed by the prophets. As a result, the relation between God's ongoing action in history and his original act of creation became more sharply delineated. The exile is seen as a divine judgment that Yahweh inflicts on Israel through other nations not in covenant, in order that his people may be chastened and restored. In doing this, Yahweh shows himself to be not only Israel's God but the God who made the earth and all who dwell in it. "It is I who by my great power and my outstretched arm have made the earth . . . and I give it to whomever seems right to me. Now I have given all these lands into the hand of Nebuchadnezzar" (Jer. 27:5-6). It is in the experience of the exile that Israel clearly perceives the integral theological connection between Yahweh's saving acts in history and his initial act of creation in the beginning. Behind the biblical account of salvation history beginning with the story of creation is Israel's experience of salvation and judgment. (See Von Rad, *Old Testament Theology,* New York: Harper, 1962, pp. 136ff.)

And what is true of Israel is also true of the Christian church. Of course, the doctrine of creation was a part of the Christian confession from the beginning; in fact, as Wingren has said, it is the first article of the Creed. But, as we have noted, the almighty Father, Maker of heaven and earth, who is confessed in the first article, is the God and Father of our Lord Jesus Christ, by whose redeeming Spirit we first learn to confess that God is our Creator, that "it is he that made us, and not we ourselves" (Ps. 100:3 KJV). For the new Israel, then, as for the original Israel, the confession of God the Creator arises out of the confession of God the Redeemer. This is the truth in Barth's approach, the implications of which, in our judgment, Wingren and others do not fully appreciate.

C. STARTING WITH NOTHING: CREATION AS
CREATIO EX NIHILO

1. INTRODUCTION

The church, we have seen, rejected the Greek dualism of God and eternal matter as impugning the divine freedom; God is not limited by matter as

Michelangelo was by marble. The church also rejected Gnostic emanation; the world did not originate out of the divine Being as an oak out of an acorn. Hence there is no correlation between God and the world; the world is not God's alter ego, his "double" (Brunner). If it were, then God would be God only in relation to the world, whereas in Scripture he is revealed as Lord of the world. The rejection of all dualistic theories of God and the world, on the one hand, and all pantheistic theories of continuity between God and the world, on the other, left the church with only one option: creation, defined as God's making something (the world) out of nothing. The church, then, has always recognized *creatio ex nihilo* as the plain implication of biblical revelation.

Meditating on the divine act of creation in the *Confessions*, Augustine includes even space and time in that which came to be, of nothing, by the divine word. "Verily, neither in the heaven, nor in the earth, did you make heaven and earth; . . . nor in the whole world did you make the whole world; because there was no place where to make it, before it was made, that it might be." The world, in other words, was not made in space but with space. So also with time. To the question, "What was God doing before he made heaven and earth?" Augustine replies: "But if before heaven and earth there was no time, why is it demanded what you then did? For there was no 'then' when there was no time."[12] Therefore God may be said to have created all things, even the "where" and the "when," of nothing, by his word alone.

The doctrine of *creatio ex nihilo* is first stated in so many words in 2 Maccabees 7:28. The thought, however, is implied throughout the Old Testament. The erudite efforts of exegetes, therefore, to show that the Hebrew root בָּרָא, as used in Genesis 1:1, does not entail the meaning of creation ex nihilo, are more academically impressive than theologically significant, since the doctrine does not rest on the *ipsissima verba* of Scripture but on its general implication. Besides, no exegesis can show that what is said in Genesis 1:1 is incompatible with creation ex nihilo. Indeed, who (or what) is there "in the beginning" but God? The first Christian thinker clearly to draw the inference from Scripture that creation is ex nihilo was probably Clement of Alexandria. The doctrine was elaborated by his contemporary Tertullian (ca. 200) and from that time on has been generally received by the church. (See Pelikan, *The Christian Tradition*, vol. I, p. 36.)

In opting for creation "of nothing," the church does not embrace the absurd; it does not deny the self-evident axiom that of nothing, nothing comes (*ex nihilo nihilo fit*). Nor, as we have seen, does it understand "nothing" in the phrase "out of *(ex)* nothing" to refer to a negative, primal, formless,

12. *Confessions*, XI [V], 7; XII [X], 12 and [XIII], 15.

amorphous, uncreated something (ὕλη ἀγγένατος). Rather, creation "of nothing" means that God spoke (called, commanded) something into being when there was nothing. In the beginning there was only God and his will to create. In creating all things God took counsel with himself alone.

Some have argued that it was to preserve the thought of *creatio ex nihilo* that the LXX chose κτίζω over δημιουργέω to translate בָּרָא. The former refers to that which is spiritual and volitional in nature, the latter to the work of the craftsman. (See W. Foerster, *TDNT*, III, κτίζω, p. 1026.) Others have noted that the sheer scope of the creative act, as described in Scripture, implies creation out of nothing. In the beginning, God made "the heavens and the earth" (אֵת הַשָּׁמַיִם וְאֵת הָאָרֶץ, Gn. 1:1), that is, "everything." The predicate of the opening sentence in the Old Testament is the equivalent of the New Testament expression "all things" (τὰ πάντα, Eph. 3:9). Again: "In six days the Lord made heaven and earth, the sea, and all that is in them" (Ex. 20:11). The Lord in this verse is the same Lord by whom the mighty angel swears in the Apocalypse, the Lord "who created heaven and what is in it, the earth and what is in it, and the sea and what is in it" (Rv. 10:6). What, then, is left that is uncreated? What did the Creator have in hand when he created?

2. "AND GOD SAID . . . AND IT WAS SO"

The Creator, we have argued, did not act upon something when he created, for there was nothing to act upon; he did not speak to someone, for there was no one to hear. The creative word was a word spoken from within himself alone. The God who is in eternal conversation with himself as a Trinity becomes, by the act of creation, the God in conversation with the creature. In this regard, it is instructive to note the way in which Scripture commonly describes how God creates. As Creator, God actualizes his will by simply speaking. He says "Let it be," and it is so (Gn. 1). "By the word of the LORD the heavens were made, and all their host by the breath of his mouth. . . . For he spoke, and it came to be; he commanded, and it stood forth" (Ps. 33:6; see also Ps. 148:1-5). In like manner, the early Christians spelled out what they understood by creation in terms of God's word: "By faith we understand that the world was created by the word of God" (Heb. 11:3).

Creation by speaking is nearer the thought of *creatio ex nihilo* than creation by doing. Figures of the latter are, indeed, used: "the heavens are the work of your hands" (Ps. 102:25 NRSV; Heb. 1:10); "I made the earth, and created humankind upon it; it was my hands that stretched out the heavens" (Is. 45:12 NRSV).[13] But, as Foerster has observed,

---

13. Westermann is surely correct in affirming that the world begins as a deed, a personal act. *Genesis 1–11* (Minneapolis: Augsburg, 1984), vol. I, p. 23. Also, it should be noted, the

it is creation by speaking, creation through the word, that is the theologically

> adequate expression (so far as such is possible) for God's act of creation. . . . creation by word underscores the wonderful, "spiritual" character of creation and the absolute transcendence of the Creator over against the creature that cannot oppose him with so much as a passive resistance of the sort "inert," raw material opposes to the process of fashioning. . . . Creation by word finds its culminating expression in *creatio ex nihilo*."[14]

Speaking of creation by word as best suited to express the meaning of *creatio ex nihilo*, we are reminded of an observation of Dorothy Sayers that a "poet is not obliged . . . to destroy the work of a Hamlet in order to create a Falstaff, as a carpenter must destroy a tree-form to create a table-form." The works of artistic imagination, therefore, are the nearest approach to creation out of nothing that we can experience at the human level. "Thus Berdyaev is able to say: 'God created the world by imagination.'"[15]

We have already identified the Word (Logos), through whom all things were made, as the eternal Son, the second person of the Godhead. (See above, Unit Three, IV, D, Addendum: Concerning the Logos, pp. 303ff. Also this Unit, III, A: Creation Is the Work of the Father Through the Son and the Spirit, pp. 446ff.) It will come, then, as no surprise to hear that theologians have associated God's creation by his word with the thought that the Creator is himself the Word. "We believe," says the *Belgic Confession,* Art. XII, "that the Father, by the Word—that is, by his Son—created of nothing the heaven, the earth, and all creatures, as it seemed good to him, giving to every creature its being . . . and several offices, to serve its Creator."

Reflecting on the power of the Word by whom all things were made, some have seen that power reflected in the accounts of Jesus' miracles. He who is himself the Word often performs his miracles by simply speaking a word. "Only say the word," replies the centurion, "and my servant will be healed." (See Heim, *Der christliche Gottesglaube und die Naturwissenschaft,* vol. VI, p. 70.) In this regard, of course, one immediately thinks of the stupendous miracle of Lazarus' resurrection reported by the fourth evangelist, who begins his gospel narrative, "In the beginning was the Word." Standing before the tomb, Jesus says: "Lazarus, come out" (Jn. 11:43), and he came

---

root עָשָׂה, "to do," "to make," is often used of God's creative activity. In fact, עָשָׂה occurs as frequently as בָּרָה in the first creation narrative, though בָּרָה is used in the lapidary first verse of the narrative.

14. "κτίζω," *TWNT,* III, p. 1011 (cf. *TDNT,* III, pp. 1011-12). Foerster also observes (op. cit., p. 1010) that word-creation stresses the radical discontinuity between Creator and creature, an inescapable, if — to the scientific mind — offensive, implication of the Christian concept of creation.

15. Dorothy Sayers, *The Mind of the Maker* (San Francisco: Harper, 1979), pp. 27-31.

out, even as God in the beginning said: "Let there be light; and there was light" (Gn. 1:3).

Finally, we must remember that the God who creates all things of nothing is not only the Logos/Son but also the Creator Spirit. It is by the "breath of his mouth," whose very name is "spirit," "breath" (רוּחַ), that the heavens were made and all their hosts (Ps. 33:6). (See above, Unit Three, IV, D, 2, c, The Relational Meaning of the Trinitarian Name: Father, Son, and Holy Spirit, pp. 287ff.)

D. WORKING WITH SOMETHING: CREATION AS *CREATIO CONTINUA*

In ancient cosmogonies and in Greek philosophy the world is eternal. According to the Bible, by contrast, the world's coming into being is an event, a divine act, a wondrous calling into existence of that which is essentially new. The whole universe is a big surprise, something absolutely astonishing. The *terminus technicus* in Scripture for the godlike act that brought the world into being is the Hebrew root *bara'* (בָּרָא), which is used in the Old Testament only of God. He alone can make something of nothing.

In keeping with this fundamental understanding of creation, theologians traditionally construed most, if not all, of the events of the first creation narrative as immediate acts of God, a series of divine fiats. The text of the first creation narrative, however, easily allows for mediate as well as immediate creation. Though it is God who commands the earth to bring forth plants, each according to its kind, it is the earth that brings them forth (Gn. 1:12). In verses 24-25, God is said to have made the beasts of the field by commanding the earth to bring forth living creatures after their kind.[16] Such a way of speaking implies not only a newness of living forms but also a continuity with the preexisting earth from which they come. In the more detailed description of how God made the man and the woman, found in the second creation narrative, the thought of using preexistent materials is explicit. God is said to have formed the man out of the dust of the ground (Gn. 2:7) and to have made the woman out of the rib of the man (Gn. 2:22).[17]

To speak of creation by the use of preexisting materials, to liken the Creator to a potter who works with clay or a carpenter who builds a

---

16. In both passages the verb occurs in the jussive of the Hiphil, "to cause to go or come out," viz., of the ground.

17. The root in Genesis 2:7 is יָצַר, "to form or fashion," as a potter of clay; in 2:22, בָּנָה, "to build or fashion," as a builder of a house.

house, is every way compatible with the usage of Scripture. The numerous living things with which the sea teems die when God takes away their breath, and they are created (בָּרָא) when he sends forth his Spirit to renew the face of the ground (Ps. 104:29-30). Creation, then, is an ongoing work of God that continues down to the present; it is *creatio continua.* Such a view of creation is not in conflict with the fundamental meaning of creation as *creatio ex nihilo.* Creation of nothing has to do with beginnings; it does not imply that the Creator's work is at an end— forever finished. The world with which Scripture is concerned, as well as the world of which science speaks, is not a fixed and static one that knows no change nor newness through change. Though it began with an act of God, it was not finished in that act. Rather, it continues, a dynamic world of process and movement, a world with a history that is called "natural" history. The processes through which the Creator works, implicit in the original creation narrative, are ongoing in time. Nature's story is one of movement, progress, and development, fulfilling the purpose of the Creator.

It is true that theologians have traditionally distinguished God's original work of creation, wherein he calls the creature into being, from his ongoing works of providence, wherein he preserves the creature in its being. Such a distinction is both scriptural and necessary. The doctrine of continuous creation is not a substitute for the doctrine of providence. However, we should not separate God's works of creation and providence in a rigidly wooden way. While Scripture warrants making a distinction between them, the doctrine of continuous creation affords the needed flexibility in relating creation and providence as aspects of the one work of the one God.

By the same token, the doctrine of continuous creation should never be made a substitute for the doctrine of creation out of nothing; rather, the two should be held in tandem. By rightly relating the two we avoid errors on both sides. On the one hand, the doctrine of creation out of nothing keeps us from thinking of creation as an eternal act of God, as though the Creator and the creature were correlatives in which the creation complements the Creator. On the other hand, the doctrine of continuous creation keeps us from thinking of creation as a single act of God in a remote past in which he not only began but finished the creation, winding it up like a cosmic clock that runs on its own momentum. Such a view of the creation is more deistic than scriptural. The verb "to create" is, indeed, basically used in Scripture in the past tense; it is in the beginning, we are told, that God created the heavens and the earth. But this use of the verb in the past tense does not exclude its meaning in the present tense. It is because God is the Lord God who made the heavens and the earth in the beginning that he can say, "I form (יָצַר) light and create (בָּרָא) darkness" (Is. 45:7) from day to day.[18]

The dialectic between the continual newness manifested in the created order (God's calling new creatures into being) and the ongoing continuity of the created order (God's providential preservation—*conservatio*—of all his creatures) is often thought to be best illustrated in the miraculous events of salvation history. In such events, to be sure, there is a striking manifestation of newness that points to the power of the Creator to work both through and seemingly apart from ordinary means. How else could one feed five thousand with five loaves and two fish (Mk. 6:38ff.)?

But when we speak of the dialectic of God's creative and providential work, we have in mind much more than the isolated instances of the miraculous. In fact, the best illustration of the interplay of the divine *creatio* and *conservatio* is perhaps the human subject, perceived as an individual (new) instance of humanity. Such a subject is, in one sense, only a particular manifestation of the genus *homo*. But in the Christian vision, the self, the "I," is more than simply a particular configuration of genetic material inherited as a member of the human species. When the psalmist speaks of his origin as an individual self, he does not thank God for making a generic humanity of which he has become a particular expression as the result of generations of procreation. He rather confesses, "*My* frame was not hidden from you, when I was being made in secret . . . in the depths of the earth" (Ps. 139:15 NRSV). While the reference is undoubtedly to his mysterious formation in the womb, such a statement should not be construed as a comment on the biology of fetal development. It is rather a confession that God the Creator was uniquely at work in making him. The psalmist means what Luther and all Christians mean when they say, "I believe God created *me* and all that exists." (See below, this Unit, VI, Creation and the Christian Life, pp. 502ff.) Interestingly, the verb the psalmist uses of his own creation (v. 15) is the same verb (עָשָׂה) used in the Genesis account of the creation of the original human pair when God said, "Let us make humankind in our image" (Gn. 1:26 NRSV).

---

18. In the usage of Scripture, God's continuing work of creation refers primarily to his work as Redeemer. This is true not only for Israel (Is. 45:8) but also for the church. "For we [Christians] are his workmanship, *created* in Christ Jesus . . ." (Eph. 2:10). This work of the Redeemer is not treated by the theologians under the doctrine of creation, however, since it concerns the central theme of the gospel. As such, it opens up a whole new world of thought, namely, redemption, which is just as big a surprise as the original creation. That is why it is called the *new* creation. We will treat this subject under the general rubric of "salvation." Barth uses "reconciliation" *(Versöhnung),* a concept introduced at the beginning of *K.D.,* IV/1.

FIRST ADDENDUM: ON THE MEANING OF GENESIS 1:2

Genesis 1:2 reads:

וְהָאָרֶץ הָיְתָה תֹהוּ וָבֹהוּ וְחֹשֶׁךְ עַל־פְּנֵי תְהוֹם וְרוּחַ אֱלֹהִים מְרַחֶפֶת
עַל־פְּנֵי הַמָּיִם

Ordinarily this verse is translated: "The earth was without form and void, and darkness was upon the face of the deep (the abyss); and the Spirit of God was moving (hovering) over the face of the waters." By way of exception, it has been rendered in the New Revised Standard Version of the Bible: "the earth was a formless void and darkness covered the face of the deep, while a wind from God [or while a mighty wind] swept over the face of the waters."

Barth calls this passage—with reason—a *crux interpretum* and ventures that its interpretation is as difficult as any in the whole Bible. We agree — hence this addendum, located at this point because the interpretation of Genesis 1:2 relates to the question of immediate versus mediate creation that we have just considered. Though interpreting the verse has long been recognized as difficult, there has been a surprising consensus— Augustine, Thomas, Luther, Calvin—on what it means. This consensus, reflected in the first translation given above and found in virtually all versions, beginning with the Septuagint, emphasizes the creative work of the Spirit of God. According to this common view, God created heaven and earth by first positing a formless, unordered, unstructured universe— a watery abyss of darkness, void and without form. This primal universe contained the potential that he summoned into actuality by his creative word and so made heaven and earth, as we read in Genesis 1:1. God's first act of creation, then, was followed by successive acts of creation, whereby in six days he shaped the formless matter that he had made of nothing into heaven and earth as a home for humankind.

Though it has an impressive pedigree, the interpretation of Genesis 1:2 as referring to formless matter *(informitas materia)* puts the theologian on the horns of a dilemma. Either God began with something independent of himself, like a potter with clay, or he created something before the first day of creation recorded in verse 3. As we have seen, the church has always rejected the former view. Unlike Plato's demiurge, God began with nothing in his hand; by his word alone he created all things. This being so, the traditional interpretation of Genesis 1:2 leaves one with the question: How could creation have begun with the calling of formless matter into being in verse 2 when verse 3 says that it began with the summons, "Let there be light?" As has often been observed, in verse 2 there is no, "Let there be darkness"; darkness is not something, but the lack of something, namely, light.[19]

Furthermore, there is the difficulty, given the traditional interpretation, that while verse 2 does not say anything at all about creation, yet God's creative activity is inevitably injected into the text by the assumption that it is God's Spirit, the *Creator Spiritus,* who moves over the face of the waters. "Spirit of God" is, indeed, the most plausible translation of רוּחַ אֱלֹהִים. But how can one associate the Creator Spirit with a watery waste that is formless and dark? Here the traditional translation appears, in context, to be an intolerable misfit.

Theologians have worked hard to make all these things come together. As for the thought that God created formless matter before the first day, Augustine reasons that in the "near nothing" of the formless earth nothing could change from one form to another. Hence there was no motion or repose and so no time; and this is why Scripture makes no mention of "days" until the creation of light in verse 3, which is therefore called the first "day" of creation.[20] As for the thought that the creative Spirit of God is present in the dark and watery waste, it is sometimes suggested that here we have the Creator in the figure of a mother bird, brooding over the primordial egg of the universe that is about to hatch. But the world was not born of God any more than it was begotten of him. The world was rather created by God, who spoke it into being. Others have suggested that the darkness and the waters needed to be harnessed and organized, and this begins, as the Spirit moves over the watery waste, with a shaft of light that scatters the darkness and inaugurates day one. But to think of creation as a harnessing and organizing of something is quite different from *creatio ex nihilo.* Such a thought reflects the mythological struggles found in Mesopotamian cosmogonies rather than the sovereign word of divine command found in Scripture.

---

19. In the new Jerusalem there is no night (Rv. 21:23; 22:5), for the new creation is "a land of pure delight" where "eternal day *excludes* the night" (Watts). How strange, then, to suppose that the first creation, seen by God as good (Gn. 1:31), should have begun with darkness!

20. See his *Confessions,* XII, 15ff., where he pursues many subtle arguments. For example, were there no sound, we could not chant. Yet there is no sound *before* we chant. This seems to us to say only that we cannot chant ex nihilo. But God can and does create ex nihilo. Thomas also is zealous to deny that formless, created matter preceded *in time* its formation into heaven and earth. Though empty, shapeless, and invisible, buried under primeval waters, this amorphous world did not lack form altogether, but only in the sense that it had not the beauty of light nor the adornment of herbs and plants. See *Summa,* vol. I, Q. 66, First Article.

In view of the problems with the traditional interpretation, we make the following suggestions concerning the possible meaning of Genesis 1:2.[21]

1. Genesis 1:1: "In the beginning God created the heavens and the earth" is a general announcement having no special relation to verse 2. Standing as it does at the beginning of the first creation narrative, it is related to all that follows, not only in verse 2 but in the entire six-day creation account as found in verses 3–31. As such, this opening sentence in the Bible is unique; no such preface is found in any other creation story of antiquity (Gunkel). It functions as a superscription of lapidary brevity, evoking the all-inclusive character of the divine act of creation (Eichrodt). The subsequent, six-day creation narrative simply unfolds what the superscription contains (as a newspaper article a good headline); it adds nothing essentially new to it.[22]

2. Genesis 1:2: "The earth was without form and void, and darkness was upon the face of the deep" is not a description of preexisting chaos that the Creator shapes into a cosmos. The whole idea of formless, or "near formless," matter is Greek rather than biblical. Adopted by Augustine in his effort to interpret Genesis 1:2, it found its way into Christian thought and so unfortunately has become a permanent feature of the theology of the church.

The effort to show that the unformed matter of verse 2 is not eternal but created, yet that there is no creative act prior in time to the first day of creation (v. 3), is so much sterile casuistry. This Augustinian misinterpretation of Genesis 1:2 is echoed in the Revised Standard Version translation of Hebrews 11:3, which reads, "what is seen was made out of things which do not appear." The negative is misplaced, in our judgment. The text should read (as in the King James): "what is seen was *not* made of things which do appear."

In 2 Peter 3:5, the reference is to the scoffers who deliberately ignore this fact, that the heavens and an earth were formed from of old out of water and by means of water (ἐξ ὕδατος καὶ δι' ὕδατος συνεστῶσα). The reference is not to the primal waters of Genesis 1:2; rather, the author is thinking of Genesis 1:6-10, which speaks of God's creating a firmament called "heaven," which separates the waters under it from the waters above it, and of dry land called "earth," which appears when the lower waters are gathered into "seas."

---

21. In making these suggestions we will reflect the argument especially of Eichrodt, *Theologie der Alten Testaments,* Teil II (Stuttgart: Klotz, 1961), particularly pp. 65ff.; and the first volume of Westermann's *Genesis 1–11,* particularly pp. 97ff. See also Von Rad, *Old Testament Theology* (New York: Harper, 1962), vol. I, p. 144.

22. To put a period at the end of Genesis 1:1 does not violate the waw-consecutive structure of the Hebrew original.

3. The language the author of the first creation narrative uses in Genesis 1:2 admittedly reflects that of Mesopotamia, especially of the Babylonian creation epic. However, as we noted above, the use of mythological language by the biblical writers is inconsequential, since the faith of Israel constitutes a new theological context that gives such language an utterly different meaning from what it has in Near Eastern mythology.[23]

4. Having started with the exalted superscription of verse 1, the author turns to his detailed account of how, specifically, God created the heavens and the earth. He begins with a description, in verse 2, of the impalpable character of the situation before creation. It is a situation devoid of all creative potential and set forth in a picture of nonexistence. Thus the stage is set for the first creative word: "Let there be light." Though the language used to draw this picture is mythological, Genesis 1:2 contrasts with neighboring mythological texts in that it shows the author's unique capacity for abstraction. He has in mind not the monstrous world of chaos, which is hostile to God, but a lifeless impalpability prior to divine creation. True, he does not have the conceptual tools adequately to express such an abstraction; but the pictorial description he gives is the very image of the utter nullity that constitutes the proper setting for creation. Thus the narrative passes from the nothingness of verse 2 to the somethingness of verse 3 (i.e., light).[24] The danger that such mythological imagery may be construed as referring to primordial, amorphous, preexistent matter is real enough, as the traditional (Augustinian) misunderstanding of this verse illustrates. Yet this danger is sufficiently overcome by the emphasis in the subsequent narrative, especially in verse 3, on creation by the divine word alone. To call light into being by simply speaking implies its *creatio ex nihilo*.[25]

5. Undoubtedly, the most controversial aspect of the interpretation we suggest is the meaning it implies for רוּחַ אֱלֹהִים in the second half of the verse, "And the רוּחַ אֱלֹהִים was moving over the face of the waters." These words have been traditionally understood as referring to the Spirit of God.

23. See this Unit, III, B, 1, pp. 450-51.
24. We use the term "nothingness" in the ordinary dictionary sense, not as the equivalent of Barth's *das Nichtige*.
25. It must be granted that to say the earth was "without form and void"—*tohu wabohu* —is not simply to say: "The earth was in a state of non-existence." While this is our understanding of the author's basic intent, the added note of the ominous is also present in what is said. As Delitzsch once remarked, there is something fearful in this pair of words. As the thought of calling something into being out of nothing is awesome, so also is the corollary thought of nonbeing, nothingness. The language of Genesis 1:2, we might add, awakens the feeling evoked by Shakespeare's line, "To be or not to be: that is the question." *Hamlet*, Act III, sc. 1, l. 47.

But it is quite within the parameters of grammatical possibility to construe רוּחַ as "wind" and אֱלֹהִים as a superlative meaning "almighty," "tempestuous."[26] Given this meaning, the text reads, "And a mighty wind was sweeping over the face of the waters." Thus we have the picture of a raging, tempestuous wind, rushing along without rest or purpose over the expanse of a dark and boundless sea.[27] In this way the author draws a picture of nonbeing; of all that is opposite to the world God brings into being when he speaks his mighty creative word: "Let there be light." Whereas "Spirit of God" jars upon the structure of the narrative, the rendering "mighty wind" does not. And so we conclude that Genesis 1:1 is the general heading or title of the first creation narrative. The author then begins his narrative, using the language of myth, to paint a vivid picture of nothingness (1:2) prior to the creation. In this way he sets the stage for the story of the creation of the world in six days, beginning with Genesis 1:3 and ending with Genesis 2:3.

When the science of geology was in a nascent stage, devout students of Scripture sometimes suggested that such phrases as "without form and void" and "darkness was upon the face of the deep" were descriptive of the primordial condition of the earth's crust. As geological studies advanced, it was further suggested that the initial creation of the world in Genesis 1:1 was followed by many geological upheavals that took place on planet earth over a long period of time. Genesis 1:2 describes the chaotic condition to which the earth was reduced due to these ancient geological upheavals. As a result of these speculations, a distinction came to be made between the original creation of the earth and the reconstitution of the earth as we now know it. It is the reconstitution of the earth that is described in the six-day creation narrative. Such an interpretation enabled one, so it was believed, to acknowledge the geological evidence that the original earth was very old and at the same time to construe the six-day creation story literally. This story referred to the reconstituting of the earth, a recreation after primeval, geological disturbances had reduced the original earth to a chaos. Thus Genesis 1:2 should not be translated: "the earth was," but "the earth became without form and void."

Whereas the apologetic motif of harmonizing Genesis and geology was ever present in this approach, a further question naturally intruded itself: Why should this have happened? Why did God destroy the original earth? A ready answer was found by many in the fall of Lucifer, a theme having an ancient pedigree in theology, though its association with a primal catastrophe in Genesis 1:2 is a recent conceit. All these diverse strands of thought are reflected in the Scofield Reference Bible

26. See Genesis 23:6, for example, where the response of the Hittites to Abraham is translated both in the KJV and the RSV: ". . . you are a mighty prince (נְשִׂיא אֱלֹהִים, literally, "prince of Elohim," i.e., God) among us. Also Exodus 9:28, where קֹלֹת אֱלֹהִים, literally, "voices of Elohim," i.e., God, is rendered "mighty thunderings."

27. In the first circle of Dante's hell, the souls of the lustful are tossed forever upon a howling wind in "a place made dumb of every glimmer of light." *The Divine Comedy*, I: Hell, Canto V, 25ff.

Jeremiah 4:23-26; Isaiah 24:1 and 45:18 clearly indicate that the earth had undergone a cataclysmic change as the result of a divine judgment. The face of the earth bears everywhere the marks of such a catastrophe. There are not wanting intimations which connect it with a previous testing and fall of angels. *The Holy Bible,* ed. by C. I. Scofield (New York: Oxford, 1917, p. 3, n. 3).

Though the 1967 edition of the Scofield Bible suggests this view as simply one of two possible interpretations, the primeval cataclysm theory still has wide acceptance in American fundamentalist and dispensational circles. Due to exegetical problems, as well as the want of scientific evidence for such a universal, primordial catastrophe, this interpretation of Genesis 1:2 has not been generally accepted. (Equally problematic, in our opinion, is the effort to harmonize Genesis 1 with modern astronomy by construing verse 2 as referring to a dark nebula that condensed into planet earth. Science and the Bible cannot be harmonized by reading either good or bad science into the Bible.)

SECOND ADDENDUM: ON THE MEANING OF "HEAVEN AND EARTH" IN SCRIPTURE AND IN THE CONFESSIONS OF THE CHURCH

Perhaps more familiar than any other in the Bible are the words, "In the beginning God created the heavens and the earth" (Gn. 1:1). Summing up their message as Christian apostles, Paul and Barnabas centuries later used the same words when addressing their hearers in Lystra: "We .. bring you good news," they cried, "that you should turn from these vain things [the worship of idols] to a living God who made the heaven and the earth" (Acts 14:15). Having said what the first article of the Creed means by the words "God" and "Maker," we pause to comment briefly on the concluding phrase: "heaven and earth." God, in the Christian confession, is said to be the Maker of "heaven and earth." In reflecting on the scope of God's creative act, we observed that the phrase "heaven and earth" means simply "everything." Starting with nothing, God created heaven and earth: he created everything that is.

There is, then, no qualitative difference between heaven and earth as there is between Creator and creature.[28] Though heaven is not earth and earth is not heaven, both are part of one and the same creation; both are given their reality by the will of God. The difference between heaven and earth is a real difference, yet it is not an ultimate but only a penultimate

28. God transcends, in other words, both heaven and earth. "The LORD is high above all nations, and his glory above the heavens!" Seated on high, he "looks far down upon the heavens and the earth" (Ps. 113:4-6).

one. It is a difference-in-likeness. Ordinarily, to be sure, we think of the difference rather than the likeness; heaven, in our thought, contrasts with earth rather than compares with it. Such likeness-in-difference and difference-in-likeness calls for a brief comment.

At times, "heaven" in scriptural usage is simply the enlargement of earth. It is the atmospheric realm of the meteorologist, the celestial expanse of the astronomer. When Job is answered out of the whirlwind with the riddles of God, "more satisfying than the solutions of men" (Chesterton), the text alludes not only to the "foundations of the earth" and "the bars and doors of the sea," but in the same breath to the "hoarfrost of heaven," the "wisdom in the clouds," and the "chains of the Pleiades" (Job 38 passim). Hence the Christian sings,

> He built the earth, he spread the sky,
>   And fixed the starry lights on high:
> He fills the sun with morning light,
>   And bids the moon direct the night. (Watts)

"Heaven and earth," then, refers to the totality of the visible universe: the land, sea, and atmosphere, with the plants and animals that live in them; and the sun, moon, and stars as well, with all their hosts. In the six days of the first creation narrative we are told that God made everything we can see, feel, taste, or touch. In this light, it is plausible to give Genesis 1:1 a rather circumscribed reference. In the first verse of the Bible, "the heavens and the earth" may be construed not as meaning all things other than God, but all visible things, since it is the visible universe with which the subsequent narrative is concerned. Genesis 1:3-31 has to do with creatures that appear in the vault of heaven, fly in the air, swim in the sea, and live on the land. They are all part of that visible realm seen by an earthly observer. In the beginning God brought forth this visible realm through six days of creative activity followed by a day of rest that ends the story of the "generations of the heavens and the earth when they were created" (Gn. 2:4a). The title, then, of the narrative (Gn. 1:1), like its signature (Gn. 2:4a), refers to the visible realm of time and space.

But while this narrower, geocentric understanding of the phrase "heaven and earth" is possible, if one considers only the content of the first creation narrative, Scripture often views heaven as more than the enlargement of earth. While both heaven and earth are part of the same creation and shall perish like a garment grown old (Heb. 1:11), while both shall be replaced with "new heavens and a new earth in which righteousness dwells" (2 Pt. 3:13), yet there is a polarity in the relationship of heaven to earth. God has given the earth to humankind as their abode, but "the heavens are the LORD's heavens" (Ps. 115:16). It is to the Father "in heaven" that Christians pray; and it was "from heaven" that the Son "came down for our salvation" to be born in Bethlehem. Heaven, then, describes not only the visible realm of time and space, but the invisible realm where saints and angels enjoy fellowship with the Creator beyond the reach of sin and death. When the writers of Scripture speak of this realm, though it is inaccessible to telescope and microscope, Christian faith does not dismiss their witness as so much infantile imagining and excessive hyperbole. To do so would be to identify with Bunyan's muckraker, whom Christiana saw as she entered the house of the Interpreter. There

> was a man that could look no way but downwards, with a muck-rake in his hand: there stood also one over his head with a celestial crown in his hand, and proffered him that crown for his muck-rake; but the man did neither look up or regard, but raked to himself the straws, the small sticks, and the dust of the floor.[29]

If the visible universe is vaster than planet earth, why should not creation as a whole be vaster than the visible universe? If the grandeur of the empirical heavens evokes awe, even in this space age, why should not this vast and mysterious realm be a paradigm that images forth a reality yet more mysterious than our present, earthly reality? While such a reality is a created reality, it is, in the Christian view of things, a reality where the incognito of this material world, which veils God's presence, is lifted. Though the Creator himself transcends all his works, though he is the God whom "the heavens and the highest heaven" cannot contain, yet he is pleased to be found in fellowship with his creation and to make heaven the "seat of his throne," his "dwelling place" and "habitation."[30]

---

29. *The Pilgrim's Progress,* part II, chap. III.
30. In this addendum we have found helpful the article *"Ciel,"* by Fenasse and Guillet, in *Vocabulaire.* For a more detailed discussion of the divine transcendence, see Unit Three, II, God Is the Holy One, pp. 189ff.

IV. Creation and the Question of Temporal Origins

A. "IN THE BEGINNING . . ." GENESIS 1:1

The offense to the modern mind given in the Christian understanding of the world begins with the opening words of the Bible. We have already touched on the reason for this offense: creation implies that the world cannot be immanently explained.[1] This offense is sharply focused when one affirms that the Christian doctrine of creation is a statement about the beginning of *all* things, since such a statement implies that all that is had a first moment; the entire universe of time and space is dated.[2] All our beginnings, by contrast, emerge out of former endings; for us a beginning is always the conclusion of what happened before on the line that we call time. But when we speak of an absolute beginning, not the beginning of this or that, but just *the* beginning, we speak of an event that is unlike any other.

Such an event cannot be tied to other events by analogy; it is neither the implication of logical analysis nor a part of the empirical cause-effect nexus. Reason would say that since there is something (a universe) there must always have been something, for of nothing nothing comes.[3] Expe-

---

1. See this Unit, I, Introduction, pp. 438-39.
2. This is not to say that a particular date of creation, such as 4004 B.C., is entailed in the thought of creation. *When* the universe began is the concern of cosmology; the concern of theology is *that* it began—by an act of God.
3. As Kant observes, creation represents a conceptual impasse because it implies a "before" that is a void. See Weber, *Dogmatik* (Neukirchen-Vluyn: Neukirchener, 1955), vol. I, p. 544, for a summary of the Kantian proof that the world had no beginning. Actually, the doctrine of creation does not imply a voidless "before." As we have argued, the doctrine is not that the world was created *in* time, but *with* time.

470

rience would say that an event that is not linked to any other as the effect of a cause would be unqualifiedly novel, an absolute singularity. Such an event, therefore, is beyond the reach of empirical observation. Hence, for the modern mind the idea of a creation of all things "in the beginning" is no more than a private religious opinion that cannot be taken seriously.

In the ancient church Origen sought to remove this "offense," so far at least as the Greek mind was concerned, with his doctrine of eternal creation. But the church rejected Origen's view as heretical because it made the creature a correlate and complement of the Creator. While not espousing Origen's views uncritically, many Protestant theologians since Schleiermacher have sought to restate the doctrine of creation in a way that leaves open the question of temporal origins. Unlike Origen, they are concerned not so much with the objections of Greek Idealism as with the data of the natural sciences, especially astronomy and cosmology. It was out of such apologetic concern that Schleiermacher argued that the question of origins is the domain of the natural sciences, not of Christian piety; the "feeling of absolute dependence" does not involve the awareness of beginnings.[4] Many theologians have followed Schleiermacher in seeking to distance themselves from a doctrine of creation that includes the traditional thought of an absolute beginning. In so doing they hope to frame a doctrine that cannot be discredited by the advances of science.[5]

Given such a liberal approach, the fundamental property of the world as created is not its origin in time but its lack of self-sufficiency. Creation affirms that the world is what it is by the will and power of a personal God. It is his will that gives the world its being and his power that sustains it in its being. To speak of creation, then, is to speak not of a temporal beginning but of an ontological relationship, a relationship of transcendence and dependence. To say that God is transcendent and the world dependent is not to say that the world is a part of God; the world has its own reality, but it is a God-given reality. And because the God who gives the world its reality is all-wise, the world is a reality that is orderly, purposeful, and ultimately good. These are the essential matters in a Christian doctrine of creation. The question of a beginning in time is indifferent.[6]

---

4. See above, this Unit, III, B, 1, pp. 450-51.

5. Even E. L. Mascall, an able spokesman for orthodox Anglicanism, reiterates the conviction that "whether the world had a beginning is profoundly unimportant for theology." Just why he is so confident that this is so is not clear other than that such a view gave him the freedom to be profoundly indifferent to the choice between a steady state (Hoyle) and a expanding model (Gamow) of the universe. See his *Christian Theology and Natural Science* (London: Longmans, 1956), chap. 4, "Creation in Theology and Science."

6. See I. G. Barbour, *Issues in Science and Religion* (Englewood Cliffs: Prentice-Hall,

One cannot doubt that the Christian understanding of creation includes much of what is said by Scheiermacher, and those who have followed him, concerning the nature of God and the world. Creation does signify the Lordship of the Creator, on the one hand, and the dependence of the creature, on the other. But the very fact that this relationship is ongoing means that it is not indifferent to time. Rather, it is the Creator's act of bringing the creature into time that grounds the relationship between them and gives it meaning. To say, with Augustine, "You have made us for yourself" is, indeed, to confess our dependency on the Creator. But the dependency we confess is a temporal dependency; we do not have a supratemporal being. To say that God has made us is to confess that our being had a first moment; that we are not only in time but that we entered into time; time began for us by the will and act of the Creator. It is just because God created us in a moment that is past that all the subsequent moments that make up our lives are qualified as the moments of a creature utterly dependent on him. Thus our life has meaning because it is the gift of the Creator who, in his eternal purpose, willed that we should be and in due time called us into being in fulfillment of his purpose.

And so it is with the world as a whole. It is because God created "heaven and earth" in a moment that is past, called "the beginning" (Gn. 1:1), that the world and all its subsequent moments called history have meaning. History is the fulfilling of the eternal purpose of him who "in the beginning" brought the temporal world into being by his word. Creation, then, is not only an ongoing relationship but an ongoing relationship that presupposes and derives its significance from a past event. It is of this past event, not a timeless, metaphysical truth, that the Bible speaks when it affirms, "In the beginning God made the heavens and the earth."

B. CONTEMPORARY COSMOLOGICAL MODELS

In our discussion of theological method, we spoke at some length about the way faith and reason are related in the doing of theology.[7] We lamented the sometimes adversarial nature of this relationship reflected especially in the conflict between theology and the natural sciences. In seeking a rapprochement, theologians have often restated the doctrines of the faith;

1966), pp. 365ff. Langdon Gilkey, in his *Maker of Heaven and Earth* (Garden City: Doubleday, 1959), reflects the same approach.

7. See above, Unit One, II, Theological Method, pp. 17ff.

but when it comes to creation there has been some restatement on the part of scientists as well. We have in mind, of course, those developments in modern astronomy that bear on the question of cosmic origins.

The church has traditionally rejected the Greek idea of eternal matter on which the Creator imposes form; we too have rejected it. (For this reason we have taken issue with the followers of Schleiermacher, who make a temporal beginning of the physical universe a matter of indifference.) The material world is not a correlate of the eternal God; the Creator creates with nothing in his hand. This aspect of the Christian doctrine of creation has, as we have seen, been especially offensive to autonomous reason. The thought of an absolute beginning confronts the mind with a seeming impasse. It implies a first event—which no one could ever observe—which would be an effect without a cause. In short, it would be an absolute singularity, a novelty than which none greater could be conceived. Little wonder, then, that such an idea never crossed the mind of the Greeks and has never found a place in the Enlightenment mind of Western civilization. But of late, the word "creation," often in quotation marks, has been creeping into the literature of the natural sciences as the evidence from astronomy increasingly indicates a first moment for the entire cosmos.[8]

The story begins with the discovery of galaxies (island universes) receding from the earth in all directions. Picking up on this intriguing development and working with the largest telescope available, Edwin Hubble discovered that the more distant the galaxies are as they move away from earth, the more rapidly they are receding.[9] Furthermore, the velocity of a receding galaxy is proportional to its present location; a galaxy 20,000,000 light-years away is receding twice as fast as one 10,000,000 light-years away. This is known as Hubble's Law and is an instance of the law of uniform expansion.[10] In the light of these data, the idea of an expanding universe was born. "It is interesting to note," says Jastrow,

> that now the first signs of irritation begin to appear in the scientific community. When de Sitter pointed out to Einstein that an expanding

8. Of the many books on this subject, perhaps the easiest to read is that of the internationally known astronomer Robert Jastrow, *God and the Astronomers* (New York: Norton, 1978). See also Paul Davies, *God and the New Physics* (New York: Simon and Schuster, 1983). The following discussion will reflect these and other sources.

9. The remoter galaxies are receding at a velocity of 600,000,000 miles an hour, well over half the velocity of light, and at least one quasar (young galaxy?) appears to be receding at 90 percent of the velocity of light!

10. This law applies to everything from the galaxies in the expanding universe to the raisins in a rising loaf of bread. Some have estimated the present diameter of the expanding universe at 28 billion light-years. Our own galaxy is a mere 100,000 light-years in diameter.

universe was a feature of the solutions of his own equations of relativity and also that it expanded in accordance with Hubble's Law, which was now coming to be known to astronomers, Einstein wrote to him saying: "I have no quarrel with your mathematics in that proof; but this circumstance [of an expanding universe] irritates me." What a funny word to use for a mathematical result. In another letter he writes concerning the notion of an expanding universe that "to admit such possibilities seems senseless." Why should the movement of the galaxies away from us and one another be labeled nonsensical by a theoretical physicist? Why the emotional content of these words? The answer is to be found in another part of the first letter when Einstein points out to de Sitter that if all the galaxies are moving away from one another, there would be what Einstein called a "singularity in time." In other words, the universe would have had a beginning.[11]

Einstein saw immediately that if the universe were uniformly expanding, then, were the paths of the galaxies traced backward in time like a movie in reverse, they would meet and commingle and so all the matter in the universe would become compressed in one place till it was so hot that it would explode.[12] Such an explosion, the so-called "Big Bang," would mark the beginning of the universe. This idea of a beginning of the universe bothered Einstein because it presupposed a personal agent who started everything. Such an assumption, Jastrow surmises, was anathema to him because he did not believe in God the Creator. He rather believed in Spinoza's God, who brought order and harmony into the universe as revealed in his own relativity equation.

When Hubble announced the law of an expanding universe, Einstein traveled all the way from Berlin to Pasadena, California, to look through the telescope on Mount Wilson and study the plates showing the "red shift" before he became convinced that Hubble was right. As the implication of Hubble's expanding universe became more widely understood, there was increasing negative reaction in the community of scientists. The idea of an expanding universe was found "hard to believe," "repugnant," "incredible," something that "leaves me cold," something that "really cannot be true." Jastrow, who quotes such protests on the part of leading astronomers, his friends among them, comments on the value-laden, emotional, subjective character of such remarks, the more surprising since they are uttered by astrophysicists, supposedly the most objective of all scientists.

11. Jastrow, "Science and the Creation," *Word and World* 4 (Fall 1984): 348.
12. The density of this primal matter defies imagination. Even the stars it threw off can be very dense indeed. The *Los Angeles Times*, 15 October 1971, reports the finding of a star whose density is forty trillion pounds per square inch, a hundred times denser than all the cars in the United States compressed into a thimble!

He attributes what he calls "this strange resistance" to the fact that science has its own religion. Among its cherished dogmatisms is the deep conviction that the order and harmony in the universe is such that every event can be explained in a rational way as the product of some previous event. Every effect must have a cause; therefore there can be no first cause. This religious faith is violated by the discovery that the world had a beginning under circumstances scientists cannot investigate because they are circumstances in which the laws of physics do not apply. This traumatic experience of encountering such a state of affairs leads scientists to "refuse to speculate"; or to trivialize the origin of the world by calling it the "Big Bang," as if the universe were a firecracker. (See Jastrow, *God and the Astronomers,* pp. 112ff.; also his "Science and the Creation," p. 351).

Some who are reluctant to accept an expanding universe have postulated a steady-state model in which the density of matter remains constant. Such a universe would be eternal, having no beginning or end. But it does require the continuous creation of new hydrogen. And so *creatio ex nihilo* must be tolerated in an ongoing, secondary way. But there is no evidence for such fresh input into the system. Rather, for the universe as a whole there is only an inexorable descent into chaos; the movement toward loss of order is irreversible. Exceptions can be seen only when we look at limited systems, and even then there is nothing that appears de novo. Entropy will finally win and the universe will reach thermodynamic equilibrium.

Others admit the universe is expanding but not that it had a first moment. They postulate an oscillating (pulsating) model in which the universe explodes, expands, and then contracts and explodes again, in a never-ending cycle. The "big bang" is followed, to use another trivializing expression, by the "big crunch." But here again one has to postulate something that is purely speculative in the light of the data. The winding down of the universe can be clearly stated; it is called the second law of thermodynamics. But how shall we describe the process of rewinding? After the locomotive has gone down the track, burning its coal and belching its steam until its boiler is cold, how can one recapture the dissipated heat energy to drive the locomotive back where it came from? Here the answer is given that as the galaxies are thrust outward by the most recent explosion, gravity holds the galaxies in tow and finally puts the brakes on until eventually they collapse together again. Thus the caldron of energy is renewed to fuel another expansion phase such as we are now in. And so the universe is eternal after all.

It is true that the expansion of the universe may be slowing and therefore gravity could eventually reverse the outward thrust of the galaxies and we would have a cosmic illustration of the principle that what goes out must come back. But there are problems. The critical factor is the density of matter. Particles of matter must be close enough together to maintain their mutual gravitational attraction. Otherwise gravity can never halt the expansive thrust. The minimum required density to halt the expansion of the universe is calculated to be one hydrogen atom in a volume of ten cubic feet. But even when scientists take into account the invisible, undetected matter in the universe, the total is more than ten times too small to reverse the outward movement of the galaxies. (See Jastrow, *God and the Astonomers,* pp. 118ff.) So as far as the universe is concerned, time is linear rather than cyclical.

Not only is the expanding universe without the problems faced by other cosmological models, but it has been further confirmed by the detection of the defused radiation emanating from the original explosion when the universe came into being.

Jastrow calls this "the clincher which has convinced almost the last doubting Thomas." Thus, the scientific pursuit of the past ends in the moment of creation. (The moment can even be dated at 20 billion years, more or less. Our sun, of course, is much younger [10 billion years] and planet earth younger still [4.5 billion years].)

The triumph of an expanding model of the universe, observes Jastrow, is an exceedingly strange development, for it confronts the scientist with an insurmountable barrier before which, it appears, no further progress will ever be possible. Thus he concludes:

> For the scientist who has lived by his faith in the power of reason, the story ends like a bad dream. He has scaled the mountains of ignorance, he is about to conquer the highest peak; as he pulls himself over the highest rock, he is greeted by a band of theologians who have been sitting there for centuries.[13]

What Einstein and other scientists have experienced as a bad dream many theologians have hailed as a breakthrough of great theological significance. Mascall refers to the almost lyrical eloquence with which Pius XII concludes his November, 1951, elocution to the pontifical Academy of Sciences. In this pronouncement, the Pope speaks of the sweeping step science has taken back across millions of centuries whereby it bears witness to "the primordial *Fiat lux* uttered in the moment when, along with matter, there burst forth from nothing a sea of light and radiation."[14]

We too find the scientific story a fascinating one.[15] Yet we greet it with something less than papal enthusiasm. Our belief in creation rests, as it always has for the church, not on science but on revelation. If one is persuaded that "the world was created by the word of God" (Heb. 11:3), which is what creation means, it is a persuasion that comes through faith in that very same word of God. The natural sciences will never take us back to the moment of creation as such. When the universe was young it was bathed in an obscuring fog of radiation that no light can penetrate, now or in the future. Thus, as God caused a deep sleep to fall on the man when he made the woman, so he has veiled the moment that he made the universe behind a curtain of mystery.[16]

13. *God and the Astronomers,* p. 116.
14. *Christian Theology and Natural Science,* pp. 151-52.
15. It has been said to be the equivalent of the news that the Montagues and the Capulets are collaborating on a baby shower. See Ted Peters, "Cosmos and Creation," *Word and World* 4 (Fall 1984): 373, quoting *Time* magazine.
16. To Pope's lines,

> Nature and nature's laws lay hid in night,
> God said: Let Newton be! and all was light;

Furthermore, were the theologian to rest her affirmation of creation on the natural sciences (i.e., on knowledge gained from the world itself), consistency would compel her to embrace a scientific view of the end of the world as well, an eschatology dismal beyond imagination and shrouded in nihilistic darkness.[17] The theologian, therefore, should never baptize any leading scientific theory as such. The intelligence that the universe is expanding, with the implication that time is moving in one direction, that the cosmos is contingent, and that it had its origin in a given moment in the past, does confirm the Christian view of origins in a most remarkable way. Yet such conclusions describe a methodological frontier of astronomy; they do not constitute a rational demonstration of the doctrine of creation.

The theologian is open to all knowledge of the world gained from the study of the world. Indeed, since nothing can be true for faith that is contrary to the data of observation, it would be folly—as past history has shown—for the theologian to be closed to such knowledge. The doctrine of creation itself teaches that this world is God's world. Truth about this world is God's truth, whether it be given by revelation or discovered by reason. There is, then, a continuity in our knowledge of the world as seen by the eye of reason and our knowledge of the world as seen by the eye of faith. Yet we cannot, in the study of theology, pursue the scientific story further at this juncture. We must leave behind the question of the emergence of quarks, particles, and atoms out of "Planck time" and come immediately to the heaven and earth of everyday experience, for this is the world with which Scripture is concerned. Having announced that God created the heavens and the earth in the beginning, the text of Genesis turns at once to speak of that creative activity in which God makes planet earth a home for humanity. We shall now reflect on this aspect of the biblical doctrine of creation.

Interestingly, not only the astrophysicists but also the particle physicists are probing the mystery of origins. Working with the largest machines on earth (the estimated cost of the proposed new supercollider is 4.4 billion dollars), they explore the smallest things on earth—quarks, leptons, gluons, and other esoterica that make up the heart of matter. (Were an atom the size of an average office building, a quark at the center of the building

---

the Christian replies,

"Not quite."

17. The eschatology of science has been appropriately called the "cold death" of the universe. Were our sun like a coal-burning furnace, releasing its energy by chemical reaction between molecules, the end would be just around the corner for our race (ca. 6,000 years). Fortunately the sun is an atomic furnace. Nonetheless, it will eventually grow cold together with all the other stars.

would be no larger than the tiniest grain of sand.) Pursuing these particles and the forces that bind them together has moved scientists back toward the time when the universe was born in a primal explosion and all the forces, united in the beginning, began to separate as energy became matter.

Physicist Harold Schilling ponders this descent from cat to organ to tissue to cell to chromosome to gene to molecule to atom to nucleus to proton to quark, in a lecture "Post-Modern Science and Man's Sense of Depth and Mystery" (McCormick Quarterly [May 1968]: 335ff.). As he leaves the macroscopic world for the microscopic, he testifies to a sense of mystery that is only deepened by the increase of knowledge. By mystery, he says, he does not refer to the yet-to-be-solved but to the unfathomable, the ineffable, the awesome, the numinous.

However, there is something not only awesome but sinister about this descent into the depths. If probing outer space has ended up as a bad dream for many scientists, the probing of inner space may end up this way for all of us. The secrets of the nucleus have given the human family not only transistors, microchips, and laser surgery, but also the bomb. Noting that Paul perceived the threat of a religious philosophy that posited ultimacy in the basic constituents of nature (τὰ στοιχεῖα τοῦ κόσμου, Col. 2:8-10), Walter Wink goes on to refer, darkly, to the "idolatry instanced by modern science, with its cryptoreligious grailquest for the ultimate particle" (Unmasking the Powers, Philadelphia: Fortress Press, 1986, p. 206, n. 3).

C. "IN SIX DAYS . . ." GENESIS 1:3-31; EXODUS 20:11

In the foregoing discussion, we noted that astronomers have uncovered empirical data implying a first moment for the universe, a development of more than common interest to theologians who, unlike the scientists, have always spoken of what God did "in the beginning." We turn now from the question of how the universe as a whole came to be to that of how the world in which we live came to be. In the discussion of this question, once again we shall be concerned with the data of science, only in this instance it is the theologians' thinking rather than the scientists' that has undergone change. Having declared that "in the beginning God made the heavens and the earth," the Bible continues with an account of how God did it in six successive days of creative activity followed by a day of rest. A great deal of time and energy has been spent seeking to determine the literary genre of this seven-day creation account. Is it poetry, parable, allegory, saga, myth?[18] Until relatively recent times, almost no one bothered about such

18. The early Genesis narratives have even been read in terms of the yin-yang relationship, the Yahwist materials representing the yin tendency, the Priestly materials, the yang. See Conrad Hyers, The Meaning of Creation: Genesis and Modern Science (Atlanta: John Knox, 1984).

a question; the first chapter of Genesis was understood, as were the rest of the early chapters of the Bible, as historical narration. On the first day God called the light into being, on the second the firmament of heaven, separating the waters from the waters, and so on. These were events, occurring in days of solar time and wrought by the power of God, even as were the deliverance of his people from Egypt and the establishing of David on the throne of Israel. Thus the world, and all that is in it, came into being in a week of time about six thousand years ago.[19]

This traditional reading of the creation account—reflected in the creeds of the church both Catholic and Protestant—would seem to be the way it was read and understood by God's ancient people, who worked for six days and rested on the Sabbath as God had done at creation (Ex. 20:4). Of course, neither in ancient Israel nor in the church did anyone ever suppose that the author of the first creation narrative based his account on the report of eyewitnesses, as Luke, the author of the third Gospel, purports to do when he joins the "many [who] have undertaken to compile a narrative of the things which have been accomplished among us" (Lk. 1:1). Everyone knew the answer to the question put to Job, "Where were you when I laid the foundation of the earth?" (Job 38:4). But though no neutral witnesses were present at creation to take notes, the form of the creation story in Scripture is clearly that of a historical narrative, like the subsequent narrative of salvation history culminating in the Incarnation and Pentecost. Genesis 1:3-31, in other words, purports to be an account of what happened when God created the world; it is concerned with real events that took place—as the classic expression goes—"in the space of six days."[20]

Today, however, few who confess the Christian doctrine of creation would suppose that the world was fashioned in a week of time some six to ten thousand years ago. Drafts of time of a vastly different magnitude

19. Whatever we may say of this traditional view, it is self-evident that the early chapters of Genesis are not written according to the recognized canons of modern historiography; the Bible does not begin (Gn. 1-11) with critical history. On this point virtually all present-day scholars agree. However, when one asks what genre, then, best describes the opening chapters of Genesis, such consensus disappears. For ourselves, we prefer the thought that the Bible begins with what might be called an introductory *Heilsgeschichte;* the form is that of an historical narrative shaped by Israel's faith in the God of the covenant. The intent of this theologized history is to show how God brought the world and humankind into being and how the subsequent human story, as it unfolds in the call of Abraham, Sarah, and their descendants, leads to the establishing of the covenant community of faith.

20. "In the beginning of time, when no creature had any being, God, by his word alone, *in the space of six days,* created all things. . . ." *The Irish Articles of Religion,* Art. 18. The *Irish Articles* appeared in 1615. The *Westminster Standards* (1647) use the same phrase, as do those confessional standards that were influenced by them. Though Galileo died in 1642, this mode of expression continued to be widely used in the church for many years.

are indicated by the findings of the natural sciences. Nor would most Christians suppose that the creation of the earth as we now know it consisted of a series of instantaneous events—creation by simple fiat. The study of geology, especially, indicates that the events spoken of in Genesis actually occurred over a long period of time as a result of processes that are still occurring today (uniformitarianism).

Within American fundamentalist circles there are those who dissent from this majority opinion and maintain the traditional view that creation occurred in six solar days about six thousand years ago. For example, many Seventh-Day Adventists, named for their observance of the seventh-day Sabbath, have followed Ellen White in seeing the choice as one between the Bible, which is God's word, and science, which is a human word. Were the days of Genesis not literal, the seventh-day Sabbath would not be literal. But if the original seventh-day Sabbath was not a literal Sabbath, then how could one be sure she was keeping the right day as the Sabbath memorial of the creation, as God enjoins us to do in the fourth commandment (Ex. 20:11)? As far as planet Earth is concerned, the data to which geologists appeal, found in the rocks and fossils, is looked upon by Adventists as the catastrophic result of the Noachic deluge. Therefore, one need not postulate long periods of time to explain such data. This view, sometimes called "flood geology," was first advocated by George McCready Price, a Seventh-Day Adventist, in a book entitled *The New Geology* (Kansas City: Pacific Press, 1923).

Members of another group who believe that the world was created in a week of time six to ten thousand years ago are known as "Scientific Creationists." Scientific Creationists challenge the generally accepted conclusions of the natural sciences—physics, astronomy, geology, and biology—especially as they bear on the question of evolution. The movement takes its name from a book of H. M. Morris entitled *Scientific Creationism*, published in 1974 by Creation-Life Publishers of San Diego, an affiliate of the Institute for Creation Research. While biblical literalism and inerrancy are essential ingredients of the Scientific Creationists' approach to Scripture, the really distinctive aspect of the literature that they publish is the claim that the very data to which science appeals yield a contrary result. The evidence is there for a "young earth" in the rocks and fossils, but it has been misinterpreted by the scientific community as a whole, including many members of that community who are confessing Christians! Oftentimes the arguments of the Creationists are fraught with difficulties evident even to those who are not scientists. There is also the problem that frequently their leading spokespersons have no specialized expertise in the areas in which they publish. It seems to be assumed that a Ph.D. in civil engineering may make one not only a good engineer but also an authority on spectroscopy and carbon dating.

We have argued that the creation story in Genesis 1 is written as historical narrative. If then we would understand it, we must begin by reading it for what it is, which is the way the church has read it for centuries. It is not to be read as a poem, like one of the psalms; nor as a fable, like Jotham's fable of the talking trees (Jgs. 9:7-15); nor as a parable, like

Nathan's parable to David (2 Sm. 12:1-6); nor as an allegory, like the story of Bunyan's Pilgrim. Nor is it to be read as a myth, like the myth of Sisyphus and the rolling stone. Greek myths give concrete expression to abstract, timeless truths. But the biblical account of creation is not about abstract timeless truths. It is rather about events in time and space. The account, therefore, takes the narrative form. Hence, the text should be read for what it is—a narrative of events occurring in time and space. Whatever problems we may have with such a narrative, we cannot resolve them by reading it as something other than what it is.

It is for this reason that we must dissent from the way many sincere Christians in the scientific community understand the creation account. So far from treating it as myth or allegory, they sometimes read it as if it were a scientific document written in prescientific language. To such a reading of the biblical story, they bring a knowledge drawn from contemporary science about the nature and origin of planet Earth, seeking to show how such knowledge harmonizes with Scripture. There is, to be sure, a striking parallel between the general sequence of events as given in Genesis and that of the geological timetable. The natural history of the planet may, in a way, be regarded as beginning, both in the Bible and in modern science, with the succession of day and night, progressing through various stages involving the gathering of the seas, the heaving of the land masses, the emergence of plant and animal life, and climaxing in the appearance of homo sapiens. For those who accept the Bible as inspired revelation, such a parallelism can hardly be a mere coincidence. Yet the approach that seeks to harmonize science and the Bible by reading the biblical narrative in terms of modern scientific thought is always in danger of failing to understand the narrative in terms of itself. When this happens, one easily reads out of the text what one has already put into it, a common hermeneutical transgression. Illustrations of this sin turn up repeatedly in the way well-meaning interpreters explain the particulars of the biblical story of creation with the help of the latest scientific data.[21]

For example, we read that on the second day God said: "Let there be a firmament between the waters to divide the waters from the waters." Attempts have been made to understand this text in terms of a vaporous canopy (waters above the firmament) that shrouded the earth in steam, creating a tropical effect as the waters condensed into rain and gathered on the earth's surface (waters below the firmament). But is it plausible to

21. See, by way of illustration, Albert van der Ziel, "Modern Version of Creation," *Journal of the American Scientific Affiliation* 33 (Sept. 1981): 172ff. The author attempts "to recast the story of creation in Genesis 1 in terms of our present knowledge of the world around us" in such a way that its "theological content" is retained.

understand such an ancient text in such modern scientific terms? In keeping with the view that Israel shared with other peoples of antiquity, is it not more likely that the "firmament" (רָקִיעַ), created on the second day, refers to the solid vault of heaven that separated the waters above it from the waters of the oceans beneath it?

To cite another example, we read that on the fourth day God made two great luminaries, the greater to rule the day and the lesser to rule the night. To construe this as meaning that the sun and moon were not created but simply made to appear on the fourth day, as the vaporous envelope around the earth condensed into clouds revealing the blue sky, is to read a great deal into the text, it would seem. Do we not do this because, living after Copernicus, we are convinced that the sun must already have been shining in the heavens long before the fourth day? Only by making such an assumption can we account, scientifically, for the succession of day and night on the first day (v. 5) and the appearing of plant life on the third day (v. 11). But again, are we not failing to read the narrative on its own terms? For us, Helmut Thielicke's thesis would seem to be nearer the mark. He argues that the creation of the heavenly bodies is noted on the fourth rather than the first day to disarm the mythology of Babylon. Having vanquished Chaos, the Babylonian god Marduk begins creation by first making the stars and giving them great influence in the world, an idea basic to astrology down to the present day. But no such view is ever countenanced in the Old Testament. Though the sun was worshipped by Israel's neighbors, it was divested of its numinous powers in Israel. In the biblical narrative of creation, therefore, the sun and all the heavenly bodies are not created first but long after the *Fiat lux* of Genesis 1:3. They do not make light; they simply bear light.[22]

When one reads the creation narrative in terms of natural science, to cite one last example, the meaning of the sabbath rest on the seventh day is that no "higher forms" have appeared since homo sapiens; with the creation of humankind the Creator's work is finished. Now this may be true, but no adequate theology of the Sabbath, central both to the faith of Israel and the church, should ever look in this direction. To do so would be to miss altogether the significance of the Sabbath of creation, the denouement of creation's story. The Sabbath symbolizes the ultimate purpose of creation; it is the rest of delight and satisfaction God takes in his creation as he gives himself in fellowship and love to the creature made in his image.[23] Only such an interpretation of the creation Sabbath reflects

---

22. *The Evangelical Faith* (Grand Rapids: Eerdmans, 1974), vol. I, pp. 100-101.

23. The Sabbath rest of the Creator obviously should not be taken literally as though the divine energies were spent in making the world. God had only to speak and it came to pass; there is no sweating Deity in the Old Testament.

the perspective from which the author of the Genesis narrative writes, a perspective that is not scientific but theological in nature.[24]

The Sabbath was the institution that determined the weekly rhythm of time in Israel. Surely, it would seem, its central place in the piety of Israel accounts for the fact that the first creation narrative has the form that it has: six days of creative work followed by a Sabbath rest. The days of Genesis are not discrete visions (Augustine) nor geological ages, for Israel knew nothing of geological time. (Nor is the geological timetable divided into six epochs or ages.) It is quite true that the Hebrew word for "day" (יוֹם) may refer to a time period of indefinite duration, as in the phrase "day of the LORD" (Am. 5:18-20). But obviously the word "day" in the Genesis narrative takes its meaning from the much older tradition of the Decalogue, specifically the fourth commandment. In this commandment, as found in Ex. 20:8-11, Israel is enjoined to observe the Sabbath because "in six days the LORD made heaven and earth . . . and rested on the seventh day; therefore the LORD blessed the sabbath day and hallowed it." In such a context, the six days of creation are plainly understood after the analogy of the days that made up Israel's week of work and rest.

Indeed, in the creation story itself the meaning of "day" is clear from the fact that "day" is identified with the light, in contrast to "night," which describes the darkness (v. 5). Such a solar meaning of the "days" of creation is also indicated by the repeated use of the phrase "there was evening and there was morning" to mark the end of one day and the beginning of the next. (The [to us] odd sequence in the phrase "evening and morning" reflects the fact that in the Old Testament the day begins at sundown.) We can only conclude, then, that the seven-day structure of the creation narrative with which the Bible begins reflects a theological rather than a scientific approach to the subject. The author is not concerned to describe how the world was made in a scientific sense, but to disclose the meaning of creation as a divine work culminating in a Sabbath rest.

The nonscientific orientation of the narrative is evidenced not only by the author's use of the sabbatical structure of time but also by the way he allocates the materials within that time frame. Eight works are compressed into six days of work. Furthermore, what we would call astronomy is spread over three days—the first, second, and fourth; geology and botany, on the other hand, share the same day—the third. And what is most surprising of all, animal and human life (zoology and anthropology) also share the same day—the sixth. Once again it seems obvious that the overriding concern of the author is the culmination of the Creator's work in the seventh-day Sabbath rest.

To recognize the theological *Tendenz* in the biblical narrative of creation not only frees one from the necessity to harmonize its content with

24. As biblical revelation unfolds, it becomes evident that this ultimate telos of creation has miscarried because of the creature's transgression. Hence the meaning of the Sabbath is largely construed in the Bible in terms not of creation, but of redemption viewed as the *restoration* of creation. God achieves, in the new creation, his purpose for the original creation. The dogmatic exposition of the Sabbath motif, therefore, belongs principally to the locus of soteriology both as a realized and as an eschatological hope. For more on the Sabbath rest of creation, see below, this Unit, V, C, God's Purpose in Creation, pp. 491ff.

contemporary science, but also enables one to perceive why God moved those who spoke under the inspiration of his Spirit to speak as they did. When God would tell his people how he made the world, he speaks of making it in six days and resting on the seventh. Thus, in what has been called a "massive" (Jenni) and "daring" (Buber) anthropomorphism, God stoops to the level of his people and identifies with them in their work. As they work six days and rest on the seventh, so also does he in his work as the Creator of all things. Of course the Israelites did not perceive the anthropomorphic character of the narrative with anything like the clarity we do; neither they nor the Christians who were the heirs of their faith knew anything of cosmic time. It was only after Copernicus and Galileo that we humans began sufficiently to penetrate the disguises of our environment as to become aware of such matters. While this awareness involves a striking paradigm shift in our empirical perception of the world, and underscores the childlike limitations of the understanding reflected in the biblical account of creation, such considerations are irrelevant to faith that grasps, in the figure of a week of work followed by a Sabbath rest, the essential mystery of the origin of all things in the will of God and the end of all things in the Sabbath rest of fellowship with him.

The prescientific simplicity of the story of God's making the world "in the space of six days" does not, then, deprive faith of the insight that the world is God's creation. In fact, it underscores the truth that the essential character of all creaturely existence is temporal. For the creature, in distinction to the Creator, time's arrow moves in one direction—from the first to the last day. But this reminder of our human finitude, the contingency of our being as creatures, is infused with hope because creation begins with the light of the first day and ends with the rest of the seventh, a Sabbath that will finally be fulfilled in that new creation where there is "no need of sun or moon to shine upon it, for the glory of God is its light, and its lamp is the Lamb" (Rv. 21:23).

Since the Israelites knew nothing of geological time, obviously they knew nothing of the geological processes that filled up that time. Hence their conceptualizing of God's work at the empirical level was quite different from our way of viewing things today. Our point, however, is that their ignorance of such matters does not alter the validity of the affirmation that the world is how it is by God's creative word. There is, then, no incongruity in one's singing, as a Christian on Sunday, about the "mighty power of God that made the mountains rise" (Watts), and speaking, as a geologist on Monday, about the plate tectonics that caused the Himalayas to heave and fall when the land mass of India collided with Asia. The problem comes, rather, when one tries to harmonize the theological statements of the Bible with the scientific statements of contemporary thought, failing to perceive that the two constitute different levels of explanation and understanding.

V. Creation and the Divine Wisdom

A. INTRODUCTION

We have defined creation as the actualizing (setting) of God's will, wherein he achieves a correspondence between what is and what he wills to be, a display of unimaginable power. Creation is also a display of God's wisdom. As we have noted, hypostatized Wisdom was the Creator's intimate Companion when heaven and earth were made.[1] Hence, it is no surprise that faith's eye has discerned in the very nature of the world a wisdom that is wondrously profound.[2]

The divine wisdom revealed in creation is evident to faith even in the way the story of the creation is told in Scripture. The "architectonic structure" (Eichrodt) of the first creation narrative underscores the unity of purpose in the Creator's manifold works, culminating in the creation of humankind in and for fellowship with himself. The Creator's word, then, is not only an expression of his will but a disclosure of his wisdom. Accordingly, the seers of Israel frequently indite the divine wisdom. All God's manifold works are made in wisdom (Ps. 104:24); by his understanding he has made the heavens (Ps. 136:5) and created the earth—not a chaos, but a home—to be inhabited by humankind (Is. 45:18). "The LORD by wisdom founded the earth; by understanding he established the heavens" (Prv. 3:19). This praise of the Creator's wisdom does not mean that the seers of Israel supposed such insight into the nature of things gave them

---

1. See above, Unit Four, III, God's Wisdom and Knowledge, pp. 369ff.
2. We prefer, in this regard, to speak of "faith's eye" rather than "reason's ear" with Addison. See his creation hymn based on Psalm 19, "The spacious firmament on high. . . ." Psalm 19, like all the nature psalms, is more an expression of Israel's faith than reason's insight. But more on this presently.

485

access to the ultimate mystery of the divine transcendence. Theirs is rather the language of reverence and worship.[3]

This reverence, evoked in the community of faith by the very nature of creation, has, interestingly enough, a sort of counterpart in the world of critical thought. Though a sense of awe and an attitude of worship belong only to those who stand within the circle of faith, unbelieving philosophers and scientists have often expressed wonder at the order and beauty manifest in the simplicities as well as the complexities of nature. If the theologian cannot dismiss the insights of reason when they challenge her faith, surely she need not ignore them when they lend credence to that faith. We shall, then, look briefly at the ways in which "nature" seems to many to point beyond itself to an Intelligence of a supermundane sort.

B. THE WORLD VIEWED AS THE PRODUCT OF MIND

Philosophers have long debated the question, Is the world the purposeful work of a beneficent Intelligence or the product of blind chance? William James calls this question the deepest of all philosophic problems.[4] The answer one gives to this question obviously determines whether one's philosophic vision is optimistic or pessimistic.

The Greeks of classical antiquity were the first to confront this choice. They used the word "cosmos" to express the beauty, order, and design they saw in the structure of the universe. The Atomists, like Leucippus and Democritus, who reduced the physical world to the random movement of indestructible particles, were the exception to this consensus. Such materialistic reductionism continues down to the present day, a possible but not especially attractive option. (See its rigorous defense in Jacques Monod's *Chance and Necessity*, New York: Knopf, 1971.) As Chesterton once quipped, Materialists understand everything in a way that means everything is not worth understanding (*Orthodoxy*, Garden City: Doubleday, 1959, p. 23).

But it is not simply the philosophers who have viewed nature as the "incarnation of thought" (Emerson); members of the scientific community have expressed similar sentiments, especially when they ponder the so-called "laws of nature." Positivistic physicists, of course, will always regard such "laws" as simply mental constructs—that is, useful fictions for cor-

---

3. See Walther Eichrodt, *Theologie des Alten Testament* (Stuttgart: Klotz, 1961), Teil 2/3, p. 70.
4. See his *The Principles of Psychology*, Great Books, vol. 53 (Chicago: Britannica, 1952), p. 5.

relating observations and making predictions.[5] But, as Eddington points out, when we probe deeply the laws of nature begin to elude us, which shows that our minds did not put them there.[6] The laws of nature, in other words, are discovered, not invented.

Furthermore, these laws are such that physical reality appears to be the product of Mind. The universe seems to have been designed, notes J. Jeans, by a pure mathematician. One may postulate a vast spectrum of conceivable universes, but our universe, capable of such complex structures as stable stars and atoms, falls within an infinitesimally small band of mathematical possibility. That is to say, the mathematical values expressed in the fundamental constants of our universe are tuned exceedingly fine. If, for example, the strong force that binds the particles in the nucleus of the atom were weakened by five percent, the nucleus could not stably exist. This would mean a universe without stars and with only a few elements more complex than hydrogen. If, on the other hand, the strong force was increased by a mere two percent, molecules, basic to all life as we know it, could not exist. Given these considerations, one can hardly resist the impression that a universe so sensitive to minor alterations in its basic numbers has been rather carefully thought out.[7]

The impression that the universe is the product of thought rather than a cosmic accident is reinforced by the second law of thermodynamics. The inexorable descent of the universe as a whole into chaos means that an extraordinary amount of order (negative entropy) must have been present at the start of things. It is this vast store of negative entropy that makes possible the cornucopia of new and varied forms in nature with all their marvelous diversity. To suppose that the universe began by accident or chance poses the question, Is it likely that it just happened to have begun in such a highly ordered state?

If the universe is simply an accident, the odds against its containing any appreciable order are ludicrously small. If the big bang was just a random event, then the probability seems *overwhelming* (a colossal understatement) that the emerging cosmic material would be in thermodynamic equilibrium, at maximum entropy, with zero order. As this is clearly not the case, it appears hard to escape the conclusion that the actual state of the universe has been

5. Michael Polanyi calls this positivistic view of physics (blind chance accounts for everything) "a massive modern absurdity." *Personal Knowledge* (Chicago: University of Chicago Press, 1958), p. 9.

6. See chapter XI, "World Building," in his *The Nature of the Physical World* (New York: Macmillan, 1929). Jaeger, *Paideia* (New York: Oxford, 1945), I, xx, claims that it was the Greek mind that first perceived what was hid to other nations, namely, that the world was governed by definite, comprehensible laws.

7. See Paul Davies, *God and the New Physics* (New York: Simon and Schuster, 1983), esp. chap. 12, "Accident or Design?" and chap. 13, "Black Holes and Cosmic Chaos."

"chosen" or "selected." . . . And if such an exceedingly improbable initial state was selected, there surely had to be a *"selector"* or *"designer"* to choose it. (Davies, ibid., pp. 167-68. Italics his. For further sources see Holmes Rolston III, "Shaken Atheism: A Look at the Fine-Tuned Universe," *The Christian Century,* 3 December 1986, pp. 1093ff.)

Though one may consider it highly improbable that the event with which our universe began was random, yet one must allow that it could have been. But statistically such an event would happen only once every $10^{10 \times 80}$ years, a mathematical figure so large that it would fill a chalkboard the size of the entire universe! Of course, such an unlikely chance event would pose no problem if one were to assume that the universe is eternal. An infinity of past time is time enough even for the most improbable event to have happened. The "brainy baboon who blew down a bassoon" would, in such an infinity of time, just possibly have "hit on a tune." But the real universe—the only one that has happened—is a mere 20 billion years old, a fleeting second in the infinite expanse of time statistically indicated for our universe to have come up in a random throwing of the cosmic dice.

What may a theologian say to these intimations of Intelligence reflected in the way the universe is? Were Thomas and Paley right after all? Is the cosmological argument a valid argument? We do not think so for reasons already mentioned.[8] Yet neither do we regard the data to which it appeals of no value. Though such data may not demonstrate the biblical teaching that the world has been made by an all-wise Creator, it surely corroborates it. The scientific description of the nature of created reality is a task, therefore, "no one will deem useless, who, in the light of grace, has read of the power, wisdom and goodness of God, the Creator, . . . in that same book of Creation appointed to us to read."[9]

The rational probing of nature's secrets by the scientist helps the believer read the book of creation with greater understanding. The truths discovered by reason as well as those given by revelation constitute the one truth about the world by which people of faith live in the world. As we have said, God is not only the God of Jerusalem but also of Athens. Yet, on the other hand, the God of Jerusalem is not worshipped in Athens, or, if he is, he is worshipped as the unknown God. And when he is made known, the Athenians laugh, for his wisdom appears to them as foolishness. Bearing this paradox in mind, we venture the following comments on the transcendent wisdom that many who do not stand in the circle of Christian

8. See above, Unit One, IV, Addendum, Concerning the Theistic Proofs, pp. 54ff.
9. Vincent de Beauvois, *Speculum Majus* in Ray C. Petry, *A History of Christianity* (Englewood Cliffs, N.J.: Prentice-Hall, 1962), p. 413.

faith, as well as those who do, have thought to discern in the natural order of the world.[10]

1. The universe, according to the Christian faith, does not arise by a timeless necessity from an impersonal Logos. However, it is only through him who is the Logos that the will of the Creator has been actualized in creation. All things, we are told, were made through the Logos (Jn. 1:3). Hence the will of the Creator is an intelligent will and the world he has made is a world amenable to reason: a cosmos, not a chaos.

2. The theologian, therefore, should gladly affirm the rational character of the universe and acknowledge the insights into the nature of this world that philosophy and science have afforded. It is to be lamented that such insights have sometimes been regarded as antithetical to the doctrines of the faith and opposed by the church, not only in the past, but even down to the present time.

3. Because creation is the actualizing of the will of an intelligent Creator, it is only reasonable that the creature made in his image (a Euclid, an Archimedes) should find nature amenable to *Geist,* yielding its secrets to reason quite apart from revelation. In fact, the Christian doctrine of creation helps one understand why mathematics, a product of pure intellect, applies so universally in the natural order.[11]

4. It would be a gross oversimplification to suppose that the Christian doctrine of creation made possible the rise of the natural sciences. In fact, as we have admitted, the church, in defending the faith, has historically resisted the progress of science. Yet it is no accident that the natural sciences have developed as they have in the "Christian" West. The doctrine that all things were created through the Logos implies that the creation has a structure that is ordered and accessible to the mind through rational analysis. While it is only by observation that we can learn what the world is like in particular, we can know a priori that it will reflect the intelligent will (wisdom) of its Maker.

> A world which is created by the Christian God will be both contingent and orderly. It will embody regularities and patterns, since its Maker is rational, but the particular regularities and patterns it will embody

---

10. In the wisdom literature of the Old Testament there is the perception of the organizing, illuminating possibilities of reason. In the New Testament, however, there is a wisdom revealed that makes foolish the wisdom of this world. The distinction between these two perspectives must not be forgotten by the dogmatician, especially at this point.

11. A striking instance is the mathematics Einstein found ready at hand to describe data beyond the reach of Euclidean geometry. In this regard, see Polanyi's argument that such a circumstance shows that the rationality that governs nature is independent of the empirical data. *Personal Knowledge,* p. 15.

cannot be predicted a priori, since he is free; they can be discovered only by examination. The world, as Christian theism conceives it, is thus an ideal field for the application of the scientific method, with its twin techniques of observation and experiment.[12]

5. To acknowledge the rational character of the natural order is not to affirm that the universe will finally prove to be self-explanatory. Such a conclusion would be the denial of the doctrine of creation. In fact, the more the universe is understood, the more mysterious it becomes. The theologian, however, must guard against the temptation to discover God whenever and wherever the data of nature have not proved amenable to rational explanation. Such a "God of the gaps" is ever in danger of being squeezed out of the world by the advance of science. The Creator God, who has revealed himself in Jesus Christ, is no such Deus ex machina.

6. Though God is the Creator, it is only as Redeemer that he is known as Creator. While the vicious attacks on Paley and the cosmological argument reveal the anti-Christian bias of many philosophers and scientists, the effort to get from a cosmic Designer to the Christian God discloses a bias in the other direction. Nature, indeed, yields impressive evidence that it is grounded in intelligent will; but this evidence is not such that the existence of the God revealed in Jesus Christ can be inferred from it. God remains veiled in his revelation in nature as well as in grace.[13]

When we speak of the veiled nature of natural revelation, we are not talking about the noetic effects of sin, a subject that will concern us at another time. We are simply noting that the nature of the world makes unbelief implausible but by no means impossible. In fact, if the evidence in nature, available to reason, were such that the highly gifted minds—the smart people—could discover God for themselves, the biblical doctrine of grace would be unhinged and falsified. God would become not the God who chooses the foolish things of the world to shame the wise (1 Cor. 1:26-29), but the God who calls the wise, according to the flesh, to confound the weak. In this regard one should recall Thielicke's comments on the testimony of the lilies of the field and the glow of stained-glass windows. (See above, Unit One, III, Speaking of God, pp. 25ff.)

---

12. E. Mascall, *Christian Theology and Natural Science* (London: Longmans, 1956), p. 132.

13. See above, Unit Two, II, Addendum: God Hidden in His Revelation, pp. 85ff.

C. GOD'S PURPOSE IN CREATION

"For," says Calvin, "as I have elsewhere said, . . . it is the first evidence in the order of nature, to be mindful that wherever we cast our eyes, all things they meet are works of God, and at the same time to ponder with pious meditation to what end God created them."[14] To the question of why God created the world, the answer has been given: that he might reveal his power, wisdom, and goodness and so bring glory to his name. None can doubt the power displayed in the universe that also witnesses in many ways to a transcendent wisdom.

> I sing the mighty power of God
> That made the mountains rise,
> That spread the flowing seas abroad,
> And built the lofty skies.
> I sing the wisdom that ordained
> The sun to rule the day;
> The moon shines full at his command,
> And all the stars obey. (Watts)

But what of the divine goodness, the *bonitas Dei?* If God's goodness is revealed to us anywhere, it must be here on earth where we live by the Creator's appointment. But the goodness we see in this present world we see only through a veil of tears. This fact has evoked the cry of the faithful, "O LORD — how long?" (Ps. 6:3). It has also challenged the dialectic of the theologians. Indeed, few questions open up larger issues of theological concern than that of the Creator's goodness in making the world.

We read in Genesis 1:31 that when God had finished his work as Creator he looked upon all that he had made "and behold, it was good" (וְהִנֵּה־טוֹב). The land was fertile, the vegetation fruitful (1:4, 12); in short, everything was suited to the purpose for which it had been made. And what was that purpose? Implied in the very sequence of the first creation narrative is the answer that God made the world in order that it might be a fit abode for humankind, the creature like himself. All God's creative acts lead up to the last, the creation of humankind.[15] If creation reflects the resolve of the Creator that there should be a world, the purpose of this resolve is that there should be another, apart from himself, with whom he may enjoy

---

14. *Institutes*, I, 14, 20.

15. This denouement of the first creation narrative is reinforced by the second narrative (Gn. 2:4-24). The latter, as Von Rad observes, makes man and woman the center around whom all creation revolves. Thus the Yahwist has the same theological perspective as P, who views the creation of the man and the woman as the apex of a cosmological pyramid. See his *Old Testament Theology* (New York: Harper, 1962), vol. I, p. 141.

fellowship, a fellowship symbolized in the Sabbath rest. The Sabbath rest is God's free and joyous satisfaction as he communes with the man and the woman whom he has made for himself. To them he reveals himself and gives himself in love, that they may in return give themselves to him as their highest good and and so bring glory to his name.[16] This is the good purpose (*telos*, goal), the *causa finalis* of creation, at least so far as the human family on planet Earth is concerned.[17]

But obviously this pristine purpose of creation has miscarried. The mutual fellowship between God and the creature has been deeply disturbed by the transgression of the creature. As a result, the ultimate purpose of creation "has become eschatological" (Weber). Creation history has become a primal history that sets the stage for redemptive history. Rather than the consummation of creation, the Sabbath rest has become a reiterated rest—the weekly Sabbath of the Jews—which by virtue of its constant repetition can never bring final rest. In fact, even the fulfillment of the Sabbath rest in Christ is a fulfillment in hope. Like the Jews, therefore, Christians repeat their Lord's Day celebration week after week. Though it is the "day of all the week the best," it is but an "emblem of eternal rest" (Newton). This is why Hebrews speaks as it does to those who have believed in Christ and so enjoy God's rest. While they have come to him who says, "I will give you rest" (Mt. 11:28), yet the author feels constrained to warn readers that they must hold the beginning of their confidence steadfast to the end if they would enter into the final rest remaining for the people of God (Heb. 3:7–4:11). In that final rest, the Sabbath of creation will be realized as the Creator fellowships with the creature, uniting in Christ both the things in heaven and the things on earth (Eph. 1:10).

Of course, creation history does not simply set the stage for redemptive history and nothing more. The world God has created has, in his larger providential purpose, a history of its own. But for the writers of Scripture, the meaning of this general history is seen from the perspective of God's purpose as Redeemer. World history, in other words, is the theater of redemptive history. It is in and through world history that God is uniquely moving to accomplish the redemption of his people and thereby to restore creation to its true and proper end. Through God's redemptive work, the Sabbath rest of the creation will be finally fulfilled in a new heaven and a new earth in which righteousness dwells. In this eschatological paradise,

---

16. In the second creation narrative this communion of Creator and creature is pictured as life in a garden where God walks with our first parents in the cool of the day (Gn. 2:8; 3:8).

17. We can know of God's purpose for the myriad other creatures in his image—angels and archangels—only as their existence impinges on his purpose for us.

a new humanity will rest at last in God their Maker. Though they die, yet they are " 'blessed indeed,' says the Spirit, 'that they may rest from their labors, for their deeds follow them' " (Rv. 14:13).[18]

It would be premature at this point to sketch even briefly the Christian doctrine of salvation. Yet we cannot speak of God's purpose in creating the world apart from his purpose to redeem the world in Christ. God's purpose in creation, according to the Christian view, is inextricably bound up with his purpose of redemption. This is not to say that the story of the original creation has been wholly superseded by the story of the new creation. Yet such questions as Why did God make the world? How did he purpose by such an act to bring glory to himself? are questions whose answers compel the theologian to go beyond the story of the original creation. Fundamentally new elements enter the picture when one asks such questions and seeks to answer them.

For one, as the story of the creation unfolds, the man and the woman disobey their Maker. As sinners they no longer enjoy God but hide from him who is their highest good (Gn. 3:8). As a result, the world God pronounced good when he created it becomes cursed, subject to futility, bound over to decay, and groaning in travail (Gn. 3:17; Rom. 8:20-22). For another, God discloses himself as the angry God who condemns the man and the woman as sinners; the change in the creature evokes a change in the Creator. But the great surprise is that in revealing himself as the Judge who condemns, God also reveals himself as the Redeemer who saves. He promises our first parents One who shall deliver them from the power of the evil one (symbolized by the serpent) to which they have succumbed (Gn. 3:15). And so, in spite of the transgression of the creature, the Creator's work is not made null and void. The creation is not reduced to nothingness, for no alien power of evil or darkness can finally frustrate the purpose of the Creator.

However, God's justice and goodness as Creator are now seen in a new light, the light of his judgment and grace as Redeemer. His provident love of the creature now becomes his redeeming love of the sinner. Thus both creation and redemption become a part of God's larger purpose, for both are the one work of the one God—Father, Son, and Holy Spirit—who works all things after the counsel of his will (Eph. 1:11). In the mystery of the divine counsel, creation is related to redemption as the means to the end. Not that creation and redemption are the same work; creation remains

18. For Christians, therefore, Augustine's *City of God* is nearer the mark than Toynbee's *Civilization on Trial* (New York: Oxford University Press, 1948), or Spengler's *Der Untergang des Abendlandes* (Munich: Beck, 1922-23).

the first article of the Creed, redemption the second. Yet it is the second article that gives meaning to the first. The meaning (purpose) of what God did in creation is revealed in what he has done, is doing, and will do in Christ. The first word about creation is Genesis 1, but the final word is John 1.

Speaking of the relation between creation and redemption, it is one thing to say that we can discern God's purpose as Creator only as the beneficiaries of his grace; it is another to say that creation itself is an act of grace. The latter way of speaking, though common enough, is, in our judgment, confusing. It tends to blur the distinction between creation and redemption. To be sure, we have no claim to our being; it is the Creator's free gift. Yet one would hardly say of her creation, in the way that she must of her redemption, "I do not deserve it." By the same token, the world God makes as Creator is not the world he makes as Redeemer. The world the Creator makes is a world he calls good. The world the Redeemer makes is a world he forgives and restores; it is good because he has made it new by his grace. The world he first made displays his power and wisdom. True, the world he makes new also displays his power and wisdom; yet it is a power revealed in weakness and a wisdom that is foolish (the cross).

It should also be noted that if one views the divine purpose for creation as fulfilled in redemption, one will not, like those of a liberal theological persuasion, construe redemption in terms of creation. That is to say, one will not understand the fatherhood of God primarily in terms of his creative act, nor our adoption whereby we become God's children primarily in terms of the image given in creation—Harnack's "infinite value of the human soul." Nor will one understand the kingdom of God as the actualizing of the potential of creation through social progress in human history. Such significant differences of theological perspective illustrate the importance of clearly distinguishing and rightly relating creation and redemption.

When we answer the question of why God made the world, in terms of what he has done to redeem the world, we cannot press this answer with the rigorous consistency of some, particularly the supralapsarians. (For a full discussion of the infra/supralapsarian controversy, see our *Election and Predestination,* Grand Rapids: Eerdmans, 1985, pp. 83ff.) Those who are in the supralapsarian school infer that since the new creation in Christ is the ultimate purpose of the first creation, the transgression of the creature (the Fall) must have been necessary in order that God might reveal his justice and grace in judging and redeeming sinners in Christ. God created all things in order that there might be creatures who, through their transgression, would become either the objects of his justice (the reprobate) or his mercy (the elect). It is true that there is a coherence in such a position that appeals to the theoretical mind. It is also true that in Ephesians 3:8-12 Paul says that in the gospel he preached there is revealed "the mystery hidden for ages in God who created all things," in order that (ἵνα of purpose) through the church the manifold wisdom of God might be made known. There can be no doubt, in view of such a passage, that in the apostle's mind redemption mysteriously fulfills and reveals the divine purpose for creation.

But when we seek to reduce this grand design to an airtight, logical system, there are many pitfalls. While supralapsarianism has appealed to some of the greatest theologians—Zwingli, Luther, Calvin, Beza—it has never been made a part of any official creed or confession, and the reason is not hard to find. Supralapsarianism affirms that the fall of humankind fulfills God's eternal purpose for his creation in the same way that redemption does. To espouse such a position implies not only that the devil is "God's devil" (as Luther and anyone who is not a metaphysical dualist would say), but that the devil is God's devil just as much as Jesus is his Christ and that the fall into sin is just as much God's work as is redemption from sin.

Barth in recent times has argued for such a rigorous supralapsarian view of the purpose of creation. However, he has sought to soften the implications by more than a furtive glance in the direction of *apokatastasis* (universalism), though he never committed himself finally to such a doctrine. But in other respects he is consistent, even speaking of the Fall as necessary.

> When confronted by Satan and his kingdom, the creature, in himself and as such, has, in creaturely freedom, no power to reject that which in his divine freedom God rejects. . . . [Der Mensch . . . hat nun einmal in seiner geschöpflichen Freiheit die Macht nicht, seinerseits zu verwerfen was Gott in seiner göttlichen Freiheit verwirft. . . .] Face to face with temptation, he cannot maintain the goodness of his creation in the divine image and foreordination to the divine likeness. (*K.D.,* II/2, p. 122; cf. *C.D.,* II/2, sec. 33.1)

Thus Augustine's description of fallen, sinful humanity as "not able not to sin" *(non posse non peccare)* becomes, for Barth, the description of humanity as originally created by God! The ability not to sin *(posse non peccare)* was never given our first parents. While we reject Barth's supralapsarianism, we would not take the opposite tack of Amyraut in his controversy with Beza. "And sin seems to have changed not only the whole face of the universe," says Amyraut, "but even the entire design of the first creation, and, if one may speak this way, seems to have induced God to adopt new counsels" ("Brief Traitte de la Predestination," as quoted by B. G. Armstrong, *Calvinism and the Amyraut Heresy,* Madison: University of Wisconsin Press, 1969, p. 181). We cannot believe, for our part, that the transgression of the creature compelled the Creator to opt for "plan B."

At the beginning of our discussion we noted that God's purpose to reveal his power, wisdom, and goodness has generally been given as the reason why he created the world. To ask how he could and would have achieved this end had humankind not fallen only invites speculation that goes beyond Scripture. We know God's purpose for his creation only as he has disclosed it to us in Israel and the church through his Son, the Lord Jesus Christ. It is enough to know that though the first heavens and earth shall pass away, God will achieve his purpose as Creator in a new creation, a creation already inaugurated in Christ and manifest in the church, the company of the redeemed (Heb. 1:10-11; Eph. 2:10).

D. THE PROBLEM OF EVIL

In the ensuing discussion we shall use the word "evil" of that which brings pain, suffering, and death to any of God's creatures. It is surprising that we should feel a need to speak of such evil when talking about the creation that manifests God's goodness. Obviously a comment is called for. In making it, we do well to remember four affirmations concerning the world that have dominated the Christian tradition.

(1) The world is God's creation and reveals his goodness as the Creator (Gn. 1:31).

(2) Yet, because of human transgression, this world is a world now "subject to futility" and "groaning in travail" (Rom. 8:20ff.).

(3) Though now under a curse, this world is being made new by God's redeeming grace in Christ (2 Cor. 5:17; Rv. 21:1).

(4) This new creation, in which righteousness dwells, will be consummated when Christ returns in glory. Then God shall dwell with humankind and be their God and they his people, beyond the reach of sin and death, in a world in which righteousness dwells (2 Pt. 3:13; Rv. 21–22).

But if these affirmations are true, may we not wait to discuss evil until we have taken up the subject of human transgression, which brings us face to face with the awesome mystery of original sin? Then the question, Is this the world God made? can be answered in the affirmative; yet this "yes" to creation can be qualified in terms of the sin that flaws our humanity and brings all nature under "bondage to decay."

The materials of biblical revelation undoubtedly lend themselves to such an approach. It is only when our first parents are confronted by their Maker with their disobedience that the biblical narrative mentions thorns and thistles, a cursing of the ground and the sentence of death (Gn. 3:17-19). Hence, theologians have traditionally assumed that the world, as originally created, corresponded to the prophets' vision of the future age of messianic redemption. In that golden age of final salvation,

> "The wolf and the lamb shall feed together,
> the lion shall eat straw like the ox. . . .
> They shall not hurt or destroy
> in all my holy mountain,"
> says the LORD. (Is. 65:25)

This is the way it also must have been in the beginning; at least so it was supposed. Before the Fall, the entire realm of nature was a peaceable kingdom.[19]

---

19. The question of how pristine lions could be vegetarian and still be lions was seldom

We now know otherwise; from the beginning of life on the planet, nature has been anything but peaceful. Rather than feeding together, carnivorous wolves have fed on herbivorous lambs and that long before homo sapiens appeared on the scene. And we recognize that this relationship of predator and prey in the animal world contributes in an essential way to the balance of nature in a limited life-support system.[20] We may even see in it a manifestation of providence, recognizing with the psalmist that when the young lions roar after their prey, they are seeking their food from God (Ps. 104:21).[21]

Yet, for Christian faith, nature's redness "in tooth and claw" can hardly be contemplated with equanimity. To be sure, many events in the natural order—like floods, earthquakes, and tornados—are quite neutral in themselves; it is only as humans are involved that we make value judgments about them. Good floods fertilize the land and bad ones ravage it by ruining crops, destroying homes, and drowning people. When it comes to sentient creatures, however, things become more difficult. Pain, suffering, and death in the animal kingdom are evils in themselves, even apart from a human presence in the world. Hence, the question of animal suffering can hardly be ignored by the theologian when she speaks of God's creation as good. To be sure, the argument against the goodness of the Creator in the light of animal suffering can be overdrawn, as when the experience of a fly caught in the spider's web is read in human terms. The entomologist J. Henri Fabre describes a bee-eating wasp as licking the tongue of her prey "in her death agony" while her own belly is being munched by a mantis. We would have to agree with Annie Dillard that such a scene is a horror show assaulting all human values and hope of a reasonable God, were we to judge insect behavior as we do human behavior. But we do not.[22] If pain and suffering do occur in the insect world, in any case we must remember

---

asked. If it was, it was no harder to accept than that the trees in Eden were without rings and Adam and Eve without navels.

20. In the plant kingdom fungi function similarly by hastening the decay of the dead. The widespread belief in the Middle Ages that they were planted by demons in the darkness of the night is obviously not good science. However, such a belief does reflect an abiding Christian conviction that death is not God's proper work, not his final purpose for his creation. See Roger Van Horsen, *The Contemporary Search for the Meaning of Creation* (unpublished doctoral thesis, Fuller Seminary, 1986), p. 301, n. 39, on the *Vestigia Trinitatis* of Erigena.

21. Here one is reminded that William Blake wrote not only of the little lamb made by One who calls himself a Lamb, but also of the "Tyger! Tyger! burning bright/In the forests of the night," framed by the same "immortal hand and eye" that made the lamb. See his "The Tyger."

22. See her *Pilgrim at Tinker Creek* (New York: Harper, 1974), pp. 63-64.

that the aerial spraying of fruit flies in California is not like the fire-bombing of Dresden.

But as we move from wasp to whale in the animal kingdom, the problem of suffering intrudes itself inescapably upon us. Here is pain and misery not like our own, to be sure, but not altogether unlike it either. Christians have always acknowledged as much by their active involvement in societies for the prevention of cruelty to animals.[23] Of course, such societies are concerned with the suffering humans inflict on animals. And, it must be admitted, there is a vast difference between the ghastly cruelty that people inflict on animals and the suffering animals inflict on one another. Nonetheless, the latter suffering is very real and all the more difficult to understand now that we know this universal reign of suffering and death antedates human sin and transgression.[24] In contemplating creation, one may be persuaded that God is a God of wisdom and power. Yet one can understand—in the light of animal suffering—why some have asked, Does he have a heart? The Christian answers this question with a resounding "Yes!" But it is not a "yes" secured by a reasoned demonstration that this is (or ever was) the best of all possible worlds.[25] The dinosaurs did nothing to deserve pain and, unlike humans, were not improved by it. The Christian "yes" to the goodness of the Creator is rather a "yes" that is learned at the foot of the cross. It is at Calvary that God reveals his "inmost heart." Here, indeed, we see that

> The love of God is broader
>   Than the measure of man's mind;
> And the heart of the Eternal
>   Is most wonderfully kind. (Faber)

But though faith in God's goodness, the confidence that he has a "kind heart," is assured in the light of the cross, such faith and assurance cannot ignore the suffering of God's lesser creatures nor treat it as a trifle. But then, what can faith say? Why should the Creator, whose fatherly care

---

23. Macaulay's sardonic remark that the Puritans opposed bear-baiting not because of the pain it brought to the bears but the pleasure it brought to people tells us more about Macaulay than it does about the Puritans.

24. It was this difficulty that explains the early reluctance of the church to accept the implication of fossils. Paleontologists were assured that such mementoes of prehistoric death were created by God and placed in the rocks!

25. The movement from the upbeat tone of Leibnitz's *Theodicy* to the bitter scorn of Voltaire's *Candide* cannot be reversed by any rational analysis of the data.

embraces even the sparrow that falls to the ground (Mt. 10:39), have made a world marked for death from the beginning?

While this specific question is never addressed by the biblical writers, they do have much to say, in a more general way, about sin and death and how they are related. They always regard death as the "wages" of sin (Rom. 6:23). In the classic instance, our first parents are said to have forfeited life for themselves and their posterity and to have come under the sentence of death because of the sin of disobedience. Through their disobedience sin entered the world, we are told, and death by sin (Gn. 3:19; Rom. 5:18-19). Death, in other words, is the result of sin. This sequence, of course, was not understood to apply to the animal kingdom as such. The writers of Scripture knew that animals do not die for their sins, for they are quite incapable of sinning. As God's creatures they surely have worth, but theirs is not a dignity and glory that can be lost through transgression of the divine will; not having been made in the image of their Maker, they cannot sin and come short of the glory of God (Rom. 3:23). They have neither a good to lose nor an evil to suffer from losing it.[26] How then does Scripture, at least by implication, understand the fact that animals, along with the human family—indeed, long before there was a human family— succumb to the grim reaper?

What little is said indicates that animal suffering and death are understood in terms of human suffering and death. Humans suffer and die because they are sinners; and for this same reason, namely, the sin of humankind, death prevails even in the animal world. As the apostle says, the "creation was subjected to futility, not of its own will but by the will of him who subjected it in hope; because the creation itself will be set free from its bondage to decay and obtain the glorious liberty of the children of God" (Rom. 8:19-21).[27] This solidarity of the lower orders of creation with the human family in the curse of death does not, however, in their case entail a temporal sequence of sin, and then death. Such a temporal sequence is meaningful only in the human family, where death is the wage sin exacts of the transgressor. When we say death reigns throughout the natural order

---

26. In the Middle Ages, it is true, members of the animal kingdom were held responsible for their offenses. Grubs that ravaged the fields were brought to court in a trial at Basel in 1478, as were rats in the great rat trial in the town of Autumn in the middle of the sixteenth century. See Friedrich Heer, *The Medieval World* (New York: The New American Library, 1962), pp. 59-60.

27. ἀλλὰ διὰ τὸν ὑποτάξαντα ἐφ' ἐλπίδι ὅτι . . . , literally, "but on account of him who subjected it, in hope that. . . ." The reference is plainly to God the Creator, not Adam the sinner.

because of the sin of humankind, we are giving the reason for, not the cause of, death in the animal kingdom.

It is important to note this distinction because of the tendency erroneously to identify "cause" and "reason." There are, indeed, times when the two terms have a proximity of meaning; yet there is a significant difference between a causal explanation and a reasoned explanation. Recognizing this difference helps one in rethinking the question of how the reign of death in nature is related to the transgression of the human family.

Traditionally it has been supposed that if the curse of death rests upon the whole order of nature due to human sin, and if in the age to come sin and death shall be no more, then there could have been no death in this present world prior to the Fall. Such a way of arguing presupposes that sin is the "cause" of death; therefore it must be antecedent to death inasmuch as a "cause" always precedes an effect. However, if sin is not the "cause" of death but the "reason" for it, such a conclusion does not necessarily follow. In our human experience, of course, there is a temporal sequence between sin and death; it is only after the transgression of our first parents that death enters the world of the human family. However, it is not possible to say that the temporal sequence of sin, then death, implies a causal relationship even in our human experience. One dies because of a hardening of the arteries with age, the loss of blood in an accident, or coronary arrest under stress. All such causes, of course, necessarily precede their effects in time. But in the Christian view of things, the reason one dies, whatever the cause, is that one is a sinner. In the teaching of Scripture, death is not caused by sin; death is the *wage* of sin.[28] As for the animal kingdom, to be sure, we cannot say that death is the wage of their sin since they have no sin. Their death is due, rather, to their solidarity with us in our condemnation and judgment as sinners.[29]

The solidarity of the animal world with sinful, suffering humanity, the groaning of the whole creation in travail (Rom. 8:22), is reflected in the cultic participation of the animals in the repentance of Nineveh at the preaching of Jonah. (See W. Heim, *Weltschöpfung und Weltende*, Hamburg: Furche-Verlag, 1952, p. 86.) To impose a fast on the beasts of the field and cover them with sackcloth (Jon. 3:7-8) is, like all ceremonial acts, irrational in itself. But such ceremonial rites symbolize in all religious and social

---

28. In other words, the cause of death, both for individuals and for species, is a scientific matter; the reason of death, a theological matter.

29. For other suggestions concerning animal suffering, see C. S. Lewis, *The Problem of Pain* (New York: Macmillan, 1961), chap. IX, "Animal Pain," pp. 177ff. We do not find speculation about the fall of Satan, animal immortality, etc., of which he speaks, especially helpful.

life the truths by which a community lives. It is this larger context that gives such ceremonial acts meaning.

If we view suffering and death throughout the creation from the perspective of a divine judgment on sinful humanity, we still face the question of why God in his eternal purpose should have chosen to make a world in which death was present from the beginning and in due course came to reign even over the creature made in his likeness. Could not an infinite wisdom have devised another way to display the divine glory? Christians may be confident that the world has its origin in the will of God and that the world is as it is because the Creator would have it so (Brunner). But when the question is pressed, Why should the Creator have made a world in which there is suffering and death? faith perceives the divine reason only through a glass darkly.

When we ask this ultimate question, we must remember what has already been said about interpreting Genesis 1 in the light of John 1, about learning of God's purpose as Creator as we see it unfolding in his work as Redeemer. If the universal reign of death in this world has any meaning that we can discern, it is only from the perspective of the new creation in Christ that we can discern it. Even then we are taught only that the presence of death in the world God made is the occasion for the display of his justice and mercy in Christ. Christ's death, as John Owen would say, is the death of death. In his death and resurrection the last enemy is finally destroyed (1 Cor. 15:26).

Faith, then, really has no final answer to the question of why a good God made a world marked by death. Faith rather lives in the hope that it shall not always be so. One day the suffering and death that has marked the creation from the beginning as the theater in which the drama of redemption is played out will be overcome in a new creation. In this new creation the wolf and the lamb shall indeed lie down together and the lion eat straw like the ox.[30] In this new creation, where none shall hurt or destroy, the rest of the creation Sabbath will be finally realized. It is this hope which gives us confidence to say with the apostle, "I consider that the sufferings of this present time are not worth comparing with the glory that is to be revealed to us" (Rom. 8:18).

---

30. Such a statement is obviously a theological, not a zoological, one.

VI. Creation and the Christian Life

In framing our doctrine of creation, we have talked about many things: ancient cosmogonies, Gnostic aeons, the expanding universe, and even the death of the dinosaurs. How does such a wide-ranging discussion bear on our being Christians day by day? When we confess the first article, how does this confession shape our understanding of God, the world, and especially ourselves and our place in the world?

As for the understanding of God, we do well as Christians to remember that for Israel it was the act of creation that came to distinguish the true God from the false gods of their neighbors. "For all the gods of the peoples are idols; but the LORD made the heavens" (Ps. 96:5). These false gods "who did not make the heavens and the earth shall perish from the earth and from under the heavens" (Jer. 10:11). Little wonder, then, that when Paul stood before the Areopagus, as a Jew who had become a Christian he summed up his message by declaring to the Athenians that he came to them in the name of "the God who made the world and everything in it" (Acts 17:24).[1] For Christians, this knowledge of God as Creator is anything but a purely theoretical judgment that incorporates a "Universal Mind" into a rational system in order to explain the nature of the universe. It is rather a knowledge that inspires reverence and leads one to exclaim with the psalmist, "Bless the LORD, O my soul! O LORD my God, you are very great" (Ps. 104:1 NRSV).

Such reverence for the Creator, of course, entails reverence for his work also. If we believe that God has "stretched out the heavens like a tent" and "set the earth on its foundations" (Ps. 104:2, 5), then there is no

---

1. By the same token it was only natural that as Jews the first Christians should address God in prayer as the "sovereign Lord who made the heaven and the earth" (Acts 4:24 NRSV).

502

"nature as such." Rather, in beholding nature one's eye is constantly elevated from the world to the God who made the world. Even a snowflake evokes the question:

> What heart could have thought thee?
> Past our devisal
> (O filigree petal!)
> Fashioned so purely,
> Fragilely, surely. . . .[2]

To speak of reverence for the creation as the work of the Creator has special meaning in the time in which we live. While the heart of the Christian confession is that God in Christ has become a part of our sinful world that he might redeem it, our confession as Christians begins with the affirmation that God created the world in the first place. The world he redeems is *his* world; he owns it. Since he made this world and put us in it, we live in the world as his tenants. To see the world as God's creation is to reject the notion of nature viewed as a neutral realm in which we may do as we please. Since the world is God's world, we have no right to destroy his property which he has entrusted to us as stewards. If, as the proverb says, to oppress the poor is to insult their Maker (Prv. 14:31), may we not also conclude that to reduce whole species to extinction is to insult *their* Maker? The traditional view that dominion over the world has been given to humankind by virtue of their creation in the divine image must await our discussion of the *imago Dei*. But all that we will say at that time, including our discussion of technology and ecology, is anticipated in, and determined by, what we are now saying as we seek to frame a Christian doctrine of creation.

Our understanding of creation determines not only how we as Christians understand God and the world but also how we understand ourselves. The doctrine of creation is not just about origins in general but about my origin in particular. When I confess the first article of the Creed, I confess, in Luther's words, that "I believe God has created *me* and all that exists. . . ."[3] In the words of the *Anglican Catechism,* I learn from the first article "to believe in God the Father who has made me and all the world." That is to say, not only the world as a whole belongs to God, but I, body and soul, in life and death, also belong to him who is my Creator and has become my faithful Savior.[4] To confess the doctrine of creation is to acknowledge my dependence on God as the One from whom I have my

---

2. Thompson, "To a Snowflake." See also chapter 8 of Annie Dillard's *Pilgrim at Tinker Creek* (New York: Harper, 1974). In this chapter, entitled "Intricacy," she reveals her magnificent obsession with the details of the natural order, the fruit of the Creator's exuberance. One wonders which is more dazzling, the creation or her description of it.

3. *Small Catechism,* Part II, The Creed, the First Article.

4. *The Heidelberg Catechism,* Q. 1.

life as a gift. This utter dependence, on my part as a creature, is true whether I acknowledge it or not. God is not the postulate of my thought but the one who postulates me by actualizing his thought in creating me. I am who I am by his will, choice, and act. This relationship of dependence on God the Creator is an indefeasible quality of my humanity.

We have rejected Schleiermacher's reduction of creation to the individual's feeling of absolute dependence. Creation is not, we have argued, simply a matter of our relationship to God. (See this Unit, III, B, 1, pp. 450-51.) Yet we readily admit to a significant element of truth in this approach of the liberal tradition. To speak of creation is not simply to postulate a remote past called "the beginning"; it is also to confess an ongoing awareness of dependence on the Creator in each individual's present. While we have not oriented the doctrine of creation toward this ongoing religious experience, we do acknowledge its important place in the doctrine. When I confess that God is the Creator, I confess that he is *my* Creator. To acknowledge that the world is his because he made it is to acknowledge that I am his because he made me. He, therefore, has an absolute claim on me as his possession. As *the* Lord of all, he is *my* Lord in particular and I am his servant. This awareness of creaturely servanthood is basic to the piety of both the Old and the New Testaments.

To say the doctrine of creation involves not only the affirmation that God made all things but also that he made me does raise questions for the theologian. If creation is understood as *creatio ex nihilo,* how is the appearing of the individual self on the stage of life an act of creation? We all know that babies do not come "from nothing." In the present day, in fact, we have gone far beyond the traditional understanding of conception and birth to probe the marvels of genetic inheritance. Surely, then, one's creation as an individual can never be considered apart from the creation of one's progenitors. When one says with Luther that in creating me God "has given me body and soul, eyes, ears and all my limbs, my reason and all my senses" *(Small Catechism),* it must be acknowledged that the Creator gives me all these not by an immediate act but in and through the process of procreation and birth.

The evidence that we are who we are by inheritance no one can doubt. Yet in the Christian view, to confess "God made me" is saying more than that he created the original protoplasm that is the basis of all living things, including Adam and Eve from whom descended A, B, and C and finally me. In Enlightenment thought, the affirmation "God made me" means that I the individual am as a living organism the functioning product of biological and sociological factors that in their sum total may be called "God."[5] But in the Christian view, I am I as the unique counterpart of a transcendent I. Though I am not an absolute I, I am an I in the presence of a Thou, an

5. See Weber, *Grundlagen* (Neukirchen-Vluyn: Neukirchener, 1955), vol. I, p. 519.

I related to my Creator in a way that transcends the cause/effect nexus. That is to say, there is that which is unique about me as an individual— the ultimate mystery of the self — which is given in my creation.[6] The continuity that marks each individual's life rests on God's preservation as the provident Father; but the new in each individual person (her face, her name, her self) is God's unique gift as the Creator. The doctrine of creation teaches me that I am I, not by my will but by the Creator's will who calls me into being. My creation is not simply something I say about myself but something God says to me. Called into being by God's mighty word and preserved in being by his care and keeping, I find the beatitude of my being in him and thereby the dignity of my being as human.

6. This is the truth on the side of the creationists in their longstanding debate with the traducianists, a debate on which we shall comment further in due time as occasion requires. It is also the truth expressed long ago by the psalmist: "I give thanks unto you, for I have wonderfully come into being under fearful circumstances, circumstances causing a shudder." Psalm 139:13, as paraphrased in the *Commentary on the Old Testament*, vol. V, of Keil and Delitzsch (Grand Rapids: Eerdmans, 1978), p. 349. We prefer the Masoretic text of this verse, followed by Keil and Delitzsch, to the LXX reading used in some modern versions.

Beginnings

A Sermon Preached by Marguerite Shuster
at Knox Presbyterian Church, Pasadena, California,
Lord's Day, January 10, 1987

In the beginning God created the heavens and the earth.

Genesis 1:1 (RSV)

Why, oh why, is there *something* and not *nothing?* There didn't have to be *something,* you know. You're cheating if you start with a cloud of hot gases or a super-dense clump of matter and say that, given enough billions upon billions of years, it just figures that eventually all the possible combinations would occur and, at long last, produce a world like ours, with people like us, who sing hymns (what a strange thing to do!) and build churches (how prodigal!) and hear preachers expound thoughts about a God who got it all going (what possible biological use are preachers?). You're cheating, I say. Maybe your argument is correct and maybe it isn't; but you're still cheating, because whoever said a cloud of hot gases or a dense clump of matter *had* to exist?

Start backwards. Throw out people and everything they feel and everything they make. Throw out plants and animals. Throw out water and earth. Throw out planets and stars. Throw out gases and solids, particles and waves. Throw out time and space. When you're left with absolute emptiness, throw out even that.[1] Now, maybe, you're getting close to talking about *nothing.* Now, maybe, you're ready to ask why *something* should

---

1. See Frederick Buechner, *The Magnificent Defeat* (San Francisco: Harper & Row, 1966), p. 21.

ever appear. For no possible necessity of logic or science, mathematics or metaphysics, could ever produce so much as an atom, so much as a proton, so much as a still tinier quark or gluon out of that nothing. Everything—absolutely everything—is gratuitous. Absolutely everything might not have been. Christians confess that everything, including ourselves, *would* not have been, if it were not that. . . .

"In the beginning God created the heavens and the earth." Those simple, majestic words of my text, which serve as a heading or title for the first 35 verses of the book of Genesis, go behind all study and theorizing about the *process* by which our universe and planet and we ourselves came to appear, and assert that apart from God none of these would exist at all. It is a statement of ultimate origins, a statement behind which we cannot go. In a famous comment ascribed to Martin Luther, someone once replied to a person who asked what God was doing before he made the world: "He was cutting switches with which to flog inquisitive questioners."[2] The remark, if harsh, had this measure of appropriateness—seeking to pry into the mind of God prior to his creative activity can teach us nothing necessary to our salvation; and the Bible does not concern itself with merely speculative matters. We do need to know, though, to what or to whom we should attribute all that we see, and whether there is anyone behind it all upon whom we can rely. Thus, these crucial, jam-packed opening words of the whole Bible tell us that God created *the heavens and the earth;* that God *created* the heavens and the earth; and that *in the beginning God* created the heavens and the earth. Let's take these three points separately.

First, God created *the heavens and the earth.* That phrase simply means "everything," the equivalent of the New Testament "all things," as in Ephesians 3:9, where it is said that "God . . . created all things." In a lovely phrase, theologians speak of God finding "cheerful diversion in making all that is." Don't you like that way of thinking about it—seeing God as delighting in making an utterly unbelievable universe, in which components of atoms in some sense act randomly, while they compose galaxies that in some sense behave lawfully? Imagine his bothering with rainbows—not just in the sky but in fishes' scales. Imagine his toying with the idea of the number of legs creatures should have, whether none, or one, like snails, or two or four or six or eight, or however many centipedes really have. Contemplate the difference between plush fur and iridescent feathers. Think of his deciding that mountains and valleys and seas are much better than a perfectly harmonious round sphere.

2. Quoted by Helmut Thielicke, *How the World Began* (Philadelphia: Fortress, 1961), p. 13.

Suppose "you are God," says Annie Dillard. "You want to make a forest, something to hold the soil, lock up solar energy, and give off oxygen. Wouldn't it be simpler just to rough in a slab of chemicals, a green acre of goo?"[3] Look instead at what he did. Look at a cactus, a daisy, an oak. And don't you suppose God must have laughed when he made giraffes and determined that for sheer power to persevere, cockroaches had something to offer? Quoting Dillard again,

> Look, in short, at practically anything—the coot's feet, the mantis' face, a banana, the human ear—and see that not only did the creator create everything, but that he is apt to create *anything*. He'll stop at nothing. There is no one standing over [the process] with a blue pencil to say, "now that one, there, is absolutely ridiculous, and I won't have it." (Ibid., p. 135)

Not just the complexity, not just the variety, not just the basic orderliness of it all, but the sheer exuberance of the creation boggles the mind.

And God saw that all of it was good—a refrain repeated throughout the creation story. Perhaps a refrain that sounds a bit too subdued for the marvel of it all. Can we, without loss of due reverence, still imagine him saying, "Wow! Look at *that!* Just *look* at that, will you?!" Garrison Keillor is fond of reminding us that it is indeed a beautiful world, and perhaps we need to love it more. God's world. He made everything—the heavens and the earth. And it was good.

Second, God *created* the heavens and the earth: the word itself is significant. This particular Hebrew verb is used only of God and is never connected with any statement of any material used in the act. Thus, in itself, it implies creation out of nothing.[4] So does the verse that follows my text, which says, "the earth was without form and void, and darkness was on the face of the deep." Here we do not have a description of some sort of primeval chaos, some amorphous "stuff" that God would take and mold. Many have interpreted the verse that way, but such interpretations go against the sense of verses 1 and 3, as well as not fitting with Hebrew thought. For the Hebrew, talk of formlessness and void was a description of a sort of desert waste and is used here as a way of speaking of the opposite of creation. And "darkness" is to be understood not as a mere phenomenon of nature but as something somehow sinister, dreadful.[5] Thus, these are mythological images for utter nothingness, images that evoke in us the dread we have of nonbeing.

3. *Pilgrim at Tinker Creek* (New York: Harper & Row, 1974), pp. 129-30.
4. Gerhard von Rad, *Genesis* (Philadelphia: Westminster, 1972), p. 49.
5. Claus Westermann, *Genesis 1–11* (Minneapolis: Augsburg, 1984), in loc.

Is it important to stress that God made the world out of nothing? Well, consider the alternative. Contemplate God making use of some material that had intrinsic limitations that he could not overcome, like a sculptor thwarted by the knots in the wood or the cracks in the marble. Or imagine a world with a dark history that would keep encroaching. As an example, Helmut Thielicke relates a Germanic creation story in which

> the world is made of the corpse of the giant Ymir: the sea of his blood, the heaven of his skull, and the clouds from his brains. But this Ymir, from whose body the world was made, was murdered by Odin and his brothers, even though they were related to Ymir through their mother and thus committed the heinous crime of killing a relative. . . . This Germanic story says that the world was made of curse-ridden matter. The world which is described thus does not bear only divine features; instead the dubious matter of which it is made is constantly breaking through. So whenever guilt and horror appear in the world. . . , it is this prenatal dowry of the world that is erupting. . . . Then is it the giant Ymir who is rising up.[6]

We could not then help ourselves, for our fate would be in our origins. We would have been constrained from the very beginning of creation by forces that are absolutely beyond us. Well, we all know that that is not the biblical view—but that is another story. Here, we are only concerned to say that God made his good creation without any such constraints as some sort of preexistent matter would impose.

All God did was speak. He said, "'Let there be light,' and there was light." As our New Testament lesson reads, "In the beginning was the Word" (Jn. 1:1). It refers, of course, to Jesus Christ, "without [whom] was not anything made that was made"; but the connection to God speaking the world into existence in Genesis is not accidental.

Creation by speaking—by Word—also makes plain the point that not only did God not use preexistent materials, but also that there is no necessary connection between God and the world. Had he not spoken, it would not have been. The world is not continuous with God, not a part of God, not even like God, any more than a table built by a carpenter is essentially like a carpenter. True, the nature of his workmanship may tell us something about the character of a carpenter, but only if we have very clearly in mind how utterly different tables and carpenters really are. And we would be hard put to explain the appearing of tables if we were unwilling to suppose the existence of anything fundamentally unlike them.

6. Thielicke, *How the World Began,* p. 21.

Well, anyway, God merely speaks and what he says happens, without effort, without resistance, without needing to have what we would consider crucial prerequisites in place. For instance, many have noticed, and protested, that God makes light before he makes the sun and moon and stars (which doesn't happen until v. 14). Every school child knows that light comes from the sun and stars. Was somebody confused here? No indeed. The stars do not create light but only bear it.[7] That was a needed reminder in those days. And I fear it is a needed reminder today. For now, as then, many believe that the stars control their destinies. Many turn to horoscopes day after day, telling themselves, perhaps, that they don't *really* believe in astrology, but reading the column nonetheless. Many attribute traits of personality to the astrological sign under which people were born. And it is but a short step from attributing such powers to the stars to seeing them as somehow divine. It's always been a temptation: Job (31:26-28) protested himself to be innocent of such idolatry when he said, "if I have looked at the sun when it shone, or the moon moving in splendor, and my heart has been secretly enticed, and my mouth has kissed my hand; this also would be an iniquity to be punished by the judges, for I should have been false to God above." He who is actually in control of the universe is no unfeeling globe like the sun. No created thing is to be worshipped or feared as if it were divine. Neither the sun nor anything else would have any of the properties it possesses had God not given it those properties; and God could just as well have given those properties to something else entirely. When God created, he was dependent upon nothing and needed to take counsel with none but himself. Poet James Weldon Johnson says it this way:

> Then God reached out and took the light in his hands,
> And God rolled the light around in his hands
> Until he made the sun;
> And he set that sun a-blazing in the heavens.
> And the light that was left from making the sun
> God gathered it up in a shining ball
> And flung it against the darkness,
> Spangling the night with moon and stars.
> Then down between
> The darkness and the light
> He hurled the world;
> And God said: That's good.[8]

---

7. Ibid., p. 33, quoting von Rad.

8. "The Creation," *God's Trombones, Seven Negro Sermons in Verse* (New York: The Viking Press, 1957), pp. 17-18.

Finally, the assertion that *in the beginning God* created the heavens and the earth. That phrase contains two components that we have everywhere assumed: that there is a God, and that there was a beginning. Neither, perhaps, can be absolutely proved. Matter could, perhaps, be eternal and everything we see be the result of chance plus vast unthinkable aeons of time. One can believe that if one wishes, but one cannot claim that it is the simplest and most reasonable view of things.

For instance, it has been calculated that to write the figure expressing the likelihood that our universe came to be by a random event would require a chalkboard as large as the entire universe.[9] At the level of physics, the forces that hold the world together are so incredibly finely tuned that infinitesimally small changes would make life as we know it wholly impossible.[10] Or, at the biological level, "We do not understand how a solitary cell, fused from two, can differentiate into an embryo and then into the systems of tissues and organs that become us, nor do we know how a tadpole accomplishes his emergence, nor even a flea," says Lewis Thomas.[11] Thus, scientists report having their "atheism shaken" at the unlikeliness of it all, of seeing "a hidden principle at work";[12] or they say, like Thomas, "It is absurd to say that a place like this place is absurd. . . . I cannot abide the notion of purposelessness and blind chance in nature, and yet I do not know what to put in its place for the quieting of my mind."[13] Apart from God, scientists are baffled.

And to say just a word on the other issue—the matter of beginnings—the Big Bang theory of the origins of the universe—the currently favored model—brings scientists what they sometimes consider "perilously close" to positing a first moment. It wouldn't have been a bang, of course, for with no atmosphere the event would have been silent, more like the Great Light, says Thomas (the light before the sun and stars again). But in any case, if the universe is uniformly expanding, as the data appear clearly to show that it is, then the likelihood that it also had a beginning, a point at which the expansion started, greatly increases.

Still, one doesn't logically *have* to posit a God, or a beginning. But it helps. And add the consideration with which we started: there could have been just nothing. Nothing at all. For all who believe, Genesis 1 tells us

9. See this unit, P. 488.
10. H. Rolston III, "Shaken Atheism: A Look at the Fine-Tuned Universe," *The Christian Century,* 3 December 1986, p. 1094.
11. 1980 Stanford Commencement Address, *Stanford Observer,* June 1980, p. 2.
12. Rolston, p. 1093.
13. Thomas, 1980 Stanford Commencement Address, op. cit.

why there is, instead, something: we ourselves, everything we love, the whole remarkable universe.

In the beginning God created the heavens and the earth. And they were good. Let us seek better to love this beautiful world, even as we seek more confidently to rest our hope and trust in the mighty God who made it and us.

Index of Subjects

Adoption, doctrine of, 309f.
Agape and Eros (*see* Love of God)
Analogia entis, 32f.; Barth's critique of, 33
Analogia relationis, 33f.
Analogical language, 30f., 323ff., 340; and the analogy of being, 32f.; meaning given by the Spirit, 39; Thomas's defense of, 31f.; Tillich's use of, 31f.
Analogy of faith, 124, 151f.
Animal suffering, 496ff.
Anthropomorphisms, 186f., 340ff.
Anthropopathisms, 399f.; Reformers' view of, 400
Antilegoumena, 96f., 101
Apathetic theology, and the Fathers, 398f.; meaning of, 176 n. 5; and nominalism, 339; rejected, 408 n. 10, 412
Apocrypha, 96, 101
Apologetics, 6; truth of Christianity argued from moral insight, 71f.
Apophatic theology, meaning of, 176 n. 5, 218f.
Apostles' Creed, rewritten, 52
Arminianism, scriptural basis of, 319f.
Ascension, and space, 419f.
Atonement, 233; anticipated in Old Testament, 407
Attributes of God, 336ff.; anthropomorphic/analogical character of, 340ff.; classification of, 344ff.; the divine faithfulness and suffering, 396ff. (*see also* Faithfulness and

Suffering of God); the divine justice/righteousness and mercy, 382ff. (*see also* Justice/Righteousness and the Mercy of God); the divine omnipresence and eternity, 413ff. (*see also* Omnipresence and Eternity of God); the divine simplicity, 346f.; the divine will and power, 348ff. (*see also* Will and Power of God); the divine wisdom and knowledge, 369ff. (*see also* Wisdom and Knowledge of God); and the figures (shepherd, star, etc.) of Scripture, 345f.; and the Nominalism and Realism debate, 338ff.; their origin in doxological statements, 341ff.; predication of, 336ff.; reductionist approach to, 339; their relation to the divine nature, 343f.

Barth's doctrine of "trinitarian recapitulation," 296f., 302
Basic postulates, 53f.
Beauty, its place in worship, 113ff.
Begetting, in the Trinity, 288f.
Bible, becomes God's word, 155 n. 68 (*see also* Scripture)
Biblical theology, 14f., 427
Black churches, names of, 178f.
Black preaching, 114f.
Black, symbolism of, 30
Black theology, meaning of, 13; and Scripture, 159
Brunner's "principle of contiguity," 21f.

agape and eros, difference between, 231f.; biblical data, 232ff.; God's love as wrath, 244ff.; Hosea's grasp of, 228f., 232f.; married love (eros) as the symbol of agape, 235ff.; relation to God's holiness, 228f.; sovereign in nature, 234f.; trinitarian nature of agape, 238f.; triumphs over justice, 233f.
Luther, freedom in biblical interpretation, 131; and the righteousness of God (Rom. 1:17), 156; as translator of the Bible, 108f.

Mammon, 185
Marks *(indicia)* of Scripture, 99
Matter, in modern physics, 279f.
Mercy of God *(see* Justice/Righteousness and the Mercy of God)
Method, theological, 17ff.
Modernity, and the *mysterium tremendum,* 192; its rejection of transcendence, 201f.; its thought forms rejected, xvi
Mysticism, 218f.; and the divine attributes, 336; and pantheism, 443f.; and space, 414 n. 4, 421; and the Spirit, 321f.
Myth, defined, 28f.

Natural revelation *(see* General revelation)
Nature psalms, 71
Neo-Personalism, 23
Nominalism and Realism, 338ff.; Nominalism condemned, 343 n. 9

Omnipotence *(see* Will and Power of God)
Omnipresence and Eternity of God, 413ff.; the divine eternity conceived as simultaneity, 426f.; the divine eternity and Easter time, 427ff.; the divine eternity, meaning of, 423ff.; the divine eternity not timelessness, 427ff.; the divine omnipresence and Easter space, 419f.; the divine omnipresence, meaning of, 414, 431; the divine omnipresence and objective space, 417f.; the divine omnipresence and the personal dimension, 417f.;

and the eternity of God, 413ff.; Incarnation (Jesus event) as paradigm of the divine omnipresence, 415ff.; Jesus' "today" embraces his past and future, 430f.; Pentecost as paradigm of the divine omnipresence, 420f.
Omniscience of God *(see* Wisdom and Knowledge of God)
Ontological argument, 55f.
Orthodox theology, meaning of, 16

Pantheism and Panentheism, 206
Paradox, essential to theology, 85; its source, 42f.
Particle physics, 477f.
Pascal's wager, 53; his *Memorial,* 173
Patience, and the Christian life, 388; patience of God, 387f.
Pentecostalism, and the subordination of the Spirit, 321f.
Personality, and God, 284
Persons, trinitarian, 283f.; Barth's "ways of being," 296f.; definition of, 286; order of, 287; relational meaning of trinitarian names, 287ff.
Pessimism, 53, 202f.
Philosophy, meaning of, 17; relation to theology, 17ff., 360f.
Positivism, 26f., 30, 36, 43, 81
Power of God *(see* Will and Power of God)
Prayer, 184 n. 16, 206, 404, 433
Preaching, and the application of Scripture, 161ff.; centrality of, 150 n. 53; and the critical study of the Bible, 118f.; relation to dogmatics, xviiif.
Primal catastrophe theory, 466f.
Principle of contiguity, 21f.; and the interpretation of Scripture, 143f.
Procession, in the Trinity, 291f.
Process theology, and eros, 232; and incarnation, 20; meaning of, 18; and the Trinity, 281f.
Progressive revelation, 144f.
"Propositional" revelation, 77
Proprietas, trinitarian doctrine of, 325
Protestant scholastics, 131f.
Providence, and continuous creation, 460f.; and natural revelation, 72
Pseudepigrapha, 96
Puritan nomenclature, 178

Index of Names

Abbott, E., 214
Abbott, W. M., 109n.
Achtemeier, E., 445
Addison, 485n.
Albertus Magnus, 176n.
Alexander, 416
Alexander the Great, 135, 429
Althaus, P., 244
Altizer, T. J. J., 203
Ambrose, 19, 24
Andrews, L., 300n.
Anselm of Canterbury, 50, 55, 56, 58,
    63, 195n., 286n., 355, 399
Aquinas, Thomas, xv, 8, 18, 24, 31, 32,
    56, 58, 74, 149, 176n., 266, 286,
    296, 304n., 307, 354, 355, 357n.,
    372, 376, 426, 432n., 441n., 453n.,
    462, 463n., 488
Arandel, 108n.
Archimedes, 376n., 489
Aristotle, 17, 18, 24, 50, 134, 198, 283,
    372, 383, 384, 396, 408n., 428, 441n.
Arius, 51, 276-77, 315
Armstrong, B. G., 495
Arnold, M., 114
Athanasius, 51, 241n., 277, 304n., 317
Athenagoras, 127
Auden, W. H., 117
Augustine, 18, 19, 51, 72, 96, 100,
    115n., 119, 124, 159n., 180, 181n.,
    239, 242n., 273, 286n., 290, 294,
    295n., 299, 304n., 306, 317, 357n.,
    372, 376, 377, 380, 396, 399, 405,

413, 414, 420, 423, 424, 426, 427,
441, 442, 456, 462-64, 472, 483,
493n., 495

Bach, 137
Baillie, D., 43
Baillie, J., 75-77, 325
Baker, 247
Baldwin, J., 178
Barbour, I. G., 471n.
Bardsley, C. W., 178
Barrett, C. K., 63n.
Barrett, E., 236-37
Barth, K., xv, 20, 33-34, 55n., 75-76,
    79, 82n., 91n., 106, 133, 168, 176,
    179n., 198, 206n., 213n., 251n.,
    263n., 266n., 274, 280, 283, 286n.,
    288n., 290n., 291, 296-97, 300n.,
    302, 305n., 307, 317, 325, 340,
    343n., 353, 358n., 374n., 377, 383n.,
    387n., 394, 400, 416n., 419n., 432n.,
    451, 454-55, 461n., 465n., 495
Bartsch, H. W., 28n., 204n.
Basil of Caesarea, 273, 291n., 450
Bates, E. S., 117
Bavinck, H., 375, 415n.
Becker, C., 202n.
Beckwith, R., 101n.
Beethoven, 81, 137, 138n.
Behanna, G., 204
Behm, J., 315
Behm, R., 13
Benedict XV, 128

Index of Scripture References

DUE

DATE DUE